The First Civic University: Birmingham 1880–1980

An Introductory History

Leverhulme Trust

Grateful acknowledgement is made to the Leverhulme Trust for its support of the initial research project, 'Higher Education and Society: a case study of the University of Birmingham, 1880–1980'.

Project Team

Directors
Eric Ives
Roy Lowe

Computing and Statistics
Leonard Schwarz

Research Fellow
Diane Drummond

Research Associates
Fiona Brown
Cindy Burgoyne
Alison Gaukroger
Don Jones

The First Civic University: Birmingham 1880–1980

An Introductory History

Eric Ives

Diane Drummond

Leonard Schwarz

THE UNIVERSITY
OF BIRMINGHAM

UNIVERSITY PRESS

First published in the United Kingdom by The University of Birmingham Press,
Edgbaston, Birmingham, BI5 2TT, UK.

ISBN 1-902459-07-5

British Library Cataloguing in Publication data
A CIP catalogue record for this book is available from the British Library

Typeset at the University of Birmingham
Printed in Great Britain by Redwood Books, Trowbridge, Wiltshire

Contents

Part Four Transformation, 1950–80

Plates

Every effort has been made to trace the copyright holders of all copyright material reproduced in this book. If a copyright holder has been inadvertently overlooked, they are asked to contact the publisher at their earliest convenience.

Frontispiece Arms of the University

Foreword

THIS IS A STORY of personal, civic and academic endeavour, of one man's beneficence in founding in Birmingham a college devoted initially to the advancement of science, of another's determination to go further and found an independent university for the City, and of many other people – lay and academic – who then and subsequently created one of the country's major institutions of teaching, scholarship and research.

Sir Josiah Mason endowed his college from his own pocket, personally supervised its construction, and controlled it thereafter with a small group of friends. It was a remarkable gift from a remarkable man.

The vision of a university was shared by a number of people but it took Joseph Chamberlain's drive and personal influence to convert the vision into reality, rejecting the easier option of becoming a junior partner in an existing federal university and creating instead an independent university in Birmingham dedicated to both teaching and research.

The year 2000 marks the centenary of Chamberlain's university. From small beginnings, it has come to play a prominent role in the massive expansion of higher education in this country. From dependence on the generosity of individuals and business in Birmingham it had to look increasingly to government for its funding only to find the real value of that support diminishing in more recent times. From enjoying complete autonomy in the conduct of its affairs it has had to contend with increasing interference from government and its agencies.

The University has weathered these ups and downs, two World Wars – during the first of which it became a hospital – and a student protest. It has carried through a building programme comparable to that of a medium-sized town. It has become one of Britain's leading centres of research, something of which Chamberlain would have been particularly proud. It is a story of creativity, frustration and perseverance; of some failures and many successes; of a thriving and vibrant institution.

The authors have written this history of the century following the foundation of Mason College, feeling that the events and personalities of the last twenty years are too close for balanced analysis and comment. Whilst they mark their disapproval of some of the trends in higher education during these years, their confidence in the University of Birmingham's ability to cope with change and to ensure its future success will be shared by all who value their association with it.

Sir Alex Jarratt
University Chancellor

The University of Birmingham: a case study

THE STUDY OF UNIVERSITIES is a late comer to the discipline of history. It received the accolade of its own specialised Oxford journal only in 1981. Historians are nothing if not reactive, and the arrival in Britain of a late interest in this subject was a response to the accelerating importance of higher education since the end of the Second World War. This is not to say that there were not earlier pioneers in the field, but in the first half of the twentieth century the typical British publication was a pious domestic history of only parochial interest. More recent scholarship in the field, too, has often gone down a cul-de-sac, in this case issue-led research, what is sometimes called 'source-mining'. Scholars pick over the material looking for data to advance or refute some particular hypothesis and this can be as misleading as it would be for an archaeologist to begin robbing graves. Sheldon Rothblatt has rightly remarked that 'the modern university is like Proteus, many things at once, and the colour or form it assumes depends upon how it is viewed or grasped', but, like the Greek deity, a university remains an entity.[1]

It is for this reason that some groups of scholars working on university history have looked to attempt a different approach. In Britain – and doubtless elsewhere – hardly any activity of a modern university can be considered in isolation; the institution is an organism which is evolving in a particular but changing context. What is necessary, therefore, are holistic studies of individual institutions over a substantial period of time. The ideal would be to study the economic, sociological, social and physical dimensions as well as teaching and research, and also to explore the way all these interrelate. Furthermore, individual universities in Britain have had very different histories and it is not adequate to treat them as examples of a single species or even in categories; if overall assessments are eventually to be possible, individual examples have to be available for comparison and contrast. Locality matters, too. The distinctiveness of a particular university can in large measure be a reflection of the part played during its initial development by symbiosis between the institution and its hinterland.

Perhaps the exemplars of the holistic approach have been the Quincentennial Studies in the History of the University of Aberdeen, the first of which appeared in 1988. At Birmingham, research was begun in 1990, funded initially by a grant from the Leverhulme Trust for a project entitled 'Higher Education and Society: a case study of the University of Birmingham, 1880–1980'. The basis for this was the very substantial archive which had just been catalogued for the University Council. This covers not only the University since its foundation in 1900 but also its predecessor, Mason College, which opened in 1880. Together, the material for both institutions adds up to nearly 300 volumes of official minutes, sixteen library bays of other bound material, 32 000 boxed documents, a massive collection of plans and drawings covering estates and buildings and 70 000 student records. The research project added to this by creating a substantial database of student records and by collecting oral and questionnaire evidence.[2] Given that size and richness, questions could be asked over a wide range of issues with real confidence that in time answers would be forthcoming. This volume is presented as a preparatory step towards seeking those answers.

A holistic agenda is challenging and far too large for any single publication. One set of questions concerns the student body. The basic data here is the number of students from year to year. From 95 full-time students on all courses in its first year, 1880–1, Mason College reached 615 in 1897–8 while the University grew from 189 full-time students taking degrees and the equivalent in 1900–1 to 8741 in 1980–1.[3]

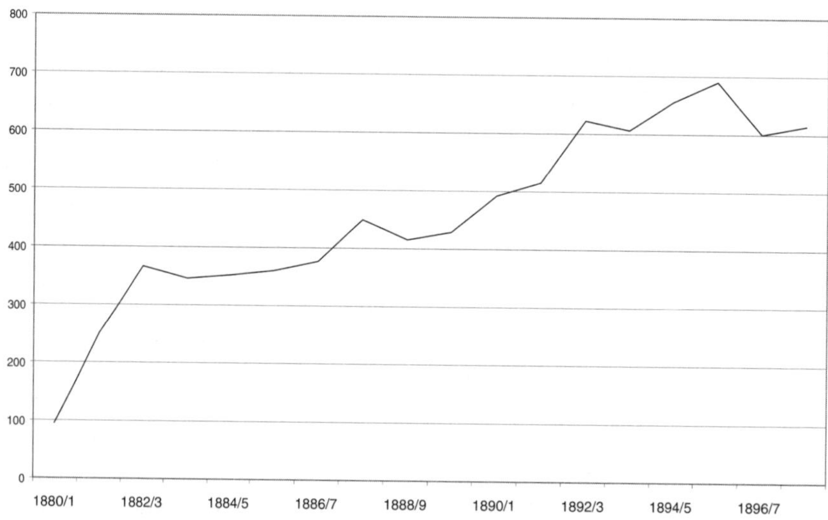

Figure 0.1 Mason College: total number of day students (all categories) 1880–98

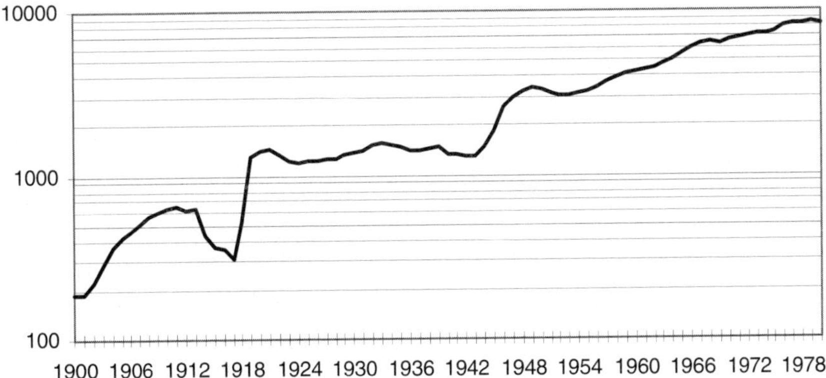

Figure 0.2 University of Birmingham: total number of systematic students 1900–80

Numbers can, of course, be refined to reveal trends: for example, by gender, faculty and study programme. Alongside numbers, it is also possible to ask questions about student origins, both geographic and social. The initial publicity for the University announced a Midland institution for Midland people, or, even narrower, a Birmingham university for Birmingham people. Yet today, in common with similar institutions, the University recruits nationally and internationally. What was the character and chronology of this change? As for social class and related issues, spasmodic data on parents, home addresses and previous education do allow some estimates to be made. Another student issue is the question of 'value-added'. What difference did study at the university make in terms, say, of employment? Joseph Chamberlain, the British statesman who was the effective founder of the University of Birmingham, described its function as training 'the captains of industry'. That expression has misled the 'decline of Britain' debate because it has been assumed that he meant 'leaders of industry'.[4] In fact Chamberlain used the term to mean not the generals but junior officers, the middle managers and technicians. Was the University successful in this respect?

A second but related set of questions arise from what students were taught. The Birmingham archive makes it possible to bring together the data of student enrolment and the detail of University and faculty prospectuses and regulations, and thus to comment on what the experience of a university course would have been at particular dates. Much of the early work of the College and University would today be done in a school, and the initial courses were broad ranging. Subsequently the move was to programmes which were progressively more highly specialised. Similarly there has been a shift from non-degree and pass-level degree courses to the almost exclusive concern with honours degrees which we find today, and a massive expansion in postgraduate work, much of it taught. The relevance of these changes to the personal, social and economic value of a university degree is obvious, and so too its link with the question of the professionalisation of society.

What it means to be a student and a 'graduate' has also changed over time. For much of its first hundred years Birmingham teaching has relied on the lecture reinforced by frequent assessments through written examinations where candidates attempt unseen question papers. It is, however, also clear that from an early date this pattern has been under challenge on the grounds that students are at a university not primarily to absorb information, but to learn how to think. Increasingly, lectures and examinations have given way to teaching methods predicated on that argument, with the result that, by 1980, the University was sending into employment and the wider society graduates with skills and expectations which were significantly different from those they would have had at the start of the century. They had also had a very different social experience, most noticeably in a change of residence (from home, via lodgings, to halls of residence, self-catering accommodation and now group occupation of private housing), and in the progressive transformation of the student guild from effectively an Edwardian club into a substantial service provider.

As well as covering students, the archive has copious documentation on the academic staff whose numbers grew tenfold in the first eighty years of the century, and also on their progressively changing roles. When the University began, policy and teaching were both dominated by the professors. Later a recognised category of lecturers began to appear. Soon these formed a majority of the staff but, although the professors no longer did most of the teaching, until the 1970s at least they continued to dominate University affairs. Research, too, is substantially documented. Before Birmingham achieved university status in 1900, J. H. Poynting, the professor of Physics, had already succeeded in calculating the weight of the world, and Joseph Chamberlain had stressed that a university was 'a place in which the work, the most important work of original research shall be continuously carried on'; the first principal of the new institution, Sir Oliver Lodge, was a pioneer of radio.[5] None of them, however, could have anticipated the emphasis on research which would come to dominate Birmingham.

Higher education thus impinges on society as students enter the university, as graduates leave, through staff and through research. Another interaction is between a university and its community, a topic of particular relevance to civic universities which were founded for particular towns or regions. That relationship was not only important in the setting up of an institution. For many years at Birmingham local direction and local control remained real and immediate. Subsequently, however, this influence has weakened, though the chronology of that has yet to be established and so too the cause. The most probable hypothesis is that the growth of a gap between university and local community reflected the fact that central government had ousted the locality as the arbiter of higher education, yet another consequence of the general national shift of power to Westminster. With that shift arrived what has become the most important change in higher education over the century, the transformation from a university which was independent to a university which is effectively treated as part of the public sector.

Interaction with the locality also involved the local economy. This was not only a matter of the substantial budget which the university spent locally, but, counting students as temporary quasi-employees, the University of Birmingham has become by far the largest enterprise in the south of the City, with all that this means. Another dimension, provided for from the outset, was that the University should service and support local industry. There was a physical interaction too. The University was the archetypal campus university in England, and has occupied the core of its current site since 1902, with successive expansions. This means that the development of the campus is part of the history of the development of the City and vice-versa. The most obvious example of this is that hospital provision in the City has been as much shaped by the need to locate the principal hospital next to the University's medical school, as by demographic considerations.

Many of these issues receive a preliminary outing in the following pages, but are necessarily not treated at length. The intention is to provide that in subsequent more detailed studies.[6] This book is an introduction to further research, and as such has two prime objectives. The first is to establish a broad narrative of the history of the University and the second to block in the pattern of growth and development and identify some of the key themes of the story. Subsequent study will refine, modify and possibly negate what is written here, but it is this book's function to make that possible.

The approach which has been adopted is to combine an overall chronological treatment with attention to themes as appropriate. The book's four sections cover the pre-university College, the early years and the trauma of the First World War, the thirty years embracing the Second World War which saw both consolidation but also increasing frustration, and finally the period from 1950 which saw huge changes take place as staff and student numbers more than doubled and as the nature of higher education in Britain was changed once and for all following the Robbins Report of 1963. As the story progresses, the focus necessarily changes from close-ups appropriate to a tiny college to the wider angle required for a major national and international institution. Some topics have deliberately been only touched on: the library, student life and society, and the history of particular faculties and departments where a number of particular studies already exist. Similarly a self-denying ordinance has substantially restricted discussion to the empirical and limited engagement in current scholarly debates.

Chapters in this book are, as indicated, the work of individual authors but I have been responsible for overall editing and coherence. Together we owe considerable debts to a number of institutions and individuals: to the Leverhulme Trust for funding the initial research and to colleagues on the project team and to those working on the database; to Dr.Ben Benedicz and Christine Penney, successively Special Collections librarians at the University and their staff for enthusiastic support and untiring effort; to Ruth Ives and David Jordan for research assistance; to Alex Jarrett, the University Chancellor, for his kindness in writing the foreword; to Professor John Grenville and Dr. John Bourne for reading the manuscript; to Tim Pearson of the Estate Management Office of the University of Birmingham; to Ian King of the National Union of Students and to Carl Chinn and innumerable other colleagues, and former colleagues and students who have shared their reminiscences or answered questions, and finally to the University Press, and to its Secretary for her efforts and her equanimity. Gratitude, however, does not imply a shifting in the responsibility for any errors.

The early years of the 21st century coincide with the centenaries of the older English civic universities. Together, their arrival marked a break-through in higher education and heralded a development, at first slow but then hectic, which by the end of the century saw the country with nearly one hundred universities and a third of its young people studying in them. In parallel with what can rightly be described as a revolution, community interest and involvement has moved from local enthusiasm in a limited number of towns and cities, to a position where higher education has become a significant element in the nation's overall educational provision and its political concerns. In any assessment of the 20th century, the story deserves to be writ large.

Notes

1 S.Rothblatt, *The Revolution of the Dons: Cambridge Society and Victorian England* (Cambridge 1968), p.15.

2 UC Database of Student Records, 1900–80, referred to subsequently as 'database'.

3 Note that the Mason College totals (as also in Figure 0.1) are for all students; the University totals (as also in Figure 0.2) are only for students registered for formal qualifications. The University total for all students in 1900–1 was 678.
As a general rule, numbers in the book have been rounded up to the nearest whole number; sums of money follow the predecimal system of twelve pence to the shilling, and twenty shillings to the pound.

4 The hypothesis that there was a causal link between having its higher education ethos dominated by a public service ethic and the decline of the British economy after 1860. For Chamberlain's remark see below p. 98.

5 See below p. 102.

6 The first of these has already appeared: J. H. Thompson's *A Centennial History of the Library of the University of Birmingham 1880–1995* (University of Birmingham 2000).

Part One

Mason College, 1880–1900

Chapter One

Josiah Mason

TWO MEN FATHERED the University of Birmingham, Josiah Mason and Joseph Chamberlain. Over the years others contributed to its growth, but the genetic inheritance has come from these two individuals. The two had much in common but in their public impact they were very different, a contrast which is reflected in their reputations – Chamberlain still a name in history, but Mason effectively forgotten, with the statue in his honour which once stood in Victoria Square, Birmingham, now lost and probably destroyed.

Josiah Mason was born on 23 February 1795, a date celebrated for many years by the University as 'Founder's Day'.[1] His birthplace was a tiny house in Mill Street, Kidderminster, a town in which the Mason family could be traced back for some generations, always very humble people.[2] Coming from such a background, there is little beyond the stories Sir Josiah Mason told privately in later life to establish the details of his childhood. His father Josiah was a bombazine weaver and, later, clerk to a carpet manufacturer. The future philanthropist was a second son and the dominant influences in his childhood were his paternal grandfather, also Josiah, and his mother Elizabeth. This eldest Josiah was also nominally a bombazine weaver but was far more in demand as a practical mechanic: 'a mender of looms and a sort of doctoring engineer of water mills'. Elizabeth Griffiths, as she had been, came from a Dudley family which enjoyed a somewhat higher level within the working classes than the Masons, and was a woman of considerable force.[3]

The young Josiah was given no proper education, but by the age of eight he could count well enough to sell cakes from door to door and to take on the laborious job of sorting copper coin for local tradesmen at a penny per £1. He tried a variety of other petty retailing, and, with help from local nonconformist Sunday schools, he learned to read and write – which allowed him to become the amanuensis in his neighbourhood. Although he subsequently practised in turn as a shoemaker, carpenter, blacksmith and housepainter, he was never properly trained for anything and at the age of nineteen ended up, inevitably, in the sheds of one of Kidderminster's numerous carpet factories.

Mason was good at carpet weaving, it paid well, and he began to subscribe to a land society, a mutual association which would eventually have given him a house. However, a future at the loom did not suit his proactive temperament and in his early twenties he moved to Birmingham to work in the gilt-toy business for his uncle Richard Griffiths, and then to marry Richard's daughter Anne in 1817. Various vicissitudes followed until, in 1822–3, through the gilt-toy trade and his nonconformist connections, he met Samuel Harrison. Harrison was a man of wide interests who earlier in life had made scientific instruments for (and played duets with) his friend, Joseph Priestley.[4] He had invented a mechanical process for making split rings and built a thriving business on it, but Harrison was by then in his sixties and looking to retire. He took to Mason and offered to sell him his Lancaster Street works by instalments. Mason seized the offer and thereby entered the ranks of the small manufacturers who then dominated the Birmingham metal trades.

Characteristically, Josiah Mason was not content to leave the business as he had bought it. First he devised a machine which would produce split rings which were bevelled rather than flat. He had his grandfather's practicality in full measure. Then he turned his attention to writing implements. One of his youthful jobs in Kidderminster Sunday schools had been to trim goose quills for those learning how to write, and he knew that a trimmed quill would go soft after less than a page. Handmade metal pens had existed since antiquity but were ruled out of ordinary use by cost. More recently steel pens and pen nibs had begun to be produced by a partly mechanised process, but to be flexible enough to write with, a nib has to be split, and no one had discovered a way to do this by machine. Mason did, and thereby was able to reduce the price from twopence (0.8p) per nib to twopence for a gross (144) – and that included a box. He secured an exclusive contract to supply this superior product to Perry & Co., the market leader, and November 1830 saw him achieving for the first time an order for 100 gross. Exporting began in 1850 and eventually Mason became the world's largest pen maker. When he sold out to Perry & Co. in 1875, his works and its workforce of 1000 were producing, in addition to pen holders, boxes and the like, 4 608 000 nibs per week and had the capacity for 5 760 000, an annual potential not far short of one for every fourth person in the world, man, woman and child.

Mason made the machines for the most secret parts of his pen-making processes himself, but when he began to look for an opportunity to invest the money he was making, he thought more of being a sleeping partner in someone else's venture. That someone else was George Richards Elkington, who, together with his cousin Henry, had taken out a patent for electroplating in 1840. The Elkingtons were short of capital but, although strongly advised against the risk, Josiah Mason was convinced that the process had a future and he invested heavily, probably in the order of £50,000.[5] Soon he was drawn into management, while the Elkingtons concentrated on developing the product. Mason was responsible for setting up a new works and showroom in Newhall Street, Birmingham, and warehouses and showrooms in Liverpool and in the City and West End of London. Two years after Mason's initial investment Prince Albert visited the firm and was presented with a spider's web which had been silver-plated by Samuel Harrison's great nephew, Alexander Parkes, who worked for the company.[6] Elkington and Mason also caused a major stir at the Great Exhibition of 1851 where their stand displayed over a hundred silver-plated items in seven glass cases plus numerous pieces in electro-bronze, with Queen Victoria herself exhibiting a plated jewel-case made by them and a gold- and silver-plated table with bas-reliefs of 'Temperance' surrounded by the gods of learning and the four elements.[7]

Electroplating was not Mason's only venture outside the world of split rings and pen nibs. He and Elkington bought out Alexander Parkes's patents for the smelting of copper, set up a plant for this at Burry Port, Llanelli, and sank a mine to supply the coal to run it.[8] Mason also went into the manufacture of nickel. In 1876, when he was eighty-one, 'Sir Josiah Mason and Alexander Parkes and Company' took out a joint patent for improving production of the metal. However, he did not go in with Parkes on the production of the first synthetic plastic, Parkesine, and, indeed, seems to have fallen out with him.[9] After splitting with Parkes, Mason had a nickel works of his own in Birches Green near Erdington, and a warehouse in Great Charles Street, Birmingham.[10] His great-nephew, Martyn Josiah Smith, ran it, but always in close consultation with the old man. As late as 1880, Martyn was writing to him from Paris about the supply of ore, and Mason is described on his death certificate as a nickel refiner.[11] The company passed to Martyn on his uncle's death.

Not all of Mason's ventures were as successful. Again with Elkington, he funded Alexander Parkes to invent the cold vulcanisation of rubber, only to decide that the patent position was problematic and sell out to competitors.[12] Ironically, he was also involved in the Birmingham Screw Co., which was set up in 1870 to challenge the industrial monopoly which Joseph Nettlefold and Joseph Chamberlain had established over mechanised screw production. Chamberlain dismissed Mason as 'an ass' but responded nevertheless with naked capitalistic strategies 'to smash the new Company' and retain a monopoly position: 'I feel certain that to let the Company get fairly in the market would be to abdicate for ever our position as Screw Kings. I do not mean to say that we might not do very well as regards money . . . but for a certainty, our sole supremacy would never be re-established.' The rival concern did last for ten years, but in 1880 was purchased by Nettlefold after Chamberlain had left the company.[13]

Mason was active in business for nearly fifty years, but it is impossible to say how great was the fortune he accumulated. It was certainly of the order of £1,000,000. He lived modestly. In 1881, after his wife's death, he was being looked after by his great-niece, with the help of a housekeeper, a cook and two housemaids.[14] He and his wife were in their fifties before they took their first foreign holiday in 1847: it was cut short by business, and they never went again. Mason lived for work. He was a tough businessman who liked nothing better than a shrewd bargain, and to the very many who did not know him he appeared something of a miser, a money-grubber born poor who was determined to die rich. It is highly doubtful whether any such reputation bothered him, but in any case it was his own fault. Mason was an extremely private person who made little impact on Birmingham society or Birmingham affairs. He had a deep Christian faith, but deliberately stood outside the City's active denominationalism – in the 1860s, when he was nearly seventy and one of the wealthiest men in the City, the Vicar of Birmingham did not recognise his name. He took no part in Birmingham politics, only once held office in a company not his own, and was no great entertainer. His taste was for private pleasures – art, music, flowers and growing grapes. Josiah Mason made no secret of his background and, despite his wealth and success, one may suspect that much of the caution and common sense of early poverty – and possibly the feeling of being an outsider – remained to the end.

By the 1850s it had been long apparent that Josiah and Anne would have no children and the question of what was to happen to his large and still-growing fortune began to loom. Nephews were now running the pen business, and although Mason was busy with Elkingtons he had the time to express the social conscience which had always made him a paternalist employer. Initially he set up in 1858 an orphanage for first twenty-five and then fifty girls in Erdington, four miles north of Birmingham, then still a village. The success of this venture encouraged him to try to form a society to establish a larger orphanage for the whole town, but that came to grief because Mason insisted on the institution being non-denominational. He thereupon decided to go it alone and in 1867 opened an orphanage for 300 children – two-thirds of them girls – and converted the earlier building to almshouses for twenty-six elderly women. He did much of the planning himself and ended up actually supervising the construction. The capital cost was £60,000 and the £200,000 endowment which Mason also provided included his own residence, Norwood House, with thirteen acres of gardens, which made him – as he liked to say – a tenant to his own charity. In recognition of his philanthropy, Gladstone proposed Mason for a knighthood in 1872 which Josiah, characteristically, asked to receive by letters patent, so avoiding a public investiture.[15]

Central to the orphanage was education, but with characteristic Mason twists. The provisions for religious instruction specifically excluded 'reference to sectarian distinctions and prejudices' – no 'catechism, formulary or articles of faith of any church or body of professing Christians'. In the wider curriculum the emphasis was on 'general or useful knowledge', with 'no instruction in any language or grammar other than the English language and the English grammar'. Literature was ignored entirely – Mason never read a novel in his life. In what today might be called his 'mission statement' Mason said that the objective of the training was to produce 'useful members of society in the position in life to which it may please

God to call them and which He may give them talents worthily to fulfil'. Most Victorians would have recognised that the first part of the sentence echoed the Anglican catechism, but the addition about talents was Mason's own. Notably, he seems to have had opportunities for girls particularly in mind, and he made special provision that young women who intended to be teachers or nurses did not have to leave the orphanage at the usual age of eighteen, but could stay on indefinitely. It was also characteristic of Mason that while he insisted on retaining authority over his seven trustees during his lifetime, he arranged that on his death the town council was to nominate seven more, with an effective provision for these to become a majority.

The year after the orphanage opened – indeed, with the legal documentation still incomplete – Mason moved to begin his greatest project, 'Sir Josiah Mason's Science College'. Legally incorporated in 1870 and taking its first students in 1880, this was an initiative very much in tune with the times. The movement to bring advanced education to Victorian Britain was at its height. Although a reformer could still speak in 1876 of 'a state of national destitution – an intellectual blight', in which fewer than 1.5% of the population received education beyond the age of eighteen, enormous progress was being made.[16] At the traditional universities of Oxford and Cambridge, reforms between 1854 and 1877 had removed discrimination against nonconformists and modernised both university life and the curriculum. More revolutionary, however, was the founding of new educational institutions in major cities. In 1825 there were two universities in England and Wales; sixty years later there were at least sixteen institutions teaching at degree level. At first the process was slow and uncertain. What is now known as University College London led the way in 1828, and in 1836 the University of London was chartered as a degree-giving body. However, Durham, set up the next year, was an Oxbridge clone and the college bequeathed to Manchester in 1851 by the will of John Owens had no degree-giving powers. Seven years later London opened its degrees to external candidates, and encouraged by this decision, the dam burst. From 1871 to 1884, colleges opened in Aberystwyth, Bangor, Bristol, Cardiff, Dundee, Leeds, Liverpool, Newcastle, Nottingham and Sheffield, as well as Birmingham. In 1880 the North acquired degree-giving rights with the setting up of the federal Victoria University. Owens was its first constituent college, joined in 1884 by Liverpool and in 1887 by Leeds. Wales was granted a federal university in 1893.

Nor was educational progress confined to such major institutions. In the first half of the century provincial medical schools had appeared to supplement the apprenticeship training traditional in the profession. Teachers began to be trained in residential colleges attached to a variety of Christian denominations, with state certification of trainees from 1846 and state support from 1849. Societies with serious – and less serious – scholarly pretensions were established in very many towns and cities. Hundreds of mechanics' institutes were opened for the working classes and also institutions to provide technical education, such as the Regent Street Polytechnic. Although the mechanics' institutes were frequently annexed by middle-class patrons, some provided a local base for another educational innovation, the University Extension movement, which was pioneered from Cambridge in and after 1867.

Josiah Mason was, therefore, not an innovator, and certainly not in Birmingham, where many examples of the educational developments of the nineteenth century could be found, and more had been tried.[17] The town was the home of one of the most prestigious learned societies, the Lunar Society, founded as long ago as 1766. In 1853 the very influential Birmingham and Midland Institute had been set up. There was Queen's College, which included a medical school. At Saltley teachers were trained for Church of England schools; Roman Catholics could read for University of London degrees at Oscott College, and Congregational ministers studied at Spring Hill, which would in 1886 move to Oxford to become Mansfield College. Attempts to provide working-class education had, however, been less successful. Although one of the earliest mechanics' institutes in England had been founded in Birmingham (in 1825) with considerable initial enthusiasm, it had had to close in 1843, as did the struggling Polytechnic ten years later.

When he turned his mind to a college of higher education Mason's first thought was to graft it on an existing stock. One possibility was the Queen's College. This had had its origin in the initiative of a local surgeon, William Sands Cox (1801–75).[18] He had himself been taught on the pupillage system at the General Hospital (established in Birmingham in 1779), but in 1825 began to give a series of systematic medical lectures in Temple Row. These led in 1828 to the foundation of the Birmingham School of Medicine and Surgery (from 1836 'The Royal School') and in 1841 an associated teaching hospital was begun under royal patronage and the presidency of Prince Albert. 'The Queen's Hospital in Birmingham' opened in 1843 and at the same time Sands Cox's school became Queen's College, with its remit broadened to include teaching in architecture, civil engineering, law, theology and the arts.

All this might appear ready-made for Josiah Mason. In reality the position was anything but promising. In a less than veiled competition with Queen's and with considerable support from the region, the staff of the General Hospital had in 1851 created 'Sydenham College' to train their own students, with purpose-built premises opened in 1858. Queen's College, meanwhile, had got into difficulties. In a city where nonconformity was strong, its ethos was very decidedly Anglican. Managing both the expanded college and the hospital proved too much for Sands Cox, but he was not prepared to share power. Chaos ensued and bankruptcy threatened. In the end Sands Cox withdrew and after a Charity Commission inquiry the college and the hospital were separated by the 1867 'Queen's College (Birmingham) Act'. The college thereafter set out to concentrate on the more moderate agenda of medicine, theology and the arts, and in 1868 logic prevailed in medical education and the rival Birmingham medical colleges combined. The name 'Sydenham' disappeared, along with most of the staff of Queen's, and in 1873 a joint clinical board was arranged for the two hospitals. The attempt to provide non-medical education at Queen's was, however, not a success. The arts were dropped in 1872, the new School of Trade and Commerce set up in 1877 only flourished temporarily, and theology also faltered.

As an alternative to Queen's, the Birmingham and Midland Institute seemed to offer a far better vehicle for Mason's proposed college.[19] In the years after its foundation it had secured strong municipal backing, a permanent site and purpose-built premises, and had made a name in two well-supported fields of activity, 'industrial' and 'general'. Indeed, the popularity of its 'industrial' classes had enabled the Institute rapidly to clear the initial capital outlay and ensure a sound financial base. It had also taken under its aegis a small and previously independent School of Design and seen it grow into the largest in the region. For its 'general' programme the Institute engaged the lions of the Victorian intellectual world. Charles Dickens gave the first of his celebrated 'readings' at one of its meetings and later became its president. Another lecturer who became president was T. H. Huxley – and his standing was such that the town invited him in 1873 to unveil the statue to Joseph Priestley. Seven years later he would be the guest speaker at the opening of Mason's college.

The Institute, therefore, was a major success, but despite this Mason turned away. Why is not clear. One possible issue was relative size. The Institute had cost £20,000 but the endowment Mason intended for the College would mean that it would not so much join the Institute as swallow it. Another possible consideration was that the success and social acceptability of the Institute's general programme would sit uneasily with Sir Josiah's emphasis on practicalities. One also suspects that personal preference played a part. Mason had the deep conviction – endorsed by his wife – that the only way to get something right was to do it himself. But whatever the explanation, within months Mason had decided, once again, to go it alone.

Given that the decision to found Mason's College belongs in the context of a very general contemporary interest in education, it would be easy to conclude that Sir Josiah's decision was Birmingham's example of the Victorian philanthropist following fashion. In reality, new educational institutions were more usually the product of collaboration within a city's elite, not the initiative of single individuals.[20] One person who did act alone was John Owens, who launched advanced education in Manchester in 1851 with a legacy of £100,000, and there are parallels between him and Mason. They were much of an age and shared a dislike of religious tests. However, the world to which Owens belonged was quite different – trading in cotton and campaigning against the Corn Laws. He was also less personally involved in his college – it was set up *post mortem* – and his endowment was insufficient for the total project.

The closer parallel is between Mason and Thomas Holloway, the founder of Royal Holloway College, now part of the University of London, even to the point of Holloway also preferring to be involved directly and not at second hand.[21] The two were of the same generation – Holloway was five years younger; he too had been humbly born, and despite a somewhat better education and being apprenticed (to a druggist), had experienced a similar struggle against obstacles – in his case as far as becoming bankrupt. Struggle was then followed, as with Mason, by great – indeed world-wide – success which again left a childless couple with the problem of disposing of a huge fortune. Holloway's endowment was probably larger than Mason's, but both were more than adequate, and the colleges opened within seven years of each other – Mason's in 1880, Holloway's in 1887. There is even some parallel in that the colleges were, for each of them, the second major venture in philanthropy. Holloway had previously built not an orphanage, but a mental hospital.

Mason, however, would certainly not have relished being compared with Holloway. Committed to the virtues of homeopathic medicine, he would have despised a fortune built not on honest manufacturing but on patent pills and ointments. Nor did Mason's retiring personality and his shunning of publicity have much in common with a man who owed everything to the ruthless advertising of his products, not their efficacy. Also, in fairness to Mason, there was a major difference in intention between his approach and that of Holloway. Sir Josiah's purpose comes out very clearly in the speech the old man wrote for the laying of the foundation stone of the College on his eightieth birthday, 23 February 1875. It was a day of intense cold and the speech, which was delivered for him, could not be given until the party had retreated to the Queen's Hotel. Mason made it clear that, as with the orphanage, the project sprang directly from his own experience, in this case of a lack of opportunity to study. It continued:

> This work, gentlemen, has been long in my mind, for I have always felt the importance of providing enlarged means of scientific instruction, on the scale required by the necessities of the town and district and upon terms which render it easily available by persons of all classes, even the humblest. The experience of my own life has long since satisfied me on this point.[22]

In other words, Mason was setting out to create an educational institution which would give Birmingham a specific provision for training in the science from which he had made his fortune and which he had had to learn the hard way.

By contrast, Holloway's educational motivation appears decidedly nebulous. Indeed, he seems to have been more concerned to erect a grand building than with its use. The Château of Chambord was the chosen model. Holloway and his favoured architect undertook a detailed survey of the Loire palace in the autumn of

1873 as the first stage to creating a home for incurables. However, in the following winter, at the request of his wife, the use of the building was changed to a college for women. Realising that he knew 'nothing or next to nothing as to the requirements or the working of a College for ladies', he then had to turn to a panel of experts for advice.[23]

Mason's emphasis on science indicates that he and Holloway also differed in another respect. The expansion in higher education in the second half of the nineteenth century was accompanied by a fierce debate about purpose. It was easy to agree that Britain needed to catch up with the Continent in the production of graduates, but much less easy to agree on whether the country needed these new graduates to be educated in the traditional liberal Oxbridge mould or with industry and commerce in mind. Cardinal Newman epitomised the first view:

> A University training . . . aims at raising the intellectual tone of society, at cultivating the public mind, at purifying the national taste, at supplying true principles to popular enthusiasm and fixed aims to public aspiration, at giving enlargement and sobriety to the ideas of the age, at facilitating the exercise of political power, and refining the intercourse of private life.[24]

This was evidently very much of what Holloway had in mind for his college: it was to be 'a University which signifies every branch of knowledge – where Anatomy, Botany, Mineralogy, Painting, Sculpture, Law, Divinity and I know not what else' would be taught.[25] The priorities for students who were to come from the 'middle and upper middle classes' are clear in the initial curriculum: Latin, Greek, French, German, mathematics, English and history, music, divinity and natural science (including zoology). Physics was added in 1891 and chemistry in 1893.[26]

Much of John Owens's thinking also approximated to the Newman position. His intention was to make available in Manchester 'instruction in the branches of learning and science usually taught in the English universities'.[27] His trustees took him literally. When they published the plan for Owens College, they stated that priority would be given to classical language and literature, mathematics and philosophy, natural and moral. They also pre-empted criticism by asserting that Manchester's importance as a commercial centre did not meant that education in classical literature was less appropriate and, further, that the endowment did not stretch to providing courses of practical instruction. 'To do so would be, in our opinion, equally inconsistent with the intentions of the testator and the best capabilities of the institution.'[28] The thinking at Bristol was similar.[29] The circular which launched the College of Science specifically endorsed 'the growing conviction that culture in all the subjects which form the staple of university teaching should be made more widely accessible'. Support for such sentiments could be found at the highest level of society. When Gladstone opened the University Extension Building in Nottingham in 1877 he warned:

> Much of the most valuable knowledge does not produce its return in the subjugation of material or the production of works of art. The knowledge of man is the knowledge which has ever been at the foundation of our old academical systems, and the higher place you can secure for instruction in the knowledge of man in your University College, the higher will the character of the College be.[30]

Against those who thought as Newman and Gladstone did were arrayed men like Thomas Huxley and Herbert Spencer:

> What knowledge is of most worth? – the uniform reply is – Science. This is the verdict on all counts. For direct self-preservation in the maintenance of life and health, the all-important knowledge is – Science. For that indirect self-preservation which we call gaining a livelihood, the knowledge of the greatest value is – Science. For the due discharge of parental functions, the proper guidance is only to be found in – Science. For the interpretation of national life, past and present, without which the citizen cannot rightly regulate his conduct, the indispensable key is – Science. Alike for the most perfect production and highest enjoyment of art in all its forms, the needful preparation is still – Science. And for purposes of discipline – intellectual, moral, religious – the most efficient study is, once more – Science.[31]

There can be no doubt which side Mason was on. The advanced education which Birmingham needed was far more practical than that envisaged by Owens or Holloway, or the University of Durham, that colony of Oxbridge values which the Anglican Church had attempted to plant in the 'barren' north of England. The stone-laying speech at Birmingham set the agenda with complete clarity. It was to provide for:

> all classes in Birmingham, in Kidderminster and in the district generally, the means of carrying on in the capital of the Midland district their scientific studies as completely and thoroughly as they can be prosecuted in the great science schools of this country and the Continent for I am persuaded that, in this way alone – by the acquisition of sound extensive and practical scientific knowledge – can England hope to maintain her position as the manufacturing centre of the world.[32]

The Foundation Deed of 1870 was even blunter in its specification:

> systematic education and instruction specially adapted to the practical, mechanical, and artistic requirements of the manufactures and industrial

> pursuits of the Midland district … to the exclusion of mere literary education and instruction, and of all teaching of theology and of subjects purely theological, which limitations the said Josiah Mason hereby declares to be fundamental.[33]

Supplementary deeds added anatomy and the Greek and Latin *languages* in 1874 and medicine and surgery in 1881.[34]

In the event this purist rigour had to be modified. Establishing the College did not mean that it was entitled to award degrees; for that a royal charter or an act of Parliament would be required. Thus the only route by which Birmingham could offer degree-level work was by linking with either the Victoria University or, more immediately, the University of London, and that meant accepting their regulations. The London regulations, in particular, called for a broad-based matriculation, and in 1881 Mason was forced to execute a further deed of variation to permit the teaching of any subject required for its degrees (or those of the Victoria University).[35] Yet while having to bend to reality, Sir Josiah's priorities were beyond doubt. As T. P. Heslop, one of the most influential of Mason's trustees, said at the laying of the foundation stone, the intention was not 'a college as once understood in this and other countries, but a college for the purpose of teaching science wholly or mainly'.[36] The original name said it all: Josiah Mason's College for the Study of Practical Science.[37]

Reverberations of the debate were certainly detectable when Mason's College was opened on Friday 1 October 1880.[38] The day was a great civic occasion and it cost the college £2272 0s 10d.[39] It began in the morning at the Town Hall. This was full long before the ceremony started, and the gathering was entertained by the Festival Choral Society and a characteristically mixed Victorian programme – 'Blest Pair of Sirens', 'My Love Is Like a Red, Red Rose' and 'The Heavens Are Telling the Glory of God'. At noon the platform party entered: Josiah Mason, the other trustees, civic dignitaries, Thomas Huxley and several academics from other civic colleges. Mendelssohn's 'Let Our Theme of Praise Ascending' followed, and then Huxley was invited to speak.

Despite his previous links with Birmingham and his scientific sympathies Huxley had not been the first choice to speak at the opening. The establishment figure, Sir John Lubbock Bt, MP, vice-chancellor of the University of London, had originally been invited, and neither Mason nor the audience can have anticipated what they were in for from his replacement.[40] It was Huxley at his most powerful. After summoning the figure of Priestley to his aid, he briefly dismissed the opinions of the 'practical men' who disdained science as speculative rubbish; the importance attached to science by such an evidently successful practical man as Mason was conclusive. Next he endorsed Mason's prohibitions on politics and religion and finally launched into his theme, 'Science and Culture'. Mason, Huxley said, was absolutely right to exclude 'literary instruction and education' from the curriculum of the College. However, he did not seek to justify this on the practical advantages of science, which were what really attracted Mason. Instead he challenged the Newman/Gladstone position head on. Education based on literature and, in particular, the classics, did have value, but the day was over when it could be the exclusive route in advanced education. 'For the attaining of real culture', Huxley declared, 'an exclusively scientific education is at least as effectual as an exclusively literary education.'[41] Indeed, he quite clearly implied that a scientific education was superior as far as the great mass of the population was concerned:

> A young Englishman in search of culture cannot do better than study the classics given ample time for learning and a destination of ordinary life or for a literary career. But for those who mean to make science their serious occupation or who have to enter early upon the business of life; for all of these, in my opinion, classical education is a mistake.[42]

He then cited one of the defenders of the virtues of literature, Matthew Arnold, the son of Arnold of Rugby and a recognised educational guru. Arnold, he said, had been right to say that the essence of culture was the criticism of life, but quite wrong to suppose that this was necessarily or even best acquired through a study of the classics. Their prominence was entirely understandable in earlier centuries but 'the distinctive character of our own times lies in the vast and constantly increasing part which is played by natural knowledge'.[43]

It was a brilliant performance, but not one which won universal assent. It was perhaps a rustle in the audience which caused Huxley to qualify his absolutism by briefly conceding that a rigorously exclusive scientific training 'will bring about a mental twist as surely as an exclusively literary training'.[44] However, this only allowed him a further swipe at Greek and Latin. Mason's College would not be turning out 'lop-sided men' because it was to teach English, French and German, 'the three greatest literatures of the modern world'.[45]

At the ensuing celebration lunch in the Queen's Hotel the feelings of many of the audience became plain. G. J. Johnson, Mason's lawyer and one of the trustees, was in the chair since the old man had retired to recoup his energies for the evening. The company numbered about 120 and was very distinguished with, as well as local dignitaries, academics from Cambridge, Glasgow, Leeds, London, Manchester, Newcastle, Oxford, Sheffield, Armagh, Dublin and Halifax (Nova Scotia), thirty-six in all. Everything went well until R. W. Dale rose to propose the second toast, 'to the College, the Founder and the Professors'.

Dr Dale was a heavyweight, minister at Carr's Lane Congregational Church, the Mecca of Birmingham nonconformity, and a veteran of the campaign for compulsory universal education.[46] The part he played in the subsequent revolt against Foster's Education Act (1870) was said to have helped to bring down the government in 1874. To make his point in reply to Huxley, Dale seized on the location chosen for the new College. Out of its windows could be seen the Free Library, the Midland Institute, the Art Gallery – literature, music, painting (applause at each): 'It was quite natural for Science in the passion and triumph of her youth to aspire to universal and undivided sway. That morning she had appeared before them like a young Caesar.'[47] But fear of science was like earlier phobias about Russia or France, or 'more recently Germany'. Huxley was not Napoleon, Tsar Nicholas or Bismarck: 'They said (not "he said" – clearly he felt the room with him) and said in Professor Huxley's presence – that the ancient kingdoms of the moral and intellectual life of man were not likely to have their legitimate frontiers driven in by the new empire of which he [Huxley] was sovereign. (Applause)'. Poetry, art, music, ethics, all remained unchallenged. Nor did Dale politely respect Huxley's agnosticism. He said bluntly: 'He believed that the august authority of righteousness, the wonder, the rapture, the awe and joy of religious faith, retained, and would continue to retain through all future centuries, their ancient place in the life of man.' The reason he welcomed the new science, as he did, was that: 'Whatever contributed to discipline and unfold the powers of man contributes to the perfection of human nature and contributes to the manifestation and glory of Him whose image he believed human nature wore. (Renewed Applause)'. The next toast was 'the Visitors', and to this Huxley was to reply, but he did so with caution, thanking Dale for pointing out matters he had not had space to include in his address.[48] He was followed by Professor Max Muller, an Oxford philosopher who could not resist attacking Huxley (whom he knew well), but did so in a way which introduced an element of high-table debate and so lightened the tone: 'Literary culture can far better dispense with physical science than physical science with literary culture, though nothing is more satisfying than the perfect combination of the two which we see in Professor Huxley.'[49] Greenwood, principal of Owens College, spoke last and avoided a sour ending to the meal by neatly raising the issue of teaching standards. These were as important as content: Birmingham had an excellent record – three of four of the country's leading scholars and divines had been taught at the Grammar School (King Edward VI's Foundation) – and Mason College was not about to abandon such quality.[50]

To read the occasion in this way depends on picking up the nuances of the speeches, but subsequent events would confirm that Mason College's commitment to science was not universally welcomed by Birmingham. All that, however, lay in the months and years ahead. The immediate future was the *conversazione* that night which would open the new College to the good and great of the town.[51] Ticket-holders arrived by carriage before a crowd of spectators, held back by barriers and a posse of police. The building had been lavishly decorated: 'Choice plants, beautiful sweet-scented flowers, rich tapestry, magnificent mirrors, luxurious furniture, costly carpets and numerous articles of vertu were to be met within one room after another, until it was easy to imagine that the Science College was not, after all, the building it was supposed to be.'[52] In all about 5000 plants were brought in, including several ten-foot-high cypress trees. The lecture rooms were transformed into 'elegant drawing rooms' and laid out for supper. The walls of the central corridor were covered in crimson baize and led to the main reception room which had Persian carpets and Turkish rugs on the floor, blue and gold tapestry on the walls, a display of Japanese bronze and vases, and a magnificent array of cloisonné and other Japanese artefacts specially made for Elkington's. On the first floor the examination hall was turned into a ballroom and so too one of the laboratories, with elaborate drapes, trophies and hothouse plants, yet 'notwithstanding the profusion of adornments, there was no haphazard or vulgar display; everything was arranged with exceptional taste, and the general effect was such as to justify and call for a most laudatory description.'[53] Sir Josiah arrived just before 8 p.m. and was escorted by the trustees to a seat on the dais in the reception room. There he produced an ornamental key and said:

> This key of my College is now mine, and I can say that the College is mine; but in a moment I shall be able to say so no longer, for I now present it, and with it the College, to my old friend Mr. Johnson, on behalf of my trustees, to be held by them in trust for the benefit of generations to come.[54]

Johnson made a brief reply and the festivities commenced.

In the chemistry theatre a band played popular light classics, a glee party performed in the physics theatre. There were numerous scientific displays for which the limited exhibition materials of the academic departments had been filled out with the help of the resources of the scientific community of the city. In biology there were fifty microscopes and a whole variety of slides lent by the Natural History and Microscopical Society, and cases of stuffed birds and specimens of insectivorous plants were lent by the surgeon, Lawson Tait. The geology museum displayed fossils and rock samples from various owners and collectors, many from the Midland Institute. Physics put on displays on magnetism, light and electricity. At 9.30 p.m. dancing commenced, followed by supper and carriages at half-past midnight.

The building which was opened in such style had taken a decade to construct. The first requirement had been to find a site. By the 1860s Birmingham had begun to develop a civic centre half a mile west of the town's historic focus on St. Martin's in the Bull Ring: a town hall, an art gallery, the Council house, a public library and the Midland Institute in close proximity. It was here that Sir Josiah wished to build his college, 'fittingly situated in the very centre of the municipal life of the city'.[55] However, the area between Edmund Street and Great Charles Street was a network of dingy courts and passageways, and the complexities of multiple ownership and the rights of tenants and sub-tenants required several years of effort by G. J. Johnson before a sufficiently large area – about an acre – could be put together at a cost of £20,000, half of the site for immediate building and the rest for future development.

The principal elevation was on Edmund Street, facing Ratcliff Place and close to the Public Library.[56] The College comprised a basement and three storeys with mezzanines on part of the front and was built in a characteristic local red brick.[57] The style was described as 'Gothic of the 13th century with details largely derived from French architecture of that period' in Portland, Bath and local stone.[58] The central gable rose to 122 feet and was surmounted by Mason's crest – a mermaid – and the façade carried the shield of arms he had adopted, along with those of the City of Birmingham and the counties of Warwickshire and Worcestershire. There were sixty main windows in the front façade with geometrical tracery, and moulded and shafted jambs with carved capitals. The red-tiled roof was pierced with quaintly designed dormer windows, ornamental chimneys and turrets. Inside, the promise of the exterior was borne out with carved capitals and geometrical tracery, ornamental glass and fine wrought iron. The main staircase was enclosed in an arcade of moulded arches on polished Aberdeen granite. Great care was also given to the quality of the workmanship. It was asserted that the College, 'solid, strong and admirably finished throughout is qualified to stand for centuries'.[59] In the event it would be allowed to stand for less than one.

The initial building had a frontage of 150 feet and a depth of 140 feet, and was essentially laid out round a basement courtyard which was divided into west and east courts by stacked corridors, which ran south to north from the main entrance and at each of the higher levels and contained the main staircase. The ground-floor rooms facing Edmund Street housed the administration and the professors' common room and also provided accommodation for the Birmingham Natural History Society, to whose collections the College had access. Opposite, across the courts, were two 'noble apartments', 48 feet by 30, the one to the west, a physics laboratory, and the other the library. The remaining face of the west court was occupied with professors' rooms and the east with reading rooms and cloakrooms for women students. The basement was just below street level, and, as well as services, provided space for storage and the accommodation of live animals, and rooms for 'special operations in physics and chemistry'.

The major room on the first floor of the southern or entrance face was the chemistry lecture theatre over the main entrance, equipped to the state of the art, raked and capable of holding 155 students. A large preparation room was next door and a further room for demonstration material. In the opposite northern block was a less elaborate but similarly sized lecture theatre for physics and a somewhat smaller one for mathematics. The rest of the floor was occupied on the east by physics and the west, biology. On the second floor, over the entrance and lit by an oriel window, was a 1700-square-foot assembly and examination hall. The rest of that floor was occupied with rooms for the science professors and 3300 square feet of science laboratory, principally for chemistry. The professor of chemistry also had his own private laboratory. At third-floor level there were mezzanines on three sides (not the east) which provided further rooms and, over the front, a large museum for the fossil collection which the College had acquired. The whole building was heated by a warm air system, and sanitation – which had much concerned Mason when designing his orphanage – was 'ample and complete'. There was also a lift.

As opened the College was equipped for both male and female students – though not for female staff. Co-education had been the goal from the start but there is evidence that the trustees envisaged providing for women as a second stage, after the teaching for men had been properly set up. Dr T. P. Heslop said at the laying of the foundation stone:

> You will be glad to hear that there is a full provision made to enable the trustees to give instructions of every kind to women, when funds will permit of such an extension after the male sex have first been provided for. The old element of domination is here, but I suppose we shall not get rid of that yet.[60]

In the event, however, the first professors insisted on equal access, although the design of the building emphasised that from the start women were regarded as a different species of student. There were special reading rooms for them and in the great chemistry theatre a separate entrance was constructed for women to enter and sit behind the men – whether because they were seen as less serious than their male counterparts or as a dangerous distraction is not clear. It is not known if such segregation was provided in the other science lecture rooms.

On the night of 1 October 1880 much of the working design of the College was deliberately disguised, and one may wonder how many of the dancers appreciated that they were in a laboratory or how many of the great and good penetrated behind the decorations. One who had no need to do so was the host, Josiah Mason. In any case he was eighty-five and very deaf and it is doubtful whether he stayed much beyond the formalities. It was, indeed, to be his last public appearance. In the following June he fell while getting out of the bath, was put to bed and died a few days later, on 16 June 1881. He was buried in the grounds of his orphanage. The memorial card bracketed his two achievements:

> *I delivered the poor that cried , and the fatherless, and him that had none to help him* [JOB xxix 12]
>
> *By the blessing of the Lord I profited, and filled my winepress like a gatherer of grapes. Consider that I laboured not for myself only, but for all them that seek learning* [ECCLESIASTICUS xxxiii 16][61]

Notes

1 Sources for Mason's life are scarce. Unless otherwise indicated the following is derived from J. T. Bunce, *Life of Josiah Mason* (Birmingham 1882; expanded edn 1890). Mason gave some account of his career when the College foundation stone was laid in 1875: *Calendar 1880–1*, pp. 129–30.
2 UA Box 3: Josiah Mason & Family.
3 Her status can be inferred from her brother's.
4 UA: Box 3. Notes by Simon Parkes.
5 UC 7/iv/7/39.
6 UA: Box 3. Notes by Simon Parkes.
7 *Great Exhibition Catalogue* (1851), i.111 and Section III Class 23.
8 UA: Box 3. Notes by Simon Parkes.
9 Ibid.
10 UA Box 3: Josiah Mason & Family.
11 Ibid.
12 UA: Box 3. Notes by Simon Parkes.
13 For the above see P. T. Marsh, *Joseph Chamberlain, Entrepreneur in Politics* (New Haven, 1994), pp. 44–8, 75–6.
14 UA Box 3: Josiah Mason & Family.
15 Ibid.
16 J. M. Sanderson, ed., *The Universities in the Nineteenth Century* (1975), p. 156.
17 C. Gill and A. Briggs, *History of Birmingham* (1952), i.394–9.
18 For the following see E. W. Vincent and P. Hinton, *The University of Birmingham, its History and Significance* (Birmingham, 1947), pp. 39–58.
19 Gill and Briggs, *History of Birmingham*, i.394–6.
20 D. R. Jones, *The Origins of Civic Universities* (1988).
21 For Holloway see C. Bingham, *The History of Royal Holloway College, 1886–1986* (1987), pp. 15–66; J. Elliott, *Palaces, Patronage and Pills* (Egham, 1996).
22 Bunce, *Mason*, p. 98.
23 Bingham, *Royal Holloway College*, pp. 42–4.
24 J. H. Newman, *The Idea of a University* (Cambridge 1931), pp. 100–1.
25 Elliott, *Palaces*, p. 34.
26 Ibid. p. 36; Bingham, *Royal Holloway College*, pp. 74–6.
27 Sanderson, ed., *Universities in the Nineteenth Century*, p. 79.
28 Ibid., pp. 91–2.
29 W. H. G. Armytage, *Civic Universities* (1955), p. 223.
30 A. C. Wood, *A History of the University College Nottingham, 1881–1948* (Oxford, 1953), pp. 18–19.
31 Herbert Spencer, *Westminster Review*, 1859 quoted in Sanderson, ed., *Universities in the Nineteenth Century*, p. 126.
32 Bunce, *Mason*, p. 129; *Calendar 1880–1*, pp. 129–30.
33 *Calendar 1881–2*, p. 26.
34 Ibid., pp. 32–4.
35 Ibid., pp. 32–5.

36 *Birmingham Daily Post*, 24 Feb. 1875.
37 *Calendar 1881–2*, p. 26.
38 For the following see *Calendar 1880–1*.
39 UC 4/ii/28, pp. 1–2. Huxley's fee was £52 10s 0d.
40 UC 4/ii/7, pp. 85, 89.
41 *Calendar 1880–1*.
42 Ibid., p. 76.
43 Ibid.
44 Ibid.
45 Ibid., p. 77.
46 *Nine Famous Birmingham Men*, ed. J. H. Muirhead (1909).
47 *Calendar 1880–1*, p. 94.
48 Ibid., p. 111.
49 Ibid., p. 113.
50 Ibid., p. 166.
51 Ibid., pp. 116–28.
52 Ibid., p. 117.
53 Ibid., p. 122.
54 Ibid., p. 123.
55 *Calendar 1899–1900*, p. xxvi.
56 *Calendar 1880–1*, pp. 130–7; *1899–1900*, pp. xxv–vi and plans.
57 *Calendar 1880–1*, pp. 130–7.
58 Ibid., p. 130.
59 *Calendar 1899–1900*, p. xxvi.
60 *Birmingham Daily Post*, 24 Feb.1875.
61 Bunce, *Mason*, pp. 148–50.

Chapter Two

The first decade

GIVEN THAT HIGHER education outside Oxbridge was in its infancy in England and Wales in 1870, Josiah Mason had very little to go on when he decided to create a science college for Birmingham. Since 1858 the University of London had made available something approaching a national mechanism for syllabus and standards – hence Mason's surrender in the matter of a broad curriculum – but there was more to a college than examinations. At Manchester, the obvious exemplar, the twenty-year-old Owens College, had only just overcome its own teething troubles and the situation of University College and King's College in London was hardly comparable with Birmingham.[1] Elsewhere, virtually all other institutions in England and Wales were equally new. Only Scotland offered tested civic models for higher education.

It is clear that from the start the size and complexity of what was involved in setting up higher education in Birmingham was seriously underestimated. Mason's original allies in the project were his doctor, James Gibbs Blake, and his solicitor, G. J. Johnson, but neither were authorities on science teaching or even higher education, although Johnson had taught law at Queen's College.[2] Mason brought in four additional trustees in 1872 and of these two did have relevant experience – George Shaw as professor of chemistry at Queen's and T. P. Heslop as a former professor of physiology there – but W. C. Aitken was chief designer for a major brass and copper concern and the fourth, J. T. Bunce, was the editor of the *Birmingham Daily Post*.[3] In February 1873 Aitken, Blake and Shaw were formed into a subcommittee (with Shaw in the chair) to advise on what the College and its departments would need.[4] Their recommendations were presented to a full meeting of trustees in the following December and demonstrate that the scheme then envisaged was minimalist to a degree.[5] They proposed to begin by teaching only chemistry, with physics being added later, plus a possibility of mathematics as well, if resources allowed. They advised that for chemistry a lecture theatre to accommodate 150 would be needed and a laboratory for 75, with a professor and two or three assistants, plus menials; physics could do with a smaller staff but would need a similar sized teaching space, plus an apparatus room. At the same meeting Mason produced a scheme design for the College which he had commissioned (apparently quite independently). The author was a local architect, Jethro A. Cossins, a competent practitioner but with no experience in education.[6] Not until the following February, when the subcommittee was strengthened (by the addition of Heslop) and given the brief to consider Cossins's plans and elevations and recommend changes, is there evidence that the size of the task was beginning to be recognised.[7]

The cautious way would have been to erect basic rooms for teaching, simply equipped, and allow experience to lead to something more complex. However, what Sir Josiah wanted was a college specifically to teach science to a high level, and that required specialised planning and state-of-the-art facilities, down to lecture rooms designed and equipped for scientific demonstration with provision for coal gas, hydrogen, oxygen and water on tap, self-ventilating fume cupboards and all the rest.[8] The committee, therefore, with Mason's approval (and no doubt his money), decided that the architect needed to visit science colleges on the Continent and report on what was required.[9] This meant holding back the start of work until the autumn; the delay, however, was worth it. The design Cossins was then able to produce was enormously successful – all except for the heating system.[10] The buildings at Birmingham were described by the principal of Owens College, Manchester as 'as complete and perfect in their arrangement for the purposes required as any buildings in this country or on the Continent'.[11] The much vaunted attention to quality was reflected in the high cost – £60,000 for construction and equipment. Civic pride described the College as 'the finest building in Birmingham'.[12]

The 'learn-as-you-go' approach evident in the basic design probably also explains why a further sixty-eight months elapsed between the laying of the foundation stone in February 1875 and the opening of the College in October 1880 with some areas still unfinished. The first suggestion was to have part of the building sufficiently completed to allow chemistry teaching to begin in October 1878, but Mason vetoed that.[13] Then Founder's Day, 23 February 1880, was proposed but that was felt to be overambitious.[14] As late as June 1879 even an opening in 1880 appeared in doubt, and only in May of that year were the trustees confident enough to announce that the college courses would commence in October.[15] As the months went by the trustees continued to take fundamental decisions piecemeal, with George Shaw the only person of real experience. In the winter of 1876–7, long before any staff appointments, three of them were sent to London on the trail of second-hand science equipment.[16] At some stage they agreed to amend their planning to include facilities for the teaching of biology as well as chemistry and physics. In May 1879, seventeen months before the eventual opening, a decision was taken to provide facilities for teaching in mathematics.[17] It was possibly only in that same month that an examination hall was incorporated in the design, following the realisation that it would be desirable to have students tested in a recognised examination, which would mean conforming to the requirements of the University of London.[18] At no time, however, does the record indicate uncertainty. The trustees very wisely agreed in March 1877 that staff should be appointed twelve months in advance of opening to advise the architect on fittings, but in the event they ignored this and took all but the final decisions themselves.[19]

Confidence in the capacity of amateur trustees to decide what was best was as evident after October 1880 as it had been during the building phase of the College. So long as Mason was alive he continued to run the Science College project with six handpicked trustees. Officially Mason was bailiff (that is, chairman), but as founder he was also allowed an effective veto on decisions.[20] However, once the College had been opened, the emphasis changed from creating assets to managing them and the trustees decided to separate their legal from their managerial responsibilities. On 23 February 1881 they set up a Council to run the College.[21] It was to meet on the first Wednesday of every month, except for August and September, the bailiff would be ex-officio president or chairman and the Council would have two committees – Finance and General Purposes, and Library, Museums and House. None of the teaching staff was included. In all this Mason was represented by his nephew Martyn Smith, but on Mason's death the Trust was enlarged in accordance with the long-term provisions he had put in place.[22] The City became substantially responsible for the College by appointing five additional trustees, with the six foundation trustees being replaced by co-option as they died or resigned. Thus in August 1881 Thomas Avery, Joseph and Richard Chamberlain, George Dixon and Richard Martineau were appointed. These were all stalwarts of the civic gospel, with strong track records in education.[23] Previously each trustee had been on the College Council, but for obvious reasons Chamberlain (and future MPs) were excused such detailed work.[24] J. G. Blake became bailiff. The House Committee quickly became the effective academic policy management of the College and library matters were hived off to a separate committee in 1887.[25]

The clear expectation of the trustees was that they would run the College like a commercial company, with a Board laying down policy and taking all decisions and with professors and porters alike engaged on short-term contracts to do what they were told. Professorial posts were advertised in July 1879 with a closing date of 31 December.[26] Four three-year appointments were offered, in chemistry, physics, biology and mathematics, at salaries of £250 plus half the fees received (with £100 guaranteed). The notice was twelve months on either side – though the actual appointments were made with six months' notice by the professor and twelve by the college or salary in lieu, 'the intention being to afford an easy and considerate means of parting with the professor in case his labours should not have been altogether satisfactory'.[27] The trustees appear to have felt themselves quite competent to select staff without specialised advice, shortlisting on the basis of applications and testimonials and then calling for interview two candidates in mathematics and one in each of the other subjects. The interviews took place on Sunday 10 January 1880.[28] M. J. M. Hill, fellow of University College London, was offered the chair of mathematics and T. W. Bridge, biology; he was professor of zoology at Trinity College Dublin. Physics went to J. H. Poynting, fellow of Trinity College, Cambridge. In the case of chemistry, the invited candidate, W. Carleton Williams from Owens College, was not appointed and the post was offered to W. A. Tilden, the science master at Clifton College, without interview. Why this was so is not clear. The suspicion must be a disagreement among the trustees, because shortly afterwards, George Shaw, their one academic and a professional chemist to boot, resigned from the trust with a degree of ill feeling.[29] It may be that he had favoured Carleton Williams and had been overridden by his colleagues, or perhaps the issue was the chemistry professor's assistant. Certainly, when Tilden was shown the applications for that post he rejected the lot and persuaded the trustees to appoint his assistant from Clifton.[30]

Lack of familiarity with the nation's embryonic academic system led the trustees astray on a number of occasions. In July 1880 they applied to be affiliated to the University of London, only to discover that affiliation had been abandoned years before.[31] Likewise in 1882 application was made to the Medical Council for recognition of the lectures at Mason College when no such recognition existed.[32] The lack of an academic network also proved a problem. In 1881 the Council applied for its courses to be recognised by the two Royal Colleges of medicine and for the London 1st MB.[33] The Physicians were partly accommodating, the Surgeons effectively said 'no' and the London University Senate replied – very reasonably – that it was inexpedient to recognise in advance courses which had yet to be evaluated or even completed.[34]

What the trustees do not seem to have done is to exploit the experience of the men they appointed. Hill, Bridge, Poynting and Tilden made up an impressive quartet but the trustees took little account of them in policy-making. The latter two were appointed from 1 July, thus giving them not the year projected but a bare three months to prepare their new departments. Bridge had to agitate in order to secure a similar concession.[35] Hill was allowed no grace at all. In September 1880, immediately upon appointment, the professors submitted to the trustees a scheme for a board of studies, but this was deferred until after the opening.[36] In the event nothing happened then, and after one term the professors themselves decided that they would have to meet each month unofficially.[37] It took a full year's experience before the Council decided that an academic board really was needed.[38]

Even after the recognition that the professors were more than operatives, the trustees were determined to keep them in their place. An application to use the College boardroom for meetings of the new Academic Board was turned down, and so too their request to be given authority to spend within approved departmental budgets. Most demeaning of all, the Council insisted that the Academic Board minute book itself must be produced for each of its meetings, not merely the papers which the professors wished to put before Council.[39] When the professors replied that their Board would keep reports and notes of uncompleted business separately from its minutes, Council informed them that it would recognise no record of their actions except that in the minute book produced each month for its inspection.[40] The result was that the Academic Board ended up keeping four registers – a record of its agenda, minutes of its private business, a record of reports received by it and the formal minutes it presented to the House Committee for Council. It took three sessions before the chairman of the Academic Board was invited even to be present when these last were scrutinised.[41] Furthermore, since the chairmanship of the Academic Board rotated annually, the potential of the post was frozen. The trustees even insisted that the bailiff, not the chairman, should give approval for functions in the student common room between 6 p.m. and 10 p.m.![42] In 1887, despite evidence that the chairman's workload was increasing, the Council rejected a proposal for a three-year term of office and an honorarium.[43] Not until 1890 did it at last admit that the College needed internal leadership by appointing Professor Robert Heath as principal.[44] Even so the post was part-time – Heath remained head of mathematics – the honorarium of £100 did not make him the highest-paid employee, he had no responsibility for finance, plant or support staff, and he only acquired further powers piecemeal.[45] Heath's first move did secure the transmutation of the Academic Board into a Senate, but professors still put individual proposals direct to Council, and Council remained very active in all fields.[46]

The trustees were not above reminding the Academic Board that the Foundation Deed (clause 50) made them responsible for the academic work of the College and in the early years they were much concerned with the College's poor examination record.[47] Even detailed decisions concerning the curriculum had to be submitted to the Council.[48] In 1881 the lecturer in French proposed that evening classes should be offered in Italian.[49] This was refused. In 1882 Edward Arber was more successful when he applied to be allowed to add history to the teaching of the English department. He was, however, told that no change would be considered in the title of his chair and that 'English history should only be taught in the class of English language and literature in so far as to illustrate such language and literature'.[50] Academic research, too, was monitored. When Poynting wished to conduct an experiment to determine the weight of the earth, he very properly applied to the Council for permission to set up his apparatus because the work involved cutting a hole in the floor of one of the college rooms. However, while approving the request and agreeing to aid professors generally in their scientific enquiries, the Council ruled that professors had to seek approval on a case-by-case basis.[51] In October 1881 the newly appointed professor of physiology, J. B.

Haycraft, fell foul of this over the need to use live animals to continue his work on the metabolism of urea.[52] Some members of the Council were broadly favourable and a proposal that the College should apply to the Home Secretary for a vivisection licence was referred to the Trustees. However, Joseph Chamberlain and George Dixon opposed this and secured a deferment of the decision until July 1882. In the interval Haycraft reduced his request to be allowed to continue with his existing government licence *ad personam* but with Chamberlain's backing and a petition from local inhabitants the application was postponed *sine die*.[53]

The initial subordination of the academics seems nowhere more obvious than in the development of the range of the College's work. In February 1881 the Council did consider suggestions from the four professors for new chairs and lectureships, but these clearly counted for little since a trustees' meeting six weeks earlier had agreed on the appointments to be made.[54] These were certainly bold. The trustees had realised, as they said later, that students would only be recruited if a virtually full range of courses was on offer.[55] So they decided to introduce for 1881-2 almost all the other subjects promised in their original publicity, which meant a chair in geology and mineralogy (with application to mining and metals), a chair in physiology (with reference to the laws of health), lectureships in French and German, and lectureships (soon upgraded to chairs) in English and Greek and Latin language, plus a chair in civil and mechanical engineering and acceptance of Tilden's offer that metallurgy should be added to his existing responsibilities.[56] Of the original prospectus, only anatomy was omitted.[57] Once again the trustees took full control of the process. Haycraft was elected to the chair of physiology, apparently without interview, and candidates for the other posts were summoned for 10 May. Charles Lapworth was appointed in geology, R. H. Smith in engineering, Nathan Bodington in classics, Eugene Joel in French and Karl Dammann in German. No candidate for the English post proved suitable, so a further interview was needed before Edward Arber was appointed.[58] In the case of these new posts the share of fees was not guaranteed, and when the four original appointees came up for renewal their guarantee was withdrawn.[59] The only one of the four potentially affected was Bridge, but the trustees applied normal commercial logic and, in effect, told him to work harder. 'We think that he must look to the success of his teaching to provide him with adequate remuneration.'

The inspired amateurism of the trustees should not, however, be set against an assumed professionalism among those appointed to the teaching staff. There was no 'blueprint' for a science college and decisions in academic matters were also made piecemeal and generally from scratch. In May 1881 the professors decided that they needed to work out regular courses of study which they could specify to students.[60] A month later it was agreed that these would have to be geared to the needs of students taking external examinations.[61] That same month saw agreement on the timing of the college day, while in October 1881 it was decided that gowns should be worn on public occasions and that any junior members of staff should be given temporary permission to use the professorial common room.[62] In 1882 it was agreed that examination results should be divided into four grades.[63] Only the first three should be published, with the firsts in order of merit, second and thirds in alphabetical order. The next year they moved to three grades, 0% to 49%, 50% to 74% and 75% and over, with both the higher categories listed in order of merit.[64] Record-keeping had, of course, to be invented from scratch.[65] In June 1881 the professors decided that they would keep a note of attendances and notify parents of absences. Clearly this proved to be too informal, and in October 1883 the Academic Board agreed on the need to keep a collective record. Two years later a continuing college register was created, backdated to October 1884.

Not only were the professors learning how to run the College as they went along, certain of them also had to learn what was expected of their new status. The behaviour of some left a good deal to be desired. The control of property was weak, especially in biology. Early in 1881 Thomas Bridge took delivery of two microscopes from a local firm on approval. He sent them back after nine months, with one of them damaged and unsaleable. The firm complained and the House Committee had to step in and buy both.[66] At the end of the year Bridge was in trouble again when his demonstrator and a student in chemistry pawned some of the department's apparatus. He tried to argue that equipment was as much his demonstrator's responsibility as his, but the Council forced him to apologise and accept that departmental heads carried full liability.[67] Orders were also given that equipment should henceforth be labelled and inventories kept.[68] Financial discipline was hard to enforce. When Haycraft was appointed in physiology two trustees were put in charge of the spending of his equipment grant 'to avoid unnecessary duplication' with items bought for other chairs.[69] Whether this reflects prior knowledge of his propensities is not known. After six months in post Haycraft was before the House Committee for overspending. It made him a further grant and recorded that the professor: 'now fully understands that the expenditure in his department must be on a more moderate scale and must be regulated by schedules submitted to the committee and reported to Council for approval'.[70] Conviction or hope, the Committee's confidence was misplaced. Haycraft produced a further stack of unpaid invoices and the Finance and General Purposes Committee was compelled to report to Council in May 1882 that: 'Whilst strongly disapproving of the action of Professor Haycraft we see no other course but to recommend payment of the accounts and we desire that his letter of apology addressed to the Bailiff may be read to the Council.'[71] The Council had laid down the rule that professors had to have equipment orders countersigned, but the reality was that once a professor had placed an order, the College was effectively obliged to pay.[72] To try stop the practice in 1882–3 the bailiff even set up his own register of cheques issued.[73]

The determination of the trustees to remain in detailed charge was undoubtedly encouraged by a growing realisation that money would be tight. At the opening of the College much was rightly made of Sir Josiah Mason's generosity, and this went well beyond the actual endowment. In the first place he had handed over capital in advance, with the result that between 1875 and 1880, £14,989 accumulated in rent and interest over and above expenditure on the building.[74] Then Mason gave £5000 to cover the cost of the opening and in the following January he cleared all outstanding bills, so allowing the trustees to invest a further £10,250. He also promised £500 a year net of tax for the rest of his life.[75] The burst of appointments in the spring of 1881 was clearly a response to this and to optimism that Mason would be followed by other benefactors. By the autumn of 1882 the endowment amounted to £191,135 0s10d, with an expectation of £25,000 more in three years and a further £15,000 when various annuities fell in.[76]

It rapidly became clear, however, that expansion was not a soft option. The principal desire of the early trustees was to build up the College's endowment, but expansion necessarily meant diverting capital to premises and plant. The building had been designed for four departments; by October 1881 it had to be adapted to accommodate eleven. Where to put Engineering, with all its heavy equipment, was a particular headache. The obvious answer might seem to be to build over more of the site, but that meant ousting tenants and adding loss of income to reduction in capital. The trustees therefore settled on adding a fourth floor to the western block, dividing or reconfiguring existing accommodation and squeezing an annexe into a corner of the site – the first of a succession of contrivings which, over the years, would turn the original symmetrical design into a rabbit warren.[77] The pressure on funds and on space was made even worse in 1882 when it became imperative to create the chair in botany and vegetable physiology to which William Hillhouse was appointed.[78] By October initial calculations were indicating that the out-turn for the financial year ending 29 September 1882 would be bad. Departmental estimates for the next session had to be slashed and the bailiff was asked to meet the science professors to explain the seriousness of the situation.[79] When the audited accounts of the college were published in February 1882 the Council was forced to admit in print that expansion was on a knife-edge. 'For the advancement of knowledge, whether of Professors or Students, all modern resources should be obtainable, unchecked by fear of insufficient income', but all that could realistically be hoped for to meet rising costs was an expanding fee income, opportunities to increase rents and income 'from other sources'.[80]

The full accounts of the College survive only from 1894, but for earlier years there are unpublished abstracts, and the Council did publish final balances. Together, these sources show that from the very beginning the College always operated at a loss. In its comments to the published balances the Council regular-

Table 2.1 Mason College: annual deficits, 1881–6 (£)[81]

Period	*Income*	*Expenditure*	*Deficit*	*Ordinary*	*Special factors*
1881-2	5476	12424	6948	841	6107
1882–3	7331	8095	764	4	1260*
1883–4	6817	8175	1358	358	1000
1884–5	7309	8450	1141	578	563
1885–6	7086	8731	1646	1075	571

Note: * £500 of the special expenditure was covered by a payment from Mason's estate.

ly pointed out that figures were affected by special expenditure on start-up and development, or (less frequently) by receipts from Mason's estate.

Unfortunately it was the total shortfall which the College had to cover, and with income effectively static or worse, the trustees turned to the £14,989 saved in the building years. By the start of the financial year September 1885 to September 1886, all that was left of this was £3066.[82] In that year exceptional expenditure was low, but the ordinary deficit leaped to £1075 and the Council publicly forecast that the reserves would soon be exhausted.[83] Thereafter the College would have to pay its way, year on year, and from 1886–7 the Council began to publish income and expenditure figures as well as balances. The position revealed for that year was certainly disturbing.[84] Expenditure (£8593) exceeded income (£7253) by a staggering 18.5%. A loss of that size was exceptional, but to the year 1890–1 the annual deficit was never less than 6%.[85]

Surprisingly, to modern eyes, the Council seems to have remained bullish despite the increasing current account deficit. Its members were well aware that the situation could not last, but they appeared determined not to impede development in the meantime. The College was encouraged to take on additional students and new work, even though these did not cover the costs involved.[86] One possible reason why financial signals never went beyond 'caution' was the size of Josiah Mason's endowment. The income this produced was, by the end of the first ten years, covering less than half of college outgoings, but the capital did provide ample collateral.[87] Moreover, the College could borrow at 4%. Thus servicing the £2482 of debt which had been accumulated by 1890–1 cost only about £100 a year.

The heavy loss on 1886–7 was, it is true, followed by severe cuts in the library and in the support for science teaching, and the trustees continued to be cautious about professorial demands for departmental improvements.[88] These are exemplified by an impassioned plea from Professor Tilden in 1889 for more funds for

Chemistry. He asserted that his department was the College's biggest earner, bringing in over 25% of day-student fees, and that it was also the most economic, costing the endowment £2 1s 5d per student against £10 a head in Engineering and Biology![89] But while damping down such arguments, the Council never gave any hint of major retrenchment or restructuring, but rather continued to draw attention to special factors: in 1888–9 it was the cost of special apparatus and for building repairs; in 1890–1 increased staff costs and, again, building.[90]

Instead of damaging economies the College put its faith in new resources. In every report from 1884–5 the Council stressed the need for further endowment and published the names of the increasing number of benefactors. An Additional Endowment Fund was set up in 1884, initially to fund scholarships.[91] This quickly reached £5000 and by 1891 had grown to £11,000.[92] In parallel with such efforts to raise funds locally, Mason College took an active part in the national campaign to secure government support for higher education in England of the sort enjoyed in the other countries of the UK.

The College's involvement began in April 1886 when Professor Tilden, then chairman of the Academic Board, attended a meeting of mainly English university colleges held at King's College London.[93] Further meetings in the summer and autumn put in hand a parliamentary campaign to be supported by public meetings and in April 1887 the Mason professors urged the College Council to act.[94] Public meetings had already been held in other towns, a deputation was about to go to government, a Commons motion was for debate in May and if Birmingham did not raise its voice soon, it would lose out. The particular importance of this to Mason College could hardly be exaggerated. Statistics prepared for the Treasury showed that where Owens College, Manchester was running an unsatisfactory 4% deficit, Mason's was up at 12%. A successful town meeting was laid on within the month and several Mason College trustees and professors (among them Joseph Chamberlain) took part in the deputation which subsequently went to the Lord President of the Council.[95] The government was persuaded to offer £15,000 and Mason College's share was £1400 in a full year which placed her third equal among the provincial colleges.[96]

If he had lived, Josiah Mason would in 1890 have been ninety-five years old. What might he have made of the College he had set up? It was still substantially under the control of the men he had appointed. Its links with the City were, as he intended, close. His magnificent building was fully used, indeed, under pressure of space, and it was staffed by men of ability (as we shall see). Striking progress had been made in starting from the concept and the funding for advanced education in Birmingham and translating both into a structured and effective institution, working virtually from scratch – an achievement which appears even more remarkable from the vantage point of a century later. Mason must, however, have been disappointed by discovering that although his had been an exceptional benefaction, the income it produced for the College was insufficient for his objectives. Not for the last time, higher education had proved to cost far more than was expected. Where Mason would also most certainly have been disturbed would be to discover that his gospel of the determinative importance of science for industry was still being substantially ignored. Thomas Huxley had, in his address at the opening of the College, flatteringly suggested that Sir Josiah's own career was demonstration enough that the age of 'practical men' who had no time for training was over. In the event Birmingham had not been persuaded.[97] As we shall see again, manufacturing had not taken full advantage from having science training available on the doorstep. The practical man was very much alive. Indeed, it was possible to argue, and not for the last time, that in an economy with a substantial sector of small trades, practicality is the only way to survive in Birmingham. And given that the ethos of industry remained stubbornly empirical, employees inevitably concurred with the priorities of their employers. The discovery that his college 'for practical science' was heavily in demand for other than science might well have shocked the old man.

Notes

1 Jones, *Origins of Civic Universities*, pp. 51–2.
2 *Calendar 1881–2*, p. 26. For Johnson see Vincent and Hinton, *University of Birmingham*, passim and C. A. Vince, *History of the Corporation of Birmingham*, iv (1923), 251; Blake was Mason's doctor: UA Box 3: Josiah Mason & Family.
3 For Shaw and Heslop see Vincent and Hinton, *University of Birmingham*, passim; for Aitken see Gill and Briggs, *History of Birmingham*, I, passim; for Bunce see Vincent and Hinton, *University of Birmingham*, Vince, *Corporation of Birmingham*, iv.377–9 and *Who was Who 1897–1915*.
4 UC 4/ii/7, p. 5.
5 Ibid., pp. 8–9.
6 Cossins was related to Mason and later built several of Birmingham's public libraries and undertook alterations to the Town Hall in 1891: Vince, *Corporation of Birmingham*, iii.167, 258.
7 UC 4/ii/7, p. 13.
8 *Calendar 1880–1*, pp. 128–37.
9 UC 4/ii/7, p. 14.
10 *Calendar 1894–5*, p. 358.
11 Ibid., *1880–1*, p. 105.
12 Ibid., p. 132.
13 UC 4/ii/7, pp. 45–6.
14 Ibid., pp. 57–8.
15 Ibid., pp. 64, 94.
16 Ibid., pp. 39–40.
17 Ibid., pp. 61–2.
18 Ibid.

19 Ibid., p. 44.
20 See above, n. 13.
21 UC 4/i/22, p. 1.
22 UC 4/ii/7, p. 188.
23 Vince, *Corporation of Birmingham*, iii, iv, passim.
24 UC 4/i/22, p. 1; 4/ii/7, p. 208.
25 UC 4/ii/8, p. 175.
26 UC 4/ii/7, p. 65.
27 UC 4/i/15, p. 137.
28 For the following see UC 4/ii/7, p. 76; for Tilden see *Dictionary of National Biography* (henceforth *DNB*), *1916–28*.
29 UC 4/ii/7, pp. 85, 87.
30 Ibid., p. 79.
31 Ibid., pp. 101–2, 105.
32 UC 4/i/22, pp. 57, 59.
33 Ibid., pp. 20, 22.
34 Ibid. pp. 42, 43, 49.
35 UC 4/ii/7, pp. 65, 87.
36 Ibid., p. 112.
37 UC 4/ii/12, p. 1.
38 UC 4/i/22, pp. 33–4.
39 UC 4/ii/8, pp. 7–9.
40 Ibid., pp. 10, 14; 4/i/22, p. 61.
41 UC 4/ii/8, p. 50.
42 Ibid., p. 38.
43 UC 4/ii/9, pp. 111–15, 121.
44 UC 4/ii/7, pp. 232–3.
45 UC 4/ii/8, p. 262; e.g. the Library: *Calendar 1892–3*, p. 356. Tilden was better paid.
46 UC 4/ii/11, pp. 121–4; 4/ii/8, p. 217; *Calendar 1891–2*, pp. 239–40. Heath was not the ablest man on the staff, and it is arguable that he was approached only because he was the current chairman of the Academic Board.
47 UC 4/ii/8–9, pp. 7, 58, 91–3.
48 UC 4/ii/8, p. 110.
49 UC 4/i/15, p. 38.
50 Ibid., p. 61.
51 UC 4/i/22, pp. 4–5; 4/ii/7, pp. 178–9.
52 UC 4/i/22, pp. 32–3; 4/ii/7, p. 189.
53 UC 1/i/3/1–2.
54 UC 4/i/22, p. 2; 4/ii/7, pp. 176–7.
55 UC 4/ii/11, p. 45; 4/ii/8, pp. 96–7.
56 UC 4/ii/7, pp. 177, 179.
57 *Calendar 1880–1*, pp. 21–2.
58 UC 4/i/22, pp. 11–13. He was not a good colleague; see below, p. 38.
59 UC 4/i/15, p. 137.
60 UC 4/ii/12, p. 3.

61 Ibid., p. 3v. The trustees had earlier considered adopting the University of London examinations entirely: UC 4/ii/7, pp. 61–2.
62 UC 4/ii/12, pp. 3v, 4v.
63 UC 4/ii/11, p. 2.
64 UC 4/ii/8, p. 44.
65 UC 4/ii/12, p. 3v; 4/ii/11, p. 9; 4/ii/9, p. 58.
66 UC 4/i/15, p. 38.
67 UC 4/i/22, pp. 35, 38, 45.
68 Ibid., p. 35.
69 Ibid., p. 18.
70 UC 4/i/15, p. 57.
71 Ibid., pp. 67, 73.
72 Ibid., p. 38.
73 UC 4/ii/28, pp. 24–5.
74 *Calendar 1889–90*, p. 228.
75 UC 4/ii/7, pp. 156, 174.
76 *Calendar 1883–4*, p. 191; UC 4/ii/7, pp. 193–6.
77 UC 4/i/15, p. 19.
78 UC 4/i/22, pp. 57–8, 60. The appointment was linked with negotiations with Queen's College.
79 UC 4/ii/28, p. 17. Cf. the moratorium on additional expenditure in 1884–5: ibid., p. 33.
80 *Calendar 1883–4*, p. 191.
81 UC i/i/6; *Calendar 1883–4*, p. 191; *1884–5*, p. 213; *1885–6*, p. 224; *1886–7*, p. 226. The *Calendar* appeared for the start of each session, hence the accounts printed are for the year ending Michaelmas, twelve months earlier. Amounts have been rounded to the nearest pound.
82 *Calendar 1886–7*, p. 226; *1887–8*, p. 239.
83 Ibid., *1887–8*, p. 239.
84 Ibid., *1888–9*, p. 265.
85 *Calendars* passim.
86 Cf. *Calendar 1889–9*, p. 265 and UC 4/ii/23, pp. 135–6, 145–6.
87 *Calendar 1899–1900*, p. xxvii..
88 Ibid., *1889–90*, pp. 228–9.
89 UC 4/i/18, Sept. 1889.
90 *Calendar 1889–9*, p. 285; *1890–1*, p. 234.
91 Ibid., *1885–6*, p. 221; *1887–8*, p. 240.
92 In 1884, £4450 was pledged and £1100 paid, plus £229 per annum: UC 4/ii/28, pp. 31–2; *Calendar 1892–3*, p. 46. However, the fund in 1898 only stood at £11,197: *1899–1900*, p. xxvii.
93 UC 4/ii/9, p.77.
94 Ibid., pp. 82, 91, 102–3.
95 Ibid., p. 105, *Calendar 1889–9*, p. 266.
96 Treasury Minute, 11 Mar. 1889.
97 See below, pp. 35–6.

Chapter Three

Towards a university

THE ADVENT OF government funding for English higher education was 'a cloud like a man's hand'. It would, however, be wrong to see it as the answer to the problems of higher education in Victorian England. Given that the Welsh colleges each received £4000 (and still could not keep out of deficit), the 1887 grant of £15,000 for England was niggardly, to say the least, and it was also only guaranteed for three years. Whatever the effect on other institutions, it certainly did not take Mason College out of the wood. The government grant of £1400 represented 14.6% of the College's total income in the first year of operation, but left the Council still facing a 6.5% shortfall.[1]

One of the first matters to which Robert Heath addressed himself on appointment as principal was the possibility of a campaign to secure an increased level of government support. He found it difficult to revive enthusiasm generally because several of the other college principals were fearful of jeopardising the possibilities of the existing grant being continued.[2] In February 1891, however, Joseph Chamberlain led a deputation to the Chancellor of the Exchequer to request an increase. The response was a call for statistics and information about the level of financial support from the Birmingham community.[3] In November 1893 a further attempt was made, but extracted only a promise that the existing grant would be continued and a request for yet more figures.[4] Eventually, however, a government commission was appointed to review the use of the existing grant. Mason College was inspected in July 1896 and the following year the grant to the College was increased to £2,700.[5]

The 1897 grant came with the proviso that £975 of the extra should be spent on staff. This allowed the Council to put all demonstrators on to £125 a year and both to raise the pay of professors and reduce their dependence on student fees.[6] What it did not do, any more than the earlier award had done, was to make the College solvent. The new grant amounted to 17.5% of revenue but left a shortfall of 15.8%. The root of the problem was the lack of sufficient financial support from the region. In 1885 the professors had begun to plan for commercial training.[7] In January of the next year the trustees asked them to devise courses for manufacturers, metallurgists, architects, teachers and other specialists.[8] In March 1886 the House Committee raised the subject of courses in agriculture.[9] In 1887 the Academic Board approved a scheme to train architects and builders.[10] Yet none of this came to anything. As the Council explained in its 1887 report, no significant donor had yet come forward to augment Mason's original gift.[11]

The Council did take the risk of launching a department of mining and colliery management in 1884. The needs of local industry seemed so obvious. The first professor was John Brown, past president of the North Staffordshire Institute of Mining and Mechanical Engineering, and his department was opened by the MP for North Staffordshire.[12] Brown resigned within the year but early reaction had been encouraging and the trustees persevered.[13] However, when their second appointee left for Australia in May 1889 the Council suspended the department.

> In doing so they cannot but express regret that, notwithstanding repeated efforts, by advertisement, by circulars addressed to all the works concerned, and by personal interviews, they have been unable to stimulate in the Midland mining district any disposition to take advantage of the means of scientific instruction for mine managers, &c., offered by the Mining Department of the College.[14]

It was not that unreasonable demands in time had discouraged students – two hours a week, timed late on Monday afternoons to minimise the loss of work-time![15] In 1895–6 Staffordshire County Council did offer £120 a year to support a chair of mining (in return for four free places), but despite the College Council's approaching Warwickshire and Worcestershire, neither county saw 'their way to make a similar grant, or in fact to make a grant at all'.[16]

The local reaction to the potential of the College was quixotic to a degree. Even when initial sponsorship was on offer interest could be very lukewarm. In 1882 George Dixon, a trustee and also a member of the Birmingham School Board, suggested two new chairs, in education and in political economy, and offered £1000 towards each.[17] The gift would have produced £80 towards a salary bill of £500, so one can understand why a subcommittee of trustees recommended that political economy should be postponed, but even when Dixon offered to put the whole £2000 to education the proposal fell through. The local teachers' association said that the time was not right. The professor of the history, theory and practice of education at St Andrews was consulted and he cast doubt on what 'a person called a Professor of Education' might do.[18] The clerk to the local School Board advised that teachers would perceive no need for instruction and would not come forward in sufficient numbers: 'there is more conceit in the world in reference to teaching than any other thing'. No professor was ever appointed. A series of ten lectures was given instead by a visiting lecturer from London.[19]

Yet while subsidised courses in mining and education were spurned, local demands were made on the College which took no regard for economic realities. Had not Mason's purpose been to provide free education to meet local needs? There were calls for scholarships, calls for fee concessions and requests for courses for specialised audiences. In 1885 a delegation from the Birmingham Trades Council called on the Council to press the College to put on evening classes to provide trade training for Birmingham artisans, inevitably at a subsidised rate.[20] The memorandum recording the Council's response to the visit is remarkably frank:

> Soon after the opening of the College it became clear that its success would largely depend on its power to afford the students a complete or nearly complete curriculum both on the Arts and Science side. The arrangements required imposed a great and unexpected burden on the financial resources at the disposal of the Trustees, the weight of which is seriously felt at the present time.

The Council accepted that there was a need in the town for good technical instruction, but the College could only take on additional evening-class work on a sound economic basis. Trade training would necessarily have to be organised broadly and involve four or five departments and must depend on extra resources becoming available. The trustees, indeed, were very ready to see someone else take on the task:

> They are equally convinced that it is not their duty to interpose any obstacle in the way of this desirable work being undertaken by any other institution possessed of the requisite means; or to divert in favour of this College, any interest that a private society may evince in the performance of such work in any other place of education.

In other words, the College could not do everything and the Council had decided to specialise in university work. The fact that the professors entered this memorandum in their report book shows how worried they had been that demands on the College would drag them away from the university objective.[21]

The fears of the professors are entirely understandable, given the problems which evening work had presented from the start. The plan for the College had envisaged a twofold mission.[22] The first was to provide 'regular systematic instruction' during the day to qualify students to pass examinations for degrees of London University or 'any profession or pursuit in which scientific knowledge can be usefully applied'. The second was to provide evening classes. This evening work was described as 'popular instruction' but that referred not to the teaching but to the audience – artisans and others who could not attend in the day. They were to be offered systematic courses in the same way as day students and in the spring session 1881 Chemistry recruited its first class of forty-nine, and Physics and Biology twenty-nine and twenty-eight students respectively.[23]

The professors, however, felt that evening work did not justify the effort involved and the Council tried to meet them first by increasing the professorial share of the evening fees for the session 1881–2 from one-half to two-thirds.[24] The staff appointed in 1881 had been told to expect to give twenty evening lectures each session and in 1881–2 at least ten subjects were offered in the autumn and eleven in the spring.[25] Attendance, however, did not increase in proportion. Only 236 students enrolled, 101 of them women, and according to figures kept by the Academic Board, five classes before Christmas and seven after had fewer than fifteen students.[26] At the end of the session the professors advised that fewer subjects should be offered for 1882–3. The Council refused the request, only to discover that evening enrolments in 1883-4 fell even further. The councillors remained adamant that evening work had to be continued in order to comply with Mason's intentions, but all they could do was to concede all the fees to the teachers, that is, to agree to run the courses at a loss.[27] Thereafter 'systematic' evening work continued but with decreasing confidence.[28] Twelve became the average size of group. Admittedly, a high fee of threepence a lecture was asked in order to avoid undercutting the Midland Institute, but even so the return to a teacher for a session of such work was only £3. By the end of the first decade it had to be accepted that Mason's vision of energetic artisans seizing the chances to train in their spare time which he had not had, was not going to be realised.

Setting a science college up from scratch was never going to be easy, but against the problems have to be set the successes. One of these was, in fact, in the contentious area of evening lectures. As we have seen, systematic evening instruction was not popular, either with students or staff, so the professors determined on a publicity drive. They proposed a new series of eight evening lectures a session which were free and truly 'popular', directed to no examination but specifically intended to create interest in study. Council replied, grudgingly, that it had 'no objection' to this, provided the systematic classes were maintained.[29] A committee of professors and local manufacturers was set up to run the new classes and invitations were issued via companies. Topics were chosen which were popular, the lectures were simple and illustrated, and proved to be an enormous success. In 1884–5 (the second session of the scheme) average attendance reached 550 and because no available hall was large enough, each lecture had to be repeated.[30] In the six years to 1888–9, total attendance reached 17 000. In that year the topics were: 'Sir Isaac Newton', 'The Atmosphere', 'A Living Machine' (the human body), 'A Grain of Mustard Seed', 'Colour', 'The Pebbles of the Fields' and 'The Forth Bridge'.[31] The lectures were eventually abandoned on blatantly chauvinistic grounds. Workmen who received tickets had begun to pass them on to their wives and daughters![32] The professors, however, discovered that they could recruit good numbers of men who would pay for evening short courses aimed at particular trade groups: master bakers, brewers, jewellers or even members of the Birmingham Fire Insurance Institute.[33] The 1891–2 course on 'Cast Iron' had an audience of 154.

An even more important development also began in the unlikely soil of 'systematic' evening work. Nearly half the early demand came from schoolteachers. This followed discussions early in 1881 with central government and the Birmingham School Board over the admission of teachers at concessionary rates or with subsidised fees, and over one hundred teachers enrolled for courses in 1881–2.[34] For some reason the scheme failed. Perhaps students chose courses with very little relevance to professional needs – the heaviest demand was for French, more than for all the sciences put together. Perhaps the standard was low; certainly the professors were complaining about this at the end of the session.[35] However, in the summer of 1884, E. A. Sonnenschein, the professor of classics, began to discuss with the School Board the possibility of a fresh approach. What emerged first was a scheme with a possible fifty takers for a two-year course exclusively for certificated teachers leading to the University of London matriculation. The fee was double the usual threepence a lecture but was paid by the School Board.[36] In February 1885 the Academic Board put a syllabus in hand.[37] Edward Arber, the professor of English, disliked Sonnenschein and was not enthusiastic – but the Council was and whipped the recalcitrant into line.[38] At the end of the year the scheme was elaborated by adding the possibility of a College certificate for two years' work in three subjects which the Council believed would encourage recruitment.[39] By 1889 active discussions were taking place for Mason to be involved in a possible college in Birmingham for the day training of elementary school teachers – as against their attending one of the existing residential colleges or not being trained at all. Existing Mason College courses would, it was felt, be entirely suitable, although a new elementary class in English would be needed 'for the women and the more backward of the men'.[40]

The publication of the 1890 Education Code provided the go-ahead. A local committee was formed (with Mason College represented), and in October forty women students enrolled in the Birmingham Day Training College for Elementary Teachers.[41] They were based in the Birmingham and Midland Institute, dined in Queen's College and had academic lectures at Mason College in three subjects in each of two years.[42] Principal Heath reported that the education students were 'as able as others and in some subjects more so' and it is clear that he was behind much of the drive for teacher training.[43] In February 1893 he pointed out that there was no facility to train men for elementary schools and none to train anyone for secondary teaching, a deficiency to be found throughout the UK.[44] What was needed was first a professor of mental and moral philosophy, which would probably mean appointing a bright Oxbridge candidate and sending him abroad to read the subject up. Then the existing Day Training College could become the nucleus of a Mason department of education. The following year Heath lowered his aim. He proposed that the College should establish a Day Training Department in elementary education for 'the majority' of its male students in the arts who were 'merely boys of quite ordinary intelligence who have acquired a certain power of passing examinations' and found it hard to find employment.[45]

Eventually, in March 1894 the principal successfully proposed that the existing day college for women should become the women's section of 'the department of education' at Mason College.[46] Funds were secured and the women moved into converted premises on Charles Street in October 1896.[47] In the same month the men's side accepted its first intake of four students.[48] As it happened, the men presented problems. Some came from a distance and this was creating a need for a residential hostel 'where students can be placed under some sort of supervision'.[49] Heath also became somewhat disillusioned on the issue of national standards. He complained in 1899 that male recruits in education were often not very able and that, because Mason College standards were high, many of its students came out with poorer certificates than if they had taken the easier route of attending a residential training college.[50]

Not all of Robert Heath's plans had as successful an outcome. One which did not take off was the proposal for an agricultural department which formed a major section of his 1894 report.[51] Earlier attempts had, he argued, failed owing to lack of funds, but County Councils had recently had finance provided specifically for this purpose, and the newly created Board of Agriculture was prepared to subsidise educational programmes. Other colleges were there already – notably Bangor – and Mason already had the staff and equipment to teach all the scientific and managerial part of a possible course. Husbandry, stock management and horticulture would need to be added but could be covered by a professor, a special lecturer and visiting lecturers. Practical demonstrations would require access to a working farm but the Corporation Farm would be ideal, backed up by the Botanical and Horticultural Society's gardens. It was, Heath pointed out not for the first time, vital to tie the College to as many of such local industries as possible, and if Mason College did not move in the near future, 'the County Councils will each be making their own arrangements, and then it will be too late'.

Along with innovation – successful and unsuccessful – there was a constant pressure within the College to raise the level and quality of academic activity. Research had been undertaken by the professors from the earliest days but by the 1890s junior members of staff were active, too. In the physics department in the year to February 1895, work was in progress on the calorific value of gas, on radiation, on fluorescence and on the electrical resistance of alloys.[52] Postgraduate research, on the other hand, faced great difficulties. Chemistry appears to have had one research scholarship and in 1893 a legacy from a Dr Aubrey Bowen of Melbourne made it possible to establish three more awards in the department (each of the first holders published within a year), plus one scholarship in metallurgy and three in engineering.[53] However, apart from special benefactions there were no funds generally available. In a first report as professor of physics, Percy Frankland wrote in 1895: 'It would immensely strengthen our position as a place of higher education if we could hold out some inducement to our students to continue their work with us after graduation.' Similar comments were made by Bridge, the professor of zoology, and he implied that he was actually turning away suitable postgraduates: 'On several occasions in the past the Professor has felt the need of such scholarships in connection with his own department and the experience of the past session has supplied an additional example of their desirability.'[54] Certainly, in the following year one of his senior undergraduates was good enough to publish a paper in the *Journal of Anatomy and Physiology* on the anatomy of the frog.[55]

The professors also kept up a constant pressure to improve facilities. In 1894 MacNeile Dixon, newly appointed to the chair of English, pointed out the serious deficiencies his subject faced in library provision and the next year the professor of French called for the purchase of a set of French classics, a selection of modern French literature (both fiction and criticism) and some up-to-date publications on linguistics.[56] The German department, meanwhile, set up its own student library of 1000 volumes which it claimed was 'the finest of its kind in the kingdom'.[57] Scientists were even more vociferous and much more expensive, even though local industry was often generous in donating particular items of equipment.[58] Not only was it necessary in existing areas of work to be 'state of the art', the whole field of science was expanding. In geology, demand came from the advent of 'petrology'. An assistant professor was appointed but space became wholly inadequate, with three classes being held in the one laboratory at the same time. There were also problems over access to the geology museum via an examination room; rectifying these cost £250, though this was partly covered by a donation of £100, collected by the professor's friends and admirers.[59] In physics, the arrival of 'electro-technics' on the syllabus was particularly expensive, developing rapidly and requiring 'complete reconstruction' of the laboratory in 1894 'if we are to retain our proper place in the educational work of the city'.[60] The Council provided £5000 for this, only to be greeted in 1895 with the warning that now the inadequate equipment for the teaching of electrical engineering was threatening the status of the College: 'It would be a grave misfortune if the teaching of Electrical Engineering were allowed to pass out of our hands, as it must if we cannot improve our equipment.'[61] By now it can have come as no surprise to College councillors that when a separate department of technical electricity was set up in 1896, they were told that 'the need for further equipment' had now become 'very pressing'.[62] The helical imperative for investment in science was well under way.

One basic consideration motivated these developments and pressures. This was the need to establish the place of Mason College both in the national higher education league and as the natural focus for higher education in the Midlands. As early as February 1882 the College contemplated a protest at being excluded from government recognition for the training for engineering posts in India.[63] In 1886 the college staked a claim to be one of the constituent colleges in the scheme for the University of London then being promoted by its Convocation.[64] Three years later the College hosted the (ultimately successful) opposition to an alternative proposal recommended by the Royal Commission on a teaching university for London.[65] This would have turned the existing University of London, with its national examination machine, into a local teaching university and left provincial colleges marginalised. In 1891–2 Mason College was active in opposing a third scheme for London, this time to give a royal charter to Gresham's College.[66] And, as we have seen, the College mobilised all its influence in Birmingham and at Westminster behind the campaign first to secure and then to increase state funding for higher education in England.

This national agenda was also clear in the attempts made to assert Mason College's standing in the 'university' sector. In September 1886 the College entertained the fourth meeting of the British Association for the Advancement of Science.[67] In the following December it played host to a meeting of the principals of 'the modern university colleges'.[68] The core activity in the teaching was, as we shall see, carefully presented as degree-related. Students not intending to take a recognised examination were registered as 'occasional' and those studying metallurgy, engineering, mining and medicine as 'technical', but those studying for examinations which could lead to an eventual degree in science or the arts were all categorised as 'university'.[69] In February 1882 the college staff proposed that in the absence of degree powers, an 'associateship of the college' should be created.[70] The non-academics were unenthusiastic at first and the proposal got past a sceptical Council only in May 1884 and in a modified form.[71] Under the regulations approved, holders of British university degrees were immediately qualified to be associates as also holders of the College's Senior Engineering Diploma. Other students of the College had to take three courses in different sections of the College in each of two years and an approved course for a third session. The Council also decided to make honorary awards of the associateship for original research, distinguished merit or special service by past members of staff. On the last ground the first curator of the geology museum was made an associate on his retirement in 1887.[72]

The associateship seems to have been generally welcomed, though the award never became the distinction for all graduates in the Midlands which was intended. Five people were elected in 1884 and by 1889 the total had only reached nineteen.[73] In 1890, however, thirty-five were elected. There was a further influx in 1893 when the rules were changed, and also in 1897 when the award was opened to medical practitioners trained at Queen's College.[74] By 1900, when the granting of a university charter and the right to confer degrees made the award unnecessary, 158 associates had been elected in all.

The goal of regional hegemony was also never far from the mind, particularly of the professors. In 1885 an Academic Board working party summed the feeling up when it reported 'that for the full development of higher education in the Midlands an independent university centre in Birmingham is desirable'.[75] This thinking accounts for the strong professorial interest in the University Extension scheme run from Cambridge. This had been pioneered in the 1870s, as we have seen, and it was anxious to expand into new territories. In 1883 a representative of Cambridge visited Birmingham to explain the programme to the House Committee, which was left in no doubt that several Mason College professors were strongly in favour.[76] Early in 1887 a college delegation went to the University to explore possibilities and the Academic Board formally advised the Council of the need to take part.[77] Between December and February 1892 the staff made a final and successful push. 'It is of vital importance that some steps should be taken by which the gradual control of the movement in the Midland district may be secured by the College.' The future depended on Mason College being 'recognized as the centre of the highest education in the Midlands'.[78] A plan was drawn up to take responsibility for Birmingham and the surrounding district (with an emphasis on the teaching of technology), while acting jointly with Cambridge in Staffordshire, Worcestershire and Warwickshire.[79] Prototype courses started in 1892 and in the following February Mason College held a large conference on University Extension in the Midlands which put the machinery in place.[80]

The biggest step which Mason College took towards this goal was to take over Birmingham's medical education. The opening of the College in 1880 had inevitably posed a question about the town's existing provision for the study of medicine at Queen's College. Why should science teaching continue to be provided there, specially for medical students, when 150 yards away there was a new college, far better equipped and teaching the very subjects medical students required? Unofficial negotiations began in November 1881 and it was agreed early in 1882 that the chairs of botany, chemistry and physiology at Queen's should go – with their current holders becoming emeritus professors of Mason College – and their respective equivalents at Mason being appointed to Queen's.[81] Classes in botany for medical students began at Mason College in the summer and the rest in the autumn.[82]

Three years later came the next moves. A further agreement was entered into for the teaching of science and two of the senior staff of Queen's became co-opted trustees of Mason.[83] Soon after, a committee of professors recommended to the Academic Board that the first step towards degree status should be for Mason and Queen's to federate, and joint discussions began in 1886 with a common mind on both sides.[84] There were, however, three obstacles. As well as its medical faculty, Queen's College taught up to twenty theology students a year and Sir Josiah had frowned on such teaching.[85] Secondly, the medical staff at Queen's, led by its dean, Bertram Windle, saw the move as a chance to secure new accommodation.[86] Finally, experience was proving that Mason College was teaching medical students at a loss. Agreement was eventually reached early 1891 and ratified by the Court of Chancery a year later. Queen's continued as a separate charity for the theologians but the medics joined Mason College in October 1892, with a mixture of new and adapted accommodation.[87]

One possible (indeed hoped-for) consequence of the amalgamation was a large increase in the number of medical students, so the changes made to the College buildings in 1892 were considerable.[88] A third court – known as the quadrangle – was laid out to the north of the original structure with a basement entry and three storeys on the west – for mechanical drawing, a natural history museum and a physiology laboratory – and on the east an extension for engineering. To the north of this was a new L-shaped block linked to the original building by raised walkways. It contained a pathology museum and raked lecture theatre holding 326 students on the ground floor, museums on the first floor devoted to public health, dentistry, anatomy and materia medica and on the third an anatomy theatre for 223 and a 2500-square-foot dissecting room.[89]

Taking in the 'Queen's Faculty of Medicine' put the coping stone on the claim of Mason College to be a university institution in waiting. Nevertheless, given the College's financial position, the step was highly imprudent. The point is very clear if a comparison is made with similar higher education establishments in the three years up to and including the union between Mason and Queen's.

Table 3.1 Mason College: income, 1890–3 (£)1[90]

1890–1		1891–2		1892–3	
Owens	31455	Owens	32127	Owens	32965
Leeds	13954	Leeds	23010	Leeds	27824
Liverpool	12020	Liverpool	13611	Liverpool	14539
Mason	10207	Newcastle	12213	Newcastle	13518
Newcastle	8961	*Mason*	10533	*Mason*	12708

The contrast is bleak, even when student numbers are taken into account.

Table 3.2 Mason College: funds available per student, 1890–3 (£)1[91]

1890–1		1891–2		1892–3	
Owens	37	Leeds	38	Leeds	42
Liverpool	33	Owens	33	Owens	32
Leeds	27	Liverpool	33	Liverpool	28
Mason	21	Newcastle	25	Newcastle	28
Newcastle	17	*Mason*	20	*Mason*	20

Birmingham was having to manage on at best 80% and at worst 48% of the capitation enjoyed by colleges elsewhere.[92]

The link with Queen's made this wooden-spoon position significantly worse. The buildings which Mason College Council agreed to erect were 'large', 'important' and very expensive – the outlay was £18,000, nearly a third as much as the cost of the original building.[93] They also cost the College £200 a year in lost rent, a fact which the Council used as one excuse for the 1892–3 deficit.[94] Outgoings increased as well. In the first year of incorporation, the gap between the College's income and its expenditure jumped by a further 5%.[95] Part of this was attributable to a commercial loan of £13,000 at 4% taken to finance the medical block and charged against the faculty. But there was also the gap between what medical students cost and what they brought in. The expenses of the rest of the College also rose because to support the move the Council decided not to charge out the running costs for the new facilities, claiming that a library extension and another lecture theatre would have been soon necessary anyway.[96]

The arrival of medicine also speeded up the merry-go-round of science funding. The premises which the medical faculty took over in 1893 were a complete suite, though there were complaints that some parts had been adapted from existing plant. Nevertheless, improvements in pharmacy teaching immediately necessitated another laboratory and a further member of staff. The faculty also gave warning of its exposure to national pressures. Recent legislation would produce a demand for a course in public health and more equipment for the bacteriological laboratory was having to be installed.[97] In 1895–6 the demand was by the examining bodies, this time for more laboratory training in physiology and the Council had to vote a special grant for additional equipment.[98] In 1897, despite the improvements of 1893, the bacteriological laboratory again needed major work – this time a quadrupling in size and fittings in order to act for the whole city – though the City Council did give a grant for apparatus.[99]

From the amalgamation of October 1892, Mason College did certainly offer teaching in 'all subjects to qualify for degrees' and Principal Heath could claim that without it 'no steps could be taken in the direction of establishing a Midland University with its centre in Birmingham'.[100] The unasked question was, could the College afford the amalgamation in the long term? From October 1892, the date of the change, to September 1898, the overall Mason College deficit rose by £11,902 and £6734 of that (56.6%) was attributable to the medical faculty.

The established practice of the medical faculty in charging entrance fees did nerve the College Council to introduce them for all students in 1893–4, but it felt that it had to sweeten the pill by setting aside one third of the proceeds to fund a 'Students' Common Rooms and Athletic Fund'.[101] Appeals for assistance were made regularly to the community, and with success – in 1893–4 £16,000 was received.[102] Requests were also made for help with specific projects, such as the call in 1897 for engineering equipment which raised over £700 for electrical and almost £2000 for civil and mechanical engineering.[103] The Council was also not above treating legacies as income – which produced a better out-turn in 1894–5.[104] Nevertheless, despite all efforts and all devices, the deficit which the College had returned every year from 1881–2 continued and grew.[105] After 1890–1 it was always (with the exception of 1894–5) in excess of 11% – indeed, often over 15%. In 1899–1900, the last year of College accounts, it reached 21%.[106]

In terms of activity the College was flourishing. Expenditure on the balance sheet increased in the fourteen years from 1886–7 to 1899–1900 from £8593 to £21,842, that is, by 154.2%. Income rose almost as fast, by 148.8% from £7253 to £18,046, but there was always a gap. It was a story which would become all too familiar to later generations of academics. What an institution of higher education did was never priced by the world at large at its real cost, however great the effort put in and however good the students and the research produced. By the end of the century trading out of deficit was becoming impossible. When the Mason College books were closed at Michaelmas 1900, the cumulative debt had reached £21,779, within a whisker – £63 – of the whole income of the year then ending.

Notes

1 *Calendar 1891–2*, p. 242.
2 UC 1/1/6, Letters.
3 *Calendar 1992–3*, p. 342; Armytage, *Civic Universities*, pp. 230–1.
4 *Calendar 1894–5*, pp. 385–6.
5 Ibid., *1897–8*, pp. 384–5.
6 Ibid., *1898–9*, pp. 399–400.
7 UC 4/ii/11, p. 85; 4/ii/9, p. 63.
8 UC 4/ii/9, p. 67.
9 Ibid., p. 73.
10 UC 4/ii/11, p. 71.
11 *Calendar 1887–8*, p. 240.
12 Ibid., *1884–5*, p. 210; *1886–7*, p. 213.
13 UC4/ii/9, p. 28; 4/ii/11, p. 47.
14 *Calendar 1890–91*, p. 233.
15 Ibid., *1884–5*, p. 163.
16 Ibid., *1896–7*, p. 396.
17 For the following see UC4/i/22, pp. 64, 239; 4/i/15, pp. 76–87.
18 J. M. D. Meiklejohn.
19 *Calendar 1883–4*.
20 UC4/ii/8, pp. 96–7.
21 UC4/ii/11, p. 45.
22 *Calendar 1880–1*.
23 Ibid., p. 164.

24 UC 4/i/22, p. 27.
25 Ibid., p. 3; 4/ii/8, p. 11. It is possible that twelve subjects were offered in each term but that two in the winter and one in the spring attracted no registrations.
26 UC 4/ii/8, p. 11; *Calendar 1883–4*, p. 196.
27 UC 4/ii/8, pp. 12, 22, 36; *Calendar 1884–5.*
28 For the following see the report for 1884–5: UC 4/ii/11, pp. 29–35.
29 UC 4/ii/8, p. 37.
30 UC 4/ii/11, pp. 84–5.
31 *Calendar 1889–90*, pp. 239–40.
32 UC 4/v/4: Morley Papers, p. 17.
33 *Calendar 1891–2*, pp. 252–3; *1892–3*, p. 354.
34 UC 4/ii/7, p. 173; 4/i/22, pp. 11, 15; 4/ii/8, p. 11.
35 UC 4/ii/7, p. 12.
36 UC 4/ii/11, pp. 36–45.
37 UC 4/ii/9, p. 17.
38 Ibid., p. 27. There were at least two public altercations between Arber and Sonnenschein: ibid., pp. 52, 72; 4/ii/8, pp. 146–7.
39 UC 4/ii/9, pp. 63–5; *Calendar 1886–7*, p. 213.
40 UC 4/ii/11, p. 112.
41 *Calendar 1891–2*, p. 241.
42 Ibid., p. 252; *1896–7*, p. 394.
43 *Calendar 1892–3.*
44 Ibid., *1893–4*, pp. 371–3.
45 Ibid., *1894–5*, pp. 379–80.
46 Ibid., *1895–6*, pp. 401–3, 419–20.
47 Ibid., *1895–6*, p. 405; *1897–8*, p. 383.
48 Ibid., *1896–7*, pp. 416–17.
49 Ibid., *1898–9*, p. 422.
50 Ibid., *1899–1900*, p. 442.
51 Ibid., *1894–5*, pp. 383–4.
52 Ibid., *1895–6*, p. 427.
53 Ibid., *1894–5*, p. 360; *1896–7*, pp. 402, 424–5; *1897–8*, pp. 393–413.
54 Ibid., *1895–6*, pp. 427, 430–1.
55 Ibid., *1896–7*, p. 427.
56 Ibid., *1895–6*, p. 423; *1896–7*, p. 420.
57 Ibid., *1896–7*, pp. 441–2.
58 But the professor of classics was also arguing the need for archaeological apparatus 'if the teaching in the College is to advance with the times': ibid., *1894–5*, p. 389.
59 Ibid., *1898–9*, pp. 432–3; *1899–1900*, pp. 426, 453–4.
60 Ibid., *1894–5*, pp. 392–3.
61 Ibid., *1895–6*, p. 426.
62 Ibid., *1897–8*, p. 411.
63 UC 4/i/22, p. 53.
64 UC 4/ii/8, p. 166.
65 UC 4/ii/11, p. 113; *Calendar 1890–1*, pp. 248–9; *1891–2*, p. 241.

66 *Calendar 1893–4*, p. 381.
67 Ibid., *1886–7*, p. 233; *1887–8*, p. 251.
68 Ibid., *1887–8*, p. 251.
69 UC 4/ii/11, p. 13; see below, p. 58.
70 UC 4/ii/8, pp. 10, 12.
71 Ibid., pp. 14, 72–4, 76; *Calendar 1884–5*, p. 49.
72 *Calendar 1888–9*, p. 273.
73 Elections are listed in the annual *Calendar.*
74 UC 4/ii/11, pp. 68–70; 4/ii/8, pp. 267–8; 4/ii/10, p. 125.
75 UC 4/ii/11, p. 73.
76 UC 4/ii/8, p. 50. The enthusiasts were Bridge, Haycraft, Joel and Sonnenschein.
77 Ibid., p. 176; 4/ii/9, pp. 100–1, 103.
78 UC 4/ii/11, pp. 126, 136, 142, 148.
79 *Calendar 1892–3*, pp. 348–9; *1893–4*, pp. 373–4.
80 Ibid., *1894–5*, pp. 381–2.
81 UC 4/i/15, p. 42; 4/i/22, pp. 38,52.
82 UC 4/1/22, p. 61.
83 UC 4/ii/11, pp. 75–7; *Calendar 1886–7*, p. 188: Oliver Pemberton, professor of surgery and Lawson Tait, gynaecology.
84 UC 4/ii/11, pp. 73–4.
85 Vincent and Hinton, *University of Birmingham*, p. 54.
86 UC 4/ii/11, p. 74.
87 *Calendar 1891–2*, p. 242; *1892–3*, p. 330; *1893–4*, p. 351. The new buildings were not completed until October 1893.
88 *Calendar 1891–2*, p. 9.
89 For the above see ibid., *1892–3*, p. 341; *1899–1900*, pp. xxix–xxx and attached plans.
90 UC 1/i/6. Tables prepared for the meeting between colleges and the Chancellor of the Exchequer, 21 Nov. 1893.
91 Calculated on the declared number of day students.
92 Except for Newcastle.
93 *Calendar 1891–2*, p. 9; *1899–1900*, p. xxix.
94 Ibid., *1894–5*, p. 364.
95 Ibid., *1893–4*, p. 359; *1894–5*, p. 362.
96 Ibid., *1894–5*, p. 363.
97 Ibid., pp. 400–1.
98 Ibid., *1896–7*, pp. 430–1.
99 Ibid., *1898–9* p. 436.
100 Ibid., *1881–2*, p. 32; *1893–4*, pp. 369–70.
101 Ibid., *1894–5*, pp. 358–9.
102 Ibid., *1895–6*, pp. 404–5.
103 Ibid., *1897–8*, p. 387; *1898–9*, p. 401.
104 Ibid., *1895–6*, pp. 404–5.
105 See 'Finance' in the annual reports of Council, *Calendars*, passim.
106 UC 4/ii/23, pp. 145–6.

Chapter Four

Staff and students

WHEN PLANNING for Mason College began in the early 1870s there was little to look to in the way of an academic profession in England. London colleges were a possible source of recruits. Oxford had its traditional way of finding teachers, but that was focused on insular needs and local intellectual interests. Cambridge, with a greater concern for mathematics and the physical sciences, offered perhaps more promising ground. Owens College, Manchester was an outside chance – a settled academic structure was beginning to develop there. Beyond that there was the market overseas and in Scotland.

Despite the fact that there was no regular academic profession – or perhaps because of it – the advertisements for the first four Mason College chairs attracted a good number and wide range of applicants.[1] Twenty-one people applied for the chemistry post, including two from abroad. Biology produced nine candidates; mathematics and physics eleven apiece. The quality was high, too. Of the applicants in physics, two had doctorates and one was a Fellow of the Royal Society (FRS). Among the unsuccessful candidates for the chemistry post, two had doctorates in science, one was a FRS, and William Ramsay would go on to a knighthood and the Nobel prize.

The most notable characteristic of those chosen by the trustees was their youth.[2] The average age of the first four was thirty and Micaiah Hill, the mathematician, was only twenty-four. The next tranche of appointments was little older. Indeed, the average age of the first nine Mason College professors (foreign nationals excluded) was thirty-two; only one was over forty.[3] This relative youthfulness is the more surprising because hardly any of them had entered higher education direct from school at the usual Victorian age of seventeen or eighteen. Many, indeed, were products of the new kind of higher education institution which they were applying to join. Micaiah Hill went up to Cambridge at the age of twenty after a spell at University College London. Bridge, originally appointed in biology, had studied at the Birmingham Midland Institute, gone to work for the director of the Museum of Zoology and Comparative Anatomy at Cambridge, become a demonstrator and then, aged twenty-two, secured a scholarship to Trinity College. J. H. Poynting, the appointee in physics, completed a London B.Sc. from Owens College, Manchester before going to Cambridge. Henry Tilden, professor of chemistry, was a pupil at Kidderminster Grammar School and at fifteen was apprenticed for five years to a London chemist. He attended various lectures in Bloomsbury and elsewhere and began to study in his own time, which included learning Greek to qualify for London matriculation. He achieved a first-class London B.Sc. at the age of twenty-six, followed by a D.Sc. three years later. Mason College professors were, therefore, in no sense conventional university products. It was said of William Hillhouse, the first professor of botany, who entered Trinity College, Cambridge, at the age of twenty-eight, that 'he was rather older than the average men of his year, in consequence he was to some extent driven into the companionship of men of senior standing, an association which stimulated his literary abilities'.[4] He co-founded the *Cambridge Review*. Only one of the early appointees seems to have made the uncomplicated transfer from school to university.[5] This was the professor of classics, the Birmingham-educated Nathan Bodington, who at the age of nineteen went from the Grammar School to Wadham College, Oxford. Robert Smith, the professor of engineering, did go direct from the Edinburgh Institute to the University of Edinburgh, but did not take a degree, and seems to have combined his undergraduate study with industrial experience as an articled pupil in pattern and fitting shops and in a drawing office.

At forty-five, Edward Arber, the professor of English language and literature, was the oldest of the early professors. Privately educated, he had no degree and between the ages of eighteen and forty-two had worked as a civil servant in the Admiralty. The most remarkable recruit, however, was Charles Lapworth, professor of geology. Born in 1842, he went to Culham Training College, became a certificated teacher and taught in Scottish schools for seventeen years from 1864. He had his first geological paper published in 1870 and in 1872 was elected to the Geological Society. He moved to Mason College in 1881 and retired in 1913, aged seventy-one, from what, by then, had become the University of Birmingham. His one and only degree was the honorary doctorate awarded by Aberdeen in 1883, though he became a Fellow (and council member) of the Royal Society and held its gold medal. He was described as 'a conspicuously unworldly creature, and seeks only the opportunity to add to his knowledge, leaving others to make fortunes. His enthusiasm makes him somewhat discursive in the lecture-room, but it is a rare privilege to attend him on a geological expedition.'[6] These expeditions were legendary, as might be expected from a man whose relaxation was visiting coal mines and water borings. In 1902 he was a member of the Royal Commission on the Coal Industry.

Another former schoolmaster was Henry Tilden, the chemist. His part-time studies had been supported by teaching chemistry freelance, but after securing his D.Sc. he worked for eight years at Clifton College as senior science master.

Bodington, too, was at one time a schoolmaster (at Manchester Grammar School and Westminster). William Hillhouse was another ex-teacher, and his career was in some ways similar to Lapworth's, though less distinguished. He went to Bedford School and at the age of seventeen became an assistant master there. He then became interested in botany, and, having helped to found the Bedfordshire Natural History Society, decided to study the subject 'more seriously' by going to Trinity College, Cambridge, which he doubled with acting as assistant curator of the University Herbarium. After graduation he was appointed lecturer in botany at both Newnham and Girton and he also lectured in the University, but he was never elected to a college fellowship. [7]

Like Hillhouse, most of the early professors had some experience in college or university teaching, but none had a great deal.[8] His amounted to a couple of years. Bridge had done a few sessions as a demonstrator at Cambridge (some while an undergraduate) and was for one year professor of zoology at the Royal College of Science in Dublin. Arber had lectured at University College London for three years. After graduating, Poynting did two years demonstrating at Owens College followed by two as a fellow of Trinity College, Cambridge while Bodington spent five years as a fellow of Lincoln College, Oxford. The only individual with significant experience at professorial level was Robert Smith, but this had been in Tokyo where, as the founding professor of civil and mechanical engineering at the Imperial University, he had established the first mechanical engineering laboratory outside the Western world. His achievement added the award of the Order of the Star of Meiji, 4th class, to what was a very varied career. When he left Edinburgh he had begun at Whitworth's in Manchester and, before going to Japan, had covered the 1873 Vienna Universal Exhibition for the periodical *Engineering*, worked as a fitter in a German machine-tool factory and then as a designer in Berlin. He returned from the East after four years to become a partner in an engineering firm in London before moving to Mason College.[9]

Because the early appointees were so young, Mason College chairs rarely came on the market, which gave the College valuable stability during the formative years. Apart from language chairs and newly established professorships in mining and philosophy, only six posts had to be filled in Arts and Science in the whole twenty years of the college, and four of these because of promotions elsewhere: Boddington went on to be principal of the Yorkshire College, Leeds and ultimately the first vice-chancellor of the later university there; Haycraft to Edinburgh; Hill to University College London and Tilden to the Royal College of Science (later Imperial College), all of which demonstrates the quality of the original selections. Their successors started at the same young age as the men they replaced and some had parallel late starts in higher education. Where they were stronger was on experience, something which reflects the gradual increase in opportunities in academic employment which was by then under way. Heath was a fellow of Trinity College, Cambridge – a distinction which he regularly cited in his Mason College correspondence. Sonnenschein had been an assistant at the University of Glasgow. Percy Frankland, appointed to succeed Tilden in 1894, had been professor of chemistry at University College, Dundee since 1888. John Henry Muirhead, the first holder of the new philosophy chair, had had a career which would not be exceptional in the early twenty-first century – six years at Glasgow followed by three years' research and eight years lecturing at Royal Holloway College and Bedford College, London.

The professors of language tended, if anything, to be better qualified than their Anglo-Saxon colleagues. Mason began with lecturerships in German and French, later raised to chairs, and five individuals held them during the life of the College, two in the German and three in the French department, which, from time to time, also put on courses in Spanish and Italian. Karl Dammann, the appointee in German, was one of only two of all the appointees in 1880 and 1881 who had a Ph.D.; he had studied at Hanover, Göttingen and Jena.[10] His successor, Hermann Georg Fiedler, held a doctorate from Leipzig.[11] The French had no time for such teutonic decorations, but Eugène Joël held the degree of B. ès Lettres, as did his successor E. Loreille, and although the next professor, Clovis Bévenot, had no degree on appointment, he had studied at Göttingen and Naples.[12]

Given the varied backgrounds of Mason College professors, it is hard to tell how far past experience of any one institution helped to shape the growth of Mason College. It has been argued that a characteristic of twentieth-century university development was the increasing hegemony of the older universities, and with Oxford so easily accessible, Birmingham might seem a very likely early colony. That, however, was not the case. Of the twenty British citizens appointed to non-medical chairs at Mason College, only three had Oxford connections – though after some years in post the professor of French did graduate BA there. Cambridge was better represented – seven men had links here. London, however, seems to have had the biggest influence. Nine professors studied at the colleges there and from the start the Mason College curriculum had been shaped by the need to prepare students for London examinations. Indeed, there was for some time a real possibility that Mason College would become an affiliated institution of the University of London – that is, until the problems of university education in the capital began to undermine the University's original role as a Victorian precursor of the Council for National Academic Awards.

The Mason College professoriate was effectively doubled when the medics of Queen's College joined in 1892 as the faculty of Medicine.[13] There were twelve professors in post including joint chairs in medicine, midwifery and surgery. Changes were no more frequent in Medicine than in Arts and Science. Seven of the twelve former Queen's College professors still occupied chairs in 1899, and six of them would still be in post when Edward VII opened the new University in 1909. Bostock Hill, professor of public health, held office from 1876 to 1919. The important common factor, however, was not continuity with Queen's College, still less academic background. Medical chairs were honorary and appointments were, in effect, shared among existing appointees in one or more of the Birmingham hospitals. For example, Arthur Foxwell, who was appointed professor of therapeutics at Mason College in 1897 and continued at the University until he died in 1909, began professionally as a pathologist at the General Hospital, become assistant physician, transferred in 1889 to the Queen's Hospital and died in post as senior physician there.[14] Robert Saundby began as assistant physician at the General and was physician there from 1885 to 1912. He also lectured in comparative anatomy at Queen's College, became professor of medicine at Mason College in 1892 and retired from the University in 1917.[15]

One group which became somewhat more important in Arts and Science over the years was the junior staff, as it was then known.[16] The size of the non-professorial establishment at any one time seems to have been determined by immediate student demand. Initially a demonstrator was appointed in chemistry, physics and biology. Gradually a rough pattern of lecturers, assistant lecturers and demonstrators emerged, both salaried and honorary, but without precise job definitions and with idiosyncrasies such as 'professor's assistant', 'assistant in the laboratory' and 'assistant professor', and with some posts being filled for a specific period only and others effectively continued year on year. From 1881 there was a lecturer in chemistry, but it was not until 1886 that the second regular lecturer was appointed, to teach metallurgy.[17] A mathematics lecturer was engaged in 1890 and from then on others were added to bring the total in Arts and Science in 1899 to nine, and there was also an assistant professor in geology. Although frequently as well qualified as the professor, a lecturer was appointed to take over much of the routine work of the department. However, it is clear that in a few cases lecturers were in post for long enough to make independent contributions to the College. Thomas Turner, a former student of the Midland Institute, was appointed demonstrator in chemistry in 1883, and in 1886 became a lecturer in the department with responsibility for teaching metallurgy. In 1890 he was given a significant pay rise and the college title 'Lecturer in Metallurgy'.[18] When he left in February 1894 to take up the post of Director of Technical Education in Staffordshire, the University Council expressed 'our deep regret that his connection with the Metallurgical Department would be severed, and our high sense of the value of his services in the past'.[19] He was particularly good with non-academic audiences. The course on precious metals which he put on for the jewellery trade in 1891 had seventy-two attenders.[20] There was, nevertheless, no suggestion of promoting him to a chair. Chairs were understood as needing to be established and it was not possible to offer him one until 1902.[21] The only promotions to chairs which did take place were, as we have seen in the Medical Faculty, determined by the special factors there.

Few lecturers stayed as long as Turner. In all fourteen lecturers completed engagements in the 1890s and ten of them were for three years or less.[22] Men moved off to a variety of posts, usually of a similar kind or in some way attached to education. For example, in 1894 one left to lecture in the Manchester Municipal Technical School and two others in 1898, one to join the staff at University College, Cardiff, and the second to become secretary of the Institute of Electrical Engineers.[23] W. A. Brockington, one of the longer serving lecturers, became principal of the Victoria Institute, Worcester in 1899. Why men were prepared to move sideways in their careers probably says something about the low salaries which were a recognised problem at Birmingham. In 1896 R. H. Housman was one of the stars of the College.[24] An Associate, a Poynting protégé and with five years' earlier experience as a demonstrator in physics, he was appointed as lecturer in charge of the newly important subject, electro-technics. Two years later he resigned to become assistant engineer at the leading Birmingham firm of Kynochs, and the comment made by the principal is revealing:

> While it is pleasant to report that an old student and a member of the staff is appointed to a position of responsibility it is with very great regret that the department has lost the services of Mr. Housman. He took up the work of his lectureship when there were very few students, and for some time practically gave his services to the College in circumstances of great discouragement. Indeed, Mr. Housman's willingness to do the work made the foundation of a separate Electrotechnical Department possible.

Lecturing at Mason College was not a career, but a stepping-off point to somewhere else.

Much the same has to be said of the demonstrators. Between 1880 and 1899 there were thirty-three completed engagements covering thirty individuals; seventeen lasted for one year and seven for two. In only three cases was the individual promoted to lecturer. They were a very mixed bunch. Some were quasi-students seeking additional qualifications and taking the job in return for fee remission. Stanley Barnes spent a postgraduate year demonstrating in physiology, on course for a career in medicine and eventually the deanship of the Medical School. Other demonstrators were already fully qualified. They were able to move on much as lecturers did, some to further demonstrating – possibly from an honorary position to a salaried one, others to a lectureship, others elsewhere. In 1889 the demonstrator in physics went to a lectureship in the University of Melbourne, and the demonstrator in engineering left to find employment in Thailand.[25]

Recruiting good staff was one essential for the success of the new College.[26] Another was building a viable intake of students – an issue in which, of course, the early professors were directly interested financially. For the opening term, autumn 1880, 53 daytime students were enrolled; there was a fall-off in the spring (42), but the summer saw 75 recruited. In all, 95 individuals studied during the day for all or part of the year. Evening work was offered for the spring term only but recruited 95 students. Since nine evening scholars also attended some day courses, the total number of individuals taught in the College in its first year was 181. Given that it had not been possible to announce the start until almost too late, this figure was encouraging.[27] In the following year (1881–2) enrolments soared to 251 day and 236 evening students, representing 462 individuals. Five years later (1886–7) the figure was 642, an annual rate of increase of just over 6%.

Initial growth could, therefore, be deemed as adequate, but the important test would be the pace of development once the College was established. Here progress was not good. In the seven years from 1886–7 to 1892–3 annual individual enrolments averaged 631 and were effectively static.[28] It looked very much as though the number of those interested in the College had reached a plateau. This makes it very difficult to substantiate William Hillhouse's assertion in 1889 that progress 'is more rapid than it has been for several years past. Our numbers far exceed those of any Provincial College, with the exception of Owens College, Manchester.'[29] Gross figures covering day and evening enrolments need, moreover, to be unpacked. The crucial statistic is the number of students studying in the daytime. Between 1886–7 and 1892–3 this did rise by 8% overall, a modest growth rate of 1.4% a year. Thereafter the rate collapsed to 0.5% a year until 1897–8, when the data series ends. With expansion in daytime study running into the sand, the statistics of evening work became vital. Evening enrolment was very volatile and could fluctuate by as much as 55% between one year and another, but the average in the twelve years from 1886–7 to 1897–8 was 337 registrations a year, with 6 years above that figure and 6 below. This meant that after the initial growth period it too had become effectively flat, but even so, and despite its unpopularity with the staff, evening work had to be kept up if the College was to present itself to the Birmingham community as a success.[30] In 1891–2 evening students provided 58% of the total registrations in Arts and Science and the figure was over 50% in every year from 1895–6 to 1897–8. Clearly, in trying to keep evening work going, the College Council was not only thinking in terms of faithfulness to Mason's intentions.

Day enrolment looks even more worrying in close-up. Recruiting 157 men in 1881–2 for what was effectively the first year of normal operation might seem encouraging, but male enrolments thereafter failed to increase significantly during the life of the College. From 1882–3 the published figures were inflated by the inclusion of the medical students from Queen's but when, from 1886–7, it is possible to strip those numbers out, recruitment of men for Arts and Science shows no advance on 1881–2 and a fluctuating record thereafter. The reality was that daytime work in the College depended to a significant extent on women students. The ninety-two enrolled in 1881–2 already represented 37.5% of all students, and although the number of female students in Arts and Science was thereafter to fluctuate, it was most often between 40% and 45% of the Faculty,

Table 4.1 Mason College: numbers of daytime male students (arts and science), 1886–92

Years	Numbers	Years	Numbers
1886–7	153	1892–3	191
1887–8	168	1893–4	181
1888–9	165	1894–5	172
1889–90	197	1895–6	179
1890–1	190	1896–7	199
1891–2	179	1897–8	196

and it could go much higher.[31] Until the 1890s women played a much smaller role in systematic evening work. Male evening enrolment reached a peak in 1891–2 and by then over three-quarters of attendances had been made by men.[32] Thereafter, however, female attendances in the evening increased considerably and from 1895–6 to 1897–8 women were in a substantial majority, and not simply because the number of male students declined at the same time. Why this should be so is not clear, but it may be connected with increasing interest among women in the possibility of training for or training to advance in a teaching career.

One of the reasons why the reality underlying the facts about recruiting attracted little attention is that for a number of years recruitment figures looked better because of the Queen's Medical School. This was outside Mason College so the students it sent were transfers, not recruits. However, they were bottoms on seats and gratefully counted accordingly. This subsidy came to an end from 1892–3 when the medics were integrated in Mason College and were counted as a separate faculty, which explains why the Faculty of Arts and Science could claim 301 male students in 1891–2 but in the next year could only muster 191. When the Medical School became a separate faculty, the Arts and Science figures did receive a limited boost from a new vocational venture, the Day Training Department which offered women a two-year course in primary teaching.[33] Unlike the quotas from the Queen's Medical School these were indeed new students, but again they were not part of the original brief of the College. When in 1897–8 the College claimed that 251 women students were studying in the day, 112 of them (45%) came from this additional source.

It can be argued that too refined an analysis of numbers gets away from the basic facts. Mason College was growing. In 1886–7 it had 748 registrations, 377 for students (including medics) for day study and 371 for evening classes. In 1897–8 there were 799 plus the registrations in Medicine, 447 day and 352 evening. This was not a dramatic advance, but it was progress in the one area plus stability in the other.[34] It also ensured that the College looked busy, and with additional building going on any passerby should have been impressed.[35] On the other hand, on a number of occasions in his annual reports Principal Heath still felt he had to gloss the figures by referring to the effect of special factors. A decade of very little core growth hardly encouraged hope of university status and trying to expand by adding further vocational courses would certainly not send out the right signals.[36] Indeed, Bertram Windle's assessment was that the only way to stimulate growth was to secure a charter first.[37] Yet whoever was right, becoming credible as a university involved much more than 'badging' an existing institution.

In his report as chairman of the Academic Board for 1884–5 Professor Lapworth reviewed the reasons which drew students to study at Mason College and the courses which were provided by the then still-youthful institution.[38] The majority of students were, he said, preparing for medical, university or other examinations 'and for these definite and rigid lecture courses are laid down'. Many others enrol 'to perfect themselves in some special scientific subject that will be of use to them in trade and business' and special courses were laid on for them, in, for example, chemical engineering. The growth of such 'systematic study' was regularly referred to by the staff as a measure of the progress of the College. In December 1897 Heath offered what would become a staple complaint of higher education over the years, that work should be measured by quality not quantity: 'The proportion of students who are taking systematic courses is increasing, so that the numbers for this session do not adequately represent the work done.'[39] However, tables published in the annual *Calendar* tell a more nuanced story.[40]

It is evident, first, that although the number of students taking systematic study did show some limited sustained growth, systematic study was not increasing as a proportion of overall College activity (see Table 4.2). The average fluctuated between 47% and 58% of the work overall.[41] The best year was 1889–90, when all three sections were strong, but that was not sustained.

One has also to recognise that much of this so-called 'systematic work' amounted to a student taking a single course in a session. In 1886–7, this was true of 221 day students (59%) and only 106 (28%) were taking three. Not until 1893–4 did as many as half the day students register for three courses in a session and there had been little further progress by 1897–8, the latest year for which data were published. Then 161 students (36%) were taking one course and 224 (50%) three courses.[42] Nor was it usual for a student to continue classes for a number of sessions. A sample cohort of students between 1892 and 1899 demonstrates that 43% of men and 56% of women attended for one session only and that only 24.1% of men and 13.8% of women attended in three consecutive sessions or more.[43] A number of students (6%) enrolled spasmodically. Some may have been prevented from attending consecutively but the more probable reason is a 'buffet' approach to what the College had on offer. Equally discouraging was the phenomenon of the eternal student who came back year after year. Frances Brown first

Table 4.2 Number and distribution of 'systematic' students 1886–98

Date	*Total no. of students*	*No. of systematic students*	*% of systematic students*	*University preparation*	*%*	*Technical*	*%*	*Engineering*	*%*
1886–7	304	141	46.4	77	25.3	26	8.6	38	12.5
1887–8	361	146	40.5	80	22.2	34	9.4	32	8.9
1888–9	301	161	53.5	90	29.9	39	13.0	32	10.6
1889–90	316	194	61.4	112	35.4	42	13.3	40	12.7
1890–1	319	182	56.1	107	32.6	45	14.1	30	9.4
1891–2	313	172	54.9	104	33.2	41	13.1	27	8.6
1892–3	329	178	54.0	87	26.4	57	17.3	34	10.3
1893–4	317	181	57.0	87	27.4	60	18.9	34	10.7
1894–5	371	164	44.2	86	23.2	48	12.9	30	8.1
1895–6	410	176	43.0	106	25.9	30	7.3	40	9.8
1896–7	328	191	58.2	100	30.5	46	14.0	45	13.7
1897–8	335	176	52.4	104	31.0	36	10.7	36	10.7
Total	4004	2062	51.5	1140	28.5	504	12.6	418	10.4

registered as a student in 1881 but still attended every year from 1892 to 1895 and again in 1898; Ada Hadley probably attended in every session from 1888 to 1899.[44]

Systematic study was, therefore, far removed from the ideal of the student who was pursuing a sequence of educational courses which led to a specific qualification. The element of it which the College set most store by was what Hillhouse in 1889 called 'the University side of the College work'.[45] He calculated that over the preceding six years the College had achieved 200 passes in University of London examinations and had gained twenty-five degrees.[46] Such success, however, has to be looked at carefully. Whatever publicity suggested, most of the academic work which Mason College undertook would today be classed as the equivalent of GCSE and A level. There were two main programmes. One was for the London matriculation. This was 'a university examination' only in the sense that the University of London required it as a certificate of general education before anyone could register for more advanced work. Very generally, however, the certificate was seen as a qualification in itself. Between 1881 and 1898 Mason College entered 176 candidates for the examination, 77 in the first half of the period and 99 in the second. The other big programme, with 154 candidates, was the examination in preliminary science. This formed part of the 1st MB requirements and again must be classed as 'secondary' education. Higher education, but even then only as it would have been understood before the advent of GCE A level, was mainly represented by candidates for the London Intermediate Level examinations, 87 in Science, 66 in Arts and 64 in Medicine.[47] Degree numbers proper amounted in the eighteen years to 1898 to only 123, 18% of the total effort put into 'university' work, 70 candidates in Science and 53 in Arts.[48]

Table 4.3 University of London examinations taken by Mason College students, 1881–98[49]

	(a) Matriculation/ preliminary science	(b) Intermediate degree	(c) Degree	Total b + c
		Arts/Science/ Medicine		
1881–9	151	25/28/24	32	109
1890–8	179	41/59/40	91	231

One caveat, however, must be made. Although secondary-level teaching remained the largest single category of work at Mason College throughout its existence, the academic staff was correct to see more advanced work increasing both absolutely and proportionately. Whereas in the first five years of its existence the

College had produced fewer than two graduates a year and spent 70% of its 'university' time on 'secondary school' work, in the last five it produced nearly ten graduates annually and secondary level work had fallen to 48%. Mason College would also have claimed that its own engineering diplomas should be added to the total as equivalent to different levels of degree. The senior diploma and the junior diploma each produced one or two passes a year.

The stress which was put on the vibrancy of the so-called 'systematic courses' was clearly in order to establish the image of the College. The emphasis also helped to obscure the very large number of Mason College students who were certainly not studying systematically. Lapworth described them as 'A third group of students [who] attend solely for the pleasure of self-culture or because they have a bias for the study of some special language or science. These form a fair proportion of the students and include some of the worst as well as some of the best and most interesting of them all.'[50] 'Fair proportion' was very much an understatement. The total of occasional students varied year on year, but only once in the twelve years 1886–7 to 1897–8 did the number fall below 40% of those registered. More often than not the figure was between 45% and 55%. As we shall see, this phenomenon of occasional attendance could be a reflection of the large number of women who registered for courses. Nor was there much sign of improvement over time. In 1897–8, 47.5% of students enrolled in Arts and Science were still 'occasional'. The existence of this large group of 'soft' students must raise issues about the level of the academic benefit being gained in Birmingham and, if recruitment in other colleges was similar, about the quality of much which passed for higher education in Britain in the late nineteenth century. A good number of students appear to have been looking for something akin to unassessed extra-mural lecturing

As well as suggesting categories of student, the registration records make it possible to discover where demand was in the curriculum and, in particular, to ask whether the College was successful in attracting takers for the scientific education Mason had intended. Judged in financial terms, the answer is 'yes'. The total of fees brought in by day teaching in 1892–3 was £3943, of which Science contributed 74%; in 1899–1900 this rose to 80%.[51] In terms of numbers of students recruited, the position was somewhat different. It is possible to determine this between 1881–2 and 1897–8 on the evidence of class enrolments, although the statistical base changes from 1892–3 when registrations for certain science subjects ceased to be inflated by the attendance of medical students from Queen's College. That said, there is no doubt that in the early years Science was taking on average two class enrolments in three. On the other hand, from 1892–3, Arts was on average almost at parity (48:52). In four of the years from 1892–3 Science had the larger class rolls and in two years Arts did, but in 1897–8 the Arts was ahead by 19%.[52]

The more dramatic fluctuations were almost certainly accounted for by the large proportion of occasional students who were, in effect, floating voters. In 1897–8, for example, enrolments for Latin rose by 71% and English language by 30% – levels not seen before – but 16% of the surge in Arts is explained by the 121 people who joined the new course on mental and moral philosophy and political economy taught by J. H. Muirhead. Nevertheless, the rise of Arts was real, to Robert Heath's evident discomposure:

> The most remarkable feature of the distribution of the students among the different departments is the large increase in almost all the departments of the Arts Faculty, and in Mathematics. The departments of Science, on the other hand, are either stationary, or exhibit a downward trend. ... The fact remains that there has been a greater demand for teaching in literary subjects than in any recent session.[53]

The effect, first, of medical students becoming a separate faculty and, second, of the shift to Arts, is very evident in a comparison between the popularity of subjects in the 1880s and the 1890s. Before 1892–3 chemistry, physics, physiology and mathematics were way out in front and even the next discipline, French, was recruiting only about half the numbers in chemistry. From 1892–3 French

Table 4.4 Mason College: popularity of subjects, Faculties of Arts and Science, 1881–98

1881–2 to 1891–2		*1892–3 to 1897–8*	
1	Chemistry*	1	FRENCH (5)
2	Physics*	2	Geology (6)
3	Physiology*	3	Maths (4)
4	Maths	4	ENGLISH LANGUAGE (8)
5	FRENCH	5	Physics (2)*
6	Geology	6	Chemistry (1)*
7	Botany*	7	GERMAN (9)
8	ENGLISH LANGUAGE	8	ENGLISH LITERATURE (11)
9	GERMAN	9	LATIN (10)
10	LATIN	10	Engineering (13)
11	ENGLISH LITERATURE	11=	Zoology (12)
12	Zoology	11=	GREEK (14)
13	Engineering	13	Botany (7)*
14	Greek	14	Metallurgy (15)
15	Metallurgy	15	Physiology (3)*

Note: Small capitals = Arts disciplines; * = subjects recruiting medical students was the subject most in demand, followed by geology, mathematics and English language. Clearly the earlier dominance of chemistry, physics and physiology was a consequence of the recruitment of Queen's College medical students, not of a heavy demand from non-medics wanting to take science *per se*. The decline in botany enrolments had the same cause, while in the 1890s physiology ceased to exist as a course taken outside medicine.

The most popular science subject in the 1890s was geology. This had taken off slowly after being introduced in 1881–2, but the 1890s were a boom time. In Arts the popularity seems to have been not just French but languages in general. Registrations in French and German averaged as many as physics, chemistry and zoology put together, while the demand for Greek and Latin together exceeded that for physics. In an otherwise worrying situation for Mason's Science College, the one advance over the two decades which would have pleased the old man was engineering. Demand for this grew steadily and moderately from its inception in 1881–2 and made a leap forward in 1896–7 when the department introduced a course in electrical engineering.

Who, then, were the students of the new College? A mass of material is available to answer this question, but with the College undergoing a constant process of evolution the archive contains much confusion and some contradiction, with bases being changed and categories altered without warning. The years of the College were also ones in which the boundaries of Birmingham were undergoing topographical extension and the area was experiencing economic change on a timescale which makes twenty years a long time. What follows, therefore, can only be the broadest of assessments.

During its first years, the College maintained a cumulative table of the names and locations of all day students. The purpose was to enable the College *Calendar* to publish evidence of a growing student body. This early data suggest that the initial intake for Arts and Science at Mason College was very substantially from inner Birmingham, that is, from within the town boundaries before the enlargement of 1891.[54] That was true of 82% of the men and all of the women listed in 1880. In the following year and in 1882 the male proportion from inner Birmingham fell to 64% and 65%, respectively, as numbers of students were recruited from the Black Country and from twenty miles elsewhere round the town. The catchment area for women appears to have been far slower to expand. In 1881, 82% were still coming from the old town and in 1882 the figure was 86%. In all these three years, only one woman was recruited from the Black Country – from Dudley.

The accumulating entries in the *Calendar* suggest that this early pattern of male recruitment was substantially maintained through the life of the College.[55] The percentage of men from Birmingham and around was always in the 80s or 90s, with the town itself and later the city making up about half. In 1898–9, for example, the overall figure for Birmingham and district was 85%, with one student in two from the centre, one in eleven from the Black Country and one in five from elsewhere within the twenty-mile radius. When men did come from outside, it was from the rest of the Midlands. Recruits from as far afield as Australia and Finland and even from northern England were exceptional. Clearly, on this *Calendar* evidence Mason College achieved a local rather than a metropolitan recruitment. For women, the annual lists continue to suggest that the range of recruitment was narrower. The great majority is always identified as coming from inner Birmingham though a handful gradually does begin to come from the Black Country and the immediate periphery. In 1888–9, for example, 87% were from Birmingham itself and ten years later the figure was still 85%.[56]

The pattern of male recruitment appears to be similar in the Medical Faculty, once names begin to be listed in the *Calendar* from 1892 – there were no women yet to disturb tradition! Taking 1898–9 as a sample, there were then 193 attenders, though they did include a number of already qualified practitioners.[57] About a third (62) are listed as 'Birmingham', which presumably means that the College had an address either in the pre-1891 town or in the wards which were added in 1891. To these can be added 25 students who came from the immediate suburbs, the largest number (17) from Handsworth.[58] One student in eight came from the heart of the Black Country (25) and nearly a quarter (45), if Smethwick, Walsall, Wednesbury and Wolverhampton are included. Adding all other locations which were within twenty miles of the Bull Ring brings the total of students accounted for to 169, 88% of the total. Very evidently the role of the Birmingham Medical School was to serve demand in the central Midlands.[59] Of those from elsewhere, although one student did come from Dublin, most again came from the outer ring of Midland counties and fewer than a half a dozen came from significantly far afield. This is not surprising given that to go to Birmingham to study still involved taking the degree elsewhere, and it may give support to Windle's fear that medicine at Birmingham was losing ground. Certainly in the list of the Queen's faculty of Medicine at transfer to Mason College there had been a somewhat higher proportion of students from a distance (19%), although the great majority again came from the Midlands overall.[60] There was particularly, both in 1892 and 1898, a number of students from mid-Staffordshire and south Derbyshire, where advantage could be taken of an easy train journey. Indeed, the railway systems were generally a factor in medical recruitment. For example, medical students from Warwickshire came from Coventry, from Shirley, Solihull, Knowle, Warwick and Leamington Spa, from Stratford-upon-Avon, and from Sutton Coldfield.[61]

The *Calendar* evidence is thus clear that by 1900, the initial inner Birmingham recruitment had expanded for men into at least the West Midlands, but less so in the case of women. Other evidence, however, muddies this clarity and suggests that the evidence of the *Calendars* should be used with caution. For example, the student register for 1893 records only 42% of intending women teachers as giving addresses in Birmingham, whereas the *Calendar* for 1898, five years later, still lists nearly two-thirds of the 112 female students in the Day Training Department as coming from the City. The register is intrinsically the more likely source to be correct and a possible explanation of the divergence is the difference between home and term-time addresses. If so, this means that although only a third of the 1898 *Calendar* total appears to come from outside the city limits, the real number could have been greater. The 1893 list includes the daughters of two cotton operatives from as far afield as Widnes, and Elizabeth Alice Roberts and Janet Hughes, whose fathers worked in the slate quarries of Blaenau Festiniog. Even the 20% in the 1898 *Calendar* who did not have a Birmingham address represented something of a national spread. One came from the Potteries, two from Burton-upon-Trent, four from London and others from Gloucestershire, Buckinghamshire, Lincolnshire, York, Kent, Essex and Lancashire. It is also germane that the few male intending teachers who came to Birmingham from outside the immediate Midland area were similarly diverse, with individuals from as far afield as Cornwall, Merthyr Tydfil and Durham and a clutch from Lancashire and Yorkshire. In the case of education students it is, therefore, clearly wise to be cautious about an overwhelmingly Birmingham make-up and, of course, the possible distorting effect of lodging addresses might extend to the Medical Faculty and more generally. If so it is possible that the student body at Mason College was not quite as restricted in origins as the *Calendar* lists suggest.

The early college registration books also include information other than name and address and course taken. The ledgers for the sessions 1892–3 and 1893–4 in particular include the age of the student, the occupation of the father and the examination or the career which the student intended.[62] Information is not complete for all students and the possibility is that collecting it may well have been unpopular. Certainly, parental details were omitted from the ledgers from the start of the 1894 session. However, despite these limitations the documents do allow something more to be said of Mason students early in the second decade of the College.

First the academic side, starting with the women. A sample, comprising all registrations in the winter term of 1893, gives the names of 184 women.[63] Only a handful of them admitted any interest in formal academic qualifications. Six were taking degrees, four BAs and two B.Sc.s. Four were entering for the Intermediate BA and one for the Intermediate B.Sc. Another was taking preliminary science, presumably with the intention of eventually going to the Elizabeth Garrett Anderson Hospital to read medicine, and there were some taking matriculation or its equivalents. The largest number, effectively half of the total (ninety) had the goal of becoming certificated teachers through the Day Training Department. In all but one case these intending teachers gave their ages and these cluster, not surprisingly, on the years eighteen to twenty.[64] A few women who list their interest as teaching were outside the Day Training Department and appear to have been experienced teachers wanting to improve their skills. One example is Lilian Lowe, aged thirty, who came to the College with her sister Janet (twenty-eight) from Hamstead Hill School, which their father ran in Handsworth, in order to learn German.[65]

With the few serious students and the trainee teachers out of the way, the 1893 list leaves us with over 40% of female students (79) who declined to indicate that they had any examination or career in mind; three-quarters of them also refused to specify their age. These registrations should probably be identified as middle-class women attending as occasional students. This conjecture is certainly supported by the few instances where a father's occupation is given: brass founder, tea merchant, auctioneer, farmer, solicitor, surgeon. Although forty-one of the seventy-nine came from Birmingham itself, thirty-two of these were from the elite district of Edgbaston, while twenty-two more came from the suburbs and a further five from further afield within a twenty-mile radius. The social patterning is obvious. Some came with friends. For example, Florence Clarke and Edith Harrold accompanied the eighteen-year-old Elizabeth Violet for classes in German; they all lived in elegant addresses in Edgbaston.[66] The nineteen-year-old Annie Dunn came in from West Bromwich with her eighteen-year-old sister Hettie to take English literature.[67] Some were as young as seventeen. Sometimes families would attend together, for example a mother, son and daughter on a geology course.[68] Wives of College staff also signed up.[69] How the bourgeois of Birmingham got on with the vocational trainees in primary education is hard to determine; even if the courses they took did not overlap, everyone shared the same common room. As we shall see, the social origins of most of the women teachers were definitely among the tradesmen and craftsmen – a china decorator, several engineers, a beer dealer, and the like. A few were from the learned poor – seven schoolmasters, a photographer, a bookseller, an organist and a verger.

When it comes to the 156 male students in the sample, the most immediate contrast is in respect of age. They started earlier, and whereas only 4% of women were seventeen and none was younger, fifteen-, sixteen- and seventeen-year-olds

Table 4.5 Mason College: examinations being prepared for by male students, winter 1893

M.Sc.	1
BA	4
B.Sc.	7
Institute of Chemistry	7
Intermediate BA	2
Intermediate B.Sc.	9
Preliminary Science	13
Matriculation	10
Other	9

made up 42% of those men whose ages are known. In other words, only a fifth of the women were under nineteen but more than half the men. An equally striking difference is over seriousness of intention. A career was mentioned by forty (25%) of those registering and sixty-two (40%) had an examination in mind. A majority of their examination work was in science and one student was reading for an M.Sc.

Among careers, the most popular was engineering, which was specified by twenty-two students, six of them particularising on electrical engineering and two even on nautical engineering. There was interest too in assaying, no doubt with Birmingham's Jewellery Quarter in mind, with a number wanting to become analytical chemists and one who wanted to follow in his father's footsteps as a manufacturing chemist. In contrast to the women, there was only one man intending to become a teacher, and he was the son of a decorator.

Table 4.6 Known parental occupation of Mason College students 1893–4

	Male students	Female students	Total
I. INDEPENDENT STATUS			
A. Professional	23	4	27
B. Government employees	4	-	4
C. Land	2	1	3
Subtotals	*29*	*5*	*34*
II. BIRMINGHAM INDUSTRY			
A. Manufacturers	19	7 (3)	26
B. Managers	6	6 (6)	12
Subtotals	*25*	*13*	*38*
III. BIRMINGHAM COMMERCE			
A. Expert consultants	4	5 (4)	9
B. Commerce	6	8 (2)	14
C. Financial sector	5	3 (1)	8
Subtotals	*15*	*16*	*31*
IV. SERVICES			
A. Construction industry	1	6 (6)	7
B. Retail trades	10	8 (6)	18
Subtotals	*11*	*14*	*25*
V. SMALL MASTERS/EMPLOYEES			
A. White-collar workers (general)	3	7 (7)	10
B. White-collar workers (skilled)	10	17 (14)	27
C. Skilled workers	5	12 (12)	17
D. Manual workers	4 (1)	8 (8)	12
Subtotals	*22*	*44*	*66*
TOTALS	102	92	194

Note: numbers of intending teachers in brackets

As well as revealing the academic profile of Mason College students, the registers for those sessions where parental occupation is recorded make it possible to say something about the social background of students, always bearing in mind that not all students supplied the information. For 1893–4, 194 students did so. Assigning these descriptions to categories is not self-evident, not least because so much of Birmingham was still dominated by small enterprises.[70] A safety-pin manufacturer from Nechells was very unlikely to be in a large way of business. Nevertheless, with due caution, the material suggests that about a quarter of male students were linked to Birmingham industry. A further 15% had fathers in the city's commerce but the largest group came from a professional background or the equivalent. Fewer than one in three were the sons of retailers or small builders or various small masters or employees. This suggests three things. First it confirms that industry was a limited source of College students. Secondly, it indicates that 66% of male students came from established backgrounds, something which is borne out by three out of four of them living in Edgbaston or one of the Birmingham suburbs, or further out in the Midlands. Thirdly, it shows that very few sons of artisans or even skilled workers made it to a college education. For female students the position was almost the opposite. The professions were almost unrepresented, and industry and commerce provided under one-third of the female students, but 63% came from the other categories. The explanation for this is clearly that teaching was beginning to offer girls an alternative to domestic service or factory work. Of the female students with fathers in category V, 93% were going for the profession.[71]

Josiah Mason would have been pleased by the use being made of his college by women looking to teach. Years earlier the regulations for his orphanage had been drawn to encourage this. Once again, however, he would have felt that there should have been more children of Birmingham industrialists registering, and more small skilled craftsmen recognising that a formal training in science for their sons was a good investment. This was the principle behind all he had done. The social snapshot provided by his College's registers merely demonstrates that relatively few of those who shared Josiah Mason's background in Midland industry thought deeply enough to share his values.

Notes

1 UC 4/ii/7, pp. 72–6.

2 For general biographical material see *DNB*, *Who Was Who*, Cheesewright, *Mirror to a Mermaid* (Birmingham, 1975) and Vincent and Hinton, *University of Birmingham*.

3 This omits Haycraft, whose age has not been established.

4 *The Mermaid, 1909–10*, p. 230.

5 With the possible exception of Haycraft.

6 UC 10/i/18, cuttings from *Birmingham Gazette* and *Birmingham Post*, 1909.

7 *The Mermaid, 1909–10*, p. 230.

8 The early career of F. J. Allen is obscure.

9 *Mason College Magazine*, xiii (1895).

10 Ibid., ix (1891).

11 Ibid., xiii (1895).

12 Ibid. viii (1890); *University Gazette* 1924–7, p. 42; UC 10/i/18, cuttings from *Birmingham Gazette* and *Birmingham Express.*

13 For the following see *Calendars*, Vincent and Hinton, *University of Birmingham*, pp. 229–30 and K. D. Wilkinson, ed., 'The History of the Birmingham Medical School', *Birmingham Medical Review* (1925). There were no chairs in dentistry.

14 Wilkinson, ed., 'History of the Birmingham Medical School', p. 65.

15 Ibid., pp. 65–6.

16 For the following see the Council Reports in the annual *Calendars.*

17 C. M. Dix was appointed in 1886 to teach Classics but appears not to have been reappointed: *Calendar 1886–7*, p. 231.

18 Ibid., *1884–5*, p. 209; *1887–8*, p. 238; *1891–2*, p. 239.

19 Ibid., *1895–6*, pp. 396–7.

20 Ibid., *1891–2*, p. 223; cf. *1889–90*, p. 241.

21 There were no personal promotions in Arts and Sciences.

22 Engagements which were still running in 1899 are excluded.

23 *Calendar 1894–5*, p. 355; *1898–9*, p. 396.

24 Ibid., *1887–8*, p. 232; *1895–6*, pp. 398–9; *1899–1900*, p. 449.

25 Ibid., *1889–90*, p. 224.

26 For statistics and tables not subsequently referenced, see *Calendars*, passim.

27 See above, p. 22.

28 The highest was 714 in 1891–2 and the lowest 575 in 1890–1. The tables published by the Council for the Faculty of Arts and Science have to be corrected for the inclusion of medical students between 1882–3 and 1891–2 and for the inclusion of day training students from 1890–1. Figures for the number of individual enrolments end in 1892–3.

29 *Calendar 1889–90*, p. 238. He was also incorrect. Leeds was a few per cent larger: UC 1/i/6.

30 See above, pp. 36–7. Government comparisons between colleges tended to ignore evening enrolments.

31 Number of female students in Arts and Science:

1886–7	151 (49.7%)	1892–3	138 (41.9%)
1887–8	193 (53.5%)	1893–4	136 (42.9%)
1888–9	136 (45.2%)	1894–5	199 (53.6%)
1889–90	119 (37.7%)	1895–6	231 (56.3%)
1890–1	129 (40.4%)	1896–7	129 (39.3%)
1891–2	134 (42.8%)	1897–8	139 (41.5%)

The exceptional figures for 1894–6 have yet to be explained.

32 2368 men: 690 women.

33 From 1890–1.

34 Evening registrations in 1886–7 were exceptional.

35 See above, p. 43.
36 *Calendar 1897–8*, p. 405; *1898–9*, p. 420; *1899–1900*, p. 440.
37 See below, chapter 6.
38 *Calendar 1885–6*, p. 235.
39 Ibid., *1898–9*, p. 420.
40 Ibid., *1888–9* p. 262 and subsequent *Calendars*.
41 Calculated on a three-year running mean.
42 In this case figures have been made uniform by omitting medical students and day training students whose registration changed over the period.
43 Frequency of registration, Mason College 1892–3 to 1899–1900

Sessions attended	Men (%)	Women (%)	Total (%)
ONE	42.9	55.7	49.3
TWO consecutively	29.5	26.1	27.8
THREE consecutively	16.1	5.2	10.6
FOUR consecutively	7.1	3.5	5.3
TWO split	1.8	3.5	2.6
THREE split	1.8	2.6	2.2
FOUR split		1.8	0.9
FIVE consecutively	0.9		0.4
SIX consecutively		0.8	0.4
SEVEN consecutively		0.8	0.4

Source: UC9/vi, Student Registers 1892–3 to 1899–1900, initials B & H (22% sample).

44 UC 9/vi.
45 *Calendar 1889–90*, p. 239; *1890–1*, p. 246; *1892–3*, p. 378.
46 Ibid., *1889–90*, p. 239.
47 Before a full degree course could begin the London Intermediate Examination had to be passed, but exemption was possible given a good enough performance in the Higher School Certificate Examination, and this became the norm with A level.
48 UC 1/i/6 shows that between 1890–1 and 1892–3, Owens College produced 173 graduates in Arts, Science and Law, Liverpool 63, Mason 36, Leeds 34 and Newcastle 29.
49 *Calendar, 1899–1900*, pp. 363 et seq.
50 Ibid., *1885–6*, p. 235.
51 UC 9/vi, Books 3, 4.
52 Total enrolments in Arts and Science, 1892–3 to 1897–8:

Year	Science	Arts
1892–3	575	448
1893–4	581	477
1894–5	536	559
1895–6	585	553
1896–7	628	492
1897–8	626	773

53 *Calendar 1899–1900*, p. 440.

54 Ibid., *1880–1*, p. 42; *1881–2*, pp. 90–2; *1882–3*, pp. 128–35.

55 The following is based on student lists in the *Calendar* for the five years 1883–4, 1888–9, 1893–4 and 1898–9.

56 From a larger 'Birmingham'. *Calendar 1899–1900*, pp. 312–17.

57 Ibid.

58 The suburbs are defined as the wards which joined the city in 1911.

59 If the Birmingham cohort is omitted entirely, 131 names remain, of which 107 fall within the twenty-mile radius. See below, p. 64.

60 *Calendar 1893–4*, pp. 282–7.

61 The railway system clearly had a significant impact on student recruitment overall.

62 UC 9/vi, Student Registers. These do not survive before the session 1892–3.

63 UC 9/vi/3, ff. 30–44.

64 Ages of intending female teachers, winter 1893:

18 years	16	22 years	6
19 years	29	23 years	1
20 years	25	25–7 years	1
21 years	9	28–30 years	2

65 UC 9/vi/3, f. 43, nos. 331, 332. Cf. f. 34, no. 95.

66 Ibid., f. 33, nos. 92–4.

67 Ibid., f. 38, nos. 207, 208.

68 Ibid., f. 36, nos. 156–8.

69 Ibid., f. 44, no. 341.

70 *Independent status*: (A) architect, army officer, 6 clerics, dental surgeon, 4 physicians, 2 professors, 7 solicitors, 5 surgeons; (B) 3 government inspectors, Home Office clerk; (C) 3 farmers. *Birmingham industry*: (A) bedstead-, bicycle-, brick-, button-, carpet-, galvanised iron-, gun-, safety pin-, and watch-manufacturer and 8 unspecified, 2 manufacturing chemists, brassfounder. brewer, 2 ironfounders, ironmaster, miller, tar distiller; (B) gas manager, furnace manager, assistant overseer (mining), 9 managers unspecified. *Birmingham commerce*: (A) analytical chemist, art director, boiler inspector, consultant brewer, 2 medical examiners, 3 surveyors; (B) agent, 3 auctioneers, beer dealer, flour-, 2 glass-, iron-merchant, 3 merchants unspecified, metalbroker, tea dealer; (C) 2 accountants, 5 banking, share broker. *Services*: (A) contractor, 6 builders; (B) 2 bakers, 2 butchers, chemist, confectioner, 5 drapers, 2 grocers, ironmonger, 3 tailors, tobacconist. *Small masters/employees*: (A) 2 cashiers, 7 clerks, secretary; (B) bailiff, bookseller, chaser, clothier, collecting agent, 7 commercial travellers, organist, photographer, 12 schoolmasters, verger; (C) blacksmith, cabinetmaker, china decorator, 7 engineers, 4 jewellers, paper maker, silversmith, toolmaker; (D) decorator, gardener, joiner, metalworker, packer, pinplate worker, 2 quarrymen, tentor, turner, weigher, wiredrawer.

71 For a different assessment based on the 1892–3 entry, see J. M. Sanderson, *Universities and British Industry* (1972), pp. 98–9.

Chapter Five

What is a university?

ACQUIRING A MEDICAL FACULTY from Queen's certainly raised the academic profile of Mason College. The subsequent path to university status was, however, neither short nor simple. Two principal difficulties lay in its path. One was obvious – finance – but behind this lay something more fundamental – uncertainty and divergence of views about what a university was.

The age-old pattern of university organisation in Western Europe was of a body of masters who taught, examined and awarded degrees. These existed as self-governing corporations that were able to own property and were substantially independent of public authority, both local and central. Such institutions were the generality on the Continent and, more immediate, were the established form in Scotland. Some, but by no means all, universities had colleges attached to them, but where these existed they were little more than convenient units in which to organise student accommodation.

In England and Wales during the nineteenth century and earlier, colleges and universities were understood quite differently. Very generally, teaching was assumed to be the province of a college, so that where a benefactor or a community wanted to provide higher education, it was a college rather than a university which was set up. That understanding reflected centuries of experience of the particular ways of Oxford and Cambridge, and it shaped all nineteenth-century expansion in higher education south of the Scottish border, with the partial exception of Durham. In this Anglocentric view a university had no teaching function at all. It existed simply as a corporation, publicly recognised (by prescription or charter), which was entitled to examine for and to award academic degrees.

The relationship between late-Victorian colleges and late-Victorian universities was, thus, strictly that of purchaser and provider. Although University College and King's College taught for its examinations, neither was a constituent part of the University of London. The charter to London allowed it to award degrees to any person who presented for examination. Even when the London colleges became institutionally linked with the University by the act of 1898 they remained the locus of most teaching. The Victoria University, chartered in 1880, did have constituent colleges – at first Owens in Manchester, and then Liverpool and the Yorkshire College at Leeds – but they remained distinct and separate institutions. Again, the way the colleges at Bangor, Aberystwyth and Cardiff obtained access to degrees was by securing a charter for a federal University of Wales in 1893. Given this background, it is understandable that Josiah Mason's 1880 deed of variation envisaged that Mason College too would secure access to degrees by joining the Victoria University or some other federal institution. Equally, it is hardly surprising that for fifteen years and more this was generally assumed be to the College's future.

Henry Tilden, the Mason College professor of chemistry, summed up the position as he saw it when he addressed the opening of the 1886–7 session.[1] He frankly admitted that there was a long way to go before access to degree-giving powers became a realistic possibility.[2] The College had too few staff and too few students; its curriculum was too restricted; it was too little known and did not stand out in the generality of 'private classes and institutions'. Nevertheless, he was clear on the eventual issue. The choice would be to become 'the centre of a new University of Birmingham and the Midlands or a constituent of some university already existent'. The current alternatives were the Victoria University and London, and Tilden openly championed London, which was at that stage exploring the possibility of recognising constituent colleges. There might, he accepted, be a third possibility: 'Some of the more ardent of my friends round this table look forward to a different consummation for our early struggles and aspirations. Nothing less than an independent University of Birmingham will satisfy them.'[3] Who this was directed to is not clear. The target may have been E. A. Sonnenschein, who would espouse similar views in later years and who had worked with him on an alliance with Queen's College.[4] But although Tilden sympathised with the aspiration, he believed that the obstacles were very severe, chiefly to do with money. If the people of Birmingham wanted a university of their own, they had only to find the funds!

Debate outside the College ranged over the same set of options. In February 1887 Dr H. W. Crosskey gave his presidential address to the Birmingham Philosophical Society entitled 'A Plea for a Midland University', in which he argued for a university on the Victoria model.[5] The Society followed this with a general discussion of the issue a fortnight later.[6] J. B. Haycraft, the Mason College professor of physiology, opened with a demonstration of both the lack of advanced education in Birmingham and the obstacles to providing it. Bertram Windle, the dean of the Queen's Medical Faculty, argued that there was activity in the region from which a federal institution might be built – which would also have to have provision for a women's college. Another Queen's professor, Dr A. H. Carter, physician at the Queen's and Children's Hospitals, was thoroughly negative. A university for the Birmingham area alone would be undesirable. It would lead to a multiplication of universities in other places and to major problems nationally over standards and the value of degrees. Already, he claimed, there were too many universities in the United Kingdom. He also saw grave practical difficulties both in creating a local university, and equally in forging links with existing federal institutions elsewhere. All he could offer was the suggestion that where particular faculties in different Midland colleges were of an adequate standard some kind of association might be possible.

The following October Birmingham was given quite another assessment when J. R. Seeley, the professor of modern history at Cambridge, addressed the Birmingham and Midland Institute.[7] Oxford and Cambridge, he declared bluntly, 'though it is the type best known to Englishmen is not yet the normal type' of university; they are 'at least as peculiar as they are ancient or illustrious'.[8] The collegiate model was not right for Birmingham and it should look instead to Scotland and Germany. But in that case, what would happen to the primary moral function which colleges were generally believed to have? Who would deliver the agenda which Arnold of Rugby had laid down for education: training 'up young men to serve God and to serve their generation'? This function Seeley completely rejected. A university was not an educational institution but a seat of learning. A school existed for its pupils; a university exists for science and learning. A professor

> is not to abandon the higher parts of [fundamental study and original research] and descend to the level of a teacher of rudiments because by doing so he may give lectures more immediately useful.
>
> In every great centre such as Birmingham there should be a body of high-class teachers, so large and so actively and methodically engaged, that they should constitute a university, at least as a university is understood in Germany.[9]

As for the option of a university as the examining body for a federation of disparate colleges, that, he said roundly, 'has long since exhausted itself'.[10] The contrast to Tilden and those who thought like him was obvious, and Seeley's voice would be heard again.[11]

Precisely when university status ceased to be a hypothetical issue at Birmingham is unclear. It was certainly not before 1888, for Joseph Chamberlain was then speaking of 'a true Midland University' as a future goal which 'every Birmingham man' should keep 'before him as one of the great objects of his life'.[12] It is not clear either who moved the subject from debate to practicality. According to Chamberlain's Founder's Day speech in 1893, the idea of a university 'for the Midland metropolis' was 'first mooted' some time previously 'with some few of my friends whom I see around me'; 'adequate endowment is the first and only remaining condition for success'.[13] He could possibly have been referring to remarks in an address he gave to the Birmingham and Midland Institute in October 1877, but these had only been aspirational in tone.[14] Henry Tilden's contention was that serious interest in university status for Mason College came mainly from the Medical Faculty, and Windle's early advocacy is beyond question.[15] The probability, therefore, is that the strategy agreed among Chamberlain and his friends was triggered by the merger of Queen's with Mason in September 1892 and encouraged by the new arrivals.

The first documented step of any campaign was taken at the December 1894 meeting of the College Senate.[16] Robert Heath, the principal, proposed that an association should be formed 'for the promotion of a Midland University' and a committee of nine was set up to take matters forward: Heath in the chair with four professors from Arts and Science – Dixon (English), Fiedler (German), Hillhouse (botany), and Poynting (physics) – and four professors from the Medical Faculty: Windle, Barling, Carter and Saundby. It is an interesting list. Medicine was substantially over-represented and there was no place for E. A. Sonnenschein, the professor of classics, although in 1885 he had pressed for the link with Queen's as a first step towards university powers and would be credited by his contemporaries and by history with a key role in the move towards a university.[17]

Over the next four months the Committee had six meetings.[18] The result was a proposal for a university which would have been little more than a Midland version of the great University of London paperchase. Its advice to the Senate in May 1895 was that it was 'desirable that the proposed university shall include all such institutions or departments of institutions in Birmingham as by their equipment and general efficiency may hereafter be considered suitable for incorporation as faculties in the university'.[19] A manuscript note by Robert Heath suggests that the Midland Institute and the Municipal School of Art were to become the faculties of Music and Art, respectively, with the Municipal Technical Schools acting as a feeder at matriculation and intermediate degree level.[20] The Senate adopted the report but rejected a rider proposed by the Committee to restrict participation to educational bodies in Birmingham. This had been proposed in the belief that neither Bristol nor Nottingham possessed 'complete teaching staffs or general equipment to justify inclusion', but clearly the prevailing opinion was that Birmingham could not go it alone. There was, however, agreement with the Committee's thinking about the practicalities of getting a charter. They proposed a general committee of notables under the presidency of Joseph Chamberlain and an executive committee headed by Thackeray Bunce, one of Mason's early trustees, with the whole campaign being launched at a special town meeting.[21] Finance was not seen as a major problem, and was grossly underestimated. Upgrading Mason College in order to be able to offer all major branches of university work could, it was said, be covered by a further £45,000 on the endowment, plus an increase in the annual Treasury grant to £2770 a year. The capital outlay to obtain the charter and provide buildings to house the university functions would be £17,000, while running expenses would require a further government grant of £2000 a year, plus the examination fees.[22]

This 1894–5 initiative apparently got nowhere. It was, perhaps, premature. Josiah Mason had stipulated that his provisions could only be changed in the two years which would follow each successive fifteenth anniversary of the first Founder's Day, so that nothing could be done at the earliest before 23 February 1896.[23] Certainly, when in May 1896 the Senate raised the issue again it did so with a difference.[24] The obvious intention now was to force the college into the Victoria University. A unanimous resolution was passed, calling the attention of the College Council to the problems caused by not being connected with any university. The government, it claimed, was favourable, the two and a half million people of the Midlands had as good a claim to a university as Manchester or Cardiff, and Birmingham, Bristol and Nottingham were alone among large urban centres in having no such provision. Access to a university would mean that student numbers would rise because medical students would no longer need to go elsewhere to get degrees and other students would not be put off by the lengthy delays of the London system. The College staff would no longer have to teach in a vacuum with no voice in course construction or examining, and no longer would they have to meet the demands of different examination boards – in medicine, as many as nine of them. There was, as Senate saw it, no alternative. The College had to secure university powers in the near future either for the Midlands or, if that would encounter insuperable difficulties, Mason had to join the Victoria University.

The College Council, however, had a different priority. Now that Mason's designated time for revision had arrived the immediate need was to incorporate the College by Act of Parliament, and so replace its trustees with a much wider and more powerful Court of Governors.[25] Council agreed, neverthless, that Bunce, G. J. Johnson and the principal should consult Joseph Chamberlain on the question of university powers and that, if he agreed, these should be applied for at the same time as the incorporation.[26] The dean of Medicine, Bertram Windle, was horrified by the prospect of waiting at least two parliamentary sessions and probably more before a new university could be formed, and he castigated Council for not grasping the seriousness of the position; before local patriotism could be whipped up to raise the necessary money, the Medical School would, on past experience, be in a bad way!

> Does not the obvious lack of enthusiasm or desire for a local University on the part of the inhabitants of the Midlands prove the truth of the statement just made as to the improbability of our securing an adequate additional endowment within any reasonable period of time? If the statement which I have quoted respecting a Midland University be true, I would respectfully

beg the Council to weigh very carefully the statements I have made before holding aloof from the Victoria University.[27]

As it happened Chamberlain could not meet a delegation – after a dramatic year as Secretary of State for the Colonies, coping with the aftermath of the Jameson Raid, he needed a holiday, and, in any case, he was preparing to go to the United States to help defuse a potential conflict over British Guiana.[28] In August 1896, therefore, Heath put the case in a letter.[29] Much of it concerned money. A university, he claimed, need not cost as much as had been suggested if it were housed in the Mason College building and was in receipt of £2000 a year from government, the figure allowed to the Victoria University. On the other hand, if setting up the University really would require a large sum of money, the Midland project was hopeless. The College had had very limited success in raising even small sums from benefactors and the General Hospital appeal then in progress was absorbing all available donations. The College Council therefore wanted to know whether Chamberlain would support an immediate bill creating a Midland university. If not, it would be driven to the 'easier though less satisfactory course' of applying to Victoria, which had the advantage of allowing immediate access to degrees on already existing regulations.

Judged by the attendance registers, Joseph Chamberlain was able to take relatively little direct part in the College trust. In the five years 1895–6 to 1899–1900 he was summoned to twenty meetings but attended only three. However, his general prestige in Birmingham and his prominence at Westminster ensured that his opinion was always decisive. His reply, by return of post, was an unequivocal 'no' to both courses of action: 'I should most strenuously oppose to the utmost of any influence that I may possess any attempt on the part of Mason College to connect itself with the Victoria University.'[30] That would be to merge Mason in another provincial institution, 'contrary to the feeling of the vast majority of Birmingham people, and I cannot believe that it has any chance of success'. As for the Midland University alternative, this was premature and 'unlikely to be successful'. Similarly with Heath's suggestion about a university on the cheap: 'I have always thought that no mistake could be greater than to start a University in a starved and cramped condition; and I believe that, properly undertaken, a successful effort might be made to obtain a large endowment.' Let the appeal for the General Hospital proceed unchallenged and wait a year or two.

This letter, dated 17 August 1896, is one of the determining documents of the University of Birmingham. It threw the immense influence of Chamberlain across the path of those who advocated a link with the Victoria University or any other outside the Midlands. More important, it also meant that one of the country's most acute and effective political and practical brains was committed to the cause. From now on the Midland university was a Chamberlain project.

Following receipt of his letter the Council went ahead only with the process of incorporation, but Clayton, Heath and Morley did go to Liverpool and Manchester to find out about the Victoria University at first hand.[31] Whether this was because not everyone was yet convinced by Chamberlain's line is not clear, but the message they came away with was that Liverpool (and, it was reported, Leeds), was extremely dissatisfied with being part of a federal university. Thus when Chamberlain met his fellow trustees and senior staff on 20 November 1896, although Heath and Windle pressed the need for urgency, the decision was to apply in two years time for powers for a new university in conjunction, it was hoped, with the colleges at Nottingham and Bristol.[32] Now, not only was the College and more importantly Chamberlain committed to a Midlands-only policy, they were committed to a date.

Securing the incorporation bill was the necessary preliminary and it duly passed into law, with a start date for a renamed Mason University College of 1 January 1898.[33] More important, November's agreement meant that what had hitherto been a concept now had to be worked up towards reality. In the process the whole issue about university identity would be sifted and a formation reached which set a pattern which has been dominant in higher education in the UK until the present day.

The accepted goal at the meeting with Chamberlain was still a federation of teaching colleges. One way of achieving this was the 1895 scheme for a university which federated the faculties of different institutions. This idea was resurrected in March 1897 in a paper by Hillhouse, the professor of botany, with the modification that postgraduate work should done under the aegis of the overall university. He showed the scheme to the professor of physics, J. H. Poynting, who liked the suggestion for postgraduates because it would raise the Midland University 'above the level of an examining body'.[34] Poynting, however, had ideas of his own which he had circulated a month earlier, under the title 'The Proposed Midland University: suggestions as to the basis of a scheme'.[35] It was a subtle piece which promoted the collegiate model of the university but began by appearing to accept something of the alternative continental model. A university, he said, had three functions: imparting learning to the younger members, pursuing research, and examining and awarding degrees. Mason College already performed the first two but the third could only be granted by the state: 'Were there any chance of a University of Birmingham alone, the simplest plan would be to identify it with Mason College, the governing body being so modified that the interests of the general community in the standards for degrees were fully preserved.' This would have produced a teaching university. Poynting, however, dismissed this as totally unrealistic: 'We certainly have no chance of obtaining a Birmingham University, and we as certainly have to look forward to the federation some day with at least Bristol and Nottingham in a Midland University.' Given this, a Midland university would have to be a corporation separate from the colleges with degree giving powers and possibly a role in funding research. All other fields of activity should be left to the colleges – that was the simplest course – and each locality would be responsible for raising the endowment for its own institution. Thus Mason College would be the university face for Birmingham, and Birmingham people would fund it, and other colleges *mutatis mutandis*. It was, he claimed, a scheme which would preserve continuity with earlier development, avoid any friction between colleges and the new University and preserve vital local freedom in 'higher teaching and higher work'.

One further proposal reached the stage of being printed. Produced by the professor of classics, E. A. Sonnenschein, it was in fact the earliest to appear, having been launched on the Senate only days after the 20 November meeting with Chamberlain.[36] It represented ideas which had incubated for over a decade and it was radical – Sonnenschein had been particularly influenced by discussions he had had with Seeley, after the latter's 1887 lecture.[37] The very title was a challenge: 'A Teaching University for the Midlands'. There were, it argued, four kinds of university in the United Kingdom: Oxbridge, which had independent teaching colleges, the Scottish model, which did not, London and the Royal Irish University, which were purely examining bodies, while Victoria and Wales were examining bodies which served federations of teaching colleges. The Midland University needed to combine features from each. Its colleges should teach but be non-residential; it should be a federation of Birmingham, Bristol and Nottingham, but its governing body should be formed collectively and power would rest at the centre. The model was Johns Hopkins and other leading universities of America and Germany. Citing Seeley's 1887 lecture, Sonnenschein also argued that the advancement of learning and the pursuit of research must be a priority of the new institution: 'The endowment of research, in close association with teaching, in all the main branches of a liberal education would give the Midland University a unique position as a national centre for post-graduate instruction.' Like Hillhouse and Poynting, Sonnenschein accepted the inevitability of a federal structure. Teaching would still take place in the various colleges. However, he envisaged two tiers of activity. University professors would be appointed to each college to teach postgraduates and conduct research in laboratories rented to them. Undergraduates would be taught by College professors. Collectively the University professors would determine University policy and act as internal examiners. College professors would be responsible for local examinations. The latter would, however, be funded so as to be free from elementary teaching and able to do university work part time. They could also be promoted to University rank, which would provide a career structure (unlike the Victoria University).

Sonnenschein's proposal was cumbersome, and the downgrading of Mason College and the prospect of first- and second-class professors positively invited opposition. Nevertheless, when he met Chamberlain at Highbury early in the New Year the professor of classics left in the belief that his scheme had the Colonial Secretary's support.[38] With this encouragement, he put three propositions to an informal meeting of Senate in March: that the new University should be a new and separate institution; that a principal object in fund-raising must be to finance research; and that all moneys raised by the appeal ought to be paid into a single fund for the University.[39] All three were all carried but this success masked considerable criticism for a proposal which 'gave all the cream to the University and left all the skim-milk to the College'.[40] Thus when on 18 May Sonnenschein proposed that the Senate should formally endorse the March vote he was not even seconded. Instead, the general principles of Poynting's paper were adopted by a large majority and sent for development to a committee of Heath, Windle, Barling, Poynting and Bridge – three scientists and two medics.[41]

The plan which this committee brought forward early in July was for a Midland version of the Victoria University, with Mason in the role of Owens College.[42] The University would not to be for Birmingham alone; the headquarters would be there but institutions from elsewhere could apply to join.

> The government of the University will, at the first, be in the hands of representatives of this City, the [i.e. Mason] College and the Midland District, who, with the Crown nominees, will form in the first instance the Court, and it will be for this body to say when the terms of admission for other institutions, laid down in the Act of Incorporation, have been fulfilled.

The University would direct courses of study and promote original research. In particular it would establish degrees in engineering, metallurgy, electro-technics and other applied sciences. The Senate would comprise the professors of the various colleges, but the University as such would not teach: 'It is clear that a University of the Federal type cannot concern itself directly with the teaching of the Students in its Colleges. This part of its work must be left in the hands of the Colleges, each of which will, therefore, in its own district act in this respect as the University.' The ordinary work of Mason College would be 'not much altered' but 'higher work' would be improved because the professors would have a voice in it. As for finance, a single committee should raise funds and decide on the division between university and college, but with the clear hint that priority would go to the latter so 'that it may be fitted to take its place as the head of the University'. It was a plan which threatened nobody and, as far as possible, endorsed the status quo. When the Senate considered it early in July, it was recommended to Council with only one vote to the contrary – Sonnenschein without doubt.

When the new session opened in October 1897 the answer to 'the university question', as it was called in Birmingham, seemed clear. A link with the Victoria University had been ruled out. The process to incorporate Mason College was in hand and achieving this would be the signal to start a move to secure a charter establishing a Midland University. This would be based in Birmingham and have central degree-awarding powers but would serve a federation of teaching colleges. The colleges to participate initially would be Mason and at least Bristol and Nottingham, and each would be responsible for its own funding. The federal pattern for higher education in England and Wales was in for powerful reinforcement.

Within weeks all this was in ruins and everyone 'in a great state of excitement'.[43] Joseph Chamberlain had announced, without warning, that 'he must have a University of Birmingham pure and simple'! And it must be under that name – otherwise 'I am out of it.' The seeds of this reversal had, all unwittingly, been sown by Chamberlain's election earlier in the year as rector of Glasgow University. In due course he had travelled north to be installed in office and on 3 November 1897 spoke to a huge gathering on the subject of 'patriotism' – not, it seems, one of his better performances. But if Chamberlain did not wholly impress Glasgow, Glasgow University very much impressed him. He left saying: 'When I go back to Birmingham I mean to have a University of my own.'[44]

No time was wasted. On 15 November Heath knew nothing about it but on the 19th he was arranging for Chamberlain to launch 'the University movement' at the first meeting of the Court of Governors of the newly incorporated College on 13 January 1898.[45] The lord mayor was due to host a celebratory lunch and this would provide an ideal opportunity to raise the subject, while the ensuing meeting of Governors could put the necessary procedures in hand. On the first Monday in December Chamberlain briefed trustees and Council on his new views and his new agenda, and on the 8th Heath, Windle, Bunce and Kenrick went to Highbury to begin to implement them.[46] The programme for 13 January 1898 worked like clockwork.[47] At lunchtime Chamberlain spoke of Mason College as at the end of possible development, given its limited financial resources and its lack of degree-giving status. What the future required was a university modelled – but not slavishly so – on Scottish examples: 'a school of universal instruction, not confined to any particular branch of knowledge but taking all knowledge in its province. A place in which those who come to teach shall continue to learn and in which the work, the most important work, of original research shall be continuously carried on under favourable circumstances.' A university like that would, he claimed, complete the advances Birmingham had made in education over the previous ten or twenty years, and earlier. Indeed, it would do more than that. To the man who above all personified the drive which had brought the town from a slum to a vibrant modern city, a university for Birmingham was the climax of that whole endeavour, enabling its citizens to see beyond the necessities of trade and commerce to 'higher aims and higher intellectual ambitions'. At the governors' meeting after lunch the business was rapidly concluded. Lord Windsor and Professor Henry Tilden, two of the new governors, proposed and seconded a motion that:

> having regard to the development of higher education in the Midlands and to the immediate requirements and prospective interests of such education, the Governors of Mason University College are of the opinion that the time has arrived for the establishment of a University in Birmingham and that the Governors will give their hearty support to the measures requisite to obtain a Royal Charter for that purpose and generally for the promotion of the object.

It was carried unanimously.[48]

It is tempting to see the vote of 13 January 1898 as a determining event in the evolution of a university for Birmingham, the moment when its character was defined as Scottish or continental rather than English. Something of that was certainly implicit in the parallel Chamberlain drew with Glasgow University, which had been 'built up, as we hope ours will be, upon a pre-existent college which has subsequently been absorbed or if you please developed into a university'. But exactly what Chamberlain intended by 'built up', 'absorbed' and 'developed' is not clear. The Secretary of State was an excellent draftsman but on the university question was known to prefer vision to detail, and that was where the devil was.[49] At the Highbury meeting on 8 December Chamberlain had himself agreed that Mason University College would be absorbed by the new University only at a later date, and that any charter had to provide for the admission of third-party institutions (as it eventually did).[50] Thus when the principal of University College, Bristol enquired of Robert Heath where Bristol now stood, Heath could still offer the private opinion that other colleges would be able to join the proposed University, although he did warn that if more money was raised than he clearly thought probable, this might change:[51] 'What we shall do afterwards depends on our success. I imagine if the promoters (Mr Chamberlain, the Lord Mayor [Alderman C. G. Beale] & others) are very successful in raising money they may wax fat and in that case I should not be surprised if they went for a University of Birmingham only.'[52]

What then did Chamberlain's 'new idea' amount to? First and foremost, as Heath informed Bristol, it was that the interests of Birmingham would now be paramount: 'At present it is a Birmingham movement and is directed to one object only, viz. to raise money from the people of Birmingham for further endowments for Higher Education and University expenses.'[53]

In Glasgow Chamberlain had seen a city which had its own university for its own people. Birmingham must have the same. Colleges could still join, but any which did would have to accept the hegemony of Birmingham. The significance of 13 January 1898 was, therefore, the rejection of the concept of a university as a federation of equals, while allowing any colleges wanting to affiliate the opportunity of dependency status. But there was more behind Chamberlain's change of direction than civic imperialism. There was, quite simply, size. Previous estimates of the funds needed to acquire and sustain degree-giving status were at a maximum, £60,000. On returning from Glasgow, Chamberlain asked Heath to produce plans to spend £200,000.[54] This figure was increased even further at the substantive discussion which Chamberlain had with Heath, Kenrick and the others on 8 December 1897. Financial projections produced by the principal had indicated that to endow additional chairs, help fund the College deficit and increase professorial support would require £150,000. A further £60,000 would be needed for buildings, including a library, and £40,000 for research fellowships and scholarships, making the appeal target £250,000 in all.[55] Since Mason had provided £230,000 in site, buildings and endowment, Chamberlain's university would be double the size of the existing College. In comparative terms it would put Birmingham on a near equality with Owens College, Manchester.[56]

Further insight into Chamberlain's thinking can be gained from the confidential and somewhat indiscreet letter which his brother-in-law George Kenrick wrote to Sonnenschein on 9 December 1897 to inform him of the revolutionary decisions of the previous week: 'It will be satisfactory to you to know that your scheme after being scouted by the Senate is now the working basis of the new idea!'[57] Kenrick was probably referring to the title rather than the detail of Sonnenschein's original paper, 'A Teaching University for the Midlands', and to the three points of principle which Senate had accepted in March 1897 and reneged on in May: that the University should be a new and separate institution, that research should be a prime objective and that all money raised should go to it and not the College. This thinking certainly corresponds to other decisions reached at the 8 December meeting. Professors would be university appointees, irrespective of whether they were supported on new university funds or existing college endowments; they would teach; research would have a high priority in both funding and the choice of staff; the financial appeal would have as its object, establishing the *University*. As for Mason University College, if the new University had effectively the same governing body, it would be easy for its endowments and activities to be taken over in due course.[58]

Following the Court on 13 January, the next stage was for the lord mayor to call a public meeting. However, planning for this only began in May with a chosen date of 1 July.[59] The reason for the interval of nearly six months was Chamberlain's conviction that, as he had said in 1893, the key to success would be the amount of money which could be raised.[60] He was, therefore, determined not to go public until he could launch the appeal with a substantial subscription list already in hand. He had promised this for the governors' meeting, but that had been premature.[61] Now a private canvass committee was organised and at the 1 July meeting Chamberlain was able to produce a list of donors who had already promised £95,580, nearly two-fifths of the sum needed.[62] The public meeting responded enthusiastically and agreed to set up the kind of structure which had been envisaged in 1895 – a general committee of well-wishers under Chamberlain, an executive committee, this time headed by Alderman Francis Corder Clayton, a management subcommittee and another to canvass funds.[63] Preliminary work for this last was already in hand to produce a number of books containing a list of potential donors which could be assigned to particular individuals to follow up. The professor of German, Georg Fiedler, was one such, but in the course of his summer holidays he set about also canvassing subscriptions in Germany.[64]

In any large appeal, the publicity created by a general canvass is probably as important or more important than the actual amount of money raised. It was so with the appeal for the new University. In public speeches Joseph Chamberlain stressed the value of subscriptions of 'a couple or three pounds', and he was no doubt delighted when the Birmingham Empire promised the proceeds of a matinée performance every year for five years![65] Yet although in the nine months after the fund was launched in July 1898 the efforts of the canvassers brought in £135,000, Chamberlain was well aware that real success would depend on finding a handful of substantial donors.[66] Where were they to be found? Birmingham had, Chamberlain knew, few men of very great wealth, so his target was the city's well-to-do.[67] Invitations to the Chamberlain house at Highbury, which had been such a successful component of party organisation in the city, were used to raise funds for the appeal. Early in July 1898 he wrote to Kenrick to say that he would be arriving in Birmingham on the 13th and leaving on holiday on the 31st: 'If in the interval I can do anything for the University by attending a committee or canvassing any Trade or individual, I am at your disposal.'[68] Chamberlain himself led the way with £2000, a significant amount for a man who was not wealthy and in days when MPs were not paid.[69] The Black Country steel magnate, Sir Charles Holcroft, came up with an initial £20,000.[70] Lord Calthorpe, Chamberlain's erstwhile electoral opponent in Birmingham, expressed an interest which in 1900 became a gift of twenty-five acres in Edgbaston.[71] That same summer Sir James Chance offered £50,000 for Engineering.[72] Charles Harding thought that it might be necessary to find as many as twenty or twenty-five such 'patriotic citizens' but he was reckoning without Chamberlain's willingness to exploit his national and international prestige.[73] His first success was with a man with whom he, as Colonial Secretary, had regular dealings, the Canadian High Commissioner Donald Smith. Smith, formerly a poor Scottish emigrant but now Lord Strathcona, had made a fortune in Canadian railways and offered £25,000.[74] Chamberlain proposed that a trust should be formed to endow the Commerce Faculty, but Strathcona insisted on anonymity. In May 1899 he offered a further £12,500 if the £250,000 target was met by June and eventually promised to increase this to a total of £50,000 overall, provided £300,000 was raised – which it was.[75]

At the same time that Chamberlain was in touch with the Canadian High Commissioner, he was also dealing with someone else from the New World who was even wealthier, the Pittsburgh steel millionaire, Andrew Carnegie.[76] He too began by offering £25,000 and ended on £50,000. Indeed, it has been suggested that Chamberlain deliberately played his two transatlantic contacts off, one against the other.[77] This, however, seems somewhat unlikely since Carnegie was very difficult to bring up to scratch because of ignorance and misconceptions about Birmingham, which he held with characteristic robustness. His first letter said that he was not much into supporting universities, but would offer £25,000 if the gift was used to help local poor boys. Chamberlain's reply elicited an offer of £50,000 but earmarked for setting up a proper scientific department: 'I wish to co-operate with you in placing Birmingham far ahead of anything in the United Kingdom, and believe me it can be done.' Given what existed at Mason College, Chamberlain replied that a brand new scientific school was not what was wanted; he needed capital in order to fund posts. Carnegie's response was most unhelpful. He would fund a scientific college. Chamberlain had money for the commercial College (the Strathcona offer). Mason College should remain as the classical side, but its buildings were useless for science. A delegation should come to see Cornell, the Steven Institute in Hoboken, Ann Arbor and Yale. 'The money must be spent, or you will get nothing.' Chamberlain returned a diplomatic – and successful answer. The suggestion of a visit was excellent, but if Carnegie insisted on a science building, money would be spent unnecessarily. Much progress in science had taken place in Britain recently and significant investment had gone into Mason College. Whether it was the suggestion of waste or the readiness to consider American examples, Carnegie's next letter was conciliatory. Money from his gift could be used to make the scientific department 'perfect', with the rest going to the endowment, so he and Chamberlain would both be satisfied. He also recommended that the School of Mines at Columbia should be added to the itinerary of the proposed visit (which he later agreed to finance).

Chamberlain attended an informal meeting on 31 August where a working party was set up to plan for the use of the Carnegie and Strathcona gifts and for the American visit.[78] On this sat Chamberlain's brother-in-law George Kenrick, his brother Arthur and his second son, Neville (a former student of Mason College) and Professors Poynting and Burstall but, perhaps significantly, not Principal Heath.[79] At a momentous meeting on 7 October the Committee decided that Carnegie was right about Mason College and that new buildings for the University were vital.[80] This set the agenda for the American trip. Kenrick, Poynting and Burstall sailed on the *Oceanic* on 1 November 1899, and in less than seven weeks, including two Atlantic crossings, they succeeded in visiting all the institutions Carnegie recommended, except Yale, plus the Massachusetts Institute of Technology (MIT), the Polytechnic at Worcester, Harvard, McGill, Toronto, Chicago, Johns Hopkins and Pennsylvania, twelve in all. They were only able to do this in the time by confining their attention to physics, chemistry and applied science, but the thirteen-page report on those areas which they published on 18 December was specific and detailed.[81] Engineering, mining and metallurgy alone would require a four-acre site. The degree course should be four years and a curriculum was proposed, along with a schedule of the facilities required to teach it. Not that this was the end of travelling. In January 1900 Burstall produced a schematic plan for engineering but was sent off to collect details of the teaching programmes at four British colleges.[82] Possibly as a result, a fuller delegation visited the University College at Sheffield in February; Neville Chamberlain, who had had to miss the *Oceanic* trip, was one of the party on this occasion.[83] The consequence of all this careful enquiry could have been predicted. In May 1900, with £330,000 now raised, Joseph Chamberlain spoke to the new University.

> The report of the committee which visited Canada and the United States has opened my eyes and I think must have opened the eyes of all who have read it. The committee found great institutions connected with a general university, real colleges of Science, occupying large spaces, in which the area was counted by many acres, fully equipped with proper buildings with the most modern and complete machinery, with the latest scientific appliances, with laboratories for every conceivable scientific purpose. And in these great colleges a training was given such as we desire to see imitated in this country, a training based, as all education ought to be, upon a foundation of general culture, but specialised in its course, highly specialised, according to the particular and separate work which each student intends to take in life. ... That is what we want and we shall not be the university which we all have in our minds until we have accomplished it.[84]

Despite success up to that point, a further £250,000 was needed. A year later this had become £500,000 and in January 1902, £1 million. This final target was never reached, but in four years Chamberlain's enthusiasm and commitment raised the equivalent of £650,000.[85]

Chamberlain's fund-raising did not always succeed, but ironically the only place where he was brushed off was at Cabinet level, where it has been said that, despite his Liberal Unionists being the minority party in a coalition, he generally enjoyed the influence of a 'co-premier'. In May 1899 he asked Hicks Beach, the Chancellor of the Exchequer, to confirm that the existing government grant would continue to be paid if Mason College was absorbed into the new institution and requested equality of treatment with the Victoria University in receiving £2000 a year extra to support university status. Hicks Beach was a Conservative and had been offered the Exchequer only after Chamberlain had refused it. The opportunity was too good to miss.[86] He replied that Mason College grant was protected to 1902. However, the payment to Victoria was a relic from the days when individual colleges were not supported and had been justified because of regional and national importance. 'I do not see how this condition could be said to be present in the case of a Birmingham University dealing with or rather absorbing a single local College only.' The University of Wales had a grant but this was justified on grounds of Welsh nationality. London University received no grant, but as its examinations were of imperial importance, the Treasury covered any losses on its fee income; in any case London offered no precedent since it had been chartered as a gesture to dissenters, a consideration no longer relevant. (Chamberlain, of course, was a dissenter). Birmingham would only be considered if it could prove that it was losing money, was unable to cover the costs of degree examinations and 'was a national institution not serving a particular locality'!

The Hicks Beach rebuff was untypical but it serves to make the point that the Chamberlain who promoted the cause of a university for Birmingham with such energy and such success was an active politician, indeed a minister who at the same time was facing decisions of the very greatest moment. When he launched the university project at the public meeting of 1 July 1898, Chamberlain's ministerial boxes were full of a tense stand-off with France over colonial rights in West and Central Africa.[87] When on 20 October he wrote to George Kenrick asking to meet the Executive Committee and also the Canvass Committee 'to see how far I can assist', it was within hours of returning to Birmingham from a 'successful trip'.[88] The plea to Hicks Beach coincided with the arrival of the Uitlanders' petition to Queen Victoria against 'ill treatment' by President Kruger's Boer government of the Transvaal. The negotiations with Carnegie punctuated the growing crisis in South Africa and when Chamberlain met to discuss the American visit, his mind must have been full of the diplomatic activity which preceded the Boer declaration of war on 9 October. That he could progress such disparate concerns simultaneously and with equal commitment is an index of the remarkable man the second founder of the University of Birmingham was.

Notes

1 UC7/iv/1, Lectures: Tilden (1886).
2 Ibid., p. 5.
3 Ibid., p. 10.
4 See above, p. 42.
5 UC7/iv/1, Lectures: Crosskey (1887). For the debates about a Midland university, see also Vincent and Hinton, *University of Birmingham*, pp. 4–7.
6 UC 7/iv/4/8: Discussion at Birmingham Philosophical Society, 24 Feb. 1887.
7 UC7/iv/1, Lectures: Seeley (1887).
8 Ibid., p. 4.
9 Ibid., p. 11.
10 Ibid., p. 14.
11 See below, p. 77.
12 28 May 1888: J. Amery, *The Life of Joseph Chamberlain*, iv (1951), p. 211. For a discussion which suggests that Chamberlain effectively dismissed developments

at Mason College, see Marsh, *Joseph Chamberlain*, pp. 443–6. The university archive indicates that from an early stage Mason College looked to Chamberlain for leadership. The nine College trustees came from the same Birmingham background as Chamberlain, and as well as Chamberlain included his brother Richard, J. T. Bunce, his close ally, and George Dixon (ibid., p. 140).

13 UC 7/iv/5/28, Lectures: Chamberlain (1893), p. 9.

14 University of Birmingham, JC4/5/96.

15 *Birmingham Daily Post*, 14 Jan. 1898.

16 UC 4/ii/10, pp. 91–2.

17 See below, pp. 77–8.

18 UC 4/ii/6, insert pp. 1–13.

19 UC 4/ii/10, pp. 95–100.

20 UC 1/i/7, undated memo headed 'Proposed Midland University'. Alternatively it could be associated with a later scheme.

21 UC 4/ii/6, insert p. 9.

22 UC 4/ii/10, p. 100.

23 UC 4/ii/11, p. 172; 1/i/3/: Clayton to Lloyd, 10 Dec.1898.

24 UC 4/ii/10, pp. 111, 118.

25 UC 4/i/24, no. 3049.

26 Ibid., nos. 3051, 3052.

27 Ibid., pp. 221–3.

28 Ibid., p. 216. The Raid had been launched on 30 December 1895. Chamberlain saw President Cleveland's secretary in September 1896 about the Venezuela Boundary Dispute.

29 UC 4/i/24, pp. 233–5.

30 Ibid., pp. 236–7.

31 UC 1/i/3/1: Clayton to Lloyd, 10 Dec. 1898.

32 Ibid.; 4/ii/7, pp. 265–6; cf. the subsequent Council (which Chamberlain attended): 4/ii/1, 6 Dec. 1897.

33 Ibid., p. 162.

34 Ibid., p. 156.

35 Ibid. p. 158.

36 Ibid. p. 160.

37 University of Birmingham: JC35/2/1.

38 E. J. Somerset, *Birth of a University* (Birmingham, 1934).

39 Ibid., p. 11; UC 4/ii/10, pp. 136–8.

40 Somerset, *Birth of a University*, p. 7.

41 UC 4/ii/10, pp. 136–8.

42 Ibid., p. 141; UC 7/iv/4/16.

43 UC 1/i/3/1:Clayton to Lloyd, 10 Dec. 1898.

44 Amery, *Joseph Chamberlain*, iv.212.

45 UC1/ii/3, pp. 307, 311–12.

46 UC4/ii/1, p. 20; Vincent and Hinton, *University of Birmingham*, pp. 15–16; UC 1/ii/3, p. 322 (assuming the latter refers to the same meeting).

47 *Birmingham Daily Post*, 14 Jan. 1898.

48 UC 4/i/21, pp. 14–15.

49 Vincent and Hinton, *University of Birmingham*, p. 25.
50 UC 1/ii/3, p. 330.
51 Ibid., p. 353.
52 Ibid., p. 354.
53 Ibid., p. 353.
54 Ibid., p. 322.
55 Ibid., pp. 330–9.
56 UC 1/i/6, memo for deputation, 27 Feb.1891.
57 Vincent and Hinton, *University of Birmingham*, pp. 15–16. One of the arguments against the Senate scheme was that it was unlikely to catch public attention: UC 9/ii/9, Somerset to Hinton, 28 Apr. 1943.
58 UC 1/ii/3, p. 330.
59 Ibid., p. 419.
60 See above, n. 13. For a discussion of the support for the appeal see D. K. Drummond, 'The University of Birmingham and the Industrial Spirit', in *History of Education* (1999), 247–63.
61 UC 1/i/3, Clayton to Lloyd, 10 Dec. 1898.
62 UC 1/ii/3, pp. 355, 358, 359, 366–7, 368, 384; UC 4/ii/6, facing p. 10.
63 UC 4/iii/9, pp. 2–4.
64 UC 4/ii/6, 10; 3/vii/10, 3.
65 Vincent and Hinton, *University of Birmingham*, p. 32; UC 4/iii/9, p. 43.
66 Vincent and Hinton, *University of Birmingham*, p. 25. For another discussion of Chamberlain's fund-raising see Marsh, *Joseph Chamberlain*, pp. 445–6, 460–2, 480–1.
67 *Birmingham Daily Post*, 14 Jan. 1898.
68 UC 1/i/3/1, Chamberlain to Kenrick, 6 Jul. 1898; cf. his active involvement in canvassing, see below, n. 87 and 1/ii/3, pp. 366–8, 384.
69 Amery, *Joseph Chamberlain*, iv.219.
70 UC 4/iii/9, pp. 38–9.
71 University of Birmingham: JC12/1/1 14, 15. This correspondence of July 1899 appears to be an anticipation of the land grant: ibid., 28.
72 Vincent and Hinton, *University of Birmingham*, p. 38.
73 UC 1/i/2, 2, 13a; Amery, *Chamberlain*, iv.217.
74 University of Birmingham: JC12/1/1/5, 9, 10, 16, 17.
75 UC 4/iii/9, pp. 38–9.
76 Ibid., pp. 26–7. For the correspondence see University of Birmingham, JC12/1/1/7, 8, 11; UC 1/i/3/1.
77 Marsh, *Joseph Chamberlain*, pp. 460–2.
78 UC 4/iii/8, p. 38; 4/iii/9, p. 47.
79 UC 4/iii/10.
80 Ibid., 7 Oct. 1899.
81 Ibid., 9 Jan. 1900.
82 Ibid., 20 Jan., 31 Jan.1900.
83 Ibid., 22 Feb. 1900.
84 Vincent and Hinton, *University of Birmingham*, p. 34.
85 Amery, *Chamberlain*, iv.218. Chamberlain had privately suggested the target of £1

million in 1899: UC 1/i/3: Chamberlain to Lloyd, 18 Jan. 1899.

86 University of Birmingham: JC12/1/1/6.

87 The Fashoda Incident.

88 UC 1/1/3/1: Chamberlain to Kenrick, 20 Oct. 1898.

Chapter Six

The struggle for the charter

THE TASK WHICH the Canvassing Subcommittee faced in raising money for the new University was huge but uncomplicated – no questions of policy, simply 'who could be persuaded to give and how much'. Simplicity most definitely did not characterise the task facing the Management Subcommittee also set up in July 1898. This had to produce substantive recommendations on what was needed to raise the range of work at Mason College to university level and on the pattern of governance which should be embodied in any charter, and neither issue was uncontentious. What did Chamberlain's 'new idea' mean when one got down to detail? How was the new institution to be, as he had said, 'built on' Mason College? How could his commitment to 'universal instruction' be squared with his emphasis on the relevance of the University to the commerce and particularly the industry of the Midlands? How was it to be governed? How was it to be managed? Who would have a voice in its operation?

Discussion of these questions exposed the fact that not all opinion in Birmingham had been convinced by Chamberlain's new vision. Open – or at least thinly veiled – scepticism was expressed by the dean of Medicine. He believed that what was now proposed would take too much time to achieve. The meeting on 13 January had been given to understand that active steps would be taken to raise funds for the University and he and Heath got together to collaborate on an appeal letter.[1] But in May 1898 Windle wrote berating the mayor and members of the prospective Canvass Committee for lack of urgency: 'The obtaining of university powers is, in no mere figure of speech, a matter of life and death to [the College] as an educational institution.'[2] Rightly or wrongly, parents expected a student to end up with a degree, and Mason College did not have the appropriate powers. His earlier letter, circulated in July 1896, had turned out to be all too true; the prophesied decline in numbers had occurred, especially in Medicine. At the start of the decade, twice the number of medical students studied in Birmingham as in Liverpool; now it was Liverpool which was twice as large. If departments were not to be cut and the quality of staff lowered, university powers had to be obtained quickly. Admittedly, the dean of Medicine did urge the latest scheme and express confidence in Chamberlain. His real belief, however, was that the federal option was still the most realistic. Success had to come in the next session of Parliament, and if degree-giving powers were not obtained in short order, the College must join the Victoria University. Heath too, although he no longer backed the Victoria option, was careful in his speeches to leave open the federal possibility, with other colleges entering the proposed University on criteria similar to those of the Victoria University.[3] The truth was that the dean was, in his heart of hearts, a college man, as was possibly Robert Heath – decidedly lukewarm about the emphasis being placed on the importance of a university for Birmingham and its district. Windle sent a copy of his broadside to the mayor to each member of the College Council with a covering note saying: 'I venture to lay these points to fellow members of Council because I think that the question of the necessity for a University from the College point of view has perhaps scarcely been clearly brought before them.'[4] Not all the trustees could be trusted to support Chamberlain either. During the summer of 1898 Charles Harding, a major subscriber to the fund, wrote to Morley, the College secretary, calling for 'an assurance that the property and Funds of Mason College are to be handed over to the new body, as part of the great scheme foreshadowed by Mr. Chamberlain in anticipation of which the public have subscribed.'[5] What he suspected is evident from a sentence later in the letter: 'I apprehend that, in any case no part of the money promised for the University could be applied to Mason University College.' In an earlier draft he had been much more direct, referring to 'a breach of trust'.

Those who were unconvinced by Chamberlain's new ideas had, indeed, good grounds for their caution. Where was the money to come from? Success seemed anything but certain. In the merry-go-round of debate about a Midlands university, how to finance development was the bottom line. Despite sixteen years of energetic publicity, 95% of the College's assets were still the result of Mason's original generosity.[6] The federalists could always bring out the clinching argument that association with other colleges was the only realistic way to fund the acquisition of degree-giving status. Windle also thought that the figures Chamberlain was now talking about were wildly excessive; all that was needed to secure a charter was £100,000.[7] The recently completed appeal for the General Hospital had been the most successful to date in the history of Birmingham, but it had raised only £150,000.[8] In the dean's view, the real goal was being lost sight of. 'A large endowment is secondary to the obtaining of university powers.'[9] The principal also urged that the whole project could be done for a very much less than Chamberlain wanted.[10] Chamberlain himself was perfectly aware of the height of the financial hurdle which he had set. A year later he would write:

> I hope to see the Endowment Fund very largely increased before long,

> although in putting the endowment at £250,000 I took what I knew was an extreme sum, and I should be content to make a start with considerably less. I am, however, thoroughly [convinced] that whatever we do should be done well. It would be better to limit in some degree the scope of the University rather than starve any branch that was finally started.[11]

Pitching the appeal target at a quarter of a million pounds had, thus, been a calculated political device, and Windle and Heath might well have been seriously offended if they had known that, in his heart of hearts, Chamberlain agreed with them about the odds!

It is at this stage in the story that one individual comes centre-stage: Edward Adolf Sonnenschein, the Mason College professor of classics. In part this is because Sonnenschein was so active in the struggles about the charter but also because much of what is known derives from his own account of events and what survives of the documents he collected at the time. There is little in the way of a corrective lens to this and it must always be remembered that the story as we have it is largely as seen through Sonnenschein's eyes. It is the case, moreover, that not all his notes were made at the time and that some of his recollections were set down twenty years after the event and after he had been soured, as other British citizens with Teutonic names, by a good deal of ill-judged abuse during the First World War. Nevertheless, McNeile Dixon, who was a close colleague from 1895 to 1904 and had first-hand knowledge of the struggle over the charter, would later write: 'Professor Sonnenschein's untiring work in connexion with the founding of the University of Birmingham has never, as far as I know, been properly acknowledged. All the best ideas incorporated in its constitution were his. The shape it took was due to him, he was the virtual architect of its constitution.'[12]

The son of an Austrian political refugee, Sonnenschein was fond of tennis and said to have been sociable 'with a fund of humour', but he was 'a devoted and single-minded grammarian' and decidedly pedantic.[13] Ernest de Selincourt, professor of English from 1908, told of a country walk in which Sonnenschein broke a long silence to ask, 'De Selincourt, what do you think about God?' Taken aback, de Selincourt took time to answer and Sonnenschein became impatient: 'Well, what *do* you think? Would you classify it as a common or as a proper noun? I can't make up my mind.' Sonnenschein was politically naïve, too. In 1902 the principal of the University had to remonstrate with his then dean of Arts for needlessly upsetting the Council by arguing about definitions. The principal conceded that he had been led on, 'but it was unwise from the point of view of keeping the members of Council patient and docile'.[14] Sonnenschein was also prickly and difficult to deal with, as we have seen.[15] It is remarkable that in 1903, when his three years as dean were approaching an end, colleagues who thought highly of him had nevertheless to organise a coup to ensure that he was not re-elected.[16]

Not, therefore, an easy man, but a man with great insight and two sacred commitments. The first was to the faculty of Arts. As long ago as 1893 Chamberlain had committed himself to expansion in that direction: 'Even now two of the most important chairs or two very important chairs in the Faculty of Arts, those of Mental and Moral Philosophy and of History and Political Economy are still unprovided for. But, gentlemen, everything comes to those who wait.'[17] However, Chamberlain also spoke, again and again, of the University being 'specially concerned in science teaching and its practical application to [local] industry and manufactures'.[18] It was, thus, easy to fear that sympathy for Arts might be sacrificed to this distinctive mission – and the more so because Science had dominated the College from the outset, even before the link with Queen's.[19] It was hardly a good omen that Heath could write a whole article on the College in October 1897 (admittedly for a technical audience) and before going on to describe Medicine, say only 'there is a complete Arts Faculty'.[20] Not that this was, in fact, the case. Provision in Mason College 'for the teaching of Arts subjects was wholly inadequate when judged of from a University point of view'.[21] Public criticism in 1897 by government commissioners of the disparity between Arts and Science had led to the appointment of Professor Muirhead and a lecturer in classics, but with a committee now appointed to determine the shape of the new University, Sonnenschein and his four Arts colleagues decided to speak out.

Letters were placed in several of the national and local papers arguing that Birmingham's claim to university status would be undermined if weakness in the faculty was not rectified.[22] Mason College statistics were ransacked and data collected from Glasgow, Edinburgh, Manchester, Liverpool and Leipzig in order to put together a highly professional case to submit to the Executive Committee.[23] It presented comparisons within Mason College between Science and Arts: staff numbers (17:7), professorial appointments (7:5),average expenditure not covered by fees (4.6:1), and space (20:1), but student load (653:771) and the professor/student ratio (1/80:1/124). External comparisons were even more damning. The disparities at Mason College were significantly greater than in any other university sampled. At Glasgow the equivalent Science/Arts comparisons were 8:10 in chairs and 1.75:1 in expenditure. Strengthening the Arts, the five professors argued, would strengthen Birmingham's claim for university status and prepare for the predictable increase in student demand: 'there appears to us to be no reason why Birmingham should not be known hereafter as a centre of humanistic as well as scientific culture to the same extent as Glasgow or Leipzig'. The paper had a bad reception when submitted on 15 September 1898. George Clayton told Bunce, the chairman of the Management Committee, that he was surprised both by the figures and by receiving it at all: 'If each department is to fight for its own hand by sending a document like this to the executive committee we shall make but little progress in a general plan for the advancement of the scheme.'[24] However, Sonnenschein produced a robust justification of 'this fuss about Arts' in the address he gave to the University Graduates Club in November. It was, he said pointedly, made necessary by the attitude of 'some persons in our midst treating the Faculty of Arts as a mere handmaid of the Faculty of Science, as though its *raison d'être* was to provide students of Science with a little light recreation and enable them to read a scientific dissertation in German or French'.[25]

One Arts professor did go it alone. On 2 November Fiedler, the professor of German, wrote to Chamberlain direct on behalf of modern languages. Sonnenschein tried to stop him in the interests of faculty solidarity.[26] So did Dixon:

> I hear from Sonnenschein that you think of writing to Chamberlain. Let me urge you most strongly not to separate yourself from the Faculty at this point. ... *Chamberlain will certainly not take up a matter of detail at the present crisis* and will only be annoyed at being troubled. He thinks we are all in agreement on the broad lines and is willing to back our interests generally. If you take up a separate attitude you will I feel do no good in your own case & seriously damage the good cause in which we all are one. You may rest assured that I shall myself second your claims when we have made sure of our position.[27]

This last was a reference to what was thought to be Fiedler's real aim, securing an assistant in German, but what he had actually had in mind was that one of the university's 'distinctive features' ought to be a school of modern languages, the first such in the country.[28] Far from being annoyed, Chamberlain welcomed Fiedler's letter and suggested that he publish that approval via the local press.[29] The motive for this was anything but disinterested. Chamberlain was intending, a week or so later, to tell the governors of Mason College of the need for 'a faculty of commercial education in connection with the University of Birmingham, in which there should be a fully-equipped school of modern languages; taught – not as they are taught now, without much system, but taught scientifically'.[30] Publicising his welcome for Fiedler's initiative thus provided an ideal trailer for the speech and, what was more, the professor was about to marry Charles Harding's daughter and Harding was both a significant contributor to the current appeal and a good prospect for the future.[31] Chamberlain's tactic was, however, unsuccessful. Fiedler had not proposed a school of modern languages as an adjunct to the upstart Commerce. Asked in January 1899 to support the 'distinctive feature' of commercial training, Harding stuck by his future son-in-law and the 'distinctive feature' of Modern Languages and when in 1902 Chamberlain tried for something else, Harding gave him the same answer.[32]

Ensuring a proper place in the new university for the faculty of Arts was one of Sonnenschein's commitments. The second and even greater was to the Chamberlain vision of a university. Indeed, Austen Chamberlain believed that his father's contacts with the grammarian were hugely significant in turning that vision into reality. Joseph Chamberlain could, he wrote to Sonnenschein's son, 'never successfully have realized the purpose he had formed as to the University's constitution without your father's intimate knowledge of University organisation and clear view of how the purpose was to be achieved'.[33] Sonnenschein had been reflecting on the problem for more than a decade. His copy of Seeley's 1887 lecture still survives, annotated: 'p.6 A true university The right model'. He lent the text to Kenrick in 1897 with considerable effect.[34] As it transpired, Chamberlain could certainly not have relied on the Management Committee which had been set up under Thackray Bunce. Sonnenschein later said that he had suspicions about it from the start because professors from the Arts Faculty were deliberately excluded and only after protest were two added (but not him).[35] It is quite possible that Sonnenschein was omitted as a potential troublemaker, but his recollection was at fault. What appears really to have happened is that when the public meeting of 1 July 1898 set up an Executive Committee, forty-three people were chosen but only six of them were academics – Heath, Poynting, Windle and three other medics. Other professors were, however, added as soon as the Committee met, including MacNeile Dixon (English) and Fiedler (German).[36] As for the smaller Management Committee itself, for this the Executive selected two professors from each faculty, plus the principal, while when an exclusive university opinion was wanted, Arts might even have the larger voice – Fiedler and the newly appointed Muirhead against Heath, Windle and Poynting.[37]

If its membership was, thus, not overtly ominous, the way the Management Committee set about its business was. Priority was given to planning how the activity of the College should be expanded; the constitutional issue of how a Chamberlain-style university would operate was put on the back burner. By November the development plan was ready.[38] It said nothing about research but did endorse the concept that Birmingham should be a teaching university and recommended that this would be best achieved by Mason College being absorbed from the outset. A blueprint was included proposing better levels of pay and an increased number of staff; three of the four new chairs and two of the six extra lectureships suggested were in the Faculty of Arts, so the September memorandum by the Arts professors appears to have had some effect. There were recommendations, too, for greater support for libraries and laboratories and for new buildings. An accompanying business plan indicated that, assuming a continuation of the existing number of students, £200,000 was the minimum figure required from the appeal. This would increase income by £5500 and so allow a total annual expenditure of £22,000. Should £50,000 more be raised, this might be spent on a university hall, a scheme very dear to Heath's heart. The report also attempted to estimate possible increases in income from the expected growth in student numbers – possibly £2500 per annum, net. The report was approved by the Executive Committee with minor modifications on 16 November.[39] Two days later the Court of Governors voted to petition for a charter and to transfer the Mason University College endowments to the new University, provided that all existing governors were given seats on its Court.[40]

All this while, however, there was no word of any university constitution, and fears were aroused that certain members of the Committee were being kept in the dark about what was going on. So from early November suspicious professors began meeting in various homes to discuss what a University of Birmingham should look like.[41] The name Sonnenschein gave to the group was 'the *boni*' and as well as his fellow Arts professors it included, so he said, four medics with some support from a fifth, Saundby, and one scientist – P. F. Frankland – although the professor of engineering did come in at the end.[42] By elimination, the contrary position was to be found among a majority of professors in Science and a majority of medics (but not all), led by Windle, the dean, and Gilbert Barling, the sub-dean.[43] Following these meetings the *boni* put their thinking together in a detailed memorandum 'Suggestions towards Constitution of Proposed University of Birmingham'.[44] This demonstrates that they had two objectives. The first was to give the University to the professoriate. There would be no principal. A chairman elected annually by Senate would act as vice-chancellor for his tenure of office (not more than three years), and thus be effectively chairman of both Court and Council.[45] All professors would have a seat on the Court. On Council a Dean and two other representatives would sit for each faculty. The second objective of the *boni* was to see residual power in the hands of the faculties rather than Council or even Senate. The latter would consist of all professors and be responsible for educational quality and for discipline, but otherwise only for matters when they concerned more than one faculty. Council was left with administration, finance and contracts of appointment.

The *boni* were, as Sonnenschein noted afterwards, 'only just in time'.[46] On 5 December the Management Committee received from the Executive Committee an instruction to start drafting a charter and a subcommittee was formed.[47] However, the next day its members received copies of an already printed draft and a notice to meet the next day at 4 p.m. to approve it! Dixon, the only member of the *boni* on the subcommittee, had not been in the secret and he was furious. His letter to Sonnenschein survives:

> I enclose the accursed thing. It stinks about as badly as anything I have ever read. Did I not say that they were all along preparing the beast? Please return it as soon as read, with comments – not on document itself.
>
> The meeting to consider it is tomorrow at 4! What a long time they give us to consider the document! They have been masticating it for months in secret, we are given a day. "O for a whip to lash the rascals naked thru' the world."[48]

The person behind this attempted putsch would appear to have been Thackray

Bunce. In the summer of 1897 Kenrick had classed him 'among those who have not very clear ideas of what universities are'.[49] A year later Harding complained of a 'good deal of vagueness' and said that it was 'the evident wish of Mr. Bunce' to promote a much smaller project than 'the public and the donors are expecting'.[50] Sonnenschein accused Bunce of packing the drafting subcommittee with those who thought as he did; 'our party were only two against six'.[51] The two were Dixon and George Kenrick. The six were Bunce, the solicitor G. J. Johnson, Heath, Windle, Poynting and Alderman Francis Corder Clayton, the treasurer of the College.

If Bunce was the manager of the coup, the ideas were those of Bertram Windle, or so Sonnenschein always said. Three of his subsequent comments have been preserved:

> Professor Windle and his friends stood not for a University of the kind which has come into being, with equal recognition of all branches of learning, but one which was to centre round the scientific interest, with the administration and control predominantly vested in the hands of the scientific staff.
>
> They had been working in the dark on a Draft Charter in which the system of government familiar to the old College and odious to us was to be perpetuated elsewhere ... perpetuating our monstrous Senate with its absolute majority of Medical votes.
>
> They hoped by adroit management to keep the practical control of the new policy in their own hands and so secure the continuance in power of the clique which had dominated the College in the past.[52]

Clayton certainly swallowed Windle's federalist arguments entire. He wrote on 10 December: 'there is a deficit of £21,000 and growing at about £2,400 pa. If we don't get U[niversity] powers the College must deteriorate or be closed or something.'[53]

The text which Bunce circulated shows how little he, Windle and their supporters accepted Chamberlain's ideas.[54] Again and again it is unreconstructedly federal and collegiate. Clause 2 even provided 'that the University shall have its seat in the City of Birmingham'. Another dealt with 'the authority of the University' – as a critic commented, 'a College idea'. One passage referred to 'students of any College of the University'. 'Scholars' from elsewhere (the word 'undergraduates' was not used) could be exempted from all but the final degree course and its associated examination. Affiliated colleges were given the right to examine on their own premises and retain control over the admission of students. A tortuous clause attempted to maintain Josiah Mason's prohibition on the teaching of theology while not putting obstacles in the way of local church colleges which were known to want to affiliate.

The scheme was also dirigiste to a degree – an uncanny prefiguring of the managerial model which Birmingham and British universities generally would be forced to adopt eighty years later.[55] The principal was described as the 'chief executive officer in all matters relative to University Studies and examinations' but was himself subject to very real external constraints, although from the locality, not, as later, from central government. The Court was overwhelmingly non-academic; the only professors on it apart from the principal and the dean of Medicine (who had entrenched representation throughout) were three persons elected by Senate. The Council was similarly lay-dominated. The five academics on the Court sat on Council by right, but although other professors might be added by the Court they had never to make up more than 20% of the membership. The Council was responsible for 'control of discipline, educational business and the internal economy of the University'. It could appoint and remove staff. The actions of the Senate were subject to its 'control and approval' and the word 'faculty' appeared only in the title of 'The Dean of the Queen's Faculty of Medicine'.

What may be called 'the Bunce agenda' is even clearer in an earlier draft (which the *boni* seem never to have discovered). This had made all university activity subject to direction not by Council but by the Court of Governors. This control went as far as the Court regulating 'the subjects, times and mode of examinations' on the advice of a General Board of Studies, so bypassing the Senate. In this text only five places on Council were proposed for professors, including the three who sat on the Court. A provision that associates of Owens College could join Convocation resurrected the old vision of 'all Midland graduates together'. For people who thought like this, the University of Birmingham was to be Mason College refounded, with degree powers and a larger endowment.

Fortunately for the *boni* Chamberlain too had been invited to the meeting of the drafting subcommittee on the 7th and the draft was not, as Dixon had expected, put to the vote.[56] Instead it was sent to faculties for comment, with Arts predictably taking twice as long as either of the others. The *boni* also went through the text line by line, and produced a memorial which Sonnenschein managed to have printed in time for the Arts professors to sign before the drafting subcommittee met again on 12 December. The text of this has not survived but a digest has.[57] It called for all professors to be on the Court of Governors, faculties to be recognised as the constituent bodies of the University on the lines of Ordinance 31 of the Scottish University Commission (each with an elected dean), faculty representation on Council, and the professorial control of teaching and discipline. Armed with this and copies of the Scottish Commission document, 'our cause', Sonnenschein said, ' triumphed'.[58]

Whatever Sonnenschein meant by 'triumphed', subsequent evidence makes it is clear that the *boni* had won only on the collegiate issue and on that only inside the drafting committee. Among the Mason councillors, Alderman J. H. Lloyd was a particularly dangerous advocate of the old College. He felt that that any university had to be federal – the dangers of going it alone were evident (he cited the examples of Aberdeen and Durham) – and as for being a model, Glasgow, he alleged, was in bad repute among those who knew. In response and despite his own misgivings, F. C. Clayton did his best to suggest that federal schemes had inherent problems and that Bristol and Nottingham could bring little strength to the project, but in the end he fell back on the need to do something about the growing Mason College deficit and on the momentum of the Chamberlain bandwagon: 'Looking at our position and specially in regard to Mr. C's views, I don't know what else is to be done.'[59] In January 1899 Chamberlain intervened in person. He wrote to Lloyd setting out his objective – 'a first-class University, inferior to none in the world' – and on the 31st invited him and others to a parlour meeting at Highbury for the afternoon of 2 February.[60] A draft of part of Lloyd's letter of refusal has survived.[61] He was not persuaded by Chamberlain's vision. Pursuing it would 'spoil a good college' and produce a second- or third-rate university. Chamberlain wrote again to persuade him to come.[62] 'It does not pledge you to anything.' Mason College 'has come practically to a standstill' and students were being lost to other institutions. As for Lloyd's doubts about the standing which a university in Birmingham could have, Chamberlain claimed to be attempting something new, not competing with Oxford and Cambridge. The traditional universities would continue to take the ablest scholars: 'Local universities appeal to a class that will never be reached by the older institutions. … What we are chiefly deficient in is the higher education of the men who take what I may call second class positions, as for instance, those of managers, advisers & experts in manufacturing and other commercial undertakings.' It was a view which he was to sum up in the famous expression, 'captains of industry'. Despite enthusiasm for a university for Birmingham Chamberlain had no expectation that 'generals' and 'colonels' would be produced there.

Chamberlain was in touch throughout with the *boni*, but there is nothing to suggest that he used the February parlour meeting to touch on the thorny issue of university governance.[63] The battle there had still to be decided. Sonnenschein believed that the December meetings of the subcommittee had secured 'the sovereign right of the professoriate' and Dixon and Kenrick apparently secured agreement that a paragraph on faculties should be included in the statutes and also some limitation on the powers of the Council over the Senate.[64] However, their attempt to get rid of the post of principal failed, which seems hardly surprising since Heath himself was present and other evidence hints that he had hopes of heading the new University. More important, they were denied further time as the Committee decided that it was ready to instruct a parliamentary draftsman, and did so on the notes made by Bunce's ally G. J. Johnson.[65] Unsurprisingly, when the draftsman (W. O. Dauckwictz) produced an outline text in February 1899, there was little comfort for Sonnenschein and others who, like

Kenrick, held that 'a university enjoys entire self-government, government by students, teachers, founders and supporters'.[66] Much of the Bunce agenda was still there.[67] The old man's influence, however, was on the wane. To the good fortune of Birmingham, illness forced him out of the chair of the drafting subcommittee a month before he died in June 1899. His place was taken by F. C. Clayton who, if not convinced that Chamberlain was right, was willing to oblige him from lack of alternative.[68]

The *boni* were well aware that matters were reaching a climax. On Sunday 21 May, Dixon, Bévenot, Fiedler and Frankland met at Sonnenschein's house in Harborne to prepare a briefing note for Joseph Chamberlain.[69] It covered professorial tenure, the constitution and powers of faculties and the powers of the Senate. The paper was then typed up and given to Neville Chamberlain the next day to pass on to his father, but deliberately left unsigned so as not to reveal the paucity of its sponsorship. The following Wednesday, 24 May, saw the first of the two crucial meetings of the Subcommittee which settled the future of the University of Birmingham. The members had in front of them a substantive version of charter and statutes based on Dauckwicz's February preliminary version.[70] The text as now redrafted did, for the first time, include the commitment to original research and the Committee strengthened this. The provision that local people should put forward a candidate for principal was dropped. An amendment was passed to give charter status to a dean for every faculty, not just a dean of Medicine. All professors were placed on the Senate and the special status of the vice-principal and dean of Medicine was cut out. The right of Council to control student discipline was dropped and its powers to review the actions of Senate relegated to statute. As for the statutes, discussion focused on the section on faculties which Dauckwicz had been asked to introduce, but which Sonnenschein said demonstrated that the draftsman did not understand what a faculty was. There was particular difficulty in fitting in the deans but since in this draft three professors were to be elected to Council by Senate, the Committee seized on the device of making one of these dean of Arts and another dean of Science! A proto-Thatcherite clause referring to the provision within faculties 'of such professors, teaching staff and instruction as shall be within the resources from time to time of the University' was dropped. Another provision under 'faculties' which went the same way provided that 'the Council shall as and when resources permit form and maintain a library and appoint a librarian and assistants'.

The meeting of 24 May thus secured major advances for the *boni*, and one final opportunity remained, the Executive Committee meeting on 31 May which was to conclude matters, and which Chamberlain would attend, armed with the *boni's* brief.[71] On 1 June Sonnenschein wrote in red ink: 'Yesterday May 31st was the great day in the history of the University, the DAY OF LIBERATION when my policy triumphed along the whole line at a meeting of the Executive Committee. At the instance of Chamberlain the draft Charter was cut to pieces.'[72] He listed four 'points secured': '(1) a sound system of tenure (2) abolition of restriction on teaching theology (3) Faculty of Commerce definitely recognised (4) Principal to be appointed by Crown for ever (not merely *pro hac vice*).' On that basis 'cut to pieces' was somewhat of an exaggeration, especially as tenure was not incorporated in either the charter or statutes. Sonnenschein may have been misinformed or perhaps the matter had been discussed rather than decided. Subsequently tenure was provided for by ordinance, although the protection of 'appointment during good behaviour' was extended only to professors and 'independent lecturers' (that is, holders of titular lectureships); lesser mortals were on three months' notice.[73] There were, however, gains beyond those Sonnenschein celebrated. Apart from the dean of Medicine, deans were to be elected as such. All professors were to sit on the Court and could comprise a quarter rather than a fifth of the Council. The first members of Senate were no longer to be nominated by Council. The concept of good cause was introduced into dismissal. Both the Guild of Graduates and the Guild of Undergraduates were given places on the Court of Governors. The research clause was redrawn widely to refer to the provision of facilities for research in 'science, literature, arts, medicine, surgery, law and especially the application of science'.

With the gains agreed on 31 May, the text of both charter and statutes was effectively in final form.[74] Only minor corrections were made in subsequent proofs before the draft was deposited with the Privy Council on 24 June.[75] However, before that happened Sonnenschein and his allies had begun to think that there was a possibility of achieving even more. In particular, they were concerned to try to have tenure recognised in statute and deans given equal prominence with the principal and vice-principal, and also concerned at the failure to spell out specifically that the University was a union of faculties.[76] All of this could be and, at least in part, eventually was covered by ordinance, but ordinances were domestic university legislation and so open to being easily repealed; rights and powers embodied in statute could only be changed with the approval of the Privy Council. Sonnenschein, Muirhead and Whitcombe, the professor of mental diseases, therefore wrote to Heath asking for a meeting of Senate to discuss the Charter.[77] When this was refused on the ground that the vacation had begun and any meeting would be 'hole and corner', they went direct to Chamberlain. He had just learned that delays on the part of the draftsman had made it impossible to get the Charter through in the 1898–9 session as intended. He therefore told the Management Committee that in the circumstances the professors: 'will do no harm by bringing forward amendments if they choose to do so. Personally I see no objection in any of their amendments and I think on the whole they are improvements, but you will no doubt consider this carefully.'[78] On 8 August Sonnenschein visited Chamberlain at the House of Commons to discuss a possible petition to the Privy Council, asking for amendments.[79] Sonnenschein's note of the meeting shows that Chamberlain did not think that these late proposals were 'absolutely necessary to secure the ends which we have in view, & with which in general he sympathises', but that he did not rule out a petition.[80] However, as always with Birmingham, Chamberlain wanted consensus rather than conflict:

> It is not impossible that we may get what we want or part of it if we proceed by way of approaching the Charter Subcommittee and the Professoriate in October. It is true that we cannot expect Mr.C. to assist us in getting our view brought forward in B'ham but if we can get the Professoriate and the Subcommittee to give us a fair hearing I think it will probably be within C's powers to get the Charter modified in accordance with such views as may be thus powerfully backed, though I have no warrant at present for saying that this will be the case. It would have to be done by C's influence at the Com[ee] of the Privy Council, where he is practically omnipotent: and I think he would not hesitate to ask if he felt that he had behind him an entente cordiale of local opinion, whereas he would not feel justified in supporting our views if coming from a small band of Professors.
>
> Here, then it appears to me lies our chance, such as it is. It must be remembered that there is an impression in B'ham that C. would rather like to see some of our points brought in, & this might predispose the Charter Sub-C. to consider them favourably, or to allow us to approach C. on the subject.

In the event there was no petition. Clearly a majority in Birmingham felt that the charter and statutes would be adequate enough and when writing in *The Times* Sonnenschein himself felt confident enough to emphasise the 'large measure' of self government to be enjoyed by faculties.[81] It would be eighty years and more before he and his colleagues would be proved to have been right in asking for charter protection for faculty powers.

One or possibly two other important questions seem to have been raised during this struggle over the university charter. The one about which there is uncertainty is 'academic freedom'. In 1920 Sonnenschein wrote that during 1898–1900 Birmingham was split over 'what some of us regarded as an essential of a proper University – academic freedom. Mr. Chamberlain was our ally in this matter, though we had to keep this private.'[82] One of the original ordinances did give professors and independent lecturers complete freedom in teaching, subject to the requirements of the hours to be worked and to quality, but there is no reference in documents of the time to this being a subject of debate.[83] It therefore seems probable that Sonnenschein was referring to university self-government rather than academic freedom as it is understood today. The other question, and this certainly was a matter for concern at the time, was continuity between the staff of Mason College and the new University. Possibly with some anxiety in his mind for the fate of particular *boni*, Sonnenschein raised the matter in his meeting with Chamberlain in August 1899, to the minister's evident amusement:

> C expressed surprise at the suggestion that the Univ. might drop some of the Professors of M.C. who 'have borne the heat & burden of the day', and declared that he for one would oppose any such action; 'the Professors of M.C.' he said 'have the same chance of being elected to Univ. chairs as I have of being re-elected for West B'ham' – that is practical certainty, unless they can be shown to have been neglecting their duties.[84]

One person who could not count on practical certainty was the principal of Mason College, Robert Heath. From the start of 1899 and probably earlier, Chamberlain was in search of someone else to lead the new institution. As he told Henry Tilden, he recognised that Heath did have a claim to being considered and did have supporters.

> I am aware that some of the leading spirits at Mason College have proposed Heath should be Principal of the new university but there is a great difference of opinion on this point. If you can give me any further suggestions or comments on these proposals I shall be much obliged and shall be ready to treat them as confidential.

However, in his opinion, the University would need to be led by a man of great academic distinction, appointed for life, and he was assuming that Heath would be offered the post of vice-principal.[85] Given the respect accorded to Chamberlain's views, it was predictable that when Heath found himself named in the draft charter it was as vice-principal, with a future which Fiedler described as handling 'the greater part of administrative work'.[86]

The search for a university principal occupied Chamberlain for many months and caused him 'infinite trouble'.[87] He consulted widely. Tilden was suggested. Butcher, professor of Greek at Edinburgh and subsequently Unionist MP for Cambridge University, was another – he was in play for a long time. In February 1900 Sonnenschein sent a list of possibles, and again in May, but by then Chamberlain thought he might have attracted interest from Oliver Lodge, professor of physics at Liverpool. The forty-nine-year-old Lodge certainly had the required 'academic distinction'. A major figure in the early development of telegraphy, he had just been awarded the Rumford medal of the Royal Society and had gained more popular notice as the inventor of a 'bellowing telephone', or loudspeaker. Chamberlain's secretary wrote to Sonnenschein on 24 May announcing success:

> Mr. Chamberlain has had an immense amount of trouble in endeavouring

> to find the right man, and several refusals, including Butcher from Edinburgh. But although it is impossible to find anyone who is absolutely ideal. it seems to Mr. Chamberlain that Professor Oliver Lodge will fulfil almost all our requirements.

Not that Lodge had been easy to get. He had rejected the first approach in the interests of continuing his research and a condition of his accepting was that Heath should do the routine work.[88]

Lodge's agreement came only just in time. The text of the charter was sealed on 24 March and received in Birmingham on 5 May.[89] 'The Birmingham University Act 1900' received the royal assent on 25 May, vesting the property of Mason University College in the new University from the start of the next autumn term and providing for the continuation of recognised medical training and hospital access. Six days later, on 31 May, the University Court of Governors met for the first time and formally took possession of the charter.[90] To exemplify the new institution the governors immediately set about acquiring a new corporate identity. The dean of Medicine was asked to consult the College of Arms to secure a design which would preserve the symbols Mason had used, but otherwise abandon the old device of the College and also *Dum Spiro Spero* ('While I Breathe I Hope') and 'Progress Through Knowledge', its old mottoes.[91] The result was a shield which effectively combined past, present and future. Two of its three sections each contained a device from the past, the two headed lion and the mermaid Mason had assumed. The third part spoke of the new present. It contained an open book, 'a charge commonly used by universities'. For the new future there was a new motto, *Per Ardua ad Alta* – 'Striving for Excellence'.[92] And to silence the uninformed who wondered why there was no crest or supporters, the Council was told that this was 'the usual custom with universities'. Birmingham was a university and it must have the distinctive image of one.[93] It is much to be regretted that in the late 1980s, a desire to appear 'modern' led the University to abandon using this expression of its inheritance and its destiny for most of its activities, and to replace it with a so-called 'logo' which makes nonsense of the heraldry and carries no message at all.

Joseph Chamberlain had three years of Cabinet office ahead of him and three further years in public life, but all dominated by party politics and with little to show for them. In terms of concrete achievement, the University of Birmingham was the last great success of his life. In many ways, too, it has been among the most substantial and enduring. A century later, despite economic subservience to the state and subordination to its philistine agenda, something still survives of his self-governing independent academic organism serving the community. More important, Chamberlain's vision of a university still remains an ideal. It is what makes – or should make – an academic career more than mere teaching or research and a university more than a standard institution in the public sector.

The greater significance of the new University was, however, not for Birmingham alone but for the country at large. The institution which Chamberlain more than any other man had created expressed a new and different understanding of 'university'. With the grant of a charter to Birmingham in May 1900 the concept of the federal University which served a group of teaching colleges received a mortal blow. What had been the received model for English higher education was effectively declared obsolete – not to be revived until 1964 in the guise of the Council for National Academic Awards. In its place was the Scottish/continental model of academic self-government balanced by support from and accountability to the community. The significance was proclaimed at the time. On the morning of first meeting of the Court of Governors, a *Times* leader described the new University as 'an institution which presents some points of difference from any University hitherto existing on English soil and which, it may be assumed, will prove better adapted to local conditions'.[94] Following Scottish and continental precedents, Birmingham University represented 'an experiment of the very highest interest to the future of University organisation in this country'. The leader was written by Sonnenschein, but others less involved and committed than he thought the same. Parliamentary papers referred to the distinctiveness of the constitution 'and the respects in which it differs from all existing Universities'.[95] Michael Sadler would later describe the struggle for a Scottish/continental-style university for Birmingham as 'a battle of national significance'.[96]

Others responded to the lead by actions rather than words. The federal pattern was proving not to be ideal and in 1901 the already dissatisfied Liverpool moved to secede from the Victoria University. Owens College also decided on independence and in 1903 both were established as independent universities on the Birmingham model. Leeds followed in 1904 and Sheffield in 1905. Bristol, denied a federal future with Birmingham, received a charter of its own in 1909. In less than a decade Chamberlain's Birmingham had become the standard pattern for British universities. By 1938-9, although nearly two-thirds of undergraduates studying in England did so at London, Oxford and Cambridge, almost three-quarters of the rest were at Birmingham and universities like it. The 'civic' model continued to dominate twentieth-century university development until well after the end of the Second World War. Indeed, by 1963–4 another tranche of English university colleges had gone down the Birmingham road to charter status and universities on the Scottish/continental civic model were responsible for 55% of all students studying in Britain.

Notes

1 UC 1/ii/3, pp. 395, 396.
2 UC 4/ii/6, facing p. 10.

3 UC 1/i//7.
4 UC 7/iv/4/16: cf. 1/ii/3, pp. 553, 555; 4/ii/6 facing p. 10; 4/iii/9 pp. 12–15, 22–3.
5 UC 1/i/2/2/6.
6 UC 12/iv/2: Speech by Chamberlain, 13 Jan. 1898.
7 Amery, *Chamberlain*, iv.217.
8 *Birmingham Daily Post*, 14 Jan. 1898, reporting Chamberlain's speech of 13 Jan.
9 UC 4/ii/6, p. 10.
10 UC 1/ii/3, p. 322: Heath to Chamberlain, 1 Dec. 1897.
11 UC 1/i/2/2/14: Chamberlain to Harding, 13 Jan. 1899.
12 University of Birmingham, JC35/2/2.
13 Vincent and Hinton, *University of Birmingham*, pp. 102–3; Cheesewright, *Mirror to a Mermaid*, p. 41; E. R. Dodds, *Missing Persons* (Oxford, 1977), p. 88.
14 UC 1/i/3/1: Lodge to Sonnenschein, 29 Jul. 1902.
15 See above, p. 77–8.
16 UC 1/i/2/2/76–8.
17 UC 7/iv/5/28, p. 6.
18 UC 1/i/3/1: Chamberlain to Lloyd, 18 Jan. 1899.
19 Somerset, *Birth of a University*, p. 8.
20 UC 7/iv/4/10.
21 UC 7/iv/4/16: 'Proposed University for Birmingham', 15 Sept. 1898.
22 Somerset, *Birth of a University*, p. 10.
23 UC 7/iv/4/16.
24 UC 4/iii/8, pp. 12–13: Clayton to Bunce, 13 Oct. 1998.
25 University of Birmingham: JC35/2/4, p. 9.
26 UC 1/i/2/2/7.
27 UC 1/i/2/2/8: the italics are authorial. The 'present crisis' was the Fashoda Incident.
28 Ibid.; cf. 3/vii/10/3: 'scheme for an honours school of modern languages'.
29 UC 1/i/2/2/9,10.
30 *The Times*, 19 Nov. 1898.
31 UC 7/iv/4: *Edgbastoniana* (Dec. 1904)
32 UC 1/i/2/2/11, 13a, 19, 20, 21.
33 University of Birmingham, JC35/2/2.
34 University of Birmingham JC35/2/1; Vincent and Hinton, *University of Birmingham*, p. 15. Sonnenschein went walking with Kenrick: UC 9/ii/9: Somerset to Hinton, 10 June 1943, p. 5.
35 Somerset, *Birth of a University*, p. 14.
36 UC 4/iii/9, pp. 2–4.
37 Ibid., p. 5; 1/ii/3, p. 476.
38 UC 4/iii/8, p. 15.
39 UC 4/iii/9, p. 15.
40 UC 4/i/21, pp. 19–20.
41 University of Birmingham, JC35/2: annotations to draft charter presented 6 Dec. 1898.

42 Sonnenschein is not entirely fair to Saundby; see his speech as President of the British Medical Association (BMA) Council to the Cardiff Medical School: UC7/iv/1, pp. 14–15: 'an objectionable makeshift is now popular, namely that of uniting together a number of different colleges, heterogeneous in essential features, situated perhaps in widely separated cities'. This had failed in Ireland, 'and it is much to be regretted that it still finds favour with our educational rulers'. It would be 'most unfortunate if the precedents of Victoria and Wales are regarded by Government as a justification for the extension of the process to other localities'.

43 For support for the *boni* from Whitcombe, another medic, see below, n. 64.

44 UC 7/iv/4/17; University of Birmingham JC35/2/4. The latter is endorsed: 'Printed Dec. 12 in order to be presented to the Management Committee but on second thoughts not actually presented. It has secured the purpose, however, of consolidating the position of the *boni*.'

45 This point is implicit in Sonnenschein's annotations to the draft of 6 Dec. 1898.

46 See Sonnenschein's annotations to the draft of 6 Dec. 1898. The dates and sequence of events do not wholly agree with the account in Somerset, *Birth of a University*.

47 UC 4/iii/8, p. 22.

48 University of Birmingham, JC 35/2 attached to the draft of 6 Dec. 1898; the italics are authorial.

49 Vincent and Hinton, *University of Birmingham*, p. 15. Note the appearance of federalism in Dec. 1897: UC 1/ii/3, p. 330.

50 UC 1/i/2/2/6.

51 University of Birmingham, JC35/2 annotation on draft of 6 Dec.1898.

52 UC 9/ii/9: Somerset to Hinton, 28 Jun. 1943.

53 UC 1/1/3: Clayton to Lloyd, 10 Dec. 1898.

54 The following is based on a comparison of the annotations on various printed texts of the charter in JC35/2 and UC 12/iv/2/4&5. There are two early drafts: the second was the one circulated for 7 Dec. 1898. For later proofs, see below, p. 98–100.

55 Somerset, *Birth of a University*, p. 14; University of Birmingham, JC12/1/1/23; see below, n. 70; Amery, *Joseph Chamberlain*, iv.213.

56 UC 4/iii/8, p. 23.

57 UC 9/ii/9: Somerset to Hinton, 18 Jun. 1943, pp. 3–4.

58 Sonnenschein used the word on several occasions, e.g. ibid., p. 5.

59 UC 1/i/3/1: Clayton to Lloyd, 10 Dec. 1898.

60 UC 1/i/3/1: Chamberlain to Lloyd, 18 Jan., 30 Jan. 1899; University of Birmingham, JC L. Add. 76: Chamberlain to H. Hinks.

61 UC 1/i/3/1: draft by Lloyd (n.d.).

62 UC 1/i/3/1: Chamberlain to Lloyd, 1 Feb. 1899.

63 Via Kenrick: Somerset, *Birth of a University*, p. 8.

64 Ibid., p. 14; University of Birmingham, JC35/2.

65 UC 4/iii/8, p. 28.

66 Vincent and Hinton, *University of Birmingham*, p. 24.

67 For the following see the five proof versions of the charter extant in UC 12/iv/2/4&5 and University of Birmingham, JC35/2, viz. (a) skeleton – presumably the text

discussed 1 Feb. 1899 [UC4/iii/8, p. 29]; (b) labelled by Sonnenschein 'Dauckwictz I', received 18 discussed 25 May [UC4/iii/8, p. 31]; (c) labelled by Sonnenschein 'Dauckwictz II', incorporating changes agreed 24 May – one copy annotated by Heath 25 May for discussion 31 May [UC4/iii/9, p. 24]; (d) labelled by Sonnenschein 'Dauckwictz III', incorporating changes agreed 31 May [UC4/iii/9, p. 24]; (e) and (f) subsequent proofs with minor corrections.

68 UC 4/iii/8, p. 31.

69 UC 9/ii/9: Somerset to Hinton, 18 June 1943, p. 5.

70 Proof (b).

71 Proof (c).

72 University of Birmingham, JC35/2. The capitals are Sonnenschein's.

73 *Ordinances*, paras. 16, 17.

74 Proof (d).

75 UC 4/iii/9, pp. 24,26.

76 See Sonnenschein's proposed emendations to proof (d).

77 UC 1/ii/3, p. 734: Heath to Sonnenschein, 20 Jul. 1899.

78 UC 4/iii/8, p. 34.

79 University of Birmingham, JC12/1/1/18.

80 University of Birmingham, JC12/1/1/19. A photograph of this document appears in Cheesewright, *Mirror to a Mermaid*, pp. 23–4, where it is wrongly associated with events before the Charter was appproved on 31 May.

81 *The Times*, 31 May 1900. For the authorship see University of Birmingham, JC35/1/1, pp. 42–6.

82 University of Birmingham, JC/2/1/1/23: Sonnenschein to [? Garvin]. 'Whether the real history of the University will ever be written, I don't know.'

83 *Ordinances* (1900), para. 20.

84 University of Birmingham, JC12/1/1/19.

85 University of Birmingham, JC12/1/1/3: Chamberlain to Tilden, 30 Jan. 1899.

86 UC 1/i/2/2/15.

87 For the following see University of Birmingham, JC12/1/1/20–2: J. Wilson to Sonnenschein 8 Feb., 16 May, 24 May 1900; JC12/1/1/25: Chamberlain to 'President' [query Brasenose, Oxf.], 11 Dec. 1899; JC L. Add., pp. 184 et seq. Chamberlain to Lodge, 2 Apr. 1900 et seq.

88 Cheesewright, *Mirror to a Mermaid*, p. 27; Vincent and Hinton, *University of Birmingham*, p. 37.

89 UC 4/iii/8, p. 42.

90 Vincent and Hinton, *University of Birmingham*, p. 33.

91 UA Council Minutes 1, pp. 85, 111.

92 Literally, 'through effort to high things'.

93 Vincent and Hinton, *University of Birmingham*, p. 70. Technically this is an achievement, not a coat of arms.

94 *The Times*, 31 May 1900.

95 Cmd. 252 of 1902, p. 71.

96 Somerset, *Birth of a University*, foreword.

Part Two

A civic university, 1900–20

Chapter Seven

A new campus

THE GRANT OF A CHARTER to an independent civic university in Birmingham was a momentous event in the history of higher education in Britain. An event of barely less significance was the receipt by Joseph Chamberlain in July 1900 of the letter from Lord Calthorpe offering the new institution twenty-five acres 'on the Bournbrook side of the Edgbaston estate ... for the new scientific department'.[1] The initial expectation of all parties in the charter debate had been that a new university would occupy the Mason College buildings. The Calthorpe gift opened an alternative, the opportunity to create, for the first time in England, a university campus. The expression is in loose usage today to mean the main part or parts of any university, but in the nineteenth century it was exclusive to the spaces of North America. In strict terms, therefore, the Birmingham campus was the first in Britain. None of the other early civics followed suit, but campus development would become the chosen pattern – and determine the siting – of virtually all subsequent university foundations until the last quarter of the twentieth century.

The genesis of the Calthorpe gift lies in the report of the team which visited North America in November 1899. Chamberlain said, as we have seen, that this 'has opened my eyes and I think must have opened the eyes of all who have read it'.[2] Although he was thinking principally of the scientific sophistication which Kenrick and the others had found there, he had also been much impressed in hearing of institutions able to occupy 'large spaces, in which the area was counted by many acres'. Nowhere in the vicinity of Mason College was there hope of finding even the four acres which would be needed for the proper development of engineering, mining and metallurgy. The Calthorpe gift offered a solution and a golden opportunity for what Chamberlain continually stressed was something new in British education. The gift, however, was not without penalty. It meant that almost from the beginning the new institution had to operate on split sites, three miles apart. For those who thought that the University ought to be in essence a science college, the split might seem unimportant, but Chamberlain's confidence was that he could keep the financial bandwagon rolling and provide accommodation progressively for all faculties to move to Bournbrook in the foreseeable future. He was not to know that the process would actually take sixty years.

Pressure from the new principal for urgently needed investment at Mason College did, nevertheless, make the chancellor rapidly aware that endorsing a new campus inevitably meant downgrading the old site.[3] It became very difficult to justify long-term investment there and the result was that donations to maintain, still less improve, the existing college buildings became extremely hard to obtain. Not that the academic move of scientists to the new site was uncomplicated either. A public dispute broke out between Poynting and Windle over the future of the teaching of science to medical students.[4] The dean of Science argued that getting a proper grounding in science made it vital for pre-clinical medical students to spend a year at Bournbrook. The dean of Medicine argued that hospital links meant that his faculty had to stay in the centre of the City long-term and in consequence members of the science staff would have to travel in to town to teach. There were more subtle dangers in the campus vision, too. The progressive shift in the academic priority from Chamberlain Square to a Birmingham suburb did nothing to sustain the interest of the City in the educational institution it had helped to create.

The site which Lord Calthorpe had given formed an approximate rectangle, 463 by 229 metres.[5] To the south it ended in two headlands separated by a re-entrant, with a drop of 50 feet down to a field used as a rifle range and then to the Bourn Brook, where it was crossed by the Bristol Road. The architects chosen were a London partnership, Aston Webb and Edward Ingress Bell, and they decided to exaggerate the contours on this side of the site to create a high curved plateau on which the main buildings would be erected. These, however, had to face north because a condition by Lord Calthorpe was that the principal access must be from that side.[6] This meant building a new road ('University Road') along the north side of the rectangle which would also serve to divide the site from the fields opposite and from the large residential properties of Edgbaston beyond. The result of all this was a semicircular layout within the rectangle, with the scarp as the circumference and the road as the diameter. This, in turn, led the architects to a concept of the University as a walled city poised impressively above the field and the brook, with most of its buildings arranged as spokes of a wheel but with a continuous block along the northern diameter with a ceremonial entrance in the middle. The final design was for nine main blocks. Two of these were at either end of the north front and seven were placed radially round the semicircle, with the central one a great ceremonial hall. Given the fall of the land, the middle radial blocks could be planned with semi-basements open to the south and the hall even with a level below that. The two blocks on the north front were completed, but, in the event, only four of the radials – the Great Hall and two teaching blocks to the west of it and another to the east. The teaching blocks each had two storeys above the semi-basement and were on a T-shaped plan, but where the foot of each T joined the semicircle there was a fourth storey, a 'pavilion' roofed by a dome with a cupola and intended to hold a museum.

Site work began in September 1901, and departments moved in to the radial blocks during the autumn of 1905.[7] The superstructure of the Great Hall itself was commenced in January 1905. Early plans show a spire over the entrance, and later a dome topped by a double cupola, but in the end that was reduced to be in proportion to the others. The was described as 'practically complete' in March 1908, although in fact not all the fittings were in place in time for Edward VII's visit on 7 July 1909.[8] By then the blocks at either end of the north front were to all intents and purposes finished and also two other buildings, the grand entrance portico for the north front, with the library above, and the great clock tower behind it.

The only early building which the King did not see was the power house, outside the main complex and far too plebeian for a royal visit.[9] It was designed by the professor of civil engineering, F. W. Burstall, as a combined industrial operation and teaching laboratory. In it the University generated its own electricity and made its own gas – another first for the new universities – but students were also able to train on something near to an operating commercial plant. Only 'near', because the power house was equipped with a much wider range of machinery than would have been found in any one industrial context. The gas-making plant supported steam generators which produced direct current twelve hours a day – at night-time, batteries took over. There were gas engines, a marine engine, a steam turbine and two other steam engines, various generators, a condensing plant and a refrigerating plant. Much of the equipment was donated by local manufacturers or supplied at a discount. When it opened in the summer of 1904, the *Birmingham Daily Post* claimed: 'The equipment of this place is absolutely unique. Certainly there is no other place like it in Great Britain, probably not in Europe.'[10] Associated with the power house were a fitting shop, a foundry and forge and a pattern shop, 762 square metres in all, capable of handling 240 students a year. Over time equipment inevitably became obsolete and it became increasingly difficult to combine teaching with supplying power to the University. Nevertheless the power house continued to function into the 1940s and was only swept away in 1954 for a new mechanical engineering building. In 1990 the replacement heating plant which had been built nearby was re-equipped to allow the University once more to generate its own electricity (with any surplus sold through the National Grid) – something of a full circle.

Another novelty which the royal party did not see was the model mine, completed in February 1905.[11] The new University, as an act of faith in local industry, had revived the department of mining in 1902, with Richard Redmayne (later Sir Richard and Chief Inspector of Mines) as professor.[12] Redmayne took advantage of the existing contours on the south side of the site to construct a mile of 'mine galleries' in brick and concrete.[13] There were different 'levels' with 'roads', one third the normal width, all contained within three-quarters of an acre. The construction was then covered with spoil from the rest of the site and landscaped into invisibility – apart from a 'motor-house' with fans of various types to ventilate the 'workings'. On a smaller scale, Civil Engineering had its need to teach water management taken into account in the design of surface drainage for the complex. Physics, too, had specialised facilities – a circular astronomical observatory and a 'transit' observatory nearby.[14]

Every new building is necessarily the result of a dialogue between client and architect. In Birmingham the client was represented by the University Building Committee which was established in February 1901.[15] Chamberlainite laymen were in a majority (as usual) – Chamberlain himself, Beale, Clayton, Kenrick and Neville Chamberlain, plus a strong ally and major benefactor, Sir John Holder. The other members were Lodge, Heath and Poynting. On the other side were the architects, Aston Webb (knighted in 1904) and Edward Ingress Bell. Bell would retire at the end of 1909, aged seventy-three, but the University remained one of Webb's clients until after the first World War. Although Sir Aston was by then in his seventies and no longer active in its affairs, his designs were still being followed.[16] Thus the central complex at Edgbaston as it is today is effectively as designed by the Webb–Bell partnership.

The design took several months to finalise. Architects presented a block plan for the Bournbrook site at the first meeting of the Building Committee in February 1901.[17] This showed six radials (not the seven in the final plan) spaced on the semicircle, provisionally allocated in anti-clockwise order to Arts and Commerce, Mining and Engineering, Engineering, Engineering again, Metallurgy and Applied Chemistry (principally the School of Brewing). Quite logically Chemistry was placed next, as the corner block at the eastern end of the University Road front, with a smaller T-shaped wing for Zoology and Physiology protruding into the courtyard and separating Chemistry from an imposing central entrance. That was only for the carriage trade and grand occasions and what was labelled 'Students' Entrance' was on the south front, in convenient walking distance from the trams along the Bristol Road. The plan for the west of the north front was a mirror image of the eastern half, with Geology and Botany matching Zoology and Physiology and Physics as the corner block, balancing Chemistry. Shown to the Council and approved, the designs were developed in considerable detail.[18] As well as its own museum, each block had a dedicated lecture theatre at the end of the ground floor but otherwise was purpose designed for its occupants. Thus where Commerce and Arts had six classrooms on the ground floor plus a room for a professor and another for his assistant, Mining and Engineering had a chemical and an electrical laboratory, a room labelled 'micrographical' (that is, microscopy), a room for research and again a room for a professor. All professors' rooms had an *en suite* toilet. Changes were also made to the proposed allocations, with the radials now assigned (anticlockwise) to Electrical Engineering, Engineering, Mining and Engineering, Metallurgy, Applied Chemistry and finally Commerce and the Arts. In another change, Physics switched places with Chemistry to the eastern end of the north front, the site it has occupied ever since.

Precisely why changes which split Chemistry and Applied Chemistry were proposed is unclear but they were probably connected with discussions about phasing the building. This, it was agreed, would be done by omitting the first and the sixth of the radials and proceeding with the four blocks symmetrically placed opposite the main entrance.[19] Anticlockwise these four proposed blocks were, somewhat confusingly, designated not '2 to 5' or 'B' to 'E' but 'A', 'B', 'C' and 'D'. Lord Calthorpe had already approved the bird's-eye plan so the Building Committee was able to give the go-ahead in July 1901, although the proposed usage was altered yet again.[20] Applied Chemistry remained in Block 'D', safely in the first phase, but Mining was moved to join Metallurgy in Block 'C' and Engineering was restricted to only two blocks ('A' and 'B'). With the non-applied sciences due for accommodation later on the road frontage, this revision meant that although Engineering and Metallurgy had less space than initially proposed, immediate building plans promised to accommodate everyone except Arts and Commerce, and Medicine, which could not move anyway.

From the outset a Great Hall was envisaged as being the focus of the site, but it was not intended to be part of the first phase, and not where it now stands. The plan approved in July placed it on the first floor of a building directly behind the north entrance, communicating with it by a 'grand staircase' built precisely where the Chamberlain Tower now stands. The hall was designed without aisles but with a curved orchestra platform at the far end, in imitation, perhaps, of the Town Hall. Four examination halls were planned for the space beneath, separated by colonnades which provided a covered way to the buildings on the semicircle.

In September 1901 all this changed. Chamberlain met Webb to consider these plans and he recommended that the Great Hall should be built as part of the first phase.[21] This was a momentous decision. It meant, first, that the hall would have to be moved to become the focus of the semicircle. This, in turn, increased the number of radial blocks required from six to seven and the first phase from four to five. Secondly, the demands of a grand ceremonial hall began to dominate development. Originally 7500 square feet, successive revisions over two months increased the Great Hall by 50% to 11 250 square feet – larger than Birmingham's own Town Hall.[22] What, however, did not grow was the sum approved for the first tranche of the main Bournbrook buildings – £229,000. The logic of quantity-survey costings rapidly became inexorable. The Great Hall was estimated at £70,000 – almost a third of the total available for it and the four blocks 'A' to 'D'. Without it, there would have been enough money to build a fifth teaching block. With it, even four became impossible. Block 'D' and Applied Chemistry had to go.[23] Outsiders described the Great Hall as 'the greatest glory' of the new University.[24] How the evicted professor of brewing described it is not recorded. One cannot imagine a university today preferring ceremonial to chemistry, still less being allowed to assess priorities in such a way. At the time critics felt that building at Edgbaston had got out of proportion – not least Oliver Lodge, Birmingham's first principal. He wanted staff and students, not bricks and mortar.[25]

The decision to build a Great Hall in the first stage was not the only influence which Chamberlain exerted on the buildings of the new University. It was Chamberlain who had selected the architects and who had the major hand in briefing them.[26] Lodge would have preferred to use local men as and when funds became available, but discussion in the Building Committee was pre-empted by Chamberlain's invitation to Webb and Bell to act! The reason for their selection was not their earlier and very successful design for Birmingham's law courts – that was never mentioned. Webb and Bell were chosen as the leading partnership of the day – architects *par excellence* of the late-Victorian establishment: consultants to the Crown agents for the Colonies, and architects of the Victoria and Albert Museum. Engaging them immediately attracted national attention to the Bournbrook project. Chamberlain was also specifically drawn to them as the architects of the Royal Naval College at Dartmouth, the largest and most prestigious recent educational building in the country.[27] When Lodge reported that local architectural circles were incensed at the choice of Webb, Chamberlain replied:

> I do not doubt there will be criticism – there would be if we were able to obtain the services of Michelangelo or Inigo Jones. But no-one can say that we have not secured a man at the very head of his profession, accepted unanimously by the Government and the House of Commons to carry out educational buildings of much greater magnitude than anything we purpose.[28]

Engaging Webb and Bell also guaranteed that the buildings at Bournbrook would be 'important in size and dignified in appearance' and so a fitting expression of Chamberlain's vision.[29] It was Chamberlain who had gone over the specifications in detail with Webb in March 1901 and endorsed the proposal for what the journal *Engineering* called 'a palatial pile'.[30] Webb himself conveyed Chamberlain's comments to the University Building Committee:

> It was desirable that this portion, when erected, should be an architectural composition complete in itself, furnished in a worthy manner, and at the same time capable of expansion in the future. The Chancellor at the same time expressing an opinion that it would be desirable to include in this first scheme the Great Hall and a Principal Entrance which would be of a dignified character'.[31]

The parallel Chamberlain liked was the medieval cathedral. When presenting Webb's designs to Court – with the aid of a magic lantern – he declared that, as with a cathedral over the centuries, the intention throughout must be to build on a scale 'worthy of the final objective'.[32] A Great Hall would announce a university; a significance which Aston Webb fully endorsed.[33] Making a ceremonial hall the focus of phase one also obliterated immediately and decisively the image of Mason's Science College. The comparisons Chamberlain made were not with Birmingham's past, but with modern universities overseas which he saw as the key to commercial vigour, especially in the USA and Germany.[34] There were more mundane considerations as well. The North American visit, which convinced him of the need to 'think big', also convinced him that Andrew Carnegie was right in saying that the original plan to accumulate endowments was psychologically wrong. We find the Chancellor soon saying, 'unless something can be shown for the money already subscribed, it will be very difficult to obtain further large sums'.[35]

Quite as remarkable as the mass and size of the first buildings at Edgbaston was the degree of artistic embellishment: ceramic friezes on the pavilions at the head of each block; another over the entrance with elaborate stonework below it; inside the Hall, the heraldic display on the ceiling and a great south window, now partly obscured by unfortunate changes made in 1966 in order to tier the seating on the platform. The ceramic friezes below the domes alone represent a substantial artistic achievement. They took twenty months to execute and cover nearly a thousand square feet. The artist was Robert Anning Bell, an associate, or even perhaps a pupil of Webb. Chamberlain knew his ceramic work in the House of Commons, as also the mosaic tympanum over the entrance to Westminster Cathedral.[36]

The friezes illustrate the function of each block – 'A' and 'B', engineering, 'C', mining and metallurgy – and the easy conclusion is that they assert the priority of science at Edgbaston. But the key point of the friezes is not that they depict science and technology, but the science and particularly the technology of the Midlands. In his great speech at the reception of the Charter in 1900, Chamberlain had announced that Birmingham would 'take some colour from its environment', and 'would practically assist the prosperity and the welfare of the district in which it is situated, by the exceptional attention which it would give to the teaching of Science in connection with its application to our local industries and manufactures'.[37] So the friezes show boilers, pistons, lathes, presses, drilling, forging, pattern-making, pipe-laying, cable-laying, bridges and colliers with a coal tub – the Midlands at work.

The importance given to 'rooting the university in the soil' is nicely illustrated by a difference over the way to complete the domes on the pavilions.[38] The initial plan was to top them with cupolas, but in June 1905, Bell suggested emblematic lead figures instead, illustrating 'Engineering', 'Electricity' and 'Mining'. At this time 'Eros' in Piccadilly Circus was the very latest thing. The proposal horrified

Chamberlain's brother-in-law, George Kenrick, chairman of the University Building Committee, and cupolas they remained![39]

Decoration on the new buildings thus expressed the conviction that there was a symbiosis between the University and the region. It also proclaimed Chamberlain's conviction that this symbiosis made Birmingham University the educational focus of the Midlands. That had been expressed already in the substantial representation of neighbouring county authorities on the Court of Governors; now it was decided to carve it in stone. The opportunity was 'the Principal Entrance of a dignified character', over which were placed the shields of Worcestershire, Shropshire, Stafford, Derby, Leicester and Warwick, a claim to tribute from all the region. Chamberlain's tactics were blatant. When Staffordshire and the City of Birmingham voted support, he announced extra building; with Worcester also assisting, he used Degree Day 1903 to criticise Warwickshire for hanging back.[40] Since Birmingham made by far the largest contribution, it might appear odd that its shield is omitted. However, as we shall see, the inside of the hall makes ample compensation.

Three of Anning Bell's ceramics thus announce a commitment to the Midlands and its industry. What of the fourth, over the main entrance, above the shields? According to the *Birmingham Daily Post*, this is emblematic of 'Learning' and 'refers to the function of the University at large'.[41] It uses the traditional formula of a ruler donating a charter and shows witnesses from Antiquity, the Middle Ages and the Renaissance watching a woman hand a wreath to a man who kneels before her throne. He wears modem academic dress, as do his supporters – an undergraduate, a master and four doctors. The message is clear. Under the eyes of the historic succession of Western culture, the Goddess of Learning hands the wreath of scholarship to the new University. This expressed the reverse side of Chamberlain's vision: his insistence that along with a distinctive Midlands character, Birmingham must embrace the ideals and values cherished by universities through the ages. As *Engineering* reported: 'It is clear that the Chamberlain ideal for the Midland University has always been a school of general culture, specialising in the faculties for training applied scientists.'[42] 'General culture', indeed, was a favourite theme in Chamberlain's speeches, as on the occasion of the second annual meeting of the Court of Governors. Speaking of the recently formed faculty of Commerce, he said that it: 'by the necessity of the case must be associated on one side with the Faculty of Arts from which it will hope to derive that general culture which must be the foundation of our education, and on the other side it is also allied to the Faculty of Science'.[43] The frieze over the main entrance thus reflects the victory of Chamberlain and Sonnenschein in the battle for the soul of higher education in Birmingham, fought out before the Charter was granted.

Birmingham's commitment to the broad definition of a university is reiterated twice more in the design for the entrance. First, below the frieze and the county shields, there is a great arch which carries the newly granted shield of arms flanked by the royal cipher, and so ostentatiously plagiarises royal foundations at Oxbridge. Secondly, and even more striking, is the sculpture over the main doorway. Early designs show a row of windows, but the notion of a frieze of representative figures soon gained ground and Henry Pegram, a somewhat stormy petrel of the artistic world, was engaged to do the carving.[44] But who was he to carve?

Answering that question aroused more passion than anything else at Edgbaston.[45] The architects proposed a series of reliefs showing Midland worthies, obviously a parallel to the ceramics showing Midland Industries. The Building Committee, however, wanted to maintain the overall theme by having figures of 'great men of all time'. Various compromise proposals followed, including a plan for nineteen figures: four 'great men' in niches – William Shakespeare, Francis Bacon, Plato and Archimedes – with local men in between.[46] Agreement was eventually reached on a scheme for nine figures in groups of three, but none at all on a revised list of names received from the architects which combined the great and the local – Mendelssohn, Virgil and Dr Johnson, Francis Bacon, Plato and Newton, Priestley, Archimedes and Watt.[47]

Oliver Lodge's paper on the problem was not his most lucid or consistent. He began by enunciating principles. It was, he wrote:

> an advantage to select Englishmen, to a great extent, and men connected with the Midland District of England, in its widest sense, as far as possible. We must further remember that the University in the future will include all branches of learning, and not merely the more technical branches which are in special evidence today; and we may hope that among the Humanities, thus dealt with, some forms of Art will not be absent.

He then launched into detail. For the centre he proposed Shakespeare, Newton and Watt – the greatest world names in literature, pure science and applied science – all Englishmen and all Midlanders. Newton actually came from Lincolnshire, and Lodge disclaimed a wish to poach on Cambridge, but the school at Grantham which Newton had attended 'was now inclined to turn its face towards Birmingham' – 'Indeed', he said, 'I have recently opened new buildings there, with that idea in mind.'

Lodge suggested that on either side the figures should be balanced, Science against the Humanities. For the one he proposed a chemist, a biologist and a physicist. Priestley and Darwin were obvious – major figures and local men – but Galileo was a departure from the principles, made necessary because the alternative, Archimedes, was 'equally great, but more shadowy'. Darwin, he recognised, might be contentious, and so he proposed reserves, either Roger Bacon or Emmanuel Kant – who was described (by, one hopes, a printers' transposition) as 'the greatest medieval philosopher'.

A humanities trio presented even greater difficulties. Lodge could find no local artists except Burne-Jones, who was 'too modern'. Dr Samuel Johnson had impeccable Midland references but insufficient 'magnitude' (*sic*). Homer was 'too impersonal and legendary', Virgil 'limited' in scope, and Lodge was left with Plato or possibly Aristotle. For the plastic arts, 'comprehensiveness' gave Leonardo da Vinci an edge over Michelangelo. For music, Webb and Bell had proposed Mendelssohn 'as having some kind of local connection' – no doubt the first performance of his *Elijah* in Birmingham Town Hall – but Charles Beale, the lay vice-chancellor, wanted either Bach or Beethoven – he had some expertise in music – and Lodge, who hadn't, opted for Beethoven because he had 'an impressive figure for sculpture'.

Unfortunately, when the principal took his careful list to a soirée of the Birmingham elite, it was torn to shreds. Plato and Aristotle? Far too remote – Francis Bacon was much preferred; Priestley was reckoned 'not to be comfortable in such a company' and was replaced by William Harvey. Faraday ousted Galileo – and a good deal of money was put on Dr Johnson. Lodge then seized on the dropping of Priestley to bring in Pasteur; he had, he admitted, entirely forgotten about the French! The more the frieze was discussed, the more the confusion. Professor Poynting produced the bizarre suggestion that Edward VII should be in the middle, flanked by Birmingham's two educational benefactors, Edward VI and Josiah Mason. Adam Smith was entered late by the faculty of Commerce and Francis Bacon wore the colours of the legal profession. Later, apparently at the decisive committee meeting, Edward VII made a strong run in the centre of the course, between Newton and Bacon (a short head in front of Shakespeare), with Faraday, Darwin and Priestley challenging Watt and Harvey on the rails.[48] It is a relief to observe the ultimate winners: Darwin, Faraday and Watt, Newton, Shakespeare and Plato, Michelangelo and Virgil, and Beethoven looking suitably impressive.

The ceramic frieze, the arch and the row of statues leave only one conclusion. The entrance to the Great Hall at Edgbaston is an explicit presentation of a 'university' image. All that is left of Josiah Mason is the mermaid in the sinister chief of the university shield; all that is left of his college is the double-headed lion in the dexter. The iconography is in deliberate tension with that of the teaching blocks – the utilitarian and limited stance of departments challenged and united by the central assertion that Birmingham University is a school of general culture in the great European tradition.

One final piece of negative evidence seals this conclusion. The entrance front makes no reference to the activity which Chamberlain stressed again and again: research – the University as a place 'in which the work, the most important work, of original research shall be continuously carried on'.[49] However this was a late omission. The initial intention had been to carve below the ceramic frieze a motto from a Chamberlain speech which listed research as one of the distinctive activities of the University, along with teaching, examining and the applying of technology.[50] The wording proposed was 'to teach, to test, to extend and to apply'.[51] The idea was dropped, but not, perhaps, because it threatened to clutter an already busy piece of carving. The phrase had no doubt sounded well from a platform, but in cold stone, 'to extend' smacked more of imperialism than extending knowledge; 'to increase', suggested as an alternative, sounded even more like 'Land of Hope and Glory'.[52] But that a motto was ever considered, confirms that the north front was intended as propaganda in stone.

Inside the main doors was the entrance hall, designed, the *Birmingham Daily Post* said: 'to give concrete expression to the desire of Mr. Chamberlain – a desire expressed at the inception of the scheme – that at the threshold of the University, students and visitors should he impressed with the importance of the work carried out there, by the nature of the surroundings'.[53] It is modelled directly on an aristocratic mansion – a perfect double cube, 50 feet square and 100 feet high, open to a domed ceiling. At first-floor level, supported on marble columns, was a circular gallery with a elegant ironwork balustrade linking eight ironwork 'standards' carrying lights and decorated with the university motto. Above, directly under the dome, is a smaller gallery. The superb marble floor and walls and later a statue of Edward VII (given by Francis Corder Clayton) completed the analogy.

Overt decoration returns in the hall itself. First the ceiling. This is one of the finest examples of the work of the Bromsgrove Guild and of its period – a barrel vault with the shields of the City and the University of Birmingham in alternating relief, white on a buff terracotta ground. Even more striking, flanked as it was by massive organ pipes and the fine woodwork of the original organ cases, is the stained-glass window at the south end of the hall.[54] A late insertion, this was donated by Sir John Holder in May 1907, and accepting it meant making structural changes to a building already part erected building.[55] But the long girder which had to be taken out was not wasted; it was given to the department of civil engineering 'to be used for experimental purposes'.[56] T. R. Spence designed the window and it has fifty-three lights. The focus, as with the north front, is the University shield. Above it, in the spandrels, we find shields of the six Midland counties on either side of a full achievement of the arms of the City of Birmingham. The window, in other words, takes up the theme of civic commitment to the Midlands University announced by the entrance front, and this was emphasised by a display of county banners down the hall on either side. The other central lights speak of private support: at the top the Calthorpe arms and Sir John Holder's own shield at the bottom, below a woman holding the Chamberlain crest.

The remaining large panels present twenty-two emblematic figures or groups of figures organised according to the faculties of the new University. The bottom row on the west is devoted to Commerce. Two rows above is the figure of 'Science'. The bottom row on the east side represents Medicine, while two rows above stands 'the Arts'. The way the window treats Science echoes precisely the friezes on blocks 'A', 'B' and 'C'. On this occasion Science is allowed an emblematic figure, but around her the viewer sees once more the Midlands at work. The only pure sciences are geology and physics – no chemistry, no mathematics. Engineering is allowed some abstract quality, but the other windows show bridge-building, forging, electroplating and mining. Nor was this merely the artist's taste for the muscular torsos of artisans. In the medical group, a window labelled 'Healing' hints at the contribution of the University in the new General Hospital. As for Commerce, the windows show practicalities: the money market, overseas trade and 'Records' – in plain terms, bookkeeping. Rooting the Arts in the locality was more difficult. The goddess herself carries a large folio; 'Literature' is there, book in hand, along with 'Languages' fluttering somewhat unconvincing scrolls in a variety of tongues. But with geometry, a local connection was again possible. It might be expected that geometry would go with science, but the design and the motto, *Docendo Discimus* ('We Learn By Teaching') shows that here is Euclid in the classroom. Science, medicine, commerce, education – the local perspective is obvious. As the *Birmingham Daily Post* was careful to point out, 'the arts and Sciences' depicted in the window were those 'practised in the University and in the City'.[57]

The south window of the Great Hall thus recapitulates much of the northern exterior but with one marked difference. Nothing very obvious echoes the frieze of 'the handing down of Learning' or the figures of 'great men of all time'. The one possibility is in the two lights which have no name and lie on either side of Geometry. On one, a man points to a book under the caption *Vincit Omnia Veritas* ('Truth Conquers All'). In the other, the motto *Sapere Aude* ('Dare To Be Wise'), appears over two figures, a listener and a speaker gesturing decisively. These two lights may well stand for the virtues of Enquiry and Courage and so express values central to research. Overall, however, the stained glass of the Great Hall retreats from the emphasis of the north front on Birmingham's rightful place in the great intellectual traditions of Europe. The window, of course, was designed after Chamberlain had experienced the stroke which took him out of public life, and it may be that this gave Webb and Bell a freer hand. Certainly it was Bell who suggested Spence, a man whose skills the *Magazine of Art* listed as architecture, painting, mosaic, metalwork, wallpaper design and relief – with no mention at all of stained glass.[58] Certainly, too, the window's more prosaic vision reflects what the architects felt privately. Webb, deferential to Chamberlain, was dismissive of the Building Committee at Birmingham, and when he spoke of the University, it was in terms of some upmarket factory.[59] It is noticeable that although Anning Bell included fifty-four figures in the departmental friezes, only four represent professionals who can be imagined to have degrees.

Whatever its iconography, the Great Hall at Bournbrook was unashamedly a prestige building, but it did have some practical use for functions and examinations. Moreover, the floor below provided ample space for a dining-room and common rooms for staff and students with a scullery, servants' hall, larder, pantry and buttery in traditional college style; a sub-basement held kitchens.[60] Utility was, however, certainly not a factor in the great clock tower which now dominates the campus. The *Birmingham Post* did suggest that it 'would be useful in connection with the Physics Department and as a record tower' and it was in fact used for Lodge's experiments with wireless.[61] However, to budget £25,000 to build a support for a radio aerial was out of all reason. There is no evidence either that the clock tower was much used as a store. Quite simply the tower was an expression of the philosophy which had created a Great Hall of such magnificence. Its purpose was impact, which was why the tower was eventually built 325 feet high – tall enough to be seen for miles around. The fact that the dial of the clock became invisible in low cloud was immaterial.

Unlike the Great Hall, a clock tower was an uncertain feature of the early plans but was clearly wanted by Chamberlain. The first proposal was to cram it in between the front of the radial blocks and a Great Hall in its originally proposed position behind the north entrance. This was clearly unrealistic and the tower disappeared, but in September 1901 the move of the Great Hall to become one of the radial blocks made more space available. Webb therefore proposed recessing the entrance and library on the north front and building the tower on top, using it for a book store – which is probably where the *Birmingham Post* got its garbled report about archives. Thanks to the non-availability of funding this plan remained dormant for some time, and fortunately so, because drawings of what was proposed have a heavy feeling, suggesting a cross between a Low Countries *beffroi* and an English church tower, topped by something reminiscent of a gazebo or at times a pagoda.

Matters changed in the autumn of 1905. Chamberlain was able to report that an anonymous donor – in fact, Sir Charles Holcroft – had offered £50,000 for a tower, with the rest going towards completing the Bournbrook site.[62] With construction now a real possibility, Webb revisited his thinking and changed the plans. A straight north front was reinstated and a clock tower located on its present site, behind the entrance but now free-standing. At the same time an entirely new design for the tower was produced. This was based on the Torre di Mangia at Siena which Chamberlain much admired, though at 99 metres, 11 metres higher than the original. Another change was less happy; the sides of 'Big Joe', as Birmingham's tower became affectionally known, were made to taper, which gave rise to a chronic problem with the run-off of rainwater. Some members of the University Council did not like the design but with Chamberlain personally committed, the Building Committee went ahead.[63] By the autumn of 1906 the foundation was being constructed, 45 cubic metres of concrete, resting on bedrock 9 metres below the surface.[64] Building the superstructure produced a major upset.[65] Virtually all the other Bournbrook contracts were let to a Birmingham man, Thomas Rowbottom, probably as priced by Webb and Bell. The tower, however, was put out to tender. Seventeen firms competed and Rowbottom was undercut by 30%. The Building Committee and the architect were clearly taken aback but after an investigation by Charles Beale and Austin Webb, the lowest bidder, Waring White, was eventually allowed the contract. Work began in the summer of 1907 and was near-enough complete by the time of the king's visit.[66] The episode certainly suggests that using fashionable architects weakened the ability of the University to secure the most competitive costings, and this suspicion is reinforced by the fact that Rowbottom became wealthy enough to make a gift of the clock for the tower, a massive 20-ton machine, with jewelled bearings and four bells, the largest weighing 6 tons 1 cwt.[67]

Holcroft's £50,000 also made it possible to proceed with the Chemistry and the Physics blocks (occupied in October 1909), but the revision of the line of the north front and the position of the tower meant that plans for the grand entrance and library had to go back to the drawing board.[68] Webb's design was changed to a rectangular building pierced by a central roadway of five vaulted archways closed with ornamental wrought-iron gates. The reading room was to be on the first floor, fitted out in oak 'on the well-known college lines' and with space for 100 000 volumes. Fortunately there was a benefactor at hand. The family of the late Charles Harding offered £10,000 and in November 1906 it approved the new design (and raised the gift to £12,000).[69] The Hardings also presented a magnificent organ for the Great Hall.[70]

With the completion of the centre and wings of the north front and the clock tower, thoughts turned to inaugurating the new site. Having a first and memorable degree day in the new Great Hall was an obvious step. This was planned for October 1909 with a list of prominent honorands. As it happened Chamberlain and the Senate fell out over the nominations.[71] Chamberlain thought Senate had put forward far too many names and that too many of them were undistinguished. He wrote:

> I think that the Honorary Degree ought to be kept for those exceptionally qualified or in other ways distinguished and that you should be careful as a University not to make it common, in which case, I am afraid, we shall have many refusals. As you know, the Universities of Oxford and Cambridge as well as those of London and Wales are agreed on this particular and I should not like to see our University taking a second place. I think that the Senate has been too liberal and I should like to reduce the list considerably.

He proposed three honorands only – A. J. Balfour, the ex-prime minister and a respected philosopher, and Sir Charles Holcroft and Lord Strathcona, the University's two major benefactors. The solution the Senate adopted was to add Chamberlain's names to its list, to produce a total of thirty-three. One of these was

Chamberlain himself, but his illness meant that he was absent from the ceremony and at least spared the sight of the unsuitable being honoured. His comment on one local peer being given an honorary LL D was: 'I like him personally and should be glad to see any honour fall to his lot but I am inclined to think that he is not suitable for academic distinction.'

Overshadowing even a degree ceremony in the Great Hall was the possibility of a royal visit. Enquiries were made and Edward VII agreed to come to open the first civic university campus in the country.[72] Although Chamberlain would be unable to be present, his seventy-third birthday, Wednesday 7 July 1909, was specifically chosen. Edward VII arrived to a royal salute at 1 p.m. on a wet and cold afternoon at Platform 3 on New Street Station, accompanied by Queen Alexandra and Princess Victoria. The emphasis of the day was what Joseph Chamberlain would have wanted, the University as a civic 'first' for Birmingham. The leader in the *Daily Post* for that morning declared: 'Birmingham people may perhaps be pardoned if they are fain to regard the visit of their sovereign to the University as the most important incident of the Royal provincial tour.'[73] Amid arches celebrating municipal gas and water provision and other earlier Birmingham achievements, the many banners proclaiming 'Prosper the University', the commemorative medals distributed in everything from gilt to pewter and the trinkets on sale all made it clear that the University was now the crown of them all.[74] Even a protocol call at the Council House did not break the mood. The lord mayor was George Kenrick, chairman of the University Building Committee, and the lady mayoress who presented a bouquet when the queen alighted from the carriage was Chamberlain's wife. A loyal address was presented and Kenrick was knighted. Lunch followed and, with the sun now out, the royal party left for Bournbrook at 3 p.m. in a carriage procession escorted by the Life Guards and the Warwickshire Yeomanry, through more decorated streets and past singing children. At the University they were met by a guard of honour of the University Officer Training Corps and received by the pro-Chancellor, Charles Beale, Francis Corder Clayton, pro-vice-chancellor and treasurer, and the principal, Oliver Lodge. The party then moved to a packed Great Hall (greeted by two verses of the National Anthem), where a bouquet was presented to the queen by Chamberlain's granddaughter, Hilda Richards, and another by Elizabeth Stephens Impey to Princess Victoria, on behalf of the women students. Lodge gave a loyal address, with a suitable reference to the absent chancellor and a ringing endorsement of the Chamberlain creed:

> We regard [our present undertaking] as capable of infinite expansion. Whilst the field of scientific research is ever widening the claims of the humaner studies become none the less imperative; and in both these branches of human activity which can only flourish side by side, we realise the need of continual development. But we believe that the work we have begun ... can

> confidently be entrusted to the generosity and to the devoted service of the generations to come.[75]

The king replied, endorsing the obligation of the undergraduates for the future, presentations followed and the king declared the buildings open. A twenty-one-gun salute commenced and the royal party left the Hall (to the overture from *Die Meistersinger*) and a tour round Civil and Electrical Engineering. Thirty-five minutes after his arrival, Edward was on his way back to New Street Station and a train leaving at 4.45 p.m.

A royal visit specifically to open the new University campus certainly underlined the national significance of what had been achieved in Birmingham. Though nobody can have known it at the time, it also marked the end of a chapter. For almost twenty years, no more building would be undertaken at Bournbrook, by which time war would have changed the world beyond recognition. This hiatus was in large measure a consequence of the conflict which broke out in August 1914, but it is clear that despite the impressive opening, the vigour which had brought the University to being was already on the wane. A crucial factor in this was the severe stroke which Chamberlain had suffered in July 1906. As we have seen, this did not prevent his being actively involved with the University through his contact with Lodge, but his incapacity drastically restricted his public life and made it much more difficult for him to exploit his local reputation or to engage in the canvassing and cajoling that had produced such substantial amounts of support for the University appeal. He continued to do what he could, but even that was ended by his death in July 1914.

Chamberlain can hardly be blamed for having a stroke, but it is germane to wonder whether he had been entirely wise to promote the Bournbrook enterprise in the way he had, against the advice of more cautious spirits on the University Council. Securing a charter for a new kind of university in Birmingham had been an enormous achievement and so, too, the initial appeal for capital, but at that point Chamberlain in effect decided to gamble on his surviving in public life. When Lodge remonstrated: 'that buildings did not constitute a university, that personnel was the greatest thing to aim for, he [Chamberlain] said, "No, spend the money now, give people something to see, and I will get the other half million without much delay."'[76] Lodge was very possibly correct to say: 'if Mr. Chamberlain had lived no doubt the rest of the endowment would have been forthcoming', but a proper risk assessment would not have committed the University to plans which depended on one man, and that man approaching the age of seventy. The chancellor argued that 'until we get to work with our new buildings we cannot expect to create another boom in the University of Birmingham' but time was against him.[77] His allies should have known better, but were either mesmerised by his legendary skill in managing Birmingham affairs or dissuaded by habitual respect from expressing any doubt. A similar criticism can be made of the priorities at Bournbrook. The public line was that 'the architects have been guided by utilitarian rather than aesthetic considerations' but Chamberlain directed too much of the capital to be spent on show.[78] If the Great Hall and the clock tower had been postponed, five radial teaching blocks could have been completed by 1909 instead of three, with a necessary result that the move of the whole University (except Medicine) from Mason College to Edgbaston must have occurred earlier than it did.

Hindsight, however, costs nothing, and whatever the problems which Chamberlain bequeathed to his creation they are long in the past. Nearly a century later the Bournbrook buildings are a source of pride to the University, one of the glories of the City of Birmingham and a monument to one of her most remarkable residents. Already in 1902 a former engineering student described what was then under construction as 'the creation of a man of marvellous personality; a statesman and a citizen of world-wide repute; a man whose word awoke an immediate echo in every portion of the civilised world'.[79] In the circumstances, the inscription at the base of the clock tower was restrained to a degree:

> THIS TOWER COMMEMORATES THE FOUNDING OF THE UNIVERSITY THROUGH THE INITIATIVE AND ACTIVE ENCOURAGEMENT OF ITS FIRST CHANCELLOR THE RIGHT HONOURABLE JOSEPH CHAMBERLAIN

Notes

1 Vincent and Hinton, *University of Birmingham*, p. 37.

2 See above, p. 84.

3 UA Council Minutes 1, p. 620: report of the Principal, 18 Dec. 1901. Although approving 'such expenditure on the new site as may seem politic and wise to those best able to judge, I would strongly deprecate a parsimonious and restrictive policy applied to a young, growing Institution'. Lodge asked for £10,000 for immediate use but Chamberlain opened a special fund which raised only £8000: ibid., p. 639; cf. University of Birmingham, JC L.Add. 197: Chamberlain to Lodge, 18 Mar. 1901, expressing opposition to diverting funds to the enlargement of Edmund St. 'but will reluctantly accept, if it is the only way to accommodate students'.

4 UC 7/iv/4/33: Poynting, 20 Mar. 1902; UC 7/iv/4/34: Windle, 3 Apr. 1902.

5 For discussions in this chapter of planning and designs see the plans and drawings in UC9/vi and Royal Institute of British Architects: Z13/1–20. Some are reproduced in Cheesewright, *Mirror to a Mermaid*, pp. 53–6.

6 UA Council Minutes 1, p. 84.

7 UA Building Committee 1/36: 26 Sep. 1901; 2/539: 20 Oct. 1905.

8 UA Building Committee 2/879: 26 Mar. 1908; 3/1040: 18 June 1909; 3/1120: 27 Oct. 1910.

9 Christine Penney, 'Per Ardua ad Alta – a short history of the University power station', UC unpublished MS (1990).

10 *Birmingham Daily Post*, 3 May 1904.
11 Vincent and Hinton, *University of Birmingham*, p. 84; completed early 1905: UC 7/ii *Council*, 1904–5, p. 19.
12 See above, p. 50.
13 For the following see *Birmingham Daily Post*, Special Supplement, 7 July 1909.
14 UC 7/ii *Building Committee* (25 Feb. 1904), p. 6; (30 Nov. 1905), p. 8.
15 UA Council Minutes 1, p. 259.
16 See below, p. 191.
17 UA Building Committee 1/1. The following is based on a comparison of the record of the Building Committee and the surviving plans and elevations.
18 UA Council Minutes 1, pp. 439–41.
19 UA Building Committee 1/19.
20 Ibid., 1/23.
21 Ibid. For an assessment which concentrates on the Great Hall see E. W. Ives, *Image of a University: The Great Hall at Edgbaston* (Birmingham, 1988).
22 UA Building Committee 1/34, 41, 57.
23 Ibid., 1/73.
24 *Birmingham Daily Post*, Supplement, 7 July 1909.
25 University of Birmingham, JC L. Add. 190, 192: Chamberlain to Lodge, 28 June, 22 Oct. 1900; UA Council Minutes 1, pp. 173–4.
26 University of Birmingham, JC L. Add. 192, 197, 201, 213, 252: Chamberlain to Lodge, 22 Oct. 1900; 13 Mar., 27 Apr., 4 Oct. 1901; 24 May 1905.
27 RIBA *Catalogue*. B, 72: T–Z130.
28 University of Birmingham, JC L. Add. 192: Chamberlain to Lodge, 22 Oct. 1900. For local complaints, see UA Council Minutes 1, pp. 329–30, 340; *Birmingham Daily Gazette*, 15, 16 Aug. 1901.
29 University of Birmingham, JC L. Add. 192: Chamberlain to Lodge, 22 Oct. 1900.
30 University of Birmingham, JC L. Add. 197: Chamberlain to Lodge, 13 Mar. 1901; C. A. Smith, 'The Birmingham University', *Engineering*, 88 (1902), p. 5.
31 UA Building Committee 1/134: Webb to Building Committee, 25 Sept. 1901; University of Birmingham, JC L. Add. 213: Chamberlain to Lodge, 4 Oct. 1901.
32 *Birmingham Daily Post*, 9 Jan. 1902; University of Birmingham, JC L. Add. 190, 192: Chamberlain to Lodge, 28 June, 22 Oct. 1900.
33 *The Builder*, 84 (1903), p.189.
34 University of Birmingham, JC 12/1/1/27: Chamberlain to unnamed addressee, 23 May 1900.
35 UA Building Committee 1/33: Chamberlain to Building Committee, 21 Sept. 1901.
36 UA Building Committee 2/527, 679, 737. For Bell see *Who Was Who, 1929–40*; RIBA *Catalogue*. B, 72; U. Thieme and F. Becker, eds., *Allgemeines Lexikon Der Bildenden Kunstler von der Antike bis zür Gegenwart* (Leipzig, 1907–50).
37 *Birmingham Daily Post*, 1 May 1900.
38 The phrase in reported in *Birmingham Daily Post*, 1 May 1899.
39 UA Building Committee 2/ 570, 585; RIBA Z13/1/9.
40 *Birmingham Daily Post*, 8 Jan. 1902.
41 Ibid., Supplement, 7 July 1909.
42 *Engineering*, 80 (1905), pp. 240–1.

43 *Birmingham Daily Post*, 8 Jan. 1902.
44 *The Builder*, 82 (1902), facing p. 442; UA Building Committee 2/535. For Pegram see *Who was Who, 1929–40*; Thieme and Becker, eds., *Lexikon*; Elfrida Manning, *Marble and Bronze: The Art and Life of Hamo Thornycroft* (1982), pp. 105,114, 180.
45 For the following see UA Building Committee 2/527, 533–5, 660, 679 and esp. UC 7/iv/8/39: report by Lodge. Pegram was paid £300 on account: Building Committee /2, p. 147.
46 RIBA Z13/1/19.
47 RIBA Z13/1/20.
48 UC 7/iv/8/39: ms. additions by Lodge.
49 Vincent and Hinton, *University of Birmingham*, p. 20.
50 *The Builder*, 82 (1902), p. 448: 'an extract from one of the Chancellor's addresses on the objects of the foundation will run across the façade'.
51 Ibid., facing p. 442.
52 RIBA Z13/1/19.
53 *Birmingham Daily Post*, Supplement, 7 July 1909.
54 For the subsequent fortunes of the platform see below, pp. 336–7.
55 UA Council Minutes 5/2691, 2692.
56 UA Building Committee 3/ 871, 874.
57 *Birmingham Daily Post*, Supplement, 7 July 1909.
58 F. H. Jackson, 'The work of T. R. Spence, designer, decorator, architect', *The Magazine of Art*, 2 ser. 1 (1903), pp. 80–4.
59 H. B. Creswell, 'Sir Aston Webb and his office', in *Edwardian Architecture and its Origins*, ed. A. Service (1975), pp. 330-1. Webb said that 'the university which ... Mr.Bell and himself were now erecting was a great assembly of huge work shops for engineering and mining and metallurgy and such like things, together with a Great Hall where the great functions which take place from time to time would be held' : *The Builder*, 84 (1903), p. 189.
60 RIBA Z13/1/13.
61 *Birmingham Daily Post*, Supplement, 7 July 1909.
62 UC 7/ii *Council* 1905–6, pp. 9–10; A. P. D. Thomson, 'The Chamberlain Tower', *University of Birmingham Historical Journal*, 4 (1954), pp. 167–79.
63 UA Building Committee 2/702.
64 UA Building Committee 2: 29 Nov. 1906, p. 3.
65 Ibid.: 31 Jan. 1907, p. 2; 30 May 1907, p. 4.
66 Ibid.: 2: 25 Apr. 1907, p. 2; 24 Sept. 1909, p. 4.
67 *Birmingham Daily Post*, Supplement, 7 July 1909.
68 For the following see ibid.
69 UA Building Committee 2/737; UC 7/ii *Council* 1905–6, pp. 10–11; Vincent and Hinton, *University of Birmingham*, p. 183.
70 Vincent and Hinton, *University of Birmingham*, p. 183.
71 UC Council Minutes 1/3481, 3492, 3525; University of Birmingham, JC L. Add. 256: Chamberlain to Lodge, 19 June 1909.
72 *Birmingham Daily Post*, Supplement, 7 July 1909; Cheesewright, *Mirror to a Mermaid*, pp. 60–5.
73 *Birmingham Daily Post*, Supplement, 7 July 1909.

74 UC 12/iv/3: Souvenir Programme.
75 Vincent and Hinton, *University of Birmingham*, p. 87.
76 Ibid., p. 35.
77 University of Birmingham, JC L. Add. 230: Chamberlain to Lodge, 22 Mar. 1902.
78 *Birmingham Daily Post*, Supplement, 7 July 1909.
79 *Engineering*, 88 (1902), p. 5.

Chapter Eight

The new University

IN SPEAKING and campaigning for the charter, Joseph Chamberlain had presented a university as the pinnacle of the Birmingham achievement, adding 'the opportunities of the highest culture' to the civic renewal which had engaged him and his allies for thirty years.[1] At the same time it was to serve the Midland region and reflect its character, which he summed up in the commitment that this new University would be 'redolent of the soil and inspired by the associations in which it exists'.[2] The vision was clear, but with the charter sealed on 24 March 1900, attention moved to practicalities. How was this sense of place and, probably more particularly, this concept of a technical and relevant educational culture to be translated into a new form of university? The answer to that question would be complex, determined by local expectations, by the form and size of sponsorship and by the relationships formed between Midlands industry and business and the University's academics, and between regional government and the new University's authorities. From the start, too, a 'player' from outside the region would have an important and growing influence on the new University's character and future: central government.

The system of government laid down in the charter certainly provided mechanisms to encourage a symbiosis between the new University and its region. The 'supreme governing body' was a large Court of Governors.[3] The City of Birmingham had five places on this (plus the mayor *ex officio*). All the Midland counties and county boroughs sent representatives and so, too, their school boards. The local MPs and bishops had seats, as did representatives of major local schools and regional educational associations. There were also some governors from further afield, but in essence the membership was intended to demonstrate ownership of the new University by the City and the Midlands region and to be a means to mobilise interest and support over the whole of the area.[4] A Court of this size could not, of course, exercise its formal power to 'regulate affairs of business'.[5] Effective authority in the University was, therefore, delegated to a Council which, as Lodge put it, 'controlled the general administration of the University and was [in sole] control of the finance and the election of professorial assistants and examiners'.[6] Once again membership was designed to be heavily representative of the City and the region, and among the Council's thirty-three (later thirty-four) members, academics were in a permanent minority. Laymen, therefore, would play a vital part in the running of the new University – as they had in Mason College. For the most part, they were local notables and members of Birmingham's tightly-knit bourgeoisie, who were being rewarded for all their hard work in raising funds for the proposed University by being asked to do yet more to aid it in its initial years. Until the end of his life Chamberlain, as chancellor, deluged Oliver Lodge, the new principal, with letters of advice and recommendation. His public pronouncements were, of course, curtailed once he suffered his stroke but the appearance in the Council lists of the names of Chamberlain, Pinsent, Martineau and Kenrick, all members of the Unitarian Chamberlain–Kenrick 'clan', guaranteed continued fidelity to the founding chancellor's vision. Charles Gabriel Beale, Chamberlain's close relative by marriage and important political ally, became the University's first vice-chancellor, at this stage the key lay post. A precise and exacting administrator, the quiet, self-effacing Beale proved himself of great worth not only in giving sterling advice to Lodge but in his astute influence on the selection of important members of staff. Margery Fry, the first warden of Birmingham's women's hostel, University House, described 'being taken by the hand by a man named Beale' who persuaded her to take up a post in the unattractively provincial civic University, and thus transformed her future.[7] As we have seen, the key post of university treasurer went to Francis Corder Clayton, another political ally of Chamberlain, and the chairmanship of the University Building Committee to George Hamilton Kenrick, Chamberlain's brother-in-law.

When the former president of Trinity, Oxford and the master of Downing made the 1901 quinquennial visit to Birmingham on behalf of the Treasury, they drew attention to these constitutional provisions as intended to introduce local representation into university affairs and appeal to 'the local patriotism of the citizens'.[8] However, their particular interest in 'the transformation into the Birmingham University' was in that 'the complete control of courses of study and examinations is vested in the Senate, *i.e.*, the teaching staff of the University, "subject to review by the Council."' This meant that the University's academic programme, also, could be 'rooted in the soil' of the Midlands. There was no outside authority to conform to. Everything could be tailored to the needs of the constituency. The inspectors were clearly surprised that Birmingham required students to attend courses and complete termly requirements before being allowed to sit for a degree, but this was almost certainly in order to continue to reassure parents.[9] They also noted that Birmingham was moving towards the model of a four-year degree, beginning with an intermediate year but ending up in the award of the MA or the M.Sc. When they visited five years later they would note that this had developed into a 'method of examination … at Birmingham in many respects peculiar to the University'.[10] They would also notice how this freedom had allowed education to be shaped to regional need.[11]

Constitutional machinery ensuring that the new University was owned locally meant nothing, however, without the money to make this possible. In broad terms, funding for the new University in the first decade continued the pattern of the old Science College. The first element in the recurrent income comprised dividends and rents. The second was student fees, and the third, fees and grants from local government or other bodies. Finally, there was the central government grant. The problem for the University was that the level of no single element of this income was assured. Indeed, the Treasury rule for grants-in-aid to colleges linked the level of any central grant to the level of funds raised from 'local' sources, on the argument that the amount raised by an institution locally in the form of endowments and gifts, local grants and student fees was an index of an institution's success and utility.[12] On the capital side the University, like the College, relied on donations, although these were now much augmented as a result of Chamberlain's famous appeal. About 40% came with conditions which could mean that the University, its buildings, schools and courses were obliged to take rather a different form to what might otherwise have been intended.[13] However, the remaining gifts carried no strings. Some of the first receipts from the 1898 appeal were applied to rescheduling the Mason College debt and the remainder was spent on buildings or invested to produce an income.[14] Most of the investments were made locally – after all, Joseph Chamberlain had declared: 'This University will stand or fall with the prosperity of the district.'[15] With the Mason College endowment, the new money meant that the University now owned property in Edmund Street, Great Charles Street and Small Heath, and invested in the City of Birmingham and local family firms such as Guest, Keen & Nettlefold, as well as the Midland Railway Co.[16]

The call for endowments continued even after the receipt of the charter, notably in 1902, although response to these later appeals was often disappointing.[17] In 1902–3 only £3850 were received, with a miserly £1700 being collected in 1903–4. Furthermore, where in the earlier appeal some 1174 individuals and 162 firms gave promptly to the cause, gifts in the period 1900–14 were spasmodic and made by the few. However donations did rise significantly towards the end of the decade – 1908 raised £70,675 – so that receipts between 1901 and 1914, although below the £335,308 raised in 1898–1900, reached a very useful £216,716. The Treasury inspectors in 1905 were very impressed at the figures subscribed, which 'demonstrate the local patriotism of the citizens of Birmingham'.[18] Thanks to Chamberlain's call for the City of Birmingham and the West Midlands to support the proposed University, Birmingham became the third best endowed of the new civic universities in England, with, in time, the most valuable range of university buildings.[19] Only the appeal to endow scholarships was disappointing.

Beneath the surface, however, the capital account presented serious problems. Funding most of the inherited Mason College deficit had meant a £50,000 mortgage with the Wesleyan & General Insurance Co., plus an overdraft facility of £100,000 from Lloyd's Bank. These had to be serviced, creating a cost of about £7000 a year to be passed to the income and expenditure account.[20] Then new donations were, as we have seen, coming in both more slowly and more spasmodically than hoped for. The cost, some said extravagance, of the Aston Webb buildings at Bournbrook was one cause of this. Chamberlain's confidence that further contributions would come flowing in once the locality had seen the glory of the buildings that were to house their civic university, proved to be misguided. Despite attempts to publicise Aston Webb's buildings as eminently practical and ideal for a university for the Midlands, people could judge with their own eyes.[21] In short, Chamberlain's initial preference for 'brains and not architecture' demonstrated a far better understanding of the Midlands psyche than his second thoughts that grand buildings would make an extra appeal to local pockets.[22] Another reason was, as we have seen, that Chamberlain's policy was essentially a gamble on his continuing to be in a position to lead and mobilise his close allies and those who at least saw a benefit in supporting his favourite cause. Lodge specifically told Lloyd George that the University's 1908 appeal failed because of Chamberlain's illness.[23] Again, it was the revenue account which was badly affected. Without new endowments coming in readily to replace money spent on building, the yield of the University's endowments was bound to suffer. Thus income from rents and interest, which was £10,627 in 1900–1 and reached a peak of £12,082 in 1903–4, by 1909–10 was producing only £7610.

The combination of heavy interest payments and falling endowment receipts was serious enough, but the revenue account was also in serious difficulties of its own. The University's opening deficiency of £1484 for 1900–1 could be dismissed as a hiccup, no doubt reflecting the start-up costs of the new status, and the next four years each returned positive balances which aggregated to a surplus of nearly £5000 at 30 September 1905. The next six years were, however, a disaster. The deficit for 1905–6 was £2683, two years later the shortfall was £13,680 and by 1910–11 the accumulated loss had reached £37,749, equivalent to more than half a year's revenue. Since the deficit leaped between 1907–8 and 1909–10 from £6590 to £32,908, one exceptional factor in the losses may have been the cost of the royal opening. However, the basic and continuing reason was the increased cost of staff necessary to meet the pretensions of a university. And this despite the fact that Birmingham's academics were poorly paid by comparison with elsewhere.[24] The problems which had faced Mason College in its final years were back with a vengeance. The Treasury inspectors wrote in 1906: 'It is not in buildings alone that the University has committed itself to a far larger and more expensive undertaking. The additions made to the teaching staff involve an increased annual expenditure of £8,397. The wages of the largely increased staff of porters, laboratory assistants, and skilled workmen are not included in this return.'[25] In its last year the College had employed twenty-seven professors and thirty-five other staff; in the years 1901–6 it had added nine new chairs and made twenty-five other appointments, with all the knock-on effect on departmental expenses and administration costs.[26] As with the Bournbrook buildings, the University was paying the price for taking a deliberate financial risk. It had 'entered into such expenditure beyond its income' in order to establish an institution fit for the future.[27] In 1912 a sinking fund was set up and the University achieved the first positive balance for seven years, but effectively the accumulated deficit was only stabilised.

That costs were the root of the University's financial problem is evident from the fact that throughout the period 1900–14, income grew year on year, beginning with £25,094 in 1900–1 and rising to an immediate pre-war total of £71,792. The rate of growth was, thus, nearly 8.5% a year, although this average masks considerable fluctuation, from 14.3% in 1904–5 to a drop of 2.3% during crisis years in 1910–11. Of the four sources of recurrent income, fee income from students attending courses and taking examinations at the University faltered in 1904–5 but consolidation of payment methods in 1906–7 stopped the decline and produced £12,500 in real terms, which by 1913–14 had risen to £17,769. Receipts by the University from local authorities and from central government accounted in 1900–1 for over a quarter of its income, each contributing just over 13%, and these too rose over the pre-war years. Birmingham City Council was always far and away the biggest local payer but was joined by Staffordshire and Worcestershire, while the Assay Office paid a portion of any profits. National government support came from various departments and funds including the Board of Education and the Ad Hoc Treasury Committee. In the last year before the war, grants from local government made up 21.5% of the University's receipts, with 25.5% coming from central government.

Achieving such increases was anything but easy. Raising fees to individual students could quickly become counterproductive. In the first place it might actually deter students from attending the University – numbers were effectively static between 1911–12 and 1913–14. Secondly, it could rapidly lose the University popular sympathy and undermine Chamberlain's claims to have established a university that would serve all classes of the community. The problem with income from local and central government was that in each case there was a political battle to fight.

City Council support for higher education in Birmingham had begun in 1899 when it voted a sum of £1500 to Mason University College via its technical instruction grant.[28] In June 1901, Chamberlain wrote to ask for the grant to become annual and at a halfpenny in the pound on Birmingham's rateable value (0.208%).[29] This grant of a halfpenny rate was not given without debate or criticism, even if Birmingham's elder statesman had made the plea. At the time of the appeal for the proposed University, people had been bombarded with calls to support good causes, from hospital funds to campaigns to establish a new bishopric. Having raised its quarter of a million pounds, the University now appeared to be asking for more. Some members of the City Council fully supported Chamberlain's call for support. Alderman Martineau, a member of the University Court and chair of the City's Technical Schools Committee, voiced the Chamberlainite idea that the University was the 'top stone of the fabric of the municipality'.[30] Whittall, a member of the City Finance Committee, suggested that as the top stone it should 'study economy'. An amendment was moved to reduce support to a farthing rate (0.104%). Fortunately for the University this was lost, but fifteen members of the City Council did vote for it, and it was agreed that the halfpenny rate should be reviewed annually.[31] The Council was careful to express its gratitude.[32] The University possibly owed its success as much to civic rivalry as to the merits of its case. As the debate was going on, the local press was alive with the news that Liverpool City Council had decided to give a halfpenny in the pound to support to the attempt of its University College to secure university status: 'one municipal stroke and the University might be founded'.[33]

This agreement between University and City was, however, called into question as early as 1904–5 by government insistence that national support could only reflect the support a university received locally. When Principal Lodge led a deputation from the universities to meet David Lloyd George, President of the Board of Trade, he was informed that he should attempt to liquidate Birmingham's debt via an increased local grant. He later recorded: 'I must tell the City that their [Treasury] support would be contingent on the equivalent of an extra half penny rate being given, and that it ought to be one penny.'[34] Asking was a task which did not please Lodge. He accepted that additional city support was the route to an increased Treasury grant, but he was already bitterly resentful of the degree of influence over the University that rate support conferred on the City's worthies, complaining that 'the citizen members of the council [are] not to regard the professors as they regarded the employees, or officials, of the city council'.[35] In the event, despite Lodge passing on Lloyd George's call to follow the lead of other provincial cities and increase its grant to the University, Birmingham City Council merely confirmed the halfpenny rate.[36]

Tension between Treasury, University and City Council became critical in 1910–11, threatening both the continued payment of the City's contribution and the possibility of an increase in grant from national government. Working-class criticism of the University and of its high costs was nothing new; the 'Workers representatives' on the City Council had resisted even the original grant in 1901.[37] However, in January 1911, when Chamberlain called on the City to increase support to the University to a penny in the pound, criticism become vehement and was taken up by more and more of the Labour councillors, who by this time were becoming numerous.[38] In their opinion, a university established to educate the sons of the working class and to inculcate 'democracy within the city' was doing nothing of the sort.[39] The poor were angry that their children were not gaining university places, and concluded that the University had been brought into existence 'for the middle-class part of the community'.[40] 'Popular' criticism also challenged the University over accepting students from outside Birmingham and the Midland region, and Chamberlain was personally attacked for encouraging foreign students to study there.[41]

To make matters between the University and the City of Birmingham even worse, a number of Birmingham ratepayers, led by an Arthur W. Wood of Edgbaston, began to ask whether rate support to the University was legal under the Technical Instruction Acts of 1889 and 1891.[42] They were spurred on by the fact that the University had not awarded all of the twenty grants made available by the City Council for 'poor' Birmingham students, only nine applicants being judged by the University as of a suitable calibre to enjoy higher education.[43] The district auditors were brought in to deal with the ratepayers, while the Board of Education was consulted as to whether the City Council had ever asked the Board's permission to award the University these grants.[44] To add to the complexity of the situation, the University was 'caught in the middle of the debate on Greater Birmingham', with the City Council attempting in that same year to extend its boundaries to include the land of the suburbs and more.[45]

The result of all this was that the City Council grant to the University was, once again, only made for one year, a difficult situation for the university authorities, who not only needed an increased income but a guaranteed income as well. A leader in the *Birmingham Daily Post* early in January 1912 advocated a way out of this impasse between the University, the Council and local citizenry. It suggested that rate support should only be increased if twenty-eight new scholarships, costing a total of between £12,320 and £16,000, were provided and awarded, and that the University should have 'more contact' with the town, especially through the Workers' Educational Association (WEA).[46] The University had begun WEA work in 1909 under earlier prompting by the Treasury, but it was less than impressed by the job. Lodge, often seen as a pioneer in early adult education, recalled that it was 'many years before more than half [of students] could reach the standard required for University entrance'.[47]

In February 1912, at the height of the crisis, the Treasury's Ad Hoc Committee paid its quinquennial visit to the University, no doubt repeating that its grants were still very much influenced by local levels of support. Between the rock of Treasury's insistence and the hard place of approaching bankruptcy the University gave in. It agreed to form a joint board for WEA work and to be more enthusiastic in providing courses. By the time that the City Council reassessed the matter of its grant to the University in February 1913, the matter was settled. The city promised £15,000 per year for an indefinite period on condition that fifteen scholarships were established and regularly allocated.[48] The University somewhat reluctantly agreed.

The year-by-year uncertainty in City Council support was, thus, resolved by 1913. The issue of the grant by central government proved to be more intractable. Mason College had received only a few thousand pounds per year from this source, but the fact that the state was willing to support higher education at all was seen to be of great importance.[49] However, the government maintained that past grants had not established a precedent, notionally being given in exceptional circumstances and then only for limited periods of time.[50] It did not accept that support of higher education was a continuing national economic responsibility.

State aid to higher education in England was much lower than in other European states, notably Germany, while, as we have seen, English colleges initially received far less per head of population than universities and university colleges did in either Scotland or Wales.[51] The 1889 grant for England of £15,000 per year certainly rose to £25,000 by 1897, £100,000 by 1906 and reached £150,000 by the outbreak of war.[52] Even so, the state support received by each institution was only one element in its overall income, though the proportion varied, depending on the availability of other sources. Birmingham was more dependent than most. The Treasury maintained that it received some 33% of all its income in 1910 from state sources, where, for example, the grant to Manchester provided only 20%.[53]

For almost two decades the grant allocation was made to individual institutions for limited periods by an Ad Hoc Advisory Committee of experts, which made long-term planning in higher education very difficult.[54] Even after the deputation made in readiness for the beginning of a new grant period in December 1901, Hicks Beach, the chancellor, and then Austen Chamberlain, the financial secretary, maintained that the grant was temporary, the giving of aid 'not implying any assumption of liability on the part of the Exchequer'.[55] In any case, to ask for increased support was not without dangers, particularly that administration of the grant would pass from Treasury control to the Board of Education, a prospect that many, including Birmingham's Oliver Lodge, saw as a potential threat to university autonomy.

Such difficulties prompted action by all the new universities and university colleges and not least the University of Birmingham, which had the largest debt in the higher education system. The result was a continuation of the late-Victorian campaign for support, which achieved success only, and even then partially, in the creation of the University Grants Committee (UGC) in 1919.[56] Throughout the campaign 'Birmingham men', both academics and politicians, played leading roles. Indeed, Birmingham's first principal, Oliver Lodge, played the most consistent role in promoting deputations to the government and in establishing close liaison between university and university college principals and vice-chancellors. In 1919 this eventually bore fruit in the formation of the Committee of Vice-Chancellors and Principals (CVCP). Lodge had taken little or no action towards the deputation in 1901, but the ambitious programme of expansion at Birmingham and the threat of financial trouble forced him to become, in effect, the co-ordinator for later deputations, advised all the while by Joseph Chamberlain.[57]

As well as deputations to lobby the Chancellor – by now relatively common – speeches and published articles kept up the pressure. Joseph Chamberlain played a leading role. Near-obsessed as he was with the Imperial question, tariff reform and Britain's relative economic decline, he saw state funding for British higher education overall as part of the remedy, just as much as the promotion of higher and technical education in the city known as the 'workshop of the World'. Systemised training for those in business and industry was vital in order to aid the Midland economy; higher education, supported by assured and increased state support, was a necessity for the national good.[58] Chamberlain pressed for this not only in speeches to Parliament and the public but on select committees on English universities and university colleges, by his efforts to persuade important individuals and through the Privy Council.[59] This was very much the case with the special examination by the Privy Council of the principle of the civic as against the federal university, completed in 1903.[60]

Chamberlain also particularly influenced a political opponent, R. B. Haldane, who in 1898 had been instrumental in securing the reorganisation of the University of London. In 1902 he told Chamberlain that he was the only person 'in a prominent position on either side of politics who sees so clearly ... the real point in the present situation or cares much about it. ... There is nothing that I should like better than to work with you and under you to remedy what seems to me to be grave shortcomings. ... I can find some time and have my hand on experts.'[61] Haldane also sent him 'his little book' comparing state provision for higher education in Britain and Germany.[62] In a letter nine months later he declared that Chamberlain was 'the only man in this country who has the combination of business and power that can make ['highest education'] live'.[63] Haldane went on to chair the important committee that produced the Treasury's Third Report on grant-in–aid to universities and university colleges that was published in April 1905. The two younger Chamberlains, Austen and Neville, also played important parts in the debate as backbenchers, supporting the University of Birmingham, and to a lesser extent, higher education nationally. Ironically, each became less enthusiastic when in office as Chancellor of the Exchequer at important junctures in state and university history – Austen between 1903 and 1905 and Neville during the period when the notorious inter-war 'Geddes Axe' began to take effect.[64] However, during a second term at the Treasury from 1919 to 1921, Austen would preside over the creation of the UGC.[65]

Lodge's involvement in this campaigning had begun in a small way in December 1903 when he simply indicated that he would be willing to join a small deputation to the Chancellor of the Exchequer to ask for a consolidation of the annual grant made to English universities. He said that he was disturbed that this had been on 'an experimental basis for years', and added that 'the sum allocated from the Imperial exchequer has never been commensurate with the worth of local effort'.[66] In the event, Lodge led the deputation.[67] He prepared it well. The principals of the grant-receiving institutions were invited to meet at King's College London on the morning of Ash Wednesday, 17 February 1904, for a preliminary meeting, but before then he sent round a circular. The deputation was to be 'small and businesslike'. Each college was to have no more than one or two representatives and they were to speak in 'short sentences'.[68] Representatives were to draw attention to the fact that the increased support which the colleges needed was 'to develop their work efficiently'. They were not to argue against the need to raise funds locally, but 'on the contrary' to suggest that 'local generosity might be stimulated by a backbone of wise government' and greater state support. They were to remind the Chancellor that their work was 'national not just local work', a point of view that, in fact, the chancellor, Austen Chamberlain, already shared.[69] This first deputation of 1904 was followed by a further one to the prime minister in July. The result, Lodge reported to the University of Birmingham's Court of Governors in 1905, was a resounding success. Not only, as we have seen, was the Treasury grant increased in 1906 to £100,000 (from £54,000) but the government agreed to make the Ad Hoc Advisory Committee permanent.[70] The principal claimed, with some exaggeration, that this was, 'one of the most important and encouraging events of that kind that has occurred in English History'.[71]

It was at this point that the Treasury Committee, chaired by the highly sympathetic Haldane, was set up, but even so Lodge remained vigilant. His concern was the power that the Treasury might assume with this increase in its grants and regular quinquennial visitations of its now permanent Advisory Committee. He therefore wrote to the heads of Manchester, Liverpool, Leeds and the two London colleges, University and King's, suggesting that they had 'better act together'.[72] He need not have feared. When Haldane's Committee reported in April 1905, the various universities and university colleges declared themselves quite happy with the principles it established.

With the increase in support and the establishment of the new and permanent Advisory Committee in 1906, there was little need for further action on the part of universities and colleges until 1910 and the next quinquennial inspection and reassessment of the Treasury's grant. Lodge, however, determined not to allow Birmingham's problems to be forgotten. At some point in 1908, Lodge, Neville Chamberlain (still at this time involved in Birmingham's municipal politics), Alfred Hughes, the dean of Arts, and Margery Fry, warden of University House, the women's hostel, went as a delegation to the Board of Education to appeal for an increased grant towards the new University's costly buildings. While waiting, Fry amused herself by 'solemnly meandering round the National Portrait Gallery' and teasing Neville Chamberlain by choosing a place where his portrait as a future prime minister would be hung.[73] In August of the same year, Lodge published an important promotional article in *The National Review* entitled 'The University of

Birmingham'. Admitting that the University's 'resources are exhausted', Lodge claimed that this 'matter is a national as well as a civic issue'. By 1909, too, the financial situation of Birmingham and of a number of other universities was being made worse by the need to provide pensions as older members of academic staff approached retirement age. Here the Treasury did listen and made a special grant in 1911.

In 1909 the secretaryship of the unofficial grouping of university and college vice-chancellors and principals passed from Lodge to Arthur C. Headlam, the principal of King's College London. With the next quinquennium approaching, the line this time was to be that higher education in Britain received far less state support than overseas and that this had resulted in a shortage of essential trained workers.[74] Germanophobia was, of course, at its height, triggered by the threat to Britain's naval superiority. In planning the deputation that was to be held on 11 February 1910, Headlam and Arthur H. D. Acland of the Board of Education suggested that only some twenty representatives attend, so that real conversation could be carried on. A preparatory meeting did take place, but the Chancellor, David Lloyd George, fell ill and the visit was postponed until after a House of Lords report on University College finances was published in March.[75]

When the delegation of vice-chancellors and principals was eventually received on 17 November, the government's attitude towards the universities and colleges had hardened. Pressure to move control of grants from the Treasury to the Board of Education was at its height, and Lloyd George was angered by the increased indebtedness of universities and colleges and their reluctance to press for more local financial support. Little wonder that Lodge recorded that he had had 'a sleepless night about the Treasury' before Acland led him and the rest of the deputation to meet Lloyd George, the chief Treasury official Sir George Murray, and Dr Frank Heath and Sir Richard Morant of the Board of Education. Despite protests that they did not wish the Treasury to pay off their deficits, preferring a grant for future work and expansion, the university and college officials met with short shrift from Lloyd George, with the Chancellor muttering in particular about the University of Birmingham's overdrafts! The meeting was made even more acrimonious by the tension that existed between officials from the Treasury and the Board of Education, who, as Lodge observed, differed greatly on how grants should be paid and who should control the paying! Lloyd George's impatience may also have been because more than half his mind must have been on the dissolution of Parliament which the Prime Minister would announce the next day.

With the meeting ending in stalemate, Lodge had no other hope than to persuade a friend who was breakfasting with Lloyd George the next morning to 'urge my contentions about our needs', and to wait for a further meeting a few days later.[76] This involved Headlam, Morant, Frank Heath, and himself, as a representative of the English universities and colleges. Morant stated that he wished to 'pin himself and his successor down to a sum', casually mentioning that the Chancellor had hinted at a total of between £20,000 and £30,000, but 'I fancy he really means £50,000'![77] A scheme of allocation was also discussed, but in Lodge's opinion it was neither on 'a scientific nor a reasoned out basis of distribution'. Lloyd George had apparently emphasised the future and need for new development, but baulked at giving support to the University for Birmingham's 'wildcat schemes'. Lodge records that the prime minister had been somewhat mollified to discover that part of the University's annual deficit was the result of paying interest on outstanding debt, although he also noticed that the citizens of Birmingham had failed to come up to expectation. Eventually the Chancellor relented and agreed to treat the University of Birmingham as a special case. However, he insisted that local support must be raised to a penny in every pound of rateable value (0.42%), a requirement which, as we have seen, helped to precipitate the crisis between the University and the City in the following year. In addition the Board of Education's 'monstrous attempt' to gain control of all state grants to universities and colleges was successful, despite Lodge's protestations that '[the Board] had better keep its hands off higher education'![78]

In the first decade of the century, therefore, the relations between English higher education and the government, and in the case of the University of Birmingham between itself, the state and local authorities, reached a low ebb. Even a fairly favourable report from the quinquennial visitors, for the first time under the auspices of the Board of Education and headed by William McCormick, failed to alleviate Lodge's gloom, not even when this was followed by the increase in Birmingham's Treasury grant, from £9900 per year to £15,500. Settlement of the City's grant in February 1913 at £15,000 per annum less fifteen scholarships still left him depressed.[79] By February the following year, Lodge was confiding in the University's Finance Committee that he had had 'the idea of resignation ... in my mind now for several years, owing to the state of funds and the expensiveness of myself'.[80] The University's income may have increased but so had costs, the millstone of debt was still round its neck and local and national government were far less sympathetic than they had been earlier in the decade.

The financial situation in these early years was, of course, of direct relevance to the teaching, research and general operation of the new University. The problem of indebtedness and inadequate revenue ensured that it was always struggling for survival. Intent on establishing new schools and disciplines, it so often found itself held back by lack of day-to-day running expenses. Nevertheless Birmingham fought, and fought successfully, to retain the vision of a university not 'like Oxford or Cambridge'.[81] It was to be an institution which should 'shape itself on [the needs] of a manufacturing town' and produce a graduate who was 'all modern and up to date and fully conscious of conditions of national prosperity', just as Chamberlain wanted![82] The result of this was an emphasis on developing applied science courses which, along with its new faculty of Commerce, made Birmingham famous, elevating subjects to degree status, often for the first time. Such

Plate 1

Plate 2

Plate 3

Plate 4

Plate 5

Plate 6

Plate 7

Plate 8

Plate 9

Plate 10

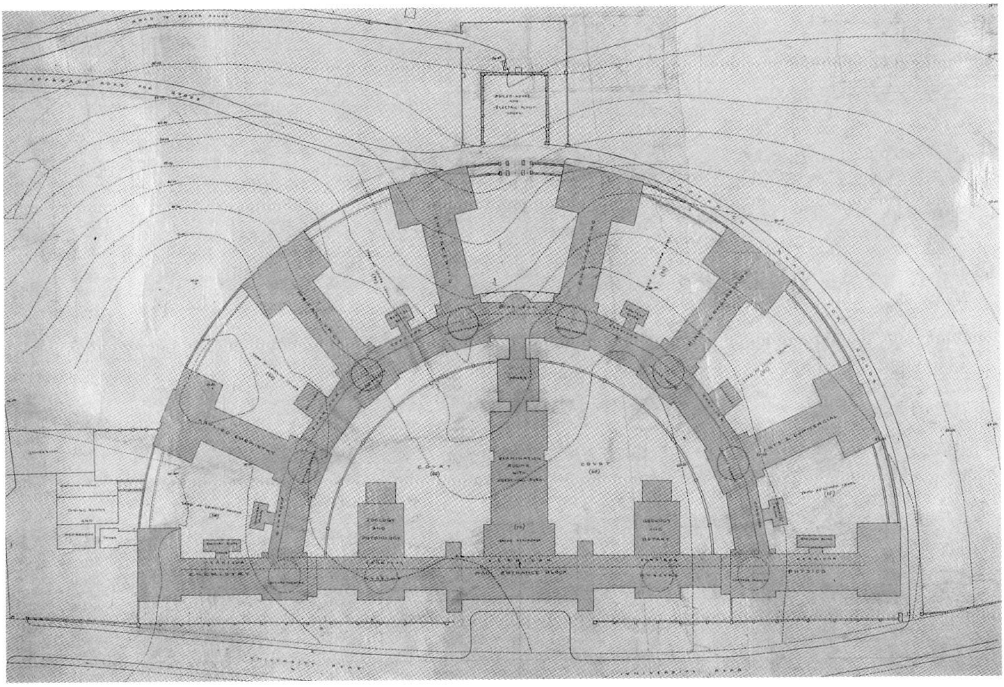

Plate 11

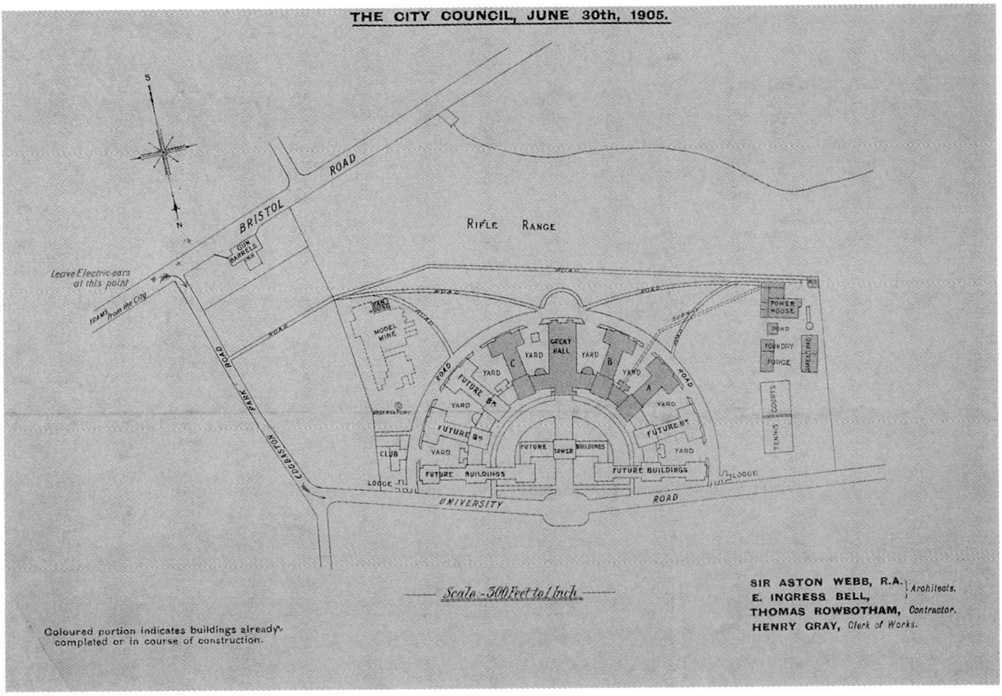
THE CITY COUNCIL, JUNE 30th, 1905.
BRISTOL ROAD
RIFLE RANGE
GUN BARRELS INN
Leave Electric cars at this point
TRAMS from the City
EDGBASTON PARK ROAD
MODEL MINE
POWER HOUSE
FOUNDRY FORGE
TENNIS COURTS
GREAT HALL
YARD
FUTURE BUILDINGS
UNIVERSITY ROAD
LODGE
CLUB
OBSERVATORY
Scale - 300 Feet to 1 Inch
SIR ASTON WEBB, R.A.
E. INGRESS BELL, Architects.
THOMAS ROWBOTHAM, Contractor.
HENRY GRAY, Clerk of Works.
Coloured portion indicates buildings already completed or in course of construction.

Plate 12

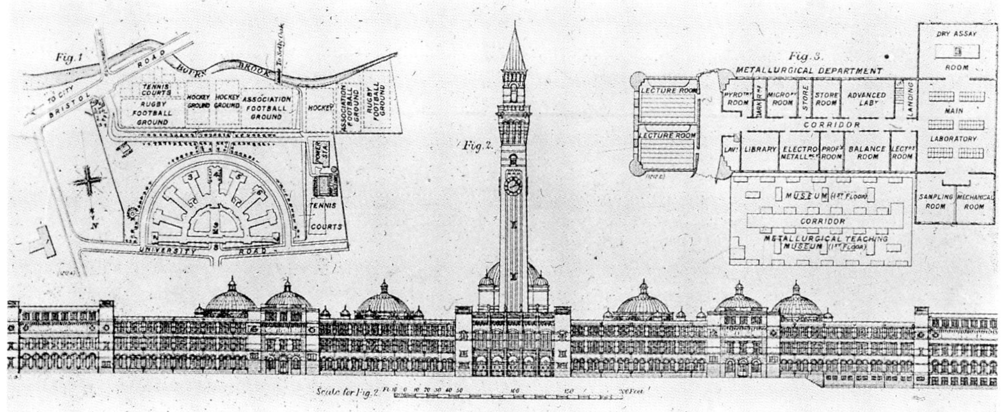

BUILDINGS OF THE BIRMINGHAM UNIVERSITY.

Plate 13

Plate 14

Plate 15

Plate 16

Plate 17

Plate 18

Plate 19

Plate 20

Plate 21

Plate 22

Plate 23

Plate 24

Plate 25

Plate 26

Plate 27

Plate 28

Plate 29

educational innovations were, inevitably, mocked by traditionalists. Oxford undergraduates liked to regale their 'peers' in the new provincial universities with the ditty:

> He gets a degree in making jam
> At Liverpool and Birmingham.[83]

The *Pall Mall Gazette* dubbed Birmingham 'a Bread and Butter University' which would follow its founder's political example and produce 'graduates in the School of Tariff and Values'.[84]

The innovative courses in practical applied science and in commerce which gave the new University its own distinctive character, even regional flavour, were in two important cases a consequence of a specific Chamberlain technique. This was to raise start-up funds by encouraging specific firms and industries to sponsor schools and courses in their own areas of interest, a strategy that in turn helped to strengthen the University's links with the locality. One such innovation was the British School of Malting and Brewing, set up in 1900 with a £28,000 grant from the Midland Association of Brewers. Again *Punch* and the *Westminster Gazette* had a field day, but brewing was no joke, having recently been transformed into one of the Midland's major industries. The School, moreover, was involved in teaching and research over a much wider area within biochemistry as its later name, the School of Brewing and Fermentation, indicates. The other novelty was the University's 'practical mining school' established in 1902–3 with encouragement from 'a great many mine owners'. With their support, legislation was secured which exempted graduates of the school from the statutory requirement for extra training in 'underground colliery management', and a centre of instruction on mine safety was in place at Birmingham by 1909.[85] This success was in marked contrast to Mason College's earlier attempts to teach mining, which had collapsed because of the lack of students and the refusal of the industry to support its courses.[86]

Mining and brewing, however, were exceptional among the famous Birmingham University courses in being innovations; most of the others were developed within departments previously established at Mason College. Indeed, staff continuity at the head of the sciences between the College and the University was complete. Metallurgy, as we have seen, had been first taught as a subsidiary of chemistry as early as 1881, and the local importance of the course and the charismatic performance of the instructor, Thomas Turner, led to his being named lecturer in the subject. However, metallurgy remained a sub-speciality within chemistry until the new University set up a chair in 1902 and brought back Turner as its first holder. A similar progression occurred with the other 'practical sciences' which made up the 'department of applied science'.[87] Thus engineering was quickly deemed by the new University to be 'far too wide for a single professor' and was split into three departments, civil, electrical and mechanical. It is also noticeable that in metallurgy and engineering, in contrast to brewing and mining, there was no element of sponsorship by the relevant industries. The Feeney Chair of Metallurgy was endowed by a newspaper proprietor and the developments in engineering were funded by a glass manufacturer and a solicitor.

The mission of 'the department of applied science' was to educate and train graduates to work in the industry of the city and the Midlands. The University's metallurgical department maintained that its chief aim was to 'be of the greatest possible benefit to the metal industry of the district' while applied chemistry claimed to be 'an enormous subject, vitally connected with all sides of the community'.[88] Similarly, the mining department had been reborn because of the 'requests of the large mining community in the Midlands'.[89] Foremost in pursuit of this mission were the professors themselves. While well qualified academically, the professors in applied science were often highly experienced practically. Both Redmayne and Cadman had worked as under-managers and managers in various pits, Redmayne actually serving an apprenticeship and gaining a Colliery Manager's Certificate, the goal of many of the mining students.[90] Frankland, while working as a demonstrator at the Royal School of Mines in London, had developed new methods of water purification and carried out monthly tests on local water supplies for the Local Government Board.[91]

The practical interests of the professors were matched by the provision on so many of these courses of practical work geared to the needs of Birmingham and the Midland industry.[92] Industrialists even had a very direct influence over what was taught when they provided machinery of a type used in their own factories. The Aston Webb buildings were designed with practical work in mind. As well as the power station and the model mine there were laboratories and workshops where undergraduates spent as much as three to four hours per week, and a 'hall of machines' with equipment including 'a cupola, furnace, casting shops, pattern shops and carpenter and drawing shops'.[93] This practical component in training proved so effective that not until the Second World War were Birmingham engineering students required to take up vacation work in order to gain experience in an engineering plant. The School of Mining likewise had a special museum of specimens, machinery parts and surveying instruments, along with models of mines. There was also an ore dressing plant for those studying metalliferous mining.

As well as the involvement of professors and undergraduates in the application of science in a local context, the University, even in these early years, began to develop a research profile in the subject. From its very foundation the University of Birmingham had been intended as a research institution, pursuing 'original research in all its branches'. However, Chamberlain himself recognised that the University had to be 'made' before it could really generate a notable research profile.[94] Nevertheless, its early academic staff did carry out serious research, building on the record already established by Mason College, once again particularly research of local relevance.[95] Bournbrook possessed what must, at that time, have been some of the best appointed and equipped buildings for scientific and technological research in the country, including, as well as the machine hall, the model mine and the power station, constant temperature rooms and more besides. In 1906 the Treasury inspectors arrived to visit Birmingham and found that in Civil Engineering, 'a testing machine, capable of exercising a pressure of 300 tons and taking a specimen for testing by compression 26 feet long, was being fitted up; it will be the largest testing machine in any university in the world'.[96] There were even postgraduates in some of the science departments. Ten doctorates in science were awarded between 1901 and 1904 alone.[97] The result of this infant activity was that in the years up to 1914 the departments of chemistry, metallurgy and mining were able to publish a significant number of research papers to add to those from Mason College days. Oliver Lodge himself was an eminent research scientist. Others, such as Burstall of mechanical engineering, with his interest in the petrol engine, and the metallurgist Thomas Turner, who tested and worked on metals produced in Midlands industry and was much in demand for his advice, had research interests that were of high significance locally.

More formal organisational links between University and industry were also established. This was to ensure that its academic work was determined by those who are 'thoroughly conversant with the educational needs of those engaged in manufacture and science'.[98] The mechanism for this was the advisory board on which local and national industrialists and businessmen would be represented. Boards were set up in brewing in 1899 and in engineering education in 1900 (chaired by Austen Chamberlain). There was also a general advisory board for the whole faculty of Science. Joseph Chamberlain was particularly keen on this device as an aid to fund-raising, for he held to the view that 'I would insist upon representation before I gave a penny' and a number of boards were set up following particularly generous gifts.[99] A more general 'advisory sub-committee' was specifically established in 1899 to enquire into the 'practical applications of science to the industries of the Midland district'. This suggested some overall goals for the University, even drawing up a list of the 'trades of the district' that could be taught as applied sciences at the Midlands' own university. By the 1920s industrial sponsorship and, with this, the number of advisory boards, had expanded to include engineering studies, coal and metal mining, mining research and oil engineering and refining (later petroleum technology).[100]

Advisory boards were not, however, the only means by which links were maintained between the industrialists of the region and Birmingham's applied courses. Many of the different professions represented at the new University had their own institutions, both locally and nationally. These bodies not only held many of their more important local and sometimes national meetings at the University (as earlier, at Mason College), but invited these 'practical professors' to address them or to take on the presidency of their institute. Perhaps the earliest example of this had been Professor Tilden's election to the local executive when the Birmingham branch of the Society of the Chemical Industry was formed in 1883.[101] By the time the University had been founded it became a mark of honour to have one of Birmingham's professors acting as president. R. A. S. Redmayne, the first holder of Birmingham's revived chair of mining, was made president of the South Staffordshire and East Worcestershire Institute of Mining Engineers.[102] His successor, John Cadman, professor of mining and later of petroleum technology, had important local connections, most notably as the Government Inspector of Mines in the Staffordshire district.[103] Thomas Turner was president of the Institute of Metals as well as a member of the Iron and Steel Institute of Staffordshire. Academic staff also moved between the University and the world outside. Turner spent eight years as Director of Technical Education in Staffordshire before returning to the Feeney Chair. Professor Redmayne resigned to become the Chief Inspector of Mines.[104]

These links brought the new applied departments of the University into close contact with local and national industrialists and kept the academics informed of the needs of industry. Professional associations also usually had a student section which often held meetings at the University and arranged visits to local factories, workshops and mines. It was normal, too, for an association to invite the student section to its annual dinner. Contacts with influential men in high places were also established by the University's academic staff. Lodge lunched regularly at the Union Club in Colmore Row, 'which I found an excellent place for getting to know the citizens of Birmingham'.[105] Further afield, he and Cadman purposely cultivated a connection with Sir Arthur Anstice, owner of both mining and metal concerns at Madeley in Staffordshire.[106] In 1909 Sir Henry Cunnyngham, Under-Secretary of State at the Home Office, came to the University to address mining students on approaches to mining research and the organisation of rescue brigades in local coalfields.[107] Such links also brought promises of vacation employment, even of future professional work for the University's graduates, and advancement and new consultancy work for professors and other members of staff. In 1909 Vice-Chancellor Beale actually suggested that the congregation day for graduates in metallurgy be moved from July to October as the date originally chosen clashed with a quarter-day in the iron industry.[108]

The story of the 'rooting' of the applied sciences into the 'soil' of the Midlands is to a significant degree paralleled by the story of the new faculty of Commerce. The original suggestion that business was a subject in which the proposed University could specialise was made by the Birmingham Chamber of Commerce in 1898.[109] It caught the local imagination and was vigorously championed by business and Joseph Chamberlain throughout the period leading up to the establishment of the Faculty in October 1902. Noting that 'this is an education which seems to have been hitherto neglected in the universities', Chamberlain and the Chamber drew up a series of proposed curricula, and through a whole series of preparatory documents proposed the form of the course and the establishment of a Board of Studies on which the Chamber would be represented.[110] Suggestions for what would constitute a useful course for young trainees in business ranged from modern languages, elements of commercial law, recent commercial history and commercial geography, to bookkeeping and engineering. With the establishment of the faculty in 1902, these close links with Birmingham commerce were strengthened. Curricula were designed to be of 'practical benefit to the future careers [of students]' and a number of the faculty's courses were set up to meet specific professional needs.[111] Thus, although Chamberlain's appeal to the nation's railway companies to sponsor a School of Railway Engineering and Economics failed miserably, the University did establish the first course in transport economics in Britain.[112]

Even more noteworthy was the faculty's 'revolutionary' course in accounting and the creation of the first UK chair in the subject in 1902. This was set up after full consultation with a committee of the Birmingham and Midland Society of Chartered Accountants. It was followed in 1906 with a chair in finance. A. W. Kirkaldy, who was appointed, established a mock office at Edmund Street where commerce students could have practical experience in such exciting work as filing![113] Courses were even 'tailor-made' for particular employers. For instance, Muntz's Metal Co. was provided with a short course that combined some of the difficulties of economics and marketing with details of elementary engineering. Once again, the University was careful to give undergraduates the opportunity to meet future potential employers. Ashley noted that taking tea after commerce's obligatory seminar brought students into contact with men of business and led to employment in a variety of local firms including Rudge, Whitworth, Avery's and the Metropolitan Wagon Co.[114] Other practical courses established in the faculty included the social studies course, begun in 1905 to cater for those in the locality who wished to serve or who were working in public and social work. This appealed especially to young women who could gain experience by working and living in the University Settlement.[115] An advisory board was established for social studies in 1905 and for commerce in 1906.

Birmingham's new ventures in the applied sciences and in commerce are often seen as model examples of liaison between university and local business and industry, and of higher education responding to economic need. It was for its new degrees in these subjects that the University of Birmingham won national recognition, even notoriety. However, while links between university, city and region were strong, they were not always as intimate as some would maintain. Advisory boards turned out in the long run to be pretty bland. Chamberlain had expected as much by saying that committees on which 'outside members' served usually ran smoothly, with little dissention; he valued them for publicity purposes.[116] Although when the applied science curricula were planned or in some cases, replanned, they were often close to what boards and professional groups suggested, design and implementation remained the responsibility of academics and not local business.[117] For instance, it was Redmayne who was responsible for 'drawing up the original scheme of mining instruction'.[118] The metallurgy curriculum did specialise in the study of metals important in local industry. Iron and brass were given special attention, as was cast iron, particularly with special reference to the silicon casting technique that was becoming increasingly important locally for the manufacture of pumps and dynamos.[119] Yet the model for both the curriculum and the methods of experiment and teaching was provided by the United States, with some influence from the German system of technical higher education.[120]

The picture of Birmingham industry and business being asked to advise but the advice being kept at one remove applies also in commerce. The Chamber, which had done so much work in forwarding the idea of a faculty of Commerce, only discovered that a professor of commerce was to be appointed by seeing the advertisement for the post in the newspaper![121] Yet what may seem cavalier conduct in this case may well have been a natural reaction to the 'lukewarmness of interest between city magnates and University staff' which became evident whenever funding was mentioned.[122] The Chamber was happy to support the idea of a Commerce Faculty but little or no financial support was forthcoming locally. Chamberlain was only able to launch Commerce with the £50,000 given by Lord Strathcona, Canadian High Commissioner and apparently once a lecturer at Mason College.[123] As for the detail, although both the Chamber of Commerce and Chamberlain constantly forwarded ideas, both the faculty and its curriculum were the creation of William Ashley, the person appointed to the commerce chair that came as such a surprise to the Chamber.[124] Thus while topics which the Chamber and Chamberlain had proposed, such as modern languages and economic history, were included, Ashley was responsible for highly innovatory elements such as a commerce 'spine' which ran through each of the degree's three years and included a vocational third year where students put themselves 'in the position of business' as they studied such subjects as 'techniques of trade' and 'advanced public finance'. Under Ashley's curriculum, even modern language courses differed from those the local business community had envisaged, offering not mere language training but a 'systematic study of literature and language'. Nor did the influence of city commerce on the University increase with the years. J. G. Smith, professor of finance from 1923, was of the opinion that there was 'no record [of the Commerce advisory board] having materially affected the fortunes of the faculty at any time'. To be fair, it had not had much opportunity. In the twenty years during which Smith was dean of the faculty, he held only two meetings of the board.[125]

The insistence of professors on a 'thus far but no further' relationship with local industry and commerce reflected something deeper than a mere confidence in their own value and a refusal to become intellectually dependent. First, although Midland business and industry were often keen that a new, more technical university should be established, allowing it too much say might quickly reduce the University to little more than a training institution for local employers, a function which Birmingham's Technical School was already doing well. Secondly, it was no simple matter to incorporate technical education within higher education. Ashley, for instance, faced a real tension in trying to ensure that his faculty was accepted as practical enough for local business, but academic enough to enter the canon of what constituted true higher education. There were, moreover, practical difficulties in incorporating the nineteenth century's 'inruption of technology' into liberal higher education. Some locals aimed too low. Thus the Birmingham Jewellers' and Silversmiths' Association drew up a full curriculum for a university course in their subject which proved to have neither content nor depth enough to merit degree status. Ashley did, however, produce within the Commerce Faculty an emollient short course in business specially for jewellers.[126] On other occasions, the problem was the reverse. The curriculum in applied chemistry was intended to encompass an 'enormous subject, vitally connected with all sides of the community' but when the local Chemical and Allied Trades Association submitted questions to the University's department of applied chemistry, they 'were so complicated and so many manufacturing and industrial issues arose out of it in regard to Birmingham work that they could not give definite information on what could be taught'.[127] A practical, specifically Midlands-orientated chemistry course was quite simply impossible to devise.[128]

By the outbreak of the First World War the work of the University of Birmingham had put applied sciences such as mining, brewing and metallurgy, along with the 'science of business', on the way towards respectability as academic disciplines. Where innovation had not been so successful was in securing a commensurate number of students. Many new courses in 'practical subjects' were poorly attended. In its first session, 1902–3, mining had ten students.[129] In the same year commerce began with eight, and over the twelve sessions up to the outbreak of war, the cumulative total of students 'primarily attached' to the faculty reached only 380.[130] Many of them, as Dudley Docker remarked, were Japanese.[131] Failure to recruit was, however, not a problem for Arts, the most underrated faculty in the new University. As Lodge remarked: 'There is an unfortunate impression abroad that Birmingham either does not possess or does not encourage a faculty of Arts.'[132] In reality the Arts departments continued to make in the new University the important contribution which they had in Mason College and, by 1910, were offering as many or more subject courses as science, from Latin, philosophy and Anglo-Saxon to new subjects such as history.

The ground of this expansion began to be laid in 1902 with the establishment of Chamberlain's long-wished-for professorship in history, a visiting appointment made permanent in 1904. In 1903 a chair of education was set up, which had been on the agenda for even longer than history. The next year it was the turn of geography, and there was also the innovative appointment of a lecturer in Spanish and Italian. The quality was there, too. Although accommodation at Edmund Street was 'cramped and overcrowded' and the library notoriously understocked, the Faculty included some notable scholars. The most senior was Sonnenschein, who as well as publishing extensively was joint founder of the Classical Association. Among others were Georg Fiedler, professor of German, the philosopher J. H. Muirhead, and the second holder of the chair of history, C. R. Beazley. There were postgraduates, too.[133] To be sure, these were fewer in number than in the sciences, but two D.Litt. degrees were awarded between 1901 and 1904. The greatest coup, however, came in 1905 when another of Chamberlain's priorities was achieved with the appointment of Sir Edward Elgar as professor of music.

Student numbers also indicate clearly that, despite publicity and popular assumptions, science was not the only thing studied at Birmingham. In 1900–1, the number of registered students was 678 and they took 1297 course between them. Over half of these (686) were in Arts. Ten years later registrations had reached 958 with (on changed definitions) 263 undergraduates recorded as taking science as against 246 in Arts and 28 in Commerce. There were a number of reasons why, despite these figures and being long established and traditionally more prestigious, Arts courses received less than their proper mention and were considered to be secondary at the new University of Birmingham. First there was publicity. Degrees in subjects such as malting, brewing and commerce were new. They invited notice and gave distinctiveness to the University. Second was the fact that sponsorship and local support, by resourcing these new disciplines, had enhanced the prestige of the professors involved. Lodge noted that the Arts professors were only 'admitted on sufferance' into the general running of the new University, and this despite all the battles they had fought and won during the years the University of Birmingham was being established.[134] Another factor was the perceived status and utility of each faculty, coupled with the gender pattern of its students. The middle classes of the Midlands sent both sons and daughters to the new University, but the boys were destined to lead local industry and enter the professions and so were sent into the faculties of Science, Medicine and Commerce. Their sisters had no such future before them and were recruited by Arts, and often, as at Mason College, attended courses as a recreation.[135]

The marginal position afforded the Arts within the Edwardian University was something which would be familiar to subsequent generations of the faculty. However, in curriculum development the faculty was the leader in the new institution.[136] At this date the accepted sequence of university study was matriculation, a first or 'intermediate' year and then two further years for a bachelor's degree at ordinary level, and this prevailed at Birmingham in science. However,

> in the Faculty of Arts there are one or two recognised courses of Honours study, namely the School of Modern Languages and other allied schools amongst which the School of English is about to be recognised. Candidates

> enter these specialised schools at the Intermediate stage and study for three years two principal subjects. At the end of three years they may receive the degree of Master of Arts without having formally received the degree of Bachelor.[137]

The Faculty itself refused to use the word 'honours' and tried to promote the term 'special', saying that 'The Master's degrees take the place of Honours schools with us, since we wish to maintain a high standard for the ordinary Bachelor's degree, and not stigmatise it as a "Pass" and distinguished from "Honours".' Another innovative feature of these special schools was that students already had to present a thesis in the third year.

The faculty of Science had no equivalent procedure, and M.Sc.s were gained after (effectively) two postgraduate years of study and either an examination or a thesis.[138] Both Science and Arts, however, had recognised that students from 'the better class of schools' had often already reached intermediate level by the time they registered and therefore risked facing a year marking time. Such students were, therefore, permitted to substitute the intermediate examination for matriculation and, if successful, to proceed immediately to second-year work and so take the degree examination after six terms. This freed the final three terms before graduation for advanced work, and allowed the student to leave with a master's degree or in the case of engineering, a B.Sc. after three, not the normal four years.

New course opportunities were not the only changes at the University in its first decade. One was the closure of evening courses from the end of the session 1899–1900, 'the Council judging that sufficient provision for the students who used to attend them is made by other institutions in the City'.[139] Though certainly unlamented at Edmund Street, this step, given the subsequent alienation between the City and the University, may have been impolitic and it certainly meant 350 fewer registrations a year. By 1906 there had been something of a retreat.[140] It was still not possible to study for a degree part-time, but a number of the technical departments were being kept open in the evenings and five courses of winter lectures were being given at minimum fees 'for working men on social and civic ideals and administration'. Another development was a slow but steady improvement in the number of students enrolled for degree programmes.[141]

In 1900–1 there were 189 'undergraduates' in the student body of 678 (28%), 46 of them reading Science, 51 Arts and 92 Medicine. After five years the figures were 419 out of 902 (46%) and after ten, 608 out of 958 (63%). One has also to remember that the remaining students were by no means all 'occasional'; the largest group belonged to the Day Training Department and was studying for diplomas and certificates in education. Recreational attendance was in terminal decline. Ironically, given the arguments of Bertram Windle, the subject which did not do so well for undergraduates after the granting of the charter was medicine.

The competition between Arts and Science was within a rising market, but numbers reading for degrees in medicine fell from ninety-one in 1900–1, which made it the largest faculty, to seventy-one in 1909–10, which put it in third place. The corollary of more undergraduates was, of course, more degree-level work. Eighteen students sat the intermediate examination in the first session of the University, eight in Arts and ten in Science. In 1909–10 there were seventy-eight and seventy-two, respectively. Increasingly, too, students persisted for the full curriculum of three or four years. In 1900–1, Science awarded twelve B.Sc.s and five M.Sc.s, Arts three BAs and two MAs. In 1909–10 there were ninety-three B.Sc.s and twenty M.Sc.s, forty-three BAs and ten MAs, plus one each in the new 'special schools' in modern languages, English and classics. Birmingham had become a true centre of 'higher' learning.

Joseph Chamberlain himself died on 2 July 1914 in his seventy-eighth year. In the fourteen years since the grant of the charter 'his' University had changed. It had moved into science premises second to none. It had established new and highly innovatory courses for its students, and proved that practical education was congruent with higher education. It had grown. Degree-level work was now its bread and butter. Research was established. The roots in the soil of the Midlands were going deep. Yet, at the same time, the University had not changed. There was still the problem of money, despite significantly enhanced public support, and if Chamberlain had not succeeded in solving it, it was hard to see any future public figure in a position to do so. However, there was also still the vision, held by men who had worked with the first chancellor of the University and by men whom he had chosen. The question was, how would his Birmingham institution and his Birmingham men perform in the maelstrom which would break over Europe a month after his death?

Notes

1 University of Birmingham, JC4/5/96, Chamberlain to the Midland Institute, 7 Oct. 1977.
2 *The Times*, 19 Nov. 1898.
3 *Calendar* (1900–1).
4 UC 7/iv/4/17: Oliver Lodge, miscellaneous file.
5 The Court totalled almost 240 people.
6 UC 7/iv/4/17: Oliver Lodge, miscellaneous file.
7 Enid Huws Jones, *Margery Fry: The Essential Amateur* (Oxford, 1966), p. 81. This teasing took place before Neville Chamberlain had entered parliamentary politics.
8 *University Colleges (Great Britain) (Grant in Aid)* (1902), p. 70.
9 UC1/ii/3: Robert Heath's letter books show that Mason College students had been closely monitored.
10 *University Colleges (Great Britain) (Grant in Aid)* (1907), p. 40.

11 See below, n. 126.
12 R. E. Humphries, 'English and Welsh Civic Universities and the State from the mid-nineteenth Century to 1914', unpublished MA thesis, University of Kent (1979), p. 82.
13 *University Colleges (Great Britain) (Grant in Aid)* (1907), p. 38.
14 UC 4/iii/9, pp. 49–50.
15 University of Birmingham, JC L. Add. 194: Chamberlain to Lodge, 26 Dec. 1900.
16 E. g. UC 7/ii *Accounts* 1911. There were also investments in German and Egyptian bonds and New South Wales stock.
17 *Birmingham Daily Post*, 8 Jan. 1902. For the following see UC 7/ii *Accounts* 1900–1 to 1913–14.
18 *University Colleges (Great Britain) (Grant in Aid)* (1907), p. 38.
19 Sanderson, *Universities and British Industry*, pp. 68–70, 78. In 1904–5 the value of Birmingham's (incomplete) buildings and equipment was estimated as £300,000, against Liverpool's £310,000 and Manchester's £400,000. As at 31 July 1920 the figure for Birmingham was £678,675 (not counting compensation due for equipment commandeered), against Manchester's £669,996 and Liverpool's £502,289: UGC, *Returns 1919–20*, pp. 21, 68, 197.
20 See below, p. 168.
21 University of Birmingham, JC L. Add. 192: Chamberlain to Lodge, 22 Oct. 1900.
22 UC 1/1/3/1–2: Chamberlain to Carnegie, 25 Sept. 1899 and 14/ii OL27: Beale to Lodge 28 April. 1901. The Treasury's Ad Hoc Committee warned in 1902 'that it is a mistake for a College to invest a large portion of its capital in buildings which cannot be readily adapted and extended to meet changing needs': *University Colleges (Great Britain) (Grant in Aid)* (1907), p. 7. Lodge quoted extracts from the Committee in his report for 1901–2, evidently to support his argument for more recurrent expenditure: UC 7/iii 1901–2, pp. 12–15.
23 UC 14/ii: OL75, Second Report to the Vice-Chancellor and Treasurer of the University of Birmingham, 18 Nov. 1911.
24 University of Birmingham, JC L. Add. 194: Chamberlain to Lodge, 26 Dec. 1900. 'We want to keep the best men and we must bring our pay more into proportion with that [elsewhere].'
25 *University Colleges (Great Britain) (Grant in Aid)* (1907), p. 38.
26 *Calendar 1899–1900*, pp. 415–16; *University Colleges (Great Britain) (Grant in Aid)* (1907), pp. 41–2.
27 UC 7/iv/4/17: Oliver Lodge, miscellaneous file.
28 *Birmingham Daily Post*, 13 June 1899.
29 UA Council Minutes 1, no. 423: Chamberlain to City Council, 5 June 1901.
30 *Birmingham Daily Post*, 31 July 1901.
31 City of Birmingham, Finance and General Purposes Committee, minute 18509, 31 July 1901; UA Council Minutes 1, no. 498, 31 July 1901. Cf. Council Minutes 1, no. 502, 3 Sept. 1901.
32 UC 7/ii *Council* 1901–2, p. 5.
33 *Birmingham Daily Post*, 14 Oct. 1901.
34 UC 7/iv/4/17: Oliver Lodge, miscellaneous file.

35 Oliver Lodge, *Past Years: An Autobiography by Sir Oliver Lodge* (London, 1931), p. 318.
36 Attention was drawn to the level of rate support given to other civic universities or university colleges, e.g. Sheffield, 1.83d in the £; Nottingham, Bristol and Southampton, 1d in the £. In each case, money was given out of local rates and excise. UC 14/ii: OL80, 'Analysis of grants given by cities to universities and University colleges'.
37 UC 14/ii: OL75. Lodge commented on this to Lloyd George when appealing for additional support in Nov. 1910.
38 Ibid.: 11 Jan. 1911 notes that Chamberlain had sent a letter from Highbury asking the Council to increase the University's support to a penny in the pound of rateable value.
39 *Birmingham Daily Post*, 24 Jan. 1911.
40 Ibid.: the speaker was Alderman Jephcott.
41 *Birmingham Daily Post*, 14 Jan. 1911.
42 PRO, ED119/1: Wood to Birmingham's Town Clerk, 26 Jan. 1911.
43 *Birmingham Gazette*, 7 Feb. 1912; note in PRO ED119/1 20 Feb. 1911.
44 PRO, ED119/1 Runciman in response to City's questions, 17 Jan. 1912.
45 *Birmingham Daily Post*, 1 Feb. 1911.
46 Ibid., 6 Feb. 1912.
47 PRO, ED119/1.
48 *Birmingham Daily Post*, 13 Feb. 1913.
49 State aid was granted to the University of London in 1836, Owens College in 1858 and to the University College of Wales during the 1880s.
50 Cf. the comments of Hicks Beach, above, pp. 84–5.
51 UC 14/ii: OL51, Oct. 1 1909, memo on grants to university colleges in England drawn up by Arthur C. Headlam.
52 Humphries, 'English and Welsh Civic Universities', p. 89.
53 UC 14/ii: OL75: 'Report to the Vice-Chancellor and Treasurer of the University of Birmingham 18 Nov. 1910'.
54 Christine Shinn, *Paying the Piper; The Development of the University Grants Committee, 1919–1946* (1986), p. 29.
55 Humphries, 'English and Welsh Civic Universities', p. 92.
56 Ibid., p. 83.
57 University of Birmingham, JC L. Add. 184 to 226: Chamberlain to Lodge, 9 Apr. 1900 to 10 Jan. 1902. Chamberlain wrote Lodge a total of at least forty-two letters in less than two years.
58 University of Birmingham, JC 12/1/1/39: Chamberlain to Haldane, 12 Mar. 1905.
59 UC 7/iv/4/17: Oliver Lodge, miscellaneous file.
60 University of Birmingham, JC12/1/1/36. For the Privy Council inquiry, see R. B. Haldane, *Autobiography* (1929), p. 146.
61 University of Birmingham, JC 12/1/1/35: Haldane to Chamberlain, 14 Aug. 1902.
62 Ibid.
63 University of Birmingham, JC 12/1/1/35: Haldane to Chamberlain, 13 Mar. 1903.
64 The Geddes Axe was initially imposed by Lloyd George's coalition government in 1922. Neville Chamberlain served as Chancellor under Stanley Baldwin, 11 Oct.

1923 to 23 Jan. 1924: R. O. Berdahl, *British Universities and the State* (Cambridge, 1959), p. 60.

65 Shinn, *Paying the Piper*, p. 33.

66 UC 14/iii/1: OL7, 15 Dec. 1903.

67 Lodge led the deputation that visited Chancellor Austen Chamberlain in Feb. 1904: Humphries, 'English and Welsh Civic Universities', p. 93.

68 UC 14/ii/1: OL8: '5th Circular to the Principals concerning a small deputation from the English Colleges to the Chancellor of the Exchequer, 17 Feb. 1904'.

69 UC 14/ii/1: OL9: Lodge 18 Feb. 1904. See UC 7/iv/6/4: 'Speech of Austen Chamberlain, Chancellor of the Exchequer, 8 Oct. 1920'.

70 See *The Times*, 18 Feb. 1904; Humphries, 'English and Welsh Civic Universities', p. 93.

71 UC 7/iii 1904–5, pp. 5–6.

72 UC 7/iv/4/17: Oliver Lodge, miscellaneous file, 4 Apr. 1905.

73 Jones, *Origins of Civic Universities*, ch. 3.

74 UC 14/ii/1: OL5, memo from Headlam, 2 Oct. 1909.

75 Ibid.: OL68, Lodge to Beale, 17 Mar. 1910. Lodge noted that Lloyd George was ill and had gone south to recuperate. He then advised Beale how to conduct the meeting with Lloyd George, Acland and Headlam, if it was called at short notice while Lodge was away; ibid.: OL69, Treasury Minute on the House of Lords report on university colleges report, 23 Mar. 1910. A further Treasury Minute of 31 Mar. 1910 recommended a special grant for making superannuation payments.

76 Ibid.: OL78, Lodge to University Council re attempt to increase the Treasury grant.

77 Ibid.: OL74.

78 Ibid.: OL68, Lodge to Beale 17 Mar. 1910.

79 *Birmingham Daily Post*, 13 Feb. 1913.

80 UC 7/iv/4/17: Oliver Lodge, miscellaneous file, Feb. 1914.

81 University of Birmingham, JC 1/1/2/1–2: Chamberlain to Carnegie.

82 *Dundee Advertiser*, 21 Nov. 1898.

83 'Why I Vote Non Placet', Oxford Broadsheet, c.1914 (Bodleian G. A. Oxon b. 141. 307), quoted in Sanderson, *Universities and British Industry*, p. 95.

84 *Pall Mall Gazette*, 19 Nov. 1898; *Daily Telegraph*, 19 Nov. 1898.

85 UC 14/ii: OL37, Cadman to Beale, 13 Jan. 1909.

86 See above, p. 35.

87 UC 8/iv/2/3: R. A. S. Redmayne, *The Mining Department of the University of Birmingham* (read to AGM Institute of Mining Engineers, Birmingham, 14 Sept. 1904).

88 UC 7/iv/4/17: Oliver Lodge, miscellaneous file.

89 *Calendar* (1905–6).

90 *University of Birmingham Magazine* (Dec. 1902).

91 *Mason College Magazine*, xvi (Nov. 1897).

92 UC 14/ii: OL37, Cadman to Beale 13 Jan. 1909 (teaching of mine safety); OL34, Thomas Turner re summer placements of metallurgy students.

93 R. H. Smith, *Engineering* (1906).

94 University of Birmingham, JC L. Add.: Michael Foster to Lodge, 17 Apr. 1900.

95 UC 7/ii: *Deans' Reports* 1900–16 passim.

96 *University Colleges (Great Britain) (Grant in Aid)* (1907), pp. 46–7.
97 *Report on the University Colleges to the Board of Education, for numbers taking postgraduate degrees* (1906). There were also twenty-five M.Sc.s in the period though the degree did not then carry a full research connotation. See below, p.
98 UC 7/iv/4/27: Birmingham Chamber of Commerce, 'Proposal for a commerce course, 1898'.
99 University of Birmingham. JC L. Add. : Chamberlain to Lodge, 22 Oct. 1900.
100 UC 8/iv/2/1: *Report of work of mining research laboratory* (1921–4); 8/iii/iv: *Report of the work of the oil engineering and refining laboratory (petroleum technology)* (1926–9.)
101 *Birmingham Daily Post*, 24 July 1883.
102 UC 7/iv/4/32.
103 Obituary, *The Times*, 2, 12 June 1941.
104 Redmayne left the professorship at Birmingham to become the Government's Chief Inspector of Mines: Sanderson, *Universities and British Industry*, p. 88. Cadman was not only appointed by a Royal Commission to carry out special research on mines in 1907–8, and as adviser on Coal Mines to the Board of Trade, but became Consultant Petroleum Advisor to the British Colonial Office. His role and position, especially through the Royal Society, grew in importance during the First World War: see below, pp. 177–81.
105 Vincent and Hinton, *University of Birmingham*, p. 75.
106 UC 14/ii: OL53, Lodge to Cadman, 19 Nov. 1909.
107 Ibid.: OL37, Cadman to Beale, 13 Jan. 1909.
108 Ibid.: OL46, Beale to Lodge, 20 May 1909.
109 For the following see B. M. D. Smith, *Business Education in the University of Birmingham, 1899–1965* (2nd edn 1990).
110 Peter Marsh, *Joseph Chamberlain and the Enterprise of Birmingham* (Birmingham, 1994), p. 13; UC 7/iv/4/27: details of Chamber of Commerce deputation, 13 Jan. 1899 and '*Report on the Curriculum in the University of Birmingham* (n.d.).
111 W. Ashley, 'The Enlargement of Economics', *The Economic Journal*, xviii (1908), p. 184.
112 For the following see S. P. Keeble, 'University Education and Business Management from the 1880s to 1950s – A Reluctant Relationship', unpublished Ph.D. thesis, London School of Economics (1984), p. 196.
113 Ibid.
114 UC 3/vii/8: Ashley, 6 Dec. 1907; Sanderson, *Universities and British Industry*, p. 211.
115 *Birmingham Daily Gazette*, 11 July 1905. For the Settlement see J. Glasby, *Poverty and Opportunity* (Studley, 1999).
116 UC 14/ii/1: Chamberlain to Lodge, 22 Oct. 1900.
117 C. A. Smith, 'Birmingham University', *Engineering* (London, 1906); University of Birmingham, JC L. Add. Chamberlain to Lodge, 13 Mar. 1901.
118 UC 8/iv/2/2: 'Report on the University of Birmingham's Mining Department', *Colliery Guardian*, 23 Apr. 1909.
119 Sanderson, *Universities and British Industry*, p. 89.
120 But cf. E. P. Hennock, 'Technological education in England, 1850–1926: the uses

of a German model', *History of Education*, 19 (1990), pp. 324–5.

121 See G. H. Wright, *Chronicles of the Birmingham Chamber of Commerce, 1813–1913* (Birmingham, 1913), p. 425, recording that the Chamber wrote to the Proposed University Campaign secretary: 'We are glad to see from advertisements in the local press that it has been definitely decided to instigate action in commerce in Birmingham.'

122 UC 7/iv/4/17: Oliver Lodge, miscellaneous file.

123 Smith, *Business Education in the University of Birmingham, 1899–1965*, n. 18; Keeble, 'University Education', p. 34.

124 Keeble, 'University Education', p. 34; UC: 'John Adamson', *Birmingham University and Commerce.*

125 Keeble, 'University Education', p. 41.

126 Birmingham Central Reference Library: 'Proposed Curriculum of the Birmingham Jewellers' and Silversmiths' Association'; Sanderson, *Universities and British Industry*, p. 196.

127 Wright, *Chronicles of the Chamber of Commerce* (1913), p. 425.

128 Sanderson, *Universities and British Industry*, p. 85.

129 UC 7/iii 1902–3, p. 12.

130 UC7/ii *Deans' Reports*, passim. *Dean of Commerce* 1913, p. 2. There are discrepancies in the source which reflect problems in categorisation. For further discussion of student numbers, see below, p.

131 R. P. T. Davenport-Hines, *Dudley Docker: The Life and Times of a Trade Warrior* (Cambridge, 1985), p. 36.

132 UC 7/iii 1900–1, p. 10.

133 *Report of the Treasury Ad Hoc Committee on Universities and University Colleges*, Parliamentary Papers (1905).

134 Lodge, *Past Times*, p. 318.

135 *University Colleges (Great Britain) (Grant in Aid)* (1902), p. 73.

136 Ibid., p. 74; (1907), pp. 39–41.

137 In Modern Languages students studied three languages, one for three years, one for two years and one for one year.

138 It was in theory possible to secure the degree in one year, but not in practice.

139 *University Colleges (Great Britain) (Grant in Aid)* (1902), p. 72.

140 Ibid. (1907), p. 40.

141 For the following see the annual reports by the principal and the deans: UC 7/ii, 7/iii.

Chapter Nine

The University in the First World War

LOOKING BACK on a first tumultuous year of war, Oliver Lodge observed in 1915: 'It was a strange war, unlike any war before it. It was a war of artillery, of machinery. We did not know it at first. We were unprepared.'[1] Although by the summer of 1914, the British nation had 'anticipated war like never before', forward planning for the waging of war and the resultant demands on manpower, on industrial production and on the need for research and scientific testing, was less than rudimentary.[2] War was expected to be fought as before in an 'ad hoc', 'free-market' fashion, with the nation depending on private enterprise for the supply of its weaponry and on voluntaryism for its troops. Systematic state intervention on an unprecedented scale only came about gradually under the demands of war, and was not fully in place until 1917.[3]

This general unpreparedness for war also affected Britain's universities. There was no real planning for how their students and staff were to be recruited to the forces, budgets maintained or research and testing capacities best utilised, an experience that in 1939 was to lead the Committee of Vice-Chancellors and Principals to settle with government the issues of university recruitment, research and finance in the event of war, well before the outbreak of hostilities.[4]

As far as the University of Birmingham was concerned, the only practical preparation for war which affected it was the decision of the War Office to requisition the brand new buildings at Bournbrook. This was in the course of implementing Haldane's 1907 Territorial and Reserve Forces Act. The Territorial Force organised in the Midlands under that legislation needed to be supported by a field ambulance and a military hospital. Therefore, one of the first actions of the newly constituted Territorial Hospital Group was to draw up plans to transform the Aston Webb buildings in the event of war into the 13th Territorial (later the First Southern) General Hospital. Brazier and Sandford, the recorders of Birmingham's history during the First World War, noted that, 'the new University buildings at Edgbaston were fixed upon as being serviceable for the provision of 520 beds'.[5] The instructions for this, sealed in envelopes from 1907, were opened on 4 August 1914, when Lieutenant Colonel F. Marsh, administrator, and Major J. E. H. Sawyer, registrar, along with a quartermaster, received orders to act. Mobilised at 7.45 p.m. on 4 August, the First Southern General hospital was ready for action within seven days.

As a result of this takeover and the wider crisis of August 1914, it was uncertain whether the new university session would commence in the following October. The first problem lay in finding accommodation. Under an arrangement with the Birmingham Education Committee agreed as late as mid-August, the departments removed to share accommodation with the city's technical school in Suffolk Street.[6] University House, the women students' hostel, had also been requisitioned to serve as a nurses' home but an alternative was found in 'Wyddrington', a house belonging to the Wilson family of the chemical firm Albright & Wilson, some of whom served on the University Council.[7] With a location on Edmund Street and nearby Suffolk Street, the University very definitely returned to the city centre, an important consideration for the local populace, but in the faculty of Science the 'work of every department' was severely hampered by a lack of accommodation.[8]

The University's undergraduates, graduates and staff responded in large numbers to the call to arms and to essential war work which many of them carried out throughout the war. Inevitably this led to a drastic reduction in the numbers of undergraduates attending, and staff teaching at the University, and to significant losses in action. Even more important, perhaps, it also created difficulties in retaining students and staff who were essential to research that was of major local and national importance. Until 1916, when manpower problems forced the government to introduce conscription, the British forces were recruited totally on a voluntary system which put enormous psychological pressure on those not in uniform. In the autumn of 1915 the universities had approached Lord Derby, who had charge of recruitment policy in the days before conscription, and were told that science professors should, with active support from their college principals, approach the government departments they were in touch with 'for protections during this present recruiting period' for both staff and students, but that medical students in the first three years of study should be encouraged to enlist.[9]

The position did improve once control over labour both for the forces and for munitions work was put in the hands of a Director-General of National Service (Neville Chamberlain) and then, after August 1917, of the more effective Ministry of National Service. Undergraduates in the third or fourth year of studying a technological subject were now supposed to be exempted from active military service in order to preserve the future's scientists, although the system could be somewhat haphazard in practice. For members of the academic and research staff the position was less clear cut. From 1914 onwards, every university had been required to make returns to the Royal Society, among whose leaders were several prominent members of the University of Birmingham.[10] These returns made it possible to identify those who were engaged in vital war work, especially in research and testing for the War Office or the Admiralty. Frequently, individual academics and members of the Royal Society or the British Association either argued that particular members of the staff of their own university might be better used than they were, or pleaded that they should not be sent to the Front.[11] In 1915, for example, Lodge sought Barling's help to press for Barlow and Anderson to be 'spared for' work at the National Physical Laboratory, either at Teddington or at its wartime branch in Birmingham, and the vice-chancellor agreed with the principal that Anderson would be more useful doing skilled work than by enlisting and taking a commission.[12] With conscription came the Reserved Occupation Scheme, working through tribunals which assessed individuals on whether their work was essential to the nation or otherwise. By definition these bodies had no specialised knowledge and some academics were even dependent upon false medical exemptions to save their work and possibly their lives.[13] Eventually, in 1917, a special Royal Society Reserved Occupations Tribunal was set up chaired by Percy Frankland, Birmingham's professor of chemistry, and this put an end to the lottery of scientists appearing before the more general tribunals.[14] For those already in the forces, personal advocacy was still needed. After the Armistice, Gilbert Shakespear of the physics department crossed to France to run some tests on airships and on the way met a young physicist, T. L. Ibbs, returning from leave; strings were then pulled to get Ibbs seconded to the University before his turn came to be demobilised.[15] There is only one possible verdict on this slowness to develop a discriminating recruitment policy. At the commencement of the Second World War Lord Derby admitted that: 'In looking back on the recruiting for which I was mainly responsible at the beginning of the last war I recognize that one of the greatest mistakes that I made was in not discriminating between the various recruits that came forward.'[16]

At the start of the war 240 of the University's undergraduates and graduates volunteered and by the beginning of 1915, some 223 students were serving in the forces. A further forty were in uniform by the end of the year.[17] By 1917 a total of 785 men had responded, some 303 graduates and 375 undergraduates.[18] The University's Officer Training Corps (OTC) formed before the war, was further enlarged by the War Office and from 1914, attendance was compulsory for male undergraduates over nineteen years of age, and consisted of fortnightly route marches and night-time tactical exercises.[19] Encouraged by the prospect of gaining a commission on entering the forces, undergraduates were further spurred on in their OTC training by the 'healthy spirit of rivalry between the University of Manchester and of Birmingham' that the chairman of the University's Military Education Committee, Neville Chamberlain, encouraged.[20] The recruitment of special forces, including some formed by leading members of the University, no doubt also led to some students joining up. Thus John Cadman, the professor of mining, together with John Norton Griffiths, formed special tunnelling companies of qualified mining men.[21] However, by 1915–16 the University's OTC was recording that its contingent was significantly under establishment, even though the age of entry had been lowered.[22] Evidently a large proportion of undergraduates who were able to join had already enlisted.

This wholesale enlistment of men had another consequence for the University. It not only drained away current undergraduates, but it deprived the University of the new intake which would have entered if peace had prevailed. Sanderson has identified some dramatic falls in the number of undergraduates attending Britain's various universities and colleges in the first year of the war.[23] Total student numbers at University College London fell by 54.7% from 2200 to 1000, and at Oxford undergraduate numbers dropped by an astounding 88%, from 3097 to 369. The reduction for Manchester was lower, but still a fall of 37%, from 1655 in 1913–14 to 1031 in 1914–15. At first sight the University of Birmingham appears to have been less affected, for the total number of students in attendance dropped by only 23.8%, from 1032 in 1913–14 to 786 a year later. However, it is not clear whether these figures compare like with like, because there are significant difficulties with the statistics. For example, if only matriculated students are counted, the fall in numbers at Birmingham becomes 30.8%. Then there is the effect of gender. Women were a tiny minority at Oxford but made up 38.5% of the student body at Birmingham. If only men are counted, the drop in registrations there between 1913–14 and 1914–15 was 35.4%, from 625 to 404.[24]

Whether or not the recruitment of undergraduates and of potential undergraduates to the University of Birmingham was initially less affected than elsewhere, by 1916–17, with the continued impact of war and the reduction of the recruitment age, teaching was in dire straits: 'practically all the Senior work of men students has largely ceased for the time, owing to absorption by the Army'.[25] Within the University, recruitment affected faculties and schools differently.[26] The number of students in the Men's Training College fell from 69 in 1914 to 47 in the following year and 23 in 1916. Male undergraduate numbers in the faculty of Medicine fell between 1913–14 and 1914–15 and although in 1915 all medical students in the ranks not yet passed for general service were returned to their studies, the recovery of numbers to pre-war levels by 1917–18 owed a good deal to an increased proportion of women.[27] In the other faculties, Arts, Commerce and Science, the number of male undergraduates fell by 67%, from 463 in 1913–14 to 152 in 1916–17. The data do not permit more precise disaggregation to individual faculties but the total of Arts undergraduates in 1917–18 was half the number in 1913–14: 120 as against 254. For students in Commerce, already a very small group, the first year of war effectively halved matriculated numbers (from 36 to 19), and by 1916–17 there were 12 left. The Science Faculty, which should have been producing the scientists and technologists that the British state and national industry so desperately needed, was nearly as hard hit. In 1913–14 matriculated numbers in Science had been 246. Registrations fell by nearly 100 in the first year of war to 149, and from 1915–16 to 1917–18 stabilised at about 90.

This decline in the number of undergraduates, especially in the sciences, began to worry members of the University comparatively early in the war. In 1915, for example, the principal drew attention to the view of the dean of Science, Percy Frankland about the current 'false economy in education and scientific training and investigation. It has certainly been one of our dangers that the country as a whole had not been wide awake in this direction.'[28] Oliver Lodge himself practically reiterated the dean's words at an education conference at the University of London on 3 January 1915, in order to call for the better utilisation of scientific personnel, and especially in the recruitment and subsequent employment of science and technology students in the wartime universities.[29] Yet, as has been seen, pressure from Frankland, Lodge and others, even at the highest levels of society and via the illustrious Royal Society, only achieved the satisfactory protection of scientific manpower from 1917.

Thus, with the exception of female students – still seen by many as ancillary – and to a small degree, medical students, year by year there were fewer and fewer undergraduates at Birmingham. There were, however, problems even in teaching those who did enrol, a problem compounded by the University being crammed into inadequate accommodation. Empty posts remained unfilled, both for financial reasons and because the government had forbidden the recruitment of any further staff until after the end of the war. Lodge noted a particular difficulty in the teaching of French once the professor had enlisted. [30]

Wartime conditions and requirements, including the 1915 provision to end the session each year on 31 March in order to free students and staff to participate in vital agricultural work, obliged the University of Birmingham, and other British universities, to award degrees under new regulations.[31] Initially, these wartime rules were simple and straightforward, permitting new graduates to have their degrees conferred on them in absentia. However, by November 1917, in the face of new rulings already published at Oxford and planned changes at the University of London, Birmingham produced a basis for awarding degrees in wartime. Periods of over six months in the services were to count towards university attendance, while undergraduates who had served their country could be exempt from taking certain subjects and sitting examinations, army or navy service being 'taken as supplying the breadth of intellectual experience expected of graduates.'[32] More positive changes were also introduced during the war years. One was the creation of the research doctorate, the Ph.D.[33] Previously, the usual means of acquiring this had been by study in Germany. Another advantageous change was the replacement in 1917 of the University of Birmingham's own matriculation examination by matriculation/entrance examinations that were administrated by a consortium of five provincial universities. It was a move which enlarged the catchment area of each participant, and the examining body became known as the Joint Matriculation Board (JMB).[34]

The largest response from Birmingham to the national 'call to arms' was inevitably from its students. The initial impact on the senior academics was minimal. This was in marked contrast to Oxford where few members of the academic staff had been left under the age of sixty.[35] The difference was because the Birmingham professoriate was well past the age for active service. Indeed, eight of the twenty-one non-medical professors would retire in 1918–19 on the ground of age. As Lodge commented in 1914: 'Of the members of the Senior Staff the only one qualified for active service in the ranks of the Allies was Professor Chatelain, whose health was not such as to encourage strong hopes of his safe return.'[36] The position was different with the non-professors and the honorary medical staff. In 1915 Lodge could list 77 engaged on military duties, including civilians, with 8 members of the office and library staff and 15 university servants and 25 members of the power station staff also serving.[37] Of course, not all staff in the forces were combatants; as we shall see, the largest group were medical men serving in the RAMC, both in the First Southern General Hospital and elsewhere. Staff members who did not join the forces were required to become members of the rifle corps, as Professor Cadman humorously recalled to an OTC 'smoker' in 1915.[38] Others, such as Professor Kirkcaldy of the Commerce Faculty and Professor Muirhead from Arts served as privates in the Warwickshire Volunteer Regiment. Nevertheless, despite a perhaps limited exposure, even at Birmingham there was still the sense of losing a generation of scholars. A particular blow was the death in the Dardanelles of H. G. J. Moseley, Ernest Rutherford's assistant in nuclear physics at the Clarendon Laboratory. He had been noted by Lodge as a potential replacement for Poynting and his loss was still remembered by university scientists in the Second World War as a symbol of the waste that the First had inflicted on the scientific community.[39]

One member of the Birmingham staff made a distinctive contribution to the war.[40] In the summer of 1914, Dr Intze, the assistant lecturer in German, was at home in Heidelberg for the long vacation. He was called up to the German army, ended the war as a captain on the Russian front suffering from shell-shock and then became involved in the political upheavals in post-Armistice Berlin. Unfortunately for them, two Birmingham students were staying with Intze when war began, one of them the son of the professor of metallurgy, Thomas Turner. They saw the war out in an internment camp.[41]

At first, casualties among Birmingham's undergraduates, graduates and staff were relatively light. The first year saw two members of staff killed in action or dead on active service along with 16 current students, while two staff and seven students had been wounded; among former students, 24 were dead and nine wounded.[42] In November 1915 *The Mermaid* recorded that both the University and the City were 'heavy with sorrow on the loss of comrades'.[43] By 1917, a total of 5 members of staff and 135 students, 3 office staff, 2 members of the library and 3 laboratory assistants had been killed, although the *Mermaid Supplement* roll of honour of undergraduates only gives a total of 115 deaths up until the end of 1917.[44] In the inevitable confusion of war, these were minimum figures. A total of 175 names of staff, students and former students is recorded on the war memorial in the entrance to the University's Great Hall, including seven members of the academic staff and nine other staff, one of whom, John Neville Marshall, had been heavily decorated, eventually winning the Victoria Cross.[45] Marshall had enlisted in the Belgian army in 1914 but by 1918 was an acting lieutenant colonel in the Irish Guards, commanding the 16th Lancashire Fusiliers. On 7 November he was responsible for successfully bridging the Sambre and Oise Canal under heavy fire but was killed in the subsequent assault.[46] The war meant domestic tragedy too. In 1915 Lodge noted that 'I have addressed a personal letter of condolence to the bereaved parents of all students, both past and present.'[47] All too soon Lodge was mourning the death of his own youngest son, Raymond, an undergraduate of the University. This loss was a profoundly disturbing for the Lodge family. The principal's spiritualist attempts to contact his dead son are carefully recorded in his published writings. Other members of staff and former staff also lost loved ones; for example, the war memorial carries the names of both Cadman and Poynting.[48]

Some historians have argued that despite losses among men from all classes in British society, it was the young members of Britain's social elites who attended public schools and universities that suffered a proportionately far greater loss of life, a consequence of their making up the 'officer class' that was subject to a significantly high casualty rate.[49] However, among Birmingham's undergraduates J. M. Winter identified the loss of life at only 14.6%. That was a level only 2% above the death rate of one in eight amongst servicemen nationally, though it was certainly high enough to be a profound shock to the University, the City of Birmingham and the Midland region that had sent so many of its sons to the new institution. By contrast, his examination of the rolls of honour at Oxford and Cambridge produced death rates amongst undergraduates of the ancient universities of 18% and 19.2% respectively. Winter explained the higher fatalities among undergraduates from the ancient universities by the twin hypotheses that Oxbridge students were quicker to the colours and thus were longer exposed to danger, and that a much higher proportion of them served as officers than did provincial undergraduates.[50] Closer analysis, however, reveals that for Birmingham the position is less than clear cut. First the data is confused, as Winter pointed out is the case elsewhere.[51] The 14.6% casualty rate for Birmingham is based on a student tally of 115 deaths at the end of 1917.[52] It appears to be confirmed by a somewhat earlier source, a draft roll of honour which apparently indicates a 13.9% death rate among students who were on the University's books at the start of the war or who were registered to perhaps 1916.[53] On the other hand, Oliver Lodge's casualty list records 135 undergraduate deaths, and this would raise the University of Birmingham's wartime death rate to 17.1%, a level far nearer the proportion suffered by Oxbridge.[54] As for the suggestion that Birmingham's students received fewer commissions, this too presents problems. In December 1914 the Council at Birmingham noted that 61 of the 176 students who enlisted (34.7%) had already been commissioned.[55] The draft roll of honour records 184 commissions out of 373 names, that is 49.3%. Certainly this figure was nowhere near the 97% of Balliol students who became officers, but it is well above the national average of 38% for commissions to students and teachers.[56] A good deal of further analysis needs to be done, but if it does turn out that Birmingham University men had a low casualty rate despite having an above average or even an average number of commissions, the answer could lie in their specialised skills. Many were medics, of whom large numbers served in base hospitals, and others were technicians, not infantrymen.[57] Perhaps redbrick scientists enjoyed longer odds than Oxbridge classicists.

Among the University's staff, two deaths were particularly poignant. The first was that of the professor of French, Henri Chatelain. As Principal Lodge had predicted, the poor man had proved to be too weak to survive the war. Coming from peasant stock, Chatelain had, on the outbreak of war in August 1914, renounced all measure of rank to serve as a private in the 4th Reserve Army amongst men of his native area. At the Front he was 'seized with a severe illness and detained in a field ambulance inside the fighting lines' for many weeks. With 'difficulty and delay' he was transferred to a hospital in Paris where he died on 19 August 1915.[58] Also recorded on the University's war memorial is the name of Rose Sidgwick, lecturer in history. A kind and immensely popular teacher, Sidgwick died at the age of forty-one, not as Chatelain did, in France, but in New York. She had gone there on a special university mission sent by the British government to promote 'good feeling and co-operation between British and American universities', only to die a victim of the influenza epidemic that raged across the world at the end of the war.[59]

Against the contribution of the University of Birmingham to the casualty lists of the First World War must be set the work of the First Southern General Hospital. The 'nucleus of officers and workers' in the hospital was made up of the University's Medical Faculty, that is, with the exception of the women of the Territorial Force Nursing Society and those in the Women's Voluntary Aid Detachment (VAD) who joined the hospital in May 1915.[60] Faculty members who were required were seconded into the Royal Army Medical Corps (Territorial Army) (RAMC(T)) and were posted to First Southern General. The Dean of Medicine, Gilbert Barling, became a Lieutenant Colonel in the RAMC(T), Chief Surgeon of the 1st and 2nd Birmingham War Hospitals and Consulting Surgeon to the Southern Command. A. S. (Stanley) Barnes, the future dean, but then a young lecturer in clinical medicine, became a Captain in the RAMC(T) in the same hospital.[61]

Lodge records that of the 67 members of staff who were serving in the forces by the end of 1915, some 52 were medical men, of whom most worked in the First Southern General Hospital, though others were in France with the RAMC.[62] Where members of the faculty remained civilians, they added honorary consultant posts at the Southern to their duties in the city hospitals.

The First Southern received its initial trainload of mainly Belgian military casualties, sick as well as wounded, on 1 September 1914, patients being brought to Birmingham by train and then ferried from Snow Hill station by ambulances and private cars with civilian drivers, a service that many of Birmingham's students provided.[63] Gradually, the hospital was extended. By the end of 1914 the University's machinery hall had been cleared of its contents and turned into a ward to increase the provision to 800 beds. Further ones were fitted into the chemistry buildings and physics housed the hospital orderlies.[64] The Harding Library became a chapel. The hospital was further extended in 1915 when wooden huts or 'open air wards', were added where 'if you did not die of your wounds you would die of the cold'. These were erected to the south and to the west of the Great Hall, bringing the total number of hospital beds up to 1000.[65] There was a parade ground, too, and in July 1915 the Bournbrook site received its second royal visit when George V came to inspect the hospital. By the end of 1915, some 30 276 soldiers had been treated in the University's Aston Webb buildings with a further 47 244 men passing through the hospital by May 1917.[66] As casualties mounted, marquees had to be set up in front of the Great Hall, and by the time the Armistice was signed in November 1918 the Southern had grown to 3293 beds.[67] Inevitably, not all the wounded recovered, and their deaths are commemorated in a marble plaque placed over the entrance to the Great Hall. The First Southern General also became the Midland centre for a total of 47 other military hospitals, including those at nearby Selly Oak and Dudley Road, and in November 1918 there were 3476 beds in these associated hospitals and 300 more patients in billets. In all Edgbaston handled about 64 000 cases and with its satellites the total was over 122 000.

In the hospital the men of the University's Medical Faculty were faced with working to save lives under very difficult circumstances. Contemporary descriptions tell of the stench caused by the necessity of draining septic wounds in that pre-antibiotic era. On the other hand, the radical medical conditions presented by many of the wounded forced the pace of surgical advance. This was particularly true for the dentists who staffed the Centre for Jaw and Facial Injuries which was set up at the hospital.[68] This was commanded by William Billington, a consultant at Queen's Hospital who was a captain in the RAMC(T), assisted by two of the Dental Hospital consultants, A. H. Parrott and Harold Round. In 1916 Round went to Paris to address an Inter-Allied conference on jaw injuries and, with the assistance of Billington and Parrott, he published 'Bone grafting in gunshot fractures of the jaw'.[69] Round later became medical adviser to the infant RAF on head and face protection for aircrew. Members of the University who had been seconded to the army's hospital service also undertook health work for Birmingham civilian hospitals and for the immediate locality. Staff in the University's zoology and botany departments were also drawn in. Some went out to 'investigate diseases amongst the troops'.[70] The professor of botany studied trench fever and the professor of soology the control of malaria in military camps. Other topics included the control of dysentery in military hospitals and the health problems of western troops in the Mesapotamian campaign; Dr Boulenger was sent there in 1916 to work as a protozoologist.[71] Finally, a contingent of Birmingham's medical staff and students, including Dr Gwynne Maitland, lecturer in Physiology, was organised into a Surgical Relief Unit under the command of Professor Morrison, and dispatched to Serbia. The original contingent returned, but Maitland recruited more staff and went back to run a typhus camp in Skopje. While there, 'the hospital and all its staff fell into the hands of the Bulgarians' but carried on their work 'under new rulers'.[72]

As well as the loss of its premises, interference in its normal activity and the sacrifice and service of its members to the nation, the war necessarily affected university finances.[73] The recurrent income fell from a total of £71,793 in 1913–14 to £62,545 in 1914–15, a drop of £9248 or some 12.9% in one year. In the next year there was a further loss of about £5000 after which income levelled out for the next two years at just under £58,000, 19% or 20% below the peacetime figure. In 1917–18 student numbers picked up slightly, but income improved only by some £1200. Along with this, of course, went a fall in the value of an hitherto stable currency, so that in real terms, university income fell even further.

The reason for the pre-inflation loss of income was the reduction in student numbers. Fee income fell by £6925 or 39% between the years 1913–14 and 1914–15. The subsequent decline was less dramatic, but the nadir came in 1916–17 at £7917, 44.6% of the pre-war figure. Further loss of income is explained by the request of the City of Birmingham for a reduction in its rate grant of £15,000 per annum. The University Council replied that it was already losing £7000 a year in student fees but nevertheless it offered a cut of £2000.[74] A consequence of a reduced income was that expenditure per student rose significantly. In 1913–14, the University spent an average of £68 0s 5d (£68.02) per student. By 1916–17 this had risen to £85 4s 0d (£85.20) per student, and that at a time when the balance in undergraduate numbers had shifted from Science to Arts, where the fees brought in were, in Principal Lodge's opinion, 'practically all profit'.[75]

Thus Birmingham, like other universities, suffered a severe reduction in its income because of the war. Unlike many of the rest, however, it did not get into financial difficulties, and this despite the fact, as will be seen, that, throughout the war, it too was carrying out costly research and testing work for the government and receiving relatively little financial compensation. The universities did work together to secure government attention to their financial problems. In 1914, the Treasury Advisory Committee on University Grants 'waited on' the Lord Commissioners of the Treasury to ask the government to give the universities they represented a total of £145,000 to compensate them for the financial losses they had incurred as the result of hostilities. Three reasons were cited: the reduction in student numbers, the costs in certain research work and the postponement of the Advisory Committee's quinquennial inspection. All this the Lord Commissioners accepted, but in doing so reminded the universities that under the current circumstances, not all institutions could hope to remain open, and that the recruitment of staff would have to be further curtailed.[76] This campaign, however, went on with little support from Birmingham and when its Council was given the opportunity to apply for special grants to meet the financial losses of 1914–15 and 1915–16, it resolved to make no claim.[77] Indeed in the annual report published for that year the Council expressed the hope that the University would manage to absorb any extra costs.[78]

The reason for this moderation was not patriotism but, as the Council freely admitted, because the military occupation of Edgbaston had substantially reduced expenditure. There was, as Professor Frankland pointed out, a long-term cost for this in the damage the occupation was doing to the premises, but in the immediate, being restricted to one site was all gain.[79] It is doubtful whether Newcastle and Southampton, where the main teaching site was commandeered, found it equally advantageous financially.[80] Thanks to the requisition, Birmingham was able to remain in credit on the income and expenditure account in every year of the war. Positive balances were returned in 1914–15, 1915–16 and 1916–17 of £2874, £2477 and £2506, respectively, while in 1917–18 the amount was £4672, largely a reflection of the improvement in fees. By Armistice Day, a current account deficit which had stood at £34,299 in 1913–14 had been more than halved.[81] The one black spot, and it was serious, was that this success did not affect the long-term capital debt of the University which had resulted from the heavy expenditure of its opening ten years. A sinking fund to redeem this was in operation throughout the period, but in 1920 the total still stood at £130,000.[82] Lodge probably had capital charges in mind when in 1918 he reported the University's deficit as £7000 per annum.[83] Grant Robertson put the cost of servicing the debt at £8000 to £9000.[84]

Despite the success of the University in achieving a better than break-even position on its annual accounts, the war revealed one unfortunate weakness in its position. Even after the agreement with the City to reduce its contribution for the duration, one-fifth of Birmingham's income came from local rate support and this made it vulnerable to local opinion, particularly dislike of German speakers on the staff. Gisbert Kapp, the half-Scottish but Austrian-born professor of electrical engineering, complained that none of his offers to contribute to national research were taken up either by the local branch of the Institute of Electrical Engineers or by Neville Chamberlain's National Service scheme. However, eventually – and, he felt, somewhat grudgingly – he was give a 'corner of his old lab' and asked to undertake fatigue tests on aircraft alloys and to develop an electrical furnace for Kynochs Ltd to produce nitric acid from the air for use in the manufacture of explosives.[85] The worst instance of vulnerability to public opinion involved Karl Wichmann, who in 1907 had succeeded Fiedler as professor of German. Although he had taken British nationality, he had done so on the outbreak of war, and in 1917 he was effectively blackmailed into resigning his chair by a vote of the City Council Finance Committee, which made continuation of its regular payment of £13,000 a year to the University subject to the University Council 'not retaining the services of any pre-war unnaturalised German'.[86] So long as a university was partially dependent financially on its local authority, as the University of Birmingham was on the City, resistance to such pressure was almost impossible.

On the other hand, the City was not acting wholly unprompted in the Wichmann case. The first sign of a problem had been that in June 1915 Wichmann resigned as the university representative both on the Coventry Education Committee and the governing body of Bablake School. Nine months later a special meeting of Senate was called to discuss a resolution moved by Professor Cadman and seconded by Burstall: 'that in the general interest of the University it is desirable that the engagement of the Professor of German should be terminated'. After a long debate the proposition was carried by fourteen to eleven and forwarded to Council. The motion had been brought under a University statute which allowed the Senate to vote to remove a professor, but did not define what was meant by 'general interest'. The concern of Cadman and Barstall could have been that the University was suffering from anti-German sentiment such had probably caused the Coventry resignation. Alternatively the cause could be bad feeling within the University. It is noticeable that Wichmannn gave up attending Senate after February 1915 but his Arts colleagues may have been more tolerant since he continued to attend faculty meetings.[87] To its credit the Council refused to endorse the professorial resolution and there matters stayed for a year, until in early June 1916 Gilbert Barling, the vice-chancellor, was summoned to meet Brigadier General Townley, Officer Commanding 7th Division. Townley informed him that an instruction had been received from the War Office to the effect that Wichmann had in future to reside at least ten miles from the centre of Birmingham. This order would effectively prevent the professor from doing his job but once again Council declined to dismiss him. Instead it endorsed a scheme by which alternative teachers were engaged and paid for by reducing Wichmann's salary from £500 per annum to £75 a quarter (£300 per annum).[88] He clearly appreciated this support for he wrote from Oxford in the following October thanking the Council for 'the manner in which [it] has dealt with the situation', and the Council renewed the arrangement in February 1917.

A month later came the ultimatum from the City. Lodge advised the Council on 7 March that the choice was now between forgoing the Birmingham grant, which would 'embarrass' every department of the University and possibly risk closure of the whole institution, and requiring Wichmann's resignation or dismissal. The Council took the hint and gave the professor six days until 13 March in which to resign or face the sack. The resignation arrived on time and the town clerk was informed. Wichmann was paid to the end of the month, plus three months' pay in lieu of notice, and the contributions he had made to superannuation were also returned to him. The public inference, of course, was that the professor of German was a security risk and it was true that he did rub shoulders with Cadman and others who were heavily engaged in war work. However, it is hard to believe that the War Office discovered this on its own or that the action of the City Finance Committee was unprompted. The families of Wichmann's professorial colleagues were suffering bereavement along with the rest of the country, and pursuing him once he had moved to Oxford looks like deliberate vindictiveness, made the more petty because Wichmann had lived in England for seventeen years and was married to the sister of his popular and thoroughly Anglicised predecessor, Professor Georg Fiedler.

Notes

1 *Birmingham Daily Post*, 18 Aug. 1915.

2 Roy McLeod and E. Kay Andrew, 'The Origins of the Department of Scientific and Industrial Research : Reflections on Ideas and Men, 1915-16', *Public Administration*, 48 (1970), p. 36.

3 See R. Lowe, 'The erosion of state intervention in Britain, 1917-24', *Economic History Review*, n. s. 31 (1978), pp. 270-286.

4 See *Birmingham Daily Post*, 20 Jan. 1939, an article on the local and University's preparation for the Second World War; PRO UGC 5/14: 'The organisation of universities for wartime services'; ibid., 5/15: 'University finances in wartime'. The latter were agreements between the University Bureau of the British Empire Committee of Vice-Chancellors and Principals and national government in 1939. In both, various university vice-chancellors comment on the ill-preparedness for war in 1914.

5 R. H. Brazier and E. Sandford, *Birmingham and the Great War, 1914-18* (Birmingham, 1921), p. 154.

6 *Birmingham Daily Post*, Monday 17 Aug. 1914. 'The University of Birmingham – the arrangements for the coming term'.

7 UC 7/iii 1914–15, p. 9.

8 Ibid., 1916–17, p. 9.

9 UC Council Minutes 10, 5495.

10 UC 7/iii 1914–15, p. 7.

11 Ibid.

12 UC 14/ii: OL149, Barling to Lodge, 28 May 1915.

13 Sanderson, *Universities*, p. 218.

14 For this and the rest of the chapter see UC 3/vii/8: Ashley's material on the war work of university staff.
15 P. B. Moon and T. L. Ibbs, *Physics at Birmingham 1880–1980* (Birmingham, 1980), p. 13.
16 *Liverpool Daily Post*, 7 July 1941: Lord Derby speaking at Liverpool University , quoted in Sanderson, *Universities*, p. 218.
17 *The Mermaid* (1915). Lodge's figures were marginally different: UC 7/iii 1914–15, pp. 11–20.
18 *The Mermaid Guild of Graduates Supplement* (Birmingham,1917).
19 UC 7/iii 1915–16, p. 18; *The Mermaid* (1914–15) p. 82.
20 *The Mermaid* (1915–16).
21 UC 7/iii 1915–16, p. 12.
22 *The Mermaid* (1915–16)
23 Sanderson, *Universities*, pp. 217–18. For Birmingham statistics see UC 7/iii 1913–14, pp. 1-2; 1917–18, pp. 1-2.
24 Between 1914–15 and 1915–16 there was a further drop of 25.7% in male students.
25 UC 7/iii 1916–17, p. 4.
26 For the following see ibid., at n. 21 above.
27 In 1913–14, 23.7%of medical students were women; in 1917–18 the percentage was 41.3.
28 UC 7/iii 1914–15, p. 5. For Frankland's detailed suggestions see UC 7/ii *Dean of Science* 1915–16, pp. 4–10.
29 UC 7/iii 1914–15, pp. 5–6.
30 Ibid., p. 4.
31 Ibid., 1915–16, p. 5.
32 Ibid., 1916–17, p. 4; 14/ii: OL172; 'Muirhead memo 24th November, 1917: Adaptation of degrees for war students'.
33 UC 7/iii 1917–18, p. 3.
34 Ibid., 1916–17, p. 3; 7/ii *Council* 1916–17, pp. 4-5; UA Council Minutes 10, 5557; 11, 5590–8.
35 Sanderson, *Universities*, p. 217.
36 UC 7/iii 1914–15, p. 10. M. Demey, the French lecturer, also enlisted. Ibid., pp. 11–20.
37 Ibid., 1915-16, pp. 15–20.
38 *The Mermaid* (1914–15).
39 For Lodge's remarks upon Moseley's death in the context of leaving Poynting's professorship open until the end of the war (inferring that many other able physicists would have met their end by then) see UC 7/iii 1914–15, p. 4. See also Sanderson, *Universities*, p. 218. Moseley's death is used as an example of the lost generation of the Great War in Richard Rhodes, *The Making of the Atomic Bomb* (New York, 1986).
40 UC 7/ii *Dean of Arts*, 1914–15, p. 4.
41 Parts of Turner's diaries are reproduced in Cheesewright, *Mirror to a Mermaid*, p. 78.
42 UC 7/iii 1914–15, pp. 11–20.

43 *The Mermaid* (1915–16), p. 1.
44 UC 7/iii 1917–18, pp. 10-13; *The Mermaid Guild of Graduates Supplement* (1917).
45 Until the 1950s the Roll of Honour was published annually in the *University Calendar.*
46 Marshall was also awarded the Military Cross and Bar and high Belgian decorations and was wounded ten times: J. Stallworthy, *Wilfred Owen* (Oxford, 1977), pp. 276-7, 285-6; R. Kipling, *The Irish Guards in the Great War* (1923), ii.237, 239; *Register of the Victoria Cross* (Cheltenham 1981, 1988), p. 837. I am indebted for these references to Dr J. M. Bourne.
47 UC 7/iii 1914–15, p. 9.
48 Poynting had died in March 1914: *DNB*.
49 J. M. Winter, *The Great War and the British People* (1985), pp. 83–99.
50 Ibid., pp. 94, 96.
51 Ibid., pp. 92–3. The principal problem is distinguishing staff and students in place in and after 1914 from those associated with the University previously. For example, J. N. Marshall was apparently not in the employment of the University at the start of the war.
52 *The Mermaid Guild of Graduates Supplement* (1917); Winter, *Great War and the British People*, pp. 94–5.
53 UC 9/vi/16: Roll of Honour.
54 UC 7/iii 1917–18, pp. 10–13.
55 UA Council Minutes 10, 5251. The Council recorded a total of 112 commissions by February 1915 (including a handful to members of staff) and 174 commissions to OTC cadets by February 1916: 7/ii *Council* 1914–15, p. 7; 1915–16, p. 2.
56 Winter, *Great War and the British People*, p. 83.
57 Medics made up 25.9% of male students at Birmingham in 1913–14. Winter, ibid., p. 96, noted the possibility that lower death rates affected officers from provincial universities serving in technical roles, but he did not comment that Oxbridge did not teach clinical medicine.
58 UV 7/iii 1914–15, p. 10.
59 Ibid., 1917–18, p. 9.
60 Brazier and Sandford, *Birmingham and the Great War*, pp. 49, 159.
61 UC 7/ii *Dean of Medicine* 1914–15, p. 8; 7/iii 1914–15, pp. 11–20.
62 UC 7/iii 1917–18, pp. 10–13.
63 For the following see Brazier and Sandford, *Birmingham and the Great War*, pp. 117, 155–92.
64 UC 7/ii *Council* 1914–5, p. 5.
65 *The Mermaid*, 2 (1917).
66 *The Mermaid*, 1 (1916), 3 (1917).
67 Brazier and Sandford, *Birmingham and the Great War*, p. 163.
68 UC 3/vii/8: Ashley, 'War Work'.
69 A. H. Round, 'Bone grafting in gunshot fractures of the jaw', in *Proceedings of the Royal Society of Medicine*, 12 (1918–19).
70 UC 7/iii 1915–16, p. 5.
71 UA Council Minutes 11, 5593.
72 UC 7/iii 1914–15, p. 7.

73 For the following see UC 7/ii *Accounts* 1912–13 to 1918–19.
74 UA Council Minutes 10, 5290, 5298.
75 Oliver Lodge, *Past Years: An Autobiography of Sir Oliver Lodge* (London, 1931), p. 318.
76 UC 14/ii: OL152: 'Circular to Universities and other institutions': Treasury chambers, Whitehall 6431/15.
77 UA Council 10, passim; 5530.
78 UC 7/ii 1915–16, p. 10.
79 UC 7/ii *Dean of Science* 1915–16, p. 1. The use of University House as a nurses' home actually brought the University an income, originally £2280 per annum but later £1300 net of charges, although that figure also covered eventual reinstatement costs and losses on the use of Wyddrington in lieu: ibid., *Council* 1913–14 p. 5; 1915–16, p. 4.
80 Sanderson, *Universities* p. 217.
81 An additional provision of £2500 was also credited. UC7/ii *Accounts* 1917–18, pp. 2–3.
82 UC 7/iii, 1920–21, p. 7. A £5500 reduction was achieved in the £50,000 mortgage in 1916–17. UC7/ii *Accounts* 1916–17, pp. 32–3. Other totals of debt were cited from time to time, e.g. the university treasurer stated £143,598 to the *Birmingham Daily Post*, 26 Feb. 1919; the *Birmingham Mail*, 14 Feb. 1921 mentioned £170,000.
83 UC 14/ii: OL180a: 'Return from the University Report to the Minister of Education on the Needs of the University of Birmingham'.
84 UC 7/iii, 1920–21, p. 7.
85 UC 3/vii/8. Kapp's problem could have been personality rather than his father's nationality: UC 10/i/18 *Birmingham Gazette and Post* (1909).
86 For the following see UC 7/ii *Council* 1914–15, p. 7; UA Council Minutes 10, 5181–2; 11, 5589, 5622, 5681, 5683–7, 5696, 5802, 5807–9, 5840–3; Senate 6, pp. 101–2; UC 10/1/18 *Cuttings* p. 1 *Birmingham Gazette & Express*, 1909; UA Arts Faculty Minutes 2, passim and 1083.
87 UA Senate Minutes 6, passim; Arts Faculty Minutes 2, passim.
88 Any balance left over was to be paid to Wichmann at the end of the session.

Chapter Ten

The University and the war effort

IF IN 1914 there was a lack of preparation in regard to the role of the university in war, the same was most definitely true of industrial organisation and the supply of essentials, most notably armaments. That the war would be a technological war had long been apparent, but the shock of war proved how correct the prophesies about Britain's industrial decline made by Joseph Chamberlain during the campaign for the charter had been. Germany had indeed made 'enormous progress in the manufacture of articles which a few years ago was the monopoly of [Britain]'. The nation discovered on the outbreak of war that it was not only dependent on 'Stuttgart firms for magnetos [and] Zeiss of Jena for optical glass' but on other firms in Germany for aniline dyes, a number of essential drugs and certain anaesthetics, deficiencies resulting from the reluctance of British industry during the late-Victorian period to move into new areas such as organic chemistry and electrical engineering.[1] Even Britain's supply of explosives was dependent on private firms, a limitation which caused the armaments crisis of 1915.

Birmingham and the Midlands were no exception to this general rule. In an area of vital importance to the production of armaments, explosives, optical glass and engineering products, most companies lagged behind Germany in their methods of production. The exceptions were a few large, leading firms, some of which, such as Kynochs and the Eliot Metal Co., were owned within the local industrial elite that had once gravitated round the Chamberlain, Beale and Lloyd network and which was highly influential in the University's government.

As with other British universities, Birmingham's involvement in the war effort, both locally and nationally, was considerable. By a bitter irony (as Brazier and Sandford noted), the fact that some of the laboratories and workshops belonging to the University were occupied by wounded soldiers did not prevent its staff from contributing to the output of munitions.[2] The University, both staff and students, also performed war work locally. That this involvement had a profound impact on the waging of war is unquestionable. H. A. L. Fisher observed that the war of 1914:

> in a degree far higher than any other conflict in the whole course of history, has been a battle of brains. It has been a war of chemists, of engineers, of physicists ... whatever university you may choose to visit, you will find it to be the scene of delicate and recondite investigations, resulting here in a more deadly explosive, there in a stronger army boot, or again in some improvement to the fast advancing technique of aerial navigation.[3]

Lodge concurred with this opinion in his report to Council for 1917–18: 'The modern Universities have amply justified their existence during the War.'[4] Professor Bragg of Leeds was to note during the 1918 deputation of university vice-chancellors and principals to the president of the Board of Education and the Chancellor of the Exchequer (a meeting that was to lead to the formation of the UGC), the universities of Britain had carried out 'an astonishing amount of work ... [with] strange and wonderful results'.[5] Bragg did not restrict this to immediate weapon development, but included work that had improved the efficiency of waging war and supported the health of the army when in the trenches, all of this work done by men 'trained in the universities and the technical institutions of this country'. In effect, the universities of Great Britain had been able to make good some of the failings in British industry that Birmingham's founder Joseph Chamberlain had predicted and which war had revealed so dramatically. In addition, the universities' war work not only made them more acceptable to the nation, but to many in the localities where they were situated, a change that was encouraged not only by the patriotic work the universities did, but in the case of Birmingham, by the development of new attitudes towards the locality and especially its working classes on the part of the University's academic staff.

Just as in the case of the recruitment and allocation of manpower, the nation had made no specific plans for wartime research in Britain's universities.[6] This was not to be the case in the Second World War, when the lessons of the First World War prompted much advanced planning on the part of government and university authorities. Initially, indeed, there is much to suggest that in 1914 the government attitude towards the universities and their work was lackadaisical. In August the War Office sent a circular round Britain's universities to enquire about research that might benefit the war effort, but failed to act on the information.[7] In the case of Birmingham the requisition of the Bournbrook site for a hospital immediately meant that for the duration of hostilities the University would be deprived of its best scientific facilities – new, large, and well-equipped. With the clearance of the engineering block to make way for hospital beds, the vital machine tools were sold somewhat indiscriminately to industry, thus liquidating one of the new University's major assets. Finally, to add insult to injury, Lodge's experimental radio mast and wireless equipment, only installed by Electrical Engineering in the spring of 1914, was dismantled by the Post Office, allegedly for security reasons. Thus, within weeks of the outbreak of hostilities, the capacity of the University to contribute to the war effort had been seriously weakened.[8] The War Office later relented to the extent of allowing the strength and materials laboratory to be used by Professor Lea, and when the power station was not fully stretched by the requirements of the hospital (a responsibility of Professor Burchall) it was possible to carry out some experiments there.[9]

Although the letting of contracts by government departments necessarily had some steering effect on scientific activity, the first truly constructive government action towards wartime research and the universities was to assign the role of allocating essential research work to two professional bodies, the British Association and the Royal Society. With confidence in a minimum of governmental intervention, it was felt that the members of these bodies, leading experts in their fields, would be best qualified to determine where specific research could be carried out. A number of specialist subcommittees were immediately set up to deal with different areas of work, notably the War Committee, the Chemical War Committee and the Natural Products Committee of the Royal Society. These were later subdivided into even more specialised committees, such as the committee that dealt with the development of storage techniques for oxygen and gas cylinders.

Although Principal Oliver Lodge had been a prominent member of the British Association from his early days in science, there is no record of research being allocated to the University of Birmingham via this body. On the other hand, the Royal Society was of great importance. The professor of chemistry, Percy Frankland, as well as chairing the Society's Reserved Occupations Committee, also chaired the Royal Society's War Committee Chemical Section. Lodge, too, was a prominent member of the Royal Society. Interviewed by the *Birmingham Daily Post* in 1915, he explained that 'the organisation of science in England is via the Special War Committee of the Royal Society'. From 'time to time', Lodge continued, 'we receive requests from the War Office and Admiralty and these are passed on to members of the committee able to deal with them' who then directed essential research work to 'laboratories of its members [which] are set busy on investigations'.[10] Essentially, the Royal Society and the members of these special committees, who from Birmingham included John Cadman, professor of mining, as well as Frankland and Lodge, acted as an advisory board and provided an allocation system for the Admiralty and War office on the assumption that they were best able to determine which universities, departments and personnel were equipped to carry out which specific research work.

The Admiralty's Board of Invention and Research was an early promoter of research work in universities, but, especially after the establishment of the Ministry of Munitions in 1915, it was joined by a large number of other official bodies, for example, the Trench Warfare Department of the Ministry of Munitions; the Air Board, later the Air Ministry; and the RAF. The government had come to realise that the war demanded many new laboratories and experimental centres and that it was impossible to establish these from scratch. Britain's universities therefore became a most valuable and useful asset to the nation. As the official *History of the Ministry of Munitions* records: 'the knowledge and equipment of the universities were utilised in many directions, as well as in respect to the evolution of new equipment and the development process and the study of methods of testing'.[11] Birmingham also undertook work for the newly formed Aircraft Establishment at Farnborough and for the Petroleum Executive. As in the case of the Royal Society, it would appear that it was prominent Birmingham men serving on the committees of these various bodies who allocated work or at least suggested which university departments were best equipped to carry out key research work. As well as his work with the Royal Society, Frankland served on a number of other committees, including the Ministry of Munitions Chemical Warfare Committee and the Admiralty Board of Invention and Research, which also had Oliver Lodge on its expert advisory panel. Adrian Brown, professor of Brewing and Malting, served on the Natural Products committee of the Royal Society.

The most illustrious of all the Birmingham men was Cadman. With a long history of service on government bodies before the war, he not only became the chairman of the Inter-Allied Petroleum Council and a member of the Chemical Sub-committee of the Scientific Advisory Committee of the Ministry of Munitions in 1916, but also served on the Trench Warfare committee on chemical warfare and the Admiralty's research committee charged with investigating chemical defence against submarines. In 1917, after serving as technical adviser to the Inter-Departmental Oil Committee, Cadman was, in the face of a crisis in oil supply, made the Director of His Majesty's Petroleum Executive, a position that made him answerable directly to Lloyd George's War Cabinet. The consequence for Birmingham was that when Cadman's own Petroleum Executive commissioned him to research into improving oil and petroleum he allocated the work to Lodge, who transformed his physics laboratory and set about investigating methods of increasing the quantity and quality of fuel and motor spirit obtainable from crude oil.

The remaining government body involved in allocating research work to Britain's universities during the war was the Department of Scientific and Industrial Research (DSIR), established in 1915 to encourage practical scientific research. As would be the case with the UGC when it was established in 1919, the DSIR was an offshoot of the Treasury and, by a nice conjunction, its chairman was William McCormick, the able administrator who would become the first chairman of the UGC. The impulse for the establishment of the DSIR was the shock felt within Britain when the outbreak of war graphically pointed out the breadth of the nation's shortcomings in science and industry. Its role was to encourage the formation of, and give grants to, 'research associations', that is, research centres established jointly between an industry and the universities which would investigate practical applications of science to that particular industry. Thus it established the British Dyestuffs Corporation and research associations in other areas such as chemicals, explosives and textiles, industries where Britain had been shown to lag far behind Germany.[12] During the war the DSIR sponsored a whole range of such research associations. In the case of Birmingham these covered emergency building techniques, especially the use of concrete; work on condenser tubes with the British Electrical and Allied Manufacturers' Association; some of Cadman's and Lodge's work on fuel research and finally, and most appropriately for Birmingham, joint research with the Institute of Mechanical Engineers into Muntz's metal, a research interest of the department of metallurgy since the late 1880s.

The DSIR, therefore, differed from all other wartime institutions involved in directing essential research work to the universities. It did not allocate specific war work to those establishments or academics that were felt most able to carry it out. Instead it was a grant-making body which gave money in support of research that was to be carried out by specific academics, teams of researchers, individual firms or industrial associations. It also sponsored postgraduate research students by providing personal grants. The creation of the DSIR laid the foundation of British governmental grants to scientific research until it became the Science Research Council in 1964. However, personal contact and influence still remained important. Redmayne, Cadman's predecessor in the Birmingham chair of mining, served on the DSIR's Fuel Research subcommittee while postgraduate grants were clearly awarded according to the merits of the departmental professor.[13] The DSIR was to prove its worth for the University of Birmingham during the immediate post-war period, especially in forming the University's school of chemistry into an internationally important centre for chemical research.

How essential war work carried out by the universities was paid for is by no means clear, apart from the DSIR, with its grants to specific research projects in universities and to 'industrial associations', and its awards of personal grants to some postgraduate research students in the sciences. Various government bodies did award contracts to universities for their research work. In addition, research carried out under the auspices of the Royal Society and the British Association was partially compensated for by additional awards to the universities made by the Advisory Committee to the Treasury in 1914–15 and again in 1918–19. Yet, as we have already seen, these supplements were hardly enough to make amends for the loss of income the universities had suffered as a result of the drastic reduction in student numbers, let alone the cost of essential wartime research.

The reality seems to be that all Birmingham generally received were letters of thanks, and that it was left to find much of the cost of its war work itself.[14] The way the University became involved in June 1915 in the search for sources of toluol is perhaps indicative. The Council was informed that the University had been selected to take part in the programme and was asked to provide the services of advanced students. A hint was given that there might be some payment to these individuals, but it was made perfectly clear that the University must provide laboratory space, gas and water gratis, although there was a further hint that to do so might improve its chances of being allocated research grants or receiving grants from the Board of Education.[15] Another example was the involvement, early in the war, of every member of the department of physics in inspecting optical instruments for the military where, as Gilbert Shakespear noted, the payment received was only 'nominal'.[16] For its main war work Physics received no state support at all and had to rely on the generosity of 'an anonymous benefactor'. There is no record of government payments to the University to cover the salaries of staff working on essential work, indeed the reverse. Gilbert Barling, in a letter to Lodge, argued that the salaries of members of staff working on government research ought to be paid by the state, but suggested that if this was not the case the University might make up the salary so that there was no loss to the individual.[17] In certain instances, where the government's call on an individual was great, some compensation was given. Such was the case with Cadman. Even before the war, his extensive work abroad brought long periods of absence from Birmingham, and Cadman himself negotiated with the Admiralty a fee to be paid to the University in compensation.[18] By 1917, however, Cadman's government work became so extensive that the university authorities were determined that the government should pay him in full, although Cadman, in a letter to Lodge, wondered if the government 'have any idea of a professor's salary'.[19] However, Cadman appears the exception to the rule that normally no direct compensation was paid.

As the toluol example indicates, many members of the University involved in military research were in fact third-year undergraduates or postgraduates. They generally received no salary and very few received grants, but their contribution was vital and not without risk. H. M. Bambury, a postgraduate, suffered an early death 'largely due' to his work for the war effort. In some cases, graduates were recalled to their old university to work on essential research. Such was the case of a young woman graduate, E. A. N. Twigg, who recalled that 'previous to the war I was a "'home" daughter'. When war came she set about replacing her colony of cats and dogs with poultry and rabbits that would provide food, only to be approached by Professor Gamble of zoology, who asked her to help the department.

As well as students who undertook research and other essential duties while continuing their courses, others worked in local munitions factories. Meticulously and proudly they wore their 'munitions buttons' which indicated that they were profitably engaged on essential war work, but despite this, some members of the local community criticised them. Many felt that student munition workers, especially young male undergraduates whose contemporaries were serving on the Front, were still doing less than their duty. 'Breaking off a degree to work in highly paid munitions' was seen by many to be no great hardship. In addition to this, there was also seasonal agricultural work for students to do outside the specially shortened university term. That women undergraduates travelled into the nearby Worcestershire countryside to go fruit picking caused great amusement to *The Mermaid*, the student magazine, one young woman going so far as to wear her father's boots over her own in order to protect her feet from the local mud.[20] There were even calls for undergraduates, especially women, to serve in a voluntary capacity abroad. Margery Fry, by this time no longer the Warden of University House but working for relief agencies on the Continent, returned in November 1914 to address students on 'Relief Work in France'.[21] Nor was the University Council left out. Despite the desperate need for teaching space it made room available in the Great Charles Street block for a civilian clothing exchange run by Mrs Gerald Kenrick.[22]

If the challenge of organising the University's contribution to the war drew a number of Birmingham's academic staff into roles of national importance, its wartime research record further marked the coming of age of this new institution in the Midlands as a place of research and learning. In 1920, Sir William Ashley, dean of the Commerce Faculty and vice-principal, collected material for a record of the University of Birmingham's war work.[23] Produced at the request of the Universities Bureau of the British Empire, which intended to publish a record of the wartime activities of each of Britain's universities and colleges in the *Universities British Empire Yearbook*, Ashley's report is impressive. The work done at Birmingham ranged from research directly concerned with the waging of war, such as the development of poisonous gases, to medical advances and social and cultural contributions. In August 1915, so the *Birmingham Daily Post* reported, some eighty members of the academic staff and students, both undergraduates and postgraduates, were involved in this essential war work.[24]

Perhaps the area of science where Britain lagged behind most in 1914 was 'coal-tar' chemistry, vital to the development and production of modern munitions. Percy Frankland and his colleagues in the department of chemistry, Dr Frederick Challenger and Dr S. R. Carter, responded immediately by forming research teams of staff, graduates and undergraduates.[25] This enabled the Birmingham department to contribute to the rapid response of British universities to the first use of poisonous gas in the German attack of 22 April 1915. Immediately the Cassel Cyanide Co. of Glasgow began to manufacture a form of gas that had been developed by Imperial College, and Birmingham's John Cadman was ordered to erect plant to produce the sulphuretted hydrogen he had been working on for some time with Chance and Hunt. By 1917, Sir James Irvine of St Andrews was producing mustard gas in his own laboratory, although this was soon after superseded by the method of production devised at Manchester and Cambridge.[26] At Birmingham itself, Professor Frankland, together with Challenger and Dr Hamilton McCrombie, carried out further research into poisonous gas, using the University's model mine to determine the amount of gas vaporised by explosive charges. McCrombie subsequently enlisted and ended the war as a major responsible for gas warfare in the 1st Army, with an MC, DSO and Croix de Guerre. Also, as

Cadman later informed Ashley, 'Professor Frankland and I organised the first field experiments on a large scale with poison gas on Cannock Chase', testing the range and spread of gases and methods of distribution. This work was one factor leading to the eventual establishment of the Porton Chemical Warfare School.

It was a Birmingham man, Dr J. R. Coates, lecturer in physical chemistry, who helped to take the work on poison gas into production. Coates, a lieutenant in the Royal Navy Reserve, was seconded, along with other Birmingham graduates, to design and build a large industrial plant for the production of anhydrous prussic acid at Stratford in East London. In 1915 he built a larger plant that produced 5 tons of this gas, sufficient to fill 360 000 shells. He also researched into how to generate smokescreens. While experimenting in poisonous gases, Frankland and Cadman also developed, as Cadman claimed, 'one of the first box respirators ever made'. In the event the two of them had to wait over a year for the military to respond to their invention, by which time the work of B. Lambert of Oxford's chemistry department and O. C. M. Davies of the University of Bristol on box respirators and the absorption by charcoal had led to the development of the first British standard gas mask.[27] Gilbert Shakespear, the senior lecturer in charge of the wartime department of physics, carried out reciprocal work on automatic gas-detection devices. As well as helping to develop gas as a weapon, the University's chemists were much engaged in research into explosives. Cadman and Frankland carried out experiments with explosives in the model mine, in Staffordshire and at the Front. Over a period of eighteen months in 1916–17 Frankland made frequent visits to the French sector of the Western Front. Cadman concluded: 'The results were useful in selecting the types of explosives to be employed in firing heavy charges in land mines.'[28]

Although arguably essential, this scientific war work produced the horrors of poison gas and modern explosives. However, not all research by the Birmingham chemists was destructive. As well as TNT and poison gas, 'coal-gas' chemistry produced aniline dye for khaki uniforms and potentially for civilian use in peace-time. Important work was undertaken in the preparation of anaesthetics such as Diethylaminoethanol, B-Eucaine and Novocaine, substances that were often not available in Britain since, before the war, Germany had held a monopoly on the production of synthetic drugs. Once again, it was Frankland's team of staff headed by Challenger and Carter with some seven to eight students who were engaged in manufacturing these drugs, along with continuing research into the production of anaesthetics. This work was organised by a chemical subcommittee of the Royal Society's war committee, on behalf of the National Health Insurance Commission. The synthesis of these essential drugs was painstaking and as dangerous, in its way, as chemistry directed to the battlefield. Challenger noted that 'the processes involved in this preparation of large quantities were both difficult and tedious, requiring the careful preparation and purification of a large number of intermediate products', and it was working in this area which cost Bambury his life. Of course Birmingham was not alone in carrying out the large-scale purification of anaesthetics and other synthetic drugs needed in war. Centres such as St Andrews led the field in drug preparation, and in all some forty universities and laboratories were engaged.[29]

Other wartime research carried out at Birmingham included that of Professor Lea and Frank Raw of civil engineering. They had the advantage of being able to use the pre-war strength and materials laboratory for work for the Air Board, the RAF and the Royal Naval Air Service on fabric materials for use in aircraft and on the strength and elasticity of various steel alloys, and later, on the development of the metal wing. Leonard J. Willis of the department was a member of the relevant government board. The research at Birmingham made possible pistons and cylinders for aero-engines using aluminium alloy. Gilbert Shakespear also contributed to aviation by producing the 'katharometer', a device for testing the permeability of cloth to gases, a key consideration in ensuring the safety of airships. When Braggs of Leeds gave praise to 'the endeavours of the universities' in this area, noting that they had 'developed the strength of structures, the form of structures, the form of the covering, [and] the varnish that covers it', an appreciable part of that praise belonged to the University of Birmingham.[30]

In the school of mechanical engineering, Professor Burstall's pre-war research into the functioning of the petrol engine made him an obvious person to be asked to work on developing carburettors and radiators. Initially, this research was undertaken for the Air Board, particularly on the problem of carburation at high altitudes, but Burstall became incensed with the Board's dilatory attitude. In 1916 he transferred his work to the Mechanical Warfare section of the Ministry of Munitions, developing carburettors and radiators for use in tanks. Drs Barlow and Keene of physics worked on underwater detection devices for use against submarines, using Barnt Green reservoir. Dr Wall of electrical engineering moved to Portsmouth to work on sound telegraphy and communication with submerged submarines. Work was done on range-finding equipment. Oliver Lodge lent his own instruments to assist research into the determination of range by sound and the future Professor Watson produced mathematical tables for the determination of distance. He also produced tables to calculate the destructive effect of explosions. Lea and Raw joined Thomas Turner, the professor of metallurgy, to develop a practical and imaginative way to use shell cases as air and gas bottles for medical and aviation use.

The research, development and, in instances such as synthetic drugs, the actual production of materials was not the only wartime activity undertaken by the University. In common with many other British universities, equally important was the humdrum work of testing locally manufactured armaments and military components. Again, this is witness to Britain's pre-war industrial weakness; quality control and research laboratories were lacking, not just in Midland factories but across the country. Testing included the physicists using Shakespear's katharometer to assess balloon fabrics. The department also monitored the quality of optical glass used in military instruments, especially important in trench warfare, and undertook the training of air and marine wireless operators. The department of metallurgy was heavily involved in ammunition testing.[31] For example, on behalf of the Inventions Department of the Ministry of Munitions it undertook the analysis of samples of the cartridge and shell cases produced at the Elliot Metal Co., Kynochs and the King's Heath Metal Co. Lea and Raw visited aircraft factories in Birmingham and Coventry, and occasionally London, to give expert advice on how to secure maximum efficiency of production in a such a new industry. Even John Cadman, despite his many other responsibilities, was called on to act as a 'troubleshooter' in plants producing goods for the Ministry of Munitions.

The most important and essential testing work was, however, once again performed by the University's chemists, who by 1915 had had to expand into both the brewing and the physiology laboratories.[32] Indeed, Professor Frankland, with the assistance of his staff, was responsible for organising the inspection and testing of all high explosive manufactured in the Midlands, including that made at the nation's first TNT factory at nearby Oldbury. In 1916 his importance was recognised by being given the official title of 'Deputy Inspector of High Explosives' – though it was carefully pointed out that the post carried no remuneration.[33] It was a daily routine for the University's laboratories, which involved the staff, particularly A. Parker, S. R. Carter and W. Wardlow, in constant travelling. Students were also involved. The *Birmingham Daily Post* of 8 March 1915 reported that the senior students under the direction of Professor Frankland were engaged in their vacations to 'manufacture high explosives for the Ministry of Munitions'.[34] Similar work within their particular areas was carried out by other provincial universities, such as Liverpool, Leeds and Manchester.[35] The Birmingham chemistry department also analysed the coal tar and benzol produced at all the Midlands gasworks. This was in the attempt to find a good source of toluene, a chemical vital in explosive propellant. Before the war, Britain had been totally dependent for this on Germany. Dr Carter tested some 4000 tar samples throughout the war.

Essential wartime work was not confined to the scientific and medical staff and students of the University or to carrying out research and testing. Adrian Brown, the professor of brewing, was responsible for organising French breweries to supply the British army with English-type beer. William Ashley was knighted in 1917 principally for his wartime work, which included serving on a whole range of nationally important committees and councils concerned with the economics of waging war. Thus from 1915 he was a leading member of the Royal Society's Wartime Food Committee, preparing papers for it and for the Board of Trade. He was also a member of committees on such diverse matters as retail coal prices, a committee on which his colleague Kirkcaldy also served, and on the cost of living and agricultural wages. As the war drew towards a climax, Ashley became involved in committees planning for the nation's future once war had ceased. One such was the committee of economists on industry after the war (again with Kirkcaldy); another was the Consumer Council, a newly formed section of the Ministry of Food. This work resulted in a number of publications, both by Ashley and Kirkcaldy. Between 1914 and 1916 Ashley produced pamphlets on matters as diverse as the economic aspect of war and German food and cotton supply. These were translated into French, Swedish and Dutch for use by their Ministries of Information. Kirkcaldy's work included such notable works as *Credit, Industry and the War* (1915), *Labour, Finance and the War* (1916) and *Industry and Finance* (1917), all for the Economic Section of the British Association.

The overall contribution to the war effort of staff from the Arts and Commerce was necessarily of more peripheral importance than that of their scientific colleagues. In the autumn of 1914 Sonnenschein represented the University at a meeting to consider news management.[36] He also served on local war pensions committees and became very concerned with the plight of refugees, aiding his father's ex-countrymen and serving on the Belgian and Serbian Refugee Committees. This work led to the publication of two important Oxford pamphlets in 1914 and 1915. Ashley served on the Birmingham Citizens' Committee along with Professor Kirkcaldy; he also provided help to the local metal industry. Frank Tillyard, professor of commercial law, chaired Birmingham's Local Munitions Tribunal, as well as adjudicating in Coventry and Worcester from 1915 to 1917 on disciplinary cases against munition workers. Professor Sonnenschein organised the lectures in Birmingham for the Imperial Studies Committee of the Royal Colonial Institute.

Other work took members of the Arts and Commerce faculties abroad, even to the Front. Both Professor C. R. de Selincourt of the English department and C. R. Beazley, professor of history, lectured to soldiers in France for the Young Men's Christian Association (YMCA). De Selincourt went over in 1917, giving a series of lectures drawn from his book, *English Poets and the National Ideal* (1915). Beazley gave a total of twenty lectures in 1918 and, with hostilities over, followed this in 1919 with a series of lectures to French universities. He also presented a series of position papers on Poland, Romania, Albania and the Ottoman Empire, as well as essays on the 'German Imperial Ideal' and German–British relations since 1870. J. H. Muirhead, the professor of philosophy, explored similar ground, publishing a book entitled *German Philosophy and the War.*

By Armistice Day in November 1918, the University of Birmingham was war-weary, its academic staff and students, buildings and equipment worn out. The University's large pre-war debt still had to be faced and the future was anything but encouraging. The remedy was, however, neither straightforward nor immediate. Oliver Lodge, who had by this time given in his notice in order to make way for a new principal in a new era, reported:

> [the University's] new and highly equipped buildings were taken over by the government and converted into the huge military hospital. Damage to fabric throughout and the special wear and tear on the power station are to be put right by the War Office; but the scientific and technical equipment, some of which has been sold, some of which has fallen into disrepair, will require heavy expenditure.[37]

Problems pressed in on every side, for while the practicalities of recommencing work in dishevelled, under-equipped buildings with still-restricted finances were difficult enough, there was the challenge of meeting future national needs, especially as revealed by the war. In particular, the war had provided major lessons for the future use of human and other resources. Previously, in the words of Professor Percy Frankland, 'an immense amount of talent is never employed to its maximum advantage to the country, the real intellectual resources of the country never being deployed into line until equal opportunity has been secured for all.' In his, and in Lodge's opinion, 'universities should be made accessible to the more talented members of the community', irrespective of their financial resources.[38] It was obvious that a new way ahead had to be found for the recruitment of undergraduates and for the general organisation of universities.

The war had also presented specific challenges. In Lodge's opinion (he was writing in 1917), it had revealed major problems for the future role of science and after the war there must be a pressure for a 'closer linking between science and industry ... . Industrial leaders can learn the value of the expert and prepare to utilise their aid.'[39] Lodge, however, went on to see further dilemmas. The lessons of war were not necessarily the lessons of peace. War and wartime research endeavour had 'prostituted science'; only certain advances in aircraft technology represented useful, non-destructive steps forward. It was, perhaps, too jaundiced a view. However destructive the contributions of universities to the development of methods for war, they were also significant for the development of technologies that brought aid to those injured by it and for the promise of material advances in the post-war era. But the issue which most worried Lodge was that this wartime effort had all been in applied science. 'It will', he wrote, 'behove us in the University vividly to remember that pure science must precede applications of science ... and that unless pure science is cultivated in the universities it is not likely to be pursued with adequate attention anywhere.'[40] What was more, Lodge feared the continuance of state aid to scientific research in the post-war era. It could, he perceptively remarked, very well bring 'constraint and formalism'.[41]

Everywhere there were problems, but the war had produced one fundamental and determinative change. Lodge wrote in his annual report for 1917–18: 'The modern universities amply justified their existence during the war. From them have emanated the instruments and devices which have enabled the country to deal with dangerous situations and solve problems of vital importance.'[42] In the process *The Times* concluded: 'our modern universities have woven themselves into the fabric of national life'.[43] Locally, the war was seen to have a great and positive effect on University–City relations, despite the fact that the City Council still enjoyed a great deal of control over the University. Lodge could write in the *Daily Post*: 'The University of Birmingham owes its origins to the inspiration of civic patriotism and it has received a fresh consecration from the courage and self-sacrifice [paid] by this generation of its sons.' The University having proved itself worthy of its beginnings and its founder, Lodge trusted that it would become 'the glory of the city and of the Midlands'.[44] The future would determine how correct he was.

Notes

1 Arguments in support of a university charter for Birmingham had pointed to many of these deficiencies more than a decade previously: UC 7/iv/4 (Oct.1898).
2 Brazier and Sandford, *Birmingham and the War*, p. 120.
3 H. A. L. Fisher, *British Universities and the War* (1917), p. xiii, quoted in Sanderson, *Universities*, pp. 214–15.
4 UC 7/iii 1918, p. 4.
5 UC 14/ii: OL178b, p. 20 – reporting the deputation by the Universities Bureau of the British Empire to the President of the Board of Trade and the Chancellor of the Exchequer, 23 Nov. 1918.
6 K. Vernon, 'Science and Technology during the Great War', in S. Constantine, M. W. Kirby and M. E. Rose (ed.), *The First World War in British History* (1995), pp. 81–105.
7 Sanderson, *Universities*, p. 218.
8 Lodge made this point forcibly: UC 7/iii 1914–15, p. 6.
9 Brazier and Sandford, *Birmingham and the War*, pp. 120–1.
10 Oliver Lodge, in *Birmingham Daily Post*, 13 Aug. 1915.
11 *Official History of the Ministry of Munitions*, ix (ii) (1920–1), pp. 60–1.
12 R. McLeod and E. K. Andrew, 'The origins of the Department of Scientific and Industrial Research', *Public Administration*, 48 (1970), p. 36; D. S. Cardwell, *The Organisation of Science* (1957), p. 171.
13 PRO DSIR 1/1.
14 UA Council Minutes 11, *passim*.
15 UA Council Minutes 10, 5383.
16 UC3/vii/8: Shakespeare to Ashley, 15 Feb. 1919.
17 UC 14/ii: OL149: Barling to Lodge, 28 May 1915.
18 Ibid.: OL133: Cadman to Lodge, 1 Dec. 1913.
19 Ibid.: OL164: Cadman to Lodge, 10 June 1917.
20 *The Mermaid*, 1915–16.
21 Ibid.
22 Brazier and Sandford, *Birmingham and the War* , p. 237.
23 UC3/vii/8.

24 *Birmingham Daily Post*, Aug. 1915.
25 Sanderson, *Universities*, p. 221.
26 Ibid., p. 222.
27 Ibid., pp. 222–3; UC3/vii/8.
28 UC3/vii/8.
29 Sanderson, *Universities*, pp. 223–4.
30 UC 14/ii: OL178b: 'Report of meeting with the President of the Board of Trade and the Chancellor of the Exchequer, 1918'.
31 Ibid., OL157: Thomas Turner to the Ministry of Munitions, 5 Apr. 1916.
32 UC 7/iii 1914–15, pp. 11–20.
33 UA Council Minutes 11, 5650.
34 *Birmingham Daily Post*, 8 Mar. 1915.
35 Sanderson, *Universities and British Industry*, p. 221.
36 UA Council Minutes 10, 5180.
37 UC 7/iii 1918–19.
38 Ibid., 1916–17, p. 8.
39 Ibid., pp. 16–17.
40 Ibid.
41 Ibid., p. 20.
42 Ibid.
43 *The Times*, 9 Jan. 1916.
44 *Birmingham Daily Post*, 13 Aug. 1915.

Part Three

The central decades, 1920–50

Chapter Eleven

The inter-war years

THE FIRST WORLD WAR was a profound shock to the British nation, the Midland region and the City of Birmingham, but to the University it was an intimate trauma. Gerard Collier, a graduate, wrote to William Ashley in October 1919 of 'the blow to the whole university community of which we are part. How is this to be healed and the community restored?'[1] In an endeavour to come to terms at least in part with the tragedy, the University's Reconstruction Committee decided to erect a war memorial to all the staff, students and servants of the University who had sacrificed their lives.[2] Aston Webb was asked to design it and the site chosen was the east wall of the entrance to the Great Hall, with Edward VII's statue being moved to the other side. The tablets were unveiled in 1922, and marked by the performance of a setting by Sir Granville Bantock, the professor of music, of a 1746 ode by William Collins which he dedicated to those 'sons of the University of Birmingham who gave their lives in the Great War'.[3] They included three women.

There were material casualties of the war also. The University had been incapacitated in plant by the War Office commandeering its Bournbrook buildings, and was left with the inevitable aftermath of military occupation. Its equipment, too, had been largely dispersed and needed to be almost completely replaced. In 1923 compensation was at last obtained to the tune of £65,433, including interest, but only after years of face-to-face deliberations with the War Office. As a result, the relationship of the University with this department of national government became severely strained, the more so in view of what the University staff and its students had given in war service.[4] Nor was the recovery and restoration of Bournbrook the only problem the University faced. Facilities at Edmund Street were cramped and poor. Student numbers, however, were predicted to rise. The answer, as always, was money, but far from there being funds available, the University was being strangled by the need to service its burden of long-term debt.

The experience of war had, however, brought about the realisation that the relationship between university, region and nation was far more complex and fundamental than the old simplicities of debt and aid. 'Scientific' war had demonstrated that Britain, along with its famous Midland industrial centre, was no longer the workshop of the world. If the nation was to correct this industrial retardation, it would need its universities. Tragically, a world-wide economic depression intervened, only to be overtaken from 1933 by gathering war clouds, which made the as yet empty spaces on the marble wall opposite the University's 1914–18 memorial seem all too ominous.

Britain's economy during the 1920s and 1930s is popularly seen as a story of unrelenting depression and unemployment. In actual fact, it was very varied, indeed contradictory.[5] Of nowhere in Britain was this more true than the industrial Midlands. The old 'staple' industries of the region – coal, metalworking and engineering – went into a serious decline, exacerbating the industrial backwardness revealed by the war.[6] In such areas there was serious unemployment and social deprivation.[7] On the other hand, elsewhere in the region there was industrial growth and an expansion of employment with the rise of new manufactures such as motor cars, artificial fibres, confectionery and electrical goods. Thus, both the chocolate firm of Cadbury's, founded during the nineteenth century but removed in 1900 to the model factory village of Bournville, not far from the University, and the Austin plant at Longbridge, established in 1905, saw a significant increase in output and workforce.[8] Other vehicle producers in the region were Wolseley, Morris, BSA and Lanchester, a concentration of demand which spawned the motor component sector, symbolised by the Joseph Lucas amalgamation in 1925 and 1926 and the colossal Fort Dunlop tyre factory which was opened in 1927.[9] Thanks to such development, much of Birmingham and the Midland region experienced relative inter-war prosperity and, overall, 'escaped the worst impact of the Great Depression'.[10]

With industrial and economic retardation on one hand, and new, technological advanced industry on the other, Birmingham and the Midlands during the immediate post-war and inter-war years certainly needed to take to heart Lodge's call for 'a closer linking between science and industry.[11] However, the extent to which the University and indeed universities could offer that expert aid would depend upon how they could recover and adjust to the new context, and that was first and foremost a matter of public money. Here the leading men of the universities (from 1919 formed into the national body, the CVCP) could take up from pre-war campaigns, but they now had that most powerful of arguments, justice.[12] Lodge, in his report to the University's Court in 1917–18, reminded the governors, and through them the region's and nation's public, that 'the modern universities amply justified their existence during the War. In them, as in the older Universities of the British Isles have been found the men of special knowledge and ability. From them have emanated the instruments and devices which have enabled the country to deal with dangerous situations and solve problems of vital importance.'[13] Lodge and his fellow principals and vice-chancellors had not been idle during the war itself – a highly favourable report had been obtained from a consultative committee of the Board of Education in 1916, but with the war drawing to some resolution they decided that the time to press their claims had returned.[14] By July 1918, Lodge was pushing hard for a meeting between university and college representatives and the government, only to be informed by Fisher, President of the Board of Education, that it was too late in the parliamentary session for such a meeting and they would have to wait until the autumn. However, Fisher did assure Lodge that 'the interests of the Universities will not in any way be prejudiced by delay', and Lodge certainly felt that Fisher had 'shown himself to have a more adequate conception [of the universities] than many of his predecessors'.[15]

The meeting was eventually called jointly by the President and the Chancellor of the Exchequer, Andrew Bonar Law, for 23 November 1918. Also in attendance were Sir William McCormick, since 1910 chairman of the Advisory Committee on the universities, A. H. Kidd, junior examiner at the Board of Education, and Sir Frank Heath.[16] Together, McCormick and Kidd had become concerned about the condition of many universities, about the anomalies in the then current government grant system, and over the probability of an ever-increasing demand for university places, and so had been working quite unofficially on 'reconstruction plans'. It was, they both realised, vital to let institutions of higher education know of the state's plans to give them aid.[17]

Thus, the stage was set for an amicable meeting in which all parties held a common opinion. In fact, there is evidence to suggest that McCormick and Kidd had prior contact with the delegation, for the statistics the university side presented on the support which foreign governments gave to their higher education systems were provided by McCormick himself. The President opened the meeting by saying that 'nothing pays a nation better than education'. 'This', Fisher declared, was 'a new era in education'; the strictures placed on the higher educational system by the Treasury would be removed and advances made:

> We need extremely generous treatment from the State at this most critical time if we are to do creditable work *for* the country and the empire... . A nation which has been spending £6,000,000 or £7,000,000 a day in wartime ought to be able to afford a grant of £2,000,000 a year for our higher education now that war is over.[18]

The universities found all they wanted in the government's proposals. A substantial increase was awarded for the next quinquennium, plus a non-recurrent grant to reimburse them for the loss of capital and equipment, for the cost of some of their research work that had occurred as a result of the war and towards the superannuation bill.[19] The University of Birmingham in consequence found its recurrent grant raised by almost three-quarters, from the £20,270 per annum it had been between 1916–17 and 1918–19, to £35,000 for 1919–20.[20] Its non-recurrent grant for the academic year 1919–20 was £23,000.

After this positive reception, central government was once again clearly the largest single source of income for English universities.[21] Thanks to the war, state support, as a proportion of the total income to higher education in England, had dropped from 33.2% in 1913–14 to 31.8% in 1920–1 (as against fee income of 34.1%). However, following the new deal with the government, state support provided 34.6% of income in 1921–2 and 36.9% in 1922–3. Grants to the University of Birmingham reached a maximum in 1921–2 of £55,000 recurrent and £5000 non-recurrent. At that point national economic difficulties obliged the coalition government to apply the 'Geddes Axe' which cut the amount awarded to the universities via the UGC by nearly 12%, from £1,358,000 to £1,201,000. However, in the application Birmingham was luckier than some because the cut was made almost entirely on non-recurrent money, leaving annual grants untouched. Thus its UGC grant remained at £55,000 and all the University 'lost' was the £5000 supplement it might have hoped for. By contrast, Liverpool, retaining its recurrent £63,800 but receiving nothing in the way of non-recurrent grant, suffered an effective cut of nearly £16,000. As for the London School of Economics, it received in 1922–3 just over a quarter of the money it had received in the year before! Matters improved in 1925–6 when the UGC grant-in-aid was increased to £1,550,000, giving Birmingham a further £10,000 per annum. The Geddes cuts may have reduced the percentage of higher education funded by the Treasury, but they did not put an end to the pleasant custom of university deputation and governmental response. A further appeal was made to the Chancellor of the Exchequer in August 1930, asking for an increased grant to the universities of some £250,000 per year, and for the rest of the decade the state footed between 34% and 36% of the British higher education bill (in England, 32% to 34%). Birmingham did slightly better, receiving between 35% and 38.5%. There was an increment of 10% from 1930–1, and a further increase from 1936–7 raised the government grant to the University in each of the three years prior to the outbreak of war to £86,500.

With the prospect of a significant increase in government funding following the November 1918 meeting, it was obvious to go on to ask whether the mechanism of grants and inspections by a permanent Advisory Committee needed revision. The universities were clear: 'No one but ourselves can have any idea of how that money can best be spent. ... Inspect freely but have absolutely no control.'[22] The outcome was the setting up on 14 July 1919 of the UGC. Chaired by McCormick and with Kidd later installed as secretary and administrator, this consisted of a team of ten academics, including Margery Fry, subsequently to be principal of Somerville College, Oxford.[23] Established, like its predecessor, under the auspices of the Board of Education, the UGC continued the quinquennial inspection of supported universities as 'a good, dignified, suitable method, giving the State sufficient control, and not too much'.[24]

The creation of the UGC and this policy of a generally much-improved grant was not the only post-war development which improved university–state relations. In the course of the war, as we have seen, the DSIR was established in order to encourage closer links between industry and research and development, whether the latter took place in the universities, or, as was often the case at a time when research was in its infancy, in various industry-sponsored laboratories. Many wanted the department to continue in the post-war era, but Oliver Lodge and Professor Bragg of Leeds were concerned that this relationship between government and university should not decline into the bureaucratic regulation which was felt to have characterised the state sponsorship of science in Germany.[25]

The result was that, once again, the government adopted a relationship 'at arm's length'. Like the UGC, the DSIR was made permanent, with interested academics and administrators at its centre, so that in effect it acted as a representative of the universities' needs. William McCormick, chairman of the UGC, also sat as chairman of the DSIR. It remained the principal body for making government grants to the sciences until the early 1960s, when it was restructured as the Science Research Council.[26] Medicine was covered by another post-war development, the setting up of the Medical Research Council (MRC). This had originated in 1913 as a 'Medical Research Committee' funded from the national insurance scheme, but in 1919 was reconstituted on the DSIR model with funds directly voted by Parliament. A third grant-making body, the Agricultural Research Council, was founded in 1931.

The creation of the UGC, DSIR and MRC, along with the funds they administered, restored the confidence of the universities, considerably battered by the ravages of war. Yet although the result was an increased level of funding for the universities, this did not put an end to the importance of 'local income'. The three other categories of revenue – fees, local authority grants and endowments – continued to be extremely important.

Student fees were increased by a quarter from October 1920 and regularly brought the University between 25% and 30% of its income throughout the inter-war period. The end of hostilities in 1918 meant the restoration of the full £15,000 per annum from the City of Birmingham, increased payments from Staffordshire and Worcestershire, and contributions from Warwickshire and two county boroughs.[27] However, these had to be set off against fee remissions, so that local authority grants provided only about 10% of net income in the early 1920s. This did improve in the 1930s to 13.5 or 14%. Making these grants, of course, guaranteed to local councils the continuation of the influence which we have seen in the case of Professor Wichmann during the First World War; any action on the part of staff and students that met (in particular) the City's displeasure risked a reduction in the University's local rate support. As early as 1915 Lodge was expressing the hope that the wartime record of the University would lead Birmingham to raise its financial support to the level of other cities and thus improve relations between the two.[28] However, the nature of 'town and gown' relations in the immediate post-war period, while an improvement upon the pre-war era, was not such as to make an increase in grant certain. The difficulties were on both sides. As Armistice Day 1919 approached, the city police approved plans by university graduates for a celebration in costume to mark their 'public joy' after a full year of peace. Permission was then withdrawn when the lord mayor, Alderman W. A. Cadbury, received a general request from the king that the occasion should be marked in 'quiet celebration'. A small group of students, gathered with the general public in Victoria Square for the 11 a.m. silence, booed the mayor as he passed, and the University came in for considerable criticism. In contrast, an Armistice Day prank by group of medical students – they removed a gun from the 'battlements' to the rear of the Aston Webb buildings and dragged it the full length of the Bristol Road to the quadrangle of the General Hospital – received no local reprimand.[29]

On the City's part, the pre-war prejudice of citizens was still evident against those who hailed from outside Birmingham but received an education at the University 'they had paid for'. For instance, Indian students reading metallurgy were treated in a highly negative and suspicious manner. Both Oliver Lodge and his successor, Grant Robertson, were quick to point out that the people of Birmingham and the Black Country should 'Take no narrow view of the university, that it shall only teach Birmingham citizens ... [the University] was a great engine for the good of Man.'[30] The principal was also critical of the city's low level of rate support. 'Why cannot we in the Midlands have a 1d rate on the same basis as our provincial universities?'[31]

The third element in local recurrent income was provided by endowments. The government was particularly anxious not to see this source of regional funding discouraged by the increase in central provision. At the meeting that founded the UGC and increased its grant, the president of the Board of Education stated, 'We shall always welcome private gifts and local support.'[32] With this in mind the lord mayor of Birmingham launched a major appeal in October 1920 to raise £500,000 for the University.[33]

In preparation for this, an appeal committee of 300 had been established by that stalwart of the original university campaign, Alderman F. C. Clayton, who returned for a second stint as university treasurer. Recognising the need to include the City's working classes and so forestall allegations of middle-class privilege, Clayton called for a wider representation than on the 1898 committee, even suggesting the co-option of a 'bricklayer and a miner'.[34] The new principal, Grant Robertson, suggested that as well as large-scale 'investors', such as local firms, the University needed locally based endowments of lesser value; he went so far as to propose that local committees of students be formed in order to raise money during the Christmas vacation. His aim was to 'convince the Midlands that here in Birmingham is their University [and] that its efficiency is of importance to the Midlands'.[35]

Nevertheless, the appeal was not without its critics. One local source hit out at the University's big ideas: 'a ragged scarlet gown or two, a darned hood or even a mortar board stuck together with seccotine, would have been infinitely more touching'.[36] However, if the University could not appeal to 'local patriotism' it could, as the *Birmingham Daily Despatch* advocated, resort to reminding local folk of economic necessity.[37] Thus its appeal to the 'merchants, agents, shopkeepers and factors' of the district posed the question: 'What should the University expect from me, who am in no way dependent on its teaching, technical or otherwise?' The answer was: 'In an industrial community which is losing ground, there can be no assured prosperity for anybody.'[38] Self-interest required them to give. Birmingham was falling behind its civic competitors.

The plainest words to the citizens of the Midlands came from the chief speaker at the meeting in the Town Hall which launched the appeal. Austen Chamberlain not only bore a charismatic Birmingham name and was a 'friend' of his father's university, but by this time was Chancellor of the Exchequer in Lloyd George's immediate post-war Coalition government.

> If the citizens of Birmingham do not care enough for their university and all that it means, if the towns and the counties round do not care for all that it means to them to give adequate support ... the Chancellor of the Exchequer will tell you flat out that if you do not value your Midland University, you cannot expect the taxpayer at large to pay for the conveniences for which you will not yourselves contribute![39]

The rebuke to the citizens of Birmingham and the Midlands appears to have had the right effect, at least in the matter of raising endowments, if not the rates. According to the *Daily Post*, the citizens of Birmingham, well-organised by an Appeal Committee of the social elite, 'straightaway uprose and donated fifty thousand', then came the people, 'generous and public spirited ... gladly casting their coins into the treasury'.[40] By February 1921 some £280,000 had been collected, and over the year 1921–2, £318,453 was raised. The result was to revolutionise the University's financial situation. In his report for 1923, the principal was able to record that 'the heart of our finance is as sound as the heart of our academic life'.[41]

Analysis of the donations and endowments raised by the 1920 appeal reveals a rather different profile of giving, and most probably of motives for giving, to that in 1898. In the earlier appeal, contributions came from a large number of firms and industrial associations, but overall the prosperous industrialists and men of commerce of Birmingham's bourgeoisie were far more generous as individuals. Likewise, in the 1908–9 appeal the £70,000 raised came from eighty-three individuals and only one firm. The 1920 appeal, however, saw a change. Far from failing to live up to expectations, the total of nearly a third of a million pounds completely eclipsed the £103,957 which was the total the University had received during the previous decade. What produced the success was not the number of individual donors, which was tiny in comparison to 1898 – 94 against 1174 – nor the number of firms contributing – 48 against 162. The difference was the size of the gifts; many donors, especially local firms, were extremely generous. There were changes, too, in the subscription lists. The old Chamberlain dynastic and Birmingham connections were, in many cases, still evident, for example, John Sturge Ltd, Stewart & Lloyd Ltd, Muntz's Metals and the Pinsents. However, some companies which had been notable givers to the original scheme of 1898 no longer appeared, such as Guest, Keen & Nettlefold Ltd, the successor to Chamberlain and Nettlefold Ltd. Instead, members of the families appear as individuals, Miss R. Nettlefold, for example. Another contrast is that in 1898 some local industrial families, such as the Barrows and the Cadburys, had kept somewhat aloof from the university scheme because of the Liberal/Liberal–Unionist split which had followed Joseph Chamberlain's activities in the 1880s. By 1920 they were reconciled and contributions came from Barrow Stores Ltd and, most generously, from Cadbury Bros Ltd. (£5000). Finally there were the new names in local industry, the Daimler Car Co., Alfred Bird & Sons Ltd, Messrs Tangye Ltd, and others.

One of the marked characteristics of the 1920 appeal was the significant amount of money donated to specific causes. Of the £280,444 received by February 1921, £147,027 went towards the general fund and £135,417, nearly as much, to earmarked projects.[42] In part this echoed Joseph Chamberlain's own pursuit of individual benefactors, but it more probably reflected the habit which a number of locally based firms and industrial associations had developed during the war years of contributing to specific university initiatives, especially research. One such instance was the endowment which the Chamber of Commerce had provided in 1916 for a lectureship in Russian language and literature.[43] Even more notable was the signal by the Cycle and Motor Cycle Manufacturers' and Traders' Union Ltd that it recognised the need for research and would sponsor a research fellowship.

This trend continued after 1918. Cadbury Bros funded a series of evening lectures in town planning by the notable Professor Ray Unwin, a worthy compliment not only to the Bournville experiment in planning, but to the City of Birmingham's radically successful approach to town planning under the chairmanship of Neville Chamberlain.[44] International companies also joined in. Two of the largest contributions to the appeal came from the Anglo-Persian Oil Co. (£25,000) and the Anglo-Saxon Petroleum Co. (£25,000), with £10,000 from the Anglo-American Co. With a further £25,000 from Lord Cowdray, the total was earmarked for Cadman's work in petroleum and oil engineering, and provided a foundation on which a Centre for Research into Oil Engineering and Refining could be established in 1926.

Two other factors encouraged this change in the pattern of endowments to the University. On a practical level, the Finance Act of 1919 allowed charities, including universities, to recover tax on donations received under covenant from firms and individuals. Secondly, the lessons of war had proved that fundamental and applied research were of great importance nationally, and the continuation of the DSIR after the war indicated the government's assessment that the need for research extended beyond the military to wider industrial development. That was certainly true of the Birmingham area. Austen Chamberlain claimed in his appeal speech of 1920 that 'In all the leading industries of the Midlands the enormous importance of well applied, persistent scientific research is widely recognised.'[45]

Thus, after some initial debate, and despite the blow of the Geddes Axe in 1922, the finances of Britain's universities, and of the University of Birmingham in particular, improved in the years between the wars, with a consequent improvement in the University's relations with its city, region and nation. All this took place at a time of continued and deepening world economic depression, when it would have been all too tempting for state and locality to call into question the support of higher education. In the event, in the twenty years from 1919–20 to 1938–9, full-time student numbers grew by almost 35% and income for the sector from all sources by 122%.[46] This is the more remarkable since the economic climate made the value of pursuing education to graduate level seem an expensive investment with a highly uncertain yield.

The end of hostilities of necessity brought changes in the University of Birmingham's government, both in its personnel and its structure.[47] With war being declared within a month of Joseph Chamberlain's death, the University had had to look for a new chancellor at the very worst moment. It had canvassed several notables without success and in 1916 the Council decided to defer making the appointment until the conflict was over.[48] The matter was, however, considered by the University's Committee of Reconstruction which was formed in 1915, and a possible candidate identified. This was Robert Cecil, Viscount Cecil of Chelwood, the parliamentary Under-Secretary for Foreign Affairs, who was already working on what would eventually become the Covenant of the League of Nations. Cecil was elected in 1918 and installed on 12 November. As a world figure and later recipient of the Nobel peace prize Cecil brought prestige to the University, but he had neither the power nor the influence in domestic politics of his predecessor. The end of the war also saw the resignation of Principal Oliver Lodge, who felt that, with the cessation of hostilities, his task for the University was finished and it was time to call in a new and younger man. Having taken what appears to have been an emotional leave of the University and its city, Lodge was followed by Charles Grant Robertson.

Other changes in the University's personnel also occurred during this era. Arthur Godlee, who sat for the City on the University Council and had become treasurer in 1914, died in 1920. Charles Gabriel Beale, the University's first vice-chancellor, had died in 1912, although his widow continued as an active life governor until 1932. George Clayton, the pro-vice-chancellor and sometime treasurer, died in 1920, as did Sir Richard Threlfall, of Albright & Wilson, one of the longest-serving governors.[49] Sir George Kenrick retired in 1935. New faces came forward, including representatives of post-war local industry, but it is noticeable that so many of the founding families that had enjoyed long links with the University simply replaced one generation on the University Court or Council by the next. The last of Chamberlain's close associates, J. H. Lloyd, held university office until 1939.

It was, however, the form and function of the University's government that saw the most significant change during the inter-war period. In 1922 Parliament passed the Solicitor's Act, which required articled clerks to attend at least one year at a university. Birmingham opened a department of legal studies within the faculty of Arts in the following year and Sir Henry Barber came forward with an offer to endow a chair. Strong student demand made it possible to establish a LLB programme and the case for a separate Law Faculty became unanswerable. This sparked off a move to revise the charter, which was given the royal assent in April 1927.[50] Apart from adding the new faculty of Law to the University, the revision changed the title and responsibilities of certain of the University's leading officers. The title of the most senior active lay officer was changed from vice-chancellor to pro-chancellor, which allowed the principal to take the style 'vice-chancellor and principal'. Non-professorial staff gained representation on Court, Council and Senate, the first crack in the monolithic authority of the professoriate.[51] Another important innovation was the appointment in 1919 of a full-time administrative registrar. Before this, the post had been an academic one held by Heath, the vice-principal, and then for one year by Professor Alfred Hughes, the dean of Arts. Ten years later, Grant Robertson was to wonder how the University had ever done 'its work without such a full-time officer and his staff'.[52] However, the appointment created a curious situation. The registrar inherited the academic administration and hence responsibility for the Senate, but, as Heath had been, was answerable directly to the principal. This left the already existing office of secretary to the University, with independent responsibilities for plant and finance and for the business of the Council and the Court of Governors. The result was that from 1919 Birmingham was unusual among British universities in having a split administrative structure, which was kept until 1988, when David Holmes was appointed to both posts.

Financial stability and increased local and national support for different areas of academic work equipped the University to cater for changing educational demand.[53] This was the result of educational improvements which followed the passing of the 1902 and 1918 Education Acts which led to better qualified candidates applying for admission. Something of this had been evident before the war and had encouraged the University to set up various 'Special Schools' for more advanced study, but in 1919 these were renamed 'Honours Schools' and regulations were introduced for the award of the degrees of BA and B.Sc. with Honours. A related development came in 1921 when the Higher School Certificate was recognised as giving partial or complete exemption from the initial Intermediate BA or B.Sc. year. Students entitled to such exemption were thus able to take honours after three years, not four. The inter-war period also saw disciplines diversify and expand. In 1921 the Muirhead Lectureship in Social Philosophy was established. In the same year the lectureship in Greek was raised to a readership and in 1924 to a chair. That year, too, a department of geography was set up under a reader, Dr Kinvig. Previously the subject had been offered within geology.

One problem that both Lodge and the new principal, Grant Robertson, faced was with subjects that had become too complex to be taught as a single discipline. Engineering had already been split before the First World War, but under the pressure of ex-service undergraduates in particular other science subjects, notably physics and chemistry, required the same treatment. A similar course of action was recommended for arts subjects, but one chair to a subject remained the rule until after the Second World War.[54] This tendency to subdivide was a product of staff initiative as well as of increased subject specialisation and student demand. For instance, the resignation of Sir John Cadman as professor of Mining in 1922 to take on the role of adviser in petroleum to the British Cabinet (in continuation of his wartime work) created, in Grant Robertson's words, 'a definite problem'.[55] Was this the time to divide the chair between the traditional coal and metal mining and the newcomer, petrol mining? The two were indeed separated, but the original proposal to hive off petroleum engineering had actually been raised by Cadman himself in consequence of his own interests (following on those of the University's first professor, Richard Redmayne).[56] An undergraduate course in oil engineering, unique in British universities, had been established in 1919 and Cadman's contacts with many British and overseas oil companies had established Birmingham as a name in the industry.[57] By the 1920s, the University was so proud of this department, with its graduates earning good salaries and enjoying varied duties, that the handbook was advocating, 'Put your lad into oil!'[58]

Other areas of study, although not new at the University, gained status by being granted chairs as a result of local, national and even international endowments. Commercial law had been taught in the faculty of Commerce from 1904 but the Barber endowment established law generally. Russian had been taught at lecturer level from 1917, but a further Chamber endowment in 1921 raised this to chair status. Italian had struggled on jointly with Spanish since before the war, but now became the beneficiary of a second Chamber endowment assisted by Mr Arthur Serena. The Serena Chair of Italian Language and Literature was also notable for a non-academic reason: it was the first Birmingham chair to be filled by a woman, Miss L. P. De Castelvecchio. Even more remarkably for the 1920s, Miss Castelvecchio, perhaps because she had much 'savoir faire' and was 'delightful in front of young people', remained in post after her marriage to the Vicar of Four Oaks.[59]

In 1925 two donations totalling nearly £40,000 enabled work to begin on a life sciences block at Bournbrook. Stanley Baldwin, Prime Minister and a former Mason College student, performed the opening ceremony in 1927 and Edmund Street was left to Arts, Medicine and Education (Commerce having moved out immediately after the war).[60] Other gifts enabled the University to innovate. This was especially true of the annual grant from the Cadbury Bournville Village Trust which funded lectures in town planning, held under the auspices of the department of civil engineering. Such provision 'formed a nucleus at any rate around which we can do something in the direction of the applied art' where Grant Robertson's dream was to have professors in specific subjects.[61] The UGC's quinquennial visitation of the University in 1924 and again in 1929 noted further developments in the courses provided. There was, in addition, a new chair in childhood diseases, while a lectureship in English language had been founded in 1920.[62] During the inter-war period the endowment of chairs also took on, for the first time, an international flavour, a generous gift from the Mitsui family of Tokyo establishing the Mitsui Chair in Finance in the faculty of Commerce in 1922–3.[63]

Just as the fortunes of the inter-war economy of the Midlands were contradictory, so the story of student recruitment between 1918 and 1939 contradicted the positive academic developments at the University of Birmingham. Initially there was hope. With the end of hostilities ex-servicemen were given special awards to enter higher education as some form of recompense for those who had served their nation well.[64] In the Easter vacation and summer term the University even accepted seventy American servicemen![65] Across Britain, 21 084 men received awards. Ex-service grants were 'weighted towards science and technology' because of the widespread concern to put an end to the dearth of chemists and other scientists that had been demonstrated by the First World War. However, the subjects that they were advised to read changed according to the assessment of the needs of the labour market. Chemistry was the 'in' subject but for several years Grant Robertson advocated the importance of biology, adding engineering in 1923![66] It is uncertain how many of these ex-servicemen entered the University of Birmingham, but 'within a few weeks of the Armistice, the University began to be flooded with demobilised servicemen'.[67]

In the event, the post-war expansion was short-lived.[68] The University reached a maximum in 1920–1 with 1822 full-time students, effectively 75% more than in 1913–14. Thereafter the student population began to fall and by 1926–7 was down to 1537. Overall numbers picked up towards the end of the decade, but the University was now beginning to admit part-timers and, although a peak of 1970 students was reached in 1931–2, only 1531 were full-time. Numbers remained of that order until the mid-1930s but 1936–7 and 1937–8 saw a decline set in which reduced numbers to 1404 full- and 354 part-time. Even given a slight improvement in full-timers thereafter, in the final year of peace the total was still only 1795, 1472 full- and 323 part-time.

The hopes of post-war Britain ensured that the faculty to benefit most after 1919 was Science, where registrations more than doubled those in Arts. The strain of post-war demand was felt particularly by chemistry, where G. T. Morgan had just taken over the chair from Professor Frankland. The pressure is well caught in F. L. Devereux's recollection of being interviewed by a Morgan 'weighed down by the threat (was it 400 ex-servicemen?) of a stampede into the then "in subject". "I suppose" – this in weary anticipation of my answer – "you want to be a chemist?" "No, Sir, I'm taking physics." "What!"– and for a fleeting moment he smiled – "Congratulations, at last someone is talking sense."'[69] Very soon, however, science numbers began to slip, reflecting a fall of 20% in four years in the number of male students. In Arts, where women comprised more than half the faculty, the reverse was true.[70] Thanks to this, Arts achieved parity with Science in the late 1920s and went ahead in the early 1930s to produce a non-Science: Science ratio of around 10:7.9.[71] A higher proportion of men now took Arts than in the post-war period, presumably because students followed their inclinations rather than looked for a career. It was Grant Robertson's opinion that 'if the lad or girl leaving school has no alternative employment, he or she will enter University rather than remain unemployed at home'.[72] With the nation's economic malaise becoming increasingly deep-seated, it was no longer possible for the University or the government to hold out the promise of work to science graduates that had once seemed so certain. Grant Robertson noted that 'Applied Science and Metallurgy have been hard hit by the conditions in the Midlands', and he offered the Cassandra warning of all academics in times of retrenchment: 'Metallurgists [he could equally have said trained people generally] cannot be produced at a moment's notice like the famous rabbits from a conjuror's hat.'[73] The non-Science:Science ratio did weaken to 10:10.7 at the end of the decade but this was only partly because of some recovery in science admissions and more because of a drop in the number of men registering to read in other faculties, possibly a reflection of improving employment prospects in the world outside.

Graduate unemployment and employment difficulties remained serious throughout the inter-war period. Government endeavours to predict national and local demands of graduate labour proved to be just as unsuccessful in peacetime as they had been in war.[74] As early as 1920 the University had responded to the post-war increase in student numbers by setting up what was the country's first 'Appointment Board', and as the nation's economy deteriorated, the Board's work became even more important. Its brief was to place graduates in teaching posts, with commercial firms and in government departments, and although others followed suit, Birmingham boasted that no other university board was as 'efficiently or cheaply run'.[75] Nevertheless, as in so many other universities, the problems of placing graduates grew worse as the depression years dragged on. In 1931, 122 out of the 342 graduates, some 35% of those registered remained without employment into the following academic year.[76] The University of Birmingham's particular dilemma lay in the fact that it was substantially geared to educating graduates to serve local industry, at a time when that local industry was in a parlous economic state. Thus in mining and petroleum engineering there was work overseas, especially in the colonies, but vacancies in the UK were very few.[77]

Such was the concern about graduate employment that the University's Guild of Students conducted a survey of graduates in 1938, which was reported to the National Union of Students. In all, 211 questionnaires were returned out of some 1000 issued, and while most reported that the individual was in post, there was general dissatisfaction and a belief that the person concerned was 'misemployed'.[78] In fact, before the Guild of Students undertook its enquiry the Birmingham Appointment Board had detected a growing improvement in graduate employment, and in 1935 reported 'more flourishing conditions than had existed since 1931'. The local economy picked up, and of those graduates who found employment the following year, 1936, Birmingham provided work for nearly a third. Come 1938–9 and the approach of war, there was a shortage of engineers.[79] Far from the British nation and its industry being failed during the inter-war years by such practical, civic universities as Birmingham, it was rather the nation's industry that failed them, until, once again, they were called upon to rescue their country in war.

Despite the unhappy economic situation, the University did not forget the lesson it had learned before the war about the need to nurture its local constituency. The University–WEA Joint Committee was active and the WEA thriving, together reaching some 2000 students.[80] The importance of this work was recognised in 1930 by the creation of a new post of Director of Extramural Studies and further investment continued through the Great Depression. When Grant Robertson retired in 1937, annual expenditure had reached £3341.[81] Sir William Ashley and his fellow Fabian, Professor Muirhead, were especially active in encouraging trade union courses at the University. These began after a special meeting between 'organised labour and the University' in the Council Room of the University in 1918.[82] The next year an Industrial Certificate department was set up, with WEA support, to provide systematic instruction for students nominated by the trade unions. Attendance was two days a week for a full academic year with the University charging no fee and wages being made up by the union. The curriculum included the economics of modern industry, social philosophy, modern history, national and local government and English literature. The links created between the University and 'the democracy' through these courses demonstrated the University's 'desire to serve all classes of the community', even if the appearance of students as volunteers helping to run the city's trams during the General Strike was resented by local workers.[83] A link between the WEA, trade unionism and the League of Nations was also established at the University through classes taught by members of the Harborne League of Nations Union, including the minister of Edgbaston Congregational Church.[84] Other courses were of a more professional kind, including not only the Cadbury-sponsored course on town planning, but others for members of the Institute of Public Administration.[85]

Improving upon a pre-war, indeed a Mason College tradition, the University *conversazione* proved to be increasingly popular. With evening dress or military uniform the expected attire, the Birmingham folk who frequented such occasions were able to observe all manner of experiments in the University's different departments, from geology to the Mining Research Centre. There they not only saw the 'atmospheric booths' in which the famous J. S. Haldane carried out his investigation of mining conditions, but 'fog-piercing lamps by Lucas Ltd', automatic signalling from the Automatic Electric Co. and a photocell from General Electric, all demonstrating the University's close links with industry.[86] The University also provided other wonders of the modern age for people of the Midlands to see. In 1927 John Logie Baird came to demonstrate his invention, the television, while some seven years later the 'first reception of television in the Provinces' took place under the auspices of the University's department of electrical engineering. The pictures produced were 'fleeting and distorted'. An ironic reminder of the University's success in wartime research was the passage of the ill-fated airship R101 over the Edgbaston campus in 1920.[87] The University also continued its important pre-war work as an important conference and cultural centre, both for the Midlands and Britain as a whole. Local branches of the English, Historical and Geographical Societies met there, as did the Anglo-French Association and British–Italian League, members from Birmingham and the Black Country enjoying the wider contacts that the University and its academic staff afforded them.[88] The University also hosted meetings of the Inter-University Metallurgical Conference and the old students' association of the Royal School of Mines.[89] University representatives sat on a number of local bodies, including the Hospital Council of the City of Birmingham, and on national and international institutions such as the National Association for the Prevention of Tuberculosis and the *Académie des Sciences de Russie*.[90]

An international reputation was built up, with the University giving exhibitions both at home and abroad, while undergraduates began to make appropriate overseas visits. Thus, John Henry Turner, a junior lecturer and son of Professor Thomas Turner, gave a demonstration of non-ferrous metals at the British Empire Exhibition in Wembley in 1923 and another on the properties of tungsten to the Imperial Mineral Resources Bureau. He also presided at a Joint Mining and Metallurgical Congress, attended by the Prince of Wales. Turner was very active during his relatively short time at the University, taking some twenty metallurgical students to the unoccupied section of Germany during the Easter vacation in 1923, for visits to metal, engineering and educational institutions in Hamburg, Hanover, Brunswick, Berlin and Silesia.[91]

One of the priorities of the University at the coming of peace was to maintain the impetus in scientific research which had been built up during the war. As we have seen, in 1917 the University of Birmingham had, in common with many other British universities, established the Ph.D. as a postgraduate research degree.[92] In 1921–2 came an equally important development as Grant Robertson, the new principal, explained:

> Our university today is keenly interested in research and is struggling under very discouraging circumstances to prosecute it. The problem of a comprehensive and coherent *policy* [*sic*] has been much discussed during the last twelve months; with the result that the Senate has under consideration for submission to the Council, a proposal to establish a Standing Joint Committee (of Senate and Council) of Research, the functions of which will be to frame a policy, co-ordinate the activities of all the Faculties, keep in close touch with outside organisations, industrial and governmental, engaged in promoting and financing research, and advise the Council as to the best disposition of funds as may be available.[93]

The Joint Committee of Research, which began work in 1922, was described as a 'wise step, which is likely to be imitated elsewhere' as, indeed, it was. It comprised not only academics but also interested lay people nominated by Council. Thus it neatly actualised the importance of research in the University and the duty of every university teacher to undertake original work, and at the same time silenced any lay councillors who still held the vulgar notion that 'research' was 'private' or some sort of optional extra to the real business of teaching. As well as producing an annual report on research activities, the academics and non-academics on the Committee collaborated to direct staff towards outside grant aid, to award small research grants directly and generally to provide encouragement.

The notion of university research rather than individual scholarship was new, and even more so the possibility of funding, so that it is no surprise that in the first year less than half the £730 voted by Council was spent.[94] However, the amount of research in progress which the Committee uncovered was distinctly promising. Its first full report demonstrated, despite problems in collecting data, that learned publication was spread over twenty departments with chemistry well in the lead. In all 114 papers and books had been published in the year, 76 single-authored and 38 co-authored and involving 83 individuals overall. Given that in 1920, 204 full-time staff plus 12 part-time professors were coping with a huge influx of ex-service students, this achievement commands respect. Nor was it a flash in the pan. By the next year the Committee reported research in progress in every discipline in Arts and Science and in two out of three departments in Commerce (accounting was the exception).[95] Only the Medical School lagged behind, with research in only three of its eleven specialities (anatomy, physiology and medicine). Grant Robertson did note that the main problem in research was recruiting sufficiently qualified staff to assist the professors, but nevertheless in 1924–5 the Committee was able to report that this output had been maintained – 85 publications in Science, 14 in Arts, 5 in Medicine and 3 in Commerce – and throughout the inter-war years the University's research work increasingly took on a national and international flavour as the level and quality of the work carried out increased.[96]

A few years later Grant Robertson suggested, somewhat curiously, that scientific advance was beginning to run out of steam: 'Thirty years ago Arts and Medicine as branches of the higher education, seemed to be stabilised; it was Science that was in a ferment. Today, it is Science that is approximately stabilised as a university function, and Arts, Medicine and Education that are in steadily increasing ferment.'[97] The opinion clearly failed to notice that physics was about to take over from chemistry as the cutting edge of science, but the vice-chancellor was certainly on target in calling for more funds to remove the dilemma inherent in all university research work: 'Which is worse – to neglect your routine work and your students and become an F.R.S. or a F.B.A. or to neglect research and grow slowly into a degenerating mediocrity?'[98] In 1932–3 the University achieved 150 publications involving over 100 members of staff.[99] When he wrote his valedictory report in 1937 Grant Robertson could note that all the civics had copied his ideas within five years of 1921, and that some of the assessment criteria developed by the Birmingham Committee of Research had been adopted by the DSIR.

As might be expected, some research continued in areas where the University had worked to good effect during the First World War. Work on aviation and oil supply continued, including the search for a artificial substitute which Lodge had led during hostilities. Professor Burstall, along with the group of postgraduates he had collected around him during the war, carried on working on the internal combustion engine, the project being sponsored by the Cycle and Motor Cycle Manufacturers'and Traders' Union Ltd. This was in addition to continuing to finance the research fellow in motorcycle engines.[100]

Other research came about because of a 'partnership of learning and industry'. Certain of these initiatives were of immediate importance to the locality, such as the establishment of the Joint Board of Research in Mental Diseases (which was co-sponsored by the City's Asylum Committee) and the Centre for Cancer Research. The story in mining was more mixed. The Coal Owners' Association Mining Research Laboratory was transferred to the University from Doncaster in 1921 under the direction of Professor J. S. Haldane and in 1924 an Executive Board of Mining Research was set up, but despite support by mine owners the laboratory found its relevance in the Midland region declining in importance. However, the fundamental research it produced under Haldane's successor, Professor Neville Moss, was of major importance for what was then still a vital industry.[101] Moss had been born in Walsall and had begun as a mining apprentice before winning a scholarship to Birmingham and taking a first-class degree. Colliery management and war service intervened before Sir John Cadman brought him back to the University in 1920 as assistant professor in Mining, and on Cadman's retirement he became head of department in 1922. Moss's most important work was on the physiological effects of working in the high temperatures experienced in deep mining. The apparatus used was an exercise bicycle which Moss rode inside a specially built heat chamber. He also foresaw the importance of the treatment of coal and established an ore-dressing laboratory in 1931. Moss became one of the recognised authorities on the industry, as Cadman had been, and when war broke out in 1939 he was immediately recruited for the war effort – as we shall see, he knew Neville Chamberlain personally.[102]

Locally sponsored research was, however, not all directed to the practical concerns of medicine or industry. Cadbury Brothers funded a research fellow in the faculty of Commerce to investigate 'the history of the last sixty years of Birmingham industry'. This resulted in the publication in 1929 of C. G. Allen's famous book, *The Industrial Development of Birmingham and the Black Country*.[103] This seminal essay in economic history was an exception in Birmingham's failure otherwise to go along with many of Britain's other provincial universities during this unfortunate era in the nation's economy in producing in-depth studies of contemporary economic and social conditions. Work in this area had to wait until the Second World War.

The inter-war years saw the consolidation of important research schools at the University. Cadman's contacts with the oil industry directed significant funding to a new oil engineering and refining building which he returned to open in 1926. An impressive facility, this was located next to the power station with three full-scale oil rigs on an adjacent site further west. At the opening, the operation of the rigs was demonstrated by students wearing their best suits![104] Oil (later chemical) engineering would eventually become the largest of the engineering departments. Even more notable was the development in chemistry. This was given a significant boost with the transfer of two of the DSIR's wartime research centres to Birmingham under the immediate post-war professor of chemistry, G. T. Morgan. W. N. Haworth took over in 1925 and in the early 1930s began planning to reconstruct the department. Thanks to a gift by A. E. Hills, a local manufacturer, it became possible to fund a completely new building, opened in 1937, with other local industries paying for new and additional equipment. In his early years in the chair, Haworth's particular interest was in the study of carbohydrates, insulin and other natural products and also in bacteria and immunisation. Later the department began to work with ICI on the chemical aspects of nuclear physics; in particular it was successful in producing metallic uranium. Nevertheless, Haworth's outstanding achievement was the synthesising of the first artificial vitamin, an achievement which was recognised in 1937 with the award of the Nobel prize for Chemistry for 'researches into the constitution of carbohydrates and Vitamin C'.[105] It gave Grant Robertson considerable pleasure to point out that Haworth had been one of the most regular applicants for funds from the Committee of Research![106] Previously the nearest the University had come to a Nobel award was when one of its graduates, F. W. Aston, took the Chemistry prize for his spectrographic identification of non-radioactive isotopes when working at Trinity College, Cambridge with Poynting's close friend, J. J. Thomson.[107]

The physics department took longer to 'take off'.[108] Poynting, who had enjoyed a considerable reputation, died in 1914 and the University committed the grave mistake of leaving the chair vacant for the duration. Gilbert Shakespear was put in charge and under him physics made a useful contribution to the University's war effort, but in the early twentieth century, a department was its professor. In 1919 S. W. J. Smith was elected to the chair of physics, bringing with him a principal interest in the magnetic properties of metallic meteorites and a considerable reputation at Imperial College, London. Smith, however, was not happy, and the department effectively split between the professor and those working with him on magnetism and those with Shakespear continuing the wartime interest in the physics of gases. Nevertheless, the department produced good work and good people, one of them Arthur Vick, later the Director of the Atomic Energy Research Establishment (AERE) at Harwell and vice-chancellor at Belfast. One of the projects he helped with was research into the upper atmosphere using wartime sound-ranging equipment, and taking advantage of artillery tests at Shoeburyness or the salutes fired when the king reviewed the fleet in the Solent.

In 1937 Smith retired early and the University decided on drastic action to re-establish the reputation of its physics department. Nuclear studies had now become the cutting edge of the discipline and the Mecca was the Cavendish Laboratory at Cambridge where Rutherford had split the atom in 1918. The Council therefore decided to go to Cambridge for a name and to spend what was necessary to bring nuclear physics to Birmingham in a big way. The individual targeted to lead this was Marcus (Mark) Oliphant, one of the most brilliant of Lord Rutherford's colleagues, an Australian who, with the team he assembled at Birmingham, would play the key part in Birmingham's contribution to the Second World War. Oliphant was eventually persuaded to leave the Cavendish by a salary of £1300 a year, a grant of £1500 to £2000 for his own research, plus an increase in the annual departmental grant to £1000 and the service of a part-time technician.[109] His memory of what he found was not complimentary: 'When I joined the University of Birmingham in 1937, the department of Physics was housed in the original Poynting Building and in some wooden huts. With the exception of an 'L' shaped laboratory set aside for the professor's use, a roomy but cluttered basement and a small ... cloakroom, there was no space whatever which could be used exclusively for research purposes.'[110] Nevertheless, a start on major nuclear research was made and parts were obtained for a nuclear accelerator which was assembled in the professorial laboratory. It achieved 300 Kv – as much as the size of the room allowed – but the approach of war meant that it was never fully developed. Lord Nuffield, meanwhile, came up with a gift of £60,000 for a physics building and the appointment of a Nuffield fellow, but the cyclotron was not completed until after the war.[111]

Underlying the increasingly impressive progress in research during these inter-war years was the success of the University in bringing to Birmingham a nucleus of staff members who were of, or would achieve, international standing. As well as Haworth and Oliphant there was Moon, who in 1935 had demonstrated the 'thermalisation' of neutrons. He was appointed to Birmingham in 1938 and would succeed Oliphant as head of the physics department in 1950. The future Lord Zuckerman was appointed to the chair of anatomy in 1938. Then there were two brilliant scholars from Europe, Rudolf Peierls and Otto Frisch. Peierls was a mathematical physicist of wide experience in Germany and later at Manchester and Cambridge. Birmingham appointed him in 1937 to a newly created chair in applied mathematics and his contribution to the work of Oliphant and his experimentalists turned out to be vital. His friend Frisch (who coined the term 'nuclear fission') was working in Denmark in 1939 with Niels Bohr, one of the leading physicists of the day, but came to Britain that summer and stayed on. He joined Oliphant's team and initially lodged with Peierls.

Frisch was not the only refugee from Nazism assisted by the University and the City of Birmingham. Birmingham was slower off the mark and not as active as other higher education centres such as the Warburg Institute at the University of London, but nonetheless it played an important international role in the rescue of refugee students and academics. The Academic Assistance Council (AAS), later known as the Society for the Protection of Science and Learning, was established nationally in 1933 to assist those whose livelihoods and lives were threatened by the advance of fascism on the Continent and Japanese imperialism in the East to escape and, after their arrival in Britain, to find academic employment and support.[112] Eric (E. R.) Dodds, the Irish professor of Greek at the University and a prominent figure in the Association of University Teachers (AUT), started to raise funds for a local AAS branch in 1935, initially to little avail: 'a strong committee (of the University's academics and city notables), has been scraping every penny out of the pockets of citizens here', he reported in May 1935. A public meeting was held at Edmund Street in October 1935 with the hope of emulating fundraising efforts at the universities of Manchester, Leeds, Newcastle and Cardiff. In addition to this, by November 1938, pressure from the AUT, notably those academics at non-professorial level, secured an end to the rule that all those employed in the universities should be naturalised British citizens, thus providing immediate openings for refugee scholars. With this, the Birmingham branch of the AAS was able to support a handful of German and Austrian academics who were already in Birmingham.[113] Others who had managed to escape to Britain found both temporary and permanent academic homes in the University. As well as Frisch, these included Nikolaus Pevsner, the future architectural historian who became temporary researcher in applied art in the faculty of Commerce.[114]

Notes

1 UC 3/vii/8: Collier to Ashley, 18 Oct. 1919.

2 UC 4/iv/7, 8 Mar. 1919.

3 UC 7/ii *Council* 1923, p. 3.

4 In 1922 Grant Robertson and the secretary had a long interview with Sir Howard Frank, chairman of the Disposals Board, representing the War Office. The following year the same report records the 'intolerable procrastination of the War Office'. However, by part-way through 1923, most of the money had been paid. Ibid., 1922–3, p. 14; 1923–4, p. 19.

5 See D. Aldcroft, *The Interwar Economy: Britain 1918–39* (1970), ch. 3.

6 There were 25 000 men employed in the South Staffordshire and Worcestershire coalfields in 1860 but by 1926 this had dropped to 6500: Gill and Briggs, *Birmingham*, ii.282.

7 Aldcroft, *Interwar Economy*, p. 78 presents regional trends in unemployment as indices of the number of insured persons in employment. Starting with a base of 100 in June 1922, for the Midlands the index rose to 111 in 1929, fell to a level of 101 in 1932 and then increased again to 132 by 1937. In contrast, the index for Wales, the worst-hit region, fell to 85 in 1929, to 69 in 1932 and in 1937 had only recovered to 86. Infant mortality rates in Birmingham in 1933 reveal huge differences between the central wards and those near the middle and outer suburbs: John Stevenson and Chris Cook, *Britain in the Depression: Society and Politics, 1929–39* (1994), p. 51.

8 Dennis Smith, 'Getting On, Just Getting By: Changing Prospects in South Birmingham', in Philip Cooke, ed., *Localities* (1988), pp. 235–66. Even by 1918, the Austin Longbridge plant employed four times as many as it had done in its pre-war days: Gill and Briggs, *Birmingham*, i. 288; M. Millar and R. A. Church, 'Motor Manufacturing', in Neil K. Buxton and Derek H. Aldcroft, eds., *British Industry Between the Wars: Instability and Industrial Development 1919–1939* (1979), pp. 179–215.

9 Buxton and Aldcroft, eds., *British Industry Between the Wars*, pp. 283–8.

10 Ibid, p. 286.

11 See above, p. 185.

12 Berdahl, *British Universities*, p. 47.

13 UC 7/iii 1917–18, p. 4.

14 UC 14/ii: OL178b. At the meeting between the vice-chancellors and principals, the Board of Education and the Chancellor of the Exchequer in November 1918,

Fisher said that this report had been made some 2½ years before.

15 Ibid.: OL176, letter to the Principals and Vice–Chancellors of the Universities and University Colleges, 26 July, 1918; 7/iii 1918–19, p. 9.

16 UC 7/iii 1918–19, p. 9; Berdahl, *British Universities*, p. 54; C. Shinn, *Paying the Piper: The Development of the University Grants Committee, 1919–1946* (1986), p. 39.

17 Shinn, *Paying the Piper*, pp. 33–4.

18 UC 14/ii: OL178b.

19 See Berdahl, *British Universities*, p. 59.

20 For this and the following paragraphs see UGC, *Returns, passim*. These figures differ marginally from those quoted elsewhere from the university accounts because of what is or is not counted as government grant, particularly payments via the Board of Education.

21 State support was higher for Scotland and Wales.

22 Details of the meeting on 23 Nov. 1918, quoted by Berdahl, *British Universities*, p. 58.

23 Shinn, *Paying the Piper*, p. 44.

24 UC 14/ii: OL178b, quoting from a university authority in answer to a circular letter sent round the universities asking if the present system of grants was satisfactory.

25 See above, p. 138.

26 Berdahl, *British Universities*.

27 UGC, *Returns 1920–21*, p. 30. Smethwick and Dudley. The Bournville Village Trust also contributed. Eventually West Bromwich, Wolverhampton and Shropshire also made grants.

28 *Birmingham Daily Post*, 18 Apr. 1915.

29 *Birmingham Daily Post*, 12 Nov. 1918.

30 Lodge, quoted in *Birmingham Evening Despatch*, 5 July 1919.

31 UC 7/iii 1924–25, pp. 30–2. Grant Robertson was no doubt also bearing in mind Austen Chamberlain's words when he made an appeal to the locality on the University of Birmingham's behalf. Ibid., 1923–4, pp. 25–6.

32 UC 14/ii: OL178b.

33 UC 7/iii 1919–20, pp. 7–8.

34 *The Mermaid*, 17 (Nov. 1920), p. 7.

35 Ibid., p. 31.

36 Ibid., p. 5.

37 *Birmingham Daily Despatch*, 4 Oct. 1920.

38 UC 7/iv/6/2a: 'An Appeal to Traders' (Birmingham, 1920).

39 UC 7/iv/6/4: 'Speech of the Chancellor of the Exchequer the Right Honourable Austen Chamberlain, 8 Oct. 1920'.

40 *Birmingham Daily Post*, 10 Oct. 1920 and *The Mermaid*, 17 (Nov. 1920), p. 70.

41 UC 7/iii 1923–24, p. 8.

42 *Birmingham Mail*, 4 Feb. 1921.

43 *Birmingham Daily Post*, 2 Aug. 1916 and UC 7/iii 1915–16, p. 13.

44 G. Cherry, *Urban Renewal and Town Planning: the Chamberlains in Birmingham* (Chamberlain Lecture, May 1994).

45 UC 7/iv/6/4; see n. 40.
46 37 081 and £3,020,499 in 1919–20; 50 002 and £6,712,067 in 1938–9.
47 For the following see *DNB*, *Who was Who* and *Who's Who in the Midlands*.
48 UC 7/ii *Council* 1916, p. 1; 1917, p. 2. Among those approached were Lord Plymouth and Arthur Balfour: UA Council Minutes 10, 5254, 5258, 5294.
49 UC 7/ii *Council* 1932–33, p. 2.
50 Ibid., 1923–4, pp. 5–7; 1926–27, p. 22.
51 Vincent and Hinton, *University of Birmingham*, ch. 11.
52 UC 7/iii 1928–9, p. 27.
53 For the following see *Calendars*.
54 UC 7/iii 1918–19, pp. 8–9.
55 Ibid., 1922–23, p. 7.
56 K. N. Moss, previously assistant professor, took the first chair and Professor R. Thompson, formerly director of land mining under the Colonial Office in Trinidad, the second.
57 *Birmingham Mail*, 2 June 1919; Armytage, *Civic Universities*, p. 259.
58 *Birmingham Mail*, 26 June 1926.
59 UC 14/ii/GR1: 2 Apr. 1921. One proviso made by the Chamber was that their incumbents should give evening lectures at the Birmingham and Midland Institute to those of the local business community who could not attend at the University during the day. On marriage she became Mrs De C. Richardson.
60 Vincent and Hinton, *University of Birmingham*, p. 96
61 UC 14/ii/GR2: 1922.
62 Professor L. G. Parsons, appointed 1929; UC 7/iv/7/11: H. Darbishire, 'Ernest De Selincourt, 1870–1943', *Proceedings of the British Academy*, 29 (1944).
63 UC 7/ii *Council* 1923–4, p. 9; UC 7/iii 1923–4, p. 18.
64 Sanderson, *Universities and British Industry*, p. 237; *Report of the Board of Education, 1918–19* (Cd. 722 of 1920).
65 UC 7/iii 1918–19, p. 7; cf. UC 7/ii *Vice Principal* 1918–19.
66 UC 7/iii 1920–21, p. 24; 1921–22, p. 8, 1922–23, p. 9.
67 UC 7/iii 1918–9, p. 7. See generally 7/ii *Report of the Vice Principal* 1918–19.
68 For the following see the annual statistics in UC 7/iii. See below, p.
69 Moon and Ibbs, *Physics at Birmingham 1880–1980*, p. 14.
70 Grant Robertson reported that the entry for Arts was larger than for Science for the first time in 1924: UC 7/iii 1924–5, p. 13.
71 This figure excludes medics and social studies students. Commerce and Law remained stable.
72 UC 7/iii 1931–2, p. 4.
73 Ibid., 1923–24, pp. 5, 9.
74 For further discussion of graduate employment, see below, p.
75 UC 7/iii 1927–8, p. 22.
76 UC 7/iv/3: 1931–32.
77 Ibid., 1934–5.
78 Birmingham Central Library, Local Studies Department: 'Problems of Graduate Unemployment at the University of Birmingham' (Birmingham, May 1938).
79 UC 7/iv/3: 1934–35; 1935–36; 1938–39.

80 UC 7/iv/6/11: 'Report of the future development of work of the Joint Committee to the Senate and Council of the University' (1928); 7/iv/7/5: *WEA Midland Division Souvenir*, 1905–26.
81 UC 7/iii 1928–9, p. 22; 1936–7, pp. 27–8.
82 UC 7/ii Vice–Principal 1918–19, p. 12; 7/iii 1921–2, pp. 26–7.
83 *Birmingham Post*, 4 Mar. 1920 and UC 7/v:*University of Birmingham Gazette* (1926–27), iii.9 'General Strike Special Edition'.
84 UC 14/ii GR3.
85 UC 14/ii GR2: 8 Oct. 1926.
86 UC 7/iv/6/15: Conversazione 1934, 1935.
87 UC 7/v *University of Birmingham Gazette* (1924–7). Baird visited on 28 Jan. 1927; the R101 visited in May 1929: UC14/ii GR1, 30 May 1929; *Birmingham Mail*, 4 Apr. 1934.
88 UC 7/iii 1921–22, p. 21; 1922–23, p. 29.
89 UC 14/ii GR1: 1923.
90 UC 7/iii 1924–25, p. 21.
91 UC 14/ii GR1: 15 Mar. 1923. The young Turner left the University to become Chief Chemist and Metallurgist of the London, Midland & Scottish Railway Co. in February 1930, where he was far better paid than in his university work. His letters record the fact that apart from the 'hard school of German wartime prison camp' (see Cheesewright, *Mirror to a Mermaid*, p. 78) he had gained much experience in industrial research, being the research metallurgist at the Metropolitan Vickers Trafford Park factory in Manchester, visiting works in the UK, France, Germany, Switzerland, Canada and the USA. He had also taught metallography at Charlottenburg. However, D. Hanson was made the Feeney Professor of Metallurgy in 1927.
92 See above, p. 162.
93 UC 7/iii 1919–20, pp. 9–11; 1920–21, pp. 8–10.
94 UC 7/ii *Research* 1921–2, p. 8
95 Ibid., 1922–3.
96 UC 7/iii 1921–2, p. 9; UC 7/ii *Research* 1924–5.
97 UC 7/iii 1928–9, p. 29.
98 Ibid., p. 31.
99 UC 7/ii *Research* 1932–33.
100 *Birmingham Daily Post*, 20 Apr. 1920.
101 Ex. inf. Helen Wickham, 'The Warrington Family' (unpublished, 1997), pp. 59–67.
102 See below, pp. 273–4, 298.
103 *Gazette*, 31 Oct. 1925; UC 7/iii 1924–25, pp. 18–19.
104 *Birmingham Daily Post*, 26 June 1926 and *Gazette*, 15 May 1930, which includes photographs.
105 A. Osterling *et al.*, eds., *Nobel: The Man and His Prizes* (The Nobel Foundation, Amsterdam, 1963), pp. 423–4.
106 UC 7/iii 1936–7, p. 22.
107 Osterling *et al.*, *Nobel*, pp. 275, 292, 377.
108 For the following see Moon and Ibbs, *Physics at Birmingham 1880–1980.*
109 UA Council Minutes 30, 3 June, 1 July 1936.
110 UA 22/8: 'Memoir by Mark Oliphant', p. 1.

111 For the circumstances of the Nuffield gift see below, p. 274.

112 N. Bentwich, *The Rescue and Achievement of Refugee Scholars: The Story of Displaced Scholars and Scientists, 1933–52* (The Hague, 1953).

113 UC 14/ii GR2: 17, 19 May, 12 Dec. 1935.

114 Ibid.: 19 Dec. 1938 and UA 22/7B: 21 May 1940. See also Rhodes, *Making of the Atomic Bomb*, p. 231.

Chapter Twelve

Charles Grant Robertson

DURING ITS FIRST FIFTY YEARS the University of Birmingham was led by three men: Oliver Lodge, Charles Grant Robertson and Raymond Priestley. When Lodge retired in 1919, aged sixty-eight, he left with an enhanced reputation as a physicist and the University on a solid enough basis to have survived the pressures of war. Muirhead wrote of him: 'It is difficult to conceive of any other position which would have given equal scope for the exercise of his great gifts as a physicist, a writer, a wise and conciliatory chairman of Senate and as a man of deep feeling, wide ranging mind and strong, resolute will.'[1] Strength and resolution were certainly qualities necessary in a man who had, on occasions, to stand up to Chamberlain! Lodge had also worked hard to secure acceptance of the University at national and local level and to see the place of its principal firmly established in Birmingham affairs.

Lodge has figured largely in the story so far. His replacement, Charles Grant Robertson, was a man of a quite different mould. A fifty-one-year-old historian – indeed, the only arts graduate amongst the nine men who have held the office of principal and vice-chancellor at Birmingham since the charter – Grant Robertson had spent all his academic life in Oxford and was a fellow of All Souls. The process of finding him took a good six months with half a dozen possibilities and more being considered. The post was in the gift of the Crown and Neville Chamberlain, as a Privy Councillor and one of those involved from the university side, appears to have been the prime mover.[2] The man to beat was the vice-principal, William Ashley. With an international standing, good links to government, the achievement of having raised the study of commerce to academic respectability and some backing from Lodge, Ashley had strong support within the University and in the senior echelons of government. However, he was the insider – which was a disadvantage with many of the Senate – and although Grant Robertson came very late into consideration, he was felt to have the edge.

Grant Robertson's career change from academic to administrator was less dramatic than it seems. True, he had just completed what for the next four decades would remain the major English-language biography of Bismarck, but it is clear that for some time he had been looking for a move into educational management. His sponsors rightly reported that 'he had and has exuberant energy' and he proved to be a very considerable success, nationally as well as in Birmingham.[3] He was largely responsible for organising the new Committee of Vice-Chancellors and Principals, held the chair for eight years, ended by acting as its 'unofficial head' and became the chronicler of the rise of the provincial universities.[4] Like Lodge, he also kept up his scholarship and maintained a considerable output. His themes became more general but he continually revised his *England under the Hanoverians*, which reached a tenth edition in 1930 and dominated the historical scholarship of eighteenth-century England for nearly forty years. Similarly, the sixth edition of his volume of eighteenth-century British constitutional documents appeared in 1935. Somewhat surprisingly, this aloof Scots bachelor with a Presbyterian background had also published a number of romantic novels. His great failing was prolixity; on one occasion his opening remarks when chairing a committee were timed at fifty-two minutes and were only that brief because of an interruption![5]

For the incumbencies of Grant Robertson and his successors, the university archive is less lively and informative. This is partly because, with the growth of an institution business becomes increasingly formalised, but also because much semi-official material appears to have been destroyed. It is clear, however, that the success of the immediate post-war appeal had significantly changed the agenda of the University's principal.[6] Gone are Lodge's anxieties about the drain which his salary placed on Birmingham's current account. In his report for 1928–9, the vice-chancellor wrote: 'I imagine our Treasurer sleeps more soundly today than ten years ago, and that if he suffers from Mr. Micawber's "misery" (because expenditure still does exceed income) it is the mere twinge that a healthy financial conscience ought to feel, compared with the prolonged agony that the accounts of 1920 must have caused.'[7] By 1930 income had risen by 40% to £202,607 and there was a surplus of £1999; in 1937 there was a further improvement to £232,690 and again a surplus (£1885).[8]

Instead of Lodge's nightmare of a mounting deficit, Grant Robertson's problem was the familiar one of all university executives, tight control of a budget where what was desirable and necessary always exceeded what was affordable. As he commented to Council at the end of his period in office:

> much has had to be denied, in each year, which would have strengthened the University as a place of higher learning; but to a Council that remembered the meaning of debt between 1907 and 1920, both in the short and the long run, debt has been rightly regarded as a greater impediment to development than the severest self-denial.[9]

One problem was the lamentable level of staff salaries. Immediately on the new principal's appointment, Council agreed to make an extra £5000 available and Grant Robertson signalled his intentions by an alteration in terminology. 'Junior staff' were henceforth to be 'non-professorial'.[10] Then, in 1921–2, non-professorial grades were introduced, although no awards were made at Grade I.[11] The pay of professors also received attention and in 1924 a retirement age of sixty-five was introduced.[12] In the session 1926–7 non-professorial grading became more complex with assistant lecturers, lecturers 'c', 'b' and 'a', and assistant professors/ readers, though regular promotions to the latter grade only began in 1929–30.[13] The salary bill also tended to go up because more staff were needed to handle the increasing sophistication of higher education which we have noted. Where the University had employed 176 non-professors in 1920, by 1936–7 there were 297 and, as we have seen, a dozen additional professorial chairs were created during Grant Robertson's time as well.[14]

Where Grant Robertson did face major financial difficulties was on the capital account. The immediate problem was Edmund Street. At the most basic level, having to work on two separate sites two and a half miles apart was horribly inefficient and divisive. Grant Robertson complained that this not only meant that he was based at Edmund Street and the vice-principal at Edgbaston, but that the already divided Senate would constantly argue as to where its meetings were to be held![15] Inevitably there was a tendency for 'two sub-universities to grow up with the Number 35 tram service acting as a frail and fatiguing hyphen [between them]'.[16] The Edgbaston–Edmund Street split was also more than geographical. Not only were conditions on the old Mason College site markedly inferior to those provided at other civic universities, such as Liverpool and Leeds, but departments which had to work there were very evidently second-class citizens within their own institution. Making even minor improvements at Edmund Street was extremely difficult, while the post-war bulge in student numbers continued. Grant Robertson's first report noted: 'it has become clearer with every month that our organisation, machinery and buildings (particularly at Edmund Street) were neither devised nor adapted to cope with such large numbers. "Reconstruction" has had to be planned and put in hand while the work of a congested university was being carried on.'[17] But beyond reconstruction there was, as the new principal was well aware, the prospect of 'many new chapters in the life, policy, aims and, I hope, public utility of our university'. His second report noted the inadequacy of the accommodation for Education and in 1921 the deans of Arts and Medicine submitted a report to Council highlighting the 'undesirable conditions under which some of the work of these departments is carried out, and the need for additional laboratories, lecture theatres and classrooms'.[18] All that transpired, however, was the purchase of ex-army huts to provide more laboratory space.[19] Not that Grant Robertson ignored the Arts; far from it. In his opinion the Arts Faculty required just as much special provision and equipment as did Science. For example, tutorials had recently been introduced in the Arts Faculty, but unlike Leeds and even more, Manchester, where the School of History had won a high reputation as a research centre, Birmingham had to teach its students in draughty corridors with no specially provided lecture theatres or seminar rooms.[20]

By the opening of the 1922 session the principal was moved to announce that congestion at Edmund Street had 'ceased to be important and has become urgent', with lectures in Arts and Medicine having to be repeated for lack of available lecture rooms.[21] The Council had two choices. One was cutting back on entries to courses taught at Edmund Street, in essence regression to pre-1914 numbers. The second was moving the life sciences to Edgbaston. This was the solution which, as we have seen, the University was able to achieve in 1927 following the success of its appeal. However, so long as the University was adjusting to the aftermath of the war and still arguing with the War Office over compensation for the requisition of Edgbaston, any move would, as Grant Robertson freely admitted, present severe financial problems, and the more so if the urgency was such as to require the erection of temporary accommodation which would have to be pulled down later. Nevertheless he could see no alternative. Something of what made him a real academic leader comes out in the vehemence with which he argued that the risk had to be taken for the sake of the country and for the future of the University itself. The biological sciences:

> have reached a point today at which their application to health, to agriculture, to industry, to imperial development and to education is increasing daily; but the value and contribution of 'applied' biological science will be largely determined by the advance in 'pure' biological science. Is the University of Birmingham to have its proper place and share in this development ?[22]

Vision did not, however, inspire the Council to act. It noted instead that the 'financial conditions existing in the country' made action impossible.[23]

Three years later the Council had to give in.[24] The 1924 visit of the UGC had made adverse comments on the congestion at Edmund Street, especially in zoology, botany and the arts. The financial situation also had improved. This was because, as we have seen, many donations to the 1920 appeal were specifically targeted and so had the effect of reducing demands on the general fund, and also because two donors had come forward for the life science buildings, offering a total of £46,000. In all £120,000 was required and part of the shortfall was met from the University's central funds and the rest from a sinking fund made possible because the UGC did increase the recurrent grant in 1925.[25]

With the life sciences accommodated at Edgbaston, the old Mason College site was left to Arts, Law, Education and Medicine (Commerce had moved out in 1920). That, in effect, split the problem of Edmund Street into two. The location of the faculty of Medicine could not be divorced from the complex issue of overall hospital provision for Birmingham. That would inevitably take time. However, all that stood between Arts and the others and the move to Edgbaston was a lack of the necessary finance. Grant Robertson became even more insistent on the need to provide modern facilities for the Arts as soon as possible. Student demand was healthy and there was what he described as a revival in humanistic studies which reflected improvements in secondary education and owed a lot to the enthusiasm and reputation of the Birmingham staff. The prospects for a move to Edgbaston became even stronger when, soon after Baldwin's visit, the Calthorpe family made the University its third gift of land, forty-one acres between the existing frontage on University Road and Pritchatts Road to the north.[26] This almost doubled the size of the campus and provided ample development land for the foreseeable future. Grant Robertson wrote:

> When the blessed day comes on which Mason College is transferred to Edgbaston, not merely will all our work be done in a single and united area but playing fields will be at the doors of the laboratories and lecture rooms. None of our provincial rivals will be better off in this respect than we shall be and most will not be nearly so well off – a fact which by itself secures our future as a university.[27]

In fact the University appears to have had its eye on this area prior to the Calthorpe offer. Grant Robertson raised the possibility of purchase as early as 1925 and a plan was commissioned for almost a mirror image of Aston Webb's original design for a semicircular university with its axis and grand front on University Road.[28] The design envisaged the axis again on University Road, but this time with eight radial blocks, with an entrance from Pritchatts Road and a ring road circling the whole site as well.

The Calthorpes, however, had different ideas. They suggested that the topography of the site called for a grand processional avenue, and the University was not in a position to say no, even had it wanted to.[29] A local architect, William Haywood, was engaged and he designed a walled semicircular concourse alongside Pritchatts Road, with entrance lodges and an impressive pair of wrought-iron gates executed by the Birmingham Guild of Handicraft. This led to a superb avenue of Lombardy poplars which ran 330 yards long and 50 feet wide to the Harding Library gates and so through the Chamberlain Tower to the steps of the Great Hall. Most regrettably the Central Avenue fell foul, as we shall see, to the Philistines of the 1960s and only the section in University Square facing the Harding (now the Law) Library survived. The concourse and the grand gates now lead to a car-park!

Other events encouraged the hope that a final move to Edgbaston would not long be delayed. The Labour government elected in the summer of 1929 made an additional grant to universities. A buyer was found for Edmund Street, though their identity is not known.[30] Agreement was also reached to launch a public appeal for a new Hospital and Medical School at Edgbaston.[31] All the while, however, the international economic situation was worsening. The buyer for Edmund Street dropped out and in October 1929 the Wall Street Crash sent a shiver through the banking world. How serious the economic setback would be was not realised immediately. Preparations went ahead for Lady Calthorpe to open the Central Avenue and in February 1930 the Senate considered plans which William Haywood presented for buildings on the rest of the new Calthorpe land. He proposed to flank the Central Avenue with rectangular blocks, not dissimilar in ground plan to the original Mason College but with wings resting to the south on University Road and extending in the north towards the ceremonial gates.[32] Senate approved and identified accommodation for Arts, Law and Education, a new library and an administrative block. It was agreed that the remainder of the forty-one acres should be reserved for academic development (but not in science) and for student residences and for sporting and other amenities. Senate therefore urged the University (that is, the Council) to 'concentrate on disposing of Mason College and the adjoining property of the University as soon as possible, and on the transfer of the departments of the University now situated in Mason College to the Edgbaston site … and that the sooner that arrangements for this transfer can be made the better will the interests of the University be served'.[33]

However, the Depression did not turn out to be short-lived as expected. Far from it: matters got worse and it was not until 1937 that with a buyer for Edmund Street once again on the scene and the contract for the new Medical School signed, Grant Robertson was able to signal that although he was retiring, the move to Edgbaston had become a real possibility once more: 'One imminent change, which I trust is at hand, the transfer of Edmund Street to Edgbaston, I hoped might come in my time.'[34] Still it was not to be. The international situation turned black and although the medics were able to begin planning to move to Edgbaston in the summer of 1938 the buyer for Edmund Street vanished. In May 1938 the registrar wrote to heads of the remaining departments effectively telling them to give up hope:

> It will be remembered that at the recent meeting of the Faculty of Arts it was reported that the negotiations for the sale of the Edmund Street site had fallen through and that it would be necessary for the Faculty to remain at Edmund Street for a further period, and that, in view of this fact, some arrangements should be made for the redistribution of the accommodation rendered vacant by the removal of the Medical Faculty to Edgbaston.
>
> Although some review of accommodation was made a year ago, it was felt that at this stage it would be more useful if Heads of Departments would make a specific case of any extension of accommodation which they desire, bearing in mind that suggestions should involve the barest mini-

> mum of structural alteration. I was therefore asked by the Faculty to invite Heads of Departments to forward to me, as early as possible, any such suggestions on the understanding that nothing should be done which is likely to prolong the stay of the Faculty at Edmund Street.[35]

The exile of the faculty of Arts still had twenty-two years to run.

Surprisingly, the part of the Edmund Street problem which Grant Robertson did succeed in solving was the one which had seemed the more intractable, what to do about the faculty of Medicine. This was the greatest single achievement of his vice-chancellorship. The transfer of science to the Edgbaston site in the early 1900s had released much-needed space for the medics at Edmund Street, in particular for forensic medicine, public health and pharmacology. However, as we have seen, the move created academic nonsense by requiring either the separation of pre-clinical medical students from the science departments which taught them or else from their seniors in the medical curriculum.[36] If Medicine had been in the same position as the Arts the obvious solution would again have been to move the faculty to Edgbaston as soon as possible. But that was not the case. Much of the teaching of clinical students took place in hospital wards, which meant that where medical students should be taught was inextricable from the wider issue of hospital provision for Birmingham. Existing clinical teaching for the Birmingham Medical School took place at two long established multidisciplinary hospitals in the city – the General and the Queen's – both within walking distance of the Medical School at Edmund Street. Moving clinical students to Edgbaston, three miles away, was clearly impractical, and still more so moving the clinicians who taught them in the hospitals, all of whom had been given honorary university contracts in 1910.

Nor was the only immediate consideration teaching access to hospital beds.[37] Both hospitals were, by the end of the First World War, in desperate need of new investment. Not that either building was old, but medical advances, for example in the use of X-rays and even more new techniques in surgery, meant that space for additional facilities was becoming vital. Demand for treatment was on the increase as well. Once the needed modernisation and expansion took place on the existing sites the transfer of the Medical School to Edgbaston could never take place. Neither hospital, however, showed any sign of wanting to move. The General and Queen's were both voluntary hospitals, that is, trusts with an independent board of governors, each with a proud tradition of funding medicine by public philanthropy and with long-standing historic rivalries. Patients, not students, were their priority. In 1922 the General set about securing an addition to its site while Queen's began building wards for another 100 patients with ancillary facilities to follow and both considered making public appeals for the necessary capital.

The salvation for the University was that neither hospital was an entirely free agent. After the First World War they, like other voluntary hospitals, had become eligible for government grants, but that was on condition that any proposal to increase beds or make a public appeal had first to be cleared by a committee advising on all the hospitals in a locality. In the case of Birmingham these included not only the General and the Queen's but the municipal hospitals (Dudley Road and Selly Oak) and some ten smaller specialised institutions. When the extension scheme for the General Hospital was put to the Hospital Council for the City of Birmingham in 1922 it did receive support, but not without a dissenting voice. Alderman W. A. Cadbury proposed that the General and the Queen's should agree to concentrate all new developments on a new joint site in the suburbs which would be large enough for many of the specialised hospitals eventually also to concentrate there. Such collaboration would clearly be much cheaper than separate development – but in 1922 the notion was dismissed as a counsel of perfection which would mean building up one new hospital while continuing to run the two existing sites in a state of gentle decline.

The idea that something more radical was needed than parallel development had, nevertheless, been sown. In July 1924 the City Council expressed considerable doubt about the expansion plans of the central hospitals, and when they came back to the Hospitals Council in 1925 opinion had hardened still further.[38] It was agreed to put development on hold 'until a full enquiry has been made through the Ministry of Health and other available sources as to the comparative cost and efficiency of general hospital extension in open suburban areas as compared with the extension on central sites'.[39] Given the planning which had taken place, the money already spent by both hospitals and the dire clinical need, this decision was greeted with fury, but when tempers had cooled the two hospitals accepted an invitation from the Hospitals Council to begin discussions on a possible Hospitals Centre. It was to be near to the University and increase the number of general hospital beds in the city to 2400 as at 1931. By the wish of each hospital, Charles Grant Robertson was elected chairman.

After a series of meetings over a period of six months, the Grant Robertson Committee reported in the autumn of 1926 much on the lines Cadbury had suggested. It proposed that the General and the Queen's should amalgamate and together set up a new Medical School Hospital adjacent to the University. As a specifically teaching institution, the Hospitals Centre, as it became known, would need to provide, in addition to medicine and surgery, all the major medical specialities until such time as the specialist hospitals could be rebuilt nearby. Each department would need to be of an efficient size and this meant that the new building would have to have a minimum of 750 beds. These, together with the existing provision in the city centre, would give the board of the amalgamated hospitals not less than 1200 beds overall, which matched calculations of the bed shortage in the city.

The Committee's report was broadly endorsed by the Hospitals Council and welcomed by the press, but there was widespread scepticism that £750,000 for the new Hospital plus £250,000 for a Medical School would ever be forthcoming. There were also objections to the size proposed. Would it not be better to start on a scale of 300 beds and add as required? – an argument which overlooked the need to provide adequate support facilities and laboratories, not merely ward space. In any case, was a large hospital what was wanted? Building two 300-bed hospitals in different parts of the city would make access easier for patients and visitors, and they would be small enough to be friendly and generate local support. As for the future of the General and the Queen's, *amour propre* disguised as financial scepticism ensured that neither was yet ready to amalgamate; indeed, many suspected that a new hospital at Edgbaston was an excuse to downgrade the older institutions. Anyone who has followed the later National Health Service debates on hospital provision for Birmingham will find these arguments all too depressingly familiar.

Progress towards a Hospitals Centre did go on. Alderman Cadbury funded visits to hospitals on the Continent and in America and even more important, at

the end of 1926, Cadbury Bros bought and gave the city 100 acres of land for hospitals, across the Worcester Canal from the University's Edgbaston site. A year later an Executive Board was set up to plan the new Centre and Grant Robertson was once again made chairman. The medics involved drew up a careful brief of the requirements of a modern hospital while the faculty specified what a Medical School would need and after a joint architectural competition, T. A. Lodge of Lanchester & Lodge was appointed to design the complex. But despite this, obstacles meant that the overall pace of progress was depressingly slow. The Ministry of Transport had a plan to run an arterial road through the Metchley site to feed traffic on to University Road. Only a threat by the University to demand reinstatement elsewhere defeated that, although at the price of opening University Road to general traffic. The two city-centre hospitals were unwilling to commit themselves to a corporate amalgamation in advance of building, and this created severe legal difficulties.

As for the University, it had to be very cautious in advancing its own academic interests in the scheme. The confidential objective of Grant Robertson and the more scientifically aware clinicians such as Stanley Barnes, the principal physician at the General and later dean of the faculty, was a University Hospital linked to the Medical School which would thus be able to promote science-based medicine by focusing on research. As Grant Robertson wrote frankly in 1928, 'Although we can't say so yet in public, this will I hope really be a University Hospital, in which the Medical Faculty of the University would have a preponderant share.'[40] The problem was that not all clinical teachers shared an agenda which would require the faculty raising its academic performance to equal that of science. As we have seen, professorial chairs in the Medical School were effectively honorary and few holders were active researchers. Grant Robertson, however, was looking forward to a time when they would be full-time posts with obligations which were standard elsewhere in the University. Another complication was that the vice-chancellor and others were also committed to the voluntary principle and saw medicine funded from the rates or taxes as anathema. This meant that the proposed new hospital could only be funded by a public appeal, but would the public accept that the interests of the Medical School should have priority over patients? What is more, any expression by the University of its wish to promote medical research could be – and was – represented as 'wanting to experiment on patients'. To make matters even more difficult, the state-of-the-art teaching hospital which Robertson and Barnes were manoeuvring towards was significantly more expensive than a normal acute hospital.

It was, thus, not until the spring of 1930 that a public appeal for funds could be launched, to be split 5:1 between the Hospitals Centre and the Medical Faculty building. The new Labour government gave it full support, along with the Conservative opposition represented by Neville Chamberlain. The result of the appeal was dramatic. In two months nearly half a million pounds were raised. Again the pattern of giving is interesting and, like the University appeal, shows both the continuity of and the changes in charitable giving in Birmingham.[41] Up to 1939 there were almost 2000 donations in all, 1600 of which were between sixpence and £49, a good number of them representing work place collections. Although companies made up over 40% of donors over £10 (including a good representation from the retail sector as well as the more traditional trades), fewer than 100 gave as much as £100. Names as famous as British Thomson Houston and Elkington's came up with only £25 and Shell-Mex BP with ten guineas. Where the difference came was with a handful of very large gifts; nearly £1 million came from thirty-six donations of £5000 and over, at least half from individuals. Sir Charles Hyde gave £30,000 and A. E. Hills £25,000. The wealth of the motor industry was to the fore. Lord Nuffield gave £198,000, the Austin Motor Co. £21,000 and Lord Austin £5000, Joseph Lucas and Sir Peter Bennett, £12,000 and £10,385. Cadbury interests were outstanding, adding £168,000 on top of the gift of the Metchley site.

With the rapid response to the appeal – by December 1931 the figure, despite the advent of the Great Depression, would reach £625,000 – all seemed to be set fair at last. Not so. Thanks to the months and months of scant progress, divisions had begun to appear at both the General and the Queen's. On the one side were those concentrating on promoting the Hospitals Centre and on the other those trying to keep existing hospital provision running in the face of financial pressure and deteriorating facilities. Then there was financial competition, even jealousy. What could the General and Queen's not do with the £600,000 allocated to the Hospitals Centre? After the 1925 moratorium the General had managed to erect a temporary casualty block, but the Queen's had been left with its extra beds and no provision to staff or service them properly. In any case, the Grant Robertson report was now five years out of date. Nearly 900 beds had been provided in the interval so there was now no shortage to justify the proposed Centre. In part to placate these critics the proposed number of beds at Edgbaston was trimmed from 750 beds to 500, but on 5 November 1931 the Board of the General Hospital formally called for the Hospitals Centre scheme to be postponed. There followed letters in the *Birmingham Post* from both hospitals supporting postponement on the ground that the scheme was too large and too expensive and was destructive of older institutions. The *Post* was owned by Sir Charles Hyde, who was President of the Queen's Hospital, and on the morning of 26 November a leading article appeared, hostile to the Edgbaston proposal. Hyde's other paper, the *Birmingham Mail*, also joined in.

One factor which it is impossible to overlook in this crisis was the existence of personal tension between those involved. Hyde was the most generous of the University's benefactors but he found it hard to take seriously a vice-chancellor 'intoxicated with the exuberance of his own verbosity'.[42] A story circulated that when Hyde gave the University £100,000 without conditions, Grant Robertson said: 'Sir Charles, your generosity leaves me speechless' and Hyde replied, 'A miracle.' Hyde's doubts about Grant Robertson were particularly vigorous when the issue was hospital policy in which Hyde had been involved for a long time. Given the ability of Hyde's papers to influence Birmingham opinion, this poor relationship with Grant Robertson was particularly dangerous.

There was also lack of confidence between Robertson and another key figure, Sir Gilbert Barling. Barling was in many ways a dinosaur. He had enjoyed a brilliant medical career and was enormously experienced. After qualifying in 1879, he been a surgeon at the General Hospital and was substantially responsible for the building of its new premises in Steelhouse Lane in 1897. He had from 1886 been professor of pathology at Queen's College and with the link with Mason College he became joint professor of surgery. Under Windle, Barling was sub-dean of the faculty and deeply involved in the struggle for the charter and he succeeded as dean in 1904. In 1912 he retired and in 1913 gave up his chair. However, instead of allowing Barling an active retirement as one of the great and good (he was only fifty-eight) the University Council appointed him vice- (later pro-)chancellor and thus the lay leader of the University (the chancellorship being first effectively and then actually vacant following the illness and death of Chamberlain). His relations with Lodge appear to have been satisfactory, but one can imagine the problems which a person with Barling's experience, prestige and authority must have presented when Grant Robertson arrived as principal. By 1931 Barling was seventy-six years old, and matters were even more difficult because he was now wearing a second hat as Chairman of the Birmingham Hospitals Council. With this weight of opinion building up on the side of the dubious or the downright hostile, it was fortunate that the Executive Board of the Hospitals Centre itself had acquired an important new supporter, Harry (later Sir Harry) Vincent, a member of the board of the Children's Hospital who took over as the

Centre's honorary treasurer in 1930. Starting from scratch, Vincent had made a fortune in the manufacture of toffee and he was able to give a cool quarter of a million pounds to the Hospitals Centre appeal, but more than that, he was a businessman's businessman. When the dust had settled, both sides would agree that it was Vincent's influence which made all the difference in the search for an acceptable resolution.

On the day that the hostile editorial appeared in the *Post,* the Executive Board of the Hospitals Centre met and picked up the gauntlet. It voted to commence building as soon as possible a first stage comprising a 500-bed hospital, 'together with the re-organised Medical School of the University which is a necessary and integral part of the Scheme'.[43] It also challenged the boards of the General and the Queen's and Gilbert Barling to join in discussions on the present and future relation of the two hospitals to the scheme and to the University, and on their position once the first instalment of the Centre was complete. The Board also instructed Grant Robertson to issue a fighting response to the critics. This appeared in the *Post* on 3 December and was followed the next day by a two-column letter of support from Barnes and doctors and surgeons at the General, the Queen's and the Children's Hospitals who backed the Centre. Despite this most of the subsequent correspondence in the Birmingham press remained hostile, even though a statement by the Board on 21 December pointed out squarely that the real issue at stake was the health strategy of the city: 'The real problem is the co-ordination of hospitals, medical school and the health services of the city as a whole. The Centre alone can achieve this.'[44]

By then, however, the Centre was definitely on the defensive. On 12 December the Medical Officer of Health had informed the *Post* that the provision for hospital services had indeed changed since the Grant Robertson Report and beds were no longer needed. The same issue included a letter from Neville Chamberlain, the embattled Chancellor of the Exchequer, stressing the national need for economy and sacrifice and suggesting that those who had contributed to the appeal should be consulted on what to do. That raised the possibility that all the moneys raised by the appeal would have to be returned, but some kind of meeting with the subscribers could clearly not now be avoided. It is, however, probable that it was at this point that Vincent said to Barnes: 'If you will stand by me on the technical side, rather than see this scheme blown sky high, I will put up all the money necessary to build a 250 bed hospital, whatever anyone else may say.'[45] The large hall of the Midland Institute was chosen for the meeting – it would hold 600 people – to be held on 4 January 1932, with the lord mayor in the chair.

In the event the consultation resolved nothing. Public interest made it necessary to restrict admission by ticket, but the consequence was that it was impossible to say who the meeting represented. Many felt that the issue was effectively pre-empted by the opening announcement of the lord mayor that some of the larger subscribers would not allow their donations to be diverted from the Centre and by the vice-chancellor reading out a legal opinion to the effect that in the event of a change in objectives, the only possible course was to return all contributions to date. Barling then came out publicly to propose the continued support of the Centre, with Vincent seconding and making the good point that such a large project would do a significant amount to relieve unemployment among the city's building workers. All this very clearly put the opposition on the back foot, but it replied with an amendment proposing postponement. Led by the powerful figure of Lord Austin and supported by the chairmen of both the General and the Queen's, it effectively put the issue in the bluntest terms – funding for the Centre or funding to keep the existing institutions functioning. In the debate which followed figures were bandied about in a highly confusing manner. Neither side gained the ascendancy and although Grant Robertson was given the last word on behalf of the Executive Board and the amendment was defeated, 214 people voted for postponement against 256 for the scheme. The Hospitals Centre had survived by a mere 42 votes.

The Hospitals Centre executive clearly could not go ahead on such a result and to break the deadlock the lord mayor was invited to call a conference to examine the whole question, especially the issue of recurrent funding. Representatives from the General, the Queen's and the Hospitals Centre Executive met with supposedly independent members and their report advocated a start to building on 1 January 1933. Although several of the 'independents' appear to have been active supporters of the Hospitals Centre, the verdict of the lord mayor's conference was accepted by both the existing hospitals, the University confirmed that the Medical School would move as part of the scheme and the campaign of press opposition faded. The start of building at last persuaded the boards of the General and the Queen's to promote an act of Parliament amalgamating the two as 'the United Hospitals', with Sir Charles Hyde becoming President.

Work on the hospital part of the complex was advanced enough for the Prince of Wales to lay the foundation stone in October 1934 and to cut the first sod on the Medical School site.[46] Building there quickly caught up with its more complicated neighbour and the Faculty was able to transfer from Edmund Street in the summer of 1938. The cost of building and equipping the new School was some £242,000, against which the University could set its share of the appeal moneys, a net figure of £118,000. The standard of building was high and was enhanced by a Dean's Room and Faculty Board Room splendidly panelled at Stanley Barnes's expense. Two features in particular attracted much contemporary comment – the dissecting room, which was named to commemorate the work of Bertram Windle, and the 200-foot-long Chamberlain Medical Museum. The School was opened in July 1938 by the duke of Gloucester, deputising for the king, who was ill, but George VI and Queen Elizabeth did come in the following March, when the queen named the now-opened hospital the 'Queen Elizabeth'. By then Barnes had achieved a further rationalisation. As we have seen, the failure to complete the 1925 expansion had left the Queen's significantly under-provided with specialist and support facilities and it was obvious that it was now the weakest of the three units. In October 1937 Barnes persuaded Hyde not to mobilise the *Post* and the *Mail* in defence of the Queen's but to allow it to become a specialist hospital. A committee was set up and as a result the Queen's was adapted as an accident hospital.

Grant Robertson continued as chairman of the executive board of the Birmingham Hospitals Centre for several years after his retirement as vice-chancellor. This took place in the summer of 1938 and he took the opportunity of his last report to survey his eighteen years of office. Among achievements to which he gave prominence was another foundation, the setting up of the Barber Institute of Fine Arts. The benefactor here was the widow of the Sir Henry Barber who had endowed the Barber chair of law in 1923. Sir Henry, who had been a Birmingham solicitor-turned-property developer, had amassed a fortune which was reported as approaching £1 million. From the time of his appointment, Grant Robertson had proclaimed the need for a chair and department of fine arts – 'as essential to a properly constituted University as Greek or Mathematics'.[47] He became friends with the childless Lady Barber and on the death of Sir Henry in 1927 she consulted him and Gilbert Barling on how to bestow her wealth.[48]

Lady Barber claimed that her husband had entertained some idea of passing his own collection to the University but in reality she was the cultured one, keenly interested in *objets d'art* and with some amateur talent as an artist and musician. Over a number of visits to Culham Court, her house in Henley-on-Thames, Grant Robertson and to a lesser extent Barling worked out plans for a trust. In December 1932 she made an initial conveyance to the University of securities producing £12,000 a year. Some was to go to the faculty of Law, and the next tranche to building an institute of fine arts with a concert hall and picture galleries, endowing the necessary appointments in fine arts and music and to providing musical recitals. The bulk of the endowment, however, was for the purchase of high-quality pictures and *objets d'art* that would be augmented on her death by the best items from Culham Court.

Lady Barber died in the following February, having made the vice-chancellor an executor and one of three life trustees of the Institute. This involved him in the detailed implementation of Lady Barber's wishes, which he interpreted with some strictness. One suspects that he was somewhat under her spell. Thus Grant Robertson insisted that the concert hall should be smaller in size than proposed because 'music is quite subsidiary to the arts in the founder's scheme' and 'the Institute is not to be, in any sense, a place of public entertainment'.[49] More damaging was the trustees' decision to reflect Lady Barber's dislike of modern painting with a clause prohibiting the purchase of any items produced later than 1899. Thanks to this restriction, which was not amended until 1967, the Institute was unable to acquire twentieth-century artworks when they were still affordable.[50] It is also the case that Grant Robertson encouraged, indeed may have been responsible for the concept that the Institute was neither to be a gallery nor a school of art but a gallery within a university context, which it was assumed would spread culture by some sort of miasmic effect. The influence of the University in Barber affairs was deliberately restricted by a rule that no more than one trustee could be employed by it. From the start, too, directors of the Institute were placed in a curiously semi-detached position. They were part-curator and collector and part-university teacher, but they had neither a university department to support them or any necessary integration with the faculty of Arts.

Robert Atkinson was the architect appointed by the trustees in 1934. He was something of a collector himself, but at that stage of his career he had no experience of designing a gallery.[51] In style, both external and internal, what he produced was very definitely of its decade and not unrelated to what Atkinson was best known for, building cinemas. For the internal design and particularly the 9000 square feet of galleries Atkinson was substantially dependent on the first director who came on the payroll in March 1935. This was Thomas Bodkin, the thirty-nine-year-old Director of the National Gallery of Ireland. Bodkin's other task was creating a collection from scratch but under Lady Barber's daunting instruction that anything he bought had to be of the 'quality required by the National Gallery and the Wallace Collection'. The decade was one of low prices in the art market and several major sales and Bodkin's first purchases were made at the Oppenheimer sale of 1936: nine drawings by various artists including Fra Bartolommeo, Guardi, Rubens, Rembrandt, Tintoretto, Tiepolo and Degas. Two years later he acquired what was thought to be his prize acquisition, Cima da Conegliano's *Crucifixion*, although modern taste might argue for another purchase of that year, Poussin's *Tancred and Ermina*. By the time that the Queen Mother formally opened the Institute in July 1939, the galleries housed sixteen paintings, thirty-one watercolours and drawings, and nineteen prints, a number of sculptures, items of furniture and *objets d'art*, plus tapestries and other items from Lady Barber's old home. Many of the minor items from Culham were, however, disposed of after the Second World War. Perhaps Bodkin's most audacious achievement was saving a 1722 statue of George I from Irish republicans. Commissioned by the Dublin Corporation from the Flemish sculptor Van Nost, it was a potent symbol of the British connection and clearly in danger of following the only other surviving royal statue in Dublin, which had been blown up on the day of the coronation of George VI in May 1937. Today it graces the front of the Barber and also embellishes the main entrance to the University.[52]

Another area where Grant Robertson's influence had a lasting impact on the University was in respect of the library. When he arrived the library staff was insufficient in number and poorly qualified; cataloguing and binding were many years in arrears.[53] Grant Robertson put himself at the head of a reorganised library committee and began a ten year struggle for improvement.[54] One of his key initiatives was the appointment of an academic librarian on a professorial salary. It was a 'first' among the newer universities and as he put it, 'we stirred indeed the waters'.[55] In 1925 the UGC made a special grant to repair 'marked deficiencies' in the collection and to assist with the backlog in cataloguing and binding.[56] By 1929/30, use of the library had quadrupled as against 1920/1 and overall expenditure increased by 150%. Spending on books and periodicals rose from £700 a year to £2100.[57] Nor did improvement stop there. Despite the economic stresses of the early 1930s, total library expenditure in 1936–7 had reached almost five times the 1920 figure with the allocation for books and binding at £3645. The vice-chancellor remarked proudly that there was 'no department of our university life, in which more has been accomplished of real value and will stand, than in the library'.[58] Success, however, created an acute space problem and a desperate need for a new library. That, however, was an impossibility, given the glaring problem of the split site.

> Books cannot be torn in two, in the manner of Solomon, between rival claimants. The Metallurgist who desires to read *The Prelude* (ed. de Selincourt), or the humanist who craves illumination on the atom has to decide whether he will sacrifice his luncheon hour (and fivepence on trams) or spend eighteen shillings from his own pocket, or (most probably) drop in disgust Wordsworth or the atom.[59]

It was, perhaps, his long Oxford experience which explains another Grant Robertson concern, the material and social life of students. University House had been opened for women students in 1904 and had moved in 1908 to its present building for which the funds were largely raised by Neville Chamberlain. Oliver Lodge had urged that something similar needed to be done for the men but an early experiment, using the former Queen's College, proved a failure. In 1921, however, a property was purchased in Augustus Road and converted into 'Chancellor's Hall'. Despite a gift of £5000 from Sir Charles Hyde, £9000 of the initial cost of £20,000 was still outstanding in September 1922; Hyde, however, made a further offer of £4500 provided the other half of the deficit was covered, as it was.[60] Surprisingly, in view of the success of University House, Chancellor's Hall did not prove a commercial success and in 1929 the UGC had to make a special grant to cover its operating losses.[61]

Providing social facilities for students was not easy either. When Grant Robertson arrived at Birmingham he found student activity in a considerable confusion.[62] Mason College had had a union of sorts and in 1905 a Club House had been opened nearby in Great Charles Street. The Guild of Students provided for in the 1900 Charter had eventually been formed in 1907 but this was based at Edgbaston As well as this geographical division, the Club had to run on subscription while the Guild occupied its premises below the Great Hall *gratis*. Not that this meant that the Guild was open to all students; it only catered for those who had matriculated. A further complication was the sexual apartheid which was the order of the day; this resulted in a number of organisations for women, separate and in competition with each other. Sporting amenities were also pretty sparse, even after the Calthorpe family had donated the former rifle range beside the Bristol Road as a sports ground.

Grant Robertson's response was to set up a Standing Joint Advisory Committee for student affairs in 1921, but sorting out the confusion and persuading vested interests to compromise took a long time.[63] Not until 1929 was he able to announce that as well as Guild finances being now properly structured and managed and the women's organisations integral to its activities, the Guild was about to fuse with the Club and thereafter all student catering would come under the University.[64] Not that everything on the student scene was peaceful. It was the era of student 'laddism' where pranks which would now be dismissed as puerile easily got out of hand. In 1928 an inter-varsity debate had to be abandoned when the doors into the galleries of the Great Hall were forced, the stewards overwhelmed and, it seems, missiles thrown into the audience. The Guild was exonerated – it had done what it could to police the event – and the only action taken was to ban debates in the Great Hall.[65] At the same time the tradition of random student misbehaviour at degree ceremonies was challenged. It was agreed that 'Rags' organised by the Guild at degree ceremonies were 'not to be dismissed' but the vice-chancellor was asked 'to post notices in prominent places during the week preceding the degree ceremony, forbidding the use by students of mechanical devices for creating noises and the discharge of squibs or other fireworks, darts etc.'[66] The notices seem to have had little success. It was left to Robertson's successor as vice-chancellor to suppress such activity following the grave offence taken by Lord Nuffield at the behaviour of students when he received an honorary degree; a motor bike appears to have been introduced into the Great Hall.

A major factor in Grant Robertson's success in straightening out at least the official activities of students was undoubtedly the prospect of a building for the Guild at Edgbaston which he later and rightly described as 'none better in the country'. He had called for such a facility in 1924 in hope rather than expectation, but in November 1925 Sir Charles Hyde gave the University his unconditional gift of £100,000, but with a clear indication that some of it should be used for 'a Students' Union at Edgbaston which should include Common Rooms for men and women students, a large room for meetings, which could be divided when required, billiard, reading and writing rooms, etc.'[67] Just over half of the Hyde donation was spent on the building, which was completed in 1930, and in 1937 the nearby St Francis Hall was opened to provide the nearest thing possible to a university chapel in an institution which was so overtly secular as Birmingham.[68] In this case the money was provided by Edward Cadbury and his wife, although the architect chosen to design it was the architect of Hyde's Guild building, Holland Hobbiss.

One of Grant Robertson's qualities was that he had a vision of education which went beyond the university sector in which he was such a dominant figure. 'A live university today, conscious of its power and opportunities cannot have too many contacts with every educational, industrial and social development everywhere.'[69] Admittedly there was an element of self-interest in this. When he arrived Grant Robertson had noted that the University's reputation in science ensured that schools sent Birmingham their best students, but that this was not so in the case of the arts. It was vital therefore to 'make humanities balance in distinction'.[70] One of his earliest actions, therefore, was to visit every secondary school in the district over two and a half years, paying equal attention to those less well known and dealing with working-class children.[71] At the same time he inaugurated an annual conference to which he invited the heads of all secondary schools in the seven Midland counties which circled Birmingham along with the relevant directors of education. By 1937 the invitation list had grown to 280 with attendances of 100 to 140, and an increasing number of public school heads were beginning to attend as well.[72] He also presided over major changes in the university provision of training in education. On the retirement of Professor Alfred Hughes in 1919 the university department was reorganised with the new professor as Director (C. W. Valentine) and two subdivisions (male and female), each under a head at readership grade.[73] When in 1927 the Board of Education announced that it was to end examining for the certification of teachers, Grant Robertson promptly took the lead in setting up a Midlands Examining Board under his chairmanship to service five colleges in the region.[74] Sadly the situation in education deteriorated badly in the early 1930s when a desperate search by the government for economies in a time of depression led to the cutting of training grants by 30%.[75] Serious financial problems followed, with the Birmingham department having to run at 100 students below efficiency. However, Grant Robertson's response was to say that education was about more than money and that he saw the underused facility to train teachers coming under strong pressure in the next five years. The contrast to the circumstances and attitudes which dominate higher education today is glaring.

In the sequence of the vice-chancellors of the University of Birmingham, Grant Robertson stands out for creativity. In one sense this would have been demanded of whoever had taken office at the end of the First World War. Lodge had managed the transition from a college to an institution which could properly be described as offering higher education, in the main. Its institutions and its ethos, were, however, substantially still those of a college and it was Grant Robertson who put in place many of what are now the defining characteristics of a university. Nor was he merely applying a standard formula, still less imitating the Oxford from which he had come and to which he returned. There were few models to follow, and in many instances, Grant Robertson was ahead of his fellow vice-chancellors and set the trend. Whether we look at a career structure for staff, student life organised on residences and by a self-governing union, at the predominance of honours degrees, the priority of research, at the revolution in plant and much else, we see behind them Sir Charles's ascetic face and his vision and ability. He would have wasted twenty years of his life if he had stayed in Oxford.

Notes

1 Vincent and Hinton, *University of Birmingham*, p. 77.
2 University of Birmingham, NC5/8/2, 3–8,10–14, 16, 17, 25, 27.
3 University of Birmingham, NC5/8/2/27.
4 *DNB 1941–51*. C. Grant Robertson, *The British Universities* (1930, 2nd edn 1944).
5 S. Barnes, *The Birmingham Hospitals Centre* (Birmingham 1952), p. 107.
6 The deficiency is partly made up in the case of vice-chancellors who chose to use their Annual Reports to discuss policy. Grant Robertson, Priestley and especially Aitken are important in this respect.
7 UC 7/iii 1928–9, p. 8.
8 Ibid., 1936–7, p. 4.
9 Ibid.
10 UA Council Minutes, 27 Nov. 1919.
11 UC 7/ii *Council* 1921–2, p. 5.
12 Ibid., 1923–4, p. 8.
13 Ibid., 1925–6, p. 20; 1936–7, p. 7.
14 UC 7/iii 1936–7, p. 6; see also p. 201.
15 Ibid., 1927–8, p. 15.
16 Ibid., 1924–5, p. 20.
17 Ibid., 1919–20, p. 5.
18 Ibid., 1920–1, p. 14; 7/ii *Council* 1922, p. 7.
19 UC 7/ii 1920–1, p. 7.
20 UC 7/iii 1921–2, p. 9, 1923–4, p. 13.
21 Ibid., 1922–3, p. 14.
22 Ibid., 1920–1, p. 24.
23 UC 7/ii 1921–2, p. 17.
24 Ibid., 1923–4, p. 21.
25 Ibid., 1924–5, p. 10; 1927–8, p. 7.
26 UC 7/iii 1927–8, p. 13.
27 Vincent and Hinton, *University of Birmingham*, p. 158.
28 UC 7/ii *Council* 1925–6, p. 7; J. W. R. Whitehand, 'Institutional site planning: the University of Bimingham, England 1900-1969', *Planning History*, 13 (1991), p. 30.
29 Ibid., pp. 29–30.
30 *Birmingham Post*, 30 Sept. 1954: reminiscences of Cecil Burton, retiring university secretary.
31 Barnes, *Hospitals Centre*, p. 69.
32 Whitehand, 'Institutional site planning', p. 30.
33 UA Senate Minutes 10, minutes 7960, 7961.

34 UC 7/iii 1936–7, p. 33; UA Council Minutes 31: 7 Apr. 1937; 32: 4 Aug. 1937, 3 Nov. 1937. The offer was from Sir Lindsay Parkinson & Co. Negotiations were difficult since the city wanted 20% of the site for road-widening and the University could not give possession until December 1938. The purchaser withdrew early in 1938 because of pressure of government contract work: Council Minutes 6 Apr.1938.

35 UC 13/i/6: 16 May 1938.

36 See above p. 112.

37 The following is based on Barnes, *Hospitals Centre* and Vincent and Hinton, *University of Birmingham*, pp. 122–33.

38 UC 16/iii: 'City Council Meeting 1 Oct.1924'.

39 Barnes, *Hospitals Centre*, p. 40.

40 UC 16/iii: Grant Robertson to Barnes, 23 Sept. 1927.

41 Barnes, *Hospitals Centre* pp. 120–31: List of contributors above £10.

42 Ibid., p. 108.

43 Ibid., p. 74.

44 Barnes, *Hospitals Centre*: Memo., 21 Dec. 1931.

45 Ibid., p. 110.

46 UC 8/ii/4/1.

47 UC 7/iii 1936–7, p. 19.

48 For the following see Vincent and Hinton, *University of Birmingham*, pp. 170–4; UC 7/iii 1936–7, pp. 19–21; T. Bodkin, *The Place of Fine Arts in the University* (Birmingham 1935); H. Miles, *Art in the University* (Birmingham, 1972); Barber Institute, *Jubilee Exhibition* (Birmingham, 1983).

49 Miles, *Art in the University*, pp. 18–19.

50 H. Miles, *Handbook of the Barber Institute* (Birmingham, 1983), p. iv.

51 P. Spencer-Longhurst, *Barber Institute of Fine Art: Handbook* (Birmingham, 1993), pp. 63–4.

52 UC 8/iii/3:1 Mar. 1938.

53 Vincent and Hinton, *University of Birmingham*, p. 185.

54 UC 7/iii 1928–9, p. 16.

55 Ibid.

56 Vincent and Hinton, *University of Birmingham*, p. 185.

57 UC 7/iii 1928–9, p. 16.

58 Ibid., 1936-7, p. 15.

59 Vincent and Hinton, *University of Birmingham*, p. 186.

60 Ibid., pp. 157, 207; UC 7/iii 1920–1, p. 17; 7/ii 1921–2, p. 7.

61 UC 7/ii *Accounts* 1929–30, p. 3.

62 UC 7/iii 1928–9, pp. 23–5.

63 Vincent and Hinton, *University of Birmingham*, p. 199.

64 UC 7/iii 1928–9, pp. 23–5.

65 UA Senate Minutes 10, 15 Feb., 21 Mar. 1928.

66 Ibid., 21 Mar. 1928.

67 Vincent and Hinton, *University of Birmingham*, pp. 157–8.

68 Ibid., p. 200.

69 Ibid., p. 164.

70 UC 7/iii 1921–2, p. 10; 1922–3, pp. 12–14.
71 Ibid., 1921–2, p. 21.
72 Ibid., pp. 116–17,163–4; 1928–9, p. 20; 1936–7, p. 23.
73 UC 7/ii *Vice-Principal* 1918–19, pp. 8–12.
74 Ibid., 1928–9, pp. 20–2.
75 Ibid., 1933–4, p. 15.

Chapter Thirteen

In an unyielding hinterland: The student body 1900–45

OCCASIONALLY – from the point of view of the historian, far too infrequently – the students of the University of Birmingham have formally complained to the university authorities. The complaints have not usually had much effect, but they shed light on areas of experience that graduates prefer to forget and that the authorities prefer to leave unrecorded. The most interesting complaints are about the learning experience. From 1911, when the students first complained, to the present day there has been a persistent pattern. A petition is sent to the Senate, usually from the Guild. It is based on an analysis of questionnaires, distributed as conscientiously as possible. These complain of excessive rote learning, especially for scientists and engineers, who have too many dictated lectures and excessive hours of work. English students complain of excessive numbers of set texts, history students of excessively long periods of time to be studied, commerce students of the excessive width of their courses. It usually comes down to overwork, rote learning, insufficient latitude and teaching in excessively large groups. Senate refers the petitions to the faculties, where they slumber.[1]

Some of these complaints are integral to a university education: on the one hand departments tend to overload their curricula and lecturers their courses, while on the other hand students insist upon extra-curricular activities and time-consuming mating rituals. But other complaints do reflect the problems of the moment. It is this that is interesting, and it is revealing that, over time, the stress of the complaints has changed. For the first fifty years of the University's existence complaints of rote learning and excessive lecturing ranked high. The complaints were not without justification, but there were reasons for this. Until the end of the Second World War the University of Birmingham was concerned, to the point of obsession, with attracting undergraduates. It was not until the 1920s that the University was fairly sure that it would be able to attract enough of them to be viable, and by the later 1930s it was definitely falling behind its competitors in this respect. As an institution that defined quality by success in examinations, the University kept a watchful eye on the examinations of its incoming students.

Initially it was happy enough to obtain students with pretty low standards of efficiency, as far as examinations were concerned. The teaching reflected this. As the level of entry rose during the inter-war years the teaching was sometimes adapted.

Sir Oliver Lodge was a believer in hard work: 'Sloth and deterioration are the inevitable consequences of the too-easy life, for it is the struggle which braces and makes men of us', was his view and one that he had the insensitivity to utter at the 1913 Speech Day of Edgbaston High School for Girls.[2] In his belief in the invigorating powers of mental exercise he was, of course, at one with his fellow professors. *Per ardua ad alta* seemed a perfect motto for a new university that had to make its way. However, the students were inclined to believe that this was overdone and in 1911 the Guild conducted the first of its conscientious surveys, held a meeting to discuss it, and concluded that 'the arrangement of work now adopted leaves much to be desired, and ... the degree courses are overcrowded':

> We may definitely state from our observations of the whole tone of the General Meeting and the terms in which the evidence has been given, that the opinion of the students as a whole is that the overcrowding of the syllabus tends to encourage 'cramming' and leaves no time for intelligent study or serious thought, or for taking any part in the corporate life of the University, and thus militates against the best interests of University education in its broadest sense.[3]

To explain its point the Guild held a special meeting which Sonnenschein, as dean of Arts, attended. A spokesman said:

> We are not making a request for less work. We come here to get a degree for a definite purpose. and Birmingham degrees have a reputation for being good degrees, and so we do not want to see the standard brought down. There is undoubtedly overcrowding in some places, and lack of proper arrangement in other places. From personal experience I know that it is possible to pass Physics II without opening a text-book and I believe this to be also possible with Chemistry. Surely the purpose of a degree should be to certify that the man or woman who holds it can do good personal work and not follow sheepwise the words of the lecturer.'[4]

A BA Finalist commented that 'a pass is fairly easy to obtain, but any attempt at specialisation is almost impossible'. The history syllabus was criticised as being too broad – in 'European history, which covers sixteen centuries, it is impossible to do the work thoroughly – only a rough outline can be obtained'. The amount of reading required for English was already then regarded as impossible to achieve. 'About eight authors are specified and we have about sixteen to do of which the most important are generally left to the very end and therefore imperfectly treated.' French, similarly, had too many texts.

Students were asked to say how much free time they had between 9.30 a.m. and 5 p.m. on weekdays and on Saturday mornings until 1 p.m. Science students had very little, and much of that was taken up travelling between Edmund Street and Edgbaston. With practicals and lectures, John Parks claimed that he had no more than six free hours; Herbert Jones (physics) had six hours; a chemist had three hours; another conscientious undergraduate had no spare time 'because there is always extra practical to be done'. When it is considered that at the end of the day these students had to travel home, perhaps to Wolverhampton or even to Burton-upon-Trent, and write up their notes, they were indeed pressed. A 'home student' who commuted from Dudley during the later 1920s spoke of a journey that usually lasted between forty-five minutes to an hour and, in foggy conditions, sometimes two hours. The trains were full of noisy commuters – she must have travelled in the cheapest class, as they were mostly factory workers with loud voices.[5] Asked whether, when they had finished writing up their lecture notes and studying them, there was any time for consulting current literature and journals or any other authorities, the usual answer was that there was not. Outside the Science faculty the work was less intense, but still demanding. Claude Naylor, a final-year commerce student, commented that 'with continuous application and doing without much leisure it is possible to get through the work, but taking the course as whole the work demanded *is* inclined to be excessive, tho' not by much'. But when asked whether he had time for general reading his answer was 'No, without any doubt.'

Some of these responses might be considered as the usual desperation of Finals students. But many of the comments came from first- or second-year students and they covered many parts of the syllabus. A first-year scientist had twelve lectures a week in addition to thirteen and a half hours of practicals; this gave her seven and a half free hours (much of which was spent travelling between Edmund Street and Bournbrook). In addition she needed between seven and ten hours a week to write out her lecture notes properly and study them and she therefore had no time to read other literature or journals, or for general reading. A zoologist who must have had a certain aptitude for the subject, as he subsequently proceeded to his M.Sc. and Ph.D., had fifteen hours of lectures in his first year and sixteen hours of practicals, leaving him with one and a half hours' spare time, excluding Friday afternoon, and no time to read anything. This burden he did not consider excessive. Arts students were not far behind. Even Sonnenschein was affected: 'They tried not to give more than 15 hours lecture per week in 1st. year and 12 hours in 2nd. and 3rd. year and he did not consider that excessive.' But several Arts students pointed out that in some cases there had been seventeen hours of lectures during the preceding year. The general situation – the wide syllabus to be covered, the tendency of the lecturers to recite 'facts', the need for set books, the stress on knowledge rather than analysis – lent itself to cramming. It is noticeable that the student questionnaire asked how much time was occupied in writing up and studying lecture notes and whether the students had time over and above this. No student replied that this was an inappropriate question, and very rarely did they have spare time. Only one student, a fifth-year medic, protested against the exercise: 'Is work excessive? No! a medical man cannot know enough – and so too much cannot be done. I am most thoroughly satisfied with the entire course and I do not think it could possibly be arranged better.' This was countered by other medical students pointing out snags such as the physics lecturer not covering the relevant parts of the medical syllabus.

So concerned were the students that they went so far as to suggest 'the extension of the time available for the courses by a *reasonable* shortening of the vacations', not a fate that the staff were disposed to undergo. In any case, despite all the trouble that they took, there is no record of either Senate or the faculties discussing the matter. What is noticeable with this appeal is the seriousness of the students, and their evident insecurity. They were very much aware that they were in a new university that had to prove itself, they were deeply concerned with their career prospects and not at all secure about them. As will be seen, they had good reasons for such concern.

In 1920 the same complaints surfaced, this time from ex-servicemen. Having survived the war they were less worried about the future, but the workload did concern them. Engineers were at lectures or in laboratories between thirty-two and thirty-five hours a week, with metallurgy Finalists peaking at thirty-seven hours and the future chairman of British Petroleum (Professor Cadman) making his petroleum engineers attend for some thirty-five hours a week. The Engineering Board responded: it recommended that it was undesirable that students should have more than thirty hours a week in lecture halls or laboratories, so it dropped the demand for accountancy for some of the Finalists, thereby reducing the weekly workload by one hour.[6]

What the early surveys did not mention were seminars. The absence of seminars until after the Second World War was a national phenomenon. 'Bruce Truscot', the Liverpool professor of Spanish who, under this pseudonym, published one of the best-informed surveys of the inter-war universities and is credited with inventing the term 'redbrick', is remarkable for his failure even to mention them.[7] The development of Honours degrees during the 1920s – a matter discussed later – did, however, lead to small Final-year groups;[8] the existence of such groups duly led to a demand that they should be extended, and a UGC report of 1936 recommended that 'lectures might be fewer and need not be compulsory if a greater use could be made of the seminar or tutorial system'.[9] The reaction to this report was revealing.[10] The Birmingham Students' Guild promptly debated a motion approving the lecture system before an audience 'considerably larger than usual'; the motion was rejected by eighty-seven votes to twenty-one. This was followed by a mass meeting of the Guild which proposed that:

1 'The main substance of the lectures' should be distributed, 'thereby dispensing with a large number of lectures which consist of mere dictation'. [Medicine and Law apparently already did this.]
2 Lectures should survey 'basic principles' rather than be 'as at present a dictation of a conglomeration of facts'.
3 'In the time thus liberated', tutorial classes consisting of not more than six students and a lecturer be instituted.
4 A joint committee of the university authorities and the Guild representatives should study the practicability of these recommendations.

They rejected proposals that the number of lectures, especially in the Science faculty, should be substantially reduced, and that attendance at lectures should be voluntary.

The questionnaires and the report duly followed. Students in the Arts and Science faculties were particularly clamorous for small tutorial classes; in Arts there was 'general complaint' about its absence in the first year and 'in some cases' in the second year. In Science 'all departments ... are strong in support of individual tuition of students, and supervision of work, which is neglected until the student reaches an advanced course, and, consequently, many students who are not in a position to obtain expensive coaching, either from the University Staff or external sources, are prevented from achieving first-class results in examinations'. If questions were asked during lectures the rest of the lecture had to be hurried; questions asked during the lecturer's free time were curtailed 'due, frequently, to the lecturer's domestic arrangements. In some cases questions are not welcomed.' Commerce and law were praised the most by their students: in commerce 'the tutorial system has been well established, individual tuition being given to every member of the Faculty, and the staff are keenly interested in the work and success of their students'. Individual departments had their characteristics: classics and geology had so few students that that the tutorial system was effectively in existence, while the lecture groups in history were too large and the lecturer sometimes inaudible. Metal mining 'alleges that [promotion] depends on the amount of research carried out by staff'. Zoology had its own departmental committee that was discussing reform with the staff. Chemistry sent an official letter saying that all was well and an unofficial letter saying the opposite; physics was too disorganised to send a reply.

The report was circulated to all heads of departments, where it disappeared in the usual fashion. There were some desultory and isolated protests: some second-year metallurgists expressed their disapproval of a lecture by vigorous stamping; two persons were sent out of the room and 'some two dozen pages of notes were recited'; another metallurgy lecturer informed his students that he himself could only avoid dictation if the entire Faculty did so. Five years later the Guild repeated its recommendation for a staff–student committee to discuss curriculum reform, particularly in the Arts Faculty.[11] Birmingham was not, of course, alone. Liverpool students conducted a similar enquiry and the National Union of Students endorsed the opinion in its 1937 and 1941 conferences; its 'Arts Commission' in 1941 passed by 141 to zero without abstentions a resolution asking that 'tutorials and seminars should be extended and that discussions should be held following on lectures'.[12] Brian Simon, who as a former president of the National Union of Students (NUS) was well informed on this matter, gave examples of Arts students having as many as twenty-three lectures a week (although Birmingham's 1936 report did not suggest that this was widespread locally); outside the Arts Faculty many students needed to complement a heavy lecture load with laboratory work and it was common for engineering students to have as many as thirty-five hours a week of lectures and laboratory work and then to have to travel home. Twenty years after Cadman matters had not changed.

But producing change was not straightforward and it is not easy to look behind these complaints and to consider the quality and the nature of teaching at this time. As any department that has been inspected under recent government practice knows, 'teaching quality' needs to be considered in the light of a large variety of factors that professors in an earlier age were freed from the necessity of recording. However, during their tour of the United States in 1899 the Mason College Science professors had been impressed at the methods of instruction that were practised. In England, they reported, the lectures *were* the basic course, making a textbook nearly unnecessary: 'Students who have been recently to a British secondary school, one of the large public schools, or indeed any other, cannot as a rule keep their attention long fixed on anything … as a rule what they chiefly learn in class work at school is a habit of inattention to what is going on.' At college 'classes ... are too slow for the quick boys, too rapid for the slower ones and too dull for all'. They did things better in the United States. The entry standards were similar to Mason College but the textbook was read before the lecture, while a 'much to be imitated portion of the system' was that credit was not dependent on concluding exams only, but also on laboratory and class work. Furthermore, 'the right to dismissal at any stage is maintained and used'.[13] But the Mason professors did not follow in these footsteps. They lacked the students, they lacked the resources, they themselves pointed out that the staff–student ratio was much more favourable in America; their students also lacked resources. Furthermore, in addition to the differences of culture and funding there were two particular types of problems that existed during the first forty or fifty years of the century.

The first problem was practical. Brian Simon, who was particularly well informed on these matters even for a former president of the National Union of

Students, and who wrote on the subject in 1943, quoted a revealing letter from a lecturer who had wished to teach underlying principles but was 'forced to the conclusion that I must become what I despised so much, a purveyor of mere information. All my theories [of what lectures should be] had assumed the facilities of the older and richer universities; without them they didn't apply. I had to turn myself into a textbook.' He had fifty or sixty students; at best a tenth of this number would be able to obtain the books that he recommended.[14] The rest could not afford them. 'It is fairly clear', said a report of the Birmingham Guild, 'that hardly anyone has got much spare money. In particular book-buying is comparatively rare because it is virtually impossible for a large number of students and uncomfortable for most of the rest.' This was frustrating to the staff but maybe not so frustrating to the students, as the Guild also concluded that 'The point of crucial importance is that students seem, in too many cases, to be interested in nothing else than the academic course leading to the degree, leading in turn it is hoped to a job.'[15] 'Four terms in the University', wrote an altruistic student in a short-lived Arts Faculty magazine in 1922,

> have convinced me that the majority of the students have forgotten that we have a life to live as well as a living to earn. They come up with the grim (and laudable) determination to work; and keep their resolution – more or less. Students take their work so seriously at to make it more a manual than a mental task. If one suggests that they should read a book which is not prescribed in the syllabus or expressly recommended by one of the staff, they stare aghast and exclaim, 'Oh, but what about the exams?'[16]

Twenty years later Brian Simon was saying much the same thing, stressing 'the tremendous pressure on the student'. To this must be added the possibly lengthy journey back home. It took until the summer of 1924 for Edmund Street's library to remain open until 6 p.m. and it was only possible to stay in the building after 7 p.m. and travel home on a quiet train if there was a social function or an evening lecture.[17] This was a common feature with the redbricks: in 1928 it was remarked that 'not Oxford or Cambridge in the vacation are as desolate of students as the buildings of a modern university at eight o'clock in the evening. University life, as university life, ends at sundown. Midnight oil must be burnt in lodgings, not in the library.'[18]

The second set of problems related to the nature of the curriculum, to the development of academic disciplines and to what were considered appropriate priorities within these disciplines. The London BA of the 1840s has been described as looking 'more like O levels in ten or a dozen subjects than the crown of a university education, and the Honours degrees like pale anticipations of A levels'.[19] The standard rose, but slowly. The underlying problem was that academic subjects as known in the twentieth century were only being created, and until such a time had arrived the knowledge and the concepts could not very well be applied, let alone percolate down to school level.[20] The nature of the exam questions in Birmingham's Arts Faculty – and other Faculties seem to have been much the same – suggests that the comparative novelty of the disciplines led to a fourfold problem. There were few textbooks, there was insufficient secondary material, and British education inherited from the nineteenth century a tradition of rote learning, which went hand in hand with a belief that facts spoke for themselves, so one needed to know many of them. The Matriculation exams taken at the age of sixteen (which were adequate for entry to Birmingham until the 1920s) stressed memory and quick recall. In addition, the students had often been woefully taught at school, either by teachers educated in this tradition or, more probably, by teachers who had not studied the subject at all so took a safe line with teaching it. By the 1920s the universities were turning out enough graduates to fill the available teaching posts in secondary schools and it is during this decade that there are some tentative indications of change, although it is not clear that for a student success necessarily came from adapting to such change. Birmingham was hardly likely to be ahead of Oxford, and a continuous complaint of Oxford's history examiners was the lack of thought expected from the students, a view supported by their external examiner in 1914 who protested that the exam answers 'had not passed through the crucible of the student's mind', but were 'neatly-made-up packets of correct opinion still in the original wrappers in which they were served'.[21] William Ashley was proud of being a former Oxford man, and one obtains the impression from his biography and exam questions that the early commerce courses at Birmingham included a great deal of cramming: Ashley considered his B.Com. to be a new subject, for which he had to write his own textbook. The questions that did involve thought, such as '"The American race is composed of the best elements of the most progressive nations of Europe." To what extent is this statement true?' put to the second-year B.Com. in 1910 might now, in a post-eugenicist age, appear somewhat alarming.

The outcome of all these problems revealed themselves in the questions set for Finals, a pattern that had been well established within Mason College and which lasted until the 1920s. The exam questions in history and English between 1890 and 1920 have common characteristics. Even a man of de Selincourt's calibre was constrained to marking scripts that answered 'not more' than nine questions in three hours, individual questions ranging from 'How did the French Revolution affect Burns, Burke, Byron, Wordsworth and Coleridge?' to 'Compare and contrast the styles of Goldsmith, Johnson, Gibbon and Burke, noting the peculiar merits and limitations of each' or, more narrowly, 'Write a note on the final e in Chaucer', but the exam questions at Newcastle, Sheffield and Glasgow were similar.[22] History had a similarly wide curriculum, with twenty minutes per question, usually highly factual, and with much use of the term 'describe', such as 'Describe the career of Cnut and mention the more memorable events in his reign and discuss its effect upon the country', 'Describe the struggle between England and France in India up to the Peace of 1763' or 'Show, with a sketch map, the territorial settlement of Germany effected by the Treaty of Westphalia.' The more demanding questions on how Louis XIV affected the balance of power in Europe or how the relationship between the European powers had been affected by colonial questions since 1870 were heavily diluted by the absence of time to answer them. They could also be avoided. By the 1920s the history Finals papers were becoming less crowded and it became more difficult for students to avoid questions involving some thought. The old questions remained, but the Pirenne thesis did not take long to appear, nor did sixteenth-century popular revolts, and by 1925 the break appears to be well under way, despite the occasional alarming question ('Why is not Pondicherri in Westphalia?'). Invitations to 'describe' became infrequent: invitations to 'examine' had taken their place.

A similar process towards analysis took place in other disciplines, but it all took time: hence the complaints of the 1940s.[23] In the particular case of history the presence of a vice-chancellor down the corridor, who occasionally gave lectures in the place of Professor Beazley when the latter was too busy to make his customary regal entrance, may have had some influence.[24] But in the case of Birmingham the problems were compounded by the insecurities of a new university. It was certainly comforting that by the later 1920s the University was well established financially, but as far as its supply of students was concerned it was not at all so sure of its ground. It worried about this to the point of obsession, and with reason.

The founders of the new universities were fairly clear what sort of institution they wanted, but they not very clear about the kinds of students they were seeking to attract. As Chamberlain put it:

> Our general idea is that a local University cannot under any circumstances – and if it could, ought not to – compete in the slightest degree with Oxford and Cambridge. We cannot give the special advantages which are offered by the older Universities and we shall deal with a class which is very different from that from which they draw the great bulk of their students. At the same time we do not want to neglect in any way the older learning and we are anxious that both in respect to this and the general culture we may not be behind such institutions as the Scottish Universities. But beyond this, we desire to systematise and develop the special training which is required by men in business and those who, either as principals or as managers and foremen, will be called upon to conduct the great industrial undertakings in the midst of which our work will be done. In fact it is our aim to do for those engaged in commerce and manufacture what is now done for the professions of law and medicine, and while giving the general education which is calculated to train the mind and broaden the sympa-

thies, we hope also to direct the instruction so as to be of practical advantage to those concerned.[25]

Although clear about the role of the institution, he was evidently not at all clear about its students. That they needed to be different was evident. How this difference should manifest itself was another matter. Chamberlain seemed to have been hoping for the best of both worlds, leaving Oxford and Cambridge to their customary clientele but having a syllabus better than either. Nor could he have had a very clear idea where his new clientele would be found. Certainly Mason College in the 1890s had not discovered it. Although it was not put on record – and in the 1890s there was no need to put on record anything so obvious, although Chamberlain very nearly said it – one of the results of university status would hopefully be that the Sciences would attract a preponderance of better qualified males, preferably of a higher social class. Arts would abandon the large numbers of young women who attended evening classes for interest and improvement and attract more of the output of the grammar schools and even of some public schools, while the students training to be teachers in the elementary schools would be marginalised. These hopes were fulfilled, but not without a great deal of labour and worry, and then not in the manner envisaged. The gamble that such students existed, a gamble necessarily taken by all the new civic universities, eventually turned out to be successful.

On the surface success came quite easily. As Chapter 4 has shown, numbers expanded and evening classes declined. Furthermore, by the end of its first decade Birmingham University was clearly a market leader in the West Midlands region, both stimulating and taking an increased supply of students. While in 1893 as many as 78% of those women students at Mason who were not training to be teachers came from Birmingham by 1910–13 this had fallen to an average of 52% of a larger number. For men this fell from 60% to less than 40%. Much of the increased supply of students came from the West Midlands, or from just outside it, but conveniently on the railway line in places such as Burton-upon-Trent.

Table 13.1 Birmingham University: duration of study by sex, 1910–13 (% of total)

Year	Male	Female
1	39	52
2	20	9
3	41	39
Total	100	100
Number	126	85

Source: Database. This table only includes students for whom there is information on years of entry and departure.

Nevertheless, the success was chequered. Some of those who would formerly have studied part-time seem to have migrated into full-time study for a period of only one or two years. The data for this is defective, the record cards which recorded students' details often failing to give the year of completion or withdrawal. Nevertheless they are indicative and Table 13.1, which is restricted to those students with full records, shows that between 1910 and 1913 as many as 39% of the men and 52% of the women studied for only one year, while only about 40% of the students studied for three years. This is lower than the figures quoted in Chapter 8,[26] which suggested a stronger trend towards the three- or four-year degree student, but it is clear that it was not until the 1920s that it could safely be assumed that students would normally come for a three-year degree. More significant was the quality of the entrants. The rise and fall of the Birmingham Matriculation exam mirrors the period of the new University's most desperate search for students. The pool of potential students was shallow. Desperate to deepen it, Birmingham rejected the invitation to co-operate with the Victoria Federation in what would eventually become the Joint Matriculation Board, and instituted its own exam. The principle was imaginative and flexible, was clearly designed to appeal to the schools and would horrify modern inspectors:

> There are no stated subjects nor published syllabuses. The papers are set by the University examiners after they have made themselves fully acquainted with the aims and methods of the teachers and the scope of their work. but the school may, if it chooses, make use of the papers set by the University for other purposes, e.g. those of the Matriculation examination.[27]

Like other Matriculation exams, this involved passing a number of papers in a variety of subject areas, thus indicating a reasonable breadth of education. The format of these papers was also similar to that of other boards: for instance, the 1903 paper required candidates to answer many questions in a short period of time – in this case ten questions in three hours. The questions, however, could not be considered as innovative as the principle of consultation, and it is difficult to avoid the suspicion that they were based on the curricula of particular schools, with much scope for memory and little for analysis. In 1903 these included:[28]

- Write a note on Shakespeare's *Sonnets* or Chaucer's *Prologue*.
- Write a sketch of the play you are presenting for examination.
- Quote a passage of five lines from any play by Shakespeare, with observations on the metre.
- Answer very briefly the following: [this was one of the ten questions]

    Who is the biographer of Dr Johnson?

    What part in politics was played by Swift?

What was Burke's attitude towards the French Revolution?

After 1910 it was only necessary to answer eight questions in three hours. These were of a similar nature:

- Give an account of the witches and of the part they took in the action of the play of Macbeth.
- Beginning immediately after the death of Polonius, tell the story of Hamlet to the end.
- Why, according to Shakespeare, did Brutus, Cassius and the other conspirators make up their minds to kill Caesar?
- Who were the chief Empire builders between 1600 and 1700?
- Illustrate from any period you like the light which contemporary literature can throw on history.
- Sketch briefly the history of *either* music *or* painting in modern times.
- Prove that the angles subtended by the equal sides of an isosceles triangle are equal.
- Describe in some detail the character of a well known hero or heroine of fiction.

There were, admittedly, more difficult questions, but there was no compulsion to answer them or to 'discuss the merits and demerits of the current Parliamentary system' in twelve minutes. The standard of questions suggest a modest entry level, which, as shown earlier in this chapter, was reflected in the methods of teaching. In Birmingham's defence, it could be argued that this was not very different from other universities, including Oxbridge, whose non-scholarship students might be selected without much pretence of academic suitability. The University was a new institution in need of students and revenue; hence its Matriculation exam.

However, the difficulty did not consist solely in the absence of sufficient pupils willing to undergo rote learning. It was more structural. The history of the Birmingham Matriculation is one of failure, and it was abandoned after the war, a warning to those who believed that the doors of the halls of learning only needed to be opened for those halls to fill. There were two problems that Birmingham needed to tackle. The first was common to all the new universities, namely that parents saw little need to keep their children at school much beyond the age of sixteen. Nationally the situation was changing, and the last third of the nineteenth century saw a great expansion in the number of those taking exams – without this expansion the new universities would have been inconceivable – but these numbers were still not great and as has been shown in earlier chapters, Birmingham manufacturers showed no great enthusiasm to send their sons to take degrees, either at Mason College or at the new University. In fact, the 1895 Royal Commission on Secondary Education showed that in many parts of England girls were more likely than boys to stay at school after the age of sixteen, a logical decision for a labour market that had far fewer tolerably paid jobs for women, and where women were likely to require more formal evidence of education than men.[29]

The other problem arose from the particular pattern of education in Birmingham. The new universities had to develop without the support of the more prestigious public schools, whose parents were willing to send their sons (and occasionally their daughters) to Oxford or Cambridge, but not elsewhere. This raised an immediate problem of supply. During the earlier 1890s only 2% of students at the Victoria University (Manchester, Leeds and Liverpool) came from the seven most prestigious public schools, compared with nearly 25% at Oxford). At Mason, and subsequently at Birmingham, the proportion was even lower. Almost two-thirds of Victoria's students were recruited from secondary schools, from technical schools or from the higher elementary schools. The social and educational backgrounds of the students studying at the various provincial university colleges would have been broadly similar.[30] The difficulty for all the provincial civic universities was to attract enough of them, and this difficulty was exacerbated in the case of Birmingham by the King Edward Foundation. At the apex of the Foundation stood the King Edward VI High Schools for Boys and for Girls; lower down stood its grammar schools. The high schools sent many pupils to Oxford and Cambridge, they had hopes of rivalling the nation's more prestigious public schools so far as this was possible for a day school; the status of the Foundation was accordingly higher than that of Mason College. The Foundation also dominated the educational market, as was clear to the Assistant Commissioner of the Board of Education in 1895:

> The effect produced by King Edward's schools upon private school enterprise in and around Birmingham is obvious and acknowledged; the foundation has practically put an end to it. What there is left it the foundation has turned into a feeder for itself. Such private schools of the ordinary kind as still exist are mostly girls' schools, and owe their existence partly to distance form the centre (as at Handsworth, Moseley, and King's Heath), many parents disliking journeys by rail or tram for their girls), partly to the objection to mixture of classes: and the boys' schools that survive are due in the main to the commercial theories of parents.[31]

Competition was dealt with by building new schools: King Edward VI Grammar School at Five Ways nearly bankrupted Handsworth Grammar School, while the other new Foundation Grammar School, situated in Aston, where 'the fee is £3 p.a. and one-third of the places are free, while the train-service is admirable',[32] vitiated the provision of other viable independent secondary schools in northern Birmingham.

Being in the King Edward Foundation, the headmasters of its grammar schools could share some of the reflected glory of its High School, in particular its High

School for Boys, priding themselves on imparting freer methods of instruction, a less rigid discipline, the 'virtues of fair play and consideration for others' and 'those old and well-tried standards of culture and humane aim which have become traditional in the secondary area'.

> Take the matter of 'sneaking'. In an Elementary School a Teacher, wishing to discover an unknown misdemeanant, ask the class 'Who did that?' and the answer comes promptly from all the class except the culprit Jones, 'Please sir, Jones did it.' In a Secondary School, under similar circumstances, every member of the class would bite his tongue out sooner than inform on the culprit, and if the question gets answered at all, it is by Jones himself saying 'I did it.'[33]

The Birmingham student database has the schools of origin of 363 students from the UK between 1900 and 1913. Only two came directly from a self-confessed higher elementary school: neither is on record as obtaining a degree.[34] The dominance of the Foundation over every other school in the Birmingham region was greater than appears from these numbers alone. The Foundation had a self-imposed recruitment limit of ten miles outside Birmingham, at any rate for its grammar schools, but this was wide enough: of the 133 boys aged 16 and over who were still at school in Birmingham in 1894, 80% were at the King Edward High School; the remainder were all at King Edward grammar schools. Of the 122 girls, 67% were at the High School, the remainder at the Foundation's grammar schools.[35] In Birmingham developments in secondary education, often enthusiastically promoted by the Chamberlainites, the 'interlocking oligarchy' who ran the city, the College and the School Board, were almost instinctively tracked to ensure that they did not conflict with the status quo. Accordingly, the higher elementary schools linked up mainly with the municipal technical college. The grammar schools forged links with Mason College (although their best pupils proceeded to the high schools and not to Mason) while the high schools had links with Oxford.[36] The situation did not change before 1914 and the expansion of secondary education, the foundations of which were laid before 1914 but most of which took place during the 1920s, required many years to make a fundamental difference.[37]

From the point of view of Mason College and the early University, the problem was that there were not enough Foundation grammar schools, while the Foundation's high schools were too successful. State schools were gradually being built, especially in the wake of the 1902 Education Act, but these did not make a significant difference until the inter-war years. The Foundation was good at selecting pupils who were good at exams: up to the age of sixteen such pupils could obtain scholarships at the High School, and they then had a realistic possibility of access to scholarships and exhibitions at Oxford and Cambridge, 'for which universities the high schools more definitely prepare than Mason college'.[38] This compelled Mason to look for gaps in the market, a process in which it had developed some expertise. It taught Greek, a prerequisite for Oxford and Cambridge, to pupils from the grammar schools and from the King Edward High School for Girls. It prepared others for science Highers and for the London Matriculation – the latter could not be passed without some arts-based courses and it was so important that Mason, like all the nineteenth-century university colleges, was compelled at an early stage to override its original curriculum and include them in its curriculum.[39] But the overriding problem was simply that there were barely sufficient qualified pupils at local schools to achieve any security in making a switch from a college compelled to teach a ragbag of courses to a university teaching a set of degree programmes. Creating a university had been a leap of faith; the students were obtained, but they were not usually very good and Birmingham was fortunate that underlying changes in society, and in particular the effects of the First World War, created the conditions for a larger student market.

In the period between the wars the nature of the recruitment problem changed. The University was now established, and came to have established patterns of entry. Education students were now more merged with the others, studying a full three-year degree programme before having their fourth year in training. Entry standards rose: Honours were introduced. But the worries about admissions and employment remained and the trends were closely monitored. National figures for the inter-war years are unexciting, with the numbers of new students admitted for the later 1930s struggling to reach 15% more than the average for 1924–9. Even this figure is deceptive: male entries were 20% above this average, female students were usually below it.[40] The inter-war years fall into three parts that in turn mirror national developments: the bulge of ex-servicemen, the difficult consolidation of the 1920s and the slow national growth of the 1930s, from which Birmingham benefited little.

For those in charge of the universities the immediate post-war period was challenging to the point of being horrendous. Nationally it began with an onrush of 26 000 ex-servicemen, with rather generous grants, to train in universities and technical institutes.[41] The problems were predictable. Sheffield, for instance, had been designed for 500 students and had 1000 (with another 1000 in evening classes), laboratories which were too full with 30 students regularly had 40.[42] King's College London, finding that temporary structures on the roof and various army huts were insufficient, was reduced to using the principal's house for teaching purposes and looked covetously at Somerset House.[43] In Birmingham the onrush was more modest, with some 700 ex-servicemen. However, this was in addition to some 1200 other students in a pre-war institution that had had little more than a thousand students.[44] The Chemistry department claimed to be able to cope with 307 students at most; in 1919 it was teaching 415.[45]

With the departure of the ex-servicemen the second phase began. Birmingham settled down to about double its pre-war number of regular matriculated under-

Table 13.2 *Birmingham University, total number of students, 1919–38 (annual average)*

Years	Science	Arts	Medicine & Dentistry	Commerce & Social Studies	Law	Total
1919–24	628	355	257	86		1326
1925–9	505	489	182	57	26	1259
1930–4	498	522	330	88	46	1484
1935–8	446	395	423	108	61	1433

Source: Database

graduate degree students, some 1200 in total. By 1925–9 the number of science and medical students had in fact more than doubled from their pre-war average, while Arts had risen 1.75 fold. The trouble was that these were very much the same figures that were reached immediately after the war, excluding the ex-servicemen. They were targets that Grant Robertson felt needed to be achieved and preferably exceeded, which he watched with some foreboding and about which he produced annual apologetic explanations to the Council. Secondary education in the region had expanded just in time to enable the University to draw on these additional resources; by the 1920s Birmingham had clearly drawn all that was possible. Grant Robertson did what he considered feasible within a tight financial regime. He appealed to a variety of local education authorities in the region for more support, he sought scholarships wherever he could find them, he did what he could to extend the site at Edgbaston, and he presided over the introduction of Honours, a significant change which needs to be considered in more detail.

The pre-war University of Birmingham had launched itself with an ingenious sales pitch. Honours degrees were spreading across the University system, but Birmingham preferred to award Bachelor degrees without Honours. Instead it gave Master's degrees. Mason College, and subsequently Birmingham, took pupils with the London Matriculation or with other Locals, and sometimes with Highers. If they lacked these the University put them through its own Matriculation exam. There was in fact little point taking a Higher Certificate. There was, however, an incentive to take the alternative, the Birmingham Intermediate Examination, taken by Birmingham's own students after their first year, but which could be taken at school. This, quite logically, enabled students to take their degree after only two years. However, they were not permitted to do so – they had to study for a third year, but were then permitted to take a Master's degree. Early efforts by Professor Fiedler to introduce Honours for his Modern Languages BA were turned down, while Birmingham could tell itself that its three-year Master's compared rather well with Bristol, which did provide Honours but insisted on Honours candidates passing their Intermediate before starting the Honours course.[46]

This scheme did not survive the 1920s, when the principle of the full-time three- (or sometimes four-) year Honours degree came of age. The growth of the Honours degree in England, and the reason why it took a different path from Scotland, is not a subject that has been examined very systematically. As a later section of this chapter will show, the demand for Honours seems to have been generated from within the educational system, not from private employers. The process began gradually in nineteenth-century Oxford and Cambridge but by 1913 over 60% of Cambridge graduates and 80% of Oxford graduates took Honours. Between 1930 and 1935 the Oxford figure rose to 90%.[47] Other English universities followed more slowly. At Bedford College for Women half the students read for the Pass degree from 1901 to 1910, a quarter during the next decade and a tenth during the 1920s.[48] Before the war some 45% of Leeds day students were reading for degrees; between the wars the proportion was around 75%. Meanwhile, the Master's degree was acquiring a more distinct meaning than in the past. Finally, and this alone would have been sufficient, the newly-created Burnham scale gave higher pay to teachers with Honours – and without an outlet into the teaching profession the Arts faculty would have lost its *raison d'être*. By the 1930s Honours were necessary in order to obtain secondary-school appointments.[49] The professor of Education, whose task was to place graduates with authorities who knew the meaning of Honours, was apologetic as early as 1913. To Staffordshire's Director of Education he wrote:

> We have in the University special schools which, although they are not called so, are essentially Honours schools ... . They involve four years work after Matriculation, and therefore represent a higher standard of maturity than the Honours School in the other modern Universities. A man who has gone through one of these Schools successfully is at least as good as a Second Class at other Universities.[50]
>
> ... We do not get at Honours, but [English] consists of a very thorough course for three years under Professor de Selincourt, and those who come through it successfully ... have such a training of proficiency in it as is usually confined to Honours students in other Universities.[51]

In an open testimonial: 'Amy Freeman '"took the first place in the Special School of Modern Languages".'[52]

Departments were keen to introduce Honours. The Science Faculty managed to keep a halfway house, permitting only their more gifted students to progress to the final Honours year, restricting the rest to the exam for a Pass degree. In the Arts Faculty the Pass degree appears to have languished during the 1920s. By 1929 Jane Milne, the tutor for women students, felt sufficiently confident of her ground to be scathing about it in her annual and confidential report to Grant Robertson. The latter who, in common with his generation, had doubts about the narrowness of an Honours degree, was sufficiently impressed for her report to be distributed to Senate and Council:

> in the hundreds of women in the Faculty of Arts we have with much more specialised ability also many women whom circumstance rather than talent have led into Honours schools, and many in the Pass School of whom the curriculum will never make good scholars. These are women who ought to be tempted to prepare for some form of civic administration, the Civil Service, etc. They ought to have in the University an encyclopaedic training, with some relation to the world of today. But I find a certain rigidity in the Pass School regulations. I have long thought that in this matter we are at fault. Our Pass course stimulates no one in prospect; indeed it damps the most ardent spirit.[53]

Across the country faculties appear to have had mixed feelings about Honours degrees and sought to find ways of combining breadth with Honours: the Arts Faculty of Liverpool, for instance, permitted students to study for Honours either in general or special studies. Milne's criticisms fell on fertile ground: during the 1930s Birmingham's Arts faculty provided Honours in 'Grouped Subjects', much to Grant Robertson's praise. It also reformed its Pass degree which, as Milne informed a headmistress in 1936, now provided a very wide choice 'and we are hoping that a good type of girl will choose it; up to the present, students with good Pass degrees and training have had some difficulty finding jobs'.[54] The hint in the Milne correspondence is that the development of Honours degrees had been more in the interest of men that it was of women, but she did not develop this theme.

The third inter-war phase dates from the 1930s. During the 1920s Grant Robertson's annual reports had been sombre or at least cautious, but during the next decade his references to student numbers became more optimistic. Already in 1933 he was showing signs of putting the slump behind him.[55] Nationally, student numbers were gently rising, and he joined the chorus of vice-chancellors who feared that more would mean worse. But his understanding of this was different from that of some of his peers. Among Birmingham's large faculties Medicine alone gave no cause for concern. It followed the national trend (with changing definitions in the early 1930s giving the illusion of a jump in numbers) and as Chapter 12 has shown, by 1938 it had a new hospital. However, as Table 13.2 shows, by the later 1930s the two largest faculties, Arts and Science, had fewer students than a decade previously. Hence Grant Robertson's insistence that he could take more, but only at the expense of lower standards of entry. During the 1920s the quality of incoming students had improved: by 1929 hardly any students arrived directly after Matriculation, while some 80% had the Higher Certificate. It was not something that he wished to lose.[56]

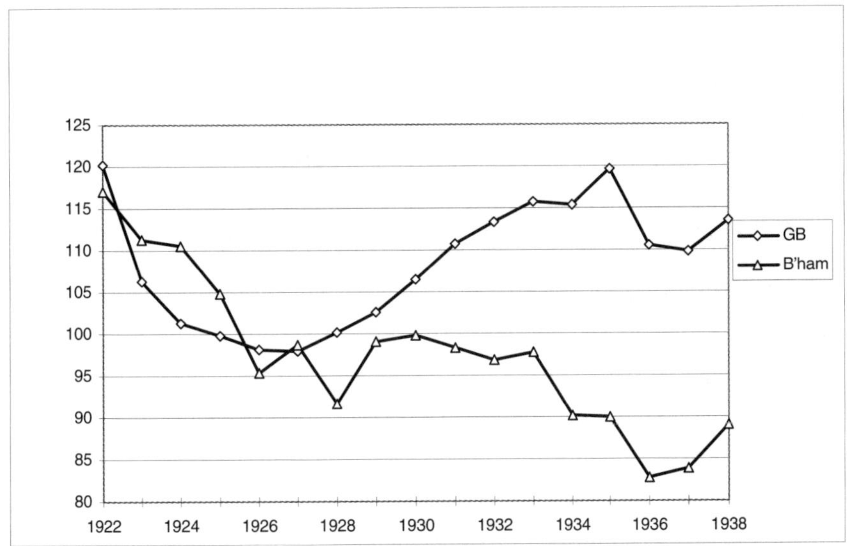

Figure 13.1 Science and technology students: Great Britain and Birmingham, 1922–38 (1924–9 = 100)

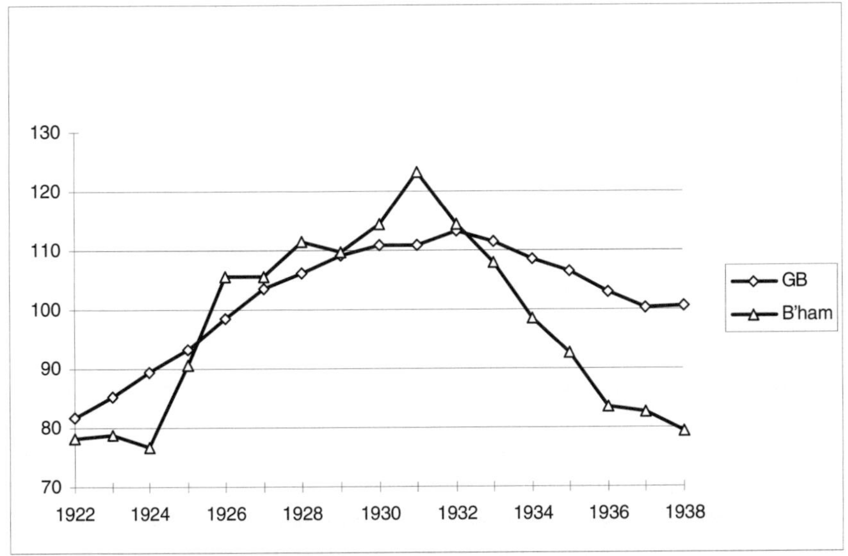

Figure 13.2 Arts students: Great Britain and Birmingham, 1922–38 (1924–9 = 100)

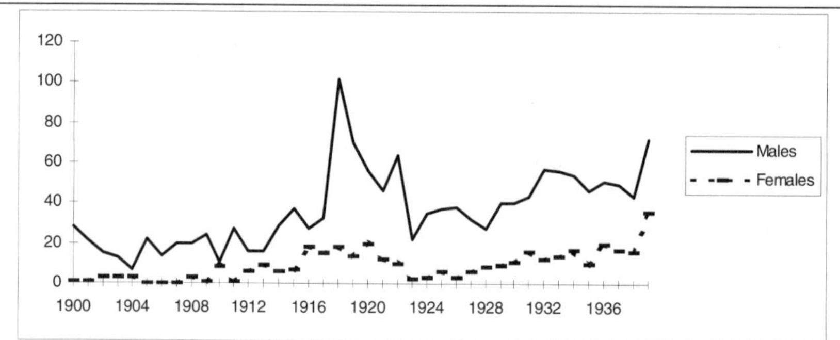

Figure 13.3 Birmingham University: MB, Ch.B. students, annual entry by sex, 1900–39

Figures 13.1 and 13.2 compare Birmingham with the national figures. The number of Birmingham's Science students followed the national trend downwards until 1926 and then continued to fall for the next decade, while the national figures rose. Birmingham's Arts students followed the national pattern of growth until 1931 and then declined. Much of the decline in arts was caused by the Board of Education's withdrawal of some of its grants for education students, but it was nevertheless a matter of some concern. The trend by sex was of less concern to a vice-chancellor, but here also there were worrying indications. Medicine, in cutting back after the initial post-war expansion, cut back even more on women, as Figure 13.3 shows, but in this respect Birmingham was not unique.[57] However, in Arts and Science the trends by sex were ominous. Comparing 1924/9 with 1935/8 the only figure that was encouraging was that of women in the Arts Faculty. This fell, but fell less, proportionately, than the national figure. However, while nationally the number of male Arts students had remained almost constant, at Birmingham their numbers fell by a third. This was not because the schools had shifted the balance of their teaching towards Science. On the contrary, while the national number of male science and engineering students rose by a fifth, at Birmingham they were stable. Women presented a different picture entirely. There were never very many of them, and as was the case everywhere, mostly they studied biology, botany and mathematics. A handful studied chemistry and physics and almost none studied engineering. In any case, while the national figures for women in the sciences were stable, in Birmingham their numbers halved. It is not easy to find a reason, and one looks instinctively for male prejudice. As far as engineering is concerned one would not need to look very far. But prejudice was not new at this time and women never had studied engineering subjects, so it does not explain this decline. In 1946 the newly arrived professor of Education was complaining to the vice-chancellor that science departments were particularly reluctant to take women.[58] It is possible that they had a point: the girls' grammar schools had worse laboratories and less specialised teachers than the boys' grammars. Though the case remains to be proved, it is conceivable that in the West Midlands – to look no further afield – the growth of Higher exams during the 1920s as a prerequisite for university entry was to the detriment of women who wished to study science. Nor was it of much assistance to boys, whose (much larger) numbers remained steady. Science does not appear to have been flourishing at the higher level of the West Midlands grammar schools during the 1930s.

None of this was much comfort for the University. Nor, by the later 1930s, could the slump be blamed. The West Midlands recovered from the slump fairly rapidly and by the later 1930s could not be considered economically depressed; indeed, this may even have discouraged students from postponing their careers by three years' study at university. The basic problem remained. The educational hinterland was insufficiently responsive and, if anything, was showing signs of contraction.

Employment prospects were inevitably another factor affecting recruitment. Before 1914 those undergraduates who went to the modern universities to study subjects outside the applied sciences had little beyond hopes that their degrees would improve their life chances. Indeed, as has been seen, many chose to leave before taking their degree. Hence their concerns, as shown in the 1911 survey. Their career expectations were highly gendered. Women would almost certainly teach, but hopefully in the better paid secondary-school sector. For men it was another matter. Systematic information on subsequent employment for Birmingham graduates does not exist before the 1920s, but there is some information about pre-war commerce students and it paints a rather bleak picture. If there was to be a new market for graduates this is where it should have been. The more forward- looking businessmen in the advanced industrial nations were advocating better training for managers; the Birmingham Chamber of Commerce even asked Chamberlain for a university course. Ashley, a former Oxford don, a professor at Harvard, a man who believed that economic history would teach students more about the world than would neoclassical economics and who was sympathetic to Chamberlain's belief in tariffs, was a high-profile 'catch' for the early B.Com. 'My experience at Harvard', he wrote, 'made me realise that the most powerful motive which led students to enter economic courses was a widespread belief that such courses would be of practical benefit in their subsequent careers.'[59]

So he designed a curriculum that was intended to be of practical benefit. It consisted of modern languages, accounting, 'applied science', business management, commerce, economic history and conspicuously avoided economic theory. Even so, he was not optimistic about the employment prospects for his graduates. He hoped that students reading for the B.Com. would have posts waiting, and did not encourage others to apply. Of the fifteen who had graduated by 1908 only half needed his help to find employment. 'The majority' of commerce graduates he wrote in 1905, 'will have openings provided for them by their families and friends; but there will always be some who have no family business backing. We do not encourage such lads to come to us unless they have more than usual ability; but when there *is* ability, we ought to receive such boys as students.'[60]

Most of these went, with Ashley's help, into local firms, usually as assistant or secretary to a manager or managing director. Ashley was cautious, well aware of the harmful demonstration effect of a poor graduate. This did not lead to large numbers of students – and certainly not women, of whom there were none in the early years – and a significant proportion of the early students on the B.Com. were foreign, quite a few of them Japanese. By 1913 he claimed to have placed thirty graduates, not many, but significantly more than other provincial universities could achieve.[61]

Table 13.3 Birmingham University: careers of ex-servicemen, October–November 1922 (% of total)

	BA	B.Com.	B.Sc. (Pure Sci)	B.Sc. (Eng)	Total
Unemployed	15.4	28.4	3.4	19.4	17.6
Teaching	79.5	12.2	44.8	4.8	29.6
Research	2.6	1.4	15.5	6.5	6.4
Government	0.0	8.1	8.6	12.9	8.2
Industry	2.6	50.0	27.6	56.5	38.2
Total	100	100	100	100	100
Number	39	74	58	62	233

Source: UC/12/ii/i

Information on students between the wars is much better. In particular we are fortunate in having systematic data on the careers of the ex-servicemen who flooded into the universities in 1919 and 1920, encouraged by quite generous grants.[62] The government wished to know whether its money had been well spent and asked for information on subsequent employment; Birmingham circulated its graduates around October and November 1922, and their answers are reproduced in Table 13.3. This was a period of rather high unemployment, at over a tenth of the labour force, although falling from an earlier peak.[63] There is clear evidence of unemployment for Arts and Commerce graduates as well as for the less outstanding of the engineers. Even so, the main outlines of the male job market are clear. Arts graduates taught. Only one Arts graduate went near industry, and then only as a rail clerk. Nearly half the Science graduates taught. Engineers did not teach. Over half the of them went into industry, as did half the B.Com. graduates and a little over a quarter of the Scientists. For the thirty-seven B.Com. students who went into industry, the 'industry' category itself is rather vague. They divided themselves up as shown in Table 13.4. Only eight went directly into manufacturing and fourteen into accountancy (accountant, audit clerk, auditor, book-keeper, cashier). Another five went into finance ('banking'). This was not, presumably, what Chamberlain or even Ashley had in mind when he created his commerce degree. It is not very different from the present pattern. A market niche had been found, but the B.Com. as early MBA had failed.

Table 13.4 *Birmingham University: careers of B.Com. ex-servicemen, October–November 1922*[64]

Accountancy	14
Advertising	2
Clerk	3
Finance	5
Manufacturing	8
Sales	5
Total	37

Source: UC 12/ii/i

At a general level it is not clear what the employers of the ex-servicemen expected. A supply of graduates on this scale was new for them. The ex-servicemen took an abbreviated degree programme, apparently taking only the first and last years of the programme.[65] This does not seem to have troubled prospective employers. More significantly, many students did not study for Honours. Scientists occasionally complained that 'the few available [jobs] appear only to be open to those with an Honours Degree and with Research', but this was unusual and seems to have been a great exaggeration. A significant proportion of B.Com. students studied for a one-year commerce certificate, others were awarded a B.Com., some with and some without Honours. It does not seem to have made much difference to their success in finding employment. Honours made little difference to BA students either. The growth of the Honours degree during the 1920s has been discussed earlier, but in 1922 the demand for it by employers outside the teaching profession was clearly not overwhelming.

Table 13.3 has a further use. It can be linked with the information in the *Register of Graduates* that was drawn up in 1932, thereby providing a base for an analysis of the employment of occupations of graduates after 1922.[66] Analyses that provide this information for different universities but do not distinguish between their Engineering, Arts and Science Faculties are rather meaningless, merely reflecting the relative size of these faculties within the individual universities.

The pattern revealed is similar to that of the ex-servicemen. Scientists had no systematic bias against industry. If they could get a job in industry they took it. Engineering graduates (invariably male) were the most successful at finding such jobs, male Science graduates were less successful, women very unsuccessful. If one could not get a job in industry, one taught. Quite a few male Science graduates taught and many more women taught, some in schools, a handful in universities. One became secretary to the professor of Botany. Of course, teaching might be a condition of obtaining a grant to attend university, but it is noticeable how infrequently the *Register* lists even male B.Sc. graduates who taught for a few years and then switched to industry.

As a result, in Birmingham and elsewhere, between the wars the teaching profession became overcrowded, as far as graduates wanting careers in secondary schools were concerned. This was made worse by the fact that during the 1920s the number of men teachers rose by 15% while the number of women teachers fell by 3%, the latter clearly caused by a fall in the number of married teachers.[67] In 1928 Vera Brittain wrote, quite unambiguously in a book advising women about careers, that the supply of teachers was excessive.[68] The UGC found it necessary to defend the situation early in 1930:

> in some subjects, for example, English and History, the supply of specialists now exceeds the demand; this is, we hope, a factor which is borne in mind by those who advise incoming students about their courses, for it appears that good teachers of Classics, Natural Science, Mathematics or Geography, rarely find much difficult in obtaining employment. The profession of school teaching is now probably better paid than most others in which any substantial number of women is employed.[69]

Nevertheless, during the 1930s the complaints continued.

As far as the Arts Faculty is concerned the employment pattern of the 1920s remained dominant. Birmingham was by no means unique in this respect. Truscot, whose *Redbrick University*, published in 1943, was one of the best-informed surveys of redbrick arts faculties to be published, saw them as ‘a kind of preparatory school to the Department of Education’, a trend exacerbated by the availability of scholarships for intending teachers from the department. In the summer of 1939 Birmingham’s dean of Arts, foreshadowing Truscot, addressed the Associated Midland Chambers of Commerce and ‘ventilated the criticism that the university Arts courses have become too much the preserve of students preparing for the teaching professions and urged the value of certain combination of Arts courses as a preparation for posts in government and industry and as a contribution towards a general philosophy of life’.[70]

Conversion, if conversion there was, came slowly: in 1953 another dean of Arts suggested that half the Arts graduates became teachers or

> enter the Christian ministry and other learned professions, become articled to solicitors or accountants, find a career in publishing, journalism, with the BBC and the like, or obtain places in the Foreign, Colonial or Home Civil Service. Not a few, an astonishing number indeed, enter industry – in the last three years some 15 to 20 % of the men and between 5 and 10 % of the women.[71]

This was better than Truscot's own experience at Liverpool during the 1930s:

> There were business appointments, but only of a mediocre kind; for the large firms which often apply to the Oxford or the Cambridge Appointments Board for promising young graduates, seem to forget that there are nine other English universities as well. What remained? For women, secretaryships and librarianships (generally ill-paid), marriage (which a gratifyingly large number of them achieve early) and – teaching. For men – teaching only.[72]

What Truscot did not realise was the importance of teaching for inter-war Science graduates, men as well as women. The Birmingham Appointments Board published annual figures during the 1930s; these are based on partial information, do not show postgraduate work, and they also fail to show the levels of unemployment among the graduates of individual subjects, a matter of some relevance during the 1930s. What they do show is the subsequent area of employment in industry or the teaching speciality (history, English, mathematics, etc.) for those who chose to teach. Graduates are not separated by their original departments. Nevertheless, provided that an area of uncertainty is accepted, broad conclusions can be drawn, in particular concerning the importance of teaching. Over 80% of Arts graduates taught, but as Table 13.5 shows, the proportion of male science graduates entering teaching between 1932 and 1938 varied between 37% and 65%, moving

Table 13.5 Birmingham University: Pure Science students entering teaching, 1932–38 (%)

	Men (%)	Women (%)	Total	Men (no.)	Women (no.)
1932–3	64.9	85.2	71.4	57	27
1933–4	43.4	94.4	56.3	53	18
1935–6	42	87.5	56.8	50	24
1936–7	37.5	82.4	46.9	64	17
1937–8	53.5	89.5	64.5	43	19

Source: Database. This is for B.Sc. students excluding Engineering, Metallurgy and Mining

inversely with the trade cycle, yet even at its lowest still employing over a third of the science graduates in the non-engineering subjects. With women the figure was always over 80%.

Graduates who taught usually hoped for a secondary school, but unemployment amongst teachers during the 1930s propelled many into elementary education. Birmingham University's Appointments Board, an optimistic organisation, claimed that 39% of the teachers trained at Birmingham between 1933 and 1938 ending up in elementary schools, and concluded that an Upper Second and a good teaching assessment mark were the two requisites for teaching in a secondary school. With Manchester returning a figure of 60% and Exeter of 80%, their figure is suspiciously low.[73]

Careers for inter-war graduates can therefore be divided into two categories. On the one hand there was teaching. Then there were other careers. The difficulties of business studies have been discussed earlier. The employment of graduates in industry during the inter-war years was carefully monitored in the annual reports of Appointments Board. One of the main functions of the Board was to foster co-operation with industry, so naturally its reports were optimistic about it. It is a matter of perspective – teaching remained very important, but the number of industrial contacts did increase. Shortly after the outbreak of war it produced a report congratulating itself on its success, listing 'some examples of the companies that had applied to them during the previous year'.[74] Of the fifty vacancies for men, eleven were in sales, while only seven had the term 'executive', 'administrative' or 'trainee' attached to them. Another five men had become 'secretaries' (usually meaning personal assistants), with uncertain career prospects. The Board could congratulate itself in a modest manner, but the belief in graduates can hardly be said to have been rampant throughout local industry.

For women, of course, it was another matter entirely. The Birmingham data suggest that during the inter-war years the advance of the woman graduate in manufacturing industry was qualitative rather than quantitative. The best opportunities seem to have been in department stores.[75] In 1929 Jane Milne compiled a list of the destinations of women science graduates who had graduated during the previous two years – much better, she claimed, than anything the Appointments Board had produced. It makes bleak reading.[76] She restricted herself to Honours graduates – the Science faculty permitted only the best of its students to progress to Honours, restricting the rest to a Pass degree. Thirteen out of fifteen mathematics graduates were teaching, one worked in the wages department at Cadbury, one had been offered a job at British Thomson Houston but had been taken ill. There were four physicists, of whom two, perhaps three, were teachers, seventeen chemists, of whom twelve taught, one was married, three held secretarial positions and one was an assistant biochemist at the Children's Hospital. Botany and zoology produced seventeen teachers, one lecturer at Studley Agricultural College, one Ph.D. student, and two graduates with quite senior positions in the local department store, Lewis's, one in charge of staff training, the other 'in charge of complaints'.[77]

This was a challenge to Milne: 'we ought therefore to encourage students of general ability to prepare for other work than teaching', she wrote – and she busied herself with this end in mind. 'Personal contact is one of the vital factors in securing employment in the present day.' Her correspondence was full of it, mostly with teachers, but in 1941 reaching to the Ministry of Economic Warfare. Nevertheless she remained very wary. In 1942, when there was an undeniable scarcity of labour in traditional men's trades, one of the older girls at George Dixon Grammar School for Girls decided that she wished to become an engineer. This caused some consternation. She had to be sent to the boys' school for her courses and the headteacher, herself soon to be a member of the University Appointments Board, was sufficiently worried to correspond with the Milne. The reply came promptly: Engineering for girls was very precarious, 'particularly without backing and money it might be a very rash qualification to take'. If she insisted on doing it, then let it be electrical engineering: 'I can only remember one woman graduate in engineering up to the present, and she found electrical research a better field than practical engineering.' The headteacher agreed and she 'therefore rather discouraged her from entertaining the idea ... . She does not want to teach ... and now she is very uncertain as to what career would be open to her. Betty still has a hankering after Civil Engineering.'[78]

As late as 1964 change remained limited. Figures 13.4, 13.5 and 13.6 compare the national employment pattern for undergraduates completing their studies in this year with the information for Birmingham. As has been argued throughout this chapter, meaningful comparisons depend on the balance of disciplines, and

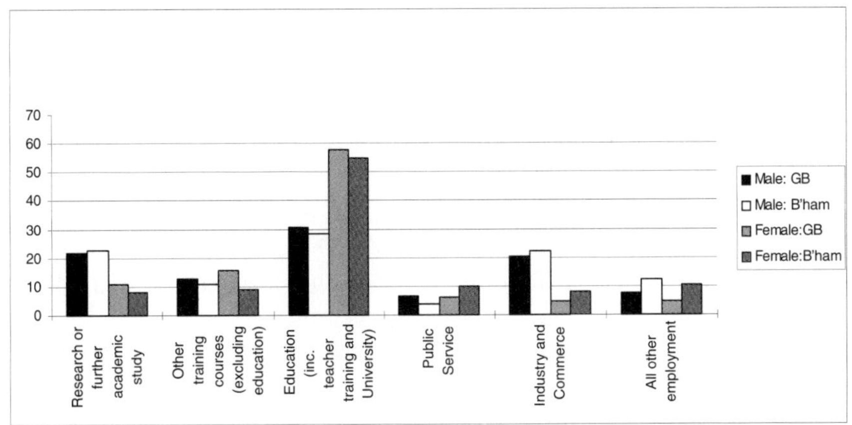

Figure 13.4 First employment of Arts, Commerce, Social Science and Law graduates, Great Britain and Birmingham, 1964

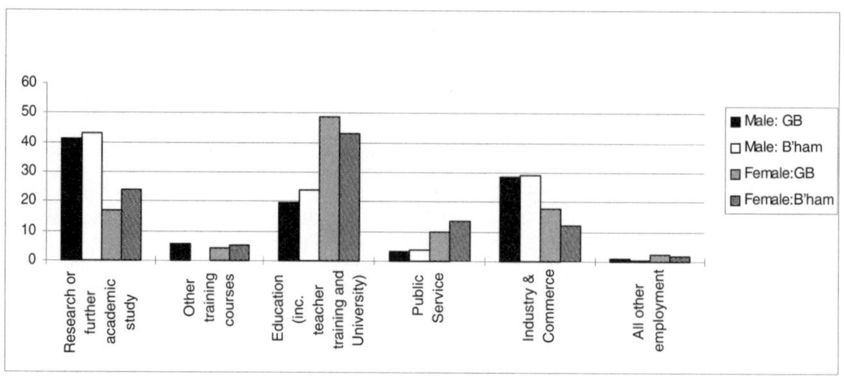

Figure 13.5 First employment of science graduates, Great Britain and Birmingham, 1964

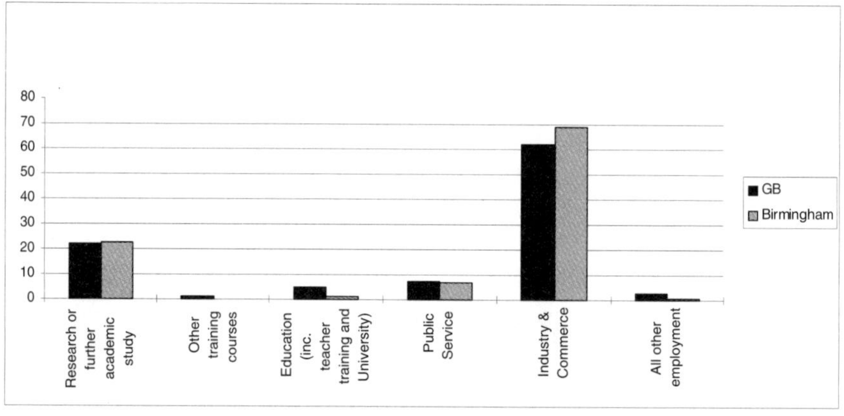

Figure 13.6 First employment of male technology graduates, Great Britain and Birmingham, 1964

the figures therefore reproduce the smallest available group of disciplines in the national statistics. Considered broadly, there are encouragingly few major differences between the national and the Birmingham statistics.

Figure 13.4 is for a combination of Arts, Commerce, Social Science and Law. Men were more than twice as likely as women to take up research or further academic study, while women were nearly twice as likely to take up teaching. Since the 1930s the proportion had dropped to 58% nationally and 55% for Birmingham, a large drop, though the figure was still high. Over a quarter of the men (31% nationally, 28% at Birmingham) were still moving into teaching. Figure 13.5 shows a similar evolution with the non-engineering sciences. The novelty is that over 40% of the men were taking higher degrees. Only 17% of women did this nationally, though in Birmingham's case the figure was 24%. Male scientists tended to take higher degrees; women scientists tended to teach. Nevertheless, looking back to the years before the war, 24% was not an insignificant proportion, and the percentage of women teaching had fallen from the pre-war levels to 43%. As a result, 29% of male scientists and only 12% of women were subsequently obtaining employment in industry and commerce.

Neither Birmingham nor the UGC considered the numbers of women in the applied sciences (that is, engineering) to be worthy of record and accordingly Figure 13.6 is restricted to male students. Teaching had never been important for this group, and only 1% of Birmingham's students chose it. Here there was little change from the inter-war pattern, with the predictable difference that only a fifth of the students took higher degrees. This was half the rate of male scientists.

To summarise, as far as the supply and employment of students was concerned, the hinterland remained unyielding. The First World War and its social consequences had given an initial boost to student numbers. The social consequences of the Second World War and the prosperity of the 1950s enabled Birmingham at last to break free from the stranglehold of the hinterland. Until then it was best summed up by Grant Robertson in 1928 in his annual report. This was Grant Robertson in his most inimitable style, in Sir Charles Hyde's words, 'intoxicated with the exuberance of his own verbosity'. The passage cited below consists of 140 words in two involved sentences, replete with double negatives and numerous sub-clauses. It was also an extremely apposite description of the student body of Birmingham University.

> The provincial Universities, compared with Oxford or Cambridge, attract few of those who either will not have to earn their own living and desire to be equipped for an unremunerated public life in some capacity, or are required by social custom to prepare, by three or four years at college, for spending an income (small or great) that they have not earned in some manner agreeable to themselves and on the windy side of the laws; and by getting through the minimum of study that a tolerant college may allow. Ninety-five % of our students come to us for a strictly professional purpose; many of them only complete their course by continuous self-sacrifice both on their part and that of their parents; many of them are only able to enter and finish because of scholarships, exhibitions and maintenance grants.[79]

Notes

1 The list of acknowledgements is long: in addition to those mentioned earlier I would like to thank Dr. Carol Dyhouse for reading an earlier draft of this chapter and of chapter 19 and for commenting on them. David Coppock generously made available the fruits of his research on Birmingham teachers; I can only regret that the constraints of space forbade me to make more use of them. Sandra Harrison somehow found the time to read a draft and suggest quite significant rearrangements, thereby earning another mention in the footnotes of history. But particular thanks must go to Alison Gaukroger who continuously and usually single-handedly inspired all those involved with the project throughout its duration, who kept the sense of wonder, and who, had fate decreed otherwise, would have written the chapters on the student body and would assuredly have written them better.

2 Janet Whitcut, *Edgbaston High School, 1876–1976* (Birmingham, 1976), p. 82.

3 UC 8/vi/1/5, Guild: report on overcrowding of syllabus, 1910–11.

4 Ibid., Report on special meeting of the Guild, 17 June 1911. 'Mr. Gordon' spokesman.

5 Olwen Johnson, *Alma Mater. A Memoir of Student Life at Birmingham University* (1940), pp. 9–10.

6 UC iv/3/31: *Sub–committee of the Engineering Board to consider the curricula of applied science students, appointed 15 October 1920.*

7 Not only a failure to mention them, but also: 'at the modern university, where the register is marked at each lecture, the theory is that 75 or 80 per cent of the maximum number of attendances is required from all candidates for examinations, the idea being to prevent the university degree from becoming an "external" one and to maintain the closest possible contact between teachers and taught': B. Truscot, *Redbrick University* (1943), p. 87.

8 Brian Simon, *A Student's View of the Universities* (1943), p. 70.

9 UGC report, 1936, p. 22 referred to in Truscot, *Redbrick*, p. 95.

10 This is taken from UC vii/4/13. Guild of Undergraduates, *Lecture System, Enquiry Report* (1936).

11 Senate Minutes 21 Oct. 1936; *Guild News*, 18 Mar., 28 Oct. 1936; Guild Council Minutes, 5 May 1941.

12 Truscot, *Redbrick*, p. 86.

13 UC 7/iv/4/11 Sir O. Lodge, *A Modern University* (reprinted from *Nature*, 21, 28 June 1900), pp. 21–3.

14 Simon, *Student's View of the Universities*, p. 68.

15 Quoted in Simon, *Student's View of the Universities*, pp. 90, 98.

16 *The Open Book.* Magazine of the Faculty of Arts. Issue 1 (of 3), 1 Dec. 1922, p. 16.

17 Johnson, *Alma Mater*, pp. 9–10; for Library: Senate Minutes 21 May 1924. By 1930 Edmund Street library was closing at 5.30: *University of Birmingham Calendar, 1930–31.*

18 H. G. G. Herklots, *The New Universities. An External Examination* (1928), p. 50; see also Truscot, *Redbrick*, p. 146; by 1943 most redbrick libraries were open 'till late evening' on at least two or three weekdays during term.

19 F. M. L. Thompson, 'The Humanities', in F. M. L. Thompson, ed., *The University of London and the World of Learning, 1836–1986* (1990), pp. 61–2.

20 Ibid., pp. 65–6; Reba N. Soffer, *Discipline and Power. The University, History, and the Making of an English Elite, 1870–1930* (Stanford, 1994), on the teaching of History at Oxford.

21 Ramsey Muir, *The School of Modern History: A Letter upon the Working of the School* (Oxford, 1914), quoted in Soffer, *Discipline and Power*, p. 138. See also ibid., p. 107 for Firth's assertion in 1907 that Oxford history students 'remained too long the passive recipients of other men's knowledge', learning 'results instead of methods; not how to find out, but what to remember'. Cambridge did a little better, however and in Manchester Tout went further still, but Tout's department was regarded as of an exceptional quality: ibid., pp. 138, 159–60.

22 Birmingham English Literature exams, 1901, 1906; John Butt, 'English at the Universities 1901–1951', *Universities Quarterly*, 5 (1951), pp. 218–24.

23 A similar chronology has been found for a variety of University English syllabi: Butt, 'English at the Universities'.

24 Johnson, *Alma Mater*, p. 9. They were considered to be much more interesting.

25 Chamberlain (to ?) 11 Dec. 1899, Chamberlain Papers, University of Birmingham quoted in Sanderson, *Universities in the Nineteenth Century*, pp. 215–16.

26 See pp. 151–2.

27 Board of Education, *Report of the Consultative Committee on Examinations in Secondary Schools* (Cd. 6004, 1911), Chaired by the Rt. Hon A. H. Dyke Acland (Acland Report), pp. 216–18.

28 UC 12/ii/7.

29 See, for example, Birmingham and some of the other regions examined by the Royal Commission on Secondary Education (Cmd. 7862–viii, 1895) (Bryce Commission), vol. 9, appendix.

30 These figures, originally in Bryce Commission, vol. 9, p. 426 have been reproduced by Roy Lowe, 'Structural change in English higher education, 1870–1920', in D. F. Müller, F. Ringer and B. Simon, eds., *The Rise of the Modern Educational System* (1987), p. 171. As for the comparison with other universities, the table of Class Enrolments in Manchester, Leeds and Liverpool produced by Jones, *Origins of Civic Universities*, p. 92 needs to be regarded with considerable caution. The figures for 1889–90 are very different from Birmingham, but Manchester does not include women, none include teachers, and it is not clear which of the courses are full-time. Bearing in mind the differences discussed below, a direct comparison may not in any case be very meaningful.

31 Bryce Commission, vol. 7. Reports of the Assistant Commissioners (1895). Cd. 7862–VI. Report of J. Massie on County of Warwick, p. 79.

32 Ibid., pp. 91, 93. Smith argues that 'by the mid-1890s a tripartite reorganisation of secondary education was developing in Birmingham': D. Smith, *Conflict and Compromise. Class Formation in English Society 1830–1914. A Comparative Study of Birmingham and Sheffield* (London 1982), pp. 213, 215; Smith, 'Social conflict in urban education', in D. A. Reeder, ed., *Urban Education in the Nineteenth Century* (1987), pp. 109, 111.

33 Quoted in Olive Banks, *Parity and Prestige in English Secondary Education* (1955),

p. 46.

34 This may be understating the case a little: a higher elementary school did not necessarily call itself thus.

35 Bryce Commission, vol. 9, Appendix, pp. 320–1, 328–9.

36 The phrase is from E. P. Hennock, 'Technological education in England, 1850–1926: the uses of a German model', *History of Education*, 19 (1990), p. 325. David Reeder, 'The reconstruction of secondary education in England, 1869–1920', in D. F. Mueller, F. Ringer and B. Simon, eds., *The Rise of the Modern Educational System. Structural Change and Social Reproduction 1870–1920* (Cambridge, 1987), p. 145; Smith, 'Social conflict in urban education'; Smith, *Conflict and Compromise*, pp. 208–24. For the Midland Institute see C. Heward, 'Education, examination and the artisans: the Department of Science and Art in Birmingham, 1853–1902', in Roy Macleod, ed., *Days of Judgement* (Driffield, 1982), pp. 45–64. Of course this is not to ignore the earlier leading role of the National Education Union in Birmingham as described by Hennock, *Fit and Proper Persons. Ideal and Reality in Nineteenth–Century Urban Government* (1973), pp. 80–103, 175–6; see Smith, *Conflict and Compromise*, pp. 173–4, 183–4, 210–14 for the interlocking system that had emerged by the 1890s, although Edgbaston High School for Girls managed to coexist well enough outside the Foundation.

37 On a national scale, David Reeder doubts whether access ratios to secondary schools increased much during the decade after the 1902 Education Act, but he is certain that the founding of new schools contributed to the expansion of the following decades, when the proportion of pupils (per thousand) population enrolled in secondary education more than doubled to reach 10.4% in 1929–30. Reeder, 'The reconstruction of secondary education in England', p. 142. Also W. E. Marsden, 'Social stratification and nineteenth-century English urban education', in R. Goodenough and W. E. Marsden, eds., *The City and Education in Four Nations* (Cambridge, 1992).

38 Bryce Commission, vol. 9, p. 6.

39 Ibid., p. 62, QQ.1748, 1793; C. Heward, 'Education, examination and the artisans', p. 63, n.40.

40 B. R. Mitchell, *British Historical Statistics* (Cambridge, 1988), p. 811.

41 *Report of Board of Education for the year 1920–21* (HMSO 1922, Cmd 1718) p. 59; G. Sherington, *English Education, Social Change and War 1911–1920* (Manchester, 1981), pp. 129–32; Sanderson, *Universities and British Industry*, pp. 237–9.

42 A. W. Chapman, *The Story of Modern University. A History of the University of Sheffield* (Oxford, 1955), p. 298.

43 F. J. C. Hearnshaw, *The Centenary History of King's College London 1828–1928* (1929), p. 468.

44 Annual Report to Council by Vice-Chancellor and Principal (henceforth *Report to Council*), *1929–30*.

45 UC 14/ii. Grant Robertson correspondence 9 Oct. 1919. Report on number of students admitted to the department of chemistry.

46 Acland Report, pp. 240–6. Between 1898 and 1902 Fiedler, professor of German, was anxious to establish an Honours school in modern languages, but was advised by Lodge to content himself with BA, rather than BA with Honours. UC Fiedler–

Harding correspondence: FH46. 24.4.1902.

47 Sheldon Rothblatt, *The Revolution of the Dons. Cambridge and Society in Victorian England* (1968; Cambridge edn 1968), p. 185; R. McWilliams-Tullberg, *Women at Cambridge. A Men's University – Though of a Mixed Type* (1975), p. 223. The 1936 figure is for Poll admissions. For Oxford: D. Greenstein, 'The Junior Members, 1900–1900: a profile', in B. Harrison, ed., *The History of the University of Oxford*, 8 (Oxford, 1994), p. 57. See also M. G. Brock and M. C. Curthoys, *The History of the University of Oxford. Vol. 16. Nineteenth Century Oxford. Pt. 1* (Oxford, 1997), pp. 358, 360: in1882–1901, 76.7% of Oxford undergraduates graduated; in1909–10 16% of these took Pass degrees. The trend in Pass degrees had been downwards since the 1860s.

48 M. J. Tuke, *A History of Bedford College for Women 1849–1937* (Oxford), p. 246.

49 L. Doreen Whiteley, *The Poor Student and the University* (1933), p. 27. See below, p. 259.

50 UC 2/i/3. Letter book of Prof. of Education (Alfred Hughes), f. 211. 16 June 1913. Hughes to G. Balfour (director of education 'Stafford').

51 Ibid., f. 79. Hughes letter book (Dorothy Holloway).

52 Ibid., f.133. 21 Feb. 1913.

53 Official report to Principal, February 1929 of Tutor for women students: UC, J.J. Milne Letter Book.

54 Milne to Headmistress of High School for Girls, Stroud, October 1936; Tuke, *Bedford College*, p. 247; *Report to Council, 1933–34.*

55 In 1933 he was optimistic, the next year he attacked the Board of Education for withdrawing finance for 100 education students, having 'pressed' him to raise the total by fifty in 1930: *Report to Council, 1933–34.*

56 Ibid., *1929–30*: 'Even in the two–year branch of the Education Department matriculation (which was not required in 1920) is taken for granted and universal, with many of the girls holding a Higher School Certificate which would entitle them to read straight away for Honours if they were staying for a three and not for a two years' course.'

57 UGC, *Report from Universities and University Colleges in receipt of the Treasury Grant Academic Year 1928–29* (HMSO, 1930), pp. 4–5. M. Tylecote, *The Education of Women at Manchester University 1883–1933* (1941), pp. 101, 118, 135. Women studied dentistry at Birmingham at the rate of one or two a year.

58 UC 3/vii/7. Jeffrys to VC (Priestley): 27 Nov. 1946.

59 W. Ashley, 'The enlargement of economics', *The Economic Journal*, 70:18 (June 1908), p. 184. He described his teaching as 'concrete, descriptive, statistical and historical' (ibid., p. 151).

60 Smith, *Business Education in the University of Birmingham*, p. 15.

61 Sanderson, ed., *Universities*, p. 211. See ibid. p. 212 for other universities.

62 Women were not entitled to the grant.

63 Unemployment among total workforce, using Feinstein's estimates, was 12.2% in 1921 and 10.8% in 1922, falling to 8.9% in 1923: C. H. Feinstein, *Statistical Tables of National Income, Expenditure and Output of the United Kingdom, 1855–1965* (Cambridge 1972), Table 128. However many of the jobs taken by graduates would have been in the non-insured workforce.

65 UC 12.ii/i. Letter by Registrar.

66 Sanderson has examined the percentage of graduates going into industry from various universities during the inter-war years: *Universities and British Industry*, p. 279. In the case of Birmingham he used the *Register of Graduates*. As a source the *Register* is problematic: it uses the information available at the time, it gives the occupations of some graduates, but often only their latest occupation. Sanderson, in an untypical moment, chose to give aggregate returns.

67 Jessica Cooke, 'Women and the Professions, 1890–1939', unpublished Ph.D. thesis, University of Sussex, 1997, pp. 53, 69.

68 Vera Brittain, *Women's Work in Modern England* (1928), p. 65.

69 UGC, *Report from Universities and University Colleges in receipt of the Treasury Grant Academic Year 1928–29* (HMSO, 1930), pp. 46–7.

70 *Report to Council, 1938–39.*

71 H. A. Cronne, in *Birmingham University and the Industrial Midlands* (reprinted from the *Birmingham Post*, November 1953), pp. 14–16.

72 Truscot, *Redbrick*, p. 153.

73 Ibid., p. 154, reference to National Union of Students, *Graduate Employment* (A report of the 1937 Congress of the NUS), pp. 17–19. Simon, *Student's View of the Universities*, p. 48. Graduates formed 67% of the male assistant teachers in secondary schools in 1920 and 94% in 1930; with women numbers advanced from 77% to 91% during the same years: *Education in England and Wales, 1920–21*, 1922 (Cmd. 1718, 1922), p. 29, para. 72 ; *Education in 1930* (Cmd. 3856, 1931), p. 157; University of Birmingham Appointments Bureau, *Report* for 1937–8.

74 Ibid., *Report* for 1938–9.

75 The question is discussed in Sanderson, *Universities and British Industry*, pp. 314–38.

76 Milne to Bosanquet, secretary of the International Federation of University Women, 14 Feb. 1929. For Milne, see Carol Dyhouse, *No Distinction of Sex? Women in British Universities 1870–1939* (1995), pp. 80, 82–4.

77 Women commerce students, who in our sample formed 40% of the total during the inter-war years (compared with none before the war), were not considered worth mentioning; the total numbers studying for the B.Com. degree were one-sixth or less of those studying Arts. Nevertheless, the first woman had been admitted to the Institute of Chartered Accountants in 1920, the number of women members creeping up to thirty-two in 1930 and eighty-four in 1940: R. Silverstone, 'Accountancy', in R. Silverstone and A. Ward, eds., *Careers of Professional Women* (1980), p. 23.

78 UC J. J. Milne, *Letter Book*: Miller, Barwell. June–July 1942. Reply from E. L. Ritchie, 2 Mar. 1943. Her stress on electrical engineering was not unique: see Ray Strachey, *Careers and Openings for Women. A Survey of Women's Employments and a Guide for Those Seeking Work* (London, 1935), p. 163: for engineers 'electrical engineering offers the best opportunity; but no girl should embark on this career, however strong her bent, unless she has either a definite opening in view, or can afford to wait for her chance. 22 women were returned as mechanical and electrical engineers and 48 as mining engineers in the Census of 1931.'

79 *Report to Council, 1927–28.*

Chapter Fourteen

The return to war

THE RETIREMENT of Birmingham's second vice-chancellor in 1938 ushered in a period of internal change for the University. In 1939, the pro-chancellor Walter Barrow, of the Cadbury-Barrow family, was replaced by E. P. Beale, the son of the University's first lay vice-chancellor, C. G. Beale. Beale's position as University treasurer was taken by Alderman S. J. Grey.[1] In the same year the retirement of Alderman J. H. Lloyd, one of the representatives of the City Council on the University Council, pro-vice-chancellor from 1921 to 1929 and deputy pro-chancellor thereafter, meant the end to an active link back to the Science College and Chamberlain's campaign for the charter.[2] Within the administration, although C. G. Burton continued as secretary, Donald Cameron, the highly experienced registrar, died suddenly at the age of fifty-one and was replaced in 1940 by George (later Sir George) Grant.[3]

Not only was change a matter of individuals. The complexion of the Court of Governors and the Council was subtly altering as well. A number of appointees with University connections took places that local industrialists, businessmen and sponsors of charity had previously held. One such was Miss E. M. Barling, daughter of Sir Gilbert Barling; another was Eric Vincent, co-author of the first history of the University. Moreover, even though familiar names and dynasties such as Wiggins, Beale, Kenrick, Barrow, Chance and Cadbury continued, with older generations replaced by younger, many no longer represented family firms but the much larger companies that had emerged during the inter-war diversification of Midlands industry.[4] At least one change was the result of business failure, the collapse on the eve of the war of the long-established family engineering firm of Tangye, ending William Tangye's more than twenty years on the University Council. Eventually in 1944, after twenty-six years, the chancellor, Lord Chelwood, would also resign. He would be replaced five months later by the Foreign Secretary Anthony Eden, MP for Warwick.[5]

In choosing Raymond Priestley to replace Grant Robertson, the University Council had selected a man with a national profile.[6] A Midlander by birth, Priestley had begun to read geology at the University of Bristol but at the end of his second year he had been recruited by Ernest Shackleton for the 1907–9 Antarctic expedition. Subsequently he had joined Scott's 1910–12 expedition and had taken part in the epic of the 'Northern Party'. He returned to Cambridge, served and was wounded in the First World War, and eventually graduated BA in 1920. Thereafter, as a fellow of Clare College, he became interested in academic administration, becoming secretary-general to the Board of the Faculty. Eventually he moved in 1935 to become vice-chancellor at Melbourne, before being elected to Birmingham.

Priestley took office at what seemed a fortunate time. When he accepted the post in the autumn of 1937 the hope was for peace and accelerating prosperity. The country and the Midlands in particular were climbing out of the absolute depths of the Great Depression. The Sudentenland crisis was hardly on the inside pages of the newspapers. The University had begun to advance again. The Medical School was nearing completion and work on the new hospital well advanced. When Priestley arrived from Melbourne in the following autumn, a majority of the country was sighing with relief at a Munich Agreement which promised 'peace in our time'. He found that Professor Mark Oliphant had now arrived from Cambridge to take over a physics department already well advanced with the designs for a cyclotron and receiving considerable material assistance from industry.[7]  Edward Cadbury was in process of endowing a chair in theology with the prospect of a faculty in due course. Student admissions were up 3%.[8] A gymnasium and associated games courts were in the course of construction and Sir Charles Hyde had promised to find the money to enlarge the Union building.

Fortune, however, was lying. A less propitious period for a vice-chancellor to take office would be hard to imagine. Priestley found himself pitched into preparations for the University to cope in wartime, and austerity would still be the order of the day when he retired after the war, in 1952. Through almost all of his fourteen years in office he was able to initiate only the most modest of developments. Post-Munich optimism was a false dawn and Priestley was a vice-chancellor who became substantially a prisoner of circumstances.

With the exposure of this supposed dawn still some months ahead, Priestley issued, within days of taking office, a memorandum on the future development of the University.[9] Predictably his most urgent priority was to transfer Arts and the other exiles from Edmund Street but this step, he was careful to point out, was less straightforward than it might seem. Not only had the expected buyer for Edmund Street dropped out 'because of the uncertainty surrounding the national future' but even if the sale had materialised the proceeds would have been insufficient to finance the move completely. In particular, the Edmund Street buildings were rate-free; those at Edgbaston were not. This meant that £100,000 of any sale receipts would have to be set aside to produce the additional £3000 a year which would be required for the revenue budget. The 'greatest single item' of Priestley's new building programme was, however, a new library at Edgbaston. This would have to be large enough to suffice for fifty years and significant enough to be the greatest ornament and the central building of the Edgbaston site. The cost would be at least £100,000, more probably as much as £150,000, and the hope was that the project was one which should appeal to a private donor who wished his name to be perpetuated.

The next objective Priestley listed was a residential hostel for (male) students. This announced a concern which would characterise the whole of his vice-chancellorship, the welfare of the student community. When he retired, the vice-president of the Guild of Students referred to his 'unwavering faith in students' and gave him the accolade, 'the students' vice-chancellor'.[10]

Lodge and Grant Robertson had previously pointed out the need for accommodation for male undergraduates living away from home but Priestley was thinking of much more than providing an alternative to lodgings which would make it easier to monitor potentially rowdy young men. As well as being less than satisfactory, the existing Chancellor's Hall was *distant*. A hostel on campus would make it possible to pass an ordinance which required students whose homes were more than ten or fifteen miles away to reside at the Edgbaston site. Birmingham would become semi-residential and so be able to achieve new and vital educational objectives.

> The presence of such a concentrated student body on the university site would immensely increase the general efficiency of the University and is of peculiar importance in the present national situation. The concentration of the students would add considerably to the University's power of developing political and social consciousness, the international outlook and a sense of citizenship in its students. We are, I think, at last, awake to the fact that the conscious training of the leaders of the future generation in these things is one of the University's chief aims.

Of course, much in this programme echoed Grant Robertson, and it may seem strange that Priestley should present a statement of the obvious in such personal terms and so soon after taking office. Indeed, he included an apology for the roughness of the memorandum on the ground that he had finished it in the early hours of Tuesday 18 October in time for a meeting called for the next day. The truth is, that he had arrived in Birmingham to a fully-fledged crisis.

The origin of this seems to have been a discussion in the University Council about the need for significant further building in physics. Neville Moss, dean of Science and professor of mining, announced that he would himself go after the money required and thereupon wrote to the Prime Minister.[11] However, in the course of his letter Moss also mentioned that the faculty had other urgent needs as well, particularly in chemistry and for the creation of research fellowships in science. Evidently impressed, Chamberlain agreed to see Moss and the outcome was a private approach by the Prime Minister to Lord Nuffield emphasising the needs of physics and saying, 'if they can get the money they have a good chance of leading the world in this Department'. Nuffield responded with a gift of £60,000 (£40,000 for the building and the rest for research fellowships), and no doubt some pleasure in upstaging Lord Austin, his commercial rival at Longbridge. Moss wanted to announce Chamberlain's involvement but the Prime Minister declined, saying that he might be able achieve more still. However, it leaked out that Moss had approached him not just for physics but for the faculty generally, and the reaction of other faculties can be imagined!

Priestley's memorandum was an early example of using personal skills famously learned in the Antarctic to calm down 'irascible professors', and not for the last time.[12] It was also a way the vice-chancellor could take control of the prime-ministerial link himself. A Chamberlain and former Birmingham student occupying Number 10, 'in a position to put in train large movements for the university's support', was an asset not to be wasted. The memorandum carried the subheading, 'with particular reference to past and future negotiations with the Prime Minister' and it defended Moss (who was good at fundraising) by stressing Chamberlain's 'unexpected intensity of interest': 'I think that this fact needs to be recognised and should offset completely any feeling that unofficial representations of one section of the university's needs have cut across the formulation of a general case to some extent.' On the other hand, since Moss had mentioned other needs to Chamberlain apart from physics, Priestley was able to say that asking for minor items undervalued the potential yield of Chamberlain's support:

> With the present national feeling of gratitude to the present Prime Minister he ought to be in a much better position to realise any plans he might adopt as his own for the development of any project that he had at heart. If we put him off by concentrating upon small objectives we might fail to take advantage of the best opportunity the University ever had.

This allowed Priestley to introduce his own priority. The proper size of project for a Prime Minister's attention was a new library.

Advancing the library project so soon was a step which Priestley probably would rather have avoided because he knew that he would not yet get universal support. A climate of hostility surrounded the existing librarian, apparently on the grounds of poor management. Priestley, however, pulled no punches.

> I am particularly anxious lest the personality of the present librarian should be allowed to prejudice the planning of the new library on the proper scale. It has clearly had some effect in the past. … The fact that the University has not the best possible librarian is, after all, the fault of those who selected him and should not, in my opinion, be allowed to prejudice

library development for a moment, or in any particular.

The vice-chancellor clearly carried opinion with him because the University Library was still high on the agenda in the New Year. In his first report to Council he pressed for a central library and then buildings to hold Arts, Commerce and Law, new administrative accommodation, a Faculty Club, and a vice-chancellor's house as well as an extension of the Union building at Edgbaston to accommodate students from the incoming faculties, and at least two hostels for men.[13] The whole would cost up to £750,000. Soon after this he prepared a formal recommendation to Council advising a large-scale public appeal.[14] It began by listing the vital capital projects which the University needed and pointing out that no adequate finance was in prospect. The current account was £3000 in deficit and having to meet large costs to get the Medical School up and running; no money could be found there. Selling Edmund Street would only release £300,000 for new building and little capital support could be expected from the UGC in view of the government's rearmament programme. On the other hand, a well prepared appeal to complete Joseph Chamberlain's scheme should, he thought, rouse civic pride generally and could include enough 'prestige' elements to attract rich individual donors. If successful, an appeal might pay completely for the new buildings at Edgbaston and allow the proceeds from the sale of Edmund Street to be invested, so providing £12,000 a year and putting the current account healthily in the black.

Priestley recognised that, given the international situation, launching an appeal would be 'an act of faith', but he felt that the timing could be right and that it was most certainly the right time to begin preparations. Nothing should deter the University short of war;

> Immediate war is much less likely than it was a few months ago, and the likelihood of war decreases on the whole with every month of the national effort at rearmament. ... For myself, I believe that if war does not come in spring or early summer it will not come at all. If war does not come, rearmament expenditure is still bound to increase steadily for a couple of years at least and a great deal of this money is being spent in and around Birmingham. A short period of prosperity in this district is, therefore, certain if peace prevails. It is equally certain, I should think, that in a few years the pinch of paying for these armaments and the return to normal peacetime expenditure will, unless the economists find some better way out than they have in the past, cause financial stringency on a national scale. This is another reason why the University should attempt to skim some of the cream while the cow is in full milk.

There was, in any case, no point in holding back, for if a war came it would produce a 'general financial tangle'.

With hindsight it is easy to label Priestley naïve, but public feeling during the winter of 1938–9 was overwhelmingly behind the policy of 'appeasement', and certainly so in both Birmingham and the University. In the city, the Chamberlain name still counted for a great deal and there was no history of vigorous anti-fascist sentiment. Support for refugees from Germany was, as we have seen, lukewarm and the area provided very few recruits for Spain. Only one graduate of the University volunteered – a local general practitioner.[15] There were Communists and anti-fascists on the university staff but John Cornford had to be brought in from Oxford to give academic weight to the Republican cause. The laymen involved with the University strongly supported the vice-chancellor's position. Within days of Chamberlain's return from Munich, Walter Barrow, the Pro-Chancellor, wrote to inform the Prime Minister that Sir Charles Hyde had given the University £10,000 to be spent at Chamberlain's direction as 'a thanksgiving offering for your untiring efforts for peace'.[16] (Chamberlain allocated it for a Physical Fitness Fund.[17]) Barrow concluded his letter: 'May I add a word of profound gratitude for all you have done, and are doing, for this country. As a personal thanksgiving my wife and I are giving the University a further £2,000 towards the costs of the Medical School.' Priestley could, thus, count on strong support but what he could not anticipate as he prepared his paper for the March meeting of the University Council was that appeasement would suddenly collapse. On the 15th of the month Hitler entered Prague. In the ensuing atmosphere the plan for an appeal was held back but Priestley and the lay officers continued to remain optimistic. As late as 21 July 1939 they requested a meeting with Chamberlain to take his advice on launching the appeal to individuals in the first instance and asked for his good offices. Six weeks later war was declared.[18]

Faced with the final collapse of his hopes, Priestley had to accept that 'development is likely to be deferred *sine die*'. His report for 1938–9 shows that the proposal for the public appeal was never put to Council; as for the extension of the Union, although funding for this was effectively already in place, it too was abandoned.[19] Most serious of all, 'our plans for the final concentration of the whole University at Edgbaston go into the discard for the time being'. Even a decision to evacuate Edmund Street if war came and leave it to its fate had to be reversed.[20] The only thing the vice-chancellor could do was to stress that unifying the campuses remained 'the University's paramount need' and to propose, in imitation of the elder Cato, that it should adopt the mantra: 'Edmund Street must go'.

> The fact that our students are aware of this overmastering need is indicated by the fact that in the first number of Guild News published after war broke out, the suggestion was made that, instead of being protected by camouflage, the roof of the University building in Edmund Street should be marked with the invitation 'bomb here'.

The advent of war in September 1939 threatened to put an immediate strain on the established rhythms of University government. In 1940 the Court of Governors delegated its powers to the Council, but Priestley did not expect 'to see much, during the war, of those industrialists of our Council who live outside Birmingham'.[21] In the event, the initial fear that voluntary work with the University government would have a low priority during hostilities proved to be far from the case. In 1941, for instance, the Council expressed concern at the news that the state of repair of the University's power station would mean the end of a practical element in the undergraduate course for the B.Sc. in electrical engineering. Their timely intervention resulted in undergraduates being offered the alternative of a summer vacation spent at Metro-Vickers, a firm with which Professor Dannatt of electrical engineering had close links and where the manager of the plant was himself a Birmingham graduate.[22] An important innovation in 1943 was the setting up of the University's first Public Relations Committee in 1943, This was followed by the appointment of Eric Vincent as a publicity officer, a shrewd move which allowed Vincent to keep press and public informed of the University's vital wartime activities.[23] Another important change that took place in the form of the University's government was an increase in the size of Senate, the vice-chancellor's concern for the welfare of the academic staff and his belief in the universities' role in preserving Western democracy happily working together to provide for the representation of non-professorial staff.[24]

War, therefore, made less of an impact on the running of the University than was expected. Where its impact was immediate and direct was in the demands for 'scientific manpower': advice and research that scientific war created in both the nation and the locality. In Birmingham, as in institutions of higher education generally, these demands began some years before the outbreak of hostilities. Britain had begun to rearm from 1935 onwards, with urgency increasing from the Munich Crisis of September 1938.[25] Birmingham and Midland industry were central to this. After the report of the Weir Committee in 1934, the building of 'shadow' aeroplane factories began in 1935–6 adjacent to existing motor-car factories at Castle Bromwich, Solihull and Cofton Hackett, and this radically transformed the industrial base of the West Midlands. This was so both in structure and unit size as these large factories were added to the existing pattern of metalwork, motor vehicles and components, armaments and electrical equipment which had already undergone a revolution in scale, economy and organisation during the inter-war period. The consequences have marked the structure of Midland industry until the present day.[26] But industrial war work was not confined to larger firms and units such as Lucas and the Austin Longbridge plant. The traditional Birmingham reliance on the smaller firm continued with some 50% of the region's 470 firms still employing fewer than 50 workers in 1944.[27] The result was that as Birmingham and the Midlands became geared up for warfare, the area was able to produce some 45% of all Britain's wartime aero-engines, 17% of her Spitfires and a whole catalogue of armaments, armoured vehicles and mechanised gun turrets, along with components without number for aeroplanes and motor vehicles.[28] As for munitions, the Midlands region, along with London and the South-East, employed the highest proportion of the nation's munitions workers – by 1941, 19.9% of them worked in the region.[29]

The war which Britain and its universities were awaiting as the 1930s came to a close was again expected to be 'war like never before'. However, in contrast to 1914, preparations had been made by the CVCP and the UGC, bodies that had not existed during the First World War, working alongside another product of that earlier conflict, the Ministry of Labour. Their key decision was that Britain's universities should continue their work throughout the war. So vital was their role in technological warfare expected to be that it was 'unthinkable that (they) should cease to function'.[30] Throughout 1938 and 1939, the CVCP and UGC worked out a series of agreements that covered practically every area of British university life. They ranged from the problem of necessary relocation and the continuation of wartime teaching and research, to how such research might be co-ordinated and supported, and to assurances that the universities would not suffer financially as a result of the falling student numbers and a suspension for the duration of the system of UGC quinquennial grants.

The first problem was how to protect the plant of this vital national resource. Universities were carefully categorised according to the danger they would face in war. Birmingham was in an area designated 'scarlet' and so was categorised as 'vulnerable'. Although well north of the Channel coast, and (at least at the commencement of hostilities) at the outer limits of the range of German bombers, the importance of Birmingham and Midland industry to the British war effort made it a very probable target. Nevertheless, there was no evacuation. The danger to the University was clearly less than to higher education institutions in London and on the south coast, and vital local industries were dependent on the continuance of Birmingham's technical support. Instead, Edgbaston became the wartime home for over two hundred medical students from King's College London.[31]

The University, with special financial support from the CVCP and UGC, prepared air-raid shelters and reinforced and protected university buildings. In all, the Edmund Street site was protected by some 10 000 sandbags, with Edgbaston needing 30 000. 'Huge semi-basement shelters in which teaching work continued' were contrived at both sites, while further shelters were provided at the University's hostels. Special precautions were taken at the newly opened Barber Institute. Much of the priceless contents was removed and packed away and a surgical post was set up in the basement, much to Bodkin's annoyance.[32] As for the statue of George I, situated in front of the Institute, this was encased in brick for the duration of the war, which students seized on as an opportunity to hoist a boat on to the top.[33] These air-raid precautions were not complete until late 1939 as the University, just as the Unionist City Council, had delayed as long as possible and beyond, in hope of a late and unexpected success of appeasement.[34] As an additional precaution some five wives of University staff, together with thirty-one children, were evacuated to the University of Toronto in Canada.

Students and staff were organised into a variety of units to protect the University and its people from a whole gamut of possible dangers.[35] There were Air-Raid Precaution squads, decontamination groups to deal with chemical or germ-based weapons, Local Defence Volunteers – later the Home Guard – and fire-watchers. Seven Home Guard units in all were drawn from the University's academic and administration staff and 'servants'. Fire-watching became a way of life for all wartime university staff. Researchers in the school of physics found nights spent on duty at the top of Chamberlain clock tower an invaluable opportunity during which they could ponder their work. In all, the Midland Fire Service trained seventy different teams at the University. The popular supposition is that Birmingham suffered relatively lightly from German air raids but in fact only London was more heavily bombed and only London and Liverpool exceeded Birmingham's 2241 killed and 6692 injured, 3010 of them seriously.[36] The first raid took place on 9 August 1940, when Erdington was hit. Sixty-five attacks followed, chiefly in November and December 1940, and January, March and April 1941, but continuing into mid-1942. University staff and students figured amongst the casualties throughout October and December 1940; some of the staff, the vice-chancellor reported, 'suffered injury in the defence of the University', though he gave no details.[37] Apparently he himself was one of the fire-watchers on the night of 11 December 1940, when Mason College and nearby buildings in the city centre were hit by three high-explosive bombs, and those on duty 'feared that they would not survive the night'.[38] Further bombs hit the University in April 1941, but without causing casualties.[39]

The University's most dramatic episode occurred during a daylight raid in the Easter vacation in 1941 when a 'stick of 14 high explosive bombs' fell on the Edgbaston campus, with incendiary devices hitting the Queen Elizabeth Medical Centre.[40] Some of these bombs quite literally bounced past the noses of staff before they hit the biology and chemistry buildings. P. B. Moon, of physics, actually entered the chemistry building to retrieve vital research notes from the safe, despite the presence of an unexploded bomb which had opened the roof and ceiling of the office to the sky. Throughout the war, although members of staff were injured, none appears to have lost their life, but some eight undergraduates were killed by enemy action, either 'at their homes, in lodgings or on the roads'.[41] Despite the peril of these bombing raids, Raymond Priestley recorded that the University's buildings emerged from war 'practically unscathed', unfortunately so as far as Edmund Street was concerned.[42]

Protecting the universities physically was one aspect of preparation for war. Even more important was 'manpower planning', both the recruitment of students to the services and the deployment of technically trained workers to industry and scientific research. This had been a major concern of the pre-war discussions between the CVCP, the UGC and the Ministry of Labour which had the responsibility for utilising the nation's manpower in wartime, a factor as crucial for Britain as industry, raw materials and investment. Together these bodies were determined that this second war would not totally destroy a further generation of university undergraduates and graduates, and that indiscriminate recruitment to the services would not denude industry and research of scientific manpower, as had occurred in the previous war. Indeed, *The Employment in War of University Men and Registration of University Staff*, which set out the agreed policy, expressly condemned the labour deployment policies of Britain's First World War governments, although, given the length of this second total war, recruitment policy could still not always be protected.[43]

Initially, the agreement provided that all Arts undergraduates over twenty years of age could be called up into the Services, whether they had completed their BA degrees or not. By the second year of war the age had fallen to eighteen.[44] Undergraduates in much needed specialist areas such as mathematics, chemistry, engineering, dentistry and medicine were permitted to continue into their final year of study, with their names being placed (depending on the degree subject) on the Central Registers of the Royal Society, the Institute of Physics and Chemistry, and the Joint Recruiting Board (JRB). Headed by the vice-chancellor of the University of Liverpool, the JRB functioned as a clearing house at both national and local levels, sending graduates to war work that would best use their abilities.[45] After September 1940, this was augmented by annual visits to the universities by Ministry of Labour officers, appointing recent graduates to posts of national importance.

As well as ensuring that the number and mix of wartime graduates was very much as the nation required, the universities established shorter wartime degree programmes to produce appropriately skilled graduates quickly. Wartime courses for students in arts, commerce, law and 'unreserved' (that is, civilian) science were restricted to one year. The remaining science courses were reduced to two years and three months and in some, thought not all, the academic year was extended to four terms.[46] Thus undergraduate life became 'a luxury consumed furtively'.[47] The war could never be forgotten. Each undergraduate was required to attend the Service Training Corps (STC) or the joint universities' Air Training Corps (ATC). In addition, the University housed an infantry training centre which men attended before entering the University. The STC had replaced a somewhat outmoded OTC, but with a similar objective, qualifying students to enter the army with an accelerated chance of a commission.[48] Each recruit to the STC had to attend at least 150 parades over two years plus a three-week training camp every summer. [49] Physical education was also made compulsory for all undergraduates.[50] Specific wartime courses were also established – in engineering, chemistry, metallurgy, radio and, at Birmingham, radiolocation or radar. Nationally, the

Hankey Committee provided some 6000 bursaries to pay undergraduate course fees and maintenance. Half of these went to those on radio courses (an index of the importance of this technology), 40% were awarded to engineering students and the remainder to chemistry.[51] The University also provided short specialist courses for British and Allied servicemen. The School of Engineering trained a total of 360 Royal Engineer cadets in addition to the 250 graduates they educated over the war years.[52]

In their aim of limiting losses among undergraduates and graduates the CVCP and UGC had partial success. This was first of all true in terms of casualties. Although some seventy-six members of staff joined the forces, the figure for undergraduates and graduates is difficult to estimate. Clearly the number was significantly larger than in the First World War, given that virtually all those who had studied at Birmingham from 1920 onwards were liable either to be conscripted or assigned to work of national importance. Nevertheless, despite that comprehensive involvement and despite the war lasting for six years instead of four, the University lost only 120 undergraduates, graduates and members of staff as against 175 in the First World War.[53] In other words, from a much larger cohort, casualties were about twenty a year instead of forty-four.

The activity of the University also suffered less in 1939–45 than in the previous war. Most obviously, the site was not requisitioned nor the equipment dispersed. Numbers also held up. As Angus Calder has put it: '(While) the First World War had denuded the universities of their pupils, the second war was kinder to them.'[54] Thanks to this careful control of recruitment, together with wartime degree regulations, the universities and the University of Birmingham in particular continued their work steadily. For many months the war had surprisingly little impact on undergraduate numbers. Priestley could write in 1941: 'We are now well into the third year of war, and the population of the civic universities has scarcely diminished.'[55] In fact, numbers at Birmingham actually rose from 1362 in the academic year 1938–9 to 1472 in 1939–40, and the fall to 1464 in the following year was insignificant. This was in contrast to the decline in student numbers nationally, where 1939–40 saw a 6.7% reduction on 1938–9 levels.[56] When the call-up age of male Arts students was lowered to eighteen, undergraduate numbers at Birmingham did fall to 1280, but they held at that level for the remainder of the war, increasing to 1410 in 1945–6. One reason why numbers at Birmingham kept up at about 94% of the 1938–9 figure was the increase in female recruitment; the vice-chancellor noted in 1943 that there were 'no fit men in Arts, Commerce or Law or unreserved Science'.[57] Given the very strict wartime emphasis on applied science degrees, Birmingham, along with other institutions of higher education, was not only 'working twenty-four hours a day' but was becoming highly vocational as a result.[58] According to Dent, British universities 'ceased to function as universities, coming to look oddly like technical colleges'.[59]

Another effect of the war was to make the student body more varied. International understanding was enhanced by the University running special courses for allied service people and for refugee students. In all, the International Student Service and Refugee committee brought a total of eighty-three students from sixteen different nations to the University. Meeting in a special club that had been formed for them, some of those in exile described their time at the University rather unfairly as 'Wait and see and make tea.' In fact, there was plenty going on, from courses in English language and literature run by the British Council to attempts to rescue a baby girl from Hungary and the family of a Jewish student from Poland.[60] On the national level, Raymond Priestley was placed in charge of 'troop education in the Midlands, working like a Trojan' in consequence.[61] Local links were also enhanced by the University setting out to provide courses for Midland workers. These were not only given by the well-established WEA, but by the University itself for specific work groups, such as the course the University ran in 1945 for the firemen of Warwickshire, Worcestershire, Shropshire and Herefordshire.[62]

The most valuable resource which the University had was, of course, its trained staff. Here again the blueprint of September 1938, *The Employment in War of University Men and the Registration of University Staff*, determined, at least in outline, how the University's teaching and research facilities and academic staff were to be utilised in war.[63] Staff were circulated and a register of possible state employment made. Although those of appropriate age who were members of faculties not vital to the scientific pursuit of war were available to be called up, in all 32 full-time and 10 part-time professors, 5 heads of department, 92 readers, 119 full-time and 150 part-time lecturers, together with 56 demonstrators remained in post throughout the war, either in a teaching or a research capacity. Many continued on past retirement age, the eventual retirement in 1945 of Valentine, the professor of education, being a notable example of this.[64] Staff numbers were also augmented by refugee academics brought to the University both before and during the war, under the auspices of the Academic Assistance Committee, among them Otto Frisch of physics.[65]

One vital role of this trained staff which it is easy to overlook is teaching. In manpower terms, turning out trained personnel was just as important to the war effort as the more exciting and intellectually rewarding research, and the University took great care to see that its teaching programmes were supported. This often took the form of a professor or head of department dividing the academic staff between those who were to devote themselves purely to teaching and a majority who were to carry out research. Both Priestley and Mark Oliphant from physics recognised the heavy load that these wartime lecturers bore, given a wide variety of courses, students of disparate ability and a four-term year. Oliphant was being no more than fair when he described this work as 'the equivalent of wartime research'.[66]

Other staff were selected for research, either in government laboratories or in the universities, the CVCP. and UGC pressing government to keep established research teams together. Research was allocated to Britain's various universities, and university personnel were posted to government work in ways very reminiscent of the First World War. Apart from certain contracts and agreements negotiated before the war, the system continued to rely on the learned societies, personal contacts between government decision-makers and university scientists of note and, if not 'gentlemanly agreements', at least 'brotherly collusion behind the scene'.[67] Again, as in the First World War, government–university links were often slow.[68]

Thanks to teaching, research, consultancies and wider cultural involvement, the University's war effort helped to integrate it with its locality and with the nation at large, just as had been the case during the First World War. As *The Times* put it, 'The don became ubiquitous in war.'[69] Inevitably the emphasis here lies on the vital work done in the faculty of Science, but it is important to note that members of Arts, Commerce and Law also contributed to Birmingham's war effort. This was a point which Raymond Priestley returned to on several occasions. Work to ensure success in combat was not all that mattered. Britain's universities in war were 'the chief repositories, exponents of that freedom of thought that has been quenched in totalitarian states'.[70] It was for the University to provide cultural and moral support for the people of the Birmingham and Midlands, visiting British and allied service personnel and those who had already found refuge in the city and its University, as they faced the long years of hard work in war. In the ultimate, therefore, Priestley saw the primary function of the University in wartime as cultural, even ethical, a living symbol of what was being fought for.

Priestley found he had to explain this message even to the members of the non-scientific faculties themselves. They must understand 'their value to the general community in the West Midlands where [they had] become an integral part of the common man's daily life'.[71] A whole array of conferences and cultural occasions had been provided for the general populace of the area. Concerts were held at the Barber Institute throughout the war. Dame Myra Hess, that musical symbol of wartime resilience, gave recitals at the Institute as President of the University Music Society.[72] 'Close associations' were built up with local education authorities and schools, with the hosting of a joint conference between the University and the headmasters and headmistresses of the Midlands area. Throughout the war, local young people were brought into contact with the University through a Midland Youth Forum, even before they became undergraduates, where they debated a wide range of matters from the war itself to the future of education. Debates on democracy furthered the idea that Britain's universities were repositories of the democratic spirit and the lord mayor of Birmingham reciprocated with a series of lectures to undergraduates on civic politics which reinforced Priestley's aim of 'relating our action to the service of the community'.[73]

On the practical level, Arts, Commerce, and to a lesser extent, Law, undertook research that was relevant to the locality both in war and in the immediate post-war era. The Second World War was not just the war of the scientist, but of the social scientist too, with region and nation being concerned about the capacity of natural, industrial and human resources to fight such a total war. For instance, Commerce and Geography collaborated on projects to determine the geographical distribution of the industrial population in Birmingham and the Black Country, so providing data for the wartime deployment of industrial workers.[74] Surveys were undertaken in regional and national planning, on industry and agriculture in the West Midlands, local road and rail transport in war, the Midland coal industry and the Birmingham area of the Ordnance Survey map.[75]

The faculty of Commerce also provided consultancy. Professor J. G. Smith, for instance, served on the local conscientious objectors tribunal. The Bureau of Russian Studies, under the directorship of Konavlov, professor of Russian language and literature, advised Birmingham business on trade with the USSR, much to the delight of the Chamber of Commerce, which had sponsored the professorship, department and bureau. Evidence of the faculty's concern for the future of the Midlands after the war was the formation of the West Midland Group on Post-War Reconstruction and Planning. Set up in 1941, this was an interesting mix of research project, local think-tank and policy maker. Under the chairmanship of Grant Robinson, the ex-vice-chancellor, the group had influence on immediate post-war development in the region, particularly when significant parts of its recommendations on the redistribution of population were carried out.

At the end of the war Priestley remarked: 'the intricate tasks of co-operation with and warfare against foreign nations demanded historical and cultural knowledge and linguistic skills as much as the fighting needed the inventions of the scientists'.[76] One example he had in mind was the recruitment of historians, social scientists and especially modern linguists for intelligence work. The war had demonstrated 'the remarkable utility of Arts studies', while also demanding that scientists 'study human history so that they have regard for human values'. Early in the war, François Lafitte, soon to be professor of French, wrote *The Internment of Aliens*, published by Penguin in 1940, which drew attention to the mismanagement and squalor of the internment camps.[77] The professor of finance, J. G. Smith, lectured on war economics. The university staff contributed to that most influential wartime medium, the British Broadcasting Corporation (BBC). In 1941 a Thomas Bodkin broadcast to the USA declared that Birmingham's population was 'bombed but blooming'![78] Priestley wrote and broadcast regularly, notably his 1943 broadcast on 'the Future of the Civic Universities' which at a dark point in the struggle turned thoughts to opportunities after the war.[79] There were also direct contributions to the well-being of British forces. The most important was arguably the work of C. W. Valentine on literacy and education within the British army. This led to a series of publications which became basic to the work of the army's education section.[80] Valentine also undertook studies of the effects of evacuation on children. At the end of the war the professor of history, Keith Hancock, was engaged to write the official history of the War Office. Some of the University's non-scientists even found an international voice. Raymond Priestley served on a Commission on Higher Education in the Colonies.[81] The Bureau of Russian Studies produced useful papers on the economy of the USSR. J. A. Hawgood, professor of modern history and government, lectured at the Royal Institute of International Affairs.[82] With a eye for the arresting phrase, he declared in his *Enigma of Germany* that 'Bismarck made the bed for Goebbels to lie on.'[83]

If the non-scientific contribution of the University of Birmingham to the morale and the thinking of the wartime nation perhaps deserves more attention than it has had, it did not differ fundamentally from that made by other universities and colleges. This was also true of much of its scientific war work. The faculty of Science was a regular agent for regionally based government bodies. Mining made reports to the Fuel Efficiency Committee. Botany carried out a soil and agricultural survey of north Warwickshire to establish data on which to maximise agricultural output in order to meet wartime food demands, and thereafter made follow-up reports to the Ministry of Agriculture and Fisheries and its agricultural executive. Metallurgy carried out more various and wide-ranging quality-control inspections for the Midlands' munitions industry than even it had done during the First World War. In all, the metallurgy laboratories tested a total of 40 000 bronze bullet and shell cases. Civil engineering tested samples from the propeller blades, aviation components, battle tanks, bridges and hangars manufactured in Midlands' shadow factories and at Fort Dunlop. Testing also led to involvement in research. Thus the School of Mechanical Engineering developed a hydraulic control mechanism for some of the gun turrets manufactured at nearby Longbridge, while Professor Dannatt of electrical engineering worked on an alternative electrical system. Science departments also undertook contract research directly for government departments and agencies. Mining, for instance, worked on the production and containment of gas for motor vehicles, the University thus having some role in creating the wartime vision of large vehicles topped with gasholders like barrage balloons! F. H. Garner, professor of oil engineering, developed a range of fuels for incendiary bombs and flame-throwers and a small flame-thrower production plant was actually set up in the University. Garner also developed the burners that were the key to the FIDO system of fog dispersion used to ensure all-weather landing visibility for aircraft. Other areas of the University's scientific work were far more humane. In the School of Chemistry, for example, although the other staff were working on problems connected with the atomic bomb, Maurice Stacey developed 'Dextran', a chemical substitute for blood plasma for use in forward casualty-dressing stations.

It would, however, be wrong to see Birmingham scientists as nose-down at the bench with no thought for the values of the war espoused by Arts, Law and Commerce. For example, Solly Zuckerman, Birmingham's professor of anatomy, became Earl Mountbatten's scientific adviser and played an important role in planning communications and transport for D-Day, work for which he received a CBE.[84] He was, however, also a publicist for scientific culture and in 1940 his *Science at War* appeared in Penguin's notable wartime science series.[85] Through their research, advisory and media work men of the Birmingham's faculty of Science certainly captured the public imagination, helping to promote further the ideal of the free spirit that was possibly crucial in bringing victory over Nazi Germany.

The University of Birmingham thus played a full part in the 1939–45 war, alongside other academic institutions. There was, however, one field where its work was distinctive and of outstanding national and international importance. This was in physics and related disciplines.[86] Priestley said later that 'the theoretical work of Professor Peierls and the advanced and experimental work of Professors Haworth and Oliphant and their teams in the Departments of Chemistry and Physics have conferred distinction upon the University, upon Birmingham and the West Midlands'.[87] He could easily have said that the work of the physics department on radar and on the atomic bomb were among the handful of scientific achievements throughout history which can genuinely be called world-shaping.

In terms both of winning the war and of post-war living, the achievement of the department of physics which mattered supremely was the discovery of how to control short radio waves by a cavity magnetron. This was significant for victory because it gave the Allies an operational advantage which the Germans could never match. Post-war, the discovery revolutionised technology, making possible everything from high-density air-traffic control to the microwave oven. The story started with the problem which Britain faced as a consequence of the advent of the aeroplane. It could no longer rely for immunity on the Channel. What was needed 'to make England an island again' was a way to detect and identify hostile incoming aircraft sufficiently early for Britain to scramble fighters and alert anti-aircraft defences.[88] In 1935 the answer was demonstrated to be the use of radio beams, and by the start of the war a defensive line of what are now known as radar stations was in place, operating on a wavelength of 1.5 metres. Early radar had excellent range but lacked resolution and the equipment was very bulky. The government had approached Oliphant at the end of 1938 about research into wavelengths of less than a metre and he was determined to get the contract.[89] He eventually succeeded, after a summer spent at the radar station at Ventnor on the Isle of Wight being introduced to the existing system.[90] The Birmingham physicists were principally nuclear scientists and none of the eight who went with Oliphant to Ventnor was familiar with radio research (and only one of those who had stayed behind), so Birmingham's success is hard to explain – though it did mean that everyone started with an open mind.[91] Since more than eighty physicists from a good number of other universities also made the trip to Ventnor, Oliphant probably won by exploiting his connections.

To find space for the project, Birmingham's newly completed Nuffield Research Laboratory was taken off nuclear research, renamed the 'Admiralty Laboratory' and made a restricted area.[92] Staff, either seconded by the University or put on the Admiralty payroll, were divided into teams and allocated one of the known or likely ways of generating radio waves as short, say, as 10 cm. The best bet was the klystron oscillator and Oliphant and his senior colleagues started to work on this. A device was quickly working at the right wavelength, but it was too bulky, too complicated and had a limited power output. Working on another of the options was a team consisting of a research fellow, J. T. Randall, and H. A. H. Boot, a research student 'who had already shown great aptitude for making electrical appliances work'.[93] Within six weeks they discovered that their assigned project was a turkey and on their own initiative began to think instead about another low-priority possibility, the magnetron.[94] This produced very little power and was highly volatile but the two wondered whether by introducing the resonators or cavities used in the klystron they would cure both problems. Oliphant gave some encouragement but could get them no money and all material had to be scrounged – some of the sealing disks required were made from halfpenny coins.[95] Given these obstacles it is surprising that the prototype was ready by December 1939, but after some teething troubles all parts worked together for the first time on 21 February 1940.[96] That the cavity magnetron produced several hundred watts of power was immediately obvious, it was certainly small and a week later Randall and Boot demonstrated that the wavelength was an incredible 9.8 cm. Moving from that point to an effective radar set took time – Randall's old company, General Electric (GEC), handled the manufacturing – but by September a submarine had been detected at seven miles. From then on the priority shifted from research to getting radar sets into the ships and aircraft engaged in the desperate Battle of the Atlantic and the magnetron effectively passed out of Birmingham hands. However, it was another member of the Physics department, James Sayers, who in August 1941 solved the one technical problem which remained, the tendency of the cavity magnetron to jump frequency.[97] The first operational success of the new radar was the destruction of a mine-laying aircraft early in April 1942 and ten days later the first U-boat was sunk. Within just over a year the German Admiralty was forced to withdraw its surviving submarines and short-wave radar was becoming available for all manner of ship and aircraft.[98] By the end of the war Britain had produced nearly a million magnetrons.[99] It was 'the most valuable English scientific invention in the Hitler war'.[100] By a bitter irony it had also been impossible for the University or any of those involved to take out a patent for it.

If the magnetron was an invention vital to the winning of the war, the other discovery of the physics department, how to produce a feasible atomic bomb, revolutionised post-war global politics and international relations. The achievement is also far more controversial. As we have seen, Professor Oliphant had been brought to Birmingham to put nuclear physics on the map. The phenomenon of nuclear fission in uranium had been identified early in 1939 and so too the theoretical possibility of developing an explosive. Oliphant calculated that one pound of uranium could in theory produce the equivalent of 50 000 tons of TNT.[101] Within months, however, it was realised that a nuclear reaction could only occur where a sufficient (or critical) mass of material was present. Rudolf Peierls, the professor of applied mathematics at Birmingham, set out to improve calculations of the amount needed and his conclusion, published in October 1939, was that the mass would have to be of the order of tons.[102] This ruled out any commercial and still more any military application of nuclear fission, and the theoretical nature of the discussion was underlined by the further discovery that what made the reaction in uranium possible was the rare 235 isotope which occurred in the metal at a concentration of only 0.7%.[103]

In the summer of 1939 the gifted nuclear physicist Otto Frisch fled to England, took refuge with Peierls (as we have seen) and was given a temporary appointment in Oliphant's department. This, of course, was wholly occupied with the top-secret radar project from which the two aliens were excluded and one day in February or March 1940 (tradition has it when they were fire-watching together) the two men began to speculate on the critical mass which would be needed to cause an explosion if pure uranium 235 was available.[104] To their surprise the answer was as little as one pound and the explosive effect equivalent to thousands of tons of TNT. The two men worked up their 'back of an envelope' calculations into a formal two-part memorandum.[105] In the first section they set out the physics and the mathematics, indicated how a critical mass could be produced to order, proposed a method of concentrating uranium 235 and drew attention to the radiation effects which would accompany and follow an explosion.[106] The second section explored the implications of 'a radioactive "super-bomb"', notably the impossibility of protection, the casualties which would follow, and the problem of radiation hazards on the battlefield.[107] It also drew attention to the possibility that Germany already had or would have the weapon and that deterrence was the only defence: 'The most effective reply would be a counter-threat with a similar bomb. Therefore it seems to us important to start production as rapidly as possible, even if it is not intended to use the bomb as a means of attack.' The introduction to the memorandum modestly described it as discussing 'a possibility which seems to have been overlooked', but Oliphant steered it to the highest level and within three weeks a committee was in being with Oliphant and later Moon, but without the aliens Peierls and Frisch![108] They were, however, admitted to a technical subcommittee in September. W. N. Haworth, professor of chemistry at Edgbaston, was also drawn in to serve as chairman of the chemical panel of Tube Alloys (the code name for the bomb project) and, with his department, to work on the chemical properties of uranium 235.[109] Radar, however, was still the priority at Birmingham and the MAUD Committee, as it was called, gave the lead research role on the atomic bomb to the University of Liverpool, to which Frisch moved.[110] Birmingham scientists continued to be involved, but mainly as individuals.

Prime ministerial approval to go ahead with an atom bomb was given in the summer of 1941 but the practical problems of developing one in Britain were immense. The Americans were brought in and in 1943 the operation was moved to North America and became the Manhattan Project.[111] While this put an end to all institutional involvement by Birmingham's department of physics, many of the staff moved with the project. Mark Oliphant went to Berkeley to work on the electromagnetic separation of isotopes and to maintain close and influential contact with the American leaders of the project.[112] Leo Szilard, the Hungaro-American physicist, said that Oliphant 'goaded' the American programme 'over the top' and into production, and suggested that a special Congressional medal was needed for 'meddling foreigners' such as Oliphant, whose all-out 'vocal determination' to 'solve the uranium problem' resulted in the bomb.[113] For his part Peierls went to a uranium separation plant in New York and then to Los Alamos, where he was joined by Frisch, Moon and others and became responsible for work on the plutonium bomb. Peierls and Frisch were together when the first device was successfully tested on 15 July 1945 and, back in England, Oliphant saw the traces on the seismograph at the University.[114]

With the successful test explosion, decision passed to the hands of politicians and the military. The reaction of the Birmingham staff to the use of the bomb in Japan was understandably mixed. Their initial motivation had been to deter and they had from the start pointed out the devastation which would follow a bomb being used. Peierls wrote later: 'Barely a month after the [Los Alamos] test came the news from Hiroshima. We knew that the war was over, and we knew that our work had contributed to the result. But with the feeling of elation there was a horror at the death and suffering that must have resulted, though we had no details yet.'[115] Such emotions became stronger after the Nagasaki explosion which Frisch would not at first credit: 'Few of us could see any moral reason for dropping a second bomb only a few days later.'[116] He appears, however, to have come to terms with his contribution to nuclear weapons, whereas Peierls became increasingly involved in attempts to mobilise the scientific community against the monster which had been unleashed. He was a member of the Atomic Scientists Association which later fused with Pugwash.[117] Oliphant declined to accept the decoration offered him (the OBE) and he, too, spoke frequently on the issues to the Association and elsewhere.[118] In discussions he regularly emphasised that the achievement of nuclear fission had a potential for good as well as bad, and it has to be said that even in 1941 the MAUD Committee had stressed this huge peacetime opportunity.[119] At the University, physics was now riding high, recognised as one of the truly international schools, but in spite of this there were doubts. In his report for 1945–6 the vice-chancellor expressed pride in the 'significant contribution' made by Birmingham staff to the evolution of the atomic bomb, but added the comment that whether this would be to the University's 'credit or discredit in the ultimate record' remained to be seen.[120] Credit it surely must be. 'Any competent nuclear scientist', said Peierls, 'would have come out with very similar answers to ours if he had been asked. ... The only unusual thing that Frisch and I did at this point was to ask these questions.'[121] The brilliance was that the two of them did ask, and ask before anyone else.

Notes

1 *Birmingham Evening Mail*, 2 Feb. 1939.
2 UC 7/ii 1938–9; Vincent and Hinton, *University of Birmingham*, p. 216.
3 UC 7/iii, p. 13.
4 E.g. Walter Chance and Alderman S. J. Grey had interests in Joseph Lucas Ltd: Cornish, *Birmingham Year Book* (1941), s. n.
5 Vincent and Hinton, *University of Birmingham*, pp. 219–20.
6 For Priestley see *DNB 1974*; R. E. Priestley, *Antarctic Adventure: Scott's Northern Party* (1914, 1974).
7 For the following see UC 7/iii 1938–9, pp. 5–6. The firms involved were Colvilles Ltd of Glasgow, and Horsley Bridge & Thos. Piggot Ltd, Tipton.
8 1643 students in Dec. 1937; 1697 in Dec. 1938.
9 UC 14/ii: Vice–chancellor's Memorandum, 17 Oct. 1938.
10 UC 7/iii 1952, p. 3.
11 For the following see the memo at n. 3; University of Birmingham, NC5/8/i/63–67; UA Council Minutes, 1/33, 28 Sept. , 7 Dec. 1938.
12 *DNB, 1974*.
13 UC 7/iii 1937–8, pp. 14–17.
14 UC 14/ii Vice–chancellor to Council, March 1939; 7/iii 1938–9, p. 3.
15 P. D. Drake, 'Labour and Spain: British Labour's response to the Spanish Civil War with special reference to ... Birmingham', unpublished Ph.D. thesis, University of Birmingham, 1977.
16 University of Birmingham NC 5/8/i/68.
17 Ibid., NC 5/8/i/70.
18 Ibid., NC 5/8/i//69.
19 UC 7/iii 1938–9, p. 2; UA Council Minutes 33, 7 Dec. 1938.
20 UA Council Minutes 33: 2 Nov. 1938, 3 May 1939.
21 UC 14/ii (1940); 7/iii 1939–40, p. 12.
22 Ibid. (1941). For Dannatt and Metro-Vickers see below, p. 277.
23 UC 14/ii (1943), (1944)
24 Ibid. (1939–40).
25 J. C. Crowther and R. Whiddington, *Science at War* (HMSO), 1947, pp. 1–30.
26 David Thoms, *War, Industry and Society: The Midlands, 1939–45* (1989), pp. 22–6; Angus Calder, *The People's War: Britain, 1939–45* (1969), p. 34. Shadow factories later became integral sections of existing car factories, e.g. Cofton Hackett became part of the Longbridge plant.

27 Calder, *The People's War*, p. 35.
28 Thoms, *War, Industry and Society*, p. 26.
29 Ibid., p. 49, Table 2. 9.
30 PRO UGC 5/14: Nov. 1938.
31 UC 7/iii 1939–40, p. 29.
32 UC 8/iii/3: Report of the Director of the Barber Institute, 1 Mar. 1940.
33 Ibid.
34 The Unionist-dominated City Council only began to make air-raid provisions in 1938. Not all precautions were completed by September 1939, but the 'Phoney War' gave the City time to finish. Part of the delay resulted from a dispute about the proportion of the cost to be met by central government: A. Sutcliffe and R. Smith, *History of Birmingham*, iii (Oxford, 1976), pp. 26–35.
35 UC 7/iv/6/24; 13/i/8.
36 Carl Chinn, *Brum Undaunted: Birmingham During the Blitz* (Birmingham, 1996), pp. 132–4.
37 UC 7/iii 1939–40, p. 14.
38 Ibid., 1945, p. 1.
39 UC 7/ii 1941, p. 11; 7/iii 1945, p. 1.
40 UC 7/iii 1945, p. 2.
41 Ibid. , 1939–40, p. 14.
42 Ibid. , 1945, p. 2: 'small in comparison with what might have happened'.
43 PRO UGC5/14: Memo, 24 Sept. 1938; Calder, *People's War*, p. 549. For the Ministry of Labour 1916–39 see Rodney Lowe, *Adjusting to Democracy; The Role of the Ministry of Labour in British Politics, 1916–39* (1986). For 1939–45 see H. M. Parker, *Manpower: A Study of Wartime Policy and Action* (HMSO, 1957).
44 UC 7/iii 1938–9, pp. 20–5; 1940–1, pp. 5–7.
45 PRO UGC5/14; Calder, People's War, pp. 547–9.
46 UC 7/ii 1940, p. 12; 7/iii 1939–40, pp. 12–13; 7/iii 1941–2, p. 2.
47 Calder, *People's War*, p. 550.
48 UC 7/iii 1939–40, pp. 17–20.
49 UC 7/iii 1939–40, p. 19.
50 The number of parades was later increased to 267: UC 7/iii 1941–3, p. 4.
51 Ibid. 1945, p. 5.
52 Ibid. , 1940–1, pp. 13–14. Birmingham was awarded ninety–five bursaries.
53 War Memorial.
54 Calder, *People's War*, p. 547.
55 UC 7/iii 1940–41, p. 1.
56 P. Gosden, 'The nationalizing of Britain's universities, 1945–65', *University of Leeds Review*, 34 (1991–2), p. 151, Table 6.
57 UC 7/iii 1942–3, p. 2.
58 Calder, *People's War*, p. 548.
59 Ibid., p. 547, quoting H. C. Dent,*The Growth of English Education, 1945–50* (1954).
60 UC 7/iv/7/9; 14/ii Box 3.
61 *Birmingham Guardian*, 10 Nov. 1939, 1 Mar. 1940.
62 UC 14/ii (1938–53).
63 PRO, UGC 5/14: memo, 24 Sept. 1938.

64 UC 7/ii 1944, p. 3; 1945, p. 3; 1946, p. 6. Valentine should have retired in September 1944 but did so in 1946.
65 *Birmingham Daily Post*, 26 Sept. 1938; N. Bentwich,*The Rescue and Achievement of Refugee Scholars, 1933–52* (The Hague, 1953).
66 UC 4/v/4: Wartime Research in the Physics School.
67 Guy Hartcup, *The Challenge of War: Science and Engineering's Contribution to World War Two* (Newton Abbot, 1970), p. 23.
68 Harry Melville, *The Department of Scientific and Industrial Research* (Oxford, 1962), p. 340.
69 *The Times*, 24 Feb. 1940.
70 *Birmingham Daily Post*, 28 Feb. 1940.
71 UC 14/ii: 22 Dec. 1943.
72 *Birmingham Daily Post*, 10 Dec. 1943
73 *Birmingham Gazette*, 3 Feb. 1944.
74 *Birmingham Evening Mail*, 17 July 1938; *Birmingham Daily Post*, 8 Mar. 1939. The overall national data was received by the 1939 Royal Commission.
75 UC 7/iii 1945, p. 6.
76 Ibid., p. 7. This year's vice-chancellor's report contains an assessment of the impact of the war on the University and the University's contribution to it.
77 F. Lafitte, *The Internment of Aliens* (1940)
78 *Birmingham Daily Post*, 1 Mar. 1941.
79 Ibid., 3 Nov. 1943; *The Listener*, 11 Nov. 1942. *The Modern University, with Special Reference to Technical Education* followed in 1945 and *The Civic Universities* in 1949.
80 E.g. *Discipline and Morale* (1942), *Principles of Army Training* (1942) and *Literacy and Army Men* (1943).
81 *Birmingham Evening Mail*, 10 Jan. 1944.
82 *Birmingham Daily Post*, 24 Apr. 1939.
83 Ibid., 1 Mar. 1941.
84 UC 7/ii 1945, p. 6; Calder, *People's War*, p. 536.
85 Calder, *People's War*, p. 533.
86 For the following see N. Wydenbach, 'The role of Birmingham University in the development of the cavity magnetron and the atomic bomb', unpublished BA dissertation, University of Birmingham (1997).
87 UC 7/iii 1945, p. 3.
88 Crowther and Whiddington, *Science at War*, p. 10.
89 S. Cockburn and D. Ellyard, *Oliphant* (Perth, Australia, 1981), p. 81, invitation prior to 11 Jan. 1939.
90 UA 22/8 'Memoir by Mark Oliphant', p. 12.
91 Institute of Electrical Engineers, A1 'Development of the Multi–Resonator Magnetron in the University of Birmingham, 1939–45'. The exception was James Sayers, recently arrived from Cambridge; see below, p. 287.
92 Moon and Ibbs, *Physics at Birmingham*, pp. 20–1.
93 Ibid.
94 H. A. H. Boot and J. T. Randall, 'Historical Notes on the Cavity Magnetron', in Institute of Electrical Engineers, *Transactions on Electronic Devices*, 23 (1976), p.

724.

95 Cockburn and Ellyard, *Oliphant*, p. 85; *Sunday Times Magazine*, 7 Sept. 1975, p. 13.

96 Institute of Electrical Engineers, A1, p. 3.

97 E. G. Bowen, *Radar Days* (1987), p. 148.

98 W. E. Burcham and E. D. R. Shearman, *Fifty Years of the Cavity Magnetron* (Birmingham 1990), p. 23.

99 Cockburn and Ellyard, *Oliphant*, p. 89.

100 C. P. Snow, *Science and Government* (Cambridge, Mass., 1961), p. 45.

101 Cockburn and Ellyard, *Oliphant*, p. 96.

102 *Proceedings of the Cambridge Philosophical Society* (1939).

103 Rudolf Peierls, *Bird of Passage* (Princeton, NJ, 1985), pp. 152–3.

104 Ibid., p. 154.

105 Cambridge, Churchill College Ms. Chad 1/28/6.

106 M. Gowing, *Britain and Atomic Energy, 1939–45* (Glasgow, 1964), p. 389; R. Clark, *Tizard* (1965), pp. 215–17.

107 Clark, *Tizard*, pp. 125–17.

108 Cockburn and Ellyard, *Oliphant*, p. 100; Rhodes, *Atomic Bomb*, pp. 239, 330.

109 Cockburn and Ellyard, *Oliphant*, p. 101; UC 7/iii 1945, p. 4.

110 O. Frisch, *What Little I Remember* (Cambridge, 1979), p. 132.

111 UC 4/v/4: 'Following a visit by Professor Oliphant and Professor Peierls to the USA in September 1943, it was decided to move the teams to America.'

112 UA 22/7B, Department of Physics.

113 Rhodes, *Atomic Bomb*, p. 372.

114 UA 22/7b: Oliphant to E. O. Lawrence at Berkeley, 3 July 1945, 'I watch the records of the seismograph in this region. I hope that it won't be long before they tell me what I want to know.'

115 Peierls, *Bird of Passage*, p. 205.

116 Frisch, *What Little I Remember*, p. 177.

117 Peierls, *Bird of Passage*.

118 UA 30/3, Staff records.

119 Cockburn and Ellyard, *Oliphant*; Churchill College, Chadwick Papers 1 28/1:Report 15 July1941.

120 UC 7/iii 1945, p. 3.

121 R. Clark, *Birth of the Bomb* (1965), p. 51.

Chapter Fifteen

Stress, hope and frustration

WHILE ITS BUILDINGS were subject to attack and its employees, notably the physicists, were making dramatic contributions to the war effort, the University of Birmingham had to be kept going as an institution. During the 1939–45 conflict, a popular catchphrase to aim at anyone who grumbled unduly about wartime problems was 'Don't you know there's a war on?' Priestley and his senior colleagues certainly did know.

Their primary problem was the impact of war on university finance. The period of buoyancy which had followed the 1920 appeal was already coming to an end before hostilities began. In 1933–4 the University had declared a surplus of £8840 – £7500 of which was allocated for the Medical School.[1] Despite an intervening increase of £10,500 in the Treasury grant, the surplus estimated for 1937–8 was £904, a consequence of increases in the salary bill at a time when student fees were in serious decline.[2] The University was also in trouble on the capital account because of its decision to build the Medical School knowing that £65,000–£70,000 of the cost was not covered, and neither were the additional running costs of £9520 a year charged to the current account.[3] Of course, with war declared, money became even tighter.[4] In the last year of peace the University had managed a surplus of £2486. In 1940–1 the loss was £1859; lack of funds forced the closure of the department of industrial hygiene and a readership in pharmacology had had to be established, unendowed.[5] In 1942 the deficit was £4345 and two years later the predicted loss was £14,000.[6]

Without government recognition of the problems of wartime, matters would have been even worse. In January 1939 the CVCP and the UGC had agreed that although in the event of war the system of quinquennial review would be suspended and student numbers would almost certainly fall, grants to the universities would be maintained during hostilities at the level already agreed for the year 1940–1, that is, at £6.5 million per annum to the country's universities overall.[7] The agreement did not kick in until the year 1940–1, with the result that Birmingham's grant from central government did fall under the existing formula from £89,096 in 1939–40 to £86,500 in 1940–1 (2.9%). Thereafter, however, that 1940–1 figure was maintained right up to 1944–5, when the government grant was increased markedly. This honouring of, indeed eventual increase in, the level of government grant to the universities was, however, not achieved by a passive reliance on the 1939 agreement, but by continuing work and representation of the university case throughout the war years. The CVCP and various MPs constantly reminded the government of the importance of the universities' role in training scientists, undertaking research, providing expert advice and contributing significantly to the progress of total war. Public opinion was mobilised by articles such as the one in *Nature* by Sir Walter Moberly, head of the UGC and one-time member of the Birmingham academic staff, rehearsing the 'immensely valuable service' the universities had performed during the First World War.[8]

The government also moved to do something about the other half of the problem, the additional war-generated costs which the universities would have to bear. This was tackled at a meeting of British university vice-chancellors, the CVCP and government in January 1940, and the result was that the UGC received increased government support towards staff salaries and the war work being carried on at the universities.[9] This, coupled with the maintenance of the basic grant, meant that once the dip in 1940–1 was past, Birmingham's total income from the state increased throughout the war years. Standing at £232,562 in 1939–40, it reached £412,432 by 1945–6. University finances were also assisted by the agreements which the UGC and CVCP had made for the payment of the salaries and superannuation of academic staff recruited to the armed forces and to government research, with universities making up the pay of members of staffs to the amount they would have received in university employ.[10] In addition, government ministries and departments often contracted with universities for research to be carried out although, as Mark Oliphant noted, such contracts often did not cover the full cost of research.[11]

The reason why, despite positive action by government, the war years created persistent difficulties for the income and expenditure account of the University of Birmingham, and indeed other British universities, was threefold: increased wartime costs which were not compensated, inflation, and loss of income, notably from student fees. Birmingham complained to the UGC that in one year alone there was a drop of a £1900 in income from undergraduate course fees. However, thanks to all this pre-planning, the position never became as serious as in the previous war, and, as Priestley explained to Council as early as 1941, the problems were not life-threatening:

> The immediate prospect is bleak. … The general situation is reflected in University finance. A deficit of £1,859 in the past University year is matched by a greater estimated deficit for this year. With the registration age reduced from 20 to 18½ and a further reduction to 18 not unlikely, and with conscription of women, the situation is likely to deteriorate. War

finance, however, is not the real cause for anxiety. The importance of the universities in war of the present type is seen and the necessity for their maintenance is obvious.[12]

Immediate financial stress was, thus, not the main thing worrying the vice-chancellor. His deeper anxiety was that war was altering the whole basis of the funding of the University:

It is the more remote future that is more nebulous and not without anxiety. In this sphere of university affairs, also, the war had altered a well-adjusted balance of resources. In the inter-war period, university income derived from three sources in roughly equal proportion – grants from government and local authorities, fees and endowments. Increase in taxation seems likely to change that balance decisively. The universities must look to the government to recognise that fact should the situation persist after the war. Income from fees today provides less than one third of the cost of university education to the paying student. This proportion must not rise; the democratic ideal demands, indeed that it must fall. There seems only one long-term answer to the problem – increase in government help, in particular help in capital development on a large scale. What the government takes with one hand it could give back with the other.

The implications of this prediction were more considerable than they may appear to a generation inured to state control and state starvation of higher education. During the 1920s and 1930s the UGC was above all else non-interventionist, insisting that the state would cover only the lesser fraction of university recurrent expenditure and would provide capital very rarely. Thus although the Committee's 1935 visit (the last before the war) congratulated the University on the 'admirable' support it received from local authorities, when Birmingham submitted a statement of its 'most pressing needs' in 1936 it was advised to approach those same local authorities for more support![13] Priestley accepted that local sources would remain important, especially for capital, and he believed that majority dependence on the state was still some years ahead. Nevertheless his message was that from this time on, Birmingham must see future solvency lying with government. Events certainly bore out his prediction. Revenue raised by the University locally, including local authority grants, declined steadily in importance from 54% of total income in 1938–9 to 38% in 1945–6 and, reciprocally, central government funding increased from 38% in the immediate pre-war years to 54% in 1945. And Birmingham was not alone. Whereas parliamentary grants had made up 34.3% of the income of British universities in 1935–6, the figure in 1946–7 was 52.7%.[14] Central government had become the principal paymaster of higher education.

One of the major casualties of the immediate financial situation was, predictably, staff pay. Priestley was well aware that the position at Birmingham was bad and the topic recurs frequently in his papers. He described as 'well-devised' a paper submitted by the local AUT in 1939.[15] This demonstrated that the minimum adequate salary for a lecturer was £500 as against a Birmingham average for non-professors of £465. Indeed, many lecturers were on £400 or less. Although efforts were made to improve these figures throughout the war, the money for an overall 7.5% rise on the salary bill was certainly not there in 1939, and thoughts turned to targeting increases by way of family allowances. These had been pioneered by the LSE, and Edward Cadbury had suggested something of the sort to Birmingham in 1936.[16] The idea aroused little debate, and a scheme was implemented in the first year of the war. It throws an interesting light on Priestley to note that he was fully aware of the inequality inherent in the scheme. Male staff benefited more than female staff because the women were much more likely to be unmarried: 'Some of the women are as good, and even better, than some of the men members of staff holding corresponding posts, and it seems quite unfair to discriminate on grounds of sex.'[17] Nevertheless, as Priestley also noted, family pressures did make male staff inefficient and the allowances had a rough effectiveness. 'There was a war on.'

The awareness of people which Priestley showed in this case is seen on other occasions. Two months after taking office he agreed to inform non-professorial staff of university decisions which might affect their 'privileges'.[18] As we have seen, in 1939 non-professors were given representation on Senate.[19] Although small in numerical terms, as a comment on the professorial monopoly of power the change was significant. By 1948 he had moved on to 'a declared policy' of bringing non-professors into all areas and all levels of university government.[20] Not that the vice-chancellor was exclusively a person of democratic sympathy. In November 1942 he prepared a powerful paper principally on professorial salaries.[21] Eight who were on the minimum of £1000 should be raised immediately by £100 and family allowances should be extended to all holders of chairs. Supplementary payments ought to be made to heads of department in science who, unlike 'professors of literary subjects', were responsible for expensive plant and large staffs. The realities of the market had also to be recognised. Appointments would have to be made above scale. Priestley anticipated that his ideas would be ignored as 'chimerical', given the increasing deficit and the prospect of several years more of conflict, but 'I do not for a moment agree that this is a correct view. . . . Nothing less will suffice. We might as well throw in our hands as try to face the post-war world with a pre-war university divided, like Gaul, into three parts, and staffed by officers whose salaries are such as business scorns to give to mediocre men.'

If there is a *leitmotif* to Priestley's vice-chancellorship it is this awareness of the future and the need to be ready. In the dark days of 1940–1 he was still adding to the pre-war development agenda – research fellowships in all faculties, especially in science, medicine, industrial research and the social sciences; a new laboratory for mechanical engineering and the funds to run it; a second attempt at industrial medicine, and with a professor this time; electrical engineering modernised and a chair in geography.[22] A year later he wrote: 'There has been an increased consciousness that the universities must not be forgotten in the planning for the post-war world. The re-planning of education is very much to the fore at present and all planning has been given an impetus by the more favourable turn taken by the war in the past months.'[23]

Priestley took the first step in post-war planning for Birmingham on 20 May 1942. He proposed to Senate the setting up of a joint committee with Council to advise on developments at Edgbaston.[24] Agreement was reached that a new committee would start from scratch, comprising pro-chancellor, treasurer, deputy treasurer, vice-chancellor, vice-principal, a representative each for Arts and Law and Neville Moss, no longer dean of Science but needed because of his expert knowledge of potential sponsors and how to approach them. At a preliminary meeting on 6 July the Committee adopted as its brief Priestley's suggestion to produce first an overall schedule of what was needed and then to move to detail as soon as possible. This was so as to be ready when potential donors appeared and to be prepared to take advantage of the thousands of demobilised men who would come on to the labour market. Clearly, the vice-chancellor expected 1919 to be repeated. The projects he listed at this stage were the familiar ones plus a swimming pool and developments in biology.

The Committee held its first substantive meeting a fortnight later, by which time the University secretary had already moved on a key issue, additional land.[25] He reported that the Calthorpe estate would not sell sites north of Pritchatts Road but that leases were a possibility. The Committee then examined pre-war plans, listed possible sponsors and asked the vice-chancellor to draft an appeal. The next meeting was not until January 1943 but this was to allow time for a great deal of detailed work to be done by specialised committees. These were set up at both Senate and faculty level.

In the Arts there was some feeling that the right way to start was to establish an overall vision for the humanities at Birmingham.[26] The vice-chancellor, however, stressed the new economic realities and that what was required was an indication of what the faculty *needed*. The faculty complied, but with a degree of feeling which was to recur. After all, this was the first prospect the Arts had ever had of purpose-built accommodation; ever since 1882 the faculty had had to exist on sufferance or by taking over space originally designed for other faculties. In 1936 the University had told the UGC that money would be needed to reallocate the rooms at Edmund Street when the medics moved out, but when that happened two years later, the University conveniently argued that no expenditure was now necessary because a sale was 'impending'.[27] Papers issuing from the vice-chancellor were certainly not such as to allay fears among the exiles in Edmund Street. The appeal memorandum which he drafted made the Library 'the very hub' of new development and gave second priority to hostels for students which 'would go far to giving the University a soul'.[28] The new accommodation for the administration, Arts, Commerce and Law came only third, and Priestley costed the whole of that at £150,000 to £200,000 (pre-war prices). Although he earmarked a further £50,000 to provide a continuing university presence in the city centre, that still left the University creaming off a surplus from the sale of Edmund Street of £150,000 (or £50,000 net of rates). The faculty would also have noticed that only one Arts department was listed for outside sponsorship: theology; no new chairs or readerships were mentioned and £15,000 was allocated for additional lectureships against £25,000 for Science.

This is not to say that Birmingham got on with planning parochially and ignored the wider context. It was inevitable that major rethinking and reconstruction would follow the end of the war, and this fuelled a debate on the overall nature of higher education in Britain which had been building up in the pre-war period. Grant Robertson himself had been an early contributor in his 1930 survey, *British Universities*. Concerns ranged from the total lack of co-ordination in an essentially makeshift system, the gap in esteem between the old universities and the new, and whether the role of the new should be local or national, to the dangers of excessive academic specialism, the place of technology in higher education, whether universities should be vocational, and whether it would be better to limit degree courses to the really able rather than turn out 'highly competent mediocrity' – Grant Robertson's particular fear.[29]

Although Priestley did not publish directly, he (together with the vice-chancellor of Manchester) was much involved in the production by Sir Ernest Simon of *The Development of British Universities*. Published in January 1944, it advocated major university expansion and positive planning at national level.[30] The pamphlet grew out of a report by the future Lord Simon which had been circulated in the previous October.[31] An appendix to this listed the various areas where national planning was needed and prefigured most of the policy issues which would dominate higher education for the rest of the century. How large should the higher education sector be? What was the optimum size and best constitution for its institutions? What of staff tenure and staff–student ratios, the academic year, student funding and graduate employment? Should institutions specialise in specific areas and avoid the kind of situation found in mining, where about twenty graduates a year were produced from the eight existing schools of mining, none of which was of an adequate size to guarantee quality? How could the glaring subject deficiencies in the existing system be remedied? Also, how was research to be funded? The easiest method was to inflate the Treasury grant by a uniform percentage, but there were other possibilities – a research fund to cover all subjects, separate funds for different groups of disciplines or else a grant specific to each institution.

Birmingham took the Simon Report very seriously and debated it at length in the Senate Development Committee.[32] It also seems to have influenced the University's reply to a concurrent request from the UGC for an indication of post-war requirements. Certainly it lay behind the vice-chancellor's reaction in January 1944 to the list of requirements put forward by the faculty of Arts.[33] This envisaged a move into temporary accommodation at Edgbaston with some accommodation in common but the rest specific to departments. On the language side, expansion in Russian was thought necessary and into linguistics; the historians required a department of political science and a chair of economic history, shared with commerce, plus lecturers in international relations and colonial studies. Ideally, theology wanted to develop into a separate faculty, but as a minimum it needed two new chairs and there were proposals for a School of Drama and for developments in psychology. The whole was costed at £300,000 at pre-war prices, in other words, the net value of Edmund Street. Priestley's response to the dean of Arts is worth quoting at length:

> I have just read through the memorandum by Shapiro and Styles [I. A. Shapiro of the English department and Philip Styles from history] on the requirements of the Faculty of Arts. The first thing that struck me was the demand for £300,000 for accommodation at pre-war prices. I should say there is not the slightest hope of our doing this or anything like it. The Faculty must pay a little more attention I think to co-ordination. With our previous rough estimate of £150,000 [for Arts] and everything else to match we have a million pound scheme in hand already and I have not the slightest doubt myself that the hostels are more important to the welfare of the University than the provision of ideal conditions for one Faculty. …
>
> As regards new developments to be financed by increased income, I think one point of view the University needs to consider is (a) what things every University needs to do well, (b) whether any other developments should necessarily be best contemplated at Birmingham. I wonder, for example, whether we are really the best university to develop Slavonic languages? I am quite sure this aspect of the problem will be raised when we come to put our requests before the University Grants Committee.[34]

Priestley had to give ground a little, and when the University response to the UGC went off in February 1944 it was impressive.[35] It placed post-war requirements in four categories: urgent, essential, desirable and 'to be funded by endowments'. First priority went to an immediate 25% salary increase for all grades of staff, to be followed by a similar rise two years later. Next came the additional staff required in the urgent category. For Science these were costed at £14,300, plus £4300 for technicians, £5400 for departmental expenses and £1100 for studentships – £26,530 a year. For the University overall the cost of 'urgent' staffing amounted to £71,422 a year which became, with the increases in salary, £106,422 in the first year and £141,422 in year three.

Table 15.1 Birmingham University: urgent current account requirements, February 1944

	£
Faculty of Science	26530
Faculty of Arts	10257
Faculty of Medicine [partial list]	15500
Faculty of Commerce	2145
Department of education	5280
Extra-mural studies	5210
Physical education	2000
Library	2000
Administration	2500
Total additional costs	*71422*
Salary increase, year 1	35000
Salary increase, year 3	35000
Grand total	*141422*

To put these figures in perspective, they have to be set against a projected post-war income of £235,500, in other words, Birmingham urgently needed a 45% increase in Treasury grant, rising to 60% with the second tranche of the rise in salary. The capital estimates were equally upbeat.

Table 15.2 Birmingham University: urgent capital requirements, February 1944

	£
War damage, arrears and temporary accommodation	105600
Buildings at Edgbaston for Arts, Commerce, etc	200000
Library	200000
Halls of residence	400000
New engineering laboratories	250000
Students' Union extension	40000
Extra-mural headquarters	50000
Total	*1140000*

Apart for £20,000 for the union extension, the University had nothing in reserve to fund these projects although, if a buyer could be found, Edmund Street was estimated to produce £400,000. If items in the other categories were added to 'urgent', the total required was £1,855,000.

That Priestley saw such sums as of necessity involving the Treasury did not prevent his private approaches for funds elsewhere. Much of the planning work in 1943 was, in fact, on an appeals brochure to enlist the self-interest of specifically local industry for improvements in Mechanical and Electrical Engineering. The response was rapid and by the end of 1944 the vice-chancellor could report seven-year covenants from Joseph Lucas and ICI worth over £20,000 a year and major progress towards £250,000 to rebuild mechanical and electrical engineering.[36] At the same time preparations were in hand to widen the appeal to the public generally, and this was launched within a week of the ending of the war with Japan in August 1945.[37] The University put its capital needs at £1,303,000, including £600,000 for residences, plus additional endowments totalling £400,000 and in the euphoria of peace donations came in quickly. By the end of the year £790,000 had been raised – nearly half the amount asked for. A year later the figure was just under £1 million and the final total was £1,125,000 gross.

This was a massive achievement, but all was not rosy. Most of the money received was earmarked for particular capital projects or for special developments. There was less than £200,000 to help the income and expenditure account where the University had accumulated its worrying wartime deficit. Despite additional UGC help, this reached £31,000 in 1946 and a special grant to clear it had to be obtained from the Treasury. Even so, the annual income and expenditure account remained in the red and by 1948 the accumulated deficit was over £11,000. The Council called for economies to eliminate this over four years but the hope was unrealistic.[38] Ex-service personnel had crowded into the University – in 1945–6 admissions raised the student population by a third – and, as Priestley said, instructions from the government to double the numbers in higher education over the next ten years meant a commitment to go to 4000 students and threatened a deficit within four years of nearly £400,000.[39] That did not materialise, but when Priestley retired in 1952 the accumulated deficit was over £70,000.

The importance given in post-war public appeals to student residences reveals an interesting development in vice-chancellorial thinking. From the start Priestley had been anxious to create the nucleus of a residential student community at Edgbaston. As early as his first report to Council his original thought of one male hostel had grown into two.[40] By 1942 his thinking was that the only students out of residence would be those living at home. Nor was he alone in this. At an early meeting of the Development Committee Professor Haworth and Professor Hanson, the professor of mining, argued an urgent case for accommodating 500 students in four hostels, three for men, one for women.[41] Since in the last year of peace the University had just under 1500 students, this would have meant one student in

Plate 30

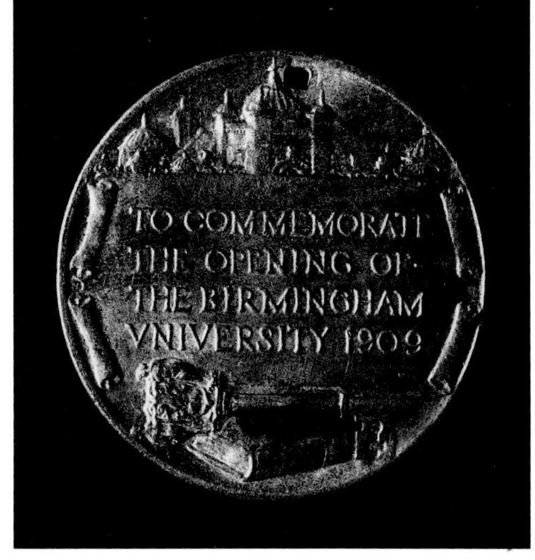

Plate 31

Plate 32

Plate 33

Plate 34

Plate 35

Plate 36

Plate 37

Plate 38

Plate 39

Plate 40

Plate 41

Plate 42

Plate 43

Plate 44

Plate 45

Plate 46

Plate 47

Plate 48

Plate 49

Plate 50

Plate 51

Plate 52

Plate 53

Plate 54

Plate 55

Strictly confidential 2

DECLASSIFIED

On the construction of a "super-bomb", based on a nuclear chain reaction in uranium.

The possible construction of "super-bombs" based on a nuclear chain reaction in uranium has been discussed a great deal and arguments have been brought forward which seemed to excluse this possibility. We wish here to point out and discuss a possibility which seems to have been overlooked in these earlier discussions.

Uranium consists essentially of two isotopes, U_{238} (99.3%) and U_{235} (0.7%). If a uranium nucleus is hit by a neutron, three processes are possible: (1) scattering, whereby the neutron changes direction and, if its energy is above about o.1 MeV, loses energy; (2) capture, when the neutron is taken up by the nucleus; and (3) fission, i.e. the nucleus breaks up into two nuclei of comparable size, with the liberation of an energy of about 200 MeV.

The possibility of a chain reaction is given by the fact that neutrons are emitted in the fission and that the number of these neutrons per fission is greater than one. The most probable value for this figure seems to be 2.3 , from two independent determinations.

However, it has been shown that even in a large block of ordinary uranium no chain reaction would take place since too many neutrons would be slowed down by inelastic scattering into the energy region where they are strongly absorbed by U_{238}.

Several people have tried to make chain reaction possible by mixing the uranium with water, which reduces the energy of the neutrons still further and thereby increases their efficiency again. It seems fairly certain, however, that even then it is impossible to sustain a chain reaction.

Plate 57

Plate 58

Plate 59

Plate 60

Plate 61

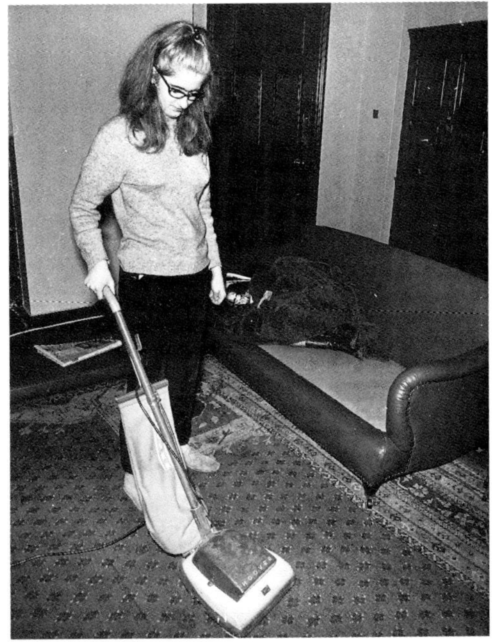

Plate 62

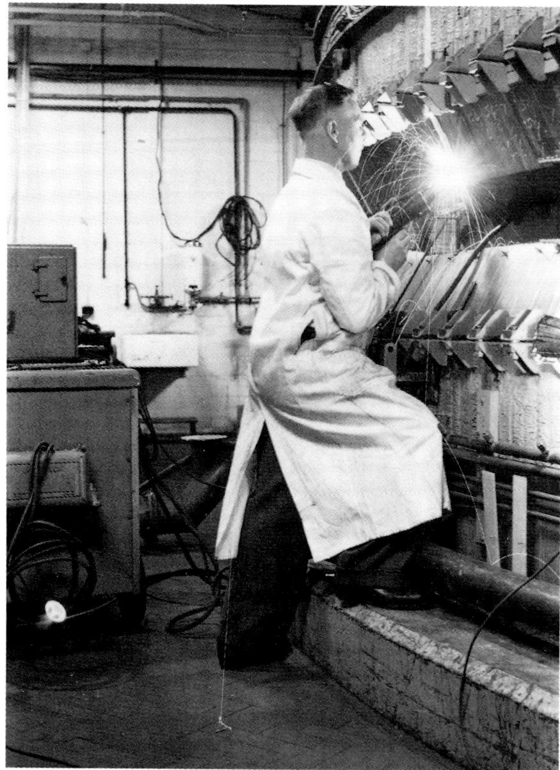

Plate 63

Plate 64

three in residence. By January 1944 Priestley was willing to cut back on space for the Edmund Street departments in order to fund hostels. On 2 February he wrote to the secretary increasing the proposed number of hostels needed to six and saying:

> As regards priority for hostels, I am more and more inclined to put them Priority 1. I still think our concentration at Edgbaston is our first need, but if elaborate buildings for Faculty and central administration involve setting back hostels for several years, then I should prefer to see us housed in temporary buildings until the hostels are set up.[42]

And to emphasise that he included himself under administration he listed his own modest space requirements, with the one essential a lavatory, 'which all my colleagues seem to have'. Later that same month he approached Sir Miles Thomas of the Austin Car Co. to see whether Lord Nuffield might help to turn Birmingham into a residential university:

> I feel sure that the proposal to take the long step towards converting Birmingham University into a residential University would appeal strongly to Lord Nuffield, and I should be grateful if you, as business associate with him and as one of his friends, will be good enough to advise us as to the best course to be taken to bring to his notice or to the notice of the appropriate foundation the needs of the University, particularly in regard to residential facilities.[43]

The definition of 'residential' which Priestley used as 'one year of three' corresponds to the view of the Committee on Post-War University Education of which he was a member. Its 1944 *Report* recommended that 'at least one year's residence in college or in a university hostel should be required of every candidate for a first degree'.[44] However, in the last year of peace Birmingham had 63% of its students living at home, so achieving residential places in a ratio of 1:3 would have meant that either the remaining students would be in residence for up to three years or that the intention was to give many home students the chance to live in. On occasions, indeed, documents do mention a residence ratio of 50:50.[45] Had Priestley been able to achieve this he would have brought about immediately after the war an accommodation position which the University was never able to achieve. It is also possible that in the different ethos of post-war society he might indeed have been able to create the academic community which Birmingham has never fully enjoyed.

In this vision staff were not overlooked.[46] The need for a vice-chancellor's residence had been in the plans from an early stage, but the AUT pressed for university housing for other members of staff as well, and it was soon accepted that this was desirable. At one level this was a straightforward matter of housing need, although few in the mid-1940s could have foreseen the housing shortage at the end of the war and the serious problem that this would pose for staff coming to Birmingham. Yet Priestley's willingness to meet the AUT on this was also again because of this ambition to form an academic community. The peak of optimism came in September 1947 when the Development Committee was presented with a plan to use the land on the north of Pritchatts Road. A road was to be built directly opposite the university gates to lead to an official residence for the vice-chancellor which would stand by itself. University Avenue would, in effect, start with the vice-chancellor and end at the Great Hall. On either side of this central road a small estate would be developed with ten houses of varying sizes, fifteen flats, a university hostel – presumably for visitors – and a community hall. The tone of the whole project was set by the fact that most houses and flats included accommodation for a residential maid! From an end-of-century point of view it may seem a blessing that nothing came of this plan for 'Oxbridge in Birmingham'. However, with the omission of the vice-chancellor's residence, the hostel and the community hall, something of the kind was eventually built at Selly Wick on a site originally earmarked for a women's hall of residence. In the long term it did not prove popular with staff and the link with university employment was abandoned in 1992.

Student hostels fared a good deal better and always ranked high on the priorities of the Development Committee. Acquiring suitable sites was the first concern. In the summer of 1943 negotiations were under way for the purchase of Winterbourne, but in the following year the house came to the University by bequest and became an annexe to the existing women students' hostel.[47] Though better than nothing, Winterbourne had no services and residents were forced to make a five-minute walk in all weathers to take meals in University House. With the war coming to an end in the summer of 1945, the Committee proceeded to appoint an architect to design the new halls, but the site issue was still not settled.[48] Final negotiations for part of what is now the Vale were only completed in March 1947, although preliminary architectural work had started some months earlier.[49] By then Wyddrington, Maple Bank and other properties in the Edgbaston Park road were under discussion and more land in the Vale was obtained from the Calthorpe estate in 1948 and 1949.[50] Meadowcroft was secured as a vice-chancellor's residence early in 1953 and Manor House, which had been secured from the Bournville Village Trust in 1952, was opened for forty students in the January 1954.[51]

Acquiring sites was no longer the simple procedure it had been before the war. The passing of the 1947 *Town and Country Planning Act* gave the City Council control over development and no property could thereafter be safely bought without first clearing the intended future use with the authorities. By 1953 the Development Committee was noting the further constraining effect of 'zoning'.[52] Even more difficulty resulted from the continuation after 1945 of wartime controls. Government licences were required for building materials (particularly steel), and given that priority went to power stations, research into atomic energy, building factories and houses and repairing war damage, Birmingham, along with other universities, found itself well down in the queue. Capital for higher education was strictly regulated in the interest of the fight against inflation, with the UGC being given a 'ration' to allocate for the sector. Labour, too, was tightly controlled and demobilisation carefully phased; the huge surplus which Priestley had expected did not materialise.

As a consequence of this, the vice-chancellor's wish to make rapid progress with the halls of residence became subject to all the frustrations of bureaucracy. Initially the University's wish for more student accommodation found little favour with the UGC.[53] Indeed, the vice-chancellor suggested that it might be wise to switch priority to extending the Students' Union building because that would benefit more students than would residences.[54] In February 1949, however, UGC policy was relaxed and universities were told that halls could be built, provided steel was used economically.[55] Two years later the UGC announced that it would allocate the greater part of its 'ration' for building to provide permanent accommodation for students, but with a proviso that the cost must not exceed a tight £1300 per place.[56] This led the University Treasurer, W. H. Newton, to question existing plans.[57] If the UGC wanted residence and if Birmingham wished to accommodate 50% of its students, ten new halls would be required. There simply was not the land available locally to achieve this on the scale planned for the Vale site. Halls certainly had to have decent amenities, but there was

> no need to emulate the spacious days of the 18th century. ... Bearing in mind that many of our students inevitably come from humble homes, and the majority of them in the future will have to live, so far as one can judge at the moment, in flats or other relatively cramped premises, it may well be that we can recede somewhat from the space originally thought to be necessary to be provided in Halls of Residence for our students.

Newton's solution was high-rise, a hall for 350 students housed in three blocks of eight storeys and more round a quadrangle, with the fourth side occupied by services, everything very basic, with lifts only from the fourth floor and all bathrooms in the basements. He seems not to have asked whether students would be willing to live in such a construction. Fortunately, despite having called for residences, the UGC had gone quiet on the University's plans, and Newton's ideas died a death.[58]

The net result of all this was that Priestley's efforts to create a substantial residential community at Edgbaston came to nothing. In his first year in office the University had 209 students in residence, 14.6% of the total. In his final year there were 330 in residence, 10.5%. Nor had he left great projects nearing completion. By 1955–6 the total was still only 353, or 11%.

What Priestley called 'the frustration of comparing progress with programme' was even more evident in academic planning.[59] In March 1947 the UGC informed Birmingham that its total labour allocation for the year would be 50 men, with a possible 128 for 1948 and 200 thereafter.[60] The University thought that 400 would have barely been adequate. Lack of bureaucratic co-ordination presented perpetual problems. In March 1947 the UGC sanctioned expenditure for building work for the department of metallurgy. [61] A year later the UGC informed the University that it now had a quota of steel available but the Ministry of Labour reported that it was as yet unable to assign an adequate workforce.[62] In February 1949 the University met the UGC and the Ministry of Works and was told that the position had now eased on labour and some building materials. However, timber and especially steel were still in short supply. Thus, while the Students' Union extension was to be allocated supplies immediately, the department of metallurgy would only return to the top of the queue for steel in second distribution for the year, two and a half years after the first go-ahead.[63] As well as delays, there were reductions in standards. The Regional Office of the Ministry of Works suggested that the internal walls of laboratories need not be plastered and that floors should be bitumastic rather than teak, which could be installed later. Buildings in concrete were more likely to be licensed than traditional constructions, which required more steel.[64] Even when permits were granted, delays occurred, and at vital points. In 1950 everything was held up because new gas and water services had to be postponed for a year because of shortage of pipe.[65] A new heating plant was the *sine qua non* of new construction and had been given the top priority in 1946.[66] When he left in 1952 Priestley grumbled that the power station and the new engineering building which had been approved in 1948 were still nothing but a steel skeleton.[67]

Problems of this kind could, perhaps, be tolerated as the aftermath of six years of war. What was less acceptable was the implicit loss of university independence. The most striking example of this was the 'rationing' of capital. The UGC control over this extended not only to grants from the Treasury but to the spending of funds raised by institutions themselves. What in theory was still a committee to act as a buffer between the institutions of higher education and the state was in reality becoming a directorate of higher education. Early in the war Priestley had complained that the University was becoming unbalanced with 'the scales steadily tipped in favour of Science, Engineering and Medicine and against Arts, Law and Commerce'.[68] Far from that balance being restored in peacetime, the increasing interference of government had the result, as he pointed out in his reports for 1948 and 1949, of throwing even more out of balance the carefully considered plans of individual institutions.[69] This was particularly the case where decisions at the centre led to privileged treatment for particular fields such as medicine, education or social science.

The biggest interference which Birmingham experienced was in the move from Edmund Street. Because this was central to the University's future, even before the war was over the Council appointed the architect Verner O. Rees to develop the Edgbaston site.[70] The matter became more urgent when in 1946 it became known that the city was promoting a private bill which would mean evacuating the old Mason College in a very few years.[71] Initial site work was about to begin between University Road and Pritchatts Road when Priestley had to announce in October 1946 that 'formal' approval would probably have to be obtained first from the UGC.[72] 'Formal' soon revealed itself as 'specific' and in 1947 only a limited amount of building was allowed for science. 'Building' is perhaps a misnomer because government control even covered the erection of the temporary huts for which some lucky departments received permission. By 1948 it had become obvious that the simultaneous construction of a new library and a new building for Arts, Commerce and Law simply would not receive approval and the Edmund Street move fell out of the list of the University's top priorities.[73] These were now the new heating plant, laboratories for mechanical and electrical engineering, work for the department of metallurgy and an extension to the Student's Union. Even in category two, priority for the Edmund Street move now came below halls of residence. The Arts Faculty pressed in vain for equal consideration but found themselves being leapfrogged by Science.[74] All that the UGC would promise was 'early consideration'. The University did restore the library/Arts building to nominal first priority in February 1949 but agreed at the same time that, provided that project was 'not interfered with', building for physics, chemistry, chemical engineering, mining, physical education, halls of residence, the Students' Union and a new wing at University House should go forward as soon as start dates were officially sanctioned.[75] In May the Medical School Library and Lecture Theatre (which had been omitted in 1938) were added to the list of 'as soon as approved'.

It was clearly sensible not to hold up feasible smaller projects in favour of one which was not. Science was certainly short of space. This was partly because student numbers in 1947–8 were 83% up on those before the war, but it was certainly not because of rapid expansion thereafter. Between 1947–8 and 1950–1, numbers in science and engineering grew by only 100, from 1304 to 1407. The other non-medical faculties could in any case argue that they had problems too. Numbers in 1947–8 were 51% up on 1938–9 and increased by 1950–1 from 1113 to 1170. The real problem with science was not students but the growing sophistication of its disciplines, both in teaching and research. Oliphant solved the problem in physics by obtaining ten trailers on long loan which he parked nearby, and he suggested that geography could be accommodated in the Chamberlain Tower.[76]

The frustration among the faculties still at Edmund Street can be imagined, and the more so because of pressure to reduce their requirements to what might secure approval. When detailed plans first made in 1946–7 were updated in 1949, Arts found that the theatre it wanted had become an over-large lecture facility and then that this would not be part of the first stage anyway.[77] The other lecture rooms showed little awareness of practicalities – one was 200 feet by a mere 72, there was no room for expansion and there were no soundproof rooms, although each professor had been provided with a personal toilet. Not that making modifications brought an end any nearer. In April 1950 the UGC again refused to issue a permit for the library/Arts building, despite an offer to build the latter in concrete.[78] Some months later it did suggest that the project should be split into three phases but the University, having rejected this initially on logistical grounds, then found that the suggestion was withdrawn.[79] In 1951 the Development Committee decided to stress to the UGC that the building was the number one priority for 1951–2 but this coincided with the announcement of the drive for student residences and a consequent reduction of UGC funding for other construction.[80] When 1951–2 came, all the University's building ration was absorbed by the new heating plant and the buildings for mechanical and electrical engineering, although extra space for the Medical School was paid for by the NHS.[81] Nor did prospects improve. When Priestley retired in the summer of 1952 the building 'ration' for Birmingham for the seventeen months from August 1952 to December 1953 had just been set at £40,000. In his report to Council for January to December 1950 he had written: '[The University] was, when I arrived from Australia, poised for the completion of the move to the new site at Edgbaston. Now thirteen years later and doubled in numbers, it is still so poised.'[82] He left when planning for the next quinquennium was well under way, expressing very little hope for the future.

Against this saga of hope deferred, the story of the detailed planning of the Edgbaston site could seem unimportant. This is not the case, because the debates which went on in and after the war were decisive in producing the north side of the Edgbaston campus of today.[83] Rees had got to work immediately on appointment and his first question was how sacrosanct was the grand vista from the Pritchatts Road gates. Told that maintaining the Avenue was 'at least a moral obligation', he produced in January 1945 a 'Plan A' which did preserve the whole Avenue but also a 'Plan B' which did not. Plan A envisaged the Arts Faculty in two blocks at right angles to the Avenue, one on each side, with an archway above linking the two. This would be directly opposite and would echo the existing entrance front on University Road. The new library was located on the west of the Avenue between the proposed Arts building and University Road with a corresponding building opposite. That was designed as three sides of a courtyard with the east to be provided by an extension of the Barber Institute. The Development Committee wanted to retain the Avenue, liked the separate library and the courtyard motif, and therefore approved Plan A. However, in the wont of committees everywhere, it proposed at the same time modifications which undermined the basic design, asking for a reduction in the academic space allocated for Arts, plus the removal of education into a building of its own and the administration into a block on the south side of University Road, which would complete the frontage between the existing library and the physics department. This last was subsequently rescinded to avoid cost.

Rees's response of 27 June 1945 was of the utmost importance for the future. He argued that the changes which the Committee had requested in the accommodation he had proposed for Arts made nonsense of the formula of two blocks linked by an archway. The balance of the complex would be upset and the focus would not be the Avenue but the new library on one side of it. Rees therefore brought forward a modified version of his Plan B which had proposed sacrificing the Avenue and which he may have preferred from the start. This set the library squarely across the Avenue in place of the Arts block and with no archway though it. Only the northern third of the Avenue would survive and it would then split to run either side of the library and down to University Road. The site of the library in Plan A became the University Refectory, and space for a 500-seat theatre was provided in the block opposite. Given the existing run of buildings on the south side of University Road, the effect of Plan B was to create a quadrangle in front of the 1909 main entrance. The Committee agreed to consult the Calthorpe family about the future of the Avenue and when Sir Fitzroy accepted the change, the concept of a 'University Quad' became accepted policy and the Central Avenue was consequently doomed. It is to Verner Rees, therefore, that the University owes the articulation of library, Arts Faculty and Staff House/Refectory around a central square and, indeed, both the library and the Arts Faculty buildings were designed by him.

It has been argued that Rees promoted Plan B more for reasons of fashion than function.[84] Avenues were characteristic of architects of the inter-war generation. On the other hand, it has to be admitted that the Avenue was an obstacle to the coherent development of the land between University Road and Pritchatts Road. Not only did it bifurcate the site, it did so on a north–south axis when the major alignment of the campus was east to west. Rees had a good point, too, in proposing the library as the one building which would have sufficient authority to confront the Aston Webb quadrant. Moreover, if retained on the western side of the Avenue, as in Plan A, the library would have required the building opposite to be of equivalent mass, something which was financially out of the question. There can be no doubt that destroying the Avenue was an act of environmental vandalism but it was probably unavoidable. It is also fair to say that Rees was not responsible for the later decision to turn what survived of the Avenue into a cul-de-sac, so producing the nonsense of the University's grand northern gateway leading nowhere.

So much of Priestley's vice-chancellorship was taken up in battling against the times that it is easy to see the period as a negative one. To do so would be unfair. The enormous effort put into planning was significant for the future, and, even more important, sustained academic vigour when it might well have sagged. It was also under Priestley's direction that the University became big business. Expenditure rose from £231,800 a year to £1,021,400 and even with post-war constraints, the annual non-recurrent expenditure was over a quarter of a million pounds. Student numbers had risen from 1400 to 3393 and teaching staff from 361 to 582, with the number of support staff rising even faster, from 250 to 587. Three times the amount was being spent on research staff as pre-war and extra-mural work had multiplied four times. New disciplines appeared in the *Calendar*. The University had taught ancient history and archaeology since 1915. Now it became a department.[85] Oil engineering and coal utilisation united to form chemical engineering.[86] Among the vice-chancellor's proudest achievements was his work for 'the medical care and physical development of the university student'. On appointment he had set up a Physical Education Committee and engaged a director, and from this came a fully-fledged department in the faculty of Arts feeding students into a half-degree course.[87] In addition, the wartime requirement for compulsory physical education was retained for all first-year students, even though some of them grumbled that getting away from compulsory sport had been the best part of leaving school!

In the immediate post-war years there was a worrying incidence of psychological problems among students. Priestley's answer was characteristic. In his address to the freshers in October 1948 he made this offer: 'If you have personal problems that seem to you to be insuperable, bring them to your friends who have more experience. Let Dr Bolton [the Medical Officer] have a chance, or the Head of your Department or your Tutor, or come to me.'[88] Personal problems are often financial problems, and Priestley was concerned to reduce the financial obstacles which defeated many would-be students. In 1943 he secured funds from local industry to finance an Industrial Scholarship scheme to enable the brightest HNC students to go on to a degree.[89] Many post-war students were supported by grants or awards but Priestley anticipated the phasing out of this funding and in 1948 started a university loan fund.[90] Typically, too, while welcoming new facilities such as the gymnasium, the vice-chancellor was anxious to see that cost would not make them inaccessible to some students. Covering the running expenses by a membership scheme or by adding to student fees were equally undesirable – 'a benefaction towards this objective would therefore be very valuable'.[91] His interest in health for all students went well beyond promoting the department of physical education, showing a keen interest in student sport or appointing a full-time medical officer from 1943.[92] It was a personal crusade by a man who had been fit enough when young to face the Antarctic twice and who believed passionately that physical and mental development went hand in hand. He even argued that the University should select for admission 'men and women of more than average intellectual ability who possess as well, in more than average measure, some or all of the qualities of initiative, enterprise, originality, perseverance, adaptability, courage, tolerance, and sense of social responsibility which will fit them to lead when their training is completed, in a difficult and complex civilisation'.[93] Not for nothing was he an active promoter of polar research.

Priestley's educational views can be described as humane and liberal. He was very much opposed to overspecialisation. Birmingham fought hard to encourage breadth in secondary education and when the Higher School Certificate was changed into GCE O and A levels, the vice-chancellor publicly expressed his regret at not being able to preserve the subsidiary subject.[94] In the University he was more successful, introducing in 1950 a Liberal Education Scheme under which the first part of every Tuesday afternoon was kept free of timetabled teaching.[95] With a variety of programmes, attendance (which was voluntary) fluctuated between a fifth and a third of all students. The vice-chancellor was equally vigorous in opposing the idea that higher education existed to provide vocational training. He accepted that technology had a proper though not an exclusive place in universities.[96] Hence he was vocal in opposing suggestions that the country needed an equivalent of the MIT; Birmingham had a great potential in that direction, if only it were supported. The object of teaching technology in a university was, however, not to train technologists:

> Industry must accept the view that the University cannot make practical engineers, production planners and industrial managers by itself. The University's primary aims must remain, on the research side, original contributions to the science of engineering; on the teaching side, the utmost possible development of the personality of the students and a sound grounding in the sciences that underlie engineering and in the basic principles of engineering science.[97]

He said much the same about training for the professions. The object there was to teach the basics, which he defined as the ability to think, read, criticise, and so forth, that is, to 'use brains and apply minds'. [98]

This did not mean that Priestley was a disciple of the 'let them teach themselves' school. In 1939 he warmly welcomed the introduction of the first tutorial system for students, initially in the faculty of Arts but obviously bound to spread.[99] In 1946 there was an upsurge in student agitation, directed at the low quality of teaching, but Priestley channelled this into the production by the Union of a report for Senate.[100] The principal target was, apparently, research students who were engaged to run laboratory sessions and other classes but were always torn between their own work and the demands of their juniors. The vice-chancellor thereupon arranged for the department of education to put on training courses. Education indeed, was one of the areas of the University which changed most in his time, and with his direct involvement. A fundamental change was the setting up in October 1947 of an Institute of Education to bring teacher training in the Midlands under the umbrella of the University, in line with recommendations of the 1944 McNair Report.[101] The Institute included the University's own department of education and sixteen or so training colleges in the region. Other important features of the Institute were a research department which opened a year later and had links into the colleges and an associated Remedial Education Centre. As for the University's existing department of education, this at first continued the traditional two-year certificate course and also taught postgraduates, but in 1951 closed the certificate course in order to concentrate on the latter.[102] Advanced professional training was also introduced for experienced non-graduate teachers and by 1953, sixty or seventy such teachers were taking one of the Diploma of Education courses.[103]

Priestley was also fully behind curriculum development elsewhere. When he left he was proud to note how eager faculties and departments were. One of the most important innovations here was the taught postgraduate course, pioneered in mechanical engineering.[104] Another was the development of diploma courses and short courses in engineering production with funds donated by Joseph Lucas. Priestley listed this as one of three particular projects where outside funds had enabled the University to innovate despite the prevailing penury of the UGC.[105] A second was the development of electronics, funded by the giants of the electrical industry – BTH, AEI, and GEC with the Austin Motor Co., Rubery Owen and others. The third on the list was in many ways the most original. A generous donation from Oliver King, a magnate of the food industry, had allowed the University to purchase a historic property in Stratford-upon-Avon and establish the Shakespeare Institute. Half a century later all three flourish.

Priestley himself was a person who inspired confidence and even affection. When he approached the retirement age of sixty-five the University Council asked him to stay on until the age of seventy. He also had considerable influence outside Birmingham. During the war he had been chairman of the Midland Joint Recruiting Board and later he chaired a royal commission on the Civil Service. He was also in demand as a sort of academic ambassador. Between 1944 and his retirement he made six major sea voyages and flew 125 000 miles at a time when in the early years enemy action was a real possibility and when air travel even in peacetime was anything but routine.[106] Much of this was a consequence of becoming a member in 1943 of the Commission for Higher Education in the Colonies and particularly of its Irvine Committee, whose report on the West Indies laid the foundation for the University College of the West Indies. This opened in 1946, with Priestley on its Council, and he was also chairman of the Imperial College of Tropical Agriculture in Trinidad. His work for education in the West Indies was, perhaps, the achievement of which he was most proud.

Notes

1 For the following see UA Council Minutes 32: 4 May 1938.
2 Ibid., 1938–9. Grant Robertson estimated the loss of fees from 1933–4 to 1936–7 as £6000, two-thirds of the increased grant: UC 7/iii 1936–7.
3 UA Council Minutes 30: 6 May 1936.
4 For the following see UC 7/ii *Council*, *passim.*
5 Ibid., 1939–40; 7/iii 1940–1, p. 16.
6 UC 7/iii 1944, p. 16; the loss on the following year to 31 July 1945 was £15,716: 7/ii *Accounts* 1945.
7 PRO UGC 5/15: 31 Jan. 1939.
8 PRO UGC 5/15.
9 PRO UGC 5/15, Jan. 1940.
10 Ibid., 17 May 1939.
11 UC 19/62/v/4: note by Oliphant on agreement with the Admiralty, 1938.
12 UC 7/iii 1940–1, pp. 20–1.
13 UA Council Minutes 29: 6 Mar., 19 Mar. 1935; 30: 6 May, 3 June 1936. Endowment income did keep up in cash terms.
14 Gosden, 'The nationalizing of Britain's universities, 1945–65', p. 146, Table 2.
15 For the following see UC 7/iii 1939–40, pp. 2–4; 1940–1, pp. 8–10.
16 UA Council Minutes 30: 1 Apr. 1936.
17 UC 14/ii (1940).
18 UA Council Minutes 33: 7 Dec. 1938.
19 See above, p.
20 UC 7/iii 1948, p. 6.
21 UA Development Committee 1: 6 Jan. 1943.
22 UC 7/iii 1940–1, pp. 21–2.
23 Ibid., 1941–2, p. 1.
24 Ibid., 1942–3, p. 12; UA Development Committee 1: 6 July 1942. Cf. 7/11 1943, p. 7; 1944, p. 8.
25 Ibid., 20 July 1942.
26 UC 17/i : Special Meeting of Faculty of Arts, 9 Dec. 1942.
27 UA Council Minutes 30: 6 May, 1936; 33: 28 Sept. 1938.
28 UA Development Committee 1: 6 Jan. 1943.
29 Grant Robertson, *British Universities*, p. 75.
30 E. Simon, *The Development of British Universities* (1944).
31 UC 17/i: 'Sir Edward Simon's report, 19 Oct. 1943'.
32 Ibid.: Senate Development Committee, 26 Nov. 1943; 18 Jan. 1944.
33 UC 17/i : 'Recommendations of the Faculty of Arts, Dec. 1943'.
34 UC 14/ii: Priestley to Wood, 6 Jan. 1944.
35 UA Development Committee 1: 28 Feb. 1944.
36 UC 7/iii 1944, pp. 11–13.
37 *Birmingham Daily Post*, 16 Aug. 1945.
38 UC 7/ii *Council* 1948, p. 7.
39 UC 7/iii 1947, pp. 2–3.

40 Ibid., 1938–9, p. 3.
41 UA Development Committee 1: 6 Jan. 1943.
42 UC 14/ii Priestley to Burton, 2 Feb. 1944.
43 Ibid., Priestley to Thomas, 9 Feb. 1944.
44 Vincent and Hinton, *University of Birmingham*, p. 205.
45 UC 7/iii 1951, p. 7.
46 For the following see UA Development Committee 1: 6 Jan. 1943, 28 Feb. 1944, 4 July 1945, 11 Sep. 1947.
47 Ibid.: 30 July 1943; Vincent and Hinton, *University of Birmingham*, p. 208.
48 UA Development Committee 1: 12 Apr. 1946.
49 Ibid.: 28 Oct., 11 Dec. 1946, 18 Feb., 24 Mar. 1947.
50 UC 7/ii *Council passim.*
51 UA Development Committee 2: 19 Mar. 1953; UC 7/ii 1951, 1952, 1954.
52 Ibid.: 19 Mar. 1953 .
53 UC 7/ii 1948, pp. 9–10, quoting UGC Report (1935–47): 'So far as the present quinquennium is concerned [1947–52], it is clear that the proportion of students living in Halls will inevitably be below that of pre–war years' [i.e. 17.5%].
54 UA Development Committee 1: 16 Mar. 1948.
55 Ibid., 2: 3 Feb. 1949.
56 Ibid., 2: 6 Mar. 1951.
57 Ibid., 2: 11 Oct. 1951.
58 Ibid., 2: 21 May 1952.
59 UC 7/iii 1949, p. 4.
60 UA Development Committee 1: 24 Mar. 1947.
61 Ibid.
62 Ibid., 1: 16 Mar. 1948.
63 Ibid., 2: 3 Feb. 1949.
64 Ibid.
65 Ibid., 2: 29 June 1950.
66 Ibid., 1: 11 June 1946.
67 UC 7/iii 1951, p. 13.
68 Vincent and Hinton, *University of Birmingham,*, p. 218.
69 UC 7/iii 1948, p. 4; 1949, p. 3.
70 UA Development Committee 1: 5 Oct. 1944.
71 Ibid., 1: 11 June 1946.
72 Ibid., 1: 28 Oct. 1946.
73 Ibid., 2: 27 Sept. 1948.
74 Ibid., 2: 20 Jan., 3 Feb. 1949.
75 Ibid., 2: 28 Feb., 19 May 1949.
76 Ibid., 2: 27 Apr. 1950.
77 Ibid., 2: 19 May 1949.
78 Ibid.,2: 15 Dec. 1949, 27 Apr. 1950.
79 Ibid., 2: 29 June 1950, 15 May 1952.
80 Ibid., 2: 29 June 1950, 6 Mar. 1951.
81 Ibid., 2: 11 Oct. 1951.
82 UC 7/iii 1950, p. 17.

83 For the following see UA Development Committee 1, 2: *passim*; UC 17/i : 'Report on Future Development, January 1945'; Whitehand, 'Institutional Site Planning', pp. 31–3.
84 Whitehand, 'Institutional Site Planning', p. 34.
85 UC 7/iii 1945, p. 7; *Calendar*, 1948–9.
86 Ibid., 1946, p. 5.
87 Ibid., p. 19; 1948, p. 35; *Calendars* passim.
88 UC 7/iii 1948, p. 39.
89 Ibid., 1950, p. 22.
90 Ibid., 1948, p. 11.
91 UC 14/ii: Vice-Chancellor's Memorandum, 17 Oct. 1938.
92 Vincent and Hinton, *University of Birmingham*, p. 202.
93 Ibid., p. 214.
94 UC 7/iii 1948, pp. 14–18.
95 Ibid., 1949, pp. 38–40; 1950, pp. 34–5.
96 Ibid., 1949, pp. 8–22; 1951, pp. 12–20.
97 Vincent and Hinton, *University of Birmingham*, pp. 98–9.
98 UC 7/iii 1951, p. 25.
99 Ibid., 1939–40, pp. 10–11.
100 Ibid., 1948, pp. 6–7.
101 Ibid., pp. 30–2.
102 Ibid., 1951, pp. 64–5.
103 Ibid., 1953, pp. 22–3.
104 Ibid., 1948, pp. 7–10.
105 Ibid., 1951, pp. 7–11.
106 Ibid., p. 2.

Part Four

Transformation, 1950–80

Chapter Sixteen

Waiting for Robbins

ALTHOUGH THE UNIVERSITY COUNCIL urged Raymond Priestley to serve as vice-chancellor for five additional years, he only agreed to stay for one. To secure a long-term replacement, Birmingham again headhunted a university vice-chancellor from the Antipodes, Robert Aitken of the University of Otago. Aitken was fifty-one, and although a New Zealander by birth, his family roots were in Scotland and he had spent almost all his career in the UK. He had come as a Rhodes scholar, worked at the London Hospital, been appointed to a readership in the British Postgraduate Medical School and from 1938 to 1948, when he returned to New Zealand, had held the regius chair of medicine at Aberdeen. He was therefore not unknown in British academic circles, and wider ones, too, as he had been much involved in planning towards the NHS, as well as in advising on German reconstruction.[1]

Aitken was, however, not immediately available and Professor H. W. Humphreys was appointed for one year. One year, in fact, is misleading because Priestley was away for much of the session 1951–2 and Humphreys, who was vice-principal at the time, had been in charge as acting vice-chancellor. A graduate of the Birmingham Dental School, Humphrey Humphreys had served in the Middle East in the First World War (his letters from the campaign have survived), been appointed to the chair of dental surgery and headship of the Dental School in 1935 and, after commanding the 7th General Hospital at Devonport in the Second World War, returned to become vice-principal in succession to Professor Mark Oliphant.[2]

Though brief, Humphreys's time in office was enormously important because it broke the deadlock over Edmund Street.[3] When his first Development Committee met in October 1952 he put before it a memorandum proposing a staged move to Edgbaston, something which Priestley and the Arts Faculty had always opposed, and so too the librarian, when it had been suggested that he could accommodate his books *pro tem* in the Great Hall.[4] Humphreys's scheme brought together four considerations: selling Edmund Street would produce capital independent of the UGC; the perhaps three years which it would take to build a library; the prospective move of mechanical engineering which would by then release lecture-room space and, finally, large houses in the vicinity of the campus which were coming on the market every few months – indeed, the University owned some already. Given these factors, it would, he argued, be possible to build the library and then, concurrently, move the books into their new home and the Arts Faculty departments out of Edmund Street into houses in Edgbaston. At the same time the builders could move from the library to start on the Arts building, and when that was occupied the houses would be released to take the remaining occupants from Edmund Street. Thereafter the University would pursue either halls of residence or permanent accommodation for Commerce and Social Science, whichever had priority. Political lobbying would be necessary to secure an appropriate allocation of building material but the scheme had significant financial merits. Government backing would be necessary only for the library, not for a total move, as previously envisaged. Moreover, at a time when the quinquennial grant was expected to be very tight, the move would not increase recurrent expenditure because Edmund Street would drop out of the equation.

As with all previous schemes, nothing came of this suggested answer to the Edmund Street problem. The Chairman of the UGC was not unimpressed but could only see £250,000 becoming available for Birmingham, and not until mechanical and electrical engineering were complete. The importance of Humphreys's memorandum was, however, that it put an end to the expectation of a single exodus from Edmund Street to a promised land of new buildings ready and waiting. From this point it became accepted that the move would be staggered and that the library would be the first stage. As a realistic acceptance of what was possible this marked a major step forward, but there was a downside. Inevitably priority for the library would tilt the balance of the University decisively in favour of Edgbaston, with the Arts departments becoming increasingly marginalised. It was prophetic that the very meeting to which Humphreys presented his memorandum agreed that the secretary's department should move out of Edmund Street and that, when Aitken came, he too should be based at Edgbaston. There seems little doubt that Science and Medicine would be more in the eye of both the new vice-chancellor and the university administration than the faculties back at Mason College and duly, when Aitken arrived, he made it clear that he saw 'the centre of gravity' of the University as now at Edgbaston.

Aitken was, however, no narrow medical scientist. A competent amateur flautist, he was keenly interested in drama and was regularly to be seen at the Shakespeare Memorial Theatre in Stratford and at the Birmingham Repertory Theatre. He became directly involved in the latter and had a major hand in the Rep's new building. He was also, as we shall see, determined that higher education must embrace breadth as well as depth. Nevertheless, it does seem that Aitken came to Birmingham with a personal agenda to promote science. He wrote in 1956:

> We are in an industrial community in a technological age. If England is to

> survive we need scientists and engineers in numbers far beyond what we have trained in the past, and those scientists and engineers will increasingly become the leaders of society in fields wider than Science and Engineering. The universities must train them. Technological society demands more and more brain work, less and less muscular effort.[5]

He was also a realist, and an acute one at that. An expansion of higher education was already in progress, with Birmingham committed to a target of 4000 by the mid-1950s, but that would not be enough – the children of the post-war 'baby boom' were already in primary school – and government emphasis in any expansion would not be on the humanities. By the time he arrived a letter had already been received from the UGC to say that a building for chemical engineering had been given an immediate go-ahead but that the library would not be in the 1954 programme.[6] 'I know that you would rather have had the Library if the two schemes had been alternatives.' The stated reasons why they were not were the cost disparity and that building for a technical department was 'easier'. Aitken, however, could read the sub-text. In his first report to Council he welcomed the start for chemical engineering as a help towards meeting the calls from industry and government for an increase in applied science.[7] He also signalled the future by redefining the ideal his predecessors had pursued of a 'balanced' university. Balance, he said, was not a matter of student intake or staff numbers but balance within the education of each student. The ideal of balance had, in any case, never been recovered in practice since the end of the war. In 1938–9 Arts, Science and Medicine and Dentistry each accounted for not far short of a third of all students. By 1947–8, when the UGC began again to publish national figures, the proportion in Arts was unchanged, but Science was at 43%; Medicine was down to 20%. In the October in which Aitken arrived, Arts had somewhat declined and Medicine increased by a few points, but the figure for students reading science and engineering remained unchanged.[8] Eventually, having half of the students at Birmingham in science was accepted as the norm.

Aitken certainly did not abandon the goal of uniting the University and he continued to see progress on the library as the key to the problem. However, his technique was to 'accelerate' immediate requirements such as chemical engineering under a UGC assurance that existing priorities would not be affected.[9] In his first term he gave strong support to Professor Moon's argument that radiation problems made it vital for physics to have more space and agreed to approach the DSIR for support, but with the proviso that there should be no prejudice to other projects.[10] A year later the UGC relaxed its rules and allowed universities to go ahead with building more quickly where they could raise part or all of the funds required locally.[11] Aitken's response was to propose that Birmingham should encourage UGC help by part-funding the halls of residence, while assuring the dean of Arts that this would in no way interfere with plans for the future of *his* faculty.[12]

In the autumn of 1954 the UGC informed Birmingham that the library would be included in its funded plans for 1955.[13] This meant that the future of the Edmund Street departments now needed serious attention. Various plans were suggested.[14] One was to stay at Edmund Street as tenants until accommodation was built. Another was to be accommodated in huts at Edgbaston. Aitken's view was that the Arts Faculty 'will probably have to move its books, and it may have to suffer a few years of discomfort before entering its own quarters, but we hope it will be sustained by the early prospect of realising a fifty-year old dream'.[15] By the end of 1955 a plan had been agreed.[16] A loan would be taken out on the security of Edmund Street and used to build a women's hall of residence on the Wyddrington (that is, the Vale) site. Then, when the library was ready, the female students in residence in University House would move to the new hall and the Arts would take over their rooms. Finally, an Arts building would be completed on UGC money and University House could revert to its traditional purpose. It was when the UGC was consulted on this that the University was made to realise how far developments since the war had eroded its initiative. It was told that no UGC money would be made available for Arts until 1958, the funds from the sale of Edmund Street had to be ploughed into the new Arts building, and Treasury finance for halls of residence was earmarked for smaller universities since there were plenty of lodgings to be had in conurbations like Birmingham. The vice-chancellor reported to the Finance and General Purposes Committee in January 1956: 'It is still open to us to contest the UGC exercise of such firm control over the moneys that will accrue from the sale of Edmund Street, but the UGC is in the position to have the last word.'[17] In other words, although the University was absolutely entitled to do what it liked with the Edmund Street assets, its need to continue to go to the UGC for help effectively meant that the Committee would in future have a veto over the University's use of its own capital. Alternatives were canvassed to little avail. The UGC, for example, would not hear of the University borrowing, and subsequently being reimbursed by the Treasury for money spent on the Arts block. It was suggested instead that a loan for £750,000 should be taken out with Lloyd's Bank, with £250,000 being used to pay for an overrun on the library (which the UGC would not cover) and the rest going to the Arts block, but even this had to be put to the government's Capitals Issues Committee.

The long-awaited move from Edmund Street thus was not plain sailing, even when approval had been received from the UGC for a start on the new library. Not until the start of the 1959–60 session was Priestley's 1938 'greatest single item' ready, and it took another year for Grant Robertson's 'blessed day' to arrive in the effective evacuation of Edmund Street. On the science side the shape of things to come was made evident by the UGC launching a Higher Technological Expansion Programme in June 1954.[18] Birmingham was enthusiastic to take part and committed itself to take 400 more students in science and engineering (+31%) over the next three to five years on the promise of an eventual £200,000 on the recurrent account. Undergraduate numbers were projected to rise by 27% and research students by 29%, but most significant was the proposed 75% growth in the new graduate courses. Recent and current building in engineering were expected to be adequate to cope with such an increase but nothing could happen until chemistry expanded, and an extension of the Hills Building was scheduled immediately. Physics, too, needed space and the more so since Professor Moon was still faced with the radiation problem. Expansion also called into question old disciplinary boundaries and setting up a department of microbiology was agreed to be essential. This opened in 1955.[19]

All was not, however, quite so promising as the reports for 1954 and 1955 suggest. There was always the suspicion that the Treasury would do as little as possible to honour its promises, and even more, there was inflation. The extra cost for the library is an example of both – an unrealistic UGC cap at £427,000 coupled with an inexorable rises in costs.[20] Inflation, indeed, was to become one of the University's great concerns and Aitken chose to highlight it in the report of his first full year in office.[21] The first big crisis had occurred in 1952, Priestley's last year, with an unfunded pay award for technician staff at a time when the quinquennial settlement for 1952–7 had been announced at an effective standstill.[22] Despite frantic economies, 1952–3 saw the accumulated deficit rise to £73,596 and put research programmes in jeopardy. Humphrey Humphreys immediately proposed to the Council that the only answer was another public appeal, and preparations were ready for Aitken to launch this in November 1953.[23] This time the appeal was not for capital but for income, pure and simple, and the target was £75,000 a year, raised on seven-year deeds of covenant.[24] Again the response was encouraging. At the end of the first year £440,000 had been given or promised, equivalent to £62,000 a year, and the University ended the financial year 1953–4 in the black, with over £10,000 going to reduce the accumulated deficit.[25] Aitken welcomed the protection the appeal had given to research but he was not entirely happy about having to appeal for immediate income. He would, it seems, have preferred to put the money into a contingency fund and so be able to undertake some discreet developments from time to time.[26] Certainly he used part of the early receipts for new lectureships. Nevertheless the appeal did enable the University to extinguish the deficit by the end of 1957–8 and build up an accumulated surplus of nearly £20,000 by the end of 1959–60.[27]

These early years of Aitken's vice-chancellorship had about them a feeling of suspended animation. So much of the planning he had inherited had yet to be implemented; the country at large was taking to the idea of higher education for the young and government wanted more graduates, especially scientists. Yet there was a reluctance to take the plunge. In 1956, however, the vice-chancellor believed that change had arrived. He designated it 'the first effective year of a great transformation'.[28] In June the first issue of a *Bulletin* led with the announcement of a provisional quinquennial bid to increase numbers over the next five years by

25% which, in the final offer became 31–41%.[29] It also announced a large building programme. Work on the library would start on 1 July and be followed by the faculty of Arts. Funding had been sorted out at last, although for a smaller building than first intended. Projects under consideration included new or additional premises for chemistry, biology, mathematics and physics, mining, Arts, Commerce, education, the extra-mural department and the Union, a swimming pool and halls of residence, the completion of the Medical School and the conversion of existing accommodation for civil engineering, Law and the administration. As a professor remarked to the vice-chancellor while watching the steel going up for the new library, 'There will be no peace on this site now for a decade.'[30] By the autumn it was clear that the expectation was that the University's income would need to increase to over £2 million and that in the first three years alone, the proposed new building would cost £4,900,000.[31] Existing plans for the development of Edgbaston would clearly be inadequate and new estate architects were engaged, Sir Hugh Casson and Partners. All this, however, proved to be premature and expansion stalled yet again. The UGC offered less capital than was needed while continuing to press for 500 more students over the sessions 1963–4, 1964–5 and 1965–6 (two-thirds of them in Science) with adjustments within the building programme.[32] The Treasury grant, not for the first time, did not live up to expectations either, and with departments overdoing their recruiting there was talk of budgeting for a deficit.[33] In the event government support was marginally increased for the later years of the quinquennium, and by accepting some worsening in the staff–student ratio the University was able to achieve and slightly exceed its agreed target of growth. Nonetheless there had been no 'great leap forward'.[34]

Looking back on development in the 1950s, including this late flurry, it is clear that while the University had grown, little had happened to change it, though Aitken anticipated that the move out of Edmund Street in the summer of 1960 would create new demands on Edgbaston and some friction, a possibility he had foreseen in 1956.[35] However, mid-way in the 1959–60 session fundamental change was threatened with the receipt of a letter from the UGC.[36] This asked the University to examine the possibility of yet further growth and on a significant scale. The first *Bulletin* of the year carried a major analysis by Aitken and a special Senate meeting was called for 3 February 1960. There were, as he saw it, only two choices and gradual development was not one of them. That would mean a future of continuous attempts to catch up. The first realistic option was to stand on a student population of 5500 for the next ten or fifteen years. Existing facilities and those already planned could sustain that level. The policy would have the advantage of offering stability after the significant 38% growth achieved in the previous twelve years. What was more, if held at 5500, the University would soon achieve its long-held desire to have residential places for at least one student in three. The alternative was a quantum leap to 7000 over the next decade with facilities in proportion. This would create the opportunity of developing in new academic areas as well as producing larger departments capable of sustaining more specialisms and stronger graduate schools. The corollary, however, was a much enlarged campus with facilities on a new scale which asked the implicit question whether 10 000 students could not be accommodated just as easily.

The result was a debate, paralleled in every other university in the country and in the press. With Kingsley Amis from University College, Swansea, summing up the issue as 'more will mean worse', it might be assumed that the core of opposition to expansion would be in the common room of Birmingham's Arts Faculty.[37] In reality opinion was widely divided. The non-professorial staff of chemical engineering wrote a collective letter opposing the suggestion. Some of them signed because they wanted stability and others because they saw no hope of the government financing the fundamental changes which growth would require. In any case, even if it was paid for, where could more accommodation, especially student accommodation be put? At the Senate meeting it was also argued strongly that additional expansion would aggravate existing problems in teaching and particularly administration. The majority opinion, however, was otherwise, The expansion of higher education was a demand from the community and it was the duty of universities to meet it. It was also widely felt that expansion was inevitable and that it was better to accept it and plan properly than to be forced by circumstances later. M. V. C. Jeffreys, the professor of education, argued for keeping the size of existing institutions and meeting demand by creating new ones, but as Aitken pointed out, the time lag in this was too great. He could also have said that such a course would cost the government more than maximising numbers on existing sites.

Speed of decision was important because of the need to get building in hand, and the Senate met on 21 March 1960.[38] It recommended that the University should offer to do more even than the UGC had asked for, a total of 7500 students by October 1971, with 54% in Science, 12% in Medicine and 31% in the other faculties (Arts 16%, 7% in Commerce and Social Science, Law 3% and Education 5%), with 200 places in reserve. Two months later, the building programme which such an expansion would necessitate was agreed to be an additional £1.25 million for the next three years and £1.5 million in each of the following two years. Again the UGC was cautious, offering £600,000 and £1.25 million, respectively, which the University calculated would mean taking 500 students fewer than proposed in science.[39] Nevertheless it went ahead in May 1960 with a public appeal to raise £1,600,000 to erect residences on what later became the Vale site. The quinquennial visit of the UGC in November maintained the optimism.[40] The University was able to set out the needs of Birmingham, and although the visitors made clear that building decisions had yet to be made, they had had no criticisms to offer, and Aitken came away convinced that in particular the case for a theatre had been successfully made. The appeal had already raised £1,400,000 which meant that with existing UGC promises the University had access to nearly £2 million. By then the government had actually authorised a limited increase in numbers and added two-thirds to the UGC capital fund for 1962 and 1963 which seemed to indicate that Birmingham might get about 75% of what it had asked for.[41] Admittedly, inflation was particularly a problem here because of the lengthy lead time between approval and work starting. Officially real costs were reckoned to amount to 12.5% above grants as announced, but Aitken calculated the true figure at 20% or more. Thus, for example, the biology building, started in 1960, came in at one-third over the quantity surveyors' estimates, and despite an additional grant from the UGC the University was left to find £125,000 to cover the rest. The income and expenditure side was also seriously affected, especially by salaries and wages, and a large deficit threatened. These factors made it necessary to apply the brake on expansion towards the target of 5500 by freezing expected posts and holding student numbers to 180 below the planned figure for October 1961. Nevertheless, the expectation was that this would be temporary. The long talked-of national expansion in higher education could not be delayed much further. In 1960 the government had set up a Committee under Lord Robbins to report on higher education and make recommendations for the future, and even as it was beginning work the UGC announced that it would recommend new universities at Canterbury, Colchester and Coventry.

In April 1962, out of the blue, the dream was shattered. The government, which had just approved cost-of-living increases of between 15% and 20% for civil servants and staff in technical and training colleges, suddenly announced a 'pay pause'. The House of Commons was informed on Wednesday 14th that the University's salary bill would be allowed to rise by only a 'norm' of 3%. Aitken rushed to add a page to a *Bulletin* already in press describing the increase as 'derisory' and looking 'like a deliberate relegation of universities to an inferior status'.[42] Even worse was the quinquennial settlement announced the same day. This was way below the estimated cost of the expansion already in hand and the government's call for that expansion to continue to be met was 'hypocritical if the escape phrase "as far as possible" had not been added'. A month later the vice-chancellor was able to publish the implications of the settlement in detail.[43] The government target for expansion was 150 000 students by 1966–7, with those at Birmingham rising to 5872. By ignoring the true cost of this, the quinquennial award would produce an annual deficiency increasing from £420,000 in 1962–3 to £1,117,000 in 1966–7. The only possible course was to reduce proposed admissions in October to the 1961 figure, make economies in the budgets of departments, the centre and the estate, place a moratorium on most new staff, worsen the staff–student ratio to 1:9 and budget for a deficit – devices which would, over time, become routine in university management.[44]

It has been said of Aitken that 'It is possible to disagree with him. It is impossible to misunderstand him.' His anger at what he saw as an act of betrayal is palpable:

> The issue of quantity versus quality is now squarely before the universities. They have royal charters. They have independence. They have, and they continue to receive, some income that is not government income. If these things mean anything, they mean that the universities have a responsibility for maintaining worthy standards in teaching and research. That requires money. There can be no better judge of the expenditure necessary to maintain worthy standards than the UGC, comprising as it does a majority of active academic people and a strong minority of administrators and men of affairs. Now for the first time, the Government has rejected the UGC's judgement, and asked for more students at less cost. The universities must, therefore, accept their responsibilities and decide themselves how many students can be worthily educated with the resources made available.[45]

It is unfortunate, given all that has happened since, that universities ducked this challenge, perhaps their last opportunity to assert a true measure of independence. Instead, astute moves at Westminster blunted the sharpness of the protest.[46] The UGC divided the complainants over pay by allocating all the money to lecturers and assistant lecturers; the government promised a rise of 10% from April 1963; the Treasury gave a promise to review quinquennial grants during 1964; capital provision for higher education which had also been slashed was marginally relaxed later in the year. Given the choice between all-out conflict and struggling on, the universities chose the latter, and not for the last time. Birmingham, which had announced it would hold the line until the review was complete, agreed that it would raise admissions in October 1963 by 200 and so reach the target of 5000, and that following the improvement on the capital side its building programme probably could keep up with the requirements of expansion.[47]

The Robbins Committee was due to publish its report on 23 October 1963. Although not 'leaked', it had been very extensively trailed, and the UGC had already anticipated it by asking Birmingham to examine its building plans in case it was asked to move to 7000 or 7500 students within a decade. This, however, was more than an issue of physical growth. It meant that the questions Aitken had posed in 1960 about the effect of a 50% increase in size were no longer theoretical. First there was the possibility of a major development in graduate studies. Next there was the chance to develop new academic fields. Expansion in the last ten years had been achieved by increasing numbers in existing disciplines – the only real innovations had been biochemistry and microbiology and the Centre for West African Studies, which had just been established on earmarked government funding following the Hayter Report on the need to encourage regional studies.[48] There was also a promise of a second Hayter Centre for Russian and East European Studies. Aitken suggested that now it would be possible both to innovate within disciplines and to introduce new ones.[49] For the former he suggested solid state physics, theatre arts, highway and traffic engineering and radio-biology. For the latter he put forward psychology, architecture and environmental planning and the possibility of less conventional academic subjects such as journalism, criminology or banking – even, perhaps, domestic science! Student accommodation would also have to be rethought. The University had acquired twenty acres across the Manor House drive. Should this land be used for halls of residence, or would it be better to build a mixture of bed-sitting rooms and self-contained flats for married students with an adjacent restaurant? Even the university administration would have to be reviewed. So far two principles had been observed, the University as a unity of interlocking parts and the overall authority of Senate in academic matters. Now there were voices calling for greater non-professorial participation, full-time deans, smaller faculties, smaller departments and more.

The publication of the Robbins Report was, without question, the most important event in British higher education in the second half of the twentieth century. Everything that has happened since has been against the analysis it presented and towards compliance with or in reaction against its recommendations. The report took as its axiom 'that courses of higher education should be available for all those who are qualified by ability and attainment to pursue them and who wish to do so', which, as Aitken explained to the University Council, changed university education from a privilege for those who could afford it to a right for all who could benefit by it.[50] It also revolutionised the role of government. No longer would its interest in higher education be limited to economic utility; once access to higher education became a citizen's right, the state would be expected to guarantee it. The vice-chancellor had no doubt of the political calculation involved.

> In a parliamentary democracy the voters have the last word, and this time they have not even needed to vote. Before the election, the parties have bid each other up in their promises to expand higher education at explosive speed. . . . Only the imminence of an election will explain the Government's action in accepting the Robbins report whole, unseen and uncriticised by Parliament and public within eighteen months of its refusal on economic grounds to sustain an expansion to 150,000 university students in 1966–67.

Given that the immediate importance of the report was electoral, Aitken saw that the future would be a struggle between universities anxious to maintain standards and governments who might not be able or willing to fund at the proper level. What he did not remark on was the implied change in the relationship between universities and government. To that point government, although already the principal paymaster of higher education, had been in a purchaser/provider relationship with universities; if, henceforth, the state was to guarantee the provision of higher education that relationship would inevitably become one of control and direction. As if to signal this, the government announced that local authorities would no longer contribute to higher education from the rates, and discussions also began on mechanisms to link higher education and government. The outcome was that although the Treasury withdrew from direct responsibility for funding development, the UGC was brought under a Ministry of Education and Science. At the same time the DSIR was broken up, leaving a group of research councils, also under Education and Science, but with 'applied' research going to a Ministry of Technology.[51]

Once the report itself was published, Aitken called a general meeting of staff for 6 November to discuss what had now become a specific invitation for Birmingham to expand over the next four sessions.[52] How many could it take? In the light of that discussion the Committee of Principals and Deans and the Senate Executive put forward proposals which were accepted by Senate on 23 November and by Council four days later. Given good leadership, devolved universities are capable of rapid responses – contrary to the view which later became an obsession at Whitehall and Westminster. And the response was brave. Provided capital and additional grant were forthcoming, Birmingham could achieve 7000 by 1967–8 with the possibility of growing to 10 000 by 1980–1 and this without any additions to current plans in medicine and dentistry, which were outside the Robbins remit. The 1960 plan to move from 5000 at October 1964 to 7500 by October 1971 had necessitated student numbers rising cumulatively at 357 a year. The target now proposed for 1967–8 would require 425.

Robert Aitken went to discuss these proposals with the UGC on 14 January 1964. The offers of universities to expand had added up to more than the numbers required, and the vice-chancellor was told that decisions would be taken on an ad hoc basis, not by scaling down across the board. In Birmingham's case discussion centred on capital costs and its requirement for between £5 and £7 million over the two years 1964 and 1965, £2 million of this being for engineering. The UGC also informed him of the position in medicine, where entry was to rise by 15%. How many students could Birmingham accept? Less palatable was the news about the theatre. Although the UGC had approved a start in 1965 and allocated funding of £250,000, the Committee had now decided that to include theatres in the construction programme for higher education would attract public criticism and so approval had been withdrawn. Aitken appealed for Birmingham to be exempt because it was already so advanced in its plans, but the Committee came back only to say that it had confirmed its decision.[53] The site for the theatre is vacant to this day.

Two months after this meeting the final post-Robbins numbers were announced.[54] For Birmingham the UGC envisaged an expansion in three years to 6050 and in four years to 6300, not 7000. This gave an overall annual increase in student numbers almost identical with that envisaged in 1960. This would on the basis of existing staff–student ratios – 1:8. in Science, 1:8.4 in Arts, 1:9.6 in

Commerce and Social Science and 1:16.1 in Law – require 122 more staff. However, breaking the figures down to detail produced an immediate instance of the implications of expansion which Aitken had stressed. In the year then current, 1963–4, postgraduate students had reached 17.2% of the total. Principals and Deans proposed that there should be a further increase, especially in graduate courses, to raise that proportion to 21% at the end of the four years to 1966–7. They also recommended that the University would now have to recognise that graduate students required more attention than undergraduates, and move from its existing 1:1 weighting to the recently adopted UGC formula of 1:3 for graduate students in Science and 1:2 in Arts. This increased the number of staff required to 164 (109 of them in Science) and raised the immediate prospect of a deficit of £100,000 unless additional income was forthcoming. Indeed, by May 1964 it was possible to estimate a deficit at the end of 1965 of £113,975.[55] The pay problem did improve, with the National Incomes Commission producing favourable salary recommendations which the government did accept, but by the time that Aitken issued his pre-sessional briefing to staff in the following October it had become crystal clear that, with the Commons dissolved and MPs on the hustings, the Treasury was quietly intent on minimising the capital costs of university expansion.[56] Its assertion was that accommodation for the national target of 197 000 students in 1967–8 had already been funded through the increases of non-recurrent grant in 1961–2, 1962–3 and 1963–4. Birmingham was allocated only £120,000 for new building starts in 1966–7 and Aitken foresaw another revision of student numbers. Aitken was particularly incensed that the Government was proposing to set up five Special Institutions of Scientific and Technological Education and Research (SISTERS) and to leave Birmingham out. The future was clearly to be the battle against political short-termism and the 'too little too late' syndrome which British higher education has been fighting ever since. Aitken's verdict on 1964 is worth recalling. It was

> a year that began confidently, with an invitation to a great endeavour, and ended in uncertainty as to whether that endeavour was really desired, or could actually be supported by the Government. Confidence arose from the sweeping optimism of the Robbins Report, the challenge of a difficult task, and the encouraging size of the first instalment of financial provision. It was fortified by the Government's acceptance of the academic salary recommendations of the National Incomes Commission, which recognised the special long-term importance to the country of university teaching and research. Confidence then began to ebb as it became apparent that financial support might not extend, beyond the hurried achievement of certain student numbers in 1967–68, to the really adequate equipment of the University to meet the needs of the students and of the country in each of its faculties. The near cessation of capital provision in [for] 1966–67 con-

firmed those fears. We are now quite uncertain as to where we go next, and 1966–67 is only next year. All we can do is to continue our planning in the hope that Go-Stop will some time be succeeded by Stop-Go. This jerky advance is wasteful of time, money, and the emotional strength of academic effort. We need to have more detailed basic planning looking ten years ahead, and we need fuller discussion between the University and the Government of the University's part in the national development.[57]

Notes

1 Obituaries in *The Times*, *Daily Telegraph* and *Guardian*.

2 Vincent and Hinton, *University of Birmingham*, p. 32; UC 7/ii *Council* 1949, p. 2.

3 For the following see UA Development Committee 2, 17 Oct. 1952.

4 Ibid., 29 June 1950; 6 Mar. 1951.

5 UC 7/iii 1956, p. 3.

6 UA Development Committee 2: Capital Building Programme Committee, 29 Sept. 1953.

7 UC 7/iii 1953, pp. 2–3.

8 Students by faculties:

	1938–9 *[pp. 12–13]*	1947–8 *[pp. 14–15]*	1953–4 *[pp. 20–1]*
Arts	545 (38%)	1113 (37%)	1014 (34%)
Science and Engineering	460 (32%)	1304 (43%)	1300 (43%)
Medicine and Dentistry	428 (30%)	595 (20%)	705 (23%)

UGC *Returns for Universities and University Colleges*:

9 UA Development Committee: Capital Programme Committee, 19 Nov. 1953.

10 Ibid.

11 Ibid., 25 Oct. 1954.

12 Ibid., 10 Dec. 1954.

13 Ibid., 25 Oct. 1954.

14 Ibid., 10 Dec. 1954.

15 UC7/iii 1954, p. 11.

16 For the following see UA Finance & General Purposes Cttee 28, nos. 12280, 12314, 12391, 12397, 12474.

17 Ibid., 12280.

18 UC 7/iii 1954, pp. 2–3, 8–9; 1956, p. 6.

19 Ibid., 1955, p. 6.

20 UA Development Cttee: Capital Building Programme Cttee, 25 Oct. 1954; Finance &General Purposes Committee 28, no. 12397.

21 UC 7/iii 1954, pp. 6–8.

22 UC 7/ii *Council* 1951, pp. 7–8; 1952, p. 8.
23 UC 7/iii 1952, p. 5.
24 Ibid.,1953, pp. 3–4; 7/ii *Council* 1953, p. 6. For the appeal document see 7/iv/7/23.
25 UC 7/iii 1954, p. 2.
26 Ibid., p. 7.
27 UC 7/ii *Accounts* 1960, p. 4.
28 UC7/iii 1956, p. 1.
29 *Bulletin* 1 (14 June 1956); 2 (15 Oct. 1956).
30 UC7/iii/1956, p. 2.
31 *Bulletin* 2 (15 Oct. 1956).
32 Ibid., 5 (29 Apr. 1957).
33 Ibid., 7 (11 Dec. 1957); UC7/iii 1957, pp. 2–5.
34 Ibid., 1961, pp. 1–3.
35 Ibid., 1957, p. 5.
36 For the following see *Bulletin* 16 (27 Jan. 1960); 17 (15 Mar. 1960); UC 7/iii 1960, pp. 3–4.
37 *Encounter*, July 1960.
38 *Bulletin* 18 (13 May 1960).
39 Ibid., 19 (30 May 1960).
40 Ibid., 21 (13 Dec. 1960).
41 Ibid., 22 (2 Feb. 1961). UC 7/iii 1961, pp. 2–4.
42 *Bulletin* 28 (29 Jan. 1962).
43 Ibid., 30 (11 Apr. 1962).
44 Ibid., 32 (2 July 1962); UC 7/iii 1961, p. 3.
45 Ibid., 28 (29 Jan. 1962).
46 Ibid., 32 (2 Jul.1962); UC 7/iii 1962, p. 3.
47 Ibid., p. 3.
48 Ibid., p. 5.
49 *Bulletin* 42 (5 Oct. 1963).
50 UC 7/iii 1963, pp. 4–9.
51 Ibid., 1964, pp. 2–3.
52 For the following see *Bulletin* 43 (4 Nov. 1963); 44 (11 Dec. 1963); UC 7/iii 1963, pp. 9–10.
53 *Bulletin* 47 (17 Mar. 1964).
54 Ibid.
55 Ibid., 48 (7 May 1964).
56 UC 7/iii 1964, p. 6; *Bulletin* 51 (8 Oct. 1964).
57 UC 7/iii 1964, p. 6.

Chapter Seventeen

Expansion

IT IS A TRIBUTE to the optimism of post-war British academics and their faith in what they were trying to do, that the decades of 'Go-Stop' did not destroy their readiness to plan for a hoped-for future. It was in 1956, the year of Aitken's expected 'great transformation', that a review of the future of the Edgbaston site had begun in earnest, and Birmingham persisted in this even when cold financial winds dispelled the heady atmosphere of hope and expectation. Casson and Conder, the partners engaged, had a reputation for imagination and Sir High Casson in particular, architect of the Festival of Britian, was then at the height of his reputation.

When the new architects produced their plans in 1957 these certainly were controversial. However, some forty years later, the principal feeling they provoke is of anticlimax. The fundamental innovation was revealed to be a 'ring road'! Nothing could have been less original. No self-respecting site plan of the late 1950s was complete without one, and Rees's earlier decision to split the Avenue so as to pass each side of the library (now under construction) had already pointed in that direction. In presenting the plan Casson and Conder claimed that their first objective was 'to preserve the character of the University's hill site', but their interest seems to have been primarily to rubbish the Aston Webb design and to do everything possible to make nonsense of it: 'The strong half-circle encloses too harshly a north facing courtyard, while its northern range, fortunately not yet completed, sets up an unfriendly, indeed almost impassable barrier against the rest of the University site.'[1] As for the Avenue, which Rees had at least preserved in part: 'The grand axis of the north approach has, since the building of the Library, become meaningless – we believe mercifully so. It has ceased to exist as a monumental conception.'[2] Even the heart of the Aston Webb complex was not respected. As late as April 1957, when the Casson–Conder plan had already been received, the University still expected Block 'D' which had been sacrificed in 1902 to be at last completed for the department of metallurgy.[3] However, the advice of the new architects was that the space should be left unfilled, and so, too, the gap between the Harding Library and the physics building. Much was made of the wish 'to improve the appearance of the University site by attention to every aspect of landscapes' and it is true that where the ex-government huts between the old library and physics have been removed the planned ornamental pool has not materialised.[4] But even if landscaping had been completed, still the gaps which Casson and Conder preserved might well equally be described as 'meaningless'.

In 1957 the initial Casson–Conder plan was presented to a meeting of Council and university staff and a similar meeting was held in November 1961 to consider progress and changes since that date. By then the shape of the central section of the north side of the campus was already evident with the Arts building, the library and, on the west side, the Student Refectory and Staff House under construction. The area had also been effectively pedestrianised following agreement with the City on closing University Road. Two sections of the ring road were complete but the meeting expressed considerable interest in the line of the remainder and in car parking. Ultimately the road was built so as to discourage kerbside parking, and on the north side it was taken through a deep cutting across and below the avenue from the Pritchatts Road gates which thus ended in mid-air. Forecourt parking spaces were to be provided for members of staff with students confined to the periphery of the site. The cost of this parking, the University learned two months later, was to be an annual charge of £3.[5] When this was announced there was particular concern to defend the provision for one student in three to bring a car on the campus:

> We believe that restriction placed upon students' cars would be undesirable except as a last resort, considering that England is more and more a vehicle owning society; the University placed inside an increasingly 'motorised' city, cannot segregate its students from the kind of life that goes on around them. Public transport, for students, already leaves much to be desired, and it seems more likely to deteriorate than to improve, following the trend seen in London and the United States.

In all fairness, it must be added that 'as a corollary' bicycle sheds were to be provided in all new buildings to encourage students to cycle in from the halls of residence.

Another issue before the November 1961 meeting was the impact on planning of the proposed increase in the size of the University to 7000 students by 1970. Aitken had already raised the issue earlier in the year.[6] Physics had recently been the beneficiary of a considerable amount of building, but further expansion was inevitable, and could only occur by trenching on the space intended for Block 'D' and metallurgy and eventually even on mining and minerals engineering in the existing Block 'C'. Where, then, were these departments to go? Casson and

Conder proposed the Bristol Road playing fields, but after persuasion they presented plans to build north of Pritchatts Road instead. The hope here was to get permission to close part of this as well.[7] The University would then have had for development a wedge-shaped site bounded by the Bristol Road, Edgbaston Park Road, Somerset Road and the canal with an exit to the west across the canal bridge on to what remained of Pritchatts Road. The city planners had expressed sympathy with the closure, although if that did not materialise the alternative was an underpass.

Four months later the Bristol Road fields were again under threat, this time for physics.[8] The architects' plan envisaged moving the Bristol Road entrance to the west with a more direct approach to the Great Hall. This would have allowed all the playing fields to the east of that entrance to be raised in level and built on, down to the line of the Bristol Road. The scheme also gave Casson and Conder an opportunity to attack the citadel of the 1909 complex: it proposed to break into the basement of the Great Hall to create a main entrance on the south side, from which a passageway would be driven under the Hall to exit in what is now Chancellor's Court, with a parallel walkway constructed outside the building: 'The way through under the Great Hall and the pedestrian route are both attempts to break down the imperforate nature of the Aston Webb range.' The Senate and Council did accept that the western part of the playing fields would have to be built on for engineering, and also the possibility of a 'sunken building' at their eastern end, but by framing the pitches that remained, the development would 'perhaps help, some day to give coherence and dignity to the southern aspect of the University, which is today impressive by its size but confused in its appearance'.[9] Fortunately that day never came.

By the end of the 1957–62 quinquennium the building programme for the next five years was effectively decided and its pace was thereafter dependent on the release of government funds and the vagaries of the construction industry, factors extraneous to the University. In 1963, however, it was felt that in the light of projected student numbers over the next ten years a further revision of the site plan was advisable. This was presented in February and divided the campus overall into fifty-eight sites split into 'already occupied', 'earmarked' or for 'future expansion'.[10] For the south side, 'a fundamental part' of the architects' proposals was still to move the Bristol Street lodge and assault the Great Hall, part of a scheme described as 'refreshing the southern aspect of the University'. In the north the assumption was that Pritchatts Road was going to be closed and its building line would disappear, along with the ornamental gates, so allowing the area to be redesigned as a whole. A number of later features appeared in different locations – the 'tall tower building', the antecedent of the Muirhead Tower, was sited between the Arts building and the Barber Institute. The architects also suggested introducing a residential block on the west side of University Square, covering the Student Refectory, and they attacked the integrity of the square itself with a proposal for a free-standing lecture theatre outside the library. Again, Aitken published this plan in the *Bulletin* with an invitation to all staff to send in comments. Fifty were received and appeared in a later *Bulletin*, along with somewhat touchy replies from the architects.[11] Thus they met the general hostility to any lessening of the spaciousness of University Square with a claim that the additional lecture theatre would make the square more interesting and a reminder that 'the great, but paradoxical truth of the English picturesque theory is that if a space cannot all be seen at once, it is felt to be a bigger space'. Comments were also received from groups, in what was clearly no public relations exercise. The Planning and Priorities Committee (which had replaced the Development Committee in 1954) instructed the architects to take all the points raised into account. It also agreed that the publication of a further plan should be put off until 1964. Clearly the Committee was also less impressed by the likelihood of Pritchatts Road closing and decided to put electrical engineering on a different site from that recommended, which would not be affected by closure or otherwise. Other buildings were relocated subsequently but with the exception of the survival both of the south side and Pritchatts Road, the site plan of 1963 essentially is that of the campus today.

Along with future planning went current building. The government continued to play fast and loose – in July 1965 the Chancellor of the Exchequer imposed a six-month pause on the letting of contracts which held up both an extension to the library and the Commerce and Social Science tower – and new buildings were frequently late, but over the quinquennium the campus changed dramatically.[12] It began with the opening of Staff House and the Student Refectory, which Aitken described as 'bold rather than graceful ... but no one has said they are dull'.[13] By 1963 the novel Ashley building for Commerce and Social Science and the Physical Education Centre were under construction and so too metallurgy and minerals engineering, the first buildings on the north part of the site.[14] The high point of activity was probably 1966, but taking the full five years to 1967, Birmingham erected twelve buildings which each cost in excess of a quarter of a million pounds and the total of all construction work, including equipment, was almost £15 million.[15]

The one blot on this success story was what was done to the Great Hall. Happily it escaped the full structural force of the Casson–Conder attack but it was betrayed by academic philistinism, much as the University's shield of arms would be betrayed two decades later. The Great Hall is a gem characteristic of its period but its acoustics are lamentable. It also has a restricted utility. Proposals to make it a dining hall had foundered on the difference between Birmingham and Oxford and it had ceased being used as an emergency gym. It was now used, essentially, only for examinations and grand university occasions. Even for these it presented problems, with a level platform which, for a growing institution, was becoming pretty restricted. By the 1960s a time had arrived when the organ needed an overhaul and the hall redecoration, and this seemed to many as an opportunity for a university where space was at a premium to do something about a major item of the building stock which was both underused and in some ways unusable.

An early idea which was circulated by the Planning and Priorities Committee in 1960 for comment was that a stepped auditorium should be built within the existing shell to provide a large lecture hall and a venue for concerts and drama.[16] Subsequently more sensitive thinking put forward a cautious alternative proposal to create a raked stage with a sound reflector but without making irreversible changes.[17] However, Planning and Priorities were still for draconian measures and in October 1964 recommended to the Senate that massive changes should be made.[18] It proposed a new stepped platform at the south end of the hall covered by a large sounding board hanging from the ceiling, angled platform walls (another suggestion to improve the acoustics), an overhaul of the organ and the repositioning of the 'show pipes'. In the main body of the hall the recommendation was to fill in the side arches and introduce a stepped floor for the rear third. This would hold 435 seats, leaving a further 800 in front at the original level. Faced with these proposals the Senate divided deeply into what Aitkens labelled as 'traditionalists' and 'functionalists'.[19] The first decision was, therefore, to send the matter back to the experts and from there the debate rolled on interminably.[20] Fortunately the proposal to make changes to the body of the hall was dropped but a general agreement on what should be done overall was not forthcoming. Eventually in 1966 a direct vote was taken and the 'traditionalists' lost.[21] The superb Edwardian organ cases were thereupon torn out and discarded, along with panelling of the platform. A tiered platform was inserted which obstructed part of the great window. The walls of the new platform were made of aluminium and acoustic plastic infill, covered with what looks like plywood, and clashed horribly with the oak elsewhere in the hall. Several sections of the vaulted ceiling became obscured by the 'vast sound canopy', also of aluminium and plastic, though thankfully that was not persisted with for long. During the lengthy discussions an additional use for the hall had been proposed – as a cinema to provide entertainment for students in the new halls of residence. This, of course, was ten years after the launching of ITV! A projection box, also in pseudo plywood, was, therefore, constructed on the gallery at the west end, protruding out into and dominating the entrance hall. Again thankfully, that excrescence was removed in 1994 though Aitken's 1966 remark that 'the experts have yet to install an efficient microphone and amplifying system' in the Great Hall remains substantially true.[22]

A much happier building achievement during Aitken's vice-chancellorship was student residences. When he arrived the university had 318 residential places for 3019 students – 10.5%.[23] At the start of the 1962–7 quinquennium the position was even worse, 432 out of 4802, only 9%.[24] However, in the final year of the quinquennium, that is, one year before he retired, 1492 students out of 6245 were in residence, a striking 23.9% from a population nearly a third greater.[25] One of the earliest developments was the acquisition of Number 9 Pritchatts Road, from which Pritchatts Park has developed. The house was fitted up for twenty-six postgraduates in bed-sits with some cooking facilities, and was intended particularly for overseas students.[26] A block providing bed-sitting rooms for a further 159 graduate students was built behind it and opened early in 1967.[27] Its name, Lucas House, marked a significant financial input from the company and the United Birmingham Hospital also put in funds. Chad Hill, the house used previously for postgraduate accommodation, had to be shut in September 1965, prior to demolition.[28]

The key to success with accommodation for undergraduates was the development of the Vale site between Edgbaston Park Road and Church Road. The land, as we have seen, was acquired in the 1950s and in 1956 Casson and Conder were engaged to advise on its development.[29] However, with adequate public funding becoming more and more unlikely, the Council decided to mark 1960, the University's Diamond Jubilee, with an 'Appeal for Halls of Residence'. This was headed by Sir Bertram Waring of Lucas, the target was £1,638,250 and primary recourse was to Midland industry, although the Guild of Graduates contributed a pump-priming £26,000. Waring was enormously successful and the Appeal raised £1,400,000 in the eight months between May and December 1960, sufficient to complete the whole Vale site. Tube Investments and Guest, Keen & Nettlefold each contributed £150,000.[30]

Construction started in 1962 with the ultimate target of three halls for women and three halls for men, 1459 student places in all.[31] The first, Ridge Hall, opened for 139 women in January 1964 and its counterpart, High Hall, admitted its first male residents from the following October.[32] By then landscaping was well under way, with water already in the three acres of the artificial lake which Casson and Conder had described as 'the only thing missing' from the site.[33] The same year saw Birmingham creating a mixed hall of residence which was claimed as a 'first' in English higher education.[34] This was achieved at University House, where a new wing was built and assigned for male students (with the original Wyddrington annexe being given up). The second pair of halls on the Vale site, Lake (men) and Wyddrington (women), were opened in the autumn of 1965 and the plan was completed in 1966–7 with Mason Hall admitting 200 women students in October and Chad Hall 350 men in the following January.[35] However, it was almost immediately agreed that the lead set at University House should be followed and the two became a single hall at the start of 1967 under the name Mason Hall.[36] If anecdote is anything to go by, places at Mason and University House became much the most sought after.

Whatever may be thought of the influence of Casson and Conder on the main campus, there can be no doubt of the quality of the environment which had been established on the Vale. The provision of student accommodation on such a scale was, however, not without problems. The University had for years wanted to offer students the experience of community, but could the new halls operate as independent colleges on the Oxbridge model? Aitken raised the possibility in 1961, but the eventual decisions was that halls should not have an academic function.[37] Members of the academic staff were brought in as (non-teaching) tutors and formed a senior common room under a president, with students in a junior common room. However, the domestic operation of the halls was placed under a joint committee of Senate and Council at which, initially, hall presidents had only the right of attendance. How to allow presidents a voice in the choice of student members raised particular complications when admission to the University was the responsibility of academic departments and the registry and became even more difficult when some halls became more popular than others. There were also more fundamental problems. In 1962 the vice-chancellor had looked ten years ahead to a university grown to 7500 students and asked where land and money for 2000 extra residential places were to come from.[38] Fashion, however, was altering. Previous generations of students who had lived in lodgings would have given their eye teeth for places in a hall, particularly of the quality found on the Vale, but no sooner had Birmingham completed that phase of its programme than student demand changed.[39] The emphasis of 'the swinging sixties' on personal freedom coupled with what was perceived to be the high cost of living in hall meant that living in a student flat became the ideal, especially among second- and third-year students. As we have seen, the possibility of providing flats was raised in 1963 following the acquisition of land near Manor Hall and this bore fruit in 1970 in the completion on the site of 105 two- and three-bedroom flats holding in all 360 students.[40]

It is not surprising that what can justly be called a revolution under Aitken in the number of students and consequently of staff at Birmingham and in the capital invested in the estate posed major problems for university management. There were two aspects of this, policy making and administration. On the first Aitken's fundamental commitment was to collegiality and to what would today be called 'ownership'. He recognised the conflict which collegiality created between paperwork and teaching and research, but he was a firm proponent of the view that decisions must be taken bottom up, that is at faculty meetings. As he told Council in 1956, it followed that 'the machinery for arriving at major decisions after due discussion, and the machinery for reaching individual minor decisions, especially those that must be consistent throughout the Faculties, must therefore be fairly elaborate; and it must be operated by academic people because it concerns academic matters or academic persons'.[41] Sir Robert's own style was first to try out a new idea or the answer to some issue in a tête-à-tête with one of his tiny handful of close confidants, generally on a Sunday morning . He would then take the matter to the Committee of Principals and Deans, where he would hear from the most influential leaders in the University what the general reaction might be. From there he would go to the Executive Committee of the Senate, which was effectively principals and deans afforced by ten of the senior professors and one representative of the non-professorial staff. 'If they agreed,' he remembered many years later, 'then I could be sure that I had the votes when it came to Senate.'[42]

This belief of Aitken's that it was vital for a vice-chancellor to carry his staff with him sometimes led to his being criticised for setting up too many specialised committees. Against this it could be argued that as well as being a mechanism to widen involvement in decision making, committees with narrow terms of reference could prevent huge agendas elsewhere and often be an economy of effort. Thus in 1955 when there was a complete overhaul of university committees, Planning and Priorities took over from an overburdened Development Committee and set up a system of subcommittees by which the professors who were to occupy a particular prospective building would take responsibility for it with the help of the relevant architect and consultants.[43] On the other hand, the burden on the professoriate did rise during Aitken's vice-chancellorship. When he arrived the ratio of non-professorial staff to professors was 5.9:1; when he left it was 7.1:1, an increase of 20%. The ratio of students to professors also rose, by 12% from 51.9:1 to 58.3:1.[44] Not that Aiken did not do all he could to grow the professoriate.[45] In his time it almost doubled. Departments were either split into subspecialities (particularly at the Medical School), or else began to have more than one named chair. 'Personal chairs' also made a gingerly appearance. The physics department thus went from two professors to six, history from two to four and the total number in engineering rose from seven to fourteen.[46] The multi-professor department and the personal chair were the first steps in a long slow road which would convert a university chair from a post responsible for one section of university activity to a rank in a promotion ladder.

On the other hand, for Aitken, 'operated by academic people' did not simply mean ownership by those holding chairs. When he arrived, non-professors were represented on faculty boards but on the Senate they had only three places, whereas every professor in the University had a seat. Aitken therefore encouraged the development of a non-professorial executive and made a point of meeting its chairman immediately before each cycle of Senate and Council meetings to go over the agenda and assess grassroots opinion.[47] Another aspect of 'ownership' was communication, again particularly to those who were not on boards and committees. The *Bulletin*, which he launched in June 1956, was not an information sheet – Priestley had met that need by founding the *University Gazette* in February 1949. The intention of the *Bulletin* was specifically to keep members of staff abreast of key issues before decisions were taken, 'and to provoke comment, correspondence and general discussion'.[48] It was also, though he did not say this, a way by which the vice-chancellor could influence opinion and offer leadership to colleagues he never met in the course of normal events. Appearing initially twice a term and later three times, it was edited by Aitken and he was the most consistent contributor.[49]

While Aitken was a determined proponent of academic consensus he was equally convinced of the importance of the University having adequate administrators whom he saw as there to 'lighten the load of the senior academics'.[50] In 1959 the salaried university bureaucracy consisted of 38 individuals, from the registrar and the secretary at the top to ten administrative assistants at the bottom. With 592 academic staff and 4366 students this gave ratios of 1:16 and 1:115 respectively. By 1967–8, when the academic staff had grown to 914 and students to 6824, the number of salaried staff in the administration had risen to 99, giving ratios of 1:9.2 and 1:69.[51]

Table 17.1 Birmingham University: total number of administrative staff, 1959–60 and 1967–8

	1959–60	1967–8
Vice-chancellor and deputy principal	0	2
Registry	14	31
Secretariat (except estate)	14	18
Estate	6	30
Catering	1	4
Lodgings and halls of residence	3	14
Total	*38*	*99*

The largest single reason for the increase was the thirty-eight additional staff in estates, catering and accommodation which together now occupied the time of more than half of the university administration. In 1959 running the University's property had required six people, but early in 1961, with the prospect of the University becoming responsible for a much greater stock of land and building, it was decided to appoint a bursar as a third major administrative officer alongside the secretary and the registrar.[52] By 1966 he had a staff of thirty. A second reason for the increase in the administration was the rise in student numbers, which fell most heavily on academic departments and therefore on the registry. Anticipating this and the prospective burden, Aitken had decided in 1960 that the right way was to decentralise: 'The registry exists to serve the academic body, and in shaping the present form of its organisation, we have tried to have this consideration always in the forefront of our thinking.'[53] The result was the setting up of a registry division to cover each faculty (or in one case two) and to work closely with academics, taking as much administrative pressure as possible off their shoulders.

Not that these faculty registries were anything other than lean and keen; for years the 1500 plus students of the faculties of Arts and Law were serviced by two people.

As Table 17.1 indicates, Aitken himself also felt the need of additional help. For over sixty years the senior management of the University had comprised a full-time vice-chancellor and principal and a part-time vice-principal who remained involved in academic work, generally as head of a department. Aitken effectively worked a seven-day week. He held main committee meetings on a Saturday morning and it was proverbial that his neat handwritten notes to staff very often bore the date 'Sunday'. Despite this, in 1963 he decided that the demands on him and the vice-principal were becoming too great and he took take advantage of the retirement of Dr Thomas Alty from the vice-chancellorship of Rhodes University at Cape Town to engage him as a full-time deputy principal.[54] Alty's arrival was particularly opportune, given the halls of residence coming on stream, and he was largely responsible for organising their administration. The reason for creating a new post rather than making the vice-principalship a full-time appointment was that vice-chancellor saw the presence of a departmental teacher at the centre of policy-making as an asset too valuable to lose, and by a congruent argument he did not want to add to the administrative load on the deans. His decision was possibly also encouraged by the fact that the link between the centre and the academic coalface was about to be weakened following the election as vice-chancellor of the University of Kent of his registrar since 1955, Dr Geoffrey Templeman, formerly a distinguished lecturer in the history department.[55] Templeman had also been particularly important in representing Birmingham over two vital academic issues of national as well as local importance. One was the development of the Northern Universities Joint Matriculation Board and the other was the setting up of the Universities Central Council for Admissions (UCCA), which took over admissions at Birmingham with a test run in 1962–3 and the real thing in 1963–4.[56]

With the huge change which took place on the Edgbaston campus during Aitken's vice-chancellorship it is tempting to annexe Sir Christopher Wren's epitaph, 'if you seek his monument, look around'. Robert Stevenson Aitken was, however, much more than a highly successful academic builder and manager. A commanding figure with an intellect to match, his success at Birmingham has been put down to his being so much more intelligent than anyone else. He was also highly disciplined; it is characteristic that when in retirement he took up gardening, vegetable production was as meticulously organised as any research project. His peers clearly appreciated his talents and personality. From 1958 to 1961 he chaired the CVCP and on retirement from Birmingham he served for five years as deputy chairman of the UGC. Aitken continued the tradition seen in Birmingham's earlier support for the setting up of the University College of North Staffordshire (later Keele), by acting as godfather to the University of Warwick.

The initial plan was for a university college at Coventry attached to Birmingham, but Aitken advised an independent initiative and smoothed the path of the promoters to the UGC. 'You may take it that Birmingham will do all it can to help if we are asked – just as we have done for Keele.' He was as good as his word, and when matters got to the stage of detail, Geoffrey Templeman attended in his place, indeed, the registrar drafted the basic academic plan. Stephen Burman, the pro-chancellor of Birmingham, was drawn in to the Warwick venture as well.[57]

On casual acquaintance Aitken appeared somewhat aloof and he was never a person to tangle with lightly nor to appear before with a brief half-mastered, but his skill with people was just as important as his intelligence. For him the distinctive character of university life was 'the mixing of the young with older people, to the advantage of both'. Students trusted him implicitly and he trusted them. In 1954 the Guild Executive took disciplinary action against a student and were forced to defend their action before 900 students at a special general meeting. Aitken stood aloof but reported with satisfaction to the Council that the near unanimous support the Executive had received totally vindicated a system where the University would only become involved in the most serious cases of student misbehaviour.[58] Many of the student officers of the Guild whom he had worked with maintained contact with him well into his retirement. When an internal candidate was elected to a chair he would find the vice-chancellor bringing the news in person. He would back ability and commitment and he wanted and could pick winners. In the session 1955-6 he attended every academic appointment board, even for assistant lecturers.[59]

The overriding intellectual concern which Aitken had was for the role of higher education in the modern world. The topic comes up again and again in his reports. In 1958, for example, Council was treated to a 1000-word essay on 'The University in a Changing Society' in which he said that 'the major problem confronting the universities in a technological society' was the extent of their responsibility 'for broadening and strengthening the foundation of education in its full sense'.[60] He recognised that this extended into 'moral and social awareness' but his immediate efforts were directed to achieving breadth in degree programmes. Aitken accepted that 'specialisation is the price of knowledge' and that the older ideal of the 'synoptic man' had had to give way to the notion of 'the expert'.[61] But he was deeply concerned about the negative side of this concentration. Typically he started with the staff. In 1953 he wrote: 'Breadth of the student's interest can be achieved only through breadth of interest on the part of the staff, and that in turn can be developed only if the Faculties work in reasonable proximity and their members have facilities for mixing both socially and academically.'[62] For this reason he placed a high priority on a new staff house:

> mere exhortation does not go far to make scientists and non-scientists mix freely and come to know each other well. It should be possible by taking

> thought now to create opportunities for this mixing to happen easily, naturally and as a matter of course. For the teaching staff this can best be accomplished in a Senior Common Room and Dining Room, commodious and pleasant, where all would be glad to sit, eat and talk.[63]

Whether this faith in the efficacy of passive facilities was justified is perhaps problematic. Cynics asked how the discovery of a shared interest in gardening or golf could assist the cross-fertilisation of cultures. What was more specific was the revival in 1957 of the inaugural lecture: 'something of an ordeal for the new professor, but at the same time it is an opportunity for him to contribute to the general education of his colleagues, and help to them to see the University and its disciplines in perspective'.[64] It is a definition which has stood the test of time.

With students there was an opportunity for more general action.[65]

> The narrowly educated scientist or engineer, historian or linguist may be well-informed, and even highly competent, in his own field, with an appropriate grasp of method and principle. He may equally well know little and care less for things lying outside the range of his immediate concern. To know little or nothing, and to want to know little or nothing, of the great issues of religion and politics, art, literature and the like is to be uneducated. ...
>
> A high proportion of our ablest young people now pass through the universities as a matter of course. This means that, before very long, they will be exercising a considerable influence in the management of our affairs as a people. It is for this reason that we cannot rest content with them merely as experts in their several fields. They must share in that broad tradition of thought and learning, with its great virtues of tolerance and width of understanding, which is the necessary foundation of our common life and free institutions.

The first move came in 1956 when a Senate committee was set up to enquire into broader education. Its report was in circulation by June and this was followed by a big debate in Senate and in the *Bulletin*.[66] The one specific outcome was establishing a 'General Collection' in the library; otherwise what emerged was essentially an exhortation to staff to give lectures which deliberately emphasised 'lateral thinking' and set examinations which attempted to test the wider implications of a subject. In January 1959 the Senate, with, one suspects, some prodding from the vice-chancellor, became more positive and called for specific proposals for action.[67] Eighteen months later, as Aitken described it, 'We judged it time to stop arguing about the best answer, but to choose what looked like one reasonably good answer and put it into effect.'[68] This was a Broader Education Programme and its pilot project was launched in the spring of the following year, 1961.[69] All the first-year students reading botany, physical metallurgy, physics, zoology, English, German and history were required to take a course entitled 'Society in a Machine Age'. It comprised ten lectures and fortnightly seminars for groups of fifteen, with each student writing a 2000-word essay. The University wheeled out some of its very best performers, the venture was rated as promising and it was decided to extend it to half the new entrants in October 1961. This time three themes were on offer, 'Crime and Punishment', 'Race' and 'The Problem of World Population'.[70] From 1962 the programme became compulsory for all first-year students. For Aitken, this attempt 'to open the windows of every student's mind to something worth studying outside the set courses for his degree' as one of the most important things he ever achieved.[71] Some students benefited enormously, yet the fact that the programme *was* outside set courses meant that others saw it as an intrusion while the limited time allotted to it meant that superficiality was always a danger. The reality was – and is – that for breadth to be taken seriously it must be integral to a degree programme, not an 'add-on'. It has, nevertheless, to be recognised that institutions which about this time attempted to encourage breadth in other ways were scarcely more successful. When Birmingham's Broader Education Programme died in 1981, this was a recognition that Aitken's objective was unattainable within modern higher education. The age had arrived when students learned more and more about less and less, and when all but a tiny minority of them considered such narrowness quite unimportant.

The campaign for broader education was directed at the University as a whole. Other academic developments in the 1950s and 1960s were necessarily more particular, but they demonstrated the opportunities both for greater specialisation and for innovation which Aitken said would come with growth. They are too numerous to be more than illustrated; much more space than is available would be needed to trace the intellectual, educational and organisational changes which took place at faculty and departmental level in these years. In education, the new regime left by Priestley developed rapidly. By 1955 one-third of students taking the Postgraduate Certificate of Education (PGCE) were being recruited from outside Birmingham.[72] Advanced courses were launched in special needs teaching and in 1960 a part-time taught M.Ed. course began.[73] That year also saw the training colleges move to a three-year course and also increase their intake, as did the University's own department.[74] Following the Robbins Report and with the prospect of a new Education building starting in 1965 it was decided to create a School of Education to incorporate both the department and the Institute, with the latter becoming one of four constituent divisions.[75] Robbins also envisaged the creation of a professional B.Ed. degree which would be open to selected training college students taking a fourth year. Birmingham therefore drew up a plan to provide teaching for such students on campus, three days a week, which would lead to an honours degree equal to that of an honours BA or B.Sc.[76]

In Science the most important teaching development was in graduate courses. Already by 1957 there were twelve of these; by 1964 there were thirty-one.[77] In order to focus B.Sc. courses on basic science, pure and applied, existing undergraduate courses with a vocational bent were upgraded to postgraduate, including Birmingham's famous and notorious course in malting and brewing.[78] Mining disappeared and so did the synchrotron.[79] A new name for the faculty from October 1965, Science and Engineering, was a recognition that 44% of undergraduates and 50% of postgraduates were now studying applied science.[80] New departments appeared, for example, microbiology in 1955; a Computing Centre in 1961 (though the machine arrived late); psychology in 1965.[81] At the same time both the breaking down of disciplinary distinctions and the increasing specialisation within disciplines led to a kaleidoscope of institutes, centres, units and schools – in 1965 for example, a School of Mathematical Sciences comprising the departments of pure mathematics, mathematical statistics and mathematical physics, and a Centre for Materials Science which brought together physics, electron physics, electronic and electrical engineering and physical metallurgy.[82]

On the other side of the campus, in Arts, history developed a different form of co-operation which was pregnant for the future, a multidepartmental school with a rotating headship.[83] There were new departments there, too, such as drama and theatre arts and the Centre for Contemporary Cultural Studies.[84] In teaching, the biggest changes were in diversifying from the single honours degree which had been the staple of the faculty for several decades. An early attempt to promote 'Honours in Grouped Subjects' had attracted few takers and a much more successful alternative was set up in 1946, a three-subject 'General Degree' which could be awarded with honours.[85] In 1959 this was replaced by 'Combined Subjects' and then in 1961 the third subject was dropped to produce the two-subject Combined Honours degree.[86] In Commerce and Social Science, too, the degree patterns were remodelled alongside what Aitken called 'growth by departmental fission'.[87] Thus in 1958 political science became a separate department and in 1959 social science and sociology were split into social study and sociology.[88] By 1965 there were departments of economics, econometrics and social statistics, industrial economics and business studies, and a newcomer, mathematical economics.[89] Specialised units also appeared, an Institute of Local Government Studies and a Centre for Urban and Regional Studies.[90] The 'Hayter Centre' for West African Studies took postgraduate students from 1965–6 and by 1968–9 was recruiting seventeen a year. Its opposite number, the Centre for Russian and East European Studies, was a year behind, but still registered a dozen, and both Centres also taught undergraduates.[91] The only faculty to escape the turmoil was Law, which took the opportunity of growth in staff and student numbers to add components to the existing curriculum such as international law or criminal law and criminology.[92] However, even here, 1965 saw the setting up of postgraduate coursework and preliminary discussion about an Institute of Judicial Administration.[93]

The one faculty whose story did not coincide with the rest was Medicine. It had always been somewhat distinct, belonging to the University but also part of the Midlands medical scene, and this split identity was accentuated by the arrival in 1948 of the NHS. The faculty's post-war development therefore took place substantially outside the normal UGC context and was affected by the Health Service as much as its parent university. The most immediate example of this, and something which Priestley had complained of loudly, was the creation of separate clinical salary scales, with all their divisive consequences.[94] Another problem, and a continuous one, was the tension between the needs of medical education and the delivery of patient services.[95] That was resolved, at least for a time, only when the Ministry of Health, after two years' consideration, accepted in 1966 the concept of a medical centre where all the specialities should be available for study.[96] Another tension was between clinical treatment and clinical research. One helpful development there came in 1954 with the setting up of centres for specialisms in various hospitals of the region, and a further significant move came in 1955 with the pioneering appointment of a registrar who spent part of his time in the department of experimental pathology, two of whose members offered reciprocal ward duties.[97]

The battle between treatment and research might not have been so significant had medical research been at the low inter-war level, but this was far from the case. In 1950 the faculty was responsible for 38% of the University's output of research papers as against 40% from Science. Ten years later the total output from Medicine had doubled and it was level-pegging with Science at 38%.[98] Some departments were created and others grew; some did both. For example, a department of neurological studies was progressively established in the late 1940s and had by 1962 acquired a Neurological Communications Research Unit.[99] New medical buildings came on stream though the first stage of the Clinical Research Block was completed in 1953 without the money to staff it, and in a number of cases research space was sacrificed to teaching.[100] In 1959 the Barnes Library opened.[101] As for student numbers, these could have been a problem in medicine, partly because of excessive demand and partly because of Ministry vacillation about expansion. However, the University's answer was to keep entry steady throughout the period and in 1957 it paid no attention when the Willink Committee recommended a reduction of 10% in the number of doctors being trained nationally![102] Dentistry was always less buoyant for numbers than medicine, but it did manage to grow towards its capacity after 1964 when, at long last, it was able to move into the new Dental Hospital in Steelhouse Lane and the name of the faculty was changed to Medicine and Dentistry.[103] The major academic challenge in medicine in these years concerned the curriculum which, although already extended from four years to six, was increasingly crammed and cramped. Fortunately legislation in 1950 obliged all prospective doctors to spend one year as a hospital resident after qualification, and this allowed the General Medical Council (GMC) to relieve programmes of the requirement to cram everything in.[104] A tutorial scheme was progressively introduced from 1951 and by 1967 lectures had been drastically reduced, and the notions of 'elective' time and continuous assessment had been adopted.[105]

Change in the University between 1953 and 1968 was, therefore, evident everywhere. However, when Robert Aitken completed his last report to the University Council in January 1968 he did not, like Grant Robertson and Priestley, indulge in reflection. The year 1967 marked the start of a new quinquennium and his concerns were for the future and particularly with the looming power of the state.[106] The first problem of the year had been over student fees. These were in theory fixed by each university but by a gentleman's agreement with the UGC they had been kept nationally uniform and were, after consultation, revised every five years and allowed for in the quinquennial grant. Robbins had recommended that the universities should receive 20% of their funds from fees (the current level was less than 8%) which would have pushed up the existing fee of £80 to nearly £250. However, instead of the expected discussion of the issue, the Secretary of State for Education and Science in Harold Wilson's first Labour government unilaterally announced in December 1966 that quinquennial grants would be calculated on the assumption that the £80 a year fee would remain unchanged, except for overseas students, who would be charged £250. The change was bitterly criticised and there were a number of strikes by students. However, at Birmingham, the protest took the form of 2500 students crowding into the Great Hall to hear speeches from students, staff, MPs and the vice-chancellor himself. The University was nevertheless forced to comply – it did not have the resources to resist the increase as Oxford and Cambridge attempted to do – but the real casualty was confidence in the government: 'Friction and impairment of confidence were brought about by an arbitrary decision, of dubious value, taken by the Secretary of State without examination of its consequences by those best placed to assess them.'[107] A second problem was a change in the funding of equipment. The UGC decided no longer to fund specific projects but to make an overall equipment grant for each institution. While this did mean greater freedom in what a university could buy, the advantage was vitiated by the grant being lower than the total of the sums previously received.

A third and even more worrying development was the advent of the Comptroller and Auditor-General. Ever since the end of the war the Public Accounts Committee had been pressing for university accounts to be under public scrutiny and with the steady increase in government funding for universities Parliament at last accepted the principle in 1967. However, instead of scrutiny being introduced, as the Committee had recommended, with some recognition of the distinctive nature of universities, the Comptroller and Auditor-General decided to treat them as government departments. Private funds as well as public money came under his scrutiny and although it was denied that he would criticise academic policy, it was stated that a view would be taken on whether academic decisions had been based on proper information. Aitken's conclusion was gloomy:

> In practice it looks as if the bounds of university freedom will be set by the personal discretion of the Comptroller and Auditor-General and his officers. The new order began on 1 January 1968. We shall adapt ourselves to it as best we can, without yielding our conviction that academic work is original, personal, creative work, too easily damaged by direction from above and by administrative constraint. Lord Radcliffe did not much exaggerate when he said: 'He who pays the piper calls the tune; and generally experience has shown that he had much better not.'[108]

The final ominous innovation was in the form of the quinquennial grant. For the first time this carried indicative numbers for science and non-science subjects and for undergraduates and graduates. Aitken welcomed this, believing that the University would still be free to admit as it chose, but it is surprising that he did not also note the potential here for much greater direction. The same thing can be said of another 1967 innovation, changing from historic costs to average costs per student. He did, however, note that, much more than before, the UGC's 1967 letter contained guidance 'but not precisely direction'.[109] Only a tiny percentage of the grant was actually earmarked but there was a clear indication of which projects had been taken into consideration in making the award and which had not. Aitken had noted that the UGC quinquennial visit in 1966 had been more like an inspection and now Birmingham was encouraged to increase library expenditure, set up a central audio-visual facility, expand in medicine and dentistry, strengthen certain scientific departments and develop advanced town planning and machine-tool technology.[110] Comparative education was, however, given the thumbs-down and so, too, Birmingham's proposal for a B.Ed. degree at Honours level taught partly by university staff. The alternative, as Aitken pointed out, was an ordinary degree taught by the colleges and 'inevitably inferior to an internal degree', and he remarked regretfully that there was more interest in 'making degrees – and the prestige attaching to them – available' than in fundamental improvements in the education which college students were offered.[111] Taken together, the developments of 1967 demonstrated how far the Wilson government was prepared to downgrade university independence and values.

Notes

1 *Bulletin* 27 (9 Dec. 1961). For Aitken's views on the problems of the Aston Webb layout, see UC 7/iii 1956, pp. 2–3; 1957, pp. 5–7.

2 Whitehand, 'Institutional site planning', p. 33.

3 *Bulletin* 5 (29 Apr. 1957).

4 Ibid., 27 (9 Dec. 1961).
5 Ibid., 28 (29 Jan. 1962).
6 UC 7/iii 1960, p. 6.
7 *Bulletin* 27 (9 Dec. 1961).
8 Ibid., 29 (16 Mar. 1962).
9 Ibid., 37 (15 Feb. 1963); UC 7/iii 1962, p. 9.
10 *Bulletin* 37 (15 Feb. 1963).
11 Ibid., 41 (8 July, 1963).
12 Ibid., 60 (2 Oct. 1965).
13 UC 7/iii 1962, p. 8.
14 Ibid., 1963, p. 2.
15 Ibid., 1967, p. 11.
16 *Bulletin* 16 (27 Jan. 1960).
17 Ibid., 40 (13 June 1963).
18 Ibid., 51 (8 Oct. 1964).
19 UC 7/iii 1966, p. 9.
20 *Bulletin* 52 (12 Nov. 1964).
21 UC 7/iii 1966, pp. 9–10.
22 Ibid., p. 9.
23 Ibid., 1955, p. 17.
24 Ibid., 1963, p. 29.
25 Ibid., 1967, p. 42.
26 Ibid., 1962, p. 10; 1963, p. 27.
27 UC 7/ii *Council* 1959, p. 13; 7/iii 1959, p. 4; 1967 p. 33.
28 Ibid., 1964, p. 29; 1965, p. 30.
29 *Bulletin* 29 (16 Mar. 1962).
30 The final total was £1,467,028. For the above see UC 7/ii *Council* 1960, p. 10; 1961, p. 12; 7/iii 1960, p. 7.
31 UC 7/iii 1962, pp. 10–11.
32 Ibid., 1964, p. 28.
33 Ibid.; Cheesewright, *Mirror to a Mermaid*, p. 115.
34 Ibid., 1963, pp. 26–7; 1964, pp. 27–8.
35 Ibid., 1965, p. 30.
36 Ibid., 1966, pp. 28–9; 1967, p. 31.
37 *Bulletin* 24 (3 July 1961); UC 7/iii 1967, pp. 31–3.
38 Ibid., 1961, p. 7.
39 Ibid., 1967, p. 33.
40 Ibid., 1969, p. 44. The eventual number of residents was 281 plus 25 married couples with children: 1970, p. 5.
41 Ibid., 1956, p. 7.
42 UC Oral History Collection: comment by Robert Aitken.
43 UC 7/iii 1956, p. 6.
44 1952–3: 63 professors, 369 non-professors, 3270 students (full- and part-time): UGC, *Returns of Universities and University Colleges 1952–3*, pp. 17, 32; *1967–8*: 117 professors, 836 non–professors, 6824 students: UC 7/iii 1968, pp. 35, 37.
45 UC 7/iii 1964, p. 11.

46 *Calendar 1953–4*; *1967–8*. In addition there was a professor of electron physics and a professor of mathematical physics in 1953–4, and a professor of electron physics and two professors of mathematical physics in 1967–8.
47 Ex inf. Professor P. A. Garrett.
48 UC 7/iii 1956, p. 8.
49 The three issues commenced with *Bulletin* 20 (8 Nov. 1962).
50 Ibid., p. 7.
51 UC 7/iii 1960, pp. 24, 26; *Calendar 1959–60*; UC 7/iii 1968, pp. 35, 37; *Calendar 1967–8*. The vice-chancellor and vice-principal are not included, nor are junior employees.
52 UC 7/iii 1960, p. 12; 7/ii 1961,p. 10; *Bulletin* 21 (13 Dec. 1960).
53 *Bulletin* 20 (3 Oct. 1960).
54 UC 7/iii 1963 p. 3; 1967, p. 32; *Bulletin* 42 (5 Oct. 1963).
55 UC 7/iii 1962, p. 11.
56 *Bulletin* 27 (9 Dec. 1961).
57 For the above see H. Rees, *A University is Born* (Coventry, 1989), pp. 13–14, 16–19, 36–7, 50, 53–4, 59–64, 67, 70.
58 UC 7/iii 1954, p. 19.
59 For the above, ex inf. Professor J. R. Allanson; Professor R. J. Knecht.
60 UC 7/iii 1958, pp. 5–8.
61 Ibid., 1955, p. 5.
62 Ibid., 1953, p. 3
63 Ibid., 1955, p. 3
64 Ibid., 1957, p. 9
65 Ibid., 1955, p. 5.
66 *Bulletin* 1 (14 June 1956); 2 (15 Oct. 1956).
67 Ibid., 13 (9 Jan. 1959).
68 UC 7/iii 1962, p. 6.
69 *Bulletin* 21 (13 Dec. 1960).
70 UC 7/iii 1961, p. 5.
71 Obituary: *Guardian*, 1997.
72 UC 7/iii 1955, p. 12.
73 Ibid., 1960, p. 18.
74 Ibid., 1962, p. 20.
75 Ibid., 1965, pp. 4, 25–6.
76 Ibid., 1966, pp. 19–22. Birmingham's proposals were rejected: 1967, p. 10; see below, p. 349.
77 Ibid., 1957, p. 10; 1964, p. 13.
78 Ibid., 1962, p. 13
79 Ibid., p. 14; Moon and Ibbs, *Physics at Birmingham 1880–1980*, p. 32.
80 UC 7/iii 1964, p. 13.
81 Ibid., 1955, p. 6; 1961, p. 14; 1962, p. 14; 1965, p. 12.
82 Ibid., 1965, pp. 11–12.
83 Ibid., 1964, p. 14.
84 Ibid., pp. 14–5.
85 Ibid., 1948, pp. 22, 42.

86 Ibid., 1959, p. 27; 1961, p. 16.
87 Ibid., 1965, p. 19.
88 Ibid., 1958, p. 12; 1959, p. 14.
89 Ibid., 1965, pp. 19–20.
90 Ibid., 1964, p. 20; 1966, p. 18. CURS developed from the West Midland Social and Political Research Unit, established in 1962: 1962, p. 18.
91 Ibid., 1965, pp. 22–3; 1968, pp. 22, 35.
92 Ibid., 1963, p. 20; 1964, p. 21.
93 Ibid., 1965 p. 22; 1967, p. 23.
94 Ibid., 1949, pp. 6–8.
95 Ibid., 1948, pp. 24–5.
96 Ibid., 1963, p. 17; 1966, pp. 14–15.
97 Ibid., 1954, pp. 12–13; 1955, p. 9.
98 UC 7/ii *Standing Committee on Research*, 1950; 1960.
99 UC 7/iii 1948, p. 26; 1949, p. 50; 1951, p. 49; 1962, p. 17.
100 Ibid., 1953, p. 13; 1961, p. 18; 1966, p. 14.
101 Ibid., 1958, p. 2; 1959, pp. 2, 12–13.
102 Ibid., 1957, p. 11.
103 Ibid., 1962, pp. 17–18; 1964, p. 19; 1965, p. 16; 1967, p. 20.
104 Ibid., 1950, pp. 47–8.
105 Ibid., 1949, pp. 48–9; 1951, pp. 46–7; 1960, p. 15–16; 1967–8, pp. 18–19.
106 For the following see ibid., 1967, pp. 1–10.
107 Ibid., p. 3.
108 Ibid., p. 6.
109 Ibid., p. 10.
110 Ibid., 1966, pp. 5–6.
111 Ibid., pp. 21–2.

Chapter Eighteen

The events of 1968

SIR ROBERT AITKEN retired at the end of September 1968. Four weeks later students lobbied the first meeting of the Senate for the new session and occupied the corridor outside his successor's office. On Thursday 27 November they took over the Great Hall and the university administration and continued a 'sit-in' until the following Thursday, 5 December. Large numbers were involved on one side or another; over 4000 students attended the final extraordinary general meeting of the Guild on 5 December which called off the protest. This represented upwards of 60% of all registered students and the meeting had to be held in the open air, outside the library. Fortunately it did not rain.

Even after thirty years it is difficult to offer a reasoned assessment of the events of the autumn term of 1968. In part this is because of the documentation.[1] Although plentiful, much of it consists of ephemeral material produced almost by the hour, rarely adequately dated, and generally issued in an attempt to react to events which had already passed on. Furthermore, it is true in Birmingham as elsewhere that in the context of a fluid protest carried on outside the normal machinery of representation and debate, the student output was anything but controlled or consistent and what had been the original issues and the focus of concern rapidly became submerged. Almost all of the material also had a deliberately propaganda purpose, and this is as true of formal pronouncements by the University as by other parties involved. As for interpretation, the difficulty here is to say more than Old Caspar,

> But what they fought each other for,
> I could not well make out.

Nor is this hindsight. The question was asked at the time by none other person than Ray Phillips, the president of the Guild, a key figure in the whole story.[2] A further problem in interpretation is the shift in opinion which has taken place since 1968. Today, after thirty years of student participation in university government, few among the staff and laity associated with Birmingham would deny that undergraduate and postgraduate involvement has been beneficial overall, has promoted good relations and has certainly not been corrosive of stability. The student case in 1968 therefore appears self-evidently sensible and the opposition to it blinkered and frankly stupid. However if we are to understand the Birmingham events, it is vital to recognise that even in the fundamentally liberal ethos of a university, the weight of opinion in 1968 was cautious about bringing students into government and decision making. Only a minority was on the side of what now appear to be the angels, and not all of them for angelic motives.

The context of the Birmingham episode was international.[3] For several years students world-wide had been flexing their muscles. From the Berkeley campus of the University of California in 1964, action had spread to other institutions in the USA. There had been disturbances in Germany, particularly in Berlin, and notably violent clashes in Japan. In 1966–7 protest reached Britain with a boycott of lectures at the LSE (and a minor sit-in by a handful of students), followed by a major sit-in which paralysed the college. In December 1967 there were brief sit-ins at the Regent Street Polytechnic and the Holborn College of Law and Commerce and in January 1968 at the new University of Aston. February 1968 saw students at Leicester 'sitting in' for several days and in the summer a sit-in which had staff support humiliated the vice-chancellor of the University of Essex. In May 1968 student agitation created serious political trouble in France, there were further disturbances in the United States (most notably at Columbia) and in Germany, as well as in Italy, Switzerland, Belgium, Austria, Spain, Latin America and East Asia. Students had also been out on the streets in Poland, as they would be later in Czechoslovakia.

Given this catalogue, Birmingham was anything but in the forefront of international student activism when trouble arrived at Edgbaston in the autumn of 1968. Indeed, the relevance of any wider context was more for the emotions it encouraged than for any ideological influence on complaints which were essentially parochial. Undoubtedly, too, there was an element of imitation. Observers noticed that student activism waxed and waned in direct proportion to the presence or absence of the press and the TV. The predominant feeling at Birmingham seems, quite simply, to have been hostility to what was seen as excessive and outmoded paternalism and a wish to enjoy the right to be heard. As the leading article of *Redbrick* (the student newspaper) put it in the emergency edition for 29 October 1968, 'It is time that the University stopped treating us like children.'[4] The Latey Report had just given official support to such ideas in its proposal to lower the age of majority from twenty-one to eighteen and, indeed, the Family Law Bill which put the change in place was published on 1 November 1968, three weeks before the 'sit-in' began. With this legislation in prospect, universities and colleges and individual members of staff would need to adjust to being no longer *in loco parentis* and the words *in statu pupillari* would take on an entirely new meaning. Students would now be adults; the long march towards their becoming customers was under way.

Related to this assertion of adulthood was the prevailing atmosphere in what would now be called 'youth culture'. Here was a generation of students which had not been taught silence by having to obey authority during years of industrial depression or war. It was also a generation substantially free from family influence in term-time. Fewer than 10% of Birmingham students now lived at home.[5] These were the years of 'flower power', of CND marches, of Vietnam War protest, of Enoch Powell's 'rivers of blood' speech, of a belief in the right, the duty, even more, the possibility of doing something practical about issues which the established democratic procedures seemed incapable of addressing. And, given this overall confidence, why should students not demand a voice in matters where they were most involved? Only a tiny minority of Birmingham students were new-left radicals who 'dreamed of a new kind of politics, a new freedom from the constraints of mundane authority, a new immediacy of personal relations, a breaking down of the requirements of the roles we were forced to occupy in everyday life'.[6] The great majority had no interest in 'deliberately structureless institutions' driven by continuing crisis. Insofar as they were political at all, the desire was to have their opinions listened to where it mattered and to be recognised as more than lecture fodder.

There were also ingredients in the Birmingham situation late in 1968 which were essentially local. One of the most important was the retirement of Sir Robert Aitken. The new vice-chancellor was another medic, Robert Brockie Hunter, the professor of *materia medica* at University of Dundee. He had served on the UGC for three years, but his experience otherwise was almost entirely in Scottish academic medicine, although he had a wider claim to fame in having served during the war as General Montgomery's doctor.[7] Hunter was a marked contrast to Aitken. Individuals remember quiet private kindnesses, but even those who worked closely with him said that he was 'rather a dour Scot', and 'a tremendously difficult man to know really well'.[8] He certainly did not have Sir Robert's 'feel' for people generally, and while Hunter stressed in public the importance of communication he seems to have understood this in terms of the doctor–patient relationship.[9] What he did often undermined what would now be called 'networking'. Thus he put an end to the vice-chancellor's regular briefing sessions with non-professorial staff.[10] The vice-chancellor's annual reports ceased to be a perceptive and wide-ranging essay on higher education, national as well as local. The *Bulletin* ceased to be the vice-chancellor's personal priority and became more of an information sheet, although to be fair, Hunter did try briefly the experiment of addressing the University on television.

In 1968 most of the other university officers were also new or relatively new in post. Stephen Burman, the enormously experienced pro-chancellor, had retired in February 1966 and been replaced by George Farmer, chairman of Rover and of the Royal Shakespeare Theatre. The deputy pro-chancellor was also new. The secretary, Harry Harris, had arrived late in 1966 and Bill Lewis took over as registrar at the end of 1967. Even the vice-principal, Fred Shotton, the professor of geology, had been in office for only two sessions. An exception to this was the University's chancellor, Antony Eden, who was a past-master at relating to students, but he was a sick man.[11] There was also a relatively inexperienced team of student officers who, in those days, took over only in August.[12] The new president also brought with him some frustrations from a year's service on the Refectory Committee, where the interests of students – the majority of users – had not always proved compatible with those of the academic, technical and clerical staff, the long-term users. Furthermore, Charles Wright, Phillips's immediate predecessor, had remained active in student politics and wielded considerable influence, although without responsibility.[13]

Another local circumstance was the antiquated constitution of the University, last revised in 1927.[14] In 1927 there had been only some 1550 students and about 115 academic staff, 39 of them professors.[15] By 1968 there were 6500 students, 117 professors and 836 non-professors.[16] The 1927 revision had retained a Court of Governors as the supreme body in law, but this consisted of over 400 people, met once a year and no longer had the immediate involvement of the years following the 1900 charter. It was the University Council which had 'the government and control of the finances of the University, and of the discipline, practical affairs, business and work of the University'. This was an overwhelmingly lay body. It comprised the chancellor (normally absent) and twenty-six lay persons (six representing the City of Birmingham), plus two graduates, the vice-chancellor and the vice-principal, the deans of the five faculties and a single representative of the non-professorial staff. The key Finance and Policy Committee had ten members, all of whom were lay. The vice-chancellor, vice-principal, deputy-principal, deans, registrar and bursar attended by invitation. On the other major committee, Planning and Priorities, the vice-chancellor, the vice-principal and the deans did sit of right but there were also seven lay members one of whom, the pro-chancellor, was chairman so that in any disagreement the academics could always be outvoted. Professors and a few non-professors did serve on various council subcommittees, but there were places for students on only the Refectory Committee and the committee which dealt with the sports fields.

At the Senate, the vice-chancellor presided over 123 professors, 4 non-professorial heads, the librarian, 4 other service providers and 3 members of the non-professorial staff.[17] No students. The Senate had thirty committees, but only a handful of non-professors served on any of them, whereas students only had seats on the Lodgings Committee, the Open Lectures Committee, the Overseas Students Committee and the Works of Art Committee, though there was a consultative committee of the Guild and the Senate made up of the vice-chancellor, 3 professors and 2 non-professors and 5 students. Faculty boards varied in size, but again holders of chairs and heads of department were dominant throughout. The Science and Engineering board had 56 against 8 non-professors; Arts had 42 against 18. Even Commerce and Social Science, which had 14 professors and 11 non-professors, had 11 more professors and heads as attached members. No student sat on any faculty board or any committee of a faculty, although Commerce and Social Science was unique in having a staff/student committee.

The constitution of the University was the status quo the students protested against. The constitution of the Guild of Undergraduates was also important in shaping that protest. Its supreme body was the Guild Council, with some 120 members elected annually by undergraduates according to departments. The running of the Guild was the responsibility of an executive of ten, two of whom, the president (male) and vice-president (by tradition always a woman) were elected by general ballot, and the rest appointed by the Guild Council.[18] The constitution did provide for the holding of general meetings of the Guild, that is, of all students, and for emergency general meetings to be called if required, but these could only recommend; the Guild Council had the final decision. During the sit-in further sorts of gathering appeared. One was the mass meeting, called by the Executive at short notice and needing to be endorsed by a formally summoned emergency general meeting. The other kind of gathering was the general assembly, called by activists but possessing no constitutional authority.

The story of the sit-in begins in the autumn term of 1966 when the Guild took up the issue of student representation on university committees.[19] The resulting document appeared in February 1968 under the title *The Student Role*. It was moderate in tone, made no blanket claims for representation, argued particular cases carefully and effectively and was well received. It was featured in the *Bulletin* and sent immediately to faculty boards for comment, and this allowed the Senate to have its report ready for the meeting of Council in May. This set up a committee to meet students and take *The Student Role* forward. At the same time a working party was preparing a memorandum on increased representation for non-professorial staff. Again, good progress was made. An interim report was completed by 12 September giving a blueprint for non-professorial staff involvement in the short term and this was accepted in full by the Senate on 20 November. The Council did likewise on 27 November with one exception, a seat on the Planning and Priorities Committee, but it did confirm that development of the University's governmental structure would continue, and so too discussions with the non-professors.[20]

The first meeting between the Council and the students had taken place on 24 June and the registrar followed this by giving instructions that in each department and faculty staff–student consultative arrangements should be implemented or strengthened ready for the next session. By then, too, there had been progress nationally. A paper on student participation which had been submitted to the CVCP by the NUS had been welcomed and discussions put in hand.[21] The Birmingham Council/Student Committee met again in September and virtually all the recommendations in *The Student Role* which affected the Senate were then agreed. What remained was to discuss links between the student body and the University Council and a date was set for this to be considered. Aitken had taken the lead at the committee meetings but Hunter had attended both and, as with the non-professorial staff, everything could be thought to be set fair.[22]

There were, however, dark clouds. In the summer term there had been the friction over the management of the Refectory – essentially over competing use. An attempt to defuse the refectory issue had been made with the setting up of a committee of enquiry. Nevertheless on 23 October some students held a meeting to press claims on that and other issues, including the admission of Czech students (following the Prague coup), and to protest against 'the obsessive tradition of secrecy in university administration'.[23] They then decamped to the Senate room but the authorities had been forewarned and the group, between 50 and 100, were stopped by security staff. The Guild president was due to attend Senate by invitation (with four colleagues) and he did speak on certain items, but then, in protest against the mobilisation of the security men, he walked out. The Senate nevertheless proposed a 50/50 committee of Senate and students to review student participation particularly at faculty level, chaired by Professor Jack Allanson. The protesters, meanwhile, sat down in the corridor outside the vice-chancellor's room but dispersed after talking to him for some time on a promise that he would meet them again at the Union.

This meeting took place on Friday 25 October and what the vice-chancellor said was subsequently repeated on the University TV service.[24] It was a plea for patience: 'I have only been here 26 days.' However, he announced that he had already set up a University Forum to be chaired by Professor J. G. Davies to encourage debate and communication. He also explained that the Senate had agreed to set up the Allanson Committee and that its composition would be two other professors, two young non-professors, four students and the chair of the postgraduate association. He also added that Senate had requested Council to undertake a similar consultation in its sphere of responsibility. Hunter pointed out, however, that Council involvement still lay in the future, that he and Farmer agreed that this would take time and that although student representatives would be invited to present their case they would not be allowed to stay for the discussion. He closed by saying: 'It seems to me that we are in a situation where great things are at stake, including the good will and perhaps the good name of the University. I am sure that everyone here is going to consider this and act in the responsible way in which Birmingham staff and students have always behaved.'[25] Hardly a confident ending.

The next session of the *Student Role* negotiating committee met on 28 October with Council representation on the agenda. It was explained that to give students full membership would require a change in the charter and statutes, but it was agreed that observer status would be possible immediately. However, the University councillors turned down the request to have students on the two key committees, Planning and Priorities and Finance and General Purposes and, moreover, refused to have students present on 30 October when the report of the negotiating committee was due to be presented to Council. The next day the students held an extraordinary general meeting at which it was agreed to demand acceptance of *The Student Role* 'in toto' by 27 November, under threat of direct action. Two additional demands were made: that all meetings of Council, Senate and their committees should be open access and that a commission with 50% student membership should be set up to consider the whole structure of university government and administration.[26]

When the members of the University Council arrived for their meeting on Wednesday 30 October they had to make their way through a crowd of 100–200 students at the entrance to the Aston Webb building. The president and six colleagues attended the Council by invitation, and in a statement Ray Phillips complained of the Council's dilatoriness and both of the pro-chancellor's absence (Sir George Farmer was abroad) and of his behaviour at the committee on the 28th. Then, demanding that *The Student Role* should be accepted in toto, the president withdrew. The Council decided that it would prepare a provisional response on *The Student Role* and on the issue of non-professorial representation, in time to go both to students and staff on 20 November, prior to being considered at the regular Council meeting on 27 November at which both groups would be represented. That weekend the vice-chancellor spoke again on TV about the committee on the 28th and the decision of the Council Meeting of the 30th:

> The Council have [*sic*] decided to do what Sir George Farmer suggested – they are going to give this matter urgent consideration and when they have reached a provisional view about it they are then going to give the Guild the opportunity, if necessary at a special meeting, of coming and discussing it with them. The Council will then take this final discussion into account before they finally decide what they are going to do.[27]

Hunter also explained that following on the meeting of the 30th he and some of the Council had gone by invitation to the Union to discuss matters.

On the following Tuesday the Guild Council came up with a further request. This was for the suspension of classes for two days to allow a 'teach-in'. When this came up for consideration by Senate on 20 November it was rejected for that term but indicated as a possibility for a weekend later in the session. However, by that time the University Forum had held its first meeting in the Students' Union, under the chairmanship of Professor Gordon Davies, the dean of Arts. On the day of the deadline, 27 November, the students held a general meeting in the Great Hall, and 150 stayed on while the president and a group from the Guild met the

University Council as arranged. The Council did not concede all that the students were demanding and 80 of the protesters thereupon stayed in the hall overnight. In the afternoon of the following day a general meeting of the Guild was held and voted for direct action, upon which about a thousand students came from the Union and took possession of the entrance to the Aston Webb building and of the Great Hall itself.

The first act of the students was to occupy the vice-chancellor's ante-room, demanding answers, and he agreed to meet them in the Great Hall, provided his rooms were vacated. The meeting was an unhappy exercise in public criticism with the dice loaded against the vice-chancellor, even to the point of the amplification being turned down when he spoke. When he returned to his office the ante-room was again invaded and he was summoned to answer more points. Eventually he did so before his office was locked and he went home. The students thereupon broke in to his office and occupied his suite and many of the administrative offices in the Aston Webb building. When the vice-chancellor arrived the following morning he found students in his office and, after making some attempt at working, he moved to the Medical School. Later that day he accused the students of having broken into his confidential files.[28]

The organisation of the sit-in was taken over by a Committee of Ten, including the president and five members of the Guild Executive.[29] General assemblies were held daily, with large attendances, and thanks to the exciting atmosphere and compelling speaking, support for the sit-in grew. Meanwhile, the Senate Executive met at the Queen Elizabeth Hospital and decided to take no action until Monday 2 December. Over the weekend the students had a well-supported teach-in which ended by resolving to continue the occupation until four principles were conceded – no victimisation, all university committees to meet in public, the right of students to a say in university government and a commission to examine the role and structure of the University. In an important gloss on the second point it was agreed that students on university committees would be mandated.

After the Senate Executive had met as arranged on 2 December a statement was issued refusing to negotiate so long as the occupation continued, but promising that there would be no disciplinary action except in cases of personal injury, damage to property, illegal acts and involvement in the opening of the university files. That afternoon a chaotic general assembly was held in the Great Hall, chaired by the prospective Labour candidate for Selly Oak (an external member of the Guild), and when it reassembled in the evening, students voted to continue the sit-in. The next day an extraordinary general meeting sought to reverse this by voting by approximately 2300 to 1500 to recommend the Guild Council to end the protest. However a subsequent unofficial meeting urged continuation and when the Guild Council met, it decided by seventy-one votes to forty-two to persist. The reaction of the pro-chancellor and vice-chancellor was to announce that normal disciplinary sanctions would be restored from 3 p.m. on Wednesday 4 December, though this was then changed to 5 p.m. to allow for another general meeting in the Great Hall.

Thursday 5 December was, as we have seen, the day of the great meeting outside the library.[30] However, it began by the dean of Science, Professor G. V. Raynor, calling his fellow deans together to formulate a moderate mediating document to put before the Senate meeting which had been called for 5 p.m. The non-professorial executive held a formal meeting at 1.15 p.m. and issued an eirenic statement urging the students to end the protest, the vice-chancellor not to pursue disciplinary measures and the Senate at its meeting to initiate discussions in a good spirit. Shortly afterwards Professor Rodney Hilton met with the dean of Arts (Gordon Davies) and a number of the Arts professors. At this, the text proposed by the deans was reformulated in time for Professor Davies to take it to a 4 p.m. meeting of the deans, this time with the vice-principal, Professor Shotton. Through all this the vice-chancellor himself was absent at a meeting in London and he did not return until fifteen minutes into the Senate meeting, by which time discussion on the deans' revised document was well under way.

By the time the Senate met the outcome of the student meeting was, of course, known. A motion to recommend an end to the sit-in pending the decision of the University on 'the four principles' had been passed by a large majority, and this time the vote was constitutionally regular. The question was, would this be enough for the Senate? The specific issue before it was whether or not a delegation of student representatives should be admitted. At about 6.45 p.m. Professor S. A. Tobias of mechanical engineering rose to speak, one of the hardest of hardliners.[31] His speech swayed the meeting, but it was *in favour* of receiving the students! They were invited in at about 7.10 p.m., and Shotton grilled the president about what the student vote had meant. The Senate, agreeing that what was being asked for was discussion, quickly approved a statement which was issued immediately the meeting closed at 7.35 p.m., and included a request to the Senate Executive to set up a committee of six to meet with six students to begin talks.

The final event of the sit-in was the meeting of the Guild Council on Friday 6 December to consider the resolution of the previous day's mass meeting.[32] By then the physical occupation was over but it was natural for the Guild to try to preserve what dignity it could. The Guild Council reaffirmed the four principles and noted that direct action had demonstrated the strength of the student body and had got discussion going. However, in order to show good faith to the university authorities and to test theirs and to give the Senate a chance to act not under duress, the resolution to stage a sit-in was withdrawn. The first meeting of the joint committee with the Senate met on the following Thursday, 12 December.[33]

The sit-in was over, but who had been responsible? The senior officers of the University were in no doubt. In an account of the affair which Bill Lewis, the registrar, prepared after the Christmas vacation, the blame is put squarely on 'a group of students, known as the Ad Hoc Group for University Reform, whose extremist attitudes were derived from a knowledge of earlier student revolts in some French, German, American and British Universities'.[34] This loose association – 'anyone who turns up' – had emerged during the disputes over the Refectory in 1967–8 and, according to the registrar, numbered about fifty to one hundred students.[35] It was, he says, 'given considerable stimulus and encouragement by a few junior members of staff, of whom the most notable was Dick Atkinson, a newly recruited Temporary Assistant Lecturer in Sociology'. An intelligent and subtle personality and a most effective speaker, Atkinson was fresh from playing an active part in the troubles at the LSE and, again according to Lewis: 'Atkinson's arrival on the Birmingham scene did much to sharpen the thinking of the extremist group which was prepared for a confrontation with the University authorities whenever a suitable opportunity presented itself.' For them *The Student Role* was now not the goal but only the starting point. Their programme was spelled out early in November: an academic assembly as the supreme body of the University and the abolition of Court, Council and Senate; autonomous departments, halls of residence controlled by the residents, the Refectory under student control; all meetings in public and Guild policy determined by general meetings.[36]

The 'Ad Hoc' group was certainly prominent in the events of the autumn term of 1968. It took the initiative in picketing the Senate on 23 October and its members formed the gauntlet through which Council members had to pass a week later.[37] It is evident, too, that at Birmingham politically minded students were well aware of the writings of the French left-wing intellectuals who supported student action in Paris.[38] It is equally clear that Atkinson, as a sophisticated sociologist and proven student activist, was very influential, particularly through his speeches. For example, it was his speech at the Guild on the evening of Monday 2 December (lasting well beyond the three minutes allowed to other speakers) which led to the 'overwhelming victory over the moderates'.[39] Atkinson also rallied the radicals after their defeat the following day and produced in support David Adelstein, the leader of the LSE students, who proceeded to address the Birmingham protesters as 'comrade students'![40] There were, too, as Lewis said, staff who supported the students' line. Judging by the signatures to a radical memorandum issued on the day the sit-in began, there were about fifty of these, the great majority assistant lecturers or temporary research staff mostly from the faculty of Commerce and Social Science and its associated centres, and from Russian and German.[41] They called for the University Court and Council to be abolished and replaced by a democratic Senate representing staff and students, with power devolved to faculties and democratic departments.

A number of the fly-sheets issued by student groups could also be described as 'far-left'. One such was the proposal for a 'free university' whose key principles were no assessment, the abolition of 'the teacher–student role relationship', overcoming artificial barriers between disciplines, complete flexibility and continual self-criticism and the choosing of topics for study by teachers and students in response to 'felt needs'.[42] There was, too, a heady political atmosphere, maintained by continuous debate and monster rallies and propaganda. There were cries of 'All power to the General Assembly', although when moderates began to win votes, authority was, typically, identified as attaching only to informed participants. 'We must not be overwhelmed by a blind show of hands.'[43]

What, however, is noticeable among all this political activism is that the students behaved with meticulous respect for the Guild Constitution and that throughout the crisis the Guild Executive did everything it could to remain in control. In particular, the sit-in was funded as a regularly approved activity of the Guild.[44] The registrar's conclusion was that the Executive was the tool of the radicals but this was not the case. Indeed, on 29 October Ray Phillips denied the accusation publicly and made it clear that involvement by the Executive was in order 'to safeguard the interests of the Guild as a whole'.[45] As late as 19 November, the Guild Council, while not withdrawing the threat to act on the 27th, sent a message to the Senate expressing regret for any previous statements which had given offence.[46]

In the event the decision to stage a sit-in represented a retreat by the students from the initial decision for a mass strike.[47] That would have brought all University teaching to a standstill where the effect of a sit-in was concentrated on the senior officers. Although the target for protest was usually described as 'the University', Phillips and his Executive never had any intention of taking radical measures to force the University to close. Indeed, the Committee of Ten made rapid arrangements to maintain security and to give middle-rank and junior staff access to necessary papers.[48] In particular there was no obstruction of the working of the finance office and no attempt to extend the sit-in to other parts of the campus, where work continued uninterrupted. The local press published lurid stories about student vandalism but publicity issued by the protesters went out of its way to stress the reasonableness of the Guild case and the responsible way the sit-in was being handled. It was even claimed that the protest was directed against the waste of taxpayers' money.[49]

That the radicals were not in complete control is clear from the story of the 'teach-in'. When, six days after threatening direct action, the Guild called for a teach-in, Lewis saw this as an underhand device to promote the commission of enquiry which the students were pressing for.[50] In reality it represented a drawing back from confrontation in direct response to a press conference given by the vice-chancellor two days before in which he had personally committed himself to working out a form and structure for the University for the twenty-first century. *Redbrick* announced that the University was likely to be sympathetic to the idea of a teach-in and had this been implemented, it is very unlikely that direct action would have received the support it did.[51]

The teach-in the students organised for the weekend of the occupation confirms the impression of moderation.[52] Discussion groups were held on the role of the student in society, teaching methods and the role of the teacher, assessment and examinations, human interrelations in the University (the concept of community, problems of size, bureaucracy and the like), the educational role of extra-curricular action in the Union, the Guild Council and self-education, broader education, the moral content of courses, the objects of education, university entry (A levels, class bias, etc.) and on where students should live. There were also discussions at faculty level. The reports produced by the groups are substantially conventional – with much hostility to excessive factual teaching and excessive specialisation and a yearning for breadth in knowledge – and demonstrate both the novelty of such issues to many students and the seriousness with which they approached them.

Given that the Ad Hoc group did not have a stranglehold on the Guild Executive, how was it that the radical policy of direct action was adopted after a single unsatisfactory meeting with Council over *The Student Role?* The problem for Ray Phillips, the president of the Guild, was that of any constitutional reformer. On the one side there were the university authorities, whose timescale was much longer than that of any student and whose 'ponderous reactions to demands for change' could easily appear to be or could in fact be a way of saying 'no'.[53] On the other side, the president had the radicals, whose argument for direct action became steadily more compelling with every delay. The crux came in the brief incursion of students into the Aston Webb building on 23 October.[54] Phillips blamed this entirely on the 'Ad Hoc' group and, with other members of the Executive, attempted to discourage the militants, but he could not condemn them publicly for supporting what was a Guild document. The vice-chancellor, however, made it clear to Phillips that he believed that he and his colleagues were in the hands of the Ad Hoc group and did not represent general student opinion. He also implied that there was no Guild support for *The Student Role*. This forced the president to call the extraordinary meeting of the Guild on 29 October to debate motions critical of the University and to demand a commission into university government, and especially the opening of all university committees. The meeting, however, developed its own head of steam and voted to demand acceptance of *The Student Role* in toto, under threat of direct action.

As he reflected on events, Phillips had no doubt why the crisis had arisen a month after virtually all student demands relating to the Senate had been conceded: 'The answer is painfully obvious. The September meeting was Sir Robert Aitken's last. Since that time Sir Robert has moved on and Dr Hunter has, after an inadequate period of initiation, assumed the vice-chancellorship.' He recognised that Hunter had taken over when the most sensitive issue in *The Student Role,* students on Council, had yet to be tackled and that the new vice-chancellor did not have the respect his predecessor had enjoyed: '[Sir Robert'sl departure, therefore, has robbed the system of its previous stability and the present vice-chancellor is struggling to find a foothold.' *Redbrick* was less sensitive and less respectful. The *Redbrick* reporter who covered Hunter's arrival in his office on Friday 29 November to find it full of students commented: 'I think there was something amiss as regards his constitution as he kept raising his boney wee eyebrows. He left shortly afterwards to do some work, in a huff.'[55] The Guild produced a news bulletin entitled *Hunter and Hunted*.[56] Even more unkind was the cartoon in *Redbrick* responding to Hunter's claim that the University had conceded 90% of *The Student Role*. It showed a patient on an operating table with his heart removed and a surgically-garbed vice-chancellor saying 'We are glad to announce that 90% of the patient will live.'[57]

It is very tempting to agree with Phillips that if Robert Aitken had still been in control, matters would not have developed as they did. Given his prestige and standing with students and his deft way with people it seems very doubtful that direct action would have become a reality. Furthermore, after fifteen years his was the leading voice on Council whereas Hunter, as the new boy, was bound to listen to the non-academics who had appointed him. This is not to say that Aitken would have had no trouble in the autumn of 1968. Harry Harris, the new secretary, has even suggested that efforts were deliberately made to delay the crisis so as to avoid confrontation during Aitken's final year in office.[58] Certainly by the 1960s friction with students was becoming a new feature of vice-chancellorial life. In 1966 Aitken had had to override the authority of the president of the Guild, 'the first example in thirteen years', and order the removal of a wall newspaper which was personally offensive about the president of Ridge Hall.[59]

Aitken's final *Bulletin* appeared on 30 September 1968 and demonstrates that he was well aware of the dangers ahead and very clear about the delicacy of handling which would be needed:

> If I may offer a concluding personal observation it is this. Discussions are proceeding in a friendly and open-minded atmosphere. There is, however, an important difference between the Guild's initial approach and that of the other members of the University. The Guild has sought to increase the student role in University affairs by introducing students forthwith into many University committees and other bodies at all levels, and by prescribing powers and terms of reference in considerable detail. As yet, however, the Guild is unfamiliar with the work actually done by those committees and other bodies and the style of their operation. It is not easy for the Guild to judge where the potential students' contribution is relevant, to appreciate that the majority of decisions are effectively taken in Departments and subordinate committees, and to understand the loss of speed and efficiency which unduly formal procedures can entail. The senior members of the University favour a gradual introduction of students into the system, first at the points where their distinctive contribution is likely to be most effective. Time and opportunity must be allowed to ena-

> ble students to learn how the system works and where these points lie; it is after all a unique system of institutional government. Time and opportunity must also be allowed for senior members long accustomed to the system in its present form, to adapt it to student participation. If the goodwill and patience already evident in this series of meetings are maintained, there is a good prospect that the University will evolve an improved system of government in which both the potentialities and the inevitable limitations of the student role will be satisfactorily recognised.[60]

Perhaps this was a hope which could only be entertained by someone of Aitken's stature and experience. But he was right in believing that an atmosphere of mutual acceptance offered the only way forward. One can note in the relevant *Bulletin* how Aitken defused possible friction over the Ridge Hall episode. Increased student assertiveness, he announced, was no bad thing, but

> if it splits a university into antagonistic camps of teachers and taught it cannot but be harmful. The task of the University therefore extends beyond academic teaching, to helping students to assert themselves in an informed, well-mannered and constructive fashion. That requires knowing them personally, gaining and keeping their confidence, and taking a firm line on what is important in university education.[61]

Characteristically he then saw the Guild officers and effected a compromise, noting the good impression the students had made.[62]

Then was the root cause of the unrest the arrival of a new vice-chancellor who knew nobody personally and had had no time to gain anyone's confidence? Was Bob Hunter's inexperience to blame? He deserved – but did not receive – a good deal of grace, given that he was, as he said more than once, very much a newcomer.[63] He also deserves considerable sympathy. Photographs of his meeting with student protesters in the Great Hall on 28 November show a man completely at sea, but how many people would have emerged unscathed from that cauldron of criticism? The registrar by his side appears equally at a loss.[64] Hunter had a particular reason to consider himself badly treated that day because he had agreed to go to the Guild at lunchtime to explain the decision of the Council on the 29th to a meeting of the new University Forum, only for the Guild president to requisition the room and, as the vice-chancellor saw it, try to bounce him into addressing a student general meeting.[65]

All allowances made, however, it has to be said that Hunter was out of his depth. When, on 23 October, he talked to the students occupying the corridor outside his office he said that he was 'mystified by their dissatisfaction'.[66] As well as his manner, the measures he took made matters much worse than they might have been. It was not wise to challenge the president to show his hand, nor was it wise to express opinions to the effect 'that the University is not democratic and that he likes it that way'.[67] There is good reason to believe that the Senate was inclined to accept the Guild's olive branch and agree a 'teach-in' until Hunter effectively made rejecting it an issue of confidence.[68] When he faced the students in the Great Hall on Thursday 28th he informed them that injury to persons, damage to property and breaches of the law would be dealt with firmly by the University.[69] When he abandoned his office the next morning he warned that there would be no official dealings with the Guild until it withdrew, but he spoiled the effect of firmness by adding 'unofficially' that if the Guild did withdraw, he would call an early meeting of Senate to discuss a teach-in and would ask Sir George Farmer whether he would call Council together to consider the idea of a commission.

The business of the vice-chancellor's papers was particularly badly handled. Occupying the administrative offices in the Aston Webb building necessarily gave students physical control of the University's files. According to the registrar's subsequent account, on the first evening of the occupation the warden of the Guild entered the vice-chancellor's room to discover that his 'files had been broken into and that a document from one of the files was being examined by a student'.[70] The vice-chancellor did not raise this when the Senate Executive met the next day but he did make the accusation soon after.[71] The Guild Executive promptly denied all knowledge or involvement in any such action and complained that the vice-chancellor should have consulted it before making such a serious accusation. The following day Hunter went further and issued a formal statement to the effect that his confidential files had been broken open and copied: 'We now know what the Executive of the Guild of Undergraduates means by direct action and no confidentiality. We also know of their total disregard for the interests of the majority of the University community.'[72] Hunter also went public and informed the UGC and various government departments that he could not guarantee the confidentiality of their communications with Birmingham.

It is a strange contrast to the dramatic nature of this announcement that the files issue soon fell from prominence. Investigation was very half-hearted and there is little or no indication of what was supposed to have been read and copied or information about broken locks. The administrative staff appear to have been able to get access to the files they required and the registrar's conclusion was that 'In general the students simply occupied offices in a manner which made normal work impossible. They used typewriters and stationery for their own purposes, played transistor radio sets and slept in the rooms.'[73] It is unlikely that the full truth about the files will ever be known but a likely construction would seem to be that a student or students were seen opening various drawers and glancing at what was inside.[74]

University pronouncements were also poorly judged. On Wednesday 4 December, after the Guild Council had refused to confirm Tuesday afternoon's vote in favour of withdrawal, George Farmer and Robert Hunter circulated a statement saying that this decision had created a new situation and that normal university discipline was being restored from 3 p.m. that afternoon.[75] This was followed by Professor Shotton, the vice-principal, telling a press conference that this meant that students might be sent down.[76] Not only (as we have seen) did the deadline have to be immediately extended to 5 p.m. because a general meeting had been called for 2.30 p.m. in the Great Hall, but the Ad Hoc group were able to cry 'victimisation', point out delightedly that the 'authorities' did not understand the Guild constitution and summon their supporters with the call, 'You must be there.'[77] The next day the vice-chancellor issued a clarification 'in view of the misinterpretation' of the Farmer/Hunter warning, saying that 'the University always recognises the right of free speech and will take no disciplinary action for the expression of opinion during the Sit In'.[78]

What made this cack-handedness less forgivable was that a similar problem had arisen two days before, over the statement which had been issued by the Senate Executive on 2 December. It had said that 'there can be' no discussions on any matters put forward by student representatives while the sit-in continued and promised that no disciplinary action would be taken 'except against those who have or may have caused injury to persons or damage to property or broken the law in any other way, and against those who have been involved in any way in obtaining access to information in University files'.[79] The next day the registrar had to issue a clarification to the effect that discussions would be resumed once the occupation was over, that although it was not in the University's hands to suspend the criminal law, it had no intention of taking advantage of the civil law of trespass and that 'may have' only applied to actions taken subsequent to the Senate Executive's announcement.[80]

This readiness among Senate Executive members to get back to negotiations and end all talk of discipline suggests that the vice-chancellor did not enjoy the wholehearted support of at least this senior academic committee. That conclusion is born out by a marked difference in tone between the statement as issued and what seems to be the text as first drafted, a corrected copy of which has survived.[81] A desire not to escalate matters was also evident at the emergency meeting of the Executive called on the first day of the sit-in.[82] Dr Hunter gave a detailed account of his actions but the members of the committee distanced themselves by noting that it was on the vice-chancellor that 'responsibility rested for assessing the situation as it developed and for initiating any action against the intruders'. The Executive's only advice to him was to do nothing until at least Monday 2 December and its only decision was to reassemble at noon that day and to charge the Guild for all damages and costs.

This reluctance to get tough did not, of course, indicate staff support for the tactics of direct action – outside the small and unrepresentative group of radical sympathisers we have noted. The non-professorial staff executive condemned the sit-in immediately, arguing that students should, as they had done, accept the Council's concessions of 27 November and come back for more another day.[83] If the graphic stories which circulated can be believed, senior staff also directly obstructed the sit-in: warnings to medical students that they would lose the character references required to enter the profession; Professor Stacey threatening to close Chemistry; Professor Tobias ranting about Nazis and browbeating a departmental meeting called to discuss the crisis.[84] The vote of Tuesday 3 December to withdraw the sit-in was achieved by Professor J. G. Davies advising the moderates not to allow taking the vote to be delayed until only the radicals remained, and by chemical and civil engineering suspending teaching for the afternoon, chemistry declaring classes non-compulsory, mechanical engineering cancelling the 2 p.m. lectures and biochemistry beginning classes at 3 p.m., not 2 p.m.[85]

It was, however, one thing to disapprove of tactics but quite another to disapprove of objectives, and here the staff were decidedly less than hawkish. Several professors and other staff maintained regular contact with the protesting students and one-sixth of the academic staff endorsed a circular which called on the students to end the sit-in and on the Senate to commit itself to student participation and reform and to further discussions.[86] The signatories represented a cross-section of the university departments and as well as moderates, included known left-wingers. We have seen how the deans took the initiative to meet the students part-way and that they were fortified by the lunchtime resolution of the non-professors calling on Senate to exempt from discipline students who had acted in pursuance of Guild policy and to begin negotiations on student participation as soon as the sit-in ended 'in the spirit of the agreement between the National Union of Students and the CVCP'.[87] Later that afternoon the staff of the physics department called for willingness on the part of the University to continue discussions.[88]

It would, nevertheless, be wrong to credit academic staff with too much wisdom. They, too, as Aitken had recognised, were on a learning curve. The *in statu pupillari* mindset was deep rooted. Thus, as well as unwisely turning down the request for an immediate 'teach-in', the Senate resolution of 20 November was worded in very much a 'we know best' fashion: 'the normal academic work of the University must take precedence in term, except on occasions at weekends when a carefully prepared programme on a non-departmental and inter-departmental basis could be provided by the University'.[89] Student participation was appropriate only at points where students had anything to contribute: 'The Senate is satisfied that the situation can be met most satisfactorily at present by the further development of staff–student relationships which were given such a high priority by the Guild.' What students needed was information: 'Once these arrangements have been fully explored the Senate will consider further ways in which students can become informed about university affairs.' All this was miles away from recognising the principle that students had a right to be consulted. By 5 December, however, Senate had learned the lesson. The statement it issued that evening reaffirmed 'its commitment to the principle of student participation and the need to consider changes in the structure of the government of the University', and declared that discussions would continue.[90]

If the Senate, despite agreeing in September on most of *The Student Role*, could still get the language so wrong in October, it is not surprising that a lay-dominated Council could be totally out of touch. Indeed, a heavy responsibility for the 1968 sit-in must rest with the University Council. Its chairman, the pro-chancellor Sir George Farmer, had no time at all for student participation. He said 'I do not accept the Student Role' in much the way that he would have rejected a trade union demand at Longbridge, and students felt that during meetings he treated them with contempt.[91] When they were given access to Council it was for only half an hour and to make a statement in strict confidence.[92] They resented Sir George being absent from Council meetings and then expecting decisions to be delayed. The main leader in the edition of *Redbrick* for 30 October pointed out that Sir George would be absent from Council that afternoon and that his business commitments understandably forced him to view the University as of second importance.[93] Other councillors made an equally bad impression. The *Redbrick* leader pointed to 'Alderman Mrs Crosskey who said last night "I'm afraid I won't be at the meeting of the University Council tomorrow. Anyone who pays good money for Stratford tickets isn't going to throw them away, least of all me."' Farmer appears to have had a considerable influence over Dr Hunter – after all he had just appointed him – and the students thought that at meetings Hunter echoed Farmer's dismissive attitude to their case.[94] The joint warning which the pro-chancellor and the vice-chancellor issued on 4 December is particularly indicative. Farmer had no authority at all to add his name to a threat of disciplinary action against students since discipline was quite specifically the responsibility of the Senate, not Council. The Senate Executive had already made it clear that the vice-chancellor's authority was quite sufficient on its own and the calling in of Farmer looks very much like Hunter needing support and doubting that he could get it from either the Senate Executive or the deans. One may note that subsequently in his 1968 report the vice-chancellor went out of his way to say that 'in his short time as Pro-Chancellor [Sir George Farmer] has established himself in the regard and affection of members of the University'.[95]

As the non-professorial staff recognised, the 90% concession made to the students by Council on 27 November was considerable, but it was made 'in a way which only added to the bad feeling'.[96] Not only was it presented as a fait accompli, with conditions, notably confidentiality, which the students were known to oppose bitterly, but July 1969 was set as the date for a further review, that is when the current student leaders would be at the end of their period of office. When the *Bulletin* published the Council resolutions on 2 December it included a reminder to staff and students that there was more to administering the University than was apparent from a reading of the charter and other basic documents.[97] Experience was needed. 'It would be very foolish to try to improve this machinery without understanding it, and the Council's decisions give considerable opportunity for gaining this understanding.' This was insisting on *in statu pupillari* with a vengeance.

It has also to be remembered that Birmingham was one of the last of the 1968 student protests, and that by then public opinion had come down against what were seen as the antics of the idle who were privileged at the expense of the community. What is more, the six places which the City of Birmingham had on the University Council meant that this hostility inevitably had an influence on university decisions. This certainly came out into the open when the sit-in began. Despite student efforts at publicity the local press was uniformly hostile. At a City Council debate on 3 December Alderman Eric Mole, leader of the Labour group, said that 'the vice-chancellor had acted in a most commendable way'.[98] There were references to students as 'hairy coconuts' and 'long-haired layabouts', and the *Birmingham Post* reported that if the sit-in continued into Friday 6th, the December Degree Congregation would be moved to the Birmingham Town Hall. The suggestion had, in fact, come from the then Lord Mayor, 'We'll have all the ceremonies down in the City and let the students see that we are not going to be upset.'[99]

So what, with the hindsight of thirty years, was the fundamental cause of the 1968 'troubles' at Birmingham? Many individuals and groups played a part, but the final assessment has to be that what precipitated the 'sit-in' was the gulf of incomprehension between the 'University' and 'the Students' and between 'the Students' and 'the University'. There is little to fault in the conclusion which Harry Cronne, professor of medieval history and former dean of Arts, offered in the *Birmingham Post* of 6 December 1968: 'Firstly, the failure of senior members of the University – to an extent unprecedented in my lifetime – to understand present-day undergraduates. Secondly, the failure of undergraduates to comprehend in any practical way the answer they have been given on the subject of the Student Role.'[100]

Accident and misunderstanding are responsible for most historical crises.

Notes

1 UC 4/iv/21 is a portfolio of unorganised and unnumbered material; 4/v/6 is a box of unnumbered material mostly in folders (lettered A–K) but some loose. Citations can, therefore, only be indicative.

2 See below, p. 364.

3 For the following see C. Crouch, *The Student Revolt* (1970).

4 UC 4/v/6 in J.

5 UC 7/iii 1968, p. 36.

6 Crouch, *Student Revolt*, p. 55.
7 *Who's Who.*
8 UC Oral History: comment by Edward Marsland.
9 *Bulletin*, 97 (11 Nov. 1968).
10 Ex inf. P. A. Garratt.
11 For Eden's skill with students, see UC Oral History: comment by Lord Hunter.
12 Ex. inf. Ian King, NUS Services.
13 UC 4/v/6: W. Lewis, *The Student Role in 1968* (January 1969), pp. 2–3 (henceforward Lewis).
14 For the following see *University Calendar*.
15 Ibid., 1927. In addition there were 101 honorary clinical lecturers, etc. A number of *sui generis* posts make an exact comparison with 1968 difficult.
16 UC 7/iii 1968, p. 37.
17 The figure of 123 professors is derived from the *University Calendar* and represents the number entitled to sit in Senate. The figure of 117 (at n. 15) represents staff numbers returned to the UGC as paid from university funds.
18 Lewis, pp. 15–16.
19 The clearest account of the chronology is found in Lewis.
20 For the non-professorial staff see the letter of P. A. Garratt, 2 Dec. 1968: UC 4/v/6 in F.
21 *Bulletin* 94 (1 July 1968).
22 Lewis, p. 3.
23 Ibid., p. 4.
24 *Bulletin* 97 (11 Nov. 1968), pp. 1–3.
25 Ibid., p. 3.
26 *Redbrick*, 30 Oct. 1968: UC 4/v/6 in J.
27 *Bulletin* 97 (11 Nov. 1968), pp. 4–5.
28 See below, p. 367.
29 The names are in Lewis, p. 16.
30 UC 4/v/6 in H. Lewis gives no details of the following.
31 See below and the paper Tobias circulated to Senate, 24 Nov. 1968: UC 4/v/6 in J.
32 For the following see UC 4/v/6 in J.
33 Lewis, p. 14.
34 This and subsequent quotations in this paragraph from Lewis are from pp. 2– 3.
35 UC 4/v/6 in J; see also *Redbrick*, 29 Oct. 1968: UC 4/v/6 in J.
36 Ibid., 8 Nov. 1968: UC 4/v/6 in J.
37 Ibid., 29 Oct., 6 Nov. 1969: UC 4/v/6 in J.
38 Ibid., 29 Oct. 1968: UC 4/v/6 in J.
39 Ibid., 3 Dec. 1968: UC 4/v/6 in G.
40 Lewis, p. 12.
41 See collective letter, 28 Nov. 1968: UC 4/v/6 in A.
42 Ibid., in D.
43 Ibid., in D & J.
44 *Redbrick*, 4 Dec. 1968: UC 4/iv/21.
45 Ibid., 29 Oct. 1968: UC 4/v/6 in J.
46 Ibid., 20 Nov. 1968: UC 4/v/6 in J.

47 'Direct Action' was not defined. Ibid., 30 Oct. 1968: UC 4/ v/6 in J.
48 Ibid., 4 Dec. 1968: UC 4/iv/21; Lewis, pp. 8– 9.
49 2 Dec. 1968: UC 4/v/6 in G. One rumour was that the students had broken into the computer room, threatening £400,000 of equipment.
50 Lewis, p. 6.
51 *Redbrick*, 6 Nov. 1968: UC 4/v/6 in J.
52 UC 4/v/6 in E and substantially elsewhere through the collection.
53 The quotation is by an unnamed observer: UC 4/v/6 in E.
54 For the following see *Redbrick*, 29 Oct. 1968: UC 4/v/6 in J.
55 Ibid., 4 Dec. 1968: UC 4/iv/21.
56 *Guild News Bulletin*, 28 Nov. 1968: UC 4/v/6 in B.
57 *Redbrick*, 4 Dec. 1968: UC 4/iv/21.
58 UC Oral History: comment by Harry Harris.
59 *Bulletin* 73 (5 Dec. 1966).
60 Ibid., 95 (30 Sept. 1968).
61 Ibid., 73 (5 Dec. 1966).
62 Ibid., 74 (9 Jan. 1967).
63 E.g. TV broadcast 26 Oct.
64 *Redbrick*, 30 Oct. 1968: UC 4/v/6 in J.
65 Special Meeting of Senate Executive, 29 Nov. 1968:UC 4/v/in D.
66 *Redbrick*, 29 Oct. 1968: UC 4/v/6 in J.
67 Ad Hoc Committee, 6 Nov. 1968: UC 4/v/6 in J.
68 Staff letter of 27 Nov. 1969: UC 4/iv/21.
69 As n. 64.
70 Lewis, p. 8.
71 Hunter did not mention the break-in to the Senate Executive on Friday 29 November but did so on Monday 2 December: Meetings of Senate Executive, 29 Nov., 2 Dec. 1968: UC 4/v/6 in D & F. The students issued a denial on 29 November 1968: UC 4/v/6 in C.
72 30 Nov. 1968: UC 4/v/6 in D.
73 Lewis, p. 8.
74 The student identified was the Guild Treasurer: UC Senate Executive, 2 Dec. 1968: UC 4/v/6 in F.
75 UC 4/iv/21.
76 Student paper, ibid.
77 Ibid.
78 UC 4/v/6 in J.
79 Ibid., in F.
80 Ibid., in G.
81 Ibid., in F.
82 Ibid., in D.
83 UC 4/iv/21.
84 See 'A reasoned opinion': ibid.; *Redbrick*, 4 Dec. 1968: UC 4/iv/21; 'Press Office', 29 Nov. 1968; UC 4/v/6 in C.
85 *Redbrick*, 4 Dec. 1968: UC 4/iv/21; 4/v/6 in G.
86 Ibid., 5 Dec. 1968: UC 4/v/6 in H.

87 UC 4/v/6 in K.
88 Ibid., in H.
89 Ibid., in F.
90 Ibid., in K.
91 Guild News Bulletin, 28 Nov. 1968: UC 4/v/6 in B.
92 UC 4/v/6 in E.
93 *Redbrick*, 30 Oct. 1968: UC 4/v/6 in J.
94 UC 4/v/6 in E.
95 UC 7/iii 1968, p. 1.
96 UC 4/v/6 in E.
97 *Bulletin* 98 (2 Dec. 1968).
98 *Birmingham Daily Post*, 4 Dec. 1968.
99 UC Oral History: comment by Lord Hunter.
100 *Birmingham Daily Post*, 6 Dec. 1968.

Chapter Nineteen

The escape from the hinterland: 1945–80

CHAPTER 13 SUGGESTED THAT until well after the Second World War changes in the background, the composition and the subsequent careers of Birmingham students remained limited. By contrast, the changes which took place from the 1950s were fundamental. The roots of these changes go back to the 1930s or earlier, but they were not obvious until much later. Student numbers expanded, Birmingham's catchment area ceased to be dominated by the West Midlands, more generous students grants became available, and the upshot was that the student generation of 1968 certainly came from further afield than any previous generation of students, and was also probably more select and socially less broadly based than any previous generation of Birmingham students. This trend has, of course, continued.

Ultimately, this is a question of social mobility, a rather technical subject liable to have the same effect on the reader as some of Grant Robertson's prose. This is not the place for a full discussion of how the patterns of social mobility revealed from the student records relate to other work on national patterns of social mobility. Some of this has been published elsewhere and it is planned to publish more in the future.[1] Instead, this chapter will touch, rather briefly, on four aspects of mobility. The first of these concerns the nature of student funding before the formal arrival of universal student grants in 1960. The second concerns geographical mobility, the third heredity and the fourth mobility between social classes. In each case the discussion needs to start with the inter-war years.

> To anyone, like myself, really behind the scenes, the result of the economic depression both on the students who can just manage, and on the many who are debarred from, a university course is unmistakably and pathetically clear. And the reduction in spending power necessarily affects the provincial universities more severely than it does Oxford and Cambridge.[2]

This was Grant Robertson in 1924, at his most pessimistic. He steadily became more optimistic. By January 1930 he did not believe that the slump was having a very serious effect: the same people could afford to come to universities but they had less money to spend when there. 'When for something like fifty or sixty per cent of our students the margin is always a narrow one, a difference of £10 or even £5 a year may have regrettable if unseen consequences.'[3] By 1937 he relieved himself of the following:

> We draw our students from all classes without any tests. In fact, most universities in Great Britain today are the only form of classless society reached anywhere in Europe. With our entrance scholarship, and the maintenance grants of our local authorities, I doubt whether there is really any boy or girl in the Midlands, qualified to benefit from a university education, who is excluded by poverty from getting it. That there is a reservoir of untapped ability, which could or ought to be tapped somehow, is quite unproved, and I can find no evidence of its existence. That we could double our numbers by lowering our standards of entry is certain. But University is not the only educational organisation in any province, and our business is to see that we intend to be a university, and not a combination of technical school and an evening institute.

The number of students might not have expanded much, but about 45% to 50% of them 'hold scholarships or grants from public funds, which enable them to take a University course' and about 48% started their education in an elementary school.[4]

Table 19.1 Percentage of undergraduates from maintained schools entering universities, autumn 1934

Birmingham	58.1
Bristol	54.3
Leeds	49.4
Liverpool	53.5
Manchester	46.7
Sheffield	60.2
Oxford	24.2
Cambridge	23.8
Total, England and Wales	*36.0*

Source: *Education in 1935* (Cmd. 5290, 1936). The data is based on year ending 31 July 1935

Viewed from within the very limited contours of the system of inter-war student finance, Grant Robertson had a point. All the universities were the beneficiaries of the expanded system of secondary education that followed the 1902 Act and which continued to expand during the inter-war years. Table 19.1 shows that the modern civic universities followed similar paths. In 1934 they were taking between 50% and 60% of their pupils from maintained schools, with Birmingham actually taking a larger proportion than the almost all the others. For those who knew the pre-1914 era this was indeed progress. In Birmingham alone the number of secondary school places outside the King Edward Foundation had expanded from 2240 in 1920 to 4800 in 1933. The database suggests that before 1914 under a fifth of Birmingham's students came from the maintained sector. By 1923–4 students from the maintained schools formed a third of the new entries, helping to fill the gap left by the ex-servicemen. The proportion rose inexorably. The suggestion from the government statistics for 1935 is that intake to the English university system was equivalent to nearly a quarter of the boys and 14% of the girls in secondary schools aged sixteen and over.[5] Britain may have had one of the smallest percentage of university entrants in the developed world, but it is plausible to claim that during the inter-war years it had the largest percentage of working-class students, with Birmingham in the vanguard.[6] However, as the falling rolls of the 1930s however made clear, the vanguard was not a desirable position to occupy.

Table 19.2 Assisted full-time students: English provincial universities excluding Oxford and Cambridge, 1928–47

Year	*No.*		*%*		
	Male	Female	Male	Female	Total
1928–9	3454	2498	45.9	65.4	52.5
1934–5	4268	1930	42.7	54.1	45.7
1935–6	4314	1808	43.1	52.9	45.6
1946–7	11397	4156	72.5	62.7	69.6

Source: For 1928/29, 1934/35: UGC Report, 1929/30–1934/35 (HMSO 1936), p.55; for 1935/36: UGC, University Development from 1935 to 1947 (HMSO, 1948), p.105, Appendix X, where assistance was defined as 'in receipt of assistance from government departments, Local Education Authorities, universities or any other bodies which met either wholly or in part University fees and maintenance charges'. The data is for England excluding London, Oxford and Cambridge.

The problem for prospective students was not that of obtaining a place at university. The problem was obtaining finance. It was tempting for universities to believe in the capacity of scholarships to support students, and of exams as objective processes for choosing such students. Some 53% of English university students obtained some form of assistance during 1928/9; the proportion had fallen to 46% by 1934 (see Table 19.2). More precisely, by 1935/6 the number of men obtaining support had risen by about a quarter, and the number of women with support had fallen by a quarter, most of the fall caused presumably by cuts in grants for intending teachers. This much was made clear by the annual government statistics. But with the significant exception of the Board of Education's carefully rationed awards for intending teachers, scholarships were administered locally, and were subject to local discretion. This is a subject on which little work has been done, but the outlines are clear enough, at least in the case of Birmingham. On the one hand there is the familiar story of heavy competition for scholarships and other funds, of hardship suffered by students and by their parents, of women signing away their lives as teachers (their phrase, often repeated) in order to have their studies at university funded by the government. It was not in fact for life, but it was for a minimum of five years, and in many but not all education authorities this also meant not marrying for five years.[7] Students who went to Birmingham before 1945 and whose parents were too poor to support them fully are, when interviewed, invariably very specific about their finances or rather the lack of them: a student with a supposedly full grant from his local education authority had a weekly allowance of six shillings and six pence from his parents, who could barely afford it, and whenever possible walked rather than took the tram. Another had a scholarship worth some £18 a year and his father had to continue working as a vicar until he was seventy-two. A student from Evesham obtained a special government grant during the early years of the war to study radio physics, a grant worth as much as a state scholarship and much easier to obtain, if one was studying physics.[8] Carol Dyhouse has recently sought out inter-war students at other universities and the stories are repeated. Nor did the education students fare any better – it was not accidental that the wardens of halls of residence had to report annually to the Board of Education on the health of such students. At Birmingham during the 1930s a student who budgeted very carefully and exercised considerable self-control was believed by the University to need about £130 a year, no mean sum, although a great deal less than Oxford or Cambridge and somewhat less than London.[9]

However, alongside the usual picture of hardship there is a much-less investigated picture of the administration of local education authority (LEA) grants for students. Within the University's catchment area there were a number of local education authorities, each of which had considerable scope for deciding how or even whether to finance its university students. Birmingham LEA was only one among many, and it could afford a measure of generosity more easily than poorer Black Country townships such as Walsall. However, it was never suggested that Birmingham's attitude to student grants was very different, in the medium run, from that of other large boroughs and Birmingham usually provided its students with some support, whether they chose to study in Birmingham or not. From an examination of its records a case can be made that by the 1930s the structure of student grants that would develop after the war was in place. A survey of 1925 praised Birmingham's policy of granting a maintenance award for every pupil that went to university, in which it was ahead of other large cities; a subsequent survey of 1933 attacked Birmingham for its rather severe ranking of parental income when deciding on the level of maintenance awards.[10] Birmingham, therefore, seems to have been fairly generous in the number of grants that it provided. Where it may have been less generous is in the amount of the grant, which was linked with parental income, and in this it may have been typical. As Grant Robertson said, £5 could make all the difference. The level of support was a problem for the students and for the University, but a larger problem for a university with a tendency towards declining numbers during the 1930s was caused by the relatively small numbers of those staying on at school beyond the age of sixteen.

After the Second World War student numbers increased rapidly and so did the number of LEA awards, which on a national scale increased from 1700 for 1937/8 to over 12 000 ten years later and to 47 000 by 1957/8. The total cost of university awards in Britain rose from £5.6 million in 1951–2 to £21.6 million in 1958–9. Being discretionary, there were wide regional disparities, but it is possible to exaggerate these, and they narrowed during the 1950s. The Anderson Report of 1960, which recommended a standardisation of procedures, confirmed that most LEAs conformed to the Ministry of Education's standard recommendations. By 1958 only one-eighth of the students applying for awards did not receive them. Indeed, the circulars of the Ministry of Education suggest widespread agreement by the earlier 1950s, and the more publicised complaints of the later 1950s tended to be based on statistics demolished by the Anderson Report or to relate to relatively minor issues such as the reluctance of some LEAs to finance students who wished to change courses. It would appear that the pre-war policies of boroughs such as Birmingham were extended and regularised, not that significant innovations were made in policy. Demand rose, and supply rose, usually more.[11] Birmingham LEA paid fees and gave means-tested maintenance allowances; the total cost of the allowances doubled between 1952 to 1956 and continued to rise thereafter. Its awards subcommittee claimed to have interviewed all those who had been offered a university place, but seem rarely to have rejected anybody, irrespective of whether their university was local or not. Despite occasional expressions of concern, Birmingham was not one of those authorities that sought to compel its grant-holders to take up teaching after qualification. In 1955 the chairman of the awards committee, Professor Jeffrys of the University's School of Education, remarked that 'it seemed that they were approaching a situation where pretty well any student who could profit from a University Course had it made financially possible for him to have one'.[12] The stable door may have been open for longer than is generally assumed: a survey of undergraduate entries for Liverpool University during the three years 1947–9 showed that 85% of home students received some sort of financial support: some 90% of Arts, Science and Engineering students, 75% of medical students and 50% of the Law students.[13]

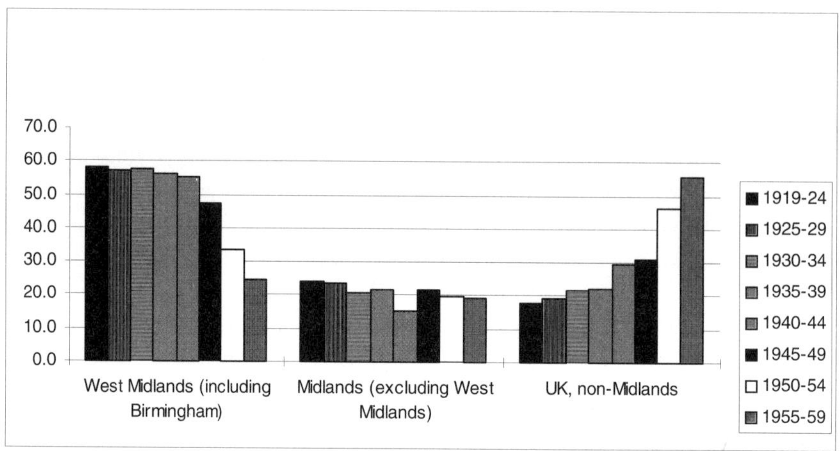

Figure 19.1 Region of origin of Birmingham University students, 1919–59 (UK nationality, UK residence)

As far as geographical mobility is concerned, the pattern is clear. Figure 19.1 shows that it was during the 1950s that the catchment area for Birmingham University widened appreciably. This, at last, was when the University could break free from the constraints of the hinterland. Immediately after the war 64% of male B.Sc. students were local while a decade subsequently the figure was a little over 29%; local Arts males fell from 73% to 19%, local Arts females from 60% to 18%. This change was by no means restricted to Birmingham, and is not a subject that has been studied much. That the catchment area of British universities widened considerably during the 1950s and 1960s is well known. This has usually been related to the universalisation of grants, which indeed appear to provide an obvious explanation. But the phenomenon is too large for any single explanation. We need to understand why there was an unprecedented and large-scale tendency for the children of professional social groups not only to study at a university but to do so at a university some distance from their parental home. For the social groups affected by it, this was a development at least as important as the much-trumpeted cultural changes of the 1960s, and much less analysed.[14] As far as grants are concerned, an analysis of the social background of the post-war students, some of which is described below, suggests that to many, although by no means all parents the grants would have acted more as a useful subsidy than as a permissive agent.

The third aspect to be discussed is that of heredity. For the modern universities in their early days, seeking to expand the market for higher education, heredity was a considerable problem. Small businessmen did not send their sons to university; they were gradually converted but as late as the 1960s the petty bourgeoisie of small proprietors and self-employed artisans were still resisting the trend, at least as far as Birmingham was concerned. There seemed to be little that could be offered to them even by the higher levels of a school, let alone by a university.[15] It was the reasonably well-to-do professions who held the key. The close connection of the universities and the professions is a fairly recent phenomenon. The great expansion of professions during the nineteenth century was carried out without excessive reliance on the universities, who restricted themselves in the main to clergy and lawyers. The traditional task of the universities has not been to create new professions (except for university teachers and, more recently, university administrators), but to train the aspiring members of those professions which had some status and wished for more. In the 1930s, and perhaps even later, the provincial universities moved around the edges of training for the new professions. It was the most they could do. The retreat of the early B.Com. from a prototype MBA was a warning of the dangers of excessive enthusiasm.[16] So was the retreat of student numbers in Birmingham during the 1930s.

If the universities were to remain viable, they needed to attract the children of the professionals. There had always been a large element of heredity in the professions. There are few published surveys of heredity, and the only systematic information on parental background that exists at Birmingham before the 1960s is for medical students.[17] Medicine was a particularly expensive subject to study, with a particularly strong culture of its own.[18] In popular belief, doctors are particularly celebrated for heredity, but little research on the matter has been published. Figure 19.2 shows the proportion of Birmingham's medical students with fathers in medically-related occupations, taking five-year averages for Birmingham from 1925/9 to 1970/4. Several conclusions are at once evident. There were never more than 30% of medical students, male or female, who had fathers in the profession,[19] and the figure was usually much less. As far as men were concerned, this proportion was falling from the 1920s until the mid-1950s, when it reached a low point of 12%. It then rose sharply. Women had a different chronology until the 1950s. As far as men were concerned it is easy to see two factors at work. The first is the national expansion of medical training, which diluted the proportion of students with fathers in the profession. The other is the status of the medical profession, which until the 1950s or 1960s was not particularly high compared with other professions.[20]

The next step, therefore, is to move away from the Medical School and to ask what the children of doctors chose to study. The data does not permit an answer to this until 1960–4, by which time the graph in Figure 19.2 had turned decisively upwards. It turns out that 54% of the sons of doctors and of medically-related professions (such as pharmaceutical chemists) studied medicine. A further 9%

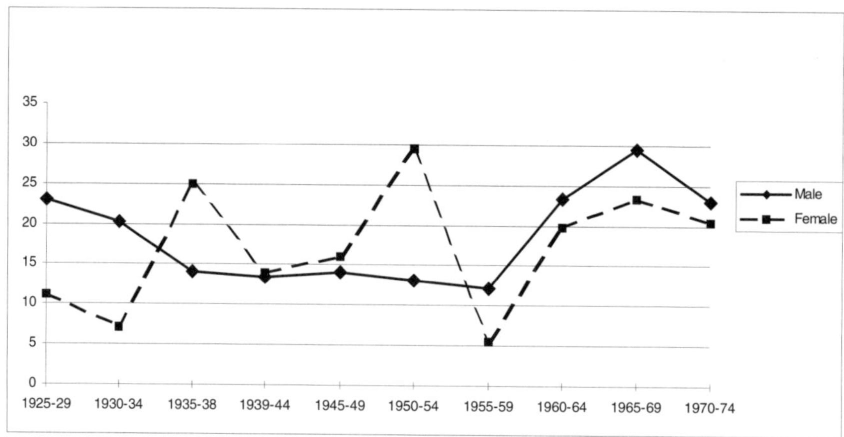

Figure 19.2 Birmingham University: percentage of MB, Ch.B. students with fathers in medically-related occupations, 1925–74

studied dentistry. The popular assumption must, therefore, be revised rather than abandoned. Most medical students were not the sons of doctors, but (outside dentistry) over half the sons of doctors chose to study medicine. With daughters the figures were a little lower, at 49% and 11% for medicine and dentistry, respectively, but the sample for daughters is too small to permit many conclusions.[21]

Table 19.3 Birmingham University: degrees studied by children of various professions, 1960–4

	Education	Medical	Engineering	Civil Service
Males				
BA	19.0	6.4	12.5	14.5
B.Sc.	41.7	12.8	66.2	53.6
Medicine	20.2	53.8	6.6	8.7
Dentistry	1.2	9.0	3.7	5.8
No.	*84*	*78*	*136*	*69*
Females				
BA	47.6	20.0	41.5	52.4
B.Sc.	12.7	8.6	26.8	26.2
Medicine	22.2	48.6	19.5	7.1
Dentistry	3.2	11.4	0.0	0.0
No.	*63*	*35*	*41*	*42*

Source: Database

Doctors, however, were not exceptional, as Table 19.3 reveals. Finding other occupations to provide a context is not a simple matter, but the table shows what can be done. It draws on parental descriptions as given by the students in their application forms. Teachers, who include academics, are clearly defined. 'Engineers' span a wide scale, as does the Civil Service. Nevertheless, the results suggest that the hereditary element among the British middle class was strong, especially for sons. If 54% of the sons of doctors were studying medicine, 66% of the sons of engineers were studying for a B.Sc. With daughters the pattern is interesting. While about half the doctors' sons and daughters had escaped into non-medical subjects, the daughters tended to study Arts subjects and the sons did not. Engineers showed a clear gender difference: less than 25% of their daughters studied for a B.Sc. and 40% were studying for a BA. Under the B.Sc. umbrella one-third of the sons of engineers were studying engineering subjects, compared with less than 5% of their daughters. The differences are intriguing, but the category is so wide that conclusions need to be drawn with care. Similarly, the 'Civil Service' is a polyglot category, including many scientific workers, but this does not explain why 54% of their sons studied for a B.Sc. and only 26% of their daughters, 52% of whom were studying for a BA. Finally, those theorists who argue in favour of the bifurcation of the professions into two groups, 'liberal professions' and others, would do well to analyse Table 19.3 in more detail, as it does not give much support to their argument. The overlap was complex and at the very least it should be redefined by gender.[22]

Social mobility, it is worth repeating, is a particularly technical subject, demanding the prior classification of the different strata of society. For those who find it too daunting, the main conclusion is that already mentioned in the introduction to this chapter: that by the 1970s the student body of Birmingham University may well have been more select and socially less broadly based than any previous generation of Birmingham students. Women undergraduates tended to come from higher social strata than men, the Science Faculty became more select during the 1960s, and the male plebeian contingent of the Arts Faculty, that is, the sons of manual workers, grew from 28% to 34%.

Table 19.4 gives the social background of Arts and Science students entering Birmingham during the years 1961–4 and 1971–4 using the Goldthorpe classification. This is preferred by sociologists to the better-known scheme of the Registrar-General. Very roughly, Classes I and II, named the service sector by Goldthorpe, comprise most white-collar occupations except for sales and routine non-manual workers, who are classified with small proprietors and lower-grade technicians in Classes III, IV and V. Classes VI and VII are manual workers. As Goldthorpe's categories are wide, Table 19.5 gives the Registrar-General's Classes I and II. Whereas Goldthorpe's classification aims at some objectivity, the Registrar-General relies much more on status. Status is elusive, but for analysing such overwhelmingly middle- and upper-class pursuits as university entry it is a useful category and is therefore included.

Table 19.4 University of Birmingham: BA and B.Sc. students, 1961–4 and 1971–4 (Goldthorpe classification)

	BA males, 1961–4	BA females, 1961–4	B.Sc. males, 1961–4	B.Sc. females, 1961–4	BA males, 1971–4	BA females, 1971–4	B.Sc. males, 1971–4	B.Sc. females, 1971–4
I, II	40.7	48.4	42.3	53.5	40.3	47.0	49.9	56.6
III, IV, V	30.2	27.9	29.2	24.4	28.2	26.9	26.2	24.2
VI, VII	29.1	23.7	28.5	22.1	34.5	26.1	23.9	19.2
No.	172	219	459	86	464	958	469	182

Source: Database

Table 19.5 University of Birmingham: BA and B.Sc. students, 1961–4 and 1971–4, (Registrar-General's 1971 classification)

	BA males, 1961–4	BA females, 1961–4	B.Sc. males, 1961–4	B.Sc. females, 1961–4	BA males, 1971–4	BA females, 1971–4	B.Sc. males, 1971–4	B.Sc. females, 1971–4
I	8.1	13.4	11.0	22.4	11.1	14.2	20.0	22.7
II	35.5	39.2	34.7	37.7	31.2	35.3	33.2	36.5
N	172	217	453	85	461	945	461	181

Source: Database

From these tables five conclusions can be drawn. The first is the difficulty of generalisation. There are differences between faculties, differences between the sexes within faculties, while separate figures (not published here) show that the Medical Faculty was different from the others. Secondly, Goldthorpe's classification permits a closer analysis of those coming from below the service classes, I and II in his system. His service classes are almost always outnumbered by the offspring of other social classes. However, a closer analysis reveals the absence of certain groups, in particular the petty bourgeoisie and the blue-collar elite. Birmingham was not unusual in this respect: a national survey conducted for the Robbins report came to similar conclusions. Other groups, including semi-skilled and skilled manual workers, made their contributions, usually about a quarter of the total. The third observation is that for the higher social classes, whether the Registrar-General's or Goldthorpe's, women consistently outnumbered men. Again, this was found by the Robbins survey for every major category of university, including Oxbridge and London.[23] The difference is particularly clear with Science during the 1960s, where the Registrar-General's Class I for women is twice the size of that for men; one recalls Professor Jeffreys's comments in 1946 on the weakness of female Science students. The wealthier parents could afford to send daughters to schools that provided an adequate Science education. Fourthly, the 1960s show a rise in the Registrar-General's Class I and a fall in his Class II. This took place across the board. In the Arts Faculty the rise does not meet statistical significance tests, but the social elevation of male science students is a remarkable conclusion to the popular view of the 1960s as a decade when traditional bonds were loosened.

Combining the Arts and Science faculties, during the 1960s the Registrar-General's Class I and II rose by two percentage points, the children of manual workers kept their proportion, and the middling groups fell. This ignores other faculties, especially Law and Medicine, so probably exaggerates the working-class presence. The student body of 1968 had a smaller working-class presence than at the start of the decade. In fact, it may have been the most select in the University's history. The process of elevation would continue. Why this should take place can only be hypothetical at this stage; the new universities of the 1960s must have had something to do with it, and the 1960s was also the decade when the Oxford men's colleges finally adopted a more formal meritocratic entry system for all applicants instead of only for those applying for scholarships. The traditional Oxbridge elite may have been pushed down.[24] And fifthly, it is clear that for a large proportion of parents the student grant on its own is unlikely to have been the single factor that propelled their children to university. As at present, when pressed the higher social classes could have afforded this without grants, if necessary. Fees, of course, would have been another matter.

During the course of the twentieth century the student bodies of the modern universities have tended to move away from their original position of geographical unity and very visible social diversity. The students of the University of Birmingham come from further afield, but on the whole are less diverse than their predecessors in Mason College. This does not mean that the social intake has widened; indeed, it may have narrowed. Visible social differences within universities have slowly declined, as they have declined within British society. However, students' memories as recorded for the project, most of them not going back much before the 1930s, do not recall Birmingham University as outstanding for its snobbery. The social mix of Chancellor's Hall, the one male hall of residence during the inter-war years, with grammar-school boys predominating, came as a considerable shock to a former Marlborough pupil in 1939.[25] It was an elitism of the grammar schools, and Birmingham's social mix reflected that of the grammar schools. As Grant Robertson pointed out, by the end of the 1920s the University would not take students without Highers, and it was difficult to obtain Highers anywhere else. The same stress on 'A' levels during the 1960s led the University to increase the proportion of the higher social classes. Social engineering was never seen as the task of the universities, either during the inter-war years or during the 1960s. The disruption of well-established teaching methods would have been too great. Nor, despite lip service by some and passionate advocacy by a few, was it strongly felt by the generation of 1968. It was a task for the schools.

Birmingham's students: the two half-centuries

'The sons and daughters of elementary school teachers are knocking on the doors of the universities clamouring for admittance', wrote Charles Masterman, a perceptive observer, in 1911 in his book *The Condition of England*. Interestingly, he made the comment in a chapter on suburban life. 'The process is only in its beginning; every year the standard improves.'[26] He was right, but the process took much longer than he anticipated. For the next half-century the suburbs grew much more than the universities and it was not until the 1950s that the suburban dwellers, increasingly the children of professional parents, began to go to university on a large scale. When they did so, their parents usually ensured that this was in a different town.

Accordingly, it was not until the 1950s that the characteristics of Birmingham's student body changed decisively. Until then most of its students had come from the West Midlands and finance even for these had been problematic. Until the1940s suitable employment after graduation could by no means be taken for granted. During the1950s grants became universal and more generous while catchment areas widened. The students in the redbricks, preponderantly grammar-school pupils and more affluent than ever before, had more confidence. Birmingham's students remained clearly different from those of Oxford or Cambridge – during the 1960s the preponderance of parents came from the Registrar-General's Social Class II, defined as 'minor professional' – but their hopes of rising to Social Class I were not unrealistic and by the 1970s an increasing proportion of students were from Social Class I. Grant Robertson's description of 1928, quoted at the end of Chapter 13, still retained some relevance. There were no silver spoons. The students from Oxford and Cambridge usually sought and obtained the more prestigious jobs. Ambitions at Birmingham were set lower: during the 1970s it was not, for instance, taken for granted that an application for the Civil Service would be for the administrative grade. The world that Grant Robertson knew had changed, if not beyond all recognition, at any rate very substantially. But it was a gradual change, and many of the roots remained.

In February 1940, five months into the war but before the fall of France, the Council of Birmingham's Guild of Undergraduates dismissed a motion that the wearing of gowns at Council meetings might be optional. Wearing gowns at such meetings 'was a custom of long standing ... it was a privilege which distinguished members of the University from students at the Technical College; the gown was a symbol of learning and authority and might tend to produce some sense of dignity and authority at Council meetings'.[27] In May 1945, less than a fortnight after VE day, Guild Council resolved to 'encourage the wearing of academic dress throughout the University'.[28] As late as 1950 a survey, conducted by the Guild, reported that students were generally in favour of academic dress, but often could not obtain it because of rationing.[29] As the students understood, gowns were symbolic. Gowns were never abolished. They symbolised the old order, and they faded away.

Notes

1 Alison Gaukroger and Leonard Schwarz, 'A university and its region: student recruitment to Birmingham 1945–75', *Oxford Review of Education*, 23 (1997), pp. 185–202.

2 *Report to Council, 1922–23.*

3 Ibid., *1929–30.*

4 Ibid., *1936–37* (probably written Jan. 1938).

5 *Education in 1935* (Cmd. 5290, 1936), Table 48. It would be wise to use this figure as only indicative until more research has been done on the categories employed in the government tables.

6 Kaelble, *Social Mobility in the Nineteenth and Twentieth Centuries: Europe and America in Comparative Perspective* (Leamington Spa, 1985), p. 72. These are based on the Glass survey which did not include a large sample of university graduates for the early 1920s. However, the conclusions, if not the precise figures, have been accepted by Harold Perkin, *The Rise of Professional Society: England since 1980* (1989), p. 247. Perkin ignores Scotland.

7 Carol Dyhouse, 'Signing the pledge? Women's investment in university education and teacher training before 1939?', *History of Education*, 26 (1997), pp. 207–23.

8 Interviews with Dr. Fred Williams and Dr. Peter Nettley.

9 UC J. J. Milne, *Letter Book*: Henman. Milne to Headmistress of Milton Mount School Crawley, Sussex 22 Oct. 1937. £130 is identical to Whiteley's authoritative survey of student scholarships and needs of 1933, which applied to Arts and Sciences: Whiteley, *Poor Student*, p. 60.

10 G. S. M. Ellis, *The Poor Student and the University* (1925), p. 36; Whiteley, *Poor Student*, pp. 49–51.

11 Gaukroger and Schwarz, 'A university and its region', p. 189; R. A. Lowe, *Education in the Post–War Years. A Social History* (1988), pp. 153–4, Sir C. Anderson, *Grants to Students* (London, HMSO, 1960, Cmnd. 1051) paras. 10–11, Political and Economic Planning (PEP), *The University Student, Selection and Awards* (1949), p. 6.

12 City of Birmingham Education Committee: *Secondary Education Minute Books* 12 Jan. 1955, p. 56.

13 Sir J. Mountford, *How They Fared: A Survey of a Three–Year Student Entry* (Liverpool, Liverpool University Press, 1956), p. 20.

14 M. Savage, 'The missing link? The relationship between spatial mobility and social mobility', *British Journal of Sociology*, 39 (1988), pp. 554–77 is a rare example.

15 Gaukroger and Schwarz, 'A university and its region', p.194.

16 For the lack of importance of university training in the 1930s see, for instance, A. M. Carr–Saunders and P. A. Wilson, *The Professions* (Oxford, 1933), pp. 365n, 378.

17 R. K. Kelsall, 'Self–recruitment in four professions', in D. V. Glass, ed., *Social Mobility in Britain* (1954), pp. 308–20 summarises the published work at the time of writing.

18 Ibid., p. 312. Kelsall's evidence suggests that teachers tended to regard medicine as a step up the ladder; lawyers did not, though they may have preferred medicine to teaching.

19 Medically related professions such as pharmaceutical chemists (one of them being the father of the novelist Francis Brett Young) have been included in this definition. At Birmingham women averaged 15% of the total numbers, male and female, that gave parental occupation between 1925 and 1934, a relatively consistent 25% between 1935 and 1959, and 33% between 1960 and 1974.

20 A. Digby, *The Evolution of British General Practice, 1850–1948* (Oxford, 1999), pp. 40–2.

21 This is similar to the figure for 'other universities' (i.e. not Oxbridge, London, Wales or Scotland) that Kelsall's survey found for the 1955–6 cohort: R. K. Kelsall, *Applications for Admission to Universities* (Association of the Universities of the British Commonwealth, 1957).

22 For instance, Perkin, *Rise of Professional Society*, chs. 8–10.

23 *Robbins Report*, App. 2B, pp. 4, 72, 92, 429.

24 This is discussed a little more fully in Gaukroger and Schwarz, 'A university and its region', pp. 197–8.

25 Interview with Mr Fred Williams.

26 C. F. G. Masterman, *The Condition of England* (1911 edn), p. 76. I would like to thank Carol Dyhouse for this reference.

27 UC Guild Minutes 12 Feb. 1940.

28 Ibid., 14 May 1945.

29 Ibid., 23 Oct. 1950.

Chapter Twenty

The Grimond Report

THE UNIVERSITY REGISTRAR ended his account of the sit-in on a hopeful note: 'At the end of 1968 the "happy academic climate" mentioned in the *Student Role* seemed a little less remote than it had done a month earlier.'[1] After what had happened it might, indeed, be expected that the new year would see a better understanding between students and the university authorities, and the report which Ray Phillips, the president of the Guild, wrote for Council was indeed remarkably emollient. It made no reference to the sit-in but stressed the value of discussion, saying particularly that 'the discussions surrounding the "Student Role" have shown the concern which students are now showing in the quality of the University community'.[2]

This positive attitude was, however, not reciprocated. The vice-chancellor's 1968 report devoted only 250 somewhat tendentious words to the sit-in, attributing it to 'the unrest which appears to be world-wide among students', and early in February the registrar's corroborating version of the sit-in was given general circulation.[3] Even more indicative was the remarkable foreword which the vice-chancellor contributed to the first *Bulletin* of the new year in which he wrote that the previous autumn would be remembered for:

> its student troubles which culminated in the occupation of the Aston Webb building for a week towards the end of term. You may be a little surprised therefore that this edition has nothing to say directly on student problems except for an article on Students' Maintenance Grants. To my mind it is refreshing and timely for us to be reminded that there are many other matters of vital importance to the University which require our attention.[4]

He also went on to reaffirm that the Council decision of 27 November 'provides an admirable basis on which to evolve a better relation with our students'. Clearly, as far as Robert Hunter was concerned, little had changed and little had been learned.

Where there had been evident progress was at department, faculty and Senate level. Before the sit-in, staff–student committees were being introduced generally in departments, and in October 1968 the faculty of Commerce had come up with the notion of reserved areas. A year later it admitted student observers to the faculty board.[5] As we have seen, the first meeting between the Senate and the students following the settlement of the sit-in took place on 12 December and a joint recommendation was ready for Senate by 16 January, proposing a working party to consider how to proceed on constitutional change.[6] However, once again the stumbling block was the Council. It was constitutionally correct, if somewhat insensitive, for Council to decide at its meeting later in the month that it would not anticipate Senate's reaction to the working party report, but when the Senate did confirm its committee's recommendation the Council then rejected it. Instead, on Hunter's advice, it set up subcommittees of Council! The promised official 'teach-in' or university symposium was held over the weekend of 15–16 March. Entitled 'The Universities Today and Tomorrow', it was well organised, with strong speakers, but what also came through clearly from staff and students alike was resentment at the vice-chancellor's rejection of the Senate's proposal. When the Senate reaffirmed its support for a working party the Council did concede the idea and called for the submission of evidence, but it also announced that the first meeting would not take place until October.

Student unhappiness with Council rumbled on through the summer. Eventually, instead of the 50% presence in discussions which they had been seeking, the composition of the working party allowed for four undergraduates and two postgraduates in a total of twenty-one, plus the vice-chancellor in the chair.[7] What, in student eyes made matters worse was that the first meeting was told it was a subcommittee of Council and so bound by Council procedure and there was no sign either of any feeling of urgency.[8] The gap in understanding was clearly as wide as ever. In his report for 1969 Robert Hunter wrote that 'the policy for student participation laid down in the Council's statement of November 1968 has been fully implemented. In addition, at Faculty and Departmental level, various arrangements have been made to extend the student contribution to University government.'[9] The pro-chancellor had, in fact, adopted a deliberate policy of attrition. Convinced by the assessment that the sit-in had been caused by dangerous radicals, he was determined that when the review body was finally set up, it would be have a brief and membership which would block them. In 1992 Lord Hunter remembered that

> George Farmer in particular wanted to take his time so although the temperature was high to start with over the monthly meetings ... Sir George Farmer [who] was a very implacable man just sat there and pushed slowly on and on until we had reached the stage where we could agree on having a degree body and terms of reference we can agree on. ... George Farmer

> was jolly good at letting them exhaust themselves or if they were very good, letting them succeed. So he had Grimond, having got them tuned in to us and all sections of the university [approved] but of course it was really us who suggested that.[10]

Whether the students were as naïve as this recollection suggests is doubtful. The president of the Guild, now M. D. A. Terry, went as far as refusing to contribute the customary Guild section to the vice-chancellor's annual report. Instead he insisted on it being presented separately:

> After the political action of last year, the Guild has found it increasingly difficult to influence decision making. It is quite clear that the University has not accepted the real meaning behind 'the Occupation'. Student representation has meant that students have been made aware of situations and decisions but the process of democratising the University has not really begun.[11]

Given such feeling, one may wonder why direct action did not become a serious danger once again. Part of the explanation is that students were in the old quandary between half a loaf and no bread. Thus the Guild formally rejected an invitation by Senate, meeting on 10 December 1969, to send two students per faculty plus two from the Guild to join the non-professorial observers on Senate.[12] Its sticking point, as during the sit-in, was the condition that observers had to accept exclusion from 'reserved' business. In the event, however, four of the fourteen observers did begin to attend, representing the faculties of Science and Engineering, and Law.[13] At the same December meeting the Senate requested the Court of Governors at its annual meeting in February to change the University ordinances so as to make it possible for students to be given voting rights, not merely to be observers. In halls of residence, too, changes made in 1969 had given students a direct input on day-to-day decisions and full representation on the Senate/Council Halls of Residence Committee.[14]

A more important reason for non-militancy on the 'student participation' issue was that it was old hat, yesterday's priority. Racism was now at the top of the student agenda. In the words of the president, the decision of the Guild to support the 'Stop the Seventy Tour Campaign' 'enabled many students to protest against the existence in Britain of teams chosen on racist grounds'.[15] If anything, however, the University of Birmingham was even more vulnerable on racism than it had been on student representation.

At the start of the decade the University had backed the development in the then Southern Rhodesia of a Medical School and teaching hospital based in Salisbury (Harare) as part of the University College of Rhodesia and Nyasaland. It was an initiative of which Birmingham was rightly proud. Robert Aitken had written in 1962:

> There is courage and high purpose in the whole enterprise, undertaken against the present background of political uncertainty. To be an international pioneer in the second half of the twentieth century may prove to be as big an adventure as to be the explorer in the nineteenth or a colonist in the earlier half of the twentieth. We have put our hands to this plough.[16]

The new School was affiliated to the University and several key appointees came from Edgbaston. There was also a regular relay of Birmingham staff to assist the new venture. Unfortunately, just as the foundation stone was laid in April 1963, 'political uncertainty' came to a climax in the break-up of the Central African Federation, and in November 1965 Ian Smith unilaterally declared Southern Rhodesia independent.[17]

The University's response was to try to ignore politics as far as possible and to maintain support for the multiracial Medical School which the region needed.[18] By 1968, 43% of the male students in the School were non-Europeans although only 28% of the women.[19] The British government argued similarly and made the School an exception to its policy of economic sanctions. Funding was still forthcoming, including support for examiners' visits from Birmingham; there was some student exchange also. To the vice-chancellor and the senior members of the Birmingham Medical School all this appeared as a refusal to be diverted by politics from meeting Central Africa's desperate need for doctors. However, the view was gaining ground among students, particularly medical students, and among committed anti-racists more generally, that these good intentions only played into the hands of a white supremacist regime. Agitation on campus began in 1969.[20] There was a brief and low-key sit-in in the spring of 1970 and in April the Council, on the advice of Senate, decided to phase out the arrangement with Salisbury. To its shame, Senate did not propose the alternative of bringing African students to study at Birmingham, though in June the vice-chancellor did visit Rhodesia to reassure existing students that they would be able to complete their training.[21]

While these immediate concerns hit the headlines, the issue of constitutional reform continued at a snail's pace. This was in part because the vice-chancellor and the Council did not give it the urgent priority the students had wanted but also because the outcome would be a remodelled university and revised charter which had to last. The students' 'quick fix' to produce a more democratic university had simply not been realistic. This was certainly recognised by the Education Committee which the Guild had set up following the sit-in and which by 1970 was grappling with issues such as the binary system, academic freedom and comprehensive education.[22]

It is also clear that while the non-professorial staff wanted some change, it , too, was both cautious and traditional. A survey conducted by the Non-Professorial Executive in the summer of 1970 showed that while only 8% approved of the status quo, only 3% wanted radical change.[23] Half of those responding voted for modest modifications, that is, an overhaul of existing procedures to produce greater flexibility and efficiency. Among the scientists, 65% held this view. The option of major structural reform and a review of learning and research to meet the changed needs of community, individual and disciplines was supported by only 30% of respondents, with Commerce and Social Science well represented.

The lack of staff support for radicalism was even more evident in what became known as 'the Atkinson Affair'.[24] Dick Atkinson, notorious for his part in the sit-in, had been on a temporary contract which expired in September 1969. He moved on to a similar post at Manchester but applied to Birmingham again when permanent positions in sociology were advertised in the spring of 1970. The appointing board in the Commerce Faculty was split over his candidature 5–4 and when the minority (mostly non-sociologists) would not accede to a recommendation to appoint (a most uncommon course), the decision was not sent back to the faculty but passed to the Academic Appointments Committee (AAC). As we have seen, Aitken had set up this committee to take the minutiae of terms and conditions of appointment out of faculty and senate agendas. Called on to decide on Atkinson, the AAC unanimously declined to appoint him and the post was left vacant. Both the reference to the Committee and the rejection were unprecedented and a furore ensued. Accusations flew that professional judgement had been set aside in favour of non-academic considerations. The faculty of Commerce and Social Science was in turmoil. Cries of 'academic freedom' led to angry meetings and the formation of a Council for Academic Freedom and Democracy and an appeal to the University Council. Tempers were not improved by Atkinson being invited to teach 'unofficially' during the session 1970–1. In June 1971 more posts were advertised in sociology and Atkinson applied yet again. This time his application was rejected by the appointing board in standard fashion but even so, Council received a second complaint alleging further impropriety. These formal complaints rumbled on to 1973, but despite them and some continuing vociferous protest, a majority of staff did not rally to Atkinson's support and his rejection stood. There is, however, an ironic coda. At the time an enquiry by the Council for Academic Freedom and Democracy accepted that the AAC had authority to act as it did by virtue of powers delegated from the Finance and Policy Committee of Council. In fact, that understanding may have been incorrect, so making the Committee's action *ultra vires*. In the first place, the constitutional right to refuse a faculty recommendation probably belonged to the full Senate and not to a committee set up to exercise one of its routine functions. Secondly, if the AAC was acting on authority delegated from a Council committee, what of the obligation on Council to act on appointments only after taking advice from Senate?

It was in the second half of 1970 that constitutional review moved from being a proposition to become a reality. Following the report of the vice-chancellor's working party the Council agreed to appoint a review body 'to consider the role, constitution and functioning of the University of Birmingham and to make recommendations to Council for any desirable changes'.[25] The person chosen to lead this was Jo Grimond, an immensely respected Liberal politician with considerable experience as a lay university officer. There were seven members representing various sections of the university plus a current science undergraduate. There were also three outsiders besides Grimond: Sir Peter Venables, the former vice-chancellor of the University of Aston, Professor Dorothy Hodgkin, the Nobel prize-winner and Sir Maurice Dean, a former permanent secretary in the Civil Service, who agreed to act as secretary. The Council had taken a long time making up its mind, but in the end no one could deny the weight of the team it had recruited.

Grimond's first step was to address a university open meeting on 20 January 1971 and this was followed by an invitation to submit evidence.[26] Thirty bodies did so, ranging from the Senate to the National and Local Government Officers' Association (NALGO), and there were forty-three individual submissions.[27] Oral evidence was taken, sometimes more than once, from sixteen groups and twenty-two individuals, including Dick Atkinson. In January 1972 the Review Body published an interim Consultative Document which elicited eighty further comments, forty-four of them from individuals. If the authority of the Review Body was beyond dispute, so too was the care it had taken to canvass opinion. The same can be said of its thoroughness. At one extreme it considered the fundamental issues which students had raised during the sit-in about the nature of higher education and at the other it went into detail about every level of university organisation. In all it made 240 recommendations.

After thirty years the comments of the Review Body on the big educational issues, the role of the university, the binary system, broader education and examinations still read judiciously and persuasively, but with an undoubted element of 'motherhood and apple pie'. On student participation, the original cause of 1968 protest, the working party did little more than endorse the practices which had grown up since the 'sit-in'.[28] There should not be a standard quota of student representatives on every committee; the recommended ratio varied from one in ten to one in four. A reserved business restriction was endorsed in line with a Privy Council directive and it was recommended that observer status should be ended.[29] Representatives should not be mandated but 'participate in the common interest of the whole University'.[30] By contrast, the section on teaching standards was positive and challenging. Teaching in the University had to be improved and the nineteen recommendations included taking teaching ability into account in making appointments and promotions, providing proper teaching training for academic staff, monitoring their teaching performance and taking note of student responses. On the matter of promotions and appointments the working party proposed that departments should be given an indirect voice in the election of professors and heads of department, that promotion to senior lecturership should be by application, and that initial appointments, salaries and probation should be both regularised and made more 'humane'.[31]

However, the undoubted heart of the Review was its constitutional sections. It rejected the argument for organising the University on a system of schools and argued that the basic unit of the University had to remain the department.[32] It was, Jo Grimond told the Council, 'the foundation of the University'.[33] He and his colleagues strongly endorsed the faculty as 'an integral part' of the university structure and 'a very important element in the participation of staff and students'.[34] They were, nevertheless, radical on the actual faculty pattern which Birmingham needed for the 1970s and beyond:

> The main criterion for a Faculty is that it should assemble related disciplines and Departments and so encourage cross-fertilisation. A Faculty should not be confined to a single discipline as this criterion would not then be met. Within a Faculty, individual disciplines have to justify their proposals before other disciplines and ... an informed critique of one discipline can be offered by other disciplines. A Faculty should not be so large as to debar effective participation by staff and students, or to make it virtually impossible for the Dean to be conversant with all that affects good government.[35]

On that basis the working party recommended splitting the faculty of Science and Engineering into four: life sciences, physical sciences, applied science and environmental science.[36] Grimond and his colleagues knew that this was very much against opinion in the existing faculty, but said bluntly that they were not convinced by the objections put forward which had not replied 'adequately' to the case they had made.[37] That their rebuke had substance is certainly suggested by the decision of the faculty in 1984 to divide into science and engineering. For the Arts, growth would make change necessary by 1980 when it should split into a faculty of Modern Languages and Literature and a faculty of Arts.[38] Law, on the other hand, failed to persuade the working party of the merits of its independence and the recommendation was that it and Commerce and Social Studies should combine in a new faculty of Law and Social Studies.[39]

Though the recommendation was that departments and faculties in this revised pattern must remain, the working party envisaged a major shift in the power structure. Heads of department would not necessarily be professors and would no longer be appointed until retirement, but would serve fixed terms and work with an elected departmental committee which included student representatives.[40] As for the faculty board, it should continue to include all relevant professors but they should make up only 50% of the total membership. The other half would be split

2:1 between non-professors and students. Reference to the arithmetic under the existing system demonstrates how radical the proposal was.[41]

Radicalism was equally evident in the changes recommended to the upper layers of the University: the Court of Governors, the University Council and the Senate. The Review Body proposed that the Council should take over from the governors as the supreme legal authority, leaving 'the Court' as a body that focused public interest on the University.[42] The Council, however, should not remain as existing and nor should the Senate. Grimond and his team recognised, first, that the old distinction between organisation and finance (the role of the Council) and academic matters (the sphere of the Senate) was no longer realistic, and, second, that with nearly 200 members the Senate was already too large to act as the charter had intended.[43] They therefore proposed a unicameral system with a single governing body of fifty members, both lay and academic, which was 'supreme in both academic and non-academic matters'.[44] In contrast with the existing Council, academics would be the largest group (twenty-three) and would have a majority over the lay members (nineteen), with the students having eight places. This new Council would be the executive in all matters and would work through two committees, Finance and General Purposes and an Academic Executive, with Principals and Deans becoming 'the Vice-Chancellor's Advisory Committee' with special responsibility to advise on the allocation of resources.[45] As for the Senate, the proposal was that it should become deliberative only. It would be reduced in size (152) and made up of members ex officio and elected representatives of professors, non-professors and students, but it would have no executive functions and would serve as a forum to consider broad policy. When this suggestion was first made in the earlier consultative document it had significant support, but the existing Senate objected strongly, arguing that it should have an increased executive status.[46] The final report did withdraw the even more radical idea that instead of a deliberative Senate there could be a larger academic assembly made up of all professors and 20% of the rest of the academic staff by election. However, Grimond and his colleagues stuck to their assessment that it was impossible for a large Senate to have *de facto* control of academic matters and that given the way higher education was developing, academic quality and cost-effectiveness had to go together.[47]

Given the passage of three decades, it is possible now to see that the Review Body identified many of the issues of fundamental importance to the University which were to emerge subsequently, and that in many ways accepting its suggestions would have made later more draconian courses unnecessary. At the time, however, the report appeared very radical. Council sent it for consideration to Senate, to the Guild of Graduates and to the Guild of Undergraduates with a view to having some, possibly interim, proposals to put to the Court of Governors at its meeting in February 1973.[48] In fact, a full response was ready in time and on Thursday 22 February the Court of Governors did vote to transfer the ultimate legal authority in the University to the Council as the Review Body had suggested, thus moving to make legality congruent with reality.[49] However, although the Council had told Grimond that because he and his colleagues had produced an agreed report with no dissenters this 'will carry much weight', it proceeded in February 1973 to recommend that all the other significant proposals affecting the Council, the Senate and the faculty structure should be turned down, and they were.[50] Since the Review Body itself had made it clear that it was recommending against entrenched interests, it is hardly unreasonable to ask what else could be expected when those interests were consulted, and said 'no'. The proposal for a unicameral government under a Council with an academic majority and a deliberative Senate was rejected entirely. Instead, the outmoded distinction between organisation and finance and academic matters was reinforced by enhancing the Senate's specific executive authority in academic matters. The number of laymen on the Council was reduced from twenty-eight to twenty-three, but instead of co-option, which had been recommended, the rights of the City Council, the Court and the Guild of Graduates to nominate were preserved. The academics were increased but only from fifteen to seventeen, that is, by 13%. As for faculties, the Council proposed that it secure a charter revision so that in future changes in faculties could be made by ordinance rather than statute, which effectively shelved the Grimond Committee proposal to split up the faculty of Science and Engineering and to merge Law and Social Studies.[51] The Court did agree in February 1974 to petition for the change in the charter which was to alter the constitution, membership and powers of the Court, the Council and the Senate and this eventually came into operation on 15 November 1975.[52] However, the only faculty change which resulted was the coming out of Education from underneath the Arts umbrella.[53] With so little accepted and so much rejected, one wonders what value the Council imagined that it had got from the £15,000 it had budgeted for the review.[54]

Not all the advice in the Grimond Report was treated in such a cavalier fashion. The recommendation for the constitution of faculty boards was approved and made standard throughout the University early in 1973.[55] A year later it was also agreed to put in place the Grimond recommendations on headships of department and on departmental committees.[56] The working party recommendations for two staffing committees were also actioned.[57] However, the approach to the Grimond Report was essentially eclectic. The proposals for the size and structure of membership for the Senate were adopted. However, to apply the figures suggested for a deliberative Senate (150) to a Senate with increased academic responsibilities was to ignore entirely the judgement of the report that an executive body of that size could not operate effectively. A similar transposition was effected with the Academic Executive, one of the two key committees that Grimond proposed. Instead of being set up to drive academic policy on behalf of the Council, it was introduced in November 1973 as a replacement for the old Senate Executive.

That had been a steering committee, but the new Executive was a body with delegated powers to take decisions on a lengthy schedule of routine academic matters.[58] The other main committee, Finance and General Purposes, continued 'virtually as before'.[59]

It is easy to be cynical about the 1971–2 Review Body and conclude that it was forced upon an unwilling university hierarchy which took care to see that very little changed as a result. The old interest groups survived. It is certainly true that the major restructuring which the Review Body designed was never seriously evaluated. It was, it can be argued, an opportunity missed. Configured in the way Grimond recommended, the University might have been better prepared for the changes which economic pressures were even then making imperative. Moving to a Senate which was consultative only would have taken out a whole layer of administration, while a shift to eight or nine smaller faculties would have provided a ready matrix for the introduction of delegated budgets. A Vice-Chancellor's Advisory Committee serving a unicameral system responsible both for finance and academic development would have been a Strategy, Planning and Resources Committee a decade and more early than it in fact was created.

On the other hand, while coherent change was not achieved, significant reforms were. Among these the enfranchisement of students rightly received the most publicity. It exemplified a fundamental shift which had taken place in the importance of and attitudes towards undergraduates and postgraduates within the university community. The effect of the change, however, remained symbolic rather than practical. Students were now consulted and had a platform to exercise influence. However, they tended to be involved only on particular issues; comparatively few were interested in making routine contributions. A reform which was much more important was the final breaking of the professorial monopoly. This was not very significant at Senate level. The ending of a guaranteed seat for every professor meant little when Senate was too large to be effective. However, it was quite different in the departments. Professors of the old school might complain that opening the university structure to non-professors only diverted staff from teaching and research into administration and politics. On the other hand, for many non-professors, the change meant empowerment and the opportunity to contribute ideas and initiatives in a new way. Indeed, it was long overdue, given the way in which, in a growing institution, initiative was increasingly coming from below. Promotion too became an issue more of open competition and less of patronage. Careers seemed more a matter of personal responsibility. The Review Body also contributed significantly to a value shift in staff thinking. Quality in teaching ceased to be a matter of personal pride and commitment and began to be seen as something to be expected. None of these changes had the glamour of a grand new constitution, but their importance cannot be gainsaid.

Notes

1 Lewis, p. 14.
2 UC 7/iii 1968, p. 31.
3 Ibid., p. 2; *Bulletin* 100 (3 Feb. 1969).
4 *Bulletin* 99 (13 Jan. 1969).
5 Ibid.,112 (2 Feb. 1970); UC 7/iii 1970, p. 12.
6 For the following see Guild Executive Account, 21 Oct. 1969: UC 4/v/6 in J.
7 *Bulletin* 108 (20 Oct. 1969).
8 See n. 6.
9 UC 7/iii 1969, pp. 5–6.
10 UC Oral History: comment by Lord Hunter.
11 UC 7/iii 1969, p. 31.
12 *Bulletin* 112 (2 Feb. 1970).
13 Ibid., 113 (23 Feb. 1979).
14 UC 7/iii 1969, p. 5.
15 Ibid., p. 31.
16 Ibid., 1962, p. 6.
17 Ibid., 1963, p. 18.
18 Ibid., 1965, p. 18; 1966, p. 15; 1967, p. 19.
19 Ibid., 1968, p. 17.
20 Ibid., 1969, p. 31.
21 UC 4/v/6 in J; UC 7/iii 1970, pp. 9, 17; 7/ii *Council* 1970, p. 25.
22 UC 7/iii 1968, p. 30; 1970, p. 17; 1971, p. 16.
23 *Bulletin* 117 (8 June 1970).
24 The principal file on this episode remains closed. The following is based on *The Report of the Committee of Enquiry, Council for Academic Freedom and Democracy* (1971): UC 19/v/7.
25 UC 7/ii *Council* 1970, p. 20.
26 *Bulletin* 123 (18 Jan. 1971); for Grimond's account of the process of the review see UC 7/ii *Council* 1972, pp. 33–5.
27 For the following see *Consultative Document prepared by the Review Body appointed by the Council of the University of Birmingham* (Birmingham, January 1972) (hereafter *Consultative Document*) and *Report of the Review Body appointed by the Council of the University of Birmingham* (Birmingham, September 1972) (hereafter *Report*). Subsequent references are to sections and paragraphs.
28 *Report*, 12, 13.
29 The Court of Governors had set up a less generous protocol for reserved areas in February 1972: *Bulletin*, 147, 28 Feb. 1972.
30 *Report*, 12.2.
31 E.g., probationary appointments should be reviewed in time for appointees to improve performance before the end of the contract.
32 *Report*, 8.2–4; 9.66–71.
33 UC 7/ii *Council* 1972, p. 33.
34 *Report*, 9.2.

35 Ibid., 9.6.
36 Ibid., 9.24–30.
37 Ibid., 9.23.
38 Growth would eventually forced Medicine and Dentistry to reconsider its structure: ibid., 9.34, 9.47.
39 Ibid., 9.39–40. Education was to remain with Arts until ready for independent faculty status: 9.43–6.
40 Ibid., 8.6–39.
41 See above, pp. 356–7.
42 *Report*, 10.
43 Ibid., 11.2.
44 Ibid., 11.25.
45 Ibid., 11.34–41.
46 *Consultative Document*, 11.6–8, 18–19.
47 *Report*, 11.21.
48 UC 7/ii *Council* 1972, p. 23; *Bulletin* 158 (2 Oct. 1972).
49 *Bulletin* 174 (26 Feb. 1972).
50 *Bulletin* 158 (2 Oct. 1972). For the following see ibid., 171 (5 Feb. 1973) and ibid., 174 (26 Feb. 1973).
51 This was expressly pointed out in *Bulletin* 174 (26 Feb. 1973); cf. also UC 7/iii 1973, pp. 3–4.
52 UC 7/iii 1974, p. 21; 1976, p. 15; *Bulletin* 202 (11 Feb. 1974).
53 Oct. 1976: UC 7/iii 1977, p. 17.
54 UC 7/ii *Accounts* 1971, p. 41; 1972, p. 47.
55 *Bulletin* 174 (26 Feb. 1973).
56 *Bulletin* 202 (11 Feb. 1974).
57 UC 7/ii *Council* 1973, pp. 23–4.
58 *Bulletin* 192 (5 Nov. 1973). The Executive had no role in policy.
59 UC 7/ii *Council* 1973, p. 23.

Chapter Twenty-one

The 1970s

IT MAY HAVE BEEN insensitive of Robert Hunter to greet the year 1969 with the remark that there were matters of vital importance to deal with other than student participation. It was, nevertheless, perfectly true. The most immediate was that 1969–70 would be the mid-year of the new quinquennium when the UGC visitation would take place and plans and aspirations begin to be put in place for the years 1972–7. The principal question was once again expansion. In preparation for the main visit several UGC subcommittees came on fact-finding visits.[1] In the summer of 1969 the UGC undertook a survey over the university system to determine whether spare capacity would be left when the current building phase ended in 1973–4. Birmingham, which in November 1969 had 6583 full-time students, replied that, with appropriate financial support, it could take 8500.[2]

Further discussion with the UGC in 1970 raised this to 9500 which, although 37% above the existing target for the end of the quinquennium (1971–2) could, it was agreed be supported by the library and most of the other facilities on campus.[3] There were, however, significant qualifications. In the first place that figure assumed that all the existing 5200 science places could be filled, although nationally there was a shortage of science applicants. What was more, a fair number of Birmingham's vacancies were in unpopular areas or in disciplines where candidates of sufficient quality were few. Growth in science, the UGC was told, would have to be governed by the need to maintain standards. It was a problem which would recur. With Arts students the issue was different. It would be possible to recruit 4300 of the right quality but the UGC agreed with the University that the number which could be accommodated in existing buildings was only 3750, so that achieving the Arts contribution to the figure of 9500 would require some new construction work. A new building would also be necessary for the physical education department. However, £200,000 of the total cost for the latter of £325,000 was reckoned as recreational and so not fundable by the UGC, while the capital required for Arts was only £170,000, so that the only really significant requirement for public capital in the next quinquennium was for medicine, which was funded separately and pencilled in at £1,754,000.[4]

That Birmingham could face the new quinquennium relatively favourably placed for teaching and research space was a consequence of the heavy investment of the previous five years.[5] Between 1968 and 1972 nine major buildings had been completed on campus at a cost of £4,411,000 plus a further £1,371,000 in connection with the Medical School and the hospitals. Virtually all of this came from the UGC apart from £266,000 from outside funds and £159,000 which was borrowed. Borrowing money to help finance academic innovation was an interesting development, and further borrowing was planned for the new quinquennium to fund the second stage of engineering production and to make a breakthrough in the important new area of post-experience work. Where expansion would produce difficulties was in student accommodation. Additional students in such numbers, 90% of whom would not be living at home, would mean finding 2700 extra beds. Finding lodgings for such a number was out of the question – the local economy was flourishing. As for the University's own stock, in 1970 Chancellor's Hall had to be closed as uneconomic, and although land was acquired to build at Maple Bank, adjoining the Vale site, funding was the major problem.[6]

Between 1968 and 1972 the UGC had provided £1,287,000 for student accommodation but a new policy had been announced which would radically alter what could be provided in future. Any further public grants for accommodation would be restricted to not more than £250 a residential place, leaving universities to borrow the rest on the money market. But if universities would have to finance residential building commercially they could be forced into providing property which building societies were prepared to accept as security, that is, flats on sites which were not integral to the campus and could thus be resold. This would call into question a cornerstone of Birmingham's residence policy, that it should provide halls which would offer the traditional style of collegiate living which people like Priestley had set such store by.

Birmingham had, of course, already committed itself to a self-catering experiment at Griffin Close, the first phase of which opened in October 1970 and, with phases two and three, would produce some 1150 places by October 1972, including some provision for postgraduates with families.[7] However, the University abandoned collegiality with reluctance. A hybrid possibility was put forward for Maple Bank: a hall of residence with a senior common room and central dining and common rooms but with the students accommodated in five-bedroom units. The scheme proved to be uneconomic and in 1971 the Council accepted the inevitable and switched to adding self-catering units on other existing sites.[8] Even these, however, became increasingly problematic as inflation pushed up the cost of borrowing. Rising costs also created revenue deficits – a £5795 surplus in 1970 became a £46,884 loss in 1971 – and despite an increase in fees, there was still a shortfall of £11,333 in 1972.[9] Very soon, too, the UGC issued instructions that universities must not subsidise student residence from public funds. And student demand went on increasing. In October 1973 there was a lodgings crisis with 100 students having to spend varying periods in temporary accommodation.[10] To make matters worse, in December 1973 the government imposed a moratorium on university residential building with the result that it was only in the second half of 1974 that work could at last begin to put flats on Maple Bank.[11] Further building followed, for example at the Triangle and the Tennis Court and in January 1979 the University began leasing Council flats.[12] Nevertheless, attempting to provide accommodation for a continually growing student population was a labour of Sisyphus. In 1964 Aitken stated that the aim was to provide residential accommodation for four-sevenths of all students.[13] In the twenty years from 1961–2 the University multiplied its residential stock eight times, but in 1980/1 there were one and a quarter as many students needing private accommodation as two decades earlier. The number in university housing was not four, but three in seven.

Discussions between the University of Birmingham and the UGC over-expansion did, of course, beg one central question. Would money be available to pay for it? Hunter was by no means convinced. He later recalled that the immediate situation in 1968–9 was not so bad, but 'there was every indication that it was going to get worse'.[14] It is unlikely, however, that even the most pessimistic of vice-chancellors could have anticipated how bad things would get or that the fifty-year-old mechanism of university support from public funds would collapse.[15]

As the first post-Robbins quinquennium approached in July 1967, the officers of the UGC had good reason to be satisfied with the national expansion of higher education thus far. Individual universities regularly grumbled that they never received as much as they needed, but overall it was demonstrable that Robbins had not been implemented on the cheap. [16] Improvements in the system had also been made. In 1966 it had proved possible to assist university planning by giving advanced warning of the size of grant for the first year of the quinquennium. The problem that funding for scientific research rarely covered infrastructure costs had been resolved by formalising the system of dual support, and a regular block grant was introduced to cover furniture and equipment.[17] Expenditure per student continued to rise. Even the problem of inflation, which had so exercised Robert Aitken, had been kept under control by making periodic additions to the quinquennial allocations. In 1967–8 'the picture on the surface could hardly have seemed happier'.[18]

Beneath the surface it was different. Despite supplementation, universities still lost. For example, Hunter calculated that over the quinquennium 1967–8 to 1971–2 Birmingham had had to absorb inflation costs of £1.5 million which were not compensated.[19] This was partly because supplementation was unpredictable and could not be planned for, but the principal reason was that it did not cover increases in university costs outside academic salaries and increased student numbers. In particular, non-academic pay was not covered and this escalated in the

1960s in consequence of inflation, government incomes policies and much more effective support-staff unionisation. In 1969, for example, technician pay went up by 28% in one year.[20] Nationally, 1958 to 1968 saw the student population and academic salaries each rise by slightly more than 100%; these other costs rose by 150%.[21] In 1970 the Department of Education and Science (DES) and the UGC did move from spasmodic supplementation to agreeing that supplementation for increases in the university cost index would be paid a year in arrears, but apart from academic salaries, only 50% of other increases in cost was guaranteed.[22] The historian of these years has written: 'The collapse of control over this area of expenditure and the reluctance of and ultimate refusal of Government to meet the consequences was the direct cause of the collapse of the traditional system of funding universities.'[23]

The UGC was fully aware of what was going on but could do very little about it. In his report for the year to 31 July 1972, the treasurer at Birmingham stressed that the UGC had only a monitoring role: 'The quinquennium has seen an increase in the complexity of the University Grants Committee machinery for ensuring that allocations of public funds to the Universities are made and spent properly. Nevertheless the allocation of recurrent income within the University remains under its own control and has been undertaken in a responsible manner.'[24] So long as the story was one of growth the UGC possessed considerable leverage, but in the event of contraction it would be left with responsibility without power. Whitehall, moreover, was becoming increasingly ready to assert direct control of higher education. Robbins had effectively made access to universities a political issue so that it became more and more difficult to argue that the sector should continue to be funded by a 'hands-off' mechanism. This feeling was accentuated by the announcement in 1965 of the 'binary line', dividing higher education into an 'autonomous' university sector and a 'public sector' controlled by local authorities and ultimately answerable to government. And the more government bypassed the UGC or handed decisions to it without consultation, the less the UGC could exercise its autonomous judgement on the sector as a whole. Formula funding in particular would leave it with merely an executive role.[25] Politicians, too, thought in crude terms of the numbers being taught, not of research and quality. As early as 1965 Robert Aitken complained of the attitude of the DES: 'The universities, for the sake of the young, have crowded them in in unsatisfactory conditions during the Robbins "emergency", and the Department, against the advice of the UGC, is saying that if they can manage that way in the emergency they can manage that way indefinitely.'[26] 'Excellence' was dismissed as a slogan to defend a 'snobbish caste-ridden hierarchical obsession with university status'.[27]

Successive national economic crises from 1965 led to a loss of 20% of the university building in the years 1967–8 to 1969–70.[28] Deflation following the devaluation of 1967 meant that in 1968 Birmingham received 3.5% of the UGC grant to counter inflation whereas in 1967–8 costs apart from salaries rose by 5.6%.[29] Expenditure per student peaked in the late 1960s but a subsequent fall in real terms thereafter produced calls for economy. The UGC warned universities in 1970 that it was under pressure to reduce costs and announced that staff–student ratios would have to rise.[30] Although in December 1972 Margaret Thatcher, then Secretary of State for Education and Science, announced that the Robbins programme was to be expanded, this was against a previous announcement that new students would be funded at only 85% of the 1971 costs.[31] Planning nevertheless went ahead for the 1972/3 to 1977/8 quinquennium. The amounts and indexing procedures were agreed but the rate of inflation was increasing at such a pace that the preliminary grant for the first year had to be adjusted within six months, which, ironically, helped Birmingham to end the financial year to 31 July 1973 £360,000 in credit.[32]

The bombshell came five months later. The 'dash for growth' which the Conservative government had begun in the summer of 1971 produced a surge in inflation which was made even worse by the decision of the Organization of Petroleum-Exporting Countries (OPEC) to push up world oil prices. By November 1973 there was a full-blown balance of payments crisis and on 17 December Anthony Barber, the Chancellor of the Exchequer, announced cuts of £1200 million in public spending to help meet 'the gravest situation by far since the end of the war'.[33] The economies included halving the university supplementation already agreed for 1974–5 and the other half was cancelled within the week, plus half of the equipment grant.[34] University building for 1974–5 was slashed by two-thirds.[35] In July 1974 the UGC did manage to secure compensation for about a third of the agreed supplementation and in November 1974 student numbers were cut by 17%.[36] However, from 1975 cash limits became the rule for all higher education funding. Academic salaries were initially the one exception, but these were included from 1976 following another mini-budget in December.[37] An additional problem in 1975 and 1976 was that the government imposed three conflicting fee changes in two years.[38] Not only did the need to revise grants already made cause havoc with the UGC system, but the UGC lost all discretion over a significant element in university incomes.[39] Effectively, formula-funding – capitation – had arrived. As the end of the supposed quinquennium approached, adjustments in higher education funding were becoming so frequent that the grant system had effectively become annual and Robert Hunter could write: 'The quinquennial system has gone for the foreseeable future.'[40]

What replaced it was the announcement of grants year by year, plus indicative projections for several years ahead, and in July 1978 the UGC did produce provisional grant figures for the three years 1979/80 to 1981/2. This was no quinquennial award, but it was at least something to plan on. However, national economics and national politics still ruled. The General Election in May 1979 brought Mrs Thatcher to power.[41] In July public spending was cut by £4000 million, with the UGC contributing 3% of its proposed grants. The cumulative effect of this and earlier decisions was to reduce funding for the university sector by 10% and on top of this it was announced in October 1980 that future government grants would assume that universities were charging overseas students full-cost fees. The impact of this change on recruitment was disastrous; Birmingham suffered a 37% loss in three years.[42] The UGC's understanding of the July figures was that these were a one-off cutback to a new baseline, and in October vice-chancellors were advised to expect level funding.[43] Two months later the government abandoned level funding and warned that there would be further cuts in resources between 1980–1 and 1983–4 of the order of 11% to 15%.[44]

How did the University of Birmingham navigate itself through the unprecedentedly stormy financial waters of the late 1960s and 1970s? It is clear that in the quinquennium 1967–8 to 1972–3 its concerns were the same as those of the UGC, the erosion of grants by inflation and the sporadic way in which compensation operated.[45] Planning was a nightmare when neither costs or the timing or level of reimbursement could be predicted. The result was that budgets had to be extremely conservative and growth in the amount spent on academic activity kept lower than it need have been. For example, the budget for 1970–1 was approved by Council in the spring and reviewed in the autumn. It was not until the following March that government announced the top-up grant for inflation, by which time it was too late to recruit additional staff. Norman Lancaster, the university treasurer, concluded his report for the year by welcoming the recently agreed DES/UGC protocol on supplementation:

> Inflation has had a dampening effect on Academic development during the first four years of the quinquennium. It is refreshing to look forward in the fifth year to the benefits arising from the action of the Government in providing supplementary grant with much greater promptitude than in the recent past. While inflation persists, prompt relief by way of additional grant will continue to be a prerequisite for the achievement of planned development.[46]

It was, therefore, principally the management of the finances which caused the problems in the 1967–8 to 1972–3 quinquennium. There were no absolute cuts, only restrictions in the rate of growth, and public funding for higher education continued to rise in real terms. In 1969–70 the net increase for Birmingham was 3.25%, in 1970–1, 3.5% and in 1971–2, 3%.[47] It is true that such percentages only kept pace with rising student numbers, left nothing for growth in research and were less than the University felt it needed to grow without sacrificing standards. However, they are figures for which vice-chancellors at the start of the twenty-first century would give their eye teeth, and are the more surprising because they comfortably exceeded the growth in the gross national product.

So far, so good, but with the start of the new quinquennium in 1972 came an ominous shift. Grants were now actually reduced by the government introducing the device of a 2% economy factor at constant prices. That was serious enough, but the percentage was an average over the university sector as a whole and Birmingham was one of the losers, ending up with an actual economy factor of 5%. This represented a 9% reduction in the grant per full-time student and the UGC was guilty enough to describe the Birmingham settlement as 'tight'.[48] Norman Lancaster, however, clearly suspected that there was worse to come and in July 1973 he took advantage of the receipt of some delayed government supplementation to create for the first time a quinquennial reserve. He put £250,000 aside so that the University would be able to grow at the agreed rate whether or not it received full compensation for inflation.[49] Five months later came the Barber 'freeze'.

The University went immediately into crisis mode, along with its sister institutions. Academic posts were frozen until at least October 1975.[50] Economies were sought everywhere. To set an example, Norman Lancaster compressed his report and accounts into four fewer pages than the year before.[51] Efficiencies in minor clerical expenditure saved £15,000![52] Questions began to be asked about flexibility and whether departments and faculties were, on financial grounds, the best form of organisation for the University, and this barely two years after the Grimond Report had roundly endorsed both as necessary academically.[53] The seeds of what would become the conflict between the University as a business run for accountants and the university as a community of scholars and teachers were beginning to germinate. The initial hope was that the situation was merely a more severe instance of the economic crises of the past. In December 1974 Robert Hunter was careful to point out that important high-cost activities such as nuclear physics and the Hayter Centres would be protected and that expansion was not at an end: 'We are at the point of abandoning substantial growth for modest growth and are endeavouring to redeploy resources from areas that have been "staffed-up" but are no longer required at the level we planned.'[54] Two years later the message was quite different:

> In many quarters, the basic assumption was that university development was really going to go on as before, although there might be minor delays. As this is not turning out to be so, we must prepare for the consequences of high tuition fees, reduction of equipment grants, the virtual disappearance of the capital building programme, the reduced level of recurrent grants and a possible 4% cut in resources in real terms in 1978.[55]

The growth in resources of higher education which had been on the up for twenty years was at an end.[56]

The verdict on Birmingham's management of the post-1973 crisis has, in accounting terms, to be highly favourable. In the four years 1973–4 to 1976–7 income fell in real terms by 10.8% and the University could not avoid going into the red after the sudden Barber cuts.[57] However, thanks to strict economies, in 1975–6 it recovered to achieve a £381,000 surplus. The next year the favourable balance was £1,289,000 and the general reserve reached £1,082,000. That gave the University room to risk deficit budgeting and a £310,000 overspend was planned to allow correction of the grosser anomalies in the policy of non-recruitment.[58] In the event, a £684,000 surplus was achieved, and the General Reserve rose further, to £1,301,000, although more than half of the year's surplus was thanks to the UGC's securing a relaxation of cash limits which brought Birmingham £349,000.[59] When the deluge at last came in 1979, with university financing hopelessly confused by the change in government and with reimbursement for the 1977–8 pay awards still outstanding and uncertain, the University was faced with a deficit of £684,000, despite making further savings of £180,000 in heat, light and power in the year.[60] However, thanks to three years of extreme prudence, it was able to cover this from reserves and still have £742,000 in hand.

The academic verdict on the economy programme is more mixed. Between 1972–3 and 1978–9 the number of full-time students grew by 18.9%, while the number of the teaching staff fell by 9%.[61] The crude staff–student ratio rose from 1:6.3 to 1:8.3. Losses were most severe amongst the tenured research staff, where numbers fell from 130 to 52. In 1970, 77.1% of university expenditure went on academic work; by 1979 the proportion was 71.8%, a fall of 5.3%, which at 1979 prices represented £1,713,200. Administrative costs declined by a similar percentage. Comparison with university costs elsewhere was also very favourable. For example, in 1975–6 academic departments more than absorbed 25% inflation, while in administration Birmingham held down costs to 24% where inflation nationally ran at 27%. Where expenditure did rise significantly was on the premises budget. In 1970 this accounted for 10.45% of expenditure but in 1978–9 that figure had risen to 17.63%, absorbing an extra £2,320,863. In principle, it is short-sighted of a scholastic management to impose excessive economies on premises and the estate, and some increase was needed to comply with new health and safety legislation. However, much of the addition to estate spending followed a deliberate decision 'to transfer expenditure temporarily into non-recurrent requirements until the national economic situation becomes more stable'.[62] It was not a view which academics necessarily shared.

One consequence of the financial pressures of the 1970s was the increased need for central management of the University. As Lord Hunter said later:

> One had to go into far more detailed budgetary control than one had in the past when money quite frankly was not such a terrible problem. One of the paradoxical situations that we had, was that we had to get a tighter control on things. And on the other hand there was a movement within the

> university for more democracy. And these were pulling in opposite directions.[63]

There was a particular need to subject research grants in science to central scrutiny and approval because of the potential knock-on effect on the university infrastructure.[64] The deans, too, had to broaden the traditional focus of the office, which had very much been on 'looking after their own'.[65] A university perspective was particularly important when it came to the allocation of funds. The non-science faculties had very limited access to outside sources of finance so that it was vital that 'there should be a little dripping off' from science and technology.[66] There was, nevertheless, 'a reluctance to have any central committee interfere with the running of the faculty and perhaps indicate where the reserves would have to go and, of course, [if there was any] idea of switching from one faculty to another, there used to be blood on the vice-chancellor's floor'.[67] The mechanism which the vice-chancellor, the treasurer and the secretary, Harry Harris, developed to get round this at least to some degree, was an 'Academic Fund for new initiatives' introduced in 1976–7.[68] Not only could the allocation of this 'Development Fund' (so called) be skewed to improve the position of the less well funded but it allowed an element of central earmarking in the way it was spent.[69]

The character of university administration was changing as well. Size was one dimension. When Hunter arrived Birmingham had 6667 students. When he left in 1981 the figure was 8741 and the prospect 10 000. There were 19% more academic staff and 34% more people employed on contract research. The most dramatic change was in the University's finances. In 1968–9 expenditure was £8,249,774; in 1981–2 it was £48,925,000. The market value of investments grew from just under £3 million to just over £17 million. No figure for the estate value is available, although in 1968 the University had owned 1876 housing units and in 1981 it owned 5919. All this meant more to be managed. The 97 salaried administrators on the main campus in 1966–7 grew to 141 in 1980–1, a 45% increase in 14 years. Administration was also more complex. New facilities had become necessary, such as administrative computing. There was greater professionalism. The lower levels of management had already moved in that direction following the recruitment by Robert Aitken of a number of ex-colonial civil servants, but in the 1970s it became the practice to give administrative staff a university perspective by rotating them between the various sectors of operation.[70]

It is ironic that external pressures should set Birmingham on the slippery slope to centralised management in the very decade which saw increased provision for staff participation in affairs of the University. Opportunities for initiative were also severely restricted by the campaign for economies. Though probably unavoidable in the emergency, the policy of disestablishing posts produced major distortions within and between departments. The faculty of Commerce reported that it had lost 13.7% of its staff.[71] Arts pointed out that one department might lose a quarter of its staff while another be unaffected.[72] Also, the policy could, in practice, only be partially enforced because of teaching requirements. There was talk that faculties could 'earn' their way out of difficulty by increasing student numbers. The Arts Faculty, for example, agreed to worsen the staff–student ratio from 1:9.5 to 1.11, which meant that the more popular departments would have to operate at a much higher figure. Commerce and Social Science followed suit. However, neither the policy of freezing posts nor of maximising recruitment were uniform in their effect over the University. In the seven years from 1972–3 to 1978–9 Science increased its students by 11.8% and cut tenured staff by 11.3%. Arts, with the problem of maintaining a number of small specialised disciplines, was forced to increase staff by 7.2% but it paid for it with a 22.7% increase in students. The faculty of Commerce and Social Science seems to have suffered most. It increased its staff by 4.7% but took in 40.3% more students, effectively an increase of a third on the workload.

The crisis of the mid-1970s must, however, not be seen in isolation. It had the effect of accentuating trends which had been building up since at least Robert Aitken's appointment. In the twenty years from 1957–8 to 1977–8 the number of full-time students rose by 130%, from 3716 to 8575, but growth had been uneven.[73] Science, the largest faculty, had expanded by only 89%. This was certainly not what was intended. Birmingham had had an expectation that half its students would take science and technology and in 1957–8 the percentage was 48.4%, sixty-one registrations below the magic 50%.[74] The position was much the same ten years later (48.7%), eighty-seven students under target. By 1977–8, however, entrants to science and engineering made up only 40% of full-time admissions and the shortfall was 883. To compensate for this, Arts and Education had grown by 178% over the period, although the most dramatic rises were in Commerce and Social Science (270%) and Law (318%). Vice-chancellors had repeatedly insisted that staff numbers must grow proportionally to maintain the 1:8 staff-student ratio which had long been regarded a vital maximum if research output and teaching standards were to be maintained.[75] In reality staff numbers rose in the period by only 96%. Over the two decades this worsened the overall staff–student ratio from 1:7 to 1:8.2, but given the uneven growth between faculties while Science and Engineering, and Medicine and Dentistry were barely affected (from 1:7.9 to 1:7.8 and from 1:6.2 to 1:6.5, respectively), Arts and Education went from 1:6.4 to 1:10.9 and Commerce and Social Science from 1:7.9 to 1:12.9.

When he began his report for 1982–3, Edward Marsland, Hunter's successor as vice-chancellor, remarked that it was 'difficult not to give the impression that all the University is concerned about is money'.[76] That is certainly also true of the history of the University in the 1970s. The significance of the financial crisis is put in sharp relief by the story of the Medical School, the one section of the University which to a demonstrable extent was able to escape the full force of the blizzard. Here the pattern of development went on much as before. The faculty had considerable advantages as against the rest of Birmingham. Medicine and Dentistry was treated as a separate category in UGC funding. Much of its work was done either jointly with or on behalf of the Health Service. The faculty also had access to the well-funded Medical Research Council and to the enormous resources of national and international medical charities. As a result, it was a very different world north of the Worcester–Birmingham canal. This is not to say that the faculty was wholly exempt from any freeze, but the responsibility which staff had to the Health Service for patient care was a powerful argument against any severe or continuing reduction in staffing. In his report for 1979, the dean of Medicine could even speak of an improved financial position and the recruitment of twelve new full-time lecturers, five on Health Service money and the rest on the University.[77] What is more, expansion in Medicine tended to be both phased and better funded, reflecting the interest of the government in the numbers of doctors and dentists in training for the Health Service. Thus in the twenty years before the 1979 election, the numbers in the faculty grew by 184%, approximately in line with the 1968 Royal Commission on Medical Education, which saw Birmingham becoming the largest Medical School in the country.[78] The number of staff provided on UGC funds rose in the period by a lower figure, 162%, a result of financial stringency in the worst years of the late 1970s when the staff–student ratio deteriorated.[79]

Where the Medical Faculty was particularly fortunate was in securing public capital. In the 1970s the Medical School took 73% of the capital funds which the UGC allowed to Birmingham.[80] It might not always be the amount wanted. Little had changed since 1964 and 1965, when the University was given £500,000, not the £1 million it has asked for to increase its intake by 50%:[81] 'The Vice-Chancellor finds himself, as usual, the embarrassed intermediary between a willing horse and a reluctant corn merchant.' Nevertheless, money was forthcoming. In 1972, when very little else was being planned, the UGC approved £500,000 for a new teaching block at the General Hospital and extra teaching space in the department of surgery, in child psychiatry, in the Children's Hospital and at Selly Oak.[82] In one sense the UGC had very little option. Having more medical students meant that additional hospitals had to be brought in to provide the required amount of clinical training, and these hospitals had to be equipped.[83] It was also possible to raise capital by bringing together different interests. When the Department of Health and Social Security (DHSS) was involved the result was not always happy. In 1972 the department had agreed to build a large psychiatric block and a smaller geriatric block on the Queen Elizabeth Hospital site and the UGC to pay for space for associated academic work, but in January 1974 the DHSS called a halt on the instructions of the Treasury.[84] There were fewer problems when the participants were substantially local, as in 1977, when the University, the Area Health Authority, the Regional Hospital Board and the UGC all agreed to do something about the teaching facilities still outstanding at the General Hospital.[85]

Charities were even more reliable, particularly when it came to research. In 1968 the Wolfson Foundation agreed to build an Automated Pathology Research facility for the study and development of automated laboratory methods. The university created a chair of clinical chemistry and then a department and the Wolfson Building was opened in May 1972 with funding for five years promised by the Department of Health[86] Computer facilities reached the Medical School and Queen Elizabeth Hospital by courtesy of the Nuffield Provincial Hospitals Trust.[87] That same trust part-funded the Health Services Research Centre in 1971.[88] Even the Medical Research Council paid to fit out part of the Neuro-communications Research Unit.[89]

As well as capital projects, trusts and charities regularly came forward to fund academic initiatives: a chair of cardiology and a senior lectureship in clinical pharmacology in 1971, a chair of ophthalmology in 1972, a senior clinical tutor in general practice and a chair of geriatric medicine in 1973.[90] A local appeal in Shropshire provided the funds in 1977 for a chair in orthopaedics based at the Robert Jones and Agnes Hunt Orthopaedic Hospital at Gobowen.[91] The following year brought funds for a sub-department of geriatrics at Selly Oak and for chairs of haematology and dermatology in 1979.[92]

The rest of the University could rightly regard the Medical School as privileged, but it would be wrong to portray the other faculties as mesmerised by the ending of the post-war expansion. What we find instead is a change in the pattern of growth. Externally imposed constraints certainly meant that initiatives and opportunities could not develop as easily or as effectively as they might, but nobody threw in the towel. Perhaps the most significant academic development of the late 1960s and early 1970s was a shift away from undergraduate teaching. This is barely detectable in Science, more so in Arts, but was particularly marked in Commerce and Social Science, where the proportion of students not studying for first degrees rose in the decade 1962–3 to 1972–3 from 13.8% to 41.1%.

Table 21.1 University of Birmingham: students in Science, Arts and Commerce registered for postgraduate/post-experience work, 1962–78 (%; last years of quinquennia)

	1962–3	1967–8	1972–3	1977–8
Science	29.8	30.4	30.5	25.0
Arts (including education)	29.5	31.2	32.5	24.6
Commerce and Social Science	13.8	29.9	41.1	30.8
Total	*28.2*	*30.6*	*32.6*	*25.8*

The beneficiary of this shift, however, was not postgraduate research, but postgraduate and post-experience courses. Over the two quinquennia, registrations rose by 194% in Arts, 212% in Science and 545% in Commerce and Social Science.

Table 21.2 University of Birmingham: postgraduate/post-experience students in Science, Arts and Social Science not registered for research (%; last years of quinquennia)

	1962–3	1967–8	1972–3	1977–8
Science	23.7	33.3	37.1	42.4
	[169:545]	[319:640]	[358:606]	[362:492]
Arts (including	69.1	71.5	74.4	70.4
education)	[239:107]	[342:136]	[464:160]	[409: 172]
Commerce and	80.8	69.4	69.2	78.0
Social Science	[42:10]	[136:60]	[229:102]	[259: 73]
Total	*40.5*	*48.8*	*54.8*	*58.3*
	[450:662]	*[797:836]*	*[1051:868]*	*[1030:737]*

Note: Numbers of registrations for non-research:research degrees in brackets.[93]

The drop in the number of research students was, in part, a consequence of a deliberate UGC cut in research-student numbers and an associated cut back in research training awards.[94] Between 1969–70 and 1978–9 the amount which the University received under this head rose by 38%, but the retail price index more than trebled.

This decline in research students had, of course, an impact on the research output of the University, a matter about which both Aitken and Hunter were most concerned, particularly as capital for non-medical building became increasingly scarce and staff–student ratios worsened. In most research projects, too, the University had to find 40% on top of any grants under the 'dual support' system, and the ability of the UGC to sustain this effectively was inevitably constrained by the overall sum which the Committee had to distribute.[95] Birmingham's biggest providers of research funds were the various Research Councils (73% in 1970–1), but as their resources also came under economic pressure, competition to secure grants became more severe.[96] It also became increasingly difficult to maintain the number of support staff as university funds tightened.[97] More ominous still, fundamental questions were being asked about the whole way of managing research support. Increased competition and concern for value for money forced Research Councils to become more directive and increasingly tempted them to judge by predicted outcomes. Government thinking was even more restrictive and favoured committing public funds, even those via the Research Councils, on 'a customer/contractor' system.[98] With such ideas abroad it was increasingly difficult to protect support for 'blue-sky' and 'fundamental' research.[99] How to measure the effect which this increasing stringency had on Birmingham is an extremely difficult problem. Counting the annual output of publications fails because forms and frequency of publication vary so much between disciplines. Calculating the number of annual starts fails because there is no such thing as a standard project. Comparing spending between projects is flawed by huge cost discrepancies. Above all, how is quality to be measured? One crude measure can be offered and this is that in the decade 1969–70 to 1978–9 the University's overall income rose by 343%, but the income from research grants and contracts rose by only 307%. In theory this could mean that the University was undertaking cheaper research; it could also mean that costs were being absorbed elsewhere, for example, by staff putting in their own resources. However, the realistic conclusion is that the amount of research being funded was falling as a proportion of overall university activity. Figures naturally fluctuated year on year but in the first two years, 1969–70 and 1970–1, research grants and contracts contributed 15.68% and 16.65% to university income, respectively; in the last two years, 1977–8 and 1978–9, the figures were 13.53% and 13.91%. In 1981–2 they would fall to 12.9%.

Instead of research students being trained in the context of a growing research funding, the new emphasis was on taught courses for postgraduates and post-experience students. Such courses were, of course, not new; the Lucas Institute for Engineering Production had been taking nearly 500 industrial executives a year for short courses since 1953.[100] In 1970 a Senate committee drew attention to the 'very-large amount of post-experience work' which was going on, and suggested that this could grow to as much as 25% of the total teaching load.[101] Although only a percentage of this was for a higher degree, the degree structure was changing, with the taught master's qualification becoming increasingly available and slowly more flexible.[102] Most programmes were begun by what the vice-chancellor called 'the "shot-in-the-arm" technique' and were thereafter expected to be self-funding but he was keen to secure recurrent funding for such work and particularly to find adequate space: 'we cannot yet see our way to finding funds for the support of those longer post-experience courses which are in the field of Government interest. Our efforts would be greatly encouraged by a Government policy about the provision of buildings for post experience activity.'[103] Encouragement was not forthcoming and in 1972 Robert Hunter announced that the University would go it alone and that substantial developments planned for in the quinquennium would be financed by borrowing.[104] This was 'an act of faith': 'in the hope that business and commerce, the departments of government concerned and the local authorities will support us as we endeavour to meet their needs'. The main areas identified for development during the quinquennium were the Institute for Local Government Studies (ILGS)and the Health Services Management Centre (HSMC), although there was a hope that substantial additional developments would prove possible in Business Management and Environmental Studies.

The ILGS had begun by training administrative officers from overseas, but by 1970 it was offering short training courses for the directors of social services departments and in 1972 added seminars for chief officers in local government.[105] The HSMC had developed out of an initiative begun jointly in January 1965 by Birmingham and the embryonic University of Aston to set up a joint Graduate Centre for Management.[106] Academically it was a success but in September 1972 the Centre was closed, with Aston taking over the activity except for courses run for the Health Service, for which Birmingham established the HSMC.[107] In 1974 a site was obtained for a post-experience centre on Edgbaston Park Road, including Park House, which was adapted for the HSMC.[108] Across the road in Garth House further post-experience facilities were provided, this time for the department of transportation and environmental planning, which in 1969 had begun providing residential courses for industrial managers.[109] The Council allocated £225,000 for the two projects in 1975–6.[110] In 1976 the University appointed Professor Leonard Minkes, a former dean of Commerce and Social Sciences, as its director of Post-Experience Studies, with a brief to promote interaction with the community and set up a Board of Post-Experience Studies to co-ordinate work in management, the social sciences, technology, medicine, education and law.

These developments were structural, but hardly a session passed without particular initiatives. The year 1971 saw Education provide a course in the teaching of maladjusted children.[111] In 1972 the Lucas Institute was able to move into purpose-built residential accommodation in Edgbaston Park Road.[112] In 1973 the faculty of Science and Engineering combined with the faculty of Commerce and Social Science to provide postgraduate courses in technological and economic studies and in industrial management.[113] In the same year the Institute of Judicial Administration in the faculty of Law began providing training courses for lay magistrates.[114] Of course, not all ventures flourished. The proposed M.Sc. courses in radiocommunications and in radar, intended for students seconded from industry, attracted fewer takers than anticipated.[115] In 1975 the ILGS courses for local government had to be suspended because of local government reorganisation.[116] In the post-1976 blizzard, too, there was a swing back to undergraduate recruitment, from 67.4% of registrations to 74.2%, with the biggest switch in Commerce and Social Science.[117] Yet overall it was research which suffered from this, with the single exception of the faculty of Arts, where research recruitment increased but taught courses declined by 11.2%. Elsewhere it was the reverse. Science and Engineering were significantly down on research, perhaps because of increased difficulty in funding, but the intake on courses was maintained. Probably for the same reason, Commerce and Social Science lost research students but here taught courses increased. Over the University as a whole, research dropped by 15.1%, but postgraduate and post-experience courses by only 2%. This certainly justified the University continuing to put considerable energy into postgraduate/post-experience courses. In 1977 the Department of Industry and the Science Research Council put forward the notion of 'teaching companies' to improve liaison between universities and industry. The department of engineering production responded immediately and a company was set up with Matrix Machine Tools.[118] In the same year Commerce and Social Science responded to an invitation by the Iranian government to provide a new Certificate in Finance. There were fifty takers. In the following year Science and Engineering, recognising 'the growing importance of post-experience work', felt it time to rationalise all its programmes on a modular basis.

There were also considerable developments in undergraduate teaching. Some of these were of the traditional kind. A new department of psychology took its first students in October 1969, the same year in which the Centre for West African Studies extended its teaching to undergraduates.[119] In 1972 Law was the first faculty in the country to make European Community law a compulsory part of the curriculum.[120] In 1977 Birmingham was one of four universities out of eight selected by the UGC to offer a four-year course in engineering and management.[121] However, as in the postgraduate and post-experience field, much of the new undergraduate development cut across traditional patterns of both activity and organisation. This did not come about by central direction. The Working Party on the Broadening of Education which had been in existence since 1969 made its final report to Senate in 1973 but once again offered little beyond exhortation.[122] Change came from below. The Computer Centre, which in 1969 had launched an M.Sc. course in computer science, joined the next year with the school of Mathematical Science to offer an undergraduate course in mathematics and computer science.[123] In 1977 it was computer science and electronic engineering.[124] A double honours system was set up to enable students to take both engineering and economics plus a substantial element of language study, and this was extended in 1974 to metallurgy and to materials science.[125] Law linked up with French and with politics; French for its part joined with sociology, and modern history with politics.[126] Arts, Commerce and Social Science and Law collaborated to set up a School of International Studies.[127] Within departments single degrees were split into attractive alternatives. Instead of an electronic and electrical engineering course which allowed some specialisation in electronics, there were courses in electronic and computer engineering, electronic and communication engineering, electronic and control engineering and in electronic and electrical engineering.[128] Faculties reviewed their degree and curriculum structures.[129] Departments collaborated to make new and exciting degree combinations: in 1978 geology and physical education, and music, drama and dance.[130] In Arts, where studying a single European language and literature was losing popularity, the faculty responded by expanding combined (that is, joint) honours courses and in October 1979 a three-subject General Honours course was initiated with a language component, which was also supported by Commerce and Social Science.[131]

All this amounted, as the vice-chancellor said, to a change in the character of Birmingham's development. In the days of expansion it had been a matter of adding new specialisms; now what was necessary was creating 'combinations of existing strong interests within the University to create new additions'. This was where the greater liberalisation of the Grimond Report had a direct impact on the core work of the university. For these new innovations to succeed, the 'essential' was 'a coming together of kindred spirits'.[132] Robert Hunter thought that existing faculty and department boundaries could present obstacles but in reality the newly liberalised system proved to be very responsive. The concept of the 'school' was particularly fruitful; this was a naturally coherent academic grouping which allowed departments to collaborate fully but also to retain a measure of initiative where necessary. It must not be confused with the later administrative 'schools' which were convenient units for assigning budgetary liability. One of the earliest and most successful academic schools was the School of History, which had been set up in 1964 and which Aitken had greeted as a mechanism which 'promises to be valuable with us'.[133] In 1969 the departments of industrial metallurgy and physical metallurgy and science of materials came together to form an experimental school which became permanent in 1972 under the name 'the School of Metallurgy and Materials'.[134]

There was considerable readiness in the University to make administration fit the academic needs, not vice versa. In 1976, following Grimond, it was agreed that it no longer made sense to run education as a specialism within Arts, so the new faculty was set up in October – and this at the height of the financial crisis.[135] Institutes, centres, units and, if necessary, departments were accommodated as it appeared sensible. Thus in August 1968 the biochemistry department in Science and Engineering, and the departments of medical biochemistry and physiological chemistry in Medicine and Dentistry came together in a biochemistry department which academically belonged to both faculties but was directly financed via Senate.[136]

Not all this development was, of course, a response to the challenge to get an academic quart out of a UGC pint pot. Much of it reflected the crumbling of demarcations between disciplines, particularly in science. Thus the disciplines of zoology, botany, genetics and microbiology came together in 1964–5 as the School of Biological Sciences, and were joined by physiology in 1970 and bacteriology in 1972.[137] Even so, in 1969 genetics found itself working on psychogenetics in collaboration with yet another department, psychology.[138] But Science was not unique. The Centre for Contemporary Cultural Studies widened its interests to a point where it no longer happily fitted in with English, its parent body, so in 1973 it became an autonomous unit answerable to the faculty of Arts.[139] Technological advances also produced collaboration. The most striking instance of this was the arrival of the 3 million volt Dynamitron particle accelerator which was financed by the UGC (together with a Radiation Centre to house it) on the understanding that it would be run jointly with the University of Aston which would have 30% use. It was opened in October 1972 with a highly impressive prospectus of its potential. The life sciences needed it to study radiation effects, civil engineers to study concrete, chemists polymers and ultra-fast chemical reactions, physicists resonance studies and neutron behaviour, metallurgists void nucleation. Geologists, archaeologists and botanists also were in the queue, and it was also proposed to provide high-quality engineering products to local manufacturers of high-quality engineering products.[140]

A less dramatic, but even more important technical provision was the installation of a mainframe computer. The first step towards this had been the appointment of a lecturer in the department of mathematical physics in 1959, but although a computer was ordered in 1961 it was not until 1965 that a machine was on site and working, and a system of services organised.[141] At this stage Computer Services were conceived of as a two-headed extra-faculty provision. It would provide practical computer facilities for users within the University and in other Midland universities and also offer academic tuition in the new discipline.[142] Nobody, however, could have predicted the speed at which both functions would develop. A new and more powerful 1906A computer became fully operational only in May 1973, but by 1976 the demand for computer time was such that it was working three shifts. As for the academic side, we have seen that computing first entered the lecture room in 1968 when what became the most popular of all the options was introduced into the mathematics curriculum. This was followed the next year by an M.Sc. course and by 1973–4 a subsidiary course was introduced for the faculty of Arts. With clear evidence of where the future was leading, the University decided in 1976 to appoint a new director for Computer Services at professorial rank and three years later Birmingham launched the first UK degree in software engineering.

Another technical innovation of which much was hoped in these years was television. As we have seen, Robert Hunter broadcast during the troubles of autumn 1968 but at that stage everything had to be improvised. A professional studio under the Great Hall was not equipped until a year later and the full facility was only completed in 1971.[143] During the rest of the decade considerable progress was made, colour arrived in the autumn of 1977 and a valuable collection of teaching material on videotape was built up and maintained in the library. However, the cost and demands of the new medium had not been fully realised. The rapid progress of the industry quickly made equipment obsolete, there were shortages of staff and too few academics had the time to learn how to input material. The 1970s did, however, make clear that television and video had considerable potential for certain areas of work, particularly routine teaching. It is ironic that the section of the university which was in a position to make most use of the new technology was the Medical School. It sponsored about half the unit's output and in 1979 the TV Service was able to provide live facilities for two international conferences on surgical procedures. Add to this the fact that the School had its own department of audio-visual aids and one is reminded that new technology only saves money for those who already have money.

How, then, are the 1970s to be assessed from the vantage point of more than two decades later? For the first seventy-five years of the life of the University the expectation, even in the darkest days, had been of progress, and it is probably true to say that a majority of staff saw the trials of the 1970s as punctuation in the story of educational advance in Britain. The day would come again. Given that we know of the approaching storm, perhaps the decade was a time when

> Alas, regardless of their doom,
> The little victims play.

Yet the 'play' of Birmingham academics in the 1970s was serious and to some purpose. The initiative liberated by the Grimond reforms revolutionised opportunity and allowed both teaching and research to be developed with a freedom not known before. The chance to innovate made the decade a golden time for many, and to innovate without, as in later years, the numbing demands of bureaucracy.  Experiment was possible without filling in a clutch of forms, risks could be taken without penalty and anomalies be allowed where they bore good fruit.

The decade was a world away from the efficiency requirements, the constant atmosphere of assessment, and the productivity norms in higher education today. Judged against criteria of that kind, the 1970s can appear years of irresponsibility where inefficiency could survive and outcomes were anything but predictable. But the University of that period was not as it was because of tradition and selfish privilege, the stereotype which politicians chose to invent. Privilege and independence were a means to an end, the living out of the principles laid down by Oliver Lodge and echoed by all his successors – that truly high-quality scholarship is not susceptible of prediction or prior assessment, and that the role of a university is to provide space, time and opportunity in which ability can grow, and that to achieve this, one has in the end to rely on individual character and motivation. Institutional values determined the spending of money, not Westminster programmes.

At the beginning of the twenty-first century this position seems hopelessly unworldly. It *was* 'ivory tower'. Taking a risk on people meant tolerating different levels of performance, and to that extent there was inefficiency. Perhaps also the ethos was more that of the lower deck than of those on the bridge who increasingly had to grapple with external elements. But when 1980 dawned, the old academic values were still very much alive at Birmingham.

Notes

1 UC 7/iii 1969, p. 7.
2 Ibid., p. 1.
3 Ibid., 1970, p. 4.
4 Ibid., 1972, p. 5.
5 Ibid., pp. 4–5.
6 UC 7/iii 1970, pp. 5–6; 1971, pp. 6–7.
7 Ibid., p. 5; 1971, p. 7.
8 Ibid., p. 6; 1972, p. 9.
9 Ibid., 1971, p. 42; 1972, p. 44.
10 Ibid., 1973, p. 5; *Bulletin*, 188 (8 Oct. 1973).
11 UC 7/iii, 1974, p. 29.
12 Ibid., 1976, p. 23; 1978, p. 34; 1979, pp. 18–19.
13 Ibid., 1964, p. 29.
14 UC Oral History: comment by Lord Hunter.
15 The following is based on J. Carswell, *Government and Universities in Britain, 1960–1980* (Cambridge, 1985).
16 Ibid., p. 63.
17 Ibid., pp. 58–60, 96.
18 Ibid., p. 96.
19 UC 7/iii 1972, p. 3.
20 Carswell, *Government*, pp. 101–2.
21 Ibid., p. 134.
22 Ibid., p. 139.
23 Ibid., p. 134.
24 UC 7/ii 1972, *Accounts*, p. 44.
25 Carswell, *Government*, pp. 113, 154–5. However, formula-funding norms were introduced by the UGC itself with the quinquennium 1967–8 to 1972–3: UC 7/iii 1967, p. 8.
26 UC 7/iii 1965, p. 7.
27 Ibid., p. 9.
28 Carswell, *Government*, p. 97.
29 UC 7/iii 1968, p. 3.
30 UGC letter: 5 May 1970.
31 Carswell, *Government*, pp. 139–40.
32 Ibid., p. 145; UC 7/ii 1973, *Accounts*, pp. 40, 46.
33 *The Times*, 17 December 1973.
34 Carswell, *Government*, p. 146.
35 Ibid., p. 152.
36 Ibid., p. 147; UC 7/iii 1974, p. 4.
37 UC 7/iii 1977, p. 47.
38 Carswell, *Government*, pp. 154–5.
39 Ibid., p. 165.
40 Ibid., p. 158; UC 7/iii 1976, p. 3.

41 UC 7/iii 1979, pp. 5, 56–7.
42 UC 7/ii *Accounts* (1982–3), p. 45.
43 M. Kogan, *The Attack on Higher Education* (1983), p. 44.
44 Ibid., p. 146.
45 Carswell, *Government*, p. 134.
46 UC 7/iii 1971, pp. 37–8.
47 Ibid., 1970, p. 36; 1971, p. 36; 1972, p. 43.
48 *Bulletin*, 173 (19 Feb. 1973).
49 UC 7/iii, 1973, p. 41.
50 Ibid., 1974, p. 5.
51 Ibid., p. 43.
52 Ex inf. the author.
53 UC 7/iii 1974, p. 3.
54 Ibid., p. 5.
55 Ibid., 1976, p. 3.
56 Carswell, *Government*, p. 158.
57 For this and the following see UC7/ii *Accounts*.
58 UC 7/iii 1978, pp. 5, 11.
59 Ibid., p. 11.
60 Ibid., 1979, pp. 56–7.
61 For the following see UGC returns reproduced in UC 7/ii *Annual Reports* and *Accounts*.
62 UC 7/iii 1976, p. 37.
63 University Oral History Collection: comment by Lord Hunter.
64 Ibid.
65 Ibid.
66 Ibid.; Aitken had said in 1965 that research income 'is saving the life of the University'. UC 7/iii 1965, p. 3.
67 University Oral History Collection: comment by Lord Hunter.
68 Ibid.; UC 7/ii 1977 *Treasurer*, p. 49.
69 University Oral History Collection: comment by Lord Hunter.
70 Ibid.: comment by A. C. Badenoch.
71 UC 7/iii 1976, p. 10.
72 Ibid., p. 9.
73 This figure ignores inter-faculty units introduced in this period.
74 UC 7/iii 1964, p. 3; 1967, p. 7.
75 Ibid.,1960, p. 4; 1961, p. 3.
76 Ibid., 1982–3, p. 5.
77 Ibid., 1979, p. 13.
78 Ibid., 1968, p. 14.
79 Between 1974–5 and 1978–9 the staff–student ratio was above 1:6.
80 UC 7/iii 1972, p. 5.
81 Ibid., 1964, p. 17; 1965, p. 17; 1966, p. 14.
82 Ibid., 1972, p. 13.
83 Ibid., 1971, p. 10; 1974, p. 11.
84 Ibid., 1966, p. 14; 1974, p. 31 The same freeze caught the tenders for the Queen

Elizabeth Hospital Centre which had originally been approved by the Ministry in 1966. Ibid., 1971, p. 26.

85 Ibid., 1972, p. 32; 1973, p. 31; 1974, p. 30; 1976, p. 24; 1977, p. 32. Much of the delay was because of DHSS deficiencies: 1973, p. 31.

86 Ibid., 1968, p. 15; 1970, p. 27; 1971, p. 11; 1972, p. 8.

87 Ibid., 1966, p. 15; 1968, p. 15.

88 Ibid., 1971, p. 26. The DHSS also contributed.

89 Ibid., p. 26.

90 Ibid., p. 11; 1972, p. 13; 1973, p. 10.

91 Ibid., 1977, p. 7.

92 Ibid., 1978, p. 34; 1979, pp. 8, 13.

93 The figure for Commerce and Social Science in 1962–3 is distorted by the very low number of research registrations.

94 *Bulletin* 143 (31 Jan. 1972); 173 (19 Feb. 1973).

95 Ibid., 143 (31 Jan. 1972).

96 Ibid., 146 (21 Feb. 1972).

97 UC 7/iii 1978, pp. 11–12.

98 Ibid., 1971, pp. 4–5.

99 Ibid., 1977, p. 22.

100 Ibid., 1972, p. 7.

101 Ibid., 1970, pp. 4–5.

102 Ibid., 1968, p. 11; 1978, p. 18.

103 Ibid., 1970, p. 5.

104 Ibid., 1972, p. 4.

105 Ibid., p. 14.

106 Ibid., 1965, p. 21; 1966, p. 5; 1967, p. 22; 1968, pp. 18–9; 1970, p. 14.

107 Ibid., 1971, p. 23; 1972, p. 17.

108 Ibid., 1969, p. 11.

109 Ibid., 1974, p. 30.

110 Ibid., 1976, p. 23.

111 Ibid., 1971, p. 13.

112 Ibid., 1972, p. 7.

113 Ibid., 1973, p. 9.

114 Ibid., p. 14.

115 Ibid., 1971, p. 9.

116 Ibid., 1974, p. 13.

117 See above, p. 412.

118 UC 7/iii 1979, pp. 4–5.

119 Ibid.,1968, p. 22; 1969, p. 11; 1972, p. 16.

120 Ibid., 1972, p. 16.

121 Ibid., 1977, pp. 5–6; 1979, p. 12. The unsuccessful universities included Oxford and Cambridge.

122 Ibid., 1973, p. 8; cf. the previous working party set up in 1956.

123 Ibid., 1970, p. 16.

124 Ibid., 1976, p. 6.

125 Ibid.,1968, p. 19; 1969, p. 11; 1974, p. 13.

126 Ibid., 1976, p. 10;1977.
127 Ibid., p. 11.
128 Ibid., p. 6.
129 E.g. Arts: ibid., 1974, p. 11; Commerce and Social Science, 1976, pp. 10–11.
130 Ibid., 1976, pp. 6, 14.
131 Ibid., p. 9; 1978, pp. 15–16.The two-subject combined honours degree was started in 1961: 1961, p. 16.
132 Ibid., 1978, p. 5.
133 Ibid., 1962, p. 14.
134 Ibid., 1969, p. 10; 1972, p. 10.
135 Ibid., 1977, p. 13.
136 Ibid.,1968, p. 13; *Calendar 1968–9*, p. 125. Other examples were the Neuro-Communications Research Unit and the two Hayter Centres. Computer Services had both an academic and a service role.
137 *Calendar 1965–6*, pp. 70–3; UC 7/iii 1970, p. 9; 1972, p. 10.
138 UC 7/iii 1969, p. 11.
139 Ibid., 1973, p. 11.
140 Ibid., 1968, pp 11–12; 1970, p. 8; 1971, p. 9; 1972, pp. 6–7.
141 Ibid., 1969, p. 20; 1961, p. 14; 1965, p. 3; *Calendar 1966–7*, p. 121. The computer, a KDFP, was upgraded in 1967 and taken out of service in 1974: UC 7/iii 1967, p. 15; 1974, p. 16.
142 For the development of computing see UC 7/iii 1969, p. 3; 1970, p. 15; 1973, p. 15; 1974, p. 16; 1976, p. 12; 1979, p. 16.
143 For the TV service see UC 7/iii 1970, p. 15; 1971, p. 14; 1972, p. 19; 1973, p. 20; 1974, p. 16; 1977, p. 19; 1978, p. 22; 1979, p. 17.

Chapter Twenty-two

Envoi: 1980 to 2000

With Birmingham completing its first hundred years as a university in the year 2000, it may seem perverse to close an introductory history twenty years earlier. Reflection, however, will show how unavoidable this is. In the first place, many of those involved in the story of the University of Birmingham in those two decades are still alive, a good number still in the service of the University or elsewhere in national life. Few ancient proverbs are more foolish than *de mortuis nil nisi bonum*. The reverse is true – only when all is dust and ashes is it possible to try to tell the truth. The only evidence for these twenty years which is so far accessible is that in the public domain; the revealing inward material remains restricted. It is also the case that many issues current in higher education and in the University of Birmingham during this period are still current. To attempt to comment would be to engage in journalism rather than history or – for those of us who have been involved – to indulge in what has only the authority of personal reflection and opinion. Friendship and shared experience are, after all, more important than the pursuit of old differences or the settling of old scores. However, the really compelling reason for silence is that to tell the story of those years at this stage would be to risk ending on a dying fall. The managerial revolution which government has forced on the universities since 1981 and which Birmingham has introduced as vigorously as any, has put an end to the University of Chamberlain and Lodge, Grant Robertson and Priestley, Aitken and Grimond. What remains is, some will feel, closer to Josiah Mason's ideal of a utilitarian knowledge factory.

The 1970s, as we have seen, had been a period of increasing financial problems for the University – indeed, for the whole of higher education. Nothing, however, had prepared it for the changes which would follow the election of May 1979 and the arrival of Thatcherism. The cuts which were announced upon the Tories taking office proved to be only interim.[1] The full intent of government was revealed when it set levels of university grants with the deliberate intention of 'slimming down' a supposedly cushioned constituent in the 'public' sector. By 1983–4, cuts imposed on Birmingham had accumulated to 17%.[2] After already effectively a decade of economy, the Thatcherite reductions left only one option. Major reductions had to be brought about in staff numbers, both academic and non-academic, partly by a programme of voluntary redundancy and partly by a freeze on all new appointments. Nor was this a temporary winter blast followed by spring. It heralded an ice age in which the resources for higher education have been permanently reduced.

The academic distortion produced by random retirements and vacancies can be imagined and so, too, the effect on staff–student ratios which vice-chancellor after vice-chancellor had sought to protect. The number of staff might fall, but the opposite was the case with the number of students the University was obliged to take. This demonstrable reduction in the amount of staff time each student could receive was trumpeted by the government as an 'efficiency' gain! The decline in state support also began to affect the academic priorities of the University as it was forced to search for other sources of income. Thus in 1982–3 the treasurer reported that post-experience work was now bringing in a surplus, but regretted that 'no new ventures came to the fore' in the year.[3] 'Income generation' became a departmental imperative. There was constitutional damage, too, as the central management of the University was obliged to assert control over every decision which might have financial consequences. With the intention of preserving coalface initiative, Birmingham grouped its departments into cost centres funded through a sophisticated system of devolved budgeting. However, in practice, continuing government under-funding reduced this to yet another mechanism by which the centre could exert financial pressure on 'academic managers', a breed which Lodge and those who followed him would not recognise. The continuing search for economies also meant the abandonment of academic utility as a yardstick. Aitken had established faculty registries as the best way to support academics; they were now abolished in the interest of supposed financial efficiency. Eventually, in 1997, faculties themselves were abolished in favour of the schools which the Grimond enquiry had firmly concluded 'cannot be a substitute for Faculties'.[4] With their disappearance went much of the representative element at Birmingham, which to Sonnenschein and Chamberlain was of the essence of a true university. The government forced the abolition of another of their criteria – academic tenure – while long-established family patterns of loyalty among support staff were undermined as employment legislation forced a shift to an impersonal, centralised staffing office.

Famine was not the only horseman responsible for this apocalypse. Another was pestilence, in the form of massively increased government interference and direction. Some regulations, such as 'health and safety', applied to the country as a whole, but most were the consequence of and were symbolised by the switch to the funding of higher education via national councils working to a political agenda, instead of via a UGC which, even in its last weakened years, had still managed to be something of a buffer between universities and the state. Another factor was the pressure of increasing numbers. The growth of the University meant that with over twice as many students, systems and structures which were appropriate for 7000 or 8000 came under increasing strain. The same was true of finance and plant. With the end of the 1990s approaching, the annual income which the University had to manage reached nearly £225 million, over eight times what it had been twenty years earlier. As for the estate, this was now valued at £536 million.[5] If the University had been quoted on the stock exchange, Birmingham would have been in the *Times* top 1000 and, like it or not, it had now to be run as a major service company.

Increasingly, too, universities came under the influence of the managerial revolution of the 1980s with its exaltation of line management and its rejection of the values enshrined in the Grimond Report. This was light years away from Aitken's dictum that in order for a university to encourage creative talents, 'the more diffuse the authority the better'.[6] The vice-chancellor, whom Sir Robert had said did not have 'any appreciable formal powers', now became the University's 'chief executive'.[7] The irony is, what was this worth? With the national system of higher education revolutionised by the abolition of the binary line and the advent of dirigiste funding councils and performance-related funding, vice-chancellors at the end of the century have less freedom and initiative than any of their predecessors.

Oliver Lodge, of course, had recognised in 1918 that the consequence of taking public money could be exactly such a development: 'He who pays the piper.' Yet what he failed to anticipate was that once Westminster began to call the tune it might rat on the obligation to pay! The reduction in government support for higher education in the 1980s and 1990s brought no 'rolling back of the frontiers of the State'. In 1918–19, the government provided 38.5% of Birmingham's income, but ministers were adamant that they were not assuming responsibility for the funding and direction of universities. In 1997–8, funding council grants provided only 32.7% of Birmingham's income, and yet ministers insisted that they had both the right and the capacity to direct higher education.[8] The state, like the Jabberwock, has claws that catch, and they do not let go.

But to lament the snows of yesteryear is to waste tears. When the Robbins Report made higher education the responsibility of the state, it rang the death-knell of university self-determination, as Robert Aitken clearly recognised. Equally, in Britain as it is, the enormous cost of the knowledge revolution could never have been funded from non-public sources. Add the discovery by politicians of votes in mass higher education, and the direction of universities by outsiders from Westminster became inevitable. It is, moreover, naïve in the extreme to imagine that traditional universities could have remained protected havens of collegiality, when business values swept to victory over the rest of national life where the accountant now is king. Statutory regulation will entertain no opt-outs. Those who live in ivory towers cannot escape conforming to the law if they wish to eat.

All this argues that it would be unrealistic and unfair to score the story of the University of Birmingham in the 1980s and 1990s as a dying coda to a great movement. Rather, the period has, in that cliché beloved by historians, to be seen as 'an age of transition', or, more accurately, 'an age of necessary translation'.[9] In the first place, painful though it was, the University took the steps necessary for it to survive and prosper in a new and unwelcome environment. Establishing strong financial control from the centre enabled it to maintain financial solvency and preserve a tiny measure of initiative. Outcomes were now closely monitored in relation to cost. A revolutionary change in 1987 was establishing unitary direction for the University, something which the Grimond Committee had argued for twenty-five years earlier. First a Strategy, Planning and Resources Committee was set up at the highest level, with authority over both the academic and the commercial and financial. Then one of its first recommendations was to unite the posts of the secretary who serviced Council, and the registrar who looked after Senate, so putting an end to a division which had grown from historical accident but had hardened into a debilitating apartheid.[10] Steps were taken to encourage a clear sense of identity and purpose, and, despite provoking a number of jokes, the new 'corporate image' – though not its unhappy 'logo' – did have a useful effect. At every level of University activity, planning became the watchword – institutional plans, academic plans, business plans. Performance indicators arrived, and so, too, the regular appraisal of members of staff.

The final decades of the twentieth century thus saw a necessary managerial reconstruction at Birmingham, but that was not all. A renewed grip was taken on research, so that pace, quality and output increased, reasserting Birmingham's position as a university in the major league. By 1993–4 the University had 4000 postgraduates, the third highest total in the UK. Thanks to this input of energy, 70% of the areas of research at Birmingham achieved ratings of 'national' and 'international' quality in the UK survey published in December 1996. Along with increased performance went increased funding. Already in the four years from 1986–7, the income from research grants and contracts had quadrupled, which, corrected for inflation, was equivalent to 70% or a growth rate of 13% per annum. For example, grants during the twenty years in medicine included £3 million for the Centre of Immunology and Cell Signalling, followed by £1.5 million for gene therapy, and in cancer studies an award of over £500,000 from the Cancer Research Fund and the opening of the purpose-built and externally funded Institute of Cancer Studies, with 160 staff, dedicated to ending the gap between laboratory research and patient care. In teaching, curriculum development flourished – in 1983 courses in race and education, in money, banking and finance, and a four-year course leading to the degree of M.Eng.; in 1988 an MA in playwriting; in 1994 an MA in history and communication. The Barber Institute set out to become nationally known and an undergraduate degree in fine arts was instituted. Novel teaching methods included the introduction by the School of

History of student-led group study and assessment, an innovation which was followed by universities elsewhere. The trend towards the crossing of disciplines accelerated. Minerals engineering amalgamated with chemical engineering; the Birmingham Business School was founded. Horizons widened, with developments in international finance, the winning against fierce opposition of the UK Institute for German Studies, and the establishment of the Japan Centre, both to develop the study of Japan and East Asia and to teach the language, particularly to students increasingly likely to work in or with Japanese-owned industries. Most recently of all, the University has entered into a strategic alliance with Westhill College of Higher Education to promote the agenda of widening access to higher education which was set out in the Dearing Report.

One particular aspect of development in the 1980s and 1990s was a turning by the University towards industry. A symbol of this was the succession to the post of chancellor of Sir Alex Jarratt. Birmingham's first three chancellors – Chamberlain, Chelwood and Eden – had been politicians. The fourth, Sir Peter Scott, had been a well-known painter, naturalist and Olympic yachtsman. Jarratt, in contrast, was a prominent businessman and former civil servant. Already Birmingham was earning more from links with industry than any other higher education institution, but in 1984 an Institute of Research and Development was launched in collaboration with the City, with the brief to transfer university expertise into industry.[11] The Institute's own building was one of the first to be erected on a University Research Park, a second innovation linking industry and higher education. Its basic purpose was to provide accommodation for high-tech companies needing easy access to academic staff and facilities and, within a decade, the Park was turning over £20 million a year. Increasingly, however, it has become the site for commercial developments sponsored by the University itself. By 1992–3, 60% of the tenant companies there had originated in this way, against an average of 25% on research parks nationally. Josiah Mason would most definitely have approved, and Chamberlain likewise!

In higher education in Britain, the period between the advent of Mrs Thatcher as prime minister and the end of the twentieth century was, in the Chinese sense, 'an exciting time'. Yet given the imperative to accommodate to a changing national context, it has been a pregnant time for Birmingham, though at some unhappy sacrifice in humane and corporate values. In the new world of higher education, the University can be confident of a future. As far as these twenty years can be judged now, they may turn out to be the necessary overture to the new score sketched out for higher education by Sir Ron Dearing. Alternatively, and the success of Birmingham thus far is witness to the importance of continuing adaptability, the decades may only serve as a bridge passage to themes as yet dimly perceived. Whichever proves to be true, the first centenary of the University of Birmingham is the hundred years between 1880 and 1980. The years 1980 to 2000 are the opening chapter of the next.

Notes

1 For the following, see above, p. 405.
2 UC 7/ii *Treasurer* 1983–4, p. 57.
3 Ibid., 1982–3, p. 54.
4 *Report of the Review Body*, p. 41: 9.3.
5 UC 7/ii *Accounts* 1977, p. 51; 1998, pp. 5–6. For the valuation see ibid., p. 28.
6 *Bulletin* 40 (13 June 1963).
7 UC 4/v/6 'Sit-in', in K.
8 UC 7/ii *Accounts*, p. 19. The recurrent grant amounted to only 29% of income. Even if full-time student fees are counted as indirect state provision, the proportion of income is only 41.9%, 3.4% higher than in the First World War.
9 For the following see UC7/ii *Annual Reports* and *Bulletin,* passim.
10 The post of secretary goes back to Morley's appointment as secretary to the Mason trustees. The post of registrar was initially an academic appointment. See above, p. 200.
11 The University of London earned more collectively, but this was a conglomerate of separate colleges.

Appendix
Plans and maps

The Evolution of the Edgbaston Plan

A As proposed 1925 (Aston Webb)
University of Birmingham Estates Management, unpublished plan May 1925

B As proposed 1928 (William Hayward)
University of Birmingham Estates Management, unpublished plan, undated

C As proposed 1945 (Verner Rees: Scheme A)
University of Birmingham Estates Management, Plan H25, Jan.1945

D As proposed 1945 (Verner Rees: Scheme B)
University of Birmingham Estates Management, Plan H24 Jan.1945

E As proposed 1957 (Casson & Conder)
University of Birmingham Estates Management, Plan H10, Apr. 1957

F As proposed 1963 (Casson & Conder)
Bulletin 37 (15 Feb.,1963)

(A–E adapted from J. W. R. Whitehand, in *Planning History* 13 (1991), pp. 29–35

A

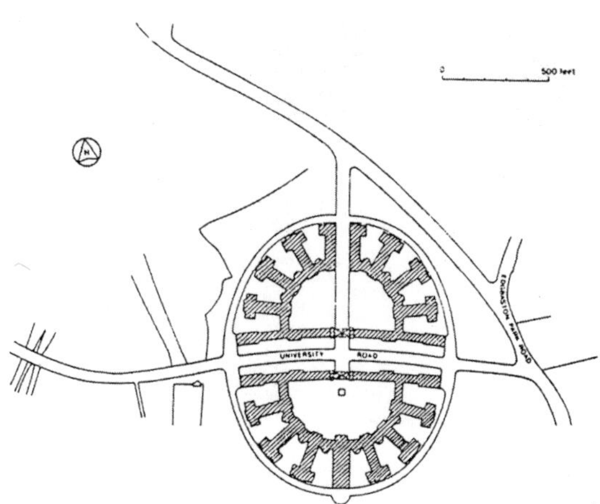

B

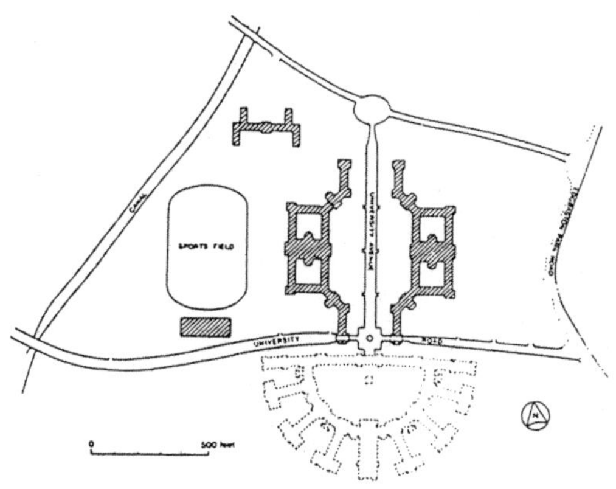

A As proposed 1925 (Aston Webb)
University of Birmingham Estates Management, unpublished plan May 1925

B As proposed 1928 (William Hayward)
University of Birmingham Estates Management, unpublished plan, undated

C

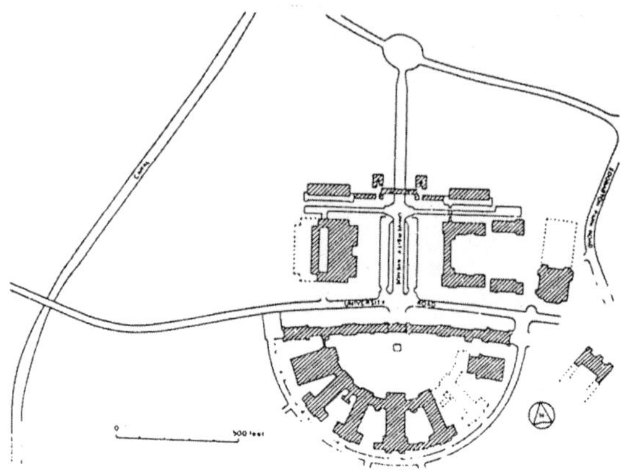

D

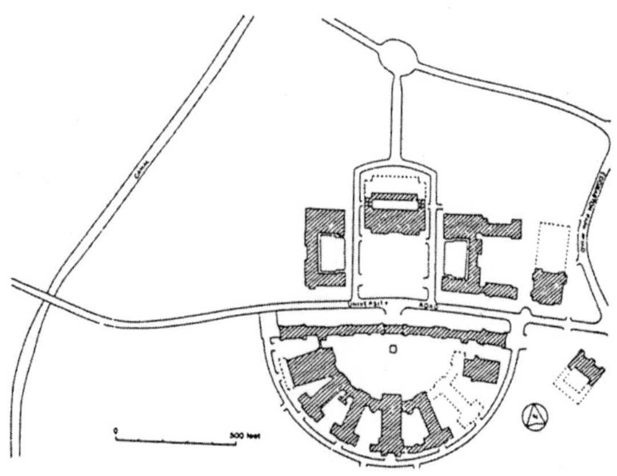

C As proposed 1945 (Verner Rees: Scheme A)
University of Birmingham Estates Management, Plan H25, Jan.1945

D As proposed 1945 (Verner Rees: Scheme B)
University of Birmingham Estates Management, Plan H24 Jan.1945

E

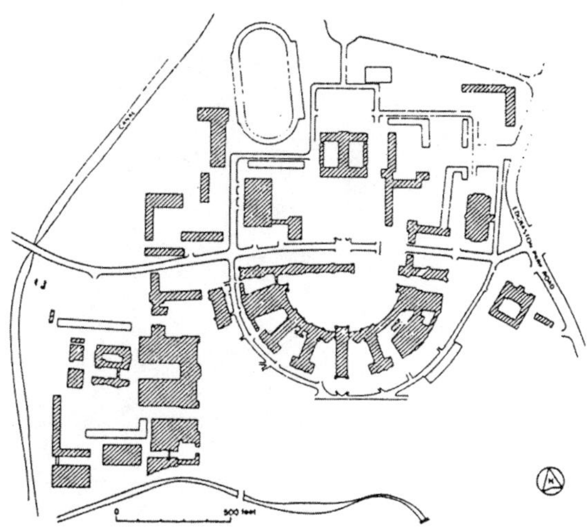

E As proposed 1957 (Casson & Conder)
University of Birmingham Estates Management, Plan H10, Apr. 1957

F

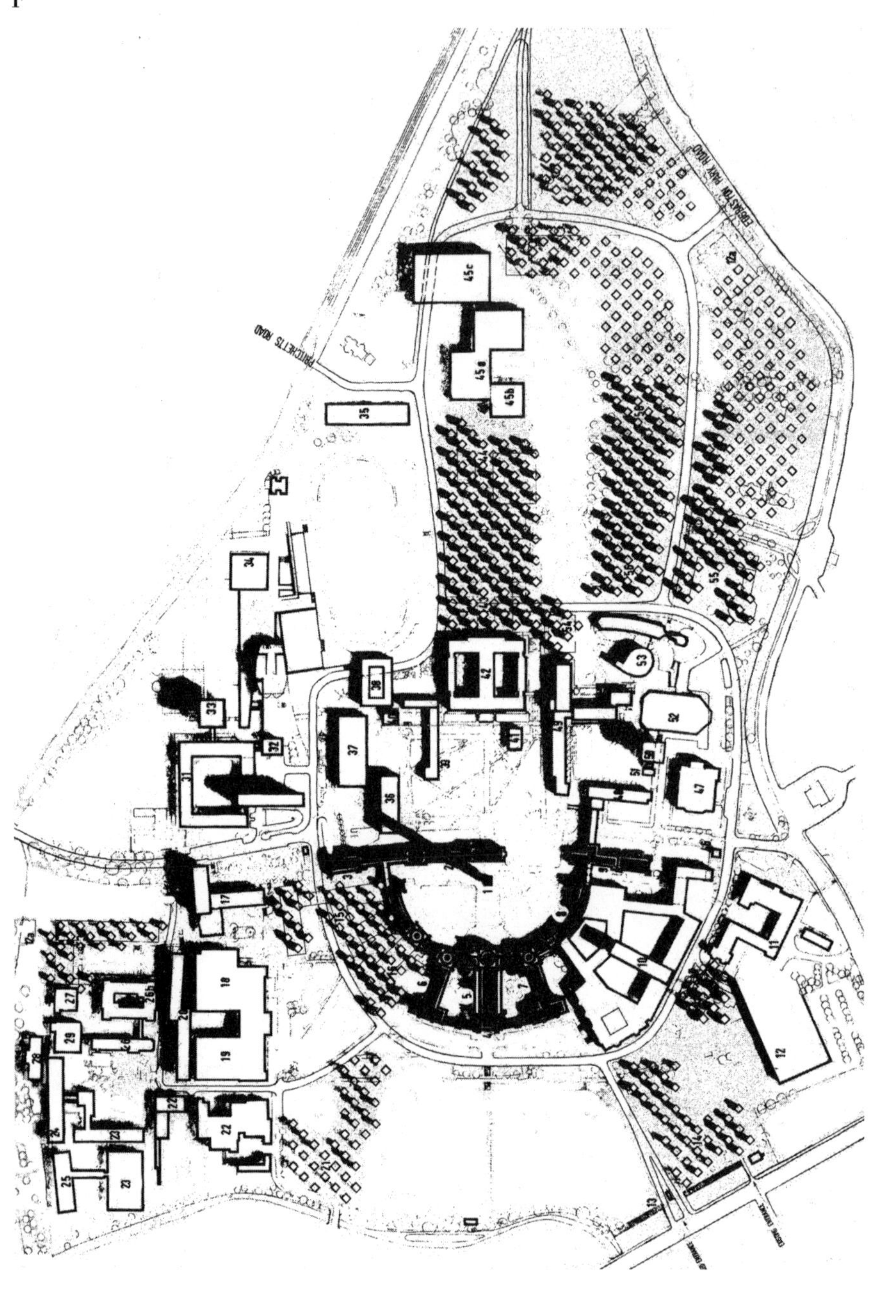

F As proposed 1963 (Casson & Conder)
Bulletin 37 (15 Feb.,1963)

The Development of the Edgbaston Campus

G 1902-1914
The broken line shows the route of the canal and railway
H 1918–1940
J 1941–1959
K 1960–1980

Key (major developments only; original usage)

1 Great Hall
2 Block A
3 Block B
4 Block C
5 Chemistry
6 Library
7 Physics
8 Power House
9 Model Mine
10 University House
11 Medical School
12 Oil Engineering
13 Mining
14 Gymnasium
15 Biology etc.
16 Chemistry
17 Physics
18 Barber Institute
19 Students' Union
20 St. Andrew's Hall
21 Clinical Research
22 Chemical Engineering
23 Civil Engineering
24 Mechanical Engineering
25 Maintenance Services
26 Chemistry
27 Biological Sciences
28 Huts
29 Huts
30 Physics
31 Westmere
32 Winterbourne

33 Library
34 Wolfson Research Centre
35 Transportation
36 University Centre
37 Staff House
38 Physical Education
39 Arts
40 Commerce & Social Science
41 Commerce & Social Science
42 Commerce & Social Science
43 Education
44 Computer Centre
45 Health Centre
46 Minerals Engineering
47 Materials Science
48 Electronic Engineering
49 Engineering Production
50 Lucas Institute
51 Radiation Centre

G

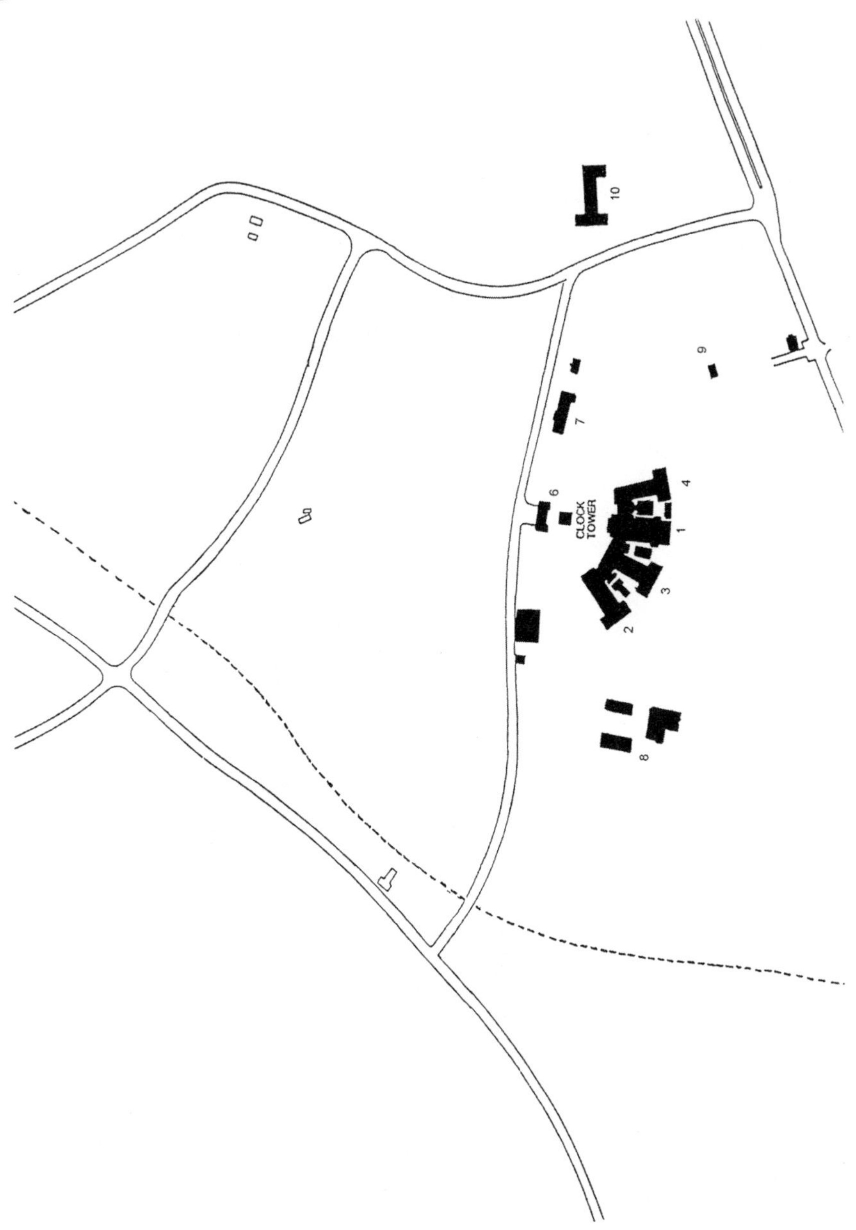

G 1902-1914
The broken line shows the route of the canal and railway

H

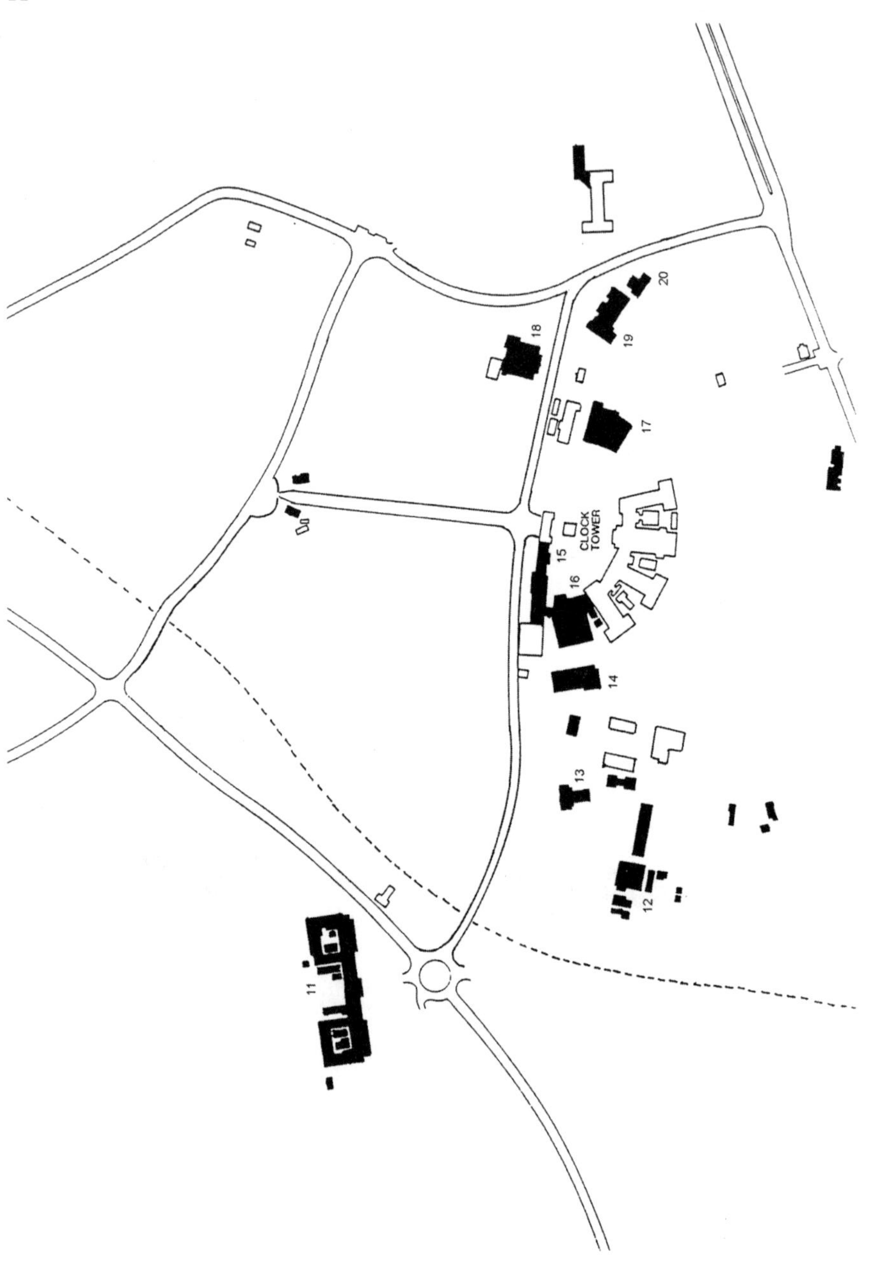

J

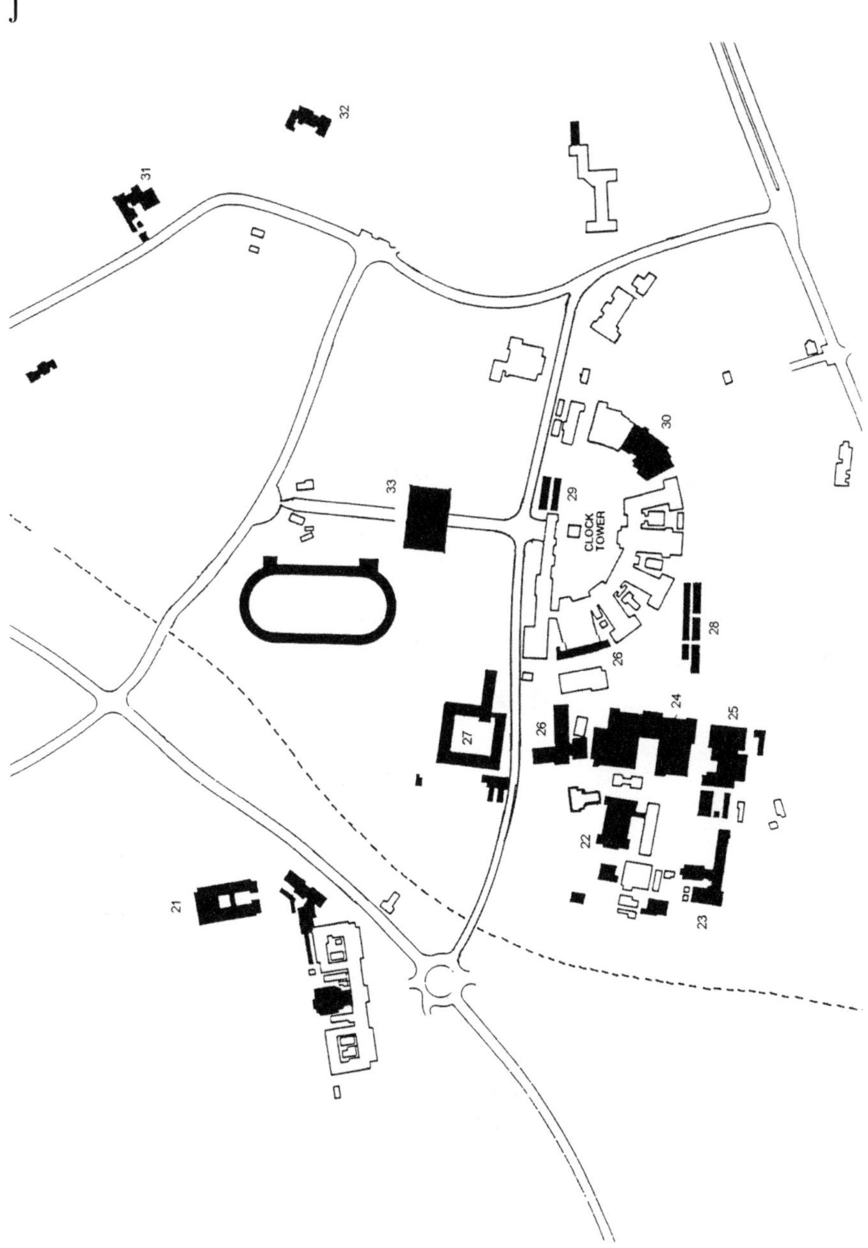

K

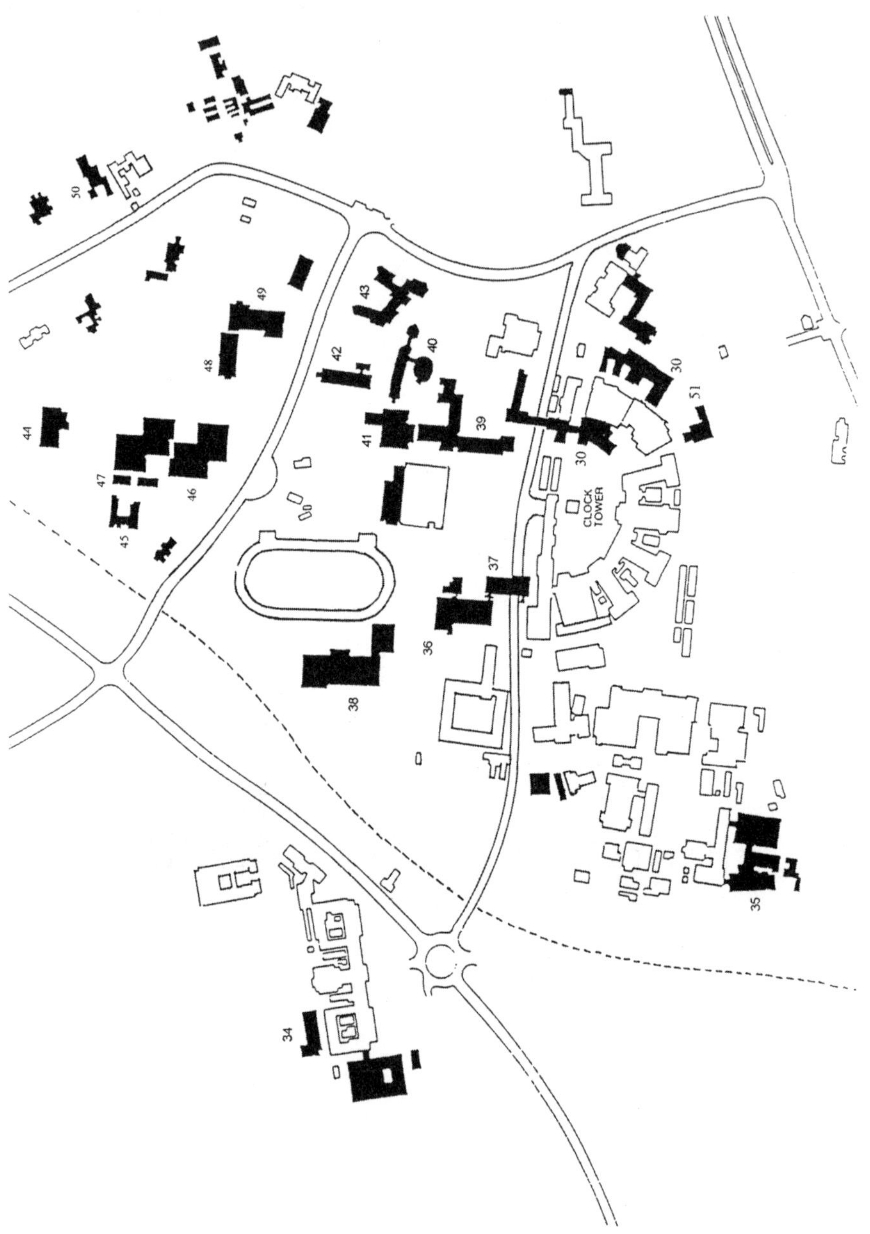
50
49
43
42
40
48
44
41
39
30
51
30
47
46
CLOCK
TOWER
45
37
36
38
35
34

The Great Hall Window

L Key: The central lights display the University arms with the arms or devices of benefactors above and below. The lights on the left represent the faculty of Medicine with the faculty of Arts above; on the right the lower lights refer to the faculty of Commerce and the upper (and some in the centre) the faculty of Science. The upper quadrants contain the shields of the six counties adjacent to the University.

Bibliography

Unpublished primary sources

Birmingham Central Library

Local Studies Department

City of Birmingham Education Committee: Secondary Education Minute Books

'Problems of Graduate Unemployment at the University of Birmingham' (Birmingham, May 1938)

'Proposed Curriculum of the Birmingham Jewellers' and Silversmiths' Association' (1906)

Birmingham Corporation

Minutes of the Finance and General Purposes Committee

Churchill College Cambridge

Chadwick Papers 1/28

Public Record Office [PRO]

DSIR Department of Scientific and Industrial Research

UGC University Grants Committee

ED Ministry of Education

University of Birmingham

University Collection (MC=*Mason College)*

1/i/2	Fiedler–Harding Letters
1/i/3/1–2	Letters: 'Proposed University'
1/i/6&7	Papers of R. S. Heath *MC*
1/ii/3	Principal's Letter Books *MC*
2/i/3	Professor of Education's Letter Book
3/vi/7–vii/2	Correspondence of the Senior Tutor for Women Students
3/vii/8	Ashley papers
3/vii/10/3	Fiedler Mss: School of Modern Languages

4/i/15	Reports to Council *MC*
4/i/18	Reports of Committees *MC*
4/i/21	Minute Book of Court of Governors *MC*
4/i/22–24	College Council Minutes *MC*
4/ii/1	University College Council Minutes *MC*
4/ii/10	Senate Minutes *MC*
4/ii/11	Reports to Academic Board *MC*
4/ii/12	Minutes of Professorial Meetings *MC*
4/ii/23	Accounts 1894–1900 *MC*
4/ii/28	Finance Committee Minutes *MC*
4/ii/6	Canvassing Committee Minutes *MC*
4/ii/7	Trustees' Minutes *MC*
4/ii/8&9	Academic Board Minutes *MC*
4/iii/10	Advisory Sub-Committee Minutes *MC*
4/iii/8	Management Sub-Committee Minutes *MC*
4/iii/9	Executive Committee Minutes *MC*
4/iv/20	Building Committee Minutes 3
4/iv/21	Events of 1968 (portfolio)
4/iv/7	Reconstruction Committee Minutes
4/v/4	Miscellaneous Items, 1910–68
4/v/6	Events of 1968 (Box)
7/ii	Annual Reports: *Accounts, Building Committee, Council, Deans', Research, Treasurer, Vice Principal*
7/iii	Annual Reports: *Principal/Vice-Chancellor*
7/iv/1	History of the University: Various Lectures
7/vi/3	Appointments Board
7/iv/4	Miscellaneous Items, 1869–1914
7/iv/5/28	Lecture by Chamberlain 1893
7/iv/6	Miscellaneous Items, 1920–63
7/iv/7	Miscellaneous Items, 1905–64
7/iv/8/39	Lodge re Great Hall entrance
7/v/1	*University of Birmingham Gazette*
8/ii/4/1	Birmingham Hospitals Centre
8/iii/3	Barber Institute, Report of Director
8/iv/2	Departments of Mining and Metallurgy
8/iv/5/3	'John Adamson' [Pseudonym of T. W. Bushill], *Birmingham University and Commerce* (1901)
8/vi/1/15	Guild report on the syllabus (1910–11)
8/vi/2	*The Open Book* (faculty of Arts)
8/vi/2/13	Guild report on the lecture system (1936)
9/ii/9	Papers of P. Hinton 28 Apr. 1943
9/vi	Student Registers 1892–3 to 1899–2000

9/vi	Site & Building Plans
9/vi/16	Roll of Honour
10/i/18	Royal Visit, 1909
12/ii/1	Higher Education for Ex-Servicemen
12/iv/2/4	Drafts of University Charter
12/iv/3	Royal Visit: Souvenir Programme
13/i/6	Faculty of Arts papers
13/i/8	ARP Committee Minutes
14/ii–14/iii	Principal's/Vice-Chancellor's Letter Books [OL, Oliver Lodge; CGR, Grant Robertson]
16/iii	Barnes papers
17/i	Development and Expansion of the University
19/v/7	Council for Freedom and Democracy

University archives

3	Josiah Mason & Family
3	Notes by Simon Parkes
22	Academic Departments
30	Staff Records

Arts Faculty Minutes
Building Committee Minutes vols. 1 & 2
Council Minutes
Development Committee Minutes
Finance & General Purposes Committee Minutes
Senate Minutes

Chamberlain Papers

JC	Papers of Joseph Chamberlain
NC	Papers of Neville Chamberlain

Published primary sources

University of Birmingham

Barber Institute, *Jubilee Exhibition* (Birmingham, 1983)
Bulletin 1956–1980
Consultative Document prepared by the Review Body appointed by the Council of the University of Birmingham (Birmingham, January 1972)
University Gazette
Mason College Calendars 1880–1 to 1899–1900
Mason College Magazine

Mermaid
Mermaid Guild of Graduates Supplement (Birmingham, 1917).
Redbrick
Register of Degrees, Diplomas and Certificates, 1900–35 (Birmingham, 1937)
Register of Graduates (Birmingham, 1932)
Report of the Committee of Enquiry, Council for Academic Freedom and Democracy (1971)
Report of the Review Body appointed by the Council of the University of Birmingham (Birmingham, September 1972)
University Gazette
University of Birmingham Magazine

Miscellaneous

Anderson, C. *Grants to Students* (Cmnd. 1051 of 1960)
Board of Education, *Reports from University Colleges participating in the grant made by Parliament* (Cmnd. 7457 of 1894; Cmnd. 8137 of 1914)
Cornish, *Birmingham Year Book* (1941)
Edgbastoniana (Dec. 1904)
Feinstein, C. H. *Statistical Tables of National Income, Expenditure and Output of the United Kingdom, 1855–1965* (Cambridge 1972)
Great Exhibition Catalogue (1851), i.111 and Section III Class 23
Ministry of Education, *Education in England and Wales, 1920–21* (Cmnd. 1718 of 1922)
Report of the Board of Education, 1918–19 (Cd.722 of 1920)
Report of the Committee under the chairmanship of Lord Robbins (Cmnd 2154 of 1963) [Robbins]
Report of the Consultative Committee on Examinations in Secondary Schools (Cmnd. 6004 of 1911) [Acland]
Report on the University Colleges to the Board of Education, for numbers taking postgraduate degrees (1906)
Royal Institute of British Architects (RIBA) *Catalogue*
Royal Commission on Secondary Education (Cmnd. 7862 of 1895) [Bryce]
UGC *Reports*
UGC *First Employment of Graduates* (1961–2 onwards)
UGC *Returns for Universities and University Colleges*
UGC *University Development 1947–52* (1953)
University Colleges (Great Britain) (Grant in Aid) (Cmd. 245 of 1897; 252 of 1902; 267 of 1907)

Newspapers and journals

Birmingham Evening Despatch

Birmingham Daily Despatch
Birmingham Daily Gazette
Birmingham Daily Post
Birmingham Guardian
Birmingham Post
Colliery Guardian
Daily Telegraph
Dundee Advertiser
Listener — *The Future of the Civic Universities* (1942); *The Modern University, with Special Reference to Technical Education* (1945); *The Civic Universities* (1949)
Pall Mall Gazette
Sunday Times Magazine
Times

Secondary sources

Aldcroft, D. *The Interwar Economy: Britain 1918–39* (1970)
Amery, J. *The Life of Joseph Chamberlain*, iv (1951)
Anderson, R. D. *Universities and elites in Britain since 1800* (Basingstoke, 1992)
Anderson, R. D. *The student community at Aberdeen, 1860–1939* (Aberdeen, 1988)
Armytage, W. H. G. *Civic Universities: aspects of a British tradition* (1955)
Ashley, A. *William James Ashley: a life* (1932)
Ashley, W. 'The Enlargement of Economics', in *The Economic Journal*, 18 (1908)
Banks, Olive, *Parity and Prestige in English Secondary Education* (1955)
Barnes, S. *The Birmingham Hospitals Centre* (Birmingham, 1952)
Bentwich, N. *The Rescue and Achievement of Refugee Scholars: The Story of Displaced Scholars and Scientists, 1933–52* (The Hague, 1953)
Berdahl, R. O. *British Universities and the State* (Cambridge, 1959)
Bingham, C. *The History of Royal Holloway College, 1886–1986* (1987)
Bodkin, T. *The Place of Fine Arts in the University* (Birmingham, 1935)
Boot H. A. H. and Randall, J. T. 'Historical Notes on the Cavity Magnetron', in *Transactions on Electronic Devices* 23 (1976)
Bowen, E.G. *Radar Days* (1987)
Brazier, R. H. and Sandford, E. *Birmingham and the Great War, 1914–18* (Birmingham, 1921)
Brittain, Vera, *Women's Work in Modern England* (1928)
Brock M. G. and Curthoys, M. C. *The History of the University of Oxford. Vol. 16. Nineteenth Century Oxford.* (Oxford, 1997)

Builder, The

Bunce, J. T. *Life of Josiah Mason* (Birmingham, 1882; expanded edition 1890)

Burcham W. E and Shearman, E. D. R. *Fifty Years of the Cavity Magnetron* (Birmingham, 1990)

Butt, John, 'English at the Universities 1901–1951', in *Universities Quarterly* 5 (1951)

Calder, Angus, *The People's War: Britain, 1939–45* (1969)

Cardwell, D. S. *The Organisation of Science* (1957)

Carr-Saunders, A. M. and Wilson, P. A. *The Professions* (Oxford, 1933)

Carswell, J. *Government and Universities in Britain, 1960–1980* (Cambridge, 1985).

Chapman, A. W. *The Story of Modern University. A History of the University of Sheffield* (Oxford, 1955)

Cheesewright, M. *Mirror to a Mermaid* (Birmingham, 1975)

Cherry, G. *Urban Renewal and Town Planning: the Chamberlains in Birmingham* (Chamberlain Lecture, May 1994).

Chinn, Carl, *Brum Undaunted: Birmingham during the Blitz* (Birmingham, 1996)

Clark, R. *Tizard* (1965)

Clark, R. W. *Birth of the Bomb* (1961)

Cockburn S. and Ellyard D. *Oliphant* (Perth, Australia, 1981)

Creswell H. B. 'Sir Aston Webb and his office', in A.Service, ed., *Edwardian Architecture and its Origins* (1975)

Crouch, C. *The Student Revolt* (1970)

Crowther J. C.and Whiddington R. *Science at War* (HMSO, 1947)

Dahrendorf, R. *LSE. A History of the London School of Economics and Political Science 1895–1995* (Oxford, 1995)

Darbishire, H. 'Ernest De Selincourt, 1870–1943', in *Proceedings of the British Academy* 29 (1944)

Davenport-Hines, R. P. T. *Dudley Docker: the life and times of a trade warrior* (Cambridge, 1985)

Dent, H. C. *The Growth of English Education, 1945–50* (1954)

Digby, A. *The Evolution of British General Practice, 1850–1948* (Oxford, 1999)

Dodds, E. R. *Missing Persons* (Oxford, 1977)

Drummond, D. K. 'The University of Birmingham and the Industrial Spirit: reasons for the local support of Joseph Chamberlain's campaign to found the University, 1897–1900', in *History of Universities* 19 (1999)

Dyhouse, Carol, 'Signing the pledge? Women's investment in university education and teacher training before 1939', in *History of Education* 26 (1997)

Dyhouse, Carol, *Girls growing up in late Victorian and Edwardian England* (1981)

Dyhouse, Carol, *No distinction of sex?* (1995)

Elliott, J. *Palaces, Patronage and Pills* (Egham, 1996)

Ellis, G. S. M. *The Poor Student and the University* (1925)

Fisher, H. A. L. *British Universities and the War* (1917)

Flexner, Abraham, *Universities: American, English, German* (Oxford, 1930)
Frisch, O. *What Little I Remember* (Cambridge, 1979)
Gaukroger, Alison and Schwarz, Leonard, 'A University and its region: student recruitment to Birmingham 1945–75', in *Oxford Review of Education* 23 (1997)
Gill, C., Briggs, A., Sutcliffe, A. and Smith, R. *History of Birmingham* (1952–76)
Glass, D. V. (ed.), *Social Mobility in Britain* (1954)
Goldthorpe, J. H. *Social mobility and class structure in modern Britain* (Oxford, 1980)
Gosden, P. H. J. H. 'The nationalizing of Britain's universities, 1945–65', in *University of Leeds Review* 34 (1991–2)
Gosden, P. H. J. H. and Taylor, A. J. (eds). *Studies in the History of a University 1874–1974. To Commemorate the Centenary of the University of Leeds* (Leeds, 1975)
Gowing, M. *Britain and Atomic Energy, 1939–45* (Glasgow, 1964)
Greenstein, D., 'The Junior Members: A Profile' in B. Harrison, ed., *The History of the University of Oxford* vol. 8 (Oxford, 1994)
Haldane, R. B. *Autobiography* (1929)
Halsey, A. H., Heath, A. F. and Ridge, J. M. *Origins and Destinations. Family, Class and Education in Modern Britain* (Oxford, 1980)
Halsey, A. H. *Decline of Donnish Dominion* (1992)
Hartcup, Guy, *The Challenge of War: Science and Engineering's contribution to World War Two* (Newton Abbot, 1970)
Hearnshaw, F. J. C. *The Centenary History of King's College London 1828–1928* (1929)
Hennock, E. P. 'Technological education in England, 1850–1926: the uses of a German model', in *History of Education* 19 (1990)
Hennock, E. P. *Fit and Proper Persons. Ideal and Reality in Nineteenth-Century Urban Government* (1973)
Herklots, H. G. G. *The New Universities. An External Examination* (1928)
Heward, C. 'Education, examination and the artisans: The Department of Science and Art in Birmingham, 1853–1902' in Roy Macleod, ed., *Days of Judgement* (Driffield, 1982)
'History of the Birmingham Medical School', ed. K. D.Wilkinson, in *Birmingham Medical Review* (1925)
Holt, J. C. *The University of Reading. The first fifty years* (Reading, 1977)
Howarth, J. 'Women', in B. Harrison, ed., *The History of the University of Oxford.* vol. viii (1994)
Howarth, J. and Curthoys, M. 'The political economy of women's higher education in late nineteenth and early twentieth-century Britain', in *Historical Research* 60 (142) (1987)
Ives, E. W. *Image of a University: the Great Hall at Edgbaston* (Birmingham,

1988)

Jackson, F. H. 'The work of T. R. Spence, designer, decorator, architect', in *The Magazine of Art*, 2 ser. 1 (1903)

Johnson, Olwen, *Alma Mater. A Memoir of Student Life at Birmingham University* (1940)

Jones, D. R. *The Origins of Civic Universities:Manchester, Leeds and Liverpool* (1988)

Jones, Enid Huws, *Margery Fry : The Essential Amateur* (Oxford, 1966)

Kaelble, H. *Social Mobility in the Nineteenth and Twentieth Centuries: Europe and America in Comparative Perspective* (Leamington Spa, 1985)

Kelsall, R. H. *Applications for Admission to Universities* (Assoc. of the Universities of the British Commonwealth, 1957)

Kelsall, R. H. *Women and Teaching* (HMSO, 1963)

Kelsall, R. H. 'Self-recruitment in four professions' in D. V. Glass, ed., *Social Mobility in Britain* (1954)

Kelsall, R. K, Poole, A. and Kuhn, A. *Graduates: the sociology of an elite* (1972)

Kipling, R. *The Irish Guards in the Great War* (1923)

Kogan, M. *The Attack on Higher Education* (1983)

Lafitte, F. *The Internment of Aliens* (1940)

Lodge, Oliver, *Past Years: An Autobiography by Sir Oliver Lodge* (London, 1931)

Lodge, Oliver, 'A Modern University', in *Nature* 21 (1900)

Lowe, R. A., *Education and social change 1964–1990* (1997)

Lowe, R. A., 'English elite education in the late nineteenth and early twentieth centuries' in W. Conze and J. Kocka, *Bildungsbürgertum im 19. Jahrhundert* (Stuttgart, 1985).

Lowe, R .A., 'Structural change in English higher education, 1870–1920' in D. F. Müller, F. Ringer and B. Simon, eds,. *The rise of the modern educational system* (1987)

Lowe, R. A., 'The transformation of higher education in England', in K. H. Jarausch, ed., *The Transformation of Higher Learning, 1860–1930* (Stuttgart, 1982)

Lowe, R. A., *Education in the post-war years. A social history* (1988)

Lowe, Rodney, *Adjusting to Democracy; The Role of the Ministry of Labour in British Politics, 1916–39* (1986)

Lowe, Rodney, 'The erosion of state intervention in Britain, 1917–24', in *Economic History Review*, n.s. 31 (1978)

Manning, Elfrida, *Marble & Bronze: the art and life of Hamo Thornycroft* (1982)

Marsden, W. E. 'Social stratification and nineteenth-century English urban education' in. R. K. Goodenow and W. E. Marsden, eds, *The city and education in four nations* (Cambridge, 1992)

Marsh, P. T. *Joseph Chamberlain, Entrepreneur in Politics* (1994)

Marsh, Peter, *Joseph Chamberlain and the Enterprise of Birmingham* (Birmingham, 1994)

Masterman, C. F. G. *The Condition of England* (ed. 1911)

McKibbin, R. *Classes and Cultures. England 1918–1951*(Oxford, 1998)

McLeod, Roy and Andrew, E. K. 'The Origins of the Department of Scientific and Industrial Research : Reflections on Ideas and men, 1915–16', in *Public Administration* 48 (1970)

McWilliams-Tullberg, R. *Women at Cambridge: a men's University – though of a mixed type* (1975)

Melville, Harry *The Department of Scientific and Industrial Research* (Oxford, 1962)

Miles H. *Art in the University* (Birmingham, 1972)

Miles, H. *Handbook of the Barber Institute* (1982)

Millar, M. and Church, R. A. 'Motor Manufacturing', in Neil K. Buxton and Derek H. Aldcroft, eds, *British Industry between the wars: instability and industrial development 1919–1939* (1979)

Ministry of Munitions, *Official History* (HMSO, 1921–2)

Mitchell, B. R., *British Historical Statistics* (Cambridge, 1988)

Moon P. B. and Ibbs, T.L. *Physics at Birmingham 1880–1980* (Birmingham, 1980)

Mountford, J. *How they fared: a survey of a three-year student entry* (Liverpool, 1956)

Mountford, J. *British Universities* (1966)

National Union of Students, *Graduate Employment: report of the Congress of the National Union of Students* (1937)

Newman, J. H. *Idea of a University* (Cambridge, 1931)

Osterling, A. ed., *Nobel: The Man and his Prizes* (Amsterdam, 1963)

Parker H. M. *Manpower: A Study of Wartime Policy and Action* (HMSO, 1957)

Peierls, R. *Bird of Passage* (Princeton N.J., 1985)

Peirels, R. *Proceedings of the Cambridge Philosophical Society* (1939)

Perkin, H. 'The recruitment of élites in British society since 1880', in *Journal of Social History* 12 (1978)

Perkin, H., *The Rise of Professional Society: England since 1880* (1989)

Political and Economic Planning, *Graduate Employment* (1956)

Political and Economic Planning, *The University Student, Selection and Awards* (1949)

Priestley, R. E. *Antarctic Adventure: Scott's Northern Party* (1914, 1974)

Proceedings of the Cambridge Philosophical Society (1939)

Redmayne, R. A. S. *The Mining Department of the University of Birmingham* (1904)

Reeder, D. 'The reconstruction of secondary education in England, 1869–1920' in D. F. Müller, F. Ringer and B. Simon, eds, *The rise of the modern educational system. Structural change and social reproduction 1870–1920* (Cambridge,

1987)
Rees, H. *A University is Born* (Coventry, 1989)
Register of the Victoria Cross (Cheltenham 1981, 1988)
Rhodes, Richard, *The Making of the Atomic Bomb* (New York, 1986)
Robertson, C. Grant, *The British Universities* (1930, 2ed. 1944)
Rothblatt, Sheldon, 'The Diversification of Higher Education in England' in K. H. Jarausch, ed., *The Transformation of Higher Learning 1860–1930* (Stuttgart, 1982)
Rothblatt, Sheldon, *The Revolution of the Dons. Cambridge and Society in Victorian England* (Cambridge, 1968)
Round, A. H. 'Bone grafting in gunshot fractures of the jaw', in *Proceedings of the Royal Society of Medicine* 12 (1919)
Sanderson, J.M. (ed.), *The Universities in the Nineteenth Century* (1975)
Sanderson, J. M. *Universities and British Industry, 1850–1970* (1972)
Savage, M., 'The missing link? The relationship between spatial mobility and social mobility', in *British Journal of Sociology* 39 (1988)
Sherington, G. *English education, social change and war 1911–1920* (Manchester, 1981)
Shinn, C. *Paying the Piper; The Development of the University Grants Committee, 1919–1946* (1986)
Simon, Brian, *A Student's View of the Universities* (1943)
Simon, E. *The Development of British Universities* (1944)
Smith C. A. 'The Birmingham University', in *Engineering* 88 (1902)
Smith, B. M. D. *Business Education in the University of Birmingham, 1899–1965* (Birmingham, 2nd. ed. 1990).
Smith, C. A. 'Birmingham University', in *Engineering* 88 (London, 1906)
Smith, D. 'Social conflict in urban education', in D.A. Reeder, ed., *Urban Education in the Nineteenth Century* (1977)
Smith, D. *Conflict and compromise. Class formation in English society 1830–1914. A comparative study of Birmingham and Sheffield* (London, 1982)
Smith, Dennis 'Getting on, just getting by: Changing prospects in south Birmingham', in Philip Cooke, ed., *Localities* (1988)
Smith, R. H. *Engineering* (1906)
Snow, C. P. *Science and Government* (Cambridge, Mass. 1961)
Soffer, Reba N. *Discipline and Power. The University, History, and the Making of an English Elite, 1870–1930* (Stanford, 1994)
Somerset, E. J. *The Birth of a University: A Passage in the Life of E. A. Sonnenschein* (Birmingham, 1934)
Spencer-Longhurst, P. *Barber Institute of Fine Art, Handbook* (Birmingham 1993)
Stallworthy, J. *Wilfred Owen* (Oxford, 1977)
Stevenson, John and Cook, Chris, *Britain in the Depression: Society and Politics, 1929–39* (1994)

Strachey, Ray, *Careers and Openings for Women. A Survey of Women's Employments and a Guide for those seeking work* (London, 1935)

Thieme, U and Becker, F (eds) *Allgemeines Lexikon Der Bildenden Kunstler von der Antike bis zür Gegenwart* (Leipzig, 1907–50)

Thomas, J. B. 'Birmingham University and teacher training: day training college to department of education', *History of Education* 21 (1992)

Thomas, J. B. *British universities and teacher education: a century of change* (Lewes, 1990)

Thompson, F. M. L. 'The Humanities', in F. M. L. Thompson, ed., *The University of London and the world of Learning, 1836–1986* (1990)

Thoms, David, *War, Industry and Society: The Midlands, 1939–45* (London, 1989)

Thomson, A. P .D. 'The Chamberlain Tower', in *University of Birmingham Historical Journal* 4 (1954)

Truscot, B. *Redbrick University* (1943)

Tuke, M. *A History of Bedford College for Women, 1849–1937* (Oxford, 1939)

Tylecote, M. *The Education of women at Manchester University 1883–1933* (Manchester, 1941)

Valentine, C. W. *Discipline and Morale*(1942)

Valentine, C. W. 'An Enquiry into the choice of the teaching profession by university students,' in *British Journal of Educational Psychology* 4 (1934)

Valentine, C. W. *Literacy and Army Men* (1943)

Valentine, C. W. *Principles of Army Training* (1942)

Vernon, K. 'Science and Technology during the Great War', in S. Constantine, M. W. Kirby and M. E. Rose, eds, *The First World War in British History* (1995)

Vince, C. A. *History of the Corporation of Birmingham* (1923)

Vincent E. W. and Hinton, P. *The University of Birmingham, its History and Significance* (Birmingham, 1947)

Whitcut, Janet, *Edgbaston High School, 1876–1976* (Birmingham, 1976)

Whitehand, J. W. R. 'Institutional site planning: the University of Bimingham, England 1900–1969', in *Planning History* 13 (1991)

Whiteley, L. Doreen, *The Poor Student and the University* (1933)

Wood, A. C. *A History of the University College Nottingham, 1881–1948* (Oxford 1953)

Wright, S.E. *Chronicles of the Birmingham Chamber of Commerce, 1813–1913* (Birmingham, 1913)

Theses

Bishop, J. M. E. 'Josiah Mason and the Foundation of Mason Science College, Birmingham'. Unpublished M.Ed. thesis, University of Birmingham (1983)

Cooke, C. 'Women and the professions, 1890–1939'. Unpublished Ph.D. thesis, University of Sussex (1997)

Drake, P. D. 'Labour and Spain: British Labour's response to the Spanish Civil War with special reference to ... Birmingham'. Unpublished Ph.D. thesis, University of Birmingham (1977)

Gibert, J. S., 'Women at the English civic universities, 1880–1920'. Unpublished Ph.D. thesis, University of North Carolina at Chapel Hill (1988)

Humphries, R. E. 'English and Welsh Civic Universities and the State from the mid-nineteenth century to 1914'. Unpublished M.A. thesis, University of Kent at Canterbury, (1979)

Keeble S. P. 'University Education and Business Management from the 1880s to 1950s – A Reluctant relationship'. Unpublished Ph.D. thesis, London School of Economics (1984)

Wydenbach N., 'The role of Birmingham University in the development of the cavity magnetron and the atomic bomb'. Unpublished B.A. dissertation, University of Birmingham (1997)

Index